The 25th
North Carolina
Troops in the Civil War

The 25th North Carolina Troops in the Civil War

History and Roster of a Mountain-Bred Regiment

CARROLL C. JONES

McFarland & Company, Inc., Publishers
Jefferson, North Carolina

> *The present work is a reprint of the illustrated case bound edition of* The 25th North Carolina Troops in the Civil War: History and Roster of a Mountain-Bred Regiment, *first published in 2009 by McFarland.*

Unless otherwise noted, all illustrations from *Harper's Weekly* were obtained from the John C. Pace Library, University of West Florida.

LIBRARY OF CONGRESS CATALOGUING-IN-PUBLICATION DATA

Jones, Carroll (Carroll C.), 1950–
The 25th North Carolina troops in the Civil War : history and roster of a mountain-bred regiment / Carroll Jones.
p.   cm.
Includes bibliographical references and index.

ISBN 978-0-7864-9555-9
softcover : acid free paper ∞

1. Confederate States of America. Army. North Carolina Infantry Regiment, 25th.   2. North Carolina—History—Civil War, 1861–1865—Regimental histories.   3. United States—History—Civil War, 1861–1865—Regimental histories.   4. North Carolina—History—Civil War, 1861–1865—Registers.   5. United States—History—Civil War, 1861–1865—Registers.   6. United States—History—Civil War, 1861–1865—Campaigns.   7. Soldiers—North Carolina—Registers. 8. North Carolina—Genealogy.   I. Title.

E573.525th .J66 2014   973.7'456—dc22   2008055746

BRITISH LIBRARY CATALOGUING DATA ARE AVAILABLE

© 2009 Carroll C. Jones. All rights reserved

No part of this book may be reproduced or transmitted in any form or by any means, electronic or mechanical, including photocopying or recording, or by any information storage and retrieval system, without permission in writing from the publisher.

Cover photograph: *The Rebel Yell*, painting by Don Troiani

Manufactured in the United States of America

McFarland & Company, Inc., Publishers
Box 611, Jefferson, North Carolina 28640
www.mcfarlandpub.com

My mother, Jimmie Hargrove, and her sisters, Nannie, Ellen, and Mildred, were born and raised within the remote recesses of Haywood County's Pigeon Valley. There they flowered bright and beautiful and lived life in its fullest. The memory of these free-spirited and unabashed granddaughters of William Harrison Hargrove (a Confederate warrior who served with the Twenty-fifth Regiment N.C.) never dims within and still serves as a beacon to guide and inspire me. It was through them that I became infused with a profound appreciation of my heritage, rooted deep in the Blue Ridge Mountains of western North Carolina. It is to them that this work is dedicated.

Acknowledgments

This first book-writing experience of mine can be likened to a walk through a dark and uncharted wilderness. By far, the more straightforward and easier route was that of researching and writing the manuscript. Once that enjoyable and rewarding trail had been blazed, the path forward was not at all clear. Blocking the way were considerable obstacles which were not easily passed. These included a humbling search for a publisher, endless hours spent reviewing and rewriting, an exploration of various archives to uncover the appropriate illustrative photographs and artwork, development of maps, and the sometimes maddening pursuit of the ever-important permissions to use the wonderful letters, art, and photographs included herein. Daunting were these new experiences for me; but along the way, many people offered a hand and served as a literary compass to guide me out of the darkness. For that assistance I am very fortunate, indeed, and to the following few I am truly grateful:

Eloise Gompf, a friend and author in her own right (*From the Mediterranean to the Jordan: Murder for Survival*), was kind enough to proof my manuscript and provide suggestions to improve the book's readability. Through several enjoyable and enlightening sessions at her residence, we reviewed the marks and comments she had carefully penciled on the endless pages. And like an anxious schoolboy listening to his teacher, I nodded deferentially as many grammatical messes were cleaned up. For these valuable lessons, as well as for her uncanny ability to unsnarl occurrences of tortured and twisted prose, my heartfelt thanks go out to Eloise.

Military history accounts are practically worthless unless accompanied by maps with which readers can gage their understanding and visualize geographic features in relation to troop positions. To illustrate the several Civil War theatres where the Twenty-fifth Regiment N.C. fought, I turned to Peter Krafft of Florida State University. He transformed my scatchings and scribblings into the several wonderful maps found in this book. Many thanks, Peter, for your professionalism and for affording me the unique opportunity to work with a true cartographer.

The rich archives and collections at several libraries were sources of valuable information and details which illuminated and helped tell the story of the Twenty-fifth Regiment's journey through the Civil War. I want to express my genuine appreciation to the many persons at the following institutions who assisted in the discovery of these treasures or generously granted permissions for their use: Hunter Library, Western Carolina University; Wilson Library, University of North Carolina; John C. Pace Library, University of West Florida; South

Caroliniana Library, University of South Carolina; Pack Memorial Public Library, Asheville, North Carolina; and the Henderson County Public Library, Hendersonville, North Carolina.

Another custodian of valuable historical knowledge and artifacts related to the Civil War and North Carolina's important role during the conflict is the North Carolina Department of Archives and History. The staff at this institution proved to be very professional and expeditious in handling my queries and requests. To them, and especially to Donna Kelly and Kim Cumber for their patience and special assistance, go my sincerest thanks.

And I managed to complete such a project only with the devotion and continuous approval and encouragement of my wife, Maria. Always supportive and critical in positive ways (like spotting those pesky clichés that inadvertently found their way into my writing), she has been and continues to be my primary source of inspiration. To her go my heart and my love.

TABLE OF CONTENTS

Acknowledgments vii
Preface 1

1. FLAMES OF SECESSION 5
2. FARMERS JOIN THE REBELLION 11
3. THE FABRIC OF THE 25TH REGIMENT N.C. 17
    The Companies of the 25th Regiment N.C. 18
4. CAROLINA COASTAL DEFENSE 33
    Defensive Duty Near Port Royal Sound 33
    Too Late to New Bern 43
5. SEVEN DAYS BATTLES AROUND RICHMOND 49
    Engagement at King's School House 52
    Battle of Malvern Hill 55
6. MARYLAND CAMPAIGN 60
    Moving North 60
    Capture of Harpers Ferry 67
    Battle of Antietam 70
7. HEIGHTS OF FREDERICKSBURG 78
8. BACK TO NORTH CAROLINA 92
    Eastern Carolina Coastal Defense. 92
    Chancellorsville 98
    Trouble in the Mountains 104
    Capture of Plymouth 106
9. RICHMOND AND PETERSBURG FRONT 114
    Battle of Drewry's Bluff 114
    Beauregard's Stopgap Defense of Petersburg 116

10. SIEGE OF PETERSBURG	121
Battle of the Crater	121
Life in the Trenches	127
Battle of the Weldon Railroad	131
Long Winter of 1864–1865	133
11. WAR ON THE HOME FRONT	141
Conscription	141
Draft Evaders, Deserters and Tories	145
Bushwhackers All	148
12. A JOURNEY ENDED	153
Fort Stedman	153
Battle of Five Forks	158
Sacred Colors	161
13. CONCLUSION	167
14. CASUALTIES OF WAR	169
Casualty Estimates: Carolina Coastal Defense	171
Casualty Estimates: The Seven Days Battles	172
Casualty Estimates: Maryland Campaign	174
Casualty Estimates: Battle of Fredericksburg	177
Casualty Estimates: Eastern North Carolina Defense	178
Casualty Estimates: Richmond and Petersburg Defense	179
Summary of Casualties	180
Desertion in the Ranks	181
15. THE COLONEL AND HIS LIEUTENANT	183
Henry Middleton Rutledge: "The Boy Colonel"	183
William Harrison Hargrove: "A Useful Citizen"	197
ROSTER OF TROOPS	213
Appendix A: Command Structure	285
Appendix B: Parolees at Appomattox	287
Appendix C: Deployment of 25th N.C. Troops During the Civil War	289
Chapter Notes	295
Bibliography	301
Index	303

Preface

There has to be an inspiration or compelling reason for someone to research and write a historical account such as this one. In my case it was a long-smoldering desire to learn more about my great grandfather's Civil War experience. Most of us who have ancestors that fought in the South's War of Independence have been able to glean bits and pieces of information that give some surety of their involvement in that horrible affair. However, other than the knowledge that a forebear belonged to a certain company or regiment and fought in one or another battle, the extent of understanding usually does not reach much further. That was not enough for me.

I knew very well that Great-Grandfather William Harrison Hargrove* joined together with some of his neighbors to form a volunteer militia group that went off to war in 1861. Accounts and stories about him that have passed down through the family have been harbored closely in remote recesses of my heart and mind for many years. Finally, with more time on my hands and daughters away at college, I endeavored to learn more about his Civil War experience.

It was a simple matter to discover in local history books the more mundane aspects of my great grandfather's Civil War record. Examples would include the name of his company and regiment and the battles or engagements credited to those Confederate military units. Yet this superficial information, although meaningful, did not satisfy my hunger to discover more details about the role he might have played in a particular martial action or the significance of that action in the overall context of the Civil War.

In my account of the 25th Regiment N.C. Infantry Troops, I have faithfully relied on a history of the regiment penned in 1901 by Lt. Garland S. Ferguson, a distinguished North Carolinian from Waynesville who was for many years after the war a lawyer, judge and state senator. Lt. Ferguson's eleven-page record afforded details and descriptions of many of the movements and engagements of his regiment, and I attempted to fill in the gaps. For reasons beyond his literary assistance, I feel a special kindred toward Garland Ferguson. It seems that he was not only a close friend of my great-grandfather after the war, as I have discovered, but he also credited Lt. William Hargrove for saving his life in one of the last desperate battles of the war.

---

*The Hargroves were not consistent in the spelling of their last name. Most of the official references in the Confederate records were to William Hartgrove. William himself after the Civil War spelled his name inconsistently. He eventually dropped the "t" in his name, as did most of his family that continue to reside in the mountains of western North Carolina.

"A Confederate soldier standing barefoot, in tattered trousers, with an Enfield rifle and his cartridge box full, was as brave a man as ever met an enemy on any field of battle in any country, or in any age" (artist Walton Taber; *Histories of the Several Regiments and Battalions from North Carolina, in the Great War 1861–1865*, vol. 3).

The readers of this story will follow the 25th Regiment N.C. through the entire Civil War drama and find descriptions or explanations of most of the major actions in which it engaged. In addition, I have tried to offer a narrative account of the war's progression to set the backdrop for the regiment's movements and actions and to offer insight into their significance. Attentive readers will learn, as I did, that the Civil War was not a pretty or glorious affair as is sometimes depicted or envisioned. Zealous soldiers marching off from their mountain communities soon lost the infectious secession fervor that had led them to war. The horrors of the battlefields, deprivations of trench warfare, and extreme suffering on the home front were too much for many of the mountain boys to bear. As a result, they fled from the army in droves, especially during the last year of the war; and it will be shown that approximately one in every five of the men who signed on with the 25th Regiment N.C. deserted or "went over to the enemy." However, we should not be too harsh or hasty in our judgments or conclusions about ancestors who resorted to this desperate act of disloyalty. Unpaid, unshod, and barely fed soldiers of the 25th N.C. confronted powerful forces other than the Yankee enemy which drove their anguished decisions so many years ago. And thoughtful readers will discern these various motive influences and likely conclude that those mountain boys were, after all, only human.

This book has been written to appeal primarily to general readers as opposed to Civil War scholars, although the latter will surely find it interesting and enlightening. The methodology undertaken to compile the tale of the exploits of the 25th North Carolina during the Civil War was neither complicated nor pretentious. It simply involved creating a skeletal structure from Lt. Garland Ferguson's historical account of the regiment's record reinforced with other dates, movements and activities taken from a synopsis of the 25th North Carolina's service contained in *North Carolina Troops, 1861–1865, A Roster*, vol. 7, *Infantry*. Using this as a framework, other information and details were overlaid and melded together in such a manner as to consolidate and add depth to the overall story. Major sources used to provide this supplemental material included the *Official Records of the Union and Confederate Armies*; Clayton Marlow's biography *Matt W. Ransom: Confederate General from North Carolina;* James McPherson's *Battle Cry of Freedom;* Shelby Foote's 3-volume treasure, *The Civil War, A Narrative;* Douglas Southall Freeman's marvelous study of the Army of Northern Virginia, *Lee's Lieutenants;* and Inscoe and McKinney's groundbreaking work, *The Heart of Confederate Appalachia: Western North Carolina in the Civil War.*

Final touches and flourishes were supported with facts and anecdotal information from various primary source accounts such as Mary Boykin Chesnut's *A Diary from Dixie* and personal correspondence obtained from library special collections. The *Special Collections — Civil War Letters* retained at Western Carolina University's Hunter Library and a collection titled *Southern Historical Collection: Documenting the American South* archived at the University of North Carolina's Wilson Library held tantalizing wartime letters from soldiers of the 25th Regiment N.C. and their families. These proved to be extremely insightful and useful for illustrating and adding a human perspective to this story.

A personal touch will be found in the final chapter of this work, where biographical sketches of Colonel Henry Middleton Rutledge, the commander of the 25th N.C., and Lt. William Hargrove are presented. These two young men from entirely different walks of life joined up to fight for the Confederacy at the beginning of the war and saw it through to the end. Their life accounts offer an interesting contrast between the colonel's privileged birthright in South Carolina's upper-crust plantation society and Lt. Hargrove's rural farming heritage founded in the midst of the Blue Ridge Mountains of Haywood County, North Carolina. And it is hoped that the reader will gain an appreciation for the challenges faced by these two stalwart Rebel soldiers at the end of the war as they each struggled to shrug off the scars and memories of the battlefields and forge new lives for themselves during the South's difficult reconstruction years.

Lastly, but perhaps most importantly, a complete roster of the names of all the soldiers who served with the 25th Regiment N.C. is appended at the end of this book. The roster information is taken directly from the seventh volume of *North Carolina Troops, 1861–1865: A Roster*, published by the North Carolina Division (now Office) of Archives and History in 1979. The data from that work has been paraphrased and reformatted with permission. For more detailed information about each soldier, you may obtain a copy of the entire book at *http://nc-historical-publications.stores.yahoo.net/125.html.*

Ultimately, my objective has been to illuminate the path blazed by the 25th Regiment N.C. through the Civil War. It is my genuine desire that the readers who retrace the steps of the mountain boys will become more aware of the considerable contributions made by their service to the Confederacy to defend the mountain homeland. And I hope that modern-day sojourners who take this journey will gain a greater appreciation of the hardships endured and sacrifices made by a courageous band of Rebels from the Land of the Sky.

1

FLAMES OF SECESSION

News of General Pierre Beauregard's attack on Charleston's Fort Sumter in April 1861 flashed across telegraph lines to nervous operators quickly scrawling messages and feeding them to an anxious public. Newspapers throughout the nation seemingly recounted every cannon shot from the South Carolina harbor's batteries and recorded the utterances of public officials and even lovely Southern belles witness to the occasion. Eventually word penetrated into the remoteness of western North Carolina's mountains and reached the small hamlets and rural settlements like Forks of Pigeon in Haywood County, where the Pigeon River boldly courses through a beautiful valley of the same name.

William Hargrove of that settlement would have learned that the Confederate cannon barrage reduced the fort's thick brick ramparts to rubble in a matter of only a couple of days, forcing the surrender of the Union troops garrisoned there. He would likely have considered this stunning news in a much different light than did most Charlestonians, Southern fire-eater politicians, and the landed gentry of the South whose way of life and economic survival were founded on the backs of subjugated men and women. Parades, hundred-gun salutes and spontaneous celebrations followed the fall of Ft. Sumter in quarters throughout the "land of Dixie" where slavery was an institution and all rights associated with owning and controlling human black beings were revered. And in all of those states, including North Carolina and the border slave states such as Virginia that had yet to secede from the United States of America, the Confederate Stars and Bars were run up at public buildings.

However, in many sections of North Carolina, and especially in the western mountains region, the response was much more subdued from a population not totally convinced that the Union must tear itself apart. Young William Hargrove and his neighbors surely deliberated and debated the significance of this historic incident at popular gathering places such as Cathey's store and nearby gristmill. As in the other western counties and the entire state, the feelings of the people in rural Haywood County were mixed regarding the secession issue.

North Carolina, one of the original thirteen colonies, remained reluctant to sever ties with an American republic whose democratic principles and form of government "the Old North State" had helped to forge. Hopeful of acts or overtones of reconciliation from the northern states, it continued to shirk the radical action of secession by choosing not to follow the lead of Deep South states such as South Carolina, Mississippi, Alabama, Georgia, Florida and Louisiana. Several months before the Fort Sumter cannonade, these cotton, rice and sugar-producing states, whose societies and economies were wholly dependent on slave

Bombardment of Fort Sumter, April 1861 (*Harper's Weekly*).

labor, had proudly and recklessly declared their independence from the Union. In Appalachian North Carolina, leaders such as Congressman Zebulon Vance from Buncombe County cautioned against such precipitous action. On his tours of the hill country during this fervid period, Vance reassured the local constituents: "We have everything to gain and nothing on earth to lose by delay, but by too hasty action we may take a fatal step we can never retrace — may lose a heritage we can never recover."[1]

Unionist loyalties pervaded the North Carolina mountains during this time frame, especially in Madison County, which shared a border with the notoriously loyal Union region of east Tennessee. This pro–Union sentiment is exemplified in the contents of a letter drafted by a Madison County resident and mailed to Mr. Balis M. Edney of Henderson County, a prominent attorney and wealthy landowner who later commanded Company A of the 25th Regiment N.C.:

> Ivy Bend, Madison Co., NC, Jan 28, 1861
> Dear Sir:
>> It is with pleasure & regret that I take this opportunity to drop you a line.
>> In the first place I am glad to let you no that the majority of our people in this country is for the union. All the countys west of the Blue Ridge is union by a large majority & my opinion is the state is from the part information that I can gether, it is set down that North Carolina is ceessian. But if it is left to the people to say, they will say diferent demagogs is a trying to so the seed of discord thruout this country. But they have faild as yet....[2]

The author of this letter was adamant when informing Mr. Edney that all of the "countys west of the Blue Ridge" were Union. Evidently the gentleman had a secure grip on the political pulse in the mountains and was convinced that the demagogs were trying to "so" the seeds of discord throughout the country. As a matter of fact, in certain sections where locals felt intimidated and even threatened by northern political antics, the seeds of discord referred to in the letter had begun to germinate and sprout.

Sympathies for the rebellious states were nourished and strengthened by Southern ultra-secessionists such as Thomas Clingman from Asheville, for many years the area's representative to Congress and at the time a senator in that august body. His inflammatory oratories stoked the smoldering fires for independence lingering in the hearts of some mountaineers and, indeed, sowed the seeds of discord. "It is not that a dangerous man has been elected to the Presidency of the United States," he said of Abraham Lincoln. "I assert that the President-elect has been elected because he was known to be a dangerous man.... [H]e declares that it is the purpose of the North to make war upon my section until its social system is destroyed, and for that he was taken up and elected. It is that great, remarkable and dangerous fact that has filled my section with alarm and dread for the future."3

Zebulon Vance was a Congressman from Asheville, North Carolina, before the Civil War and governor of North Carolina during the war. He strove diligently, but in vain, to keep his native state from heeding the secession calls of Southern fire-eater politicians. This photograph was taken in 1862 on the occasion of his inauguration as governor (North Carolina Department of Archives and History, Raleigh).

Most of the inhabitants of western North Carolina's mountains at that time grew corn and wheat crops and subsisted on small farms and plots of land. Because there were very few slave owners, no real motive existed to support the advocates of slavery rights. The stubborn mountaineers were an independent lot — clannish and tending to mind their own business. Secluded in the deep mountain hollows and valleys, they possessed a mentality more respectful of a man's independence and individual rights than the authority of government and law enforcement, which was of little use to some.

Yet, many of these descendants of Scots-Irish, German and English pioneers, who began settling in the area after the Revolutionary War, were disgusted by the rhetoric and demands of Northern coalitions of abolitionists, Black Republicans and Copperheads. The highlanders figured that these parties had no right, nor did the federal government for that matter, to dictate what property a man might possess, be it corn liquor, real property or human contraband. Throughout western North Carolina there were undoubtedly those whose blood ran hot for secession and others who were just as adamant for the Union and believed that the United States should not or could not be constitutionally dissolved. But it seems likely that the majority of the population hemmed within the mountain walls were fence sitters, quietly

Acts of secession by the Southern states were attended with celebrations such as this one in Savannah, Georgia (Library of Congress).

minding their own business and waiting for future events to play out. Though they certainly entertained the notions espoused by the likes of Congressman Vance or Senator Clingman, these independent mountain people would make their minds up in their own good time.

In February of 1861, prior to the eruption at Fort Sumter, Joseph Cathey of Haywood County had reached no hard decisions of his own in regard to secession. A prominent businessman and leader in his county and the Forks of Pigeon community where he resided, Cathey waited to learn the course on which newly elected President Abraham Lincoln would steer the country. In the letter below, Cathey wrote to a local newspaper editor, the Reverend Siler, to clarify his position on secession:

> Hominy Creek N.C. Feb. 22nd 1861
> Rev. L.F. Siler
>
> Dear sir
>
> In the last No. of your paper I see published the proceedings of a meeting held at Waynesville on the 8th inst. as communicated to you In which I am made to say that I was in favor of N.C. sesceding with a view to reconstruction &c. I did say I was identified with the South as stated in the communication, and I further said that N.C. would not have her convention in session until after Lincoln would be in office, and would have indicated his policy, which if it should be to Carry out the Chicago platform, and we should fail to get an ajustment on the Crittenden plan, or the Virginia plan, or otherwise, then I thought Virginia and all the Border slave states would go out of the union, and I would then be for N.C. going out as stated in the Communication you published....[4]

Cathey points out in the letter that the comments he made at an earlier meeting in Waynesville on February 8, 1861, regarding his position on secession were misrepresented in the

Left: Jefferson Davis was elected as the first president of the Confederate States of America and served in that capacity through the entire Civil War (Library of Congress). *Right:* Abraham Lincoln, president of the United States during the Civil War, called for troops after the fall of Fort Sumter to put down the southern insurrection (Library of Congress).

Reverend Siler's paper. Cathey states that he is not in favor of secession at the time but he identifies himself with the South. He advocates that North Carolina should not have a secession convention until after President-Elect Lincoln takes office and clearly indicates his policies. Senator John J. Crittenden's proposed compromise to reinstate the 36° 30' demarcation line of latitude for the limits of slavery was one of the pivotal issues important to Cathey. Another was whether or not Lincoln would begin instituting the planks of his Republican Party's "Chicago Platform." It is reasonable to believe that many other western North Carolinians were of the same mind as Cathey, a man they looked up to and respected. They were on the fence, so to speak, and the swing in balance between pro–Union sentiment and a thirst for secession seemed to hinge on the imminent actions of the soon-to-be inaugurated Abraham Lincoln.

For those Southern states, including North Carolina, that still claimed allegiance to the Union, the cannon fire at Ft. Sumter did not set alight the tinder that would kindle the flames of secession. That spark was effectively struck by President Lincoln. On April 15, 1861, in response to the blatant act of Southern defiance manifested at Ft. Sumter, the president issued a proclamation calling for 75,000 militiamen to be enlisted into national service for ninety days to put down an insurrection "too powerful to be suppressed by the ordinary course of judicial proceedings."[5] All across the South, people were outraged at this aggressive response by the president, and the resulting groundswell reaction against his policy and the Union was immediate. James Gentry, an Ashe County merchant, had resisted the fire-eaters' persuasions and, until Lincoln's bellicose action, had patiently waited for events to unfold. At this point, however, he was able to view the matter much more clearly. "We are now all for an inde-

Confederate soldiers on the move (*The Illustrated Confederate Reader* by Rod Gragg).

pendent Confederacy," he wrote to his father-in-law. "We watch and wait men are out now. We have great [sic] reasons to fall out with Lincoln than you secessionists. While we are watching & waiting he was undermining for our subjugation, but now we are for separation and against all sorts of compromise. Death or victory is our motto."[6]

The governor of Kentucky swiftly discharged a letter to Washington, D.C., stating that Kentucky "will furnish no troops for the wicked purpose of subduing her sister Southern States."[7] A bitter unionist from North Carolina wrote that "the Union sentiment [in North Carolina] was largely in the ascendant and gaining strength until Lincoln prostrated us. He could have adopted no policy so effectual to destroy the Union."[8] Before April closed, Virginia and Arkansas quickly convened assemblies where ordinances of secession were drafted and passed. Likewise, Tennessee and North Carolina held secession conventions in May and voted to declare independence from the Union. A participant at North Carolina's convention wrote, "This furor, this moral epidemic, swept over the country like a tempest, before which the entire population seemed to succumb."[9]

These hurried and fateful decisions cleaved the Union in the spring of 1861. Partisans of neither side in those early excited days could have foreseen the horrific and tortuous path that lay ahead for the stumbling and divided country. Nor could they have predicted a war with such tragic consequences—the repercussions of which would endure and prostrate the South long after the War for southern independence was ended.

2

FARMERS JOIN THE REBELLION

Even before North Carolina voted for secession, the legislature authorized Governor John W. Ellis to raise and organize ten regiments of state troops in anticipation of a war that must soon be fought against President Lincoln's trespassers. Convention delegates hurriedly made it official that North Carolina would join the Confederate States of America and dissolved all formal relationships with the United States government. Thereafter, volunteer regiments began forming as confidence and ardor abounded throughout the Confederate States and expectations grew higher for a brief fight and brilliant victory — one that most certainly would result in glory and independence from the tyrannical Northerners.

Popular opinion in those early jubilant days was reflected in a boast that "one Confederate soldier could whip ten Yankees." This estimation was bandied about sufficiently to become a truism to many and helped the Southerners rationalize their disadvantage in resources, including the great disparity in available manpower between the North and the South. North Carolinian Edmund W. Jones was one of the early enlistees responding to Governor Ellis' summons for troops and wrote, "I have not brought myself to believe that there will be much fighting. The courage of the North will evaporate after awhile, and the southern states permitted to go in peace."[1] The mountaineer Carolinians were certainly swallowed up by this prewar euphoria as well. Prideful of their beautiful mountain country and with a keen sense of patriotism for their state, many of the mountain men and boys were anxious to defend their homeland and families. And those not tainted with the fervor soon got caught up anyway in society's powerful political currents and were swept away to war along with the rest. When the governor's call for volunteers reached Haywood and the surrounding mountain counties, farmers, their sons, and other young men and boys were ready. In droves they shucked their hoes and ploughs and poured out of the valleys and off the ridges to join up with their neighbors for the fight.

In May 1861 these men began mustering and forming themselves into local militia companies of approximately 100 or more troops each. Expecting a war of short duration and little fighting, all those highlanders volunteered their services for twelve months, ample time in their minds to dispatch Lincoln's invaders back to their own land. Lt. Garland S. Ferguson, who penned a history of the 25th Regiment N.C. in 1901, wrote of the situation: "There were few slave owners, 90 per cent of the men [being] farmers or farmer's sons, and fully 80 per cent were homeowners. The majority of the men composing the regiment had been Union men until President Lincoln's Proclamation."

Men of stature in the communities and those with known high intellect and integrity were elected captains to lead the military units. West of the Blue Ridge, ten companies of volunteers were organized. Hailing from nine western North Carolina counties and the northern region of Georgia, these ten companies were as follows:

Company	Location	Captain
Company A	Henderson County	Balis M. Edney
Company B	Jackson County	Thaddeus D. Bryson
Company C	Haywood County	Samuel C. Bryson
Company D	Cherokee County	John W. Francis
Company E	Transylvania County	Francis W. Johnstone
Company F	Haywood County	Thomas Isaac Lenoir
Company G	Georgia; Clay/Macon/Cherokee counties	William S. Grady
Company H	Buncombe/Henderson counties	Frederick R. Blake
Company I	Buncombe County	George W. Howell
Company K	Buncombe County	Charles M. Roberts

John W. Moore records in his *Roster of North Carolina Troops in the War Between the States* the names of some 1,673 men that appeared on the rolls and muster sheets of these companies during the Civil War. Moore's work reveals that Appalachian highlanders almost exclusively comprised this population.[2] Approximately 21 percent of the mountaineers were of Buncombe County origin, while troop contributions from Haywood and Henderson counties amounted to about 18 percent each. Jackson, Cherokee, and Transylvania counties each furnished about 10 percent of the total number of soldiers making up the ten companies. And the counties of Clay, Macon and Madison combined to supply 3 percent of the soldiers. Interestingly, the state of Georgia added roughly 8 percent of the troops. Over the years, historians have drawn scant attention to the fact that Georgia made the significant contribution of some 136 men to the ranks of the companies which would eventually unite to form the 25th Regiment N.C.—a reality which the data in Moore's *Roster* clearly illuminates.

One Confederate is equal of ten Yankees! (artist: David Silvette; courtesy Freeman-Victorius Framing Shop, Charlottesville, Virginia).

From May until July of 1861 the rolls of the different companies were quickly filled and the volunteers began gathering and learning the fundamentals of military drill and organized command. Each company elected its own officers by a democratic process, and the fledgling soldiers slowly learned to demonstrate deference and obedience to the authority of these leaders. At times this was certainly difficult to do, especially when the orders were being barked by one's own brother or best friend, or possibly a neighbor harboring a long-pent-up grudge.

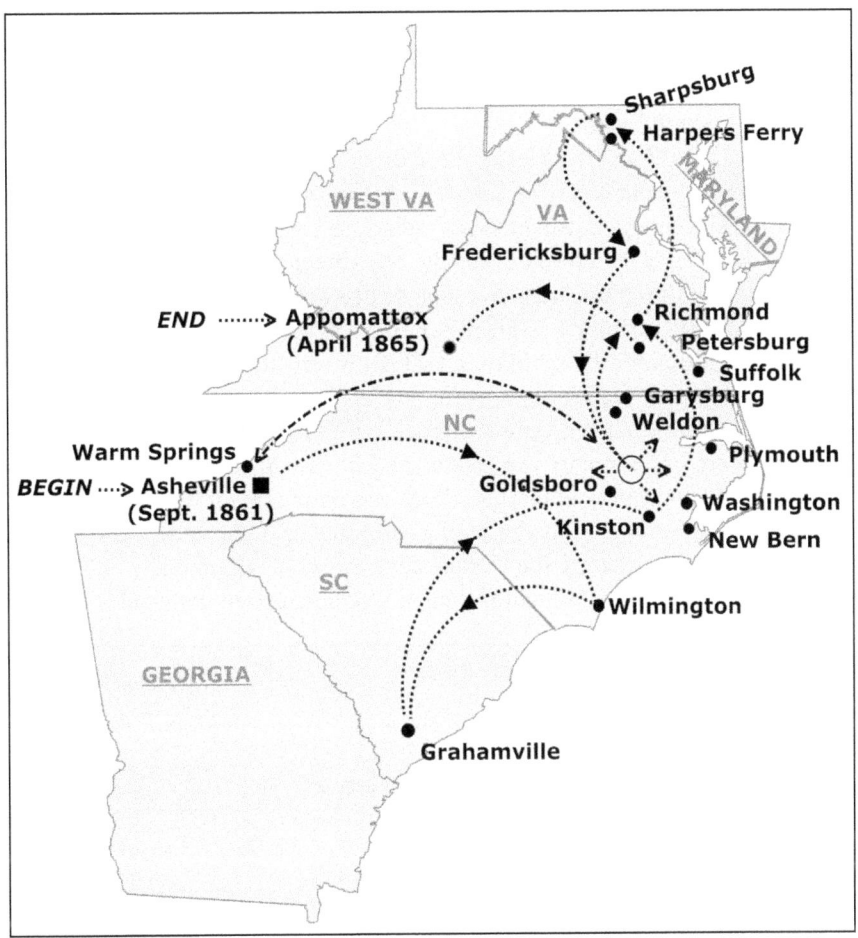

The journey of the 25th Regiment N.C. through the Civil War (Carroll Jones).

The volunteer companies were celebrated and honored in their local communities, and the soldiers earned the respect and appreciation of their friends, neighbors and citizens. Though definitely proud of their passionate commitment, these men likely held cloudy visions of what lay ahead and surely were apprehensive about their prospects. Once the requisite manpower levels were achieved in the individual companies and the captains judged the boys to be ready, the raw recruits marched off en masse to an unknown destiny from small rural crossroads and towns filled with cheering crowds of friends, speech-making politicos, and proud families. They climbed over mountains, forded streams and trod the turnpikes to Asheville, the largest town in the North Carolina highlands. At the Confederate Camp Patton (located immediately east of Charlotte Street with Chestnut Street passing east-west through it)[3] and Camp Clingman, the ten mountain volunteer companies assembled and began to organize. "As each successive company took its position in camp the guard line was extended and the civilian began to do duty and learn the step and maneuvers of the soldier."[4]

Elsewhere across the Union and the Confederate States of America, other citizens were also responding quickly to the nation-changing events and organizing for war. Late in July 1861 initial military movements and posturing by the North and the South had brought two large armies together in northern Virginia near Washington, D.C. In the vicinity of a railroad junction known as Manassas, along Bull Run Creek, the first battle of Bull Run was fought on July 21, 1861. Though evenly fought throughout most of the day, the clash ended in a rout of the Northern army by the Confederate forces under the command of generals Pierre G.T. Beauregard and Joseph Johnston.

This first great conflict of the war would serve to inspire the South and instill in its people an even higher degree of confidence, even certainty, that their independence could soon be won. On the Northern side, the military setback sent shock waves throughout the land and prompted President Lincoln to call for the recruitment of more troops. He also sought a new commander for the Union army and soon settled on the young general George McClellan. A confident McClellan quickly assumed command of the Army of the Potomac and would spend the coming nine months rebuilding that army and preparing it for the next major conflict in the eastern war theatre.

When details of the Bull Run victory reached Camp Patton in Asheville, the officers and men encamped there undoubtedly were elated and filled with some degree of gratification. After all, this great victory proved that the North was no match for the boys in gray and further inspired them to hurry their preparations and training. Otherwise, they just might not get a chance at the Yankees before the Union called the whole thing off.

By the middle of August 1861, all of the ten aforementioned companies had arrived in

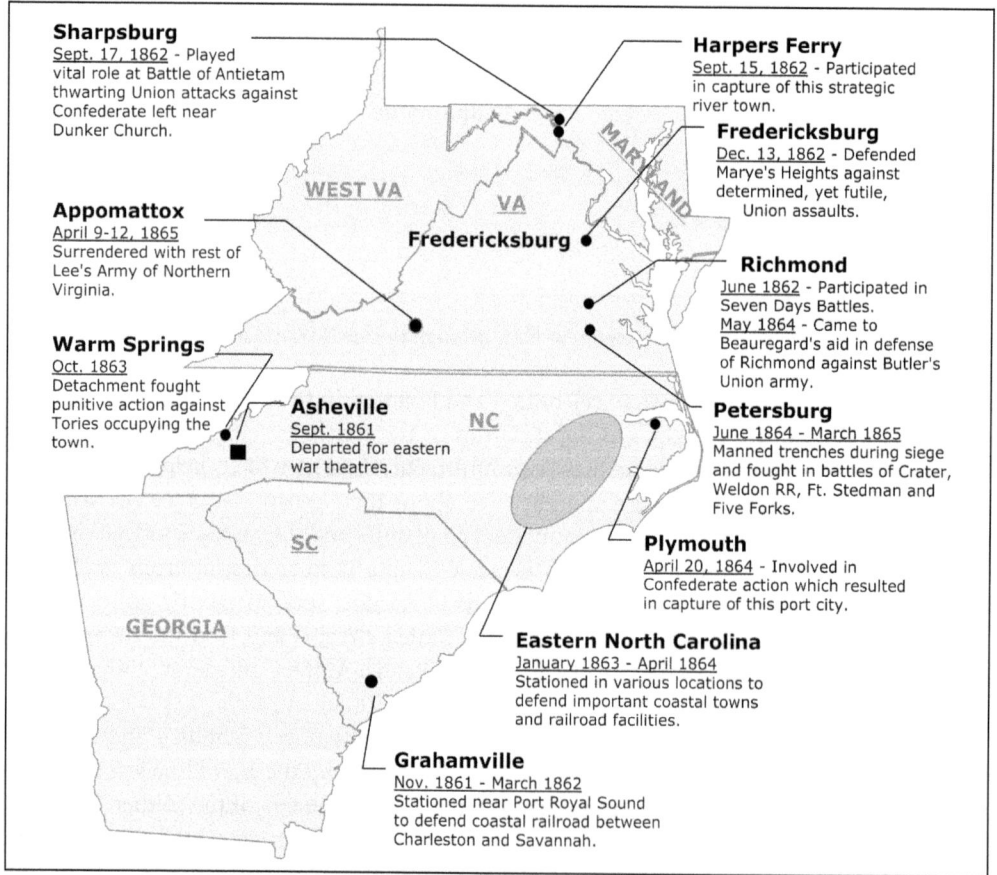

Major theaters of operation where the 25th Regiment N.C. fought and served during the Civil War (Carroll Jones).

Left: Lieutenant Garland Sevier Ferguson was from Waynesville, North Carolina, and at age 18 enlisted in Company F of the 25th Regiment N.C. He served gallantly through the entire war and was wounded three times. In 1901 Judge Ferguson penned a history of the regiment (North Carolina Department of Archives and History, Raleigh). *Right:* Thomas L. Clingman, a lawyer, congressman, and secessionist from Asheville, North Carolina, was elected as the first colonel of the 25th Regiment N.C. He was later promoted to brigadier general (Library of Congress).

camp and were assimilated into a nascent military regiment. The collection of companies was given the designation of 15th Volunteers, North Carolina, but soon would be appended to the Confederate States of America as the 25th Regiment N.C. Infantry Troops. Regimental field officers were elected by a vote of the commissioned company officers, and the staff was appointed by the new colonel. The first Field and Staff appointed to command the 25th Regiment N.C. is given below.

Colonel	Thomas L. Clingman
Lieutenant Colonel	St. Clair Dearing
Major	Henry M. Rutledge
Adjutant	Wesley N. Freeman
Quartermaster	William H. Bryson
Commissary	John W. Walker
Surgeon	Dr. Solomon S. Satchwell
Asst. Surgeon	Dr. George W. Fletcher
Sergeant Major	James C.L. Gudger
Quartermaster Sergeant	Clinton A. Jones
Commissary Sergeant	Julius M. Young
Drum Major	Peter M. Rich

The Honorable Thomas Clingman, a politician and statesman and longtime resident of Asheville, was elected colonel of the regiment. He had been one of the first Southern politicians to voice a strong secession stand in Congress and had led the forces for independence in the western Carolina mountains. Prior to the war, Colonel Clingman's political pursuits included several terms representing North Carolina in the United States House of Representatives and United States Senate. Interestingly, Senator Clingman's noteworthy career in politics did not escape controversy in the public arena. It seems that he became embroiled in a disagreement with William Yancey, another prominent politician from Alabama, which eventually culminated in an affair of honor, or a duel. Obviously, Clingman lived beyond the incident, as did the other duelist. Apparently "satisfaction of honor" was restored to both gentlemen and the business concluded before the authorities arrived on the scene.

In another instance, the "Prince of Politicians," as Clingman was referred to, became entangled in a bitter dispute with Dr. Elisha Mitchell regarding their competing claims of being the first to measure the altitude of the highest mountain in the East. That mountain, which would later be named for Dr. Mitchell, claimed the life of the renowned scientist when he fell to his death attempting to verify his measurements. Clingman, who was a scientist in his own right, surveyed and measured many mountains in western North Carolina and one still bears his name. Clingman's Dome rises high in the sky along the western border of the state.

Although not a professional soldier, Clingman, who had served as an aide at the Battle of Bull Run, possessed leadership skills and charisma sufficiently impressive to persuade fellow company officers to vote in his favor to lead the regiment. However, the officers of the ten companies recognized the need for military training and experience in the regimental command structure. To achieve that leadership balance, they elected St. Clair Dearing as their lieutenant colonel, second in command to Colonel Clingman. Prior to the war, Lieutenant Colonel Dearing was a regular officer in the U.S. Army. At the outset of hostilities, he resigned his commission to fight and defend his native state of North Carolina. Henry Middleton Rutledge, a young man born to wealth and privilege in the South Carolina low country and a seasonal resident of Flat Rock in Henderson County, North Carolina, was elected major. His youthful energy, loyalty and fearlessness in the face of the enemy would serve the regiment well in the horrific battles to come.

A historical account of the regiment written long after the war by Lt. Garland S. Ferguson of Company F described how the new officers forged the raw companies of mountaineers into a regiment to be reckoned with: "Under the mild discipline of the Colonel and skillful training and accurate drill of the Lieutenant Colonel and Major, the regiment was soon thoroughly drilled and disciplined, on duty."[5] It is noteworthy that Lt. Ferguson added the qualifying words "on duty" to the record. His clarification offers a hint that the discipline of the soldiers may not have extended to the off-duty hours spent in camp. The veracity of this is indeed revealed in another part of the lieutenant's historical record, where he states, "The men had been accustomed to independence of thought and freedom and had elected for their company officers their neighbors and companions and had no idea of giving up more of their personal liberty than should be necessary to make them effective soldiers—obedient on duty, independent off."

Obedient on duty and independent off duty, the soldiers worked hard at camps Patton and Clingman in nervous anticipation of exciting action and events yet to unfold. Soon they were ready to go to war, and on September 18, 1861, Colonel Clingman gave orders to strike camp. The 25th Regiment N.C. packed up and marched off from Asheville toward a rising sun and a cloud of uncertainty.

3

THE FABRIC OF
THE 25TH REGIMENT N.C.

During the spring and summer of 1861, farmers, farmers' sons and a scattering of men from other professions swarmed into communities and towns spread across western North Carolina to volunteer their services to the State of North Carolina. Although farming was certainly the occupational pursuit of most of the volunteers who eventually formed the 25th Regiment N.C., the Confederate service records indicate that highlanders from all walks of life enlisted in those early fervent days. Their occupations were registered as farmer, miner, merchant, lime burner, wagoner, millwright, carpenter, mechanic, doctor, printer, laborer, musician, schoolboy, blacksmith, minister, and postmaster. All were motivated by an overwhelming sense of responsibility and urgency to defend their homeland from invasion and secure certain of their unalienable rights which they perceived threatened.

These mountaineers—not yet soldiers—joined with neighbors and kin to form volunteer companies of 100 or more troops each. At camps Patton and Clingman in Asheville, ten of these companies were melded into a cohesive military unit that soon became identified as the Confederate 25th Regiment N.C. Infantry Troops. Later, after the Conscription Act of 1862 was enacted by the Confederate congress, more mountain men either voluntarily signed up with the 25th Regiment or were impressed and sent to the front by Confederate authorities to serve in one of the regiment's various companies.

The small individual companies were the fabric from which the Confederate army was formed and facilitated both the command and mobility of the regiments, brigades, divisions and great armies that were assembled. Commanders realized the importance of the company organization, which allowed friends, neighbors, countrymen and kindred to remain united in the same military outfit. In this way, the soldiers were able to support and encourage one another in the camps and on the march. In battle they could bravely charge side by side against enemy positions or come to the aid of brethren. There was, of course, the realization that any signs or acts hinting of a deficiency in courage would quickly reach the families and neighbors back home. However, a soldier's morale and courage were innately enhanced and fears and impulses of cowardice more easily overcome upon seeing kinsmen and friends face down the terrors and horrors of war. Thus, the individual companies gained their strength from such personal relationships and interactions and were the resilient and sturdy fabric from which the 25th Regiment N.C. was fashioned.

The Companies of the 25th Regiment N.C.

As previously mentioned, the 25th Regiment N.C. Troops was comprised predominantly of men from the westernmost counties of North Carolina. The following graph and table depict the county origins of the troops that served with the regiment throughout the Civil War, as well as the troop contribution levels of the various counties and states. As can be seen, a majority of the soldiers hailed from the western North Carolina counties of Buncombe, Haywood and Henderson. The men from these three counties comprised approximately 57 percent of the entire regiment. The counties of Jackson, Cherokee and Transylvania were roughly equal contributors at a lower tier level, with their combined total amounting to slightly more than 28 percent of the regiment's soldiers. Clay, Macon and Madison counties supplied 3 percent of the forces that served during the war with the 25th Regiment N.C.

Disputing the notion that the 25th Regiment N.C. was entirely a western North Carolina military unit are the 136 men from north Georgia and the few troops that hailed from South Carolina, Tennessee and Virginia who fought with the North Carolina highlanders. Many of the early Georgia volunteers made their way to Macon County in July 1861, where they enlisted and formed Company G — the Highland Guards. Following passage in the Confederate congress of the highly unpopular Conscription Law in April 1862, more Georgians enlisted in the Confederate army at Athens and made the long trip to eastern North Carolina, where they were mustered into the 25th N.C. Over the years, historians have glossed over the important contributions that the state of Georgia made to bolster the fighting strength of the 25th Regiment N.C.

The information that follows offers additional details and insight into the ten mountain companies from which the 25th Regiment N.C. was created. This data was extracted from John W. Moore's *Roster of North Carolina Troops* published in 1882 by act of the North Carolina General Assembly.[1] The extant Confederate records from which Moore compiled his work were incomplete and inadequate (and still are) and contained significant gaps, especially those for the last one and one-half years of the war. This lapse is not surprising considering that the Confederate war department clerks were yanked

Rebs (Library of Congress; artist Alfred Rudolf Waud).

3. The Fabric of the 25th Regiment N.C.

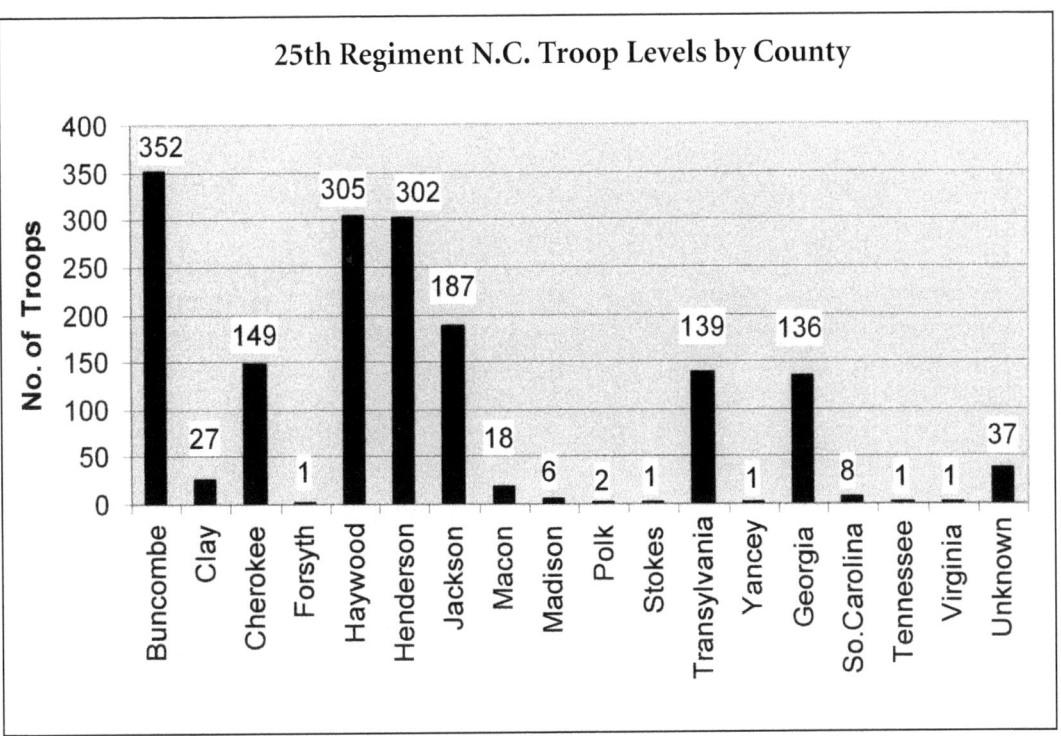

25th Regiment N.C. Troop Levels

County/State	Company										Regiment Total
	A	B	C	D	E	F	G	H	I	K	
Bumcombe	7				3	5		48	158	131	352
Clay							27				27
Cherokee				147	1		1				149
Forsyth	1										1
Haywood			184		1	119	1				305
Henderson	170		2		14			112		4	302
Jackson		183	1			1	1		1		187
Macon		3		4			10		1		18
Madison					2					4	6
Polk					2						2
Stokes				1							1
Transylvania	2				137						139
Yancey									1		1
Georgia				1	1		133		1		136
South Carolina					1		7				8
Tennessee	1										1
Virginia				1							1
Unknown		2		4	5	12	10	2	2		37
Total	181	188	188	157	167	137	190	162	163	140	1673

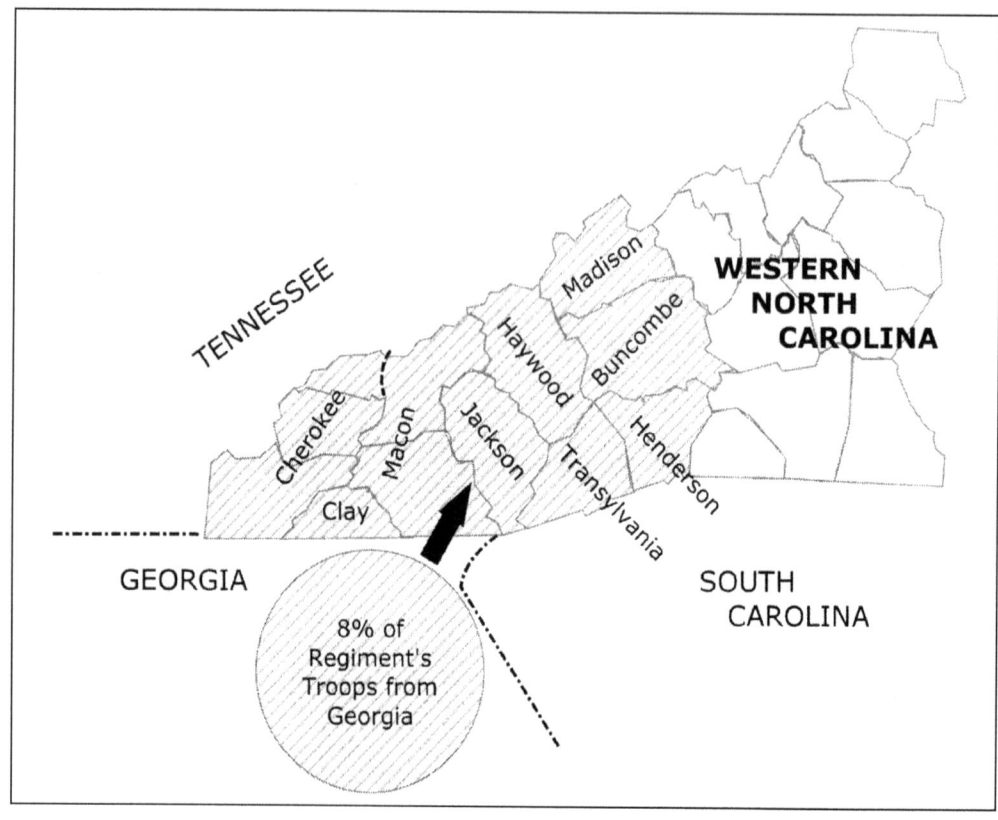

Origins of 25th Regiment N.C. Troops (Carroll Jones).

from their desks and sent out to man Richmond's defensive fortifications, alongside troops from the 25th Regiment N.C., and to defend the Confederate capital. An effort has been made to adjust or correct apparent errors in the data Moore assembled with information recorded by the regimental historian, Garland Ferguson, and with that contained in the more recent publication *North Carolina Troops, 1861–1865, a Roster,* vol. 7, *Infantry.*[2]

Company A — Edney Greys

The company known as the *Edney Greys* was raised in Henderson County and was enlisted at Edneyville on May 15, 1861. It was then mustered into state service and assigned to the 25th Regiment N.C. as Company A. The men of this company came from the counties listed below.

Company A — County Makeup

County	No. of Troops	% of Company
Henderson	170	94.0
Buncombe	7	4.0
Transylvania	2	1.0
Forsyth	1	0.5
Tennessee	1	0.5
Total	181	100.0

As can be seen, Company A was formed almost exclusively from Henderson County troops; throughout the war, approximately 181 soldiers were assigned to its command. Of the unit's soldiers, approximately 94 percent were Henderson County residents and 4 percent were out of Buncombe County. All of the following commissioned officers, with the exception of John B. Edney, were listed as Henderson County residents:

Captains

Edney, Baylis M.	Elected captain on May 15, 1861; declined to stand for reelection and resigned about May 10, 1862.
Love, Matthew N.	Elected 1st lt. on May 15, 1861; elected captain on April 30, 1862; wounded at Malvern Hill and Fredericksburg; promoted to major on Nov. 5, 1864; later promoted to lieutenant colonel; paroled at Appomattox on April 9, 1865.
Plumblee, Johns S.	Elected 1st lt. on April 30, 1862; elected captain on Nov. 9, 1864; killed at Five Forks on April 1, 1865.

Lieutenants

Cooper, Andrew	Elected 3rd lt. on April 30, 1862; died at Petersburg about Aug. 9, 1862.
Edney, John B.	Elected 3rd lt. in Dec. 1862; paroled at Appomattox on April 9, 1865 (was from Buncombe County).
Edney, John C.	Elected 3rd lt. on May 15, 1861; defeated for reelection on April 30, 1862.
Freeman, Joseph H.	Elected 2nd lt. on May 15, 1861; defeated for reelection on April 30, 1862.
Maxwell, Andrew C.	Elected 3rd lt. on Aug. 14, 1862; court-martialed and cashiered on Nov. 12, 1862.
Poor, Julius A.	Elected 2nd lt. on April 30, 1862.

Company B — Jackson Guards

This company, known as the *Jackson Guards*, was raised in Jackson County and was enlisted at Webster on May 30, 1861. It was then mustered into state service and assigned to the 25th Regiment N.C. as Company B. The men of this company came from the counties listed below.

Company B — County Makeup

County	No. of Troops	% of Company
Jackson	183	97.0
Macon	3	2.0
Unknown	2	1.0
Total	188	100.0

Note that of the total of 188 soldiers listed on the regimental rolls who served with Company B during the war, 97 percent were Jackson County residents. All of the commissioned officers were Jackson County natives or were living there at the time of their enlistment. These officers are listed below.

Captains

Bryson, Thaddeus D.	Elected captain on May 30, 1861; declined to stand for reelection and discharged on April 30, 1862.

Boone, Harlen A.	Elected 2nd lt. on June 7, 1861; elected captain on April 28, 1862; present and accounted for until June 1863, when reported absent on detached service; resigned on July 23, 1864, probably due to poor health.
Rogers, David	Elected 1st lt. on April 28, 1862; elected captain in March–Dec. 1864; wounded at Ft. Stedman and later captured at hospital.

Lieutenants

Dillard, Lynch M.	Elected 1st lt. on May 30, 1861; resigned Feb. 14, 1862.
Fisher, Lucius F.	Elected 3rd lt. on May 30, 1861; defeated for reelection on April 28, 1862.
Long, Samuel M.	Elected 3rd lt. on July 26, 1862; killed at Fredericksburg on Dec. 13, 1862.
Moss, William W.	Elected 3rd lt. on April 28, 1862; deserted June 30, 1864, and went over to enemy about April 1, 1865; took Oath of Allegiance at Knoxville, Tennessee.
Norton, David	Elected 3rd lt. on Dec. 29, 1862; resigned on Jan. 3, 1865; other records indicate he was dropped from rolls for desertion on Feb. 12, 1865.
Rice, Isaac	Elected 1st lt. on March 6, 1862; defeated for reelection about April 28, 1862.
Shelton, Samuel P.C.	Elected 2nd lt. on April 28, 1862; resigned on July 16, 1862, with no reason given.

Company C — Haywood Invincibles

Company C, known as the *Haywood Invincibles*, was raised in Haywood County and was enlisted at Waynesville on May 31, 1861. It was then mustered into state service and assigned to the 25th Regiment N.C. as Company C. The men of this company came from the counties listed below.

Company C — County Makeup

County	No. of Troops	% of Company
Haywood	184	98.0
Henderson	2	1.0
Jackson	1	0.5
Virginia	1	0.5
Total	188	100.0

As can be seen, out of the approximately 188 men who served in Company C during the war, about 98 percent, or all but 4, were from Haywood County. The company's commissioned officers listed below also hailed from Haywood, and it should be noted that this officer corps appears to have suffered little turnover through the four years of war. When compared with the other companies and the numbers of officers who served in those units, Company C is remarkable in its command stability.

Opposite: 1. Colonel Thomas L. Clingman; 2. Colonel Henry M. Rutledge; 3. Captain Thaddeus D. Bryson, Co. B; 4. Captain James A. Blalock, Co. F; 5. Captain James M. Cathey, Co. F; 6. First Lieutenant W. Pink Welch, Co. C; 7. First Lieutenant and Adjutant James C. L. Gudger (North Carolina Department of Archives and History, Raleigh).

Captains

Bryson, Samuel C.   Elected captain on May 31, 1861; promoted to major on April 30, 1862; later promoted to Lieutenant Colonel.

Freeman, Wesley N.   Elected 2nd lieutenant on May 31, 1861; promoted to acting adjutant on Aug. 21, 1861; elected captain on April 30, 1862.

Lieutenants

Hawkins, Joseph B.   Elected 3rd lt. on Jan. 1, 1865; captured at Ft. Stedman on March 25, 1865.

Shelton, Stephen J.   Elected 3rd lt. on May 31, 1861; elected 2nd lt. on Aug. 20, 1861; elected 1st lt. sometime in 1864; wounded at Ft. Stedman on March 25, 1865, and hospitalized; returned to duty on April 2, 1865.

Smith, Lewis J.   Elected 3rd lt. on April 30, 1862; elected 2nd lt. on April 28, 1863; wounded at the Crater in Petersburg on July 30, 1864; wounded at Ft. Stedman on March 25, 1865, and later captured at hospital around April 3, 1865.

Welch, William Pink   Elected 1st lt. on May 31, 1861; detailed as an engineer about May 20, 1864.

Company D — George's Guards

This company known as *George's Guards* was raised in Cherokee County and was enlisted at Valley Town on June 1, 1861. It was then mustered into state service and assigned to the 25th Regiment N.C. as Company D. The men of this company came from the counties listed below.

Company D — County Makeup

County	No. of Troops	% of Company
Cherokee	147	93.6
Macon	4	2.5
Unknown	4	2.5
Stokes	1	0.6
Georgia	1	0.6
Total	157	100.0

Note that from the total of 157 troops that served with Company D during the Rebellion, roughly 94% were from Cherokee County. Macon sent 4 soldiers into the company's service. All the commanding officers who served in Company D were from Cherokee County and these men are listed below.

Captains

Francis, John W.   Elected captain on June 1, 1861; promoted to major on May 17, 1862.

Tatham, Leander B.   Elected captain on May 17, 1862; captured at Ft. Stedman on March 25, 1865.

Lieutenants

Cromwell, Zadoc R.   Elected 2nd lt. on April 28, 1862; elected 1st lt. on May 21, 1862; died at Richmond on July 25, 1862 of "fever."

Halsey, Andrew D.	Elected 2nd lt. on July 17, 1862; court-martialed about Sept. 24, 1864; returned to duty in Jan.–Feb. 1865; deserted to the enemy about Feb. 24, 1865.
Herbert, William H.	Elected 1st lt. on June 1, 1861; defeated for reelection on April 28, 1862.
Patterson, James L.	Wounded at King's School House on June 25, 1862; elected 3rd lt. on Aug. 12, 1862; deserted and dropped from company rolls on Dec. 11, 1864.
Setser, Emanuel G.	Elected 3rd lt. on April 30, 1862; elected 1st lt. on May 21, 1862; resigned in May or Aug., 1864; listed as deserter and dropped from company rolls on Dec. 16, 1864.
Strange, William J.	Elected 3rd lt. on June 1, 1861; discharged on April 30, 1862, for reasons unknown.

Company E — Transylvania Volunteers

This company known as the *Transylvania Volunteers* was raised in Transylvania County and was enlisted at Brevard on June 17, 1861. It was then mustered into state service and assigned to the 25th Regiment N.C. as Company E. The men of this company came from the counties listed below.

Company E — County Makeup

County	No. of Troops	% of Company
Transylvania	137	82.0
Henderson	14	8.4
Unknown	5	3.0
Buncombe	3	1.8
Madison	2	1.2
Polk	2	1.2
Cherokee	1	0.6
Haywood	1	0.6
Georgia	1	0.6
South Carolina	1	0.6
Total	167	100.0

As can be seen, a high proportion of men from Transylvania County comprised Company E. Approximately 82 percent of the entire company contingent of 167 troops that served during the war hailed from Transylvania. Henderson County added another 8 percent of the troops. All but two of the commissioned officers serving in Company E throughout the war were from Transylvania County. Listed below are the officers who commanded in Company E.

Captains

Johnstone, Francis W.	Elected captain on June 15, 1861; defeated for reelection on April 28, 1862.
Young, Ephriam E.	Elected 3rd lt. on June 15, 1861; elected captain on April 30, 1862; died at Kinston on June 22, 1862, of "fever."
Graves, William H.	Detailed as acting adjutant in March–April 1862; elected 1st lt. about

1. First Lieutenant Stephen J. Shelton, Co. C; 2. First Lieutenant William H. Hartgrove, Co. F; 3. Third Lieutenant Joseph T. Cathey, Co. F; 4. Second Lieutenant Garland S. Ferguson, Co. F; 5. First Sergeant John W. Norwood, Co. C (North Carolina Department of Archives and History, Raleigh).

April 28, 1862; elected captain on June 22, 1862; killed at Petersburg about Oct. 15, 1864 (was from Henderson County).

Lieutenants

Deaver, James P.	Elected 3rd lt. about April 30, 1862; elected 1st lt. on June 22, 1862; discharged on July 16, 1862, by reason of being under age; reenlisted and elected 3rd lt. on May 12, 1863.
England, William M.	Elected 3rd lt. in March–Dec., 1864; wounded at Five Forks on April 1, 1865, and later captured at hospital in Amelia Springs, Virginia, on April 9, 1865; died in hospital at Ft. McHenry about May 10, 1865, of "pneumonia following amputation."
Henley, Abram L.	Elected 3rd lt. on Aug. 11, 1862; elected 2nd lt. on May 12, 1863; wounded with gunshot to head and hospitalized at Richmond about July 1863; resigned on Oct. 10, 1863 (was from Henderson County).
Miller, Andrew J.	Elected 1st lt. on June 15, 1861; declined to stand for reelection and was discharged on April 30, 1862; later served as assistant quartermaster (captain) of the 25th Regiment N.C.
Mull, Peter K.	Elected 3rd lt. on Dec. 4, 1863; elected 2nd lt. in March–Dec. 1864; paroled at Appomattox on April 9, 1865.
Neely, Matthew J.	Elected 3rd lt. on July 23, 1862; elected 2nd lt. on Aug. 1, 1862; resigned on Feb. 26, 1863, for unknown reasons.
Osborn, Charles L.	Elected 2nd lt. on July 23, 1862; elected 1st lt. on Aug. 1, 1862; transferred on Feb. 10, 1865, to 65th Regiment N.C. Troops (cavalry).
Robinson, John C.	Elected 2nd lt. on June 15, 1862; declined to stand for reelection about April 30, 1862, and was discharged; later served as assistant commissary of subsistence (2nd lt.) of the 25th Regiment.
Shipman, Andrew	Elected 3rd lt. about April 30, 1862; elected 2nd lt. on June 22, 1862; elected 1st lt. on July 16, 1862; died near Drewry's Bluff on Aug. 1, 1862, of disease.

Company F — Haywood Highlanders

This company known as the *Haywood Highlanders* was raised in Haywood County and was enlisted at Forks of Pigeon in that county on June 29, 1861. It was then mustered into state service and assigned to the 25th Regiment N.C. as Company F. The men of this company came from the counties listed below.

Company F — County Makeup

County	No. of Troops	% of Company
Haywood	119	86.9
Unknown	12	8.8
Buncombe	5	3.6
Jackson	1	0.7
Total	137	100.0

Note that the majority of soldiers that made up Company F were from Haywood County. In fact, approximately 87 percent of the troops that served in that unit during the war were Haywood residents, and it is suspected that several of those in the "Unknown" category were from Haywood. This "Unknown" category is simply a compilation of those soldiers where no county was designated in Moore's *Roster of North Carolina Troops*. All of the commissioned officers who served in Company F were from Haywood County with the exception of one. The company officers who commanded in Company F are listed below.

Captains

Lenoir, Thomas Isaac	Elected captain on June 29, 1861; declined to stand for reelection on April 28, 1862, and resigned.
Cathey, James M.	Elected 3rd lt. on June 29, 1861; elected Captain on April 28, 1862; killed at the Crater in Petersburg on July 30, 1864.
Blalock, James A.	Elected 2nd lt. on April 28, 1862; elected 1st lt. in November 1863; elected captain on Aug. 16, 1864.

Lieutenants

Blalock, Ethelred H.	Elected 1st lt. on June 29, 1861; defeated for reelection on April 28, 1862.
Burnett, James A.	Elected 2nd lt. on June 29, 1861; declined to accept reelection as 2nd lt. on April 28, 1862; later served as 2nd lt. of Company I, 62nd Regiment N.C.
Cathey, Joseph T.	Elected 3rd lt. on April 28, 1862; died in hospital at Wilson on Sept. 8, 1863, of "febris typhoides."
Ferguson, Ebed J.	Elected 3rd lt. about Dec. 4, 1863; killed at Drewry's Bluff about May 16, 1864.
Ferguson, Garland S.	Wounded at Drewry's Bluff on May 14, 1864; elected 2nd lt. about Aug. 16, 1864; wounded at Globe Tavern on Aug. 21, 1864; wounded at Ft. Stedman on March 25, 1865, and hospitalized and later captured on April 3, 1865.
Hartgrove, William H.	Elected 1st lt. on Aug. 16, 1864; captured at Five Forks on April 1, 1865.
Hyatt, Thaddeus C.S.	Elected 1st lt. on April 28, 1862; killed at Warm Springs in Madison County, N.C., about Oct. 26, 1863.
Wright, William M.	Elected 2nd lt. on Sept. 10, 1863; resigned on Jan. 21, 1864, for unknown reasons (was from Buncombe County).

Company G — Highland Guards

This company known as the *Highland Guards* was raised in Clay and Macon counties, North Carolina, and at Athens, Georgia. It was enlisted at Franklin on July 8, 1861, and was then mustered into state service and assigned to the 25th Regiment N.C. as Company G. The men of this company came from the counties listed below.

Company G — County Makeup

County	No. of Troops	% of Company
Georgia	133	70.0
Clay	27	14.2
Macon	10	5.3
Unknown	10	5.3
South Carolina	7	3.7
Cherokee	1	0.5

Haywood	1	0.5
Jackson	1	0.5
Total	190	100.0

As can be seen, a total of 133 soldiers who served in Company G came from the state of Georgia. Macon and Clay counties contributed 37 soldiers to the company's roster and South Carolina added another 7 troops. Approximately 10 names listed without county affiliation are included in the "Unknown" category. All of the commissioned officers of Company G listed below were Georgians with the exception of two.

Captains

Grady, William S.	Elected captain on July 8, 1861; promoted to major on Dec. 18, 1862.
Hayes, John R.	Elected 1st lt. on July 8, 1861; elected captain on Dec. 18, 1862; resigned about May 31, 1864, for unknown reasons.
Phinizy, John M.	Elected 2nd lt. on July 8, 1861; elected captain about May 31, 1864; reported absent without leave about Jan.–Feb. 1865.

Lieutenants

Edmonston, Rufus A.	Elected 3rd lt. on Jan. 4, 1862; defeated for re-election on April 28, 1862.
Hunnicutt, Thomas H.	Elected 3rd lt. in 1864; wounded at Ft. Stedman on March 25, 1865, and hospitalized at Petersburg, where he was captured by the enemy on April 3, 1865.
Jackson, Benjamin F.H.	Elected 3rd lt. on April 30, 1862; elected 2nd lt. on Dec. 18, 1862; elected 1st lt. in March–Dec. 1864; hospitalized at Danville, Virginia, about Oct. 2, 1864, with gunshot wound to head; later captured at Greenville, South Carolina, on May 12, 1865.
Marr, William J.	Elected 2nd lt. in 1864; reported wounded and in Richmond hospital on Feb. 23, 1865; later captured in hospital on April 3, 1865 (was from Clay County).
Netherland, Georgia M.	Elected 3rd lt. on Dec. 29, 1862; wounded at Malvern Hill on July 1, 1862; resigned on June 7, 1864, because he had been wounded twice and was incapacitated.
Walker, John W.	Elected 3rd lt. on July 8, 1861; appointed assistant commissary of subsistence (captain) on Nov. 27, 1861 (was from South Carolina).

Company H — Cane Creek Rifles

This company known as the *Cane Creek Rifles* was raised in Buncombe and Henderson counties and was enlisted in Henderson County on July 15, 1861. It was then mustered into state service and assigned to the 25th Regiment N.C. as Company H. The men of this company came from the counties listed below.

Company H — County Makeup

County	No. of Troops	% of Company
Henderson	112	69.1
Buncombe	48	29.6
Unknown	2	1.2
Total	162	100.0

Note that Company H was composed of good proportions of troops from both Henderson and Buncombe counties. Approximately 112 of the soldiers, or 69 percent, were from Henderson County. Buncombe supplied 48 troops, or 30 percent, of the company forces, and there were 2 soldiers with no county affiliation given. The commissioned officer corps consisting of men from both counties is shown below.

Captains

Blake, Frederick R.	Elected captain on July 15, 1861; defeated for reelection on April 30, 1862 (was from Henderson County).
Cunningham, Solomon	Elected 2nd lt. on July 15, 1861; elected captain on April 30, 1862; wounded at Malvern Hill on July 1, 1862; wounded at Fredericksburg on Dec. 13, 1862; died in Richmond hospital on Dec. 15, 1862, of wounds (was from Henderson County).
Young, Thomas J.	Elected 1st lt. on April 30, 1862; elected captain on Dec. 15, 1862; paroled at Appomattox on April 9, 1865 (was from Buncombe County).

Lieutenants

Blake, Walter	Elected 2nd lt. on Nov. 16, 1861; defeated for reelection on April 30, 1862 (was from Henderson County).
Byers, Joseph R.	Elected 2nd lt. on April 30, 1862; elected 1st Lt. on Dec. 15, 1862; paroled at Appomattox on April 9, 1865 (was from Henderson County).
Clayton, William L.	Elected 3rd lt. on July 15, 1861; declined to stand for reelection on April 30, 1862 and discharged (was from Buncombe County).
Fletcher, George W.	Elected 1st lt. on July 15, 1861; appointed assistant surgeon on Aug. 15, 1861 (was from Henderson County).
Lane, Thomas P.	Elected 3rd lt. on April 30, 1862; elected 2nd lt. in Jan.–Feb. 1863; resigned on July 10, 1864 (was from Henderson County).
Reid, John	Elected 3rd lt. on Dec. 29, 1862; court-martialed and later resigned on Sept. 12, 1864; records list him as a deserter on Oct. 5, 1864 (was from Henderson County).

Company I — Pisgah Guards

This company known as the *Pisgah Guards* was raised in Buncombe County and was enlisted in that county on July 22, 1861. It was then mustered into state service and assigned to the 25th Regiment N.C. as Company I. The men of this company came from the counties listed below.

Company I — County Makeup

County	No. of Troops	% of Company
Buncombe	158	96.9
Unknown	2	1.2
Jackson	1	0.6
Macon	1	0.6
Georgia	1	0.6
Total	163	100.0

Buncombe County soldiers almost exclusively comprised Company I. Of the total of 163 soldiers that served in Company I through the war approximately 158, or 97 percent of them, were from Buncombe. Not surprisingly, all of the officers of Company I were from Buncombe; they are listed below.

Captains

Howell, George W.	Elected captain on July 22, 1861; resigned on April 12, 1862, by reason of disability.
Morgan, William Y.	Elected 1st lt. on July 22, 1861; elected captain on April 16, 1862; promoted to major on Jan. 1, 1865.
Thrash, Augustus B.	Elected 1st lt. on April 16, 1862; elected captain on Jan. 1, 1865; wounded at Ft. Stedman on March 25, 1865, and later captured on April 3, 1865, in hospital.

Lieutenants

Howell, Foster B.	Elected 3rd lt. on July 22, 1861; resigned on March 22, 1863, for unknown reasons; reenlisted in company later as private on Nov. 1, 1863.
Luther, Andrew A.	Elected 2nd lt. on July 22, 1861; declined to stand for reelection on April 27, 1863, and discharged; reenlisted in company later as private about April 28, 1863.
Moore, Robert P.	Elected 3rd lt. on May 11, 1863; elected 2nd lt. in Nov.–Dec. 1863.
Morris, Thomas L.	Elected 2nd lt. on April 28, 1862; hospitalized at Petersburg with gunshot wound to arm about April 1, 1865; captured in hospital at Petersburg on April 3, 1865.

Company K — Black Mountain Guards

This company known as the *Black Mountain Guards* was raised in Buncombe County and enlisted at Democrat on July 23, 1861. It was then mustered into state service and assigned to the 25th Regiment N.C. as Company K. The men of this company came from the counties listed below.

Company K — County Makeup

County	No. of Troops	% of Company
Buncombe	131	93.6
Henderson	4	2.9
Madison	4	2.9
Yancey	1	0.7
Total	140	100.0

Predominantly Buncombe County men comprised Company K. Of the total of 140 soldiers who served in the company throughout the war, about 131 of these, or 94 percent, were native to Buncombe. The remaining 9 troops were supplied by Henderson, Madison and Yancey counties. The entire officer corps which came from Buncombe County is listed below.

Captains

Roberts, Charles M.	Elected captain on July 23, 1861; promoted to major and transferred to 69th Regiment N.C. about Feb. 14, 1864.

Burlison, Jesse M. Elected 3rd lt. on April 30, 1862; elected 2nd lt. in Nov.–Dec. 1862; wounded at Fredericksburg on Dec. 13, 1862; elected 1st lt. on April 20, 1863; reported under arrest in July–Aug. 1863; reported absent on furlough in Sept.–Oct. 1863; reported under arrest in Nov.–Dec. 1863; elected captain on March 23, 1864; reported absent without leave in Nov.–Dec. 1864; reported under arrest in Jan.–Feb. 1865; captured by enemy at Ft. Stedman on March 25, 1865.

Lieutenants

Anders, John Elected 2nd lt. on April 30, 1862; resigned on Oct. 30, 1862.

Barnard, Jobe D. Elected 1st lt. on July 23, 1861; defeated for reelection on April 30, 1862.

Buckner, Ninevah T. Elected 3rd lt. on July 23, 1861; defeated for reelection on April 28, 1862.

Garrison, Thomas M. Elected 2nd lt. on May 25, 1864.

Gentry, Joseph R. Elected 3rd lt. on July 27, 1863; resigned on Jan. 6, 1864.

Hensley, James A. Elected 2nd lt. on July 23, 1861; defeated for reelection on April 28, 1862; continued to serve with company at rank of private.

Patterson, James R. Elected 3rd lt. in Jan.–July 1864; wounded at the Crater in Petersburg on July 30, 1864; retired to the Invalid Corps prior to April 9, 1865.

Ray, James M. Elected 1st lt. on April 28, 1862; dropped from the rolls of the company after June 1863 for unknown reasons.

Wilson, William B. Elected 3rd lt. on Dec. 29, 1862; elected 2nd lt. in July–Aug. 1863; elected 1st lt. about March 23, 1864; present or accounted for until Jan.–Feb. 1865, when he was reported absent without leave.

4

CAROLINA COASTAL DEFENSE

Defensive Duty Near Port Royal Sound

The 25th Regiment N.C. departed from Asheville on September 18, 1861, and marched by way of the Swannanoa Gap across the Blue Ridge Mountain range and down the eastern slopes into Morganton, at that time the nearest railroad point, approximately seventy miles away. Upon reaching Morganton's Icard Station, the western terminus of the North Carolina Western Railroad, most of the boys stared for the first time in wonderment at a steam locomotive and railroad train. It is easy to imagine the mountaineers boarding the railcars and the whooping and hollering and laughter that filled the air as they headed down the tracks to North Carolina's capital city, Raleigh.

The train route passed through the towns of Statesville, Salisbury, Lexington, Greensboro, and Hillsboro, and at each of these places the steam engine was halted in order to fill the boiler with water and the tender with firewood. Arriving in Raleigh, the regiment disembarked and pitched camp for a couple of days while waiting to be issued uniforms. Prior to their arrival, there had been some confusion between the state and Confederate governments over which entity was to supply the soldiers' clothing. With the realization that winter was fast approaching, the North Carolina Legislature directed Governor Adjutant General James Martin to provide uniforms and shoes for all of North Carolina's troops. Soon every textile mill in the Tarheel State was producing cloth to be turned into winter clothing for the soldiers. A historian later wrote the following tribute to the state officials and to the women of the Confederacy for their valiant efforts to clothe the soldiers during that first winter:

> The unpleasant truth must be stated that the Government did not realize what was ahead of it, and lacked energy to supply the troops from the beginning.... Everything that could be made available in the State for clothing the troops was purchased, and the factories cheerfully furnished every yard of cloth they could. Major Devereux and his assistants were quite busy collecting and Captain Garrett equally so manufacturing. As fast as the articles were received every effort was made by all the officers of the department to furnish the troops with clothing before the severe weather of winter set in. With the large and valuable help given by the ladies of the State, who furnished blankets, quilts and carpets to be cut up into the size of small quilts and lined, and many other articles, the troops of North Carolina were clothed during the first winter of the war in such manner as to prevent much suffering.[1]

Confederate troops leaving for the front (*The Illustrated Confederate Reader* by Rod Gragg).

In the brief stopover, the mountain boys received brand new uniforms, which very likely had been manufactured there in Raleigh. Proudly donning this military attire, the men of the 25th N.C. continued their journey along the rails from Raleigh to Goldsboro. At that railroad juncture, the regiment entrained and headed south along the Wilmington & Weldon Railroad to the port city of Wilmington, situated on North Carolina's coastline. Here, their final destination, the weary troops piled off the train and went into camp on September 29, 1861, at Camp Davis near Mitchell's Sound. Within a few days, arms and muskets were issued to the soldiers, whereupon drilling and training in the effective use of this essential war equipment became an obsession with the officers and the men of the regiment.

Wilmington, North Carolina, was throughout the Civil War an important center of commerce and transportation for the Confederacy. Its location on the Cape Fear River provided a deepwater port that could easily be defended and provided a haven for blockade runners attempting, with frequent success, to slip through the Union's blockading fleet. Vital military supplies and domestic goods brought through the naval cordon by swift steam-powered ships during the dark of night were immediately shipped by rail to military depots and Southern commercial centers. The manifest of one of these sleek speedy vessels reveals the veritable treasures routinely smuggled into the South. It recorded 10,000 Enfield rifles, a million cartridges, two million percussion caps, 400 barrels of powder, and a quantity of cutlasses, revolvers, and other badly needed materials of war.[2]

Because of its strategic importance to the "southern cause" Wilmington was considered a primary target for a northern amphibious assault and demanded protection. The Cape Fear District of the Confederate Department of North Carolina was organized to insure that Wilmington remained in Confederate control, and the 25th Regiment N.C. was assigned for a short period to bolster the defense forces securing the port.

It is a certainty that few if any of the mountain boys had ever before beheld the ocean or seen boats plying through the water, with or without sails. At Camp Davis, one soldier from Company B wrote home about this country where he was stationed:

> I and all of the Redgment is in campt near the see cost not more than 2 hundred yards from the Beach you can stay in the encampment and See all the Steam Boats and steam ships Running all the time it is a grand seen to see all the Steamers Running up and Down to and fro. you may stand on the Beach and look as far as your Eys can see and it is nothing But one world of water. We have the See Breeses which is as helthy as the are up whare you live. The water that we have is the very worst of water. Such as you never Drank in your Life.[3]

Depicted in this artwork is the Battle of Port Royal Sound, where a Union armada attacked and captured the strategic South Carolina harbor on November 7, 1861. The location would soon become a base of operations for the Federal fleet blockading Charleston, Savannah and other important Confederate coastal cities and facilities (*The War with the South: A History of the Great American Rebellion* by Robert Tomes).

The men could stand on the beach and look as far as their "Eys" could see and it was "nothing but one world of water." They were obviously overwhelmed with the vastness of the ocean and the sight of steam boats plying to and fro, but it appears that they were not overly enamored with the drinking water available to them at their encampment on the coast of North Carolina.

The 25th Regiment N.C. would not remain long in Wilmington. Relatively inactive while stationed there, the troops were involved in no military actions and for the most part applied their energies to continuous drilling and training in the use of their muskets. In early November it became apparent to Confederate authorities that a huge Union invasion fleet was sailing toward the coast of South Carolina. Colonel Clingman and his regiment were ordered to Charleston, South Carolina, to assist in containing the powerful amphibious force. The 25th N.C. was assigned to the 4th Military District of South Carolina; and on November 5, 1861, the regiment's men boarded the cars for Charleston.

Concerned with the state of affairs in South Carolina and Georgia, Confederate President Jefferson Davis dispatched General Robert E. Lee on November 6, 1861, to South Carolina to take over command of the coastal defenses along the central and South Atlantic seashore. Since the beginning of the war, the Federals had been making assaults and feints up and down the seaboard, and the critical railroads running along the southern Atlantic coastline were particularly vulnerable. Rumors prevailed that a Federal expedition was being planned to capture Port Royal. Possessing a wide bay with deep water and ideally located mid-

Photograph of Fort Beauregard, located on the north side of the entrance to Port Royal Harbor (Library of Congress).

Photograph of Fort Walker, located on the south side of the entrance to Port Royal Harbor (Library of Congress).

way between Charleston and Savannah, Port Royal was a place of high strategic value that could be used as a Union base of operations and as a coaling station to supply the blockading fleet patrolling the entrances to the important coastal cities. In addition, this fortified naval base could facilitate the assembly of powerful infantry forces to attack the Charleston & Savannah Railroad and threaten the regional coastal towns.

Fortune did not pursue General Lee to South Carolina. On November 7, 1861, the very day that he arrived and assumed his new command, a Union armada of no fewer than 80 ships steamed into Port Royal Sound and bombarded its two protective forts into submission within just a few hours. With the fall of Fort Walker and Fort Beauregard the Union naval forces gained complete control of Port Royal and its Hilton Head Island. The stronghold quickly

Photograph of the Federal dock facility at Hilton Head Island, South Carolina (Library of Congress).

became a coaling station, supply depot and repair shop for the Federal's South Atlantic blockading squadron. In addition, the surrounding Beaufort District was one of the richest and most populated in the region and afforded the North a grand theatre for its anti-slavery experiments.[4] Soon Hilton Head Island boasted its own hospital, church, printing office, bakery and theater. Although the heat was oppressive at times and malaria-carrying mosquitoes swarmed in abundance, the Yankees who served at Port Royal thought of it as "the sunny side of the soldier's life."[5]

Lee quickly established his headquarters in the small town of Coosawhatchie near Port Royal Sound and began inspecting the defense lines and fortifications along the South Carolina, Georgia and Florida coastlines. In December 1861, after assessing the Southern defen-

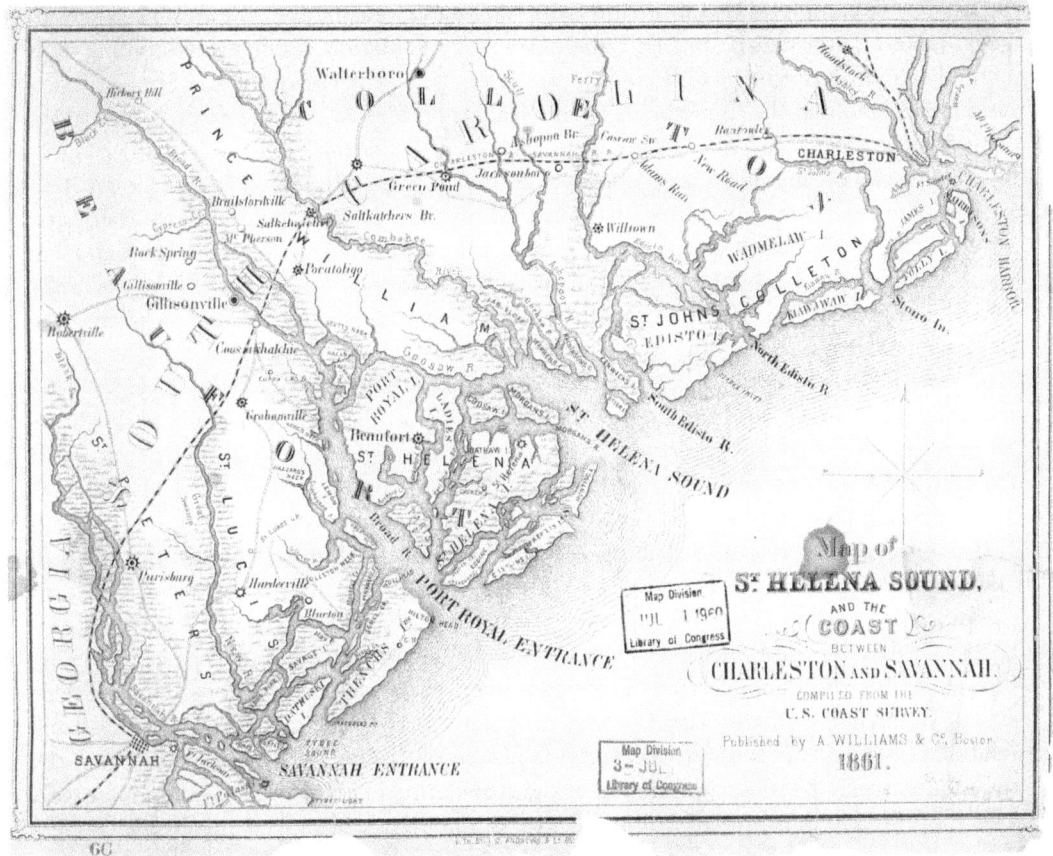

This 1861 map illustrates the area surrounding Port Royal Sound in South Carolina and includes Grahamville. The 25th Regiment N.C. was stationed near Grahamville for approximately five months (Library of Congress).

sive preparations and making a determination of the enemy's strength, he wrote to the South Carolina governor, Francis Pickens, summarizing his findings: "The strength of the enemy, as far as I am able to judge, exceeds the whole force that we now have in the state. It can be thrown with great celerity against any point, and far outnumbers any force we can bring against it in the field."[6]

One of General Lee's first acts was the establishment of the new Department of North Carolina–South Carolina–Georgia–Florida, which was assigned responsibility for defending the coastal areas of those states. Orders were given to concentrate the limited number of Confederate forces at strategic defensive points along the coastline. From these considered positions of troop concentrations, the Confederate defense garrisons were poised to quickly respond to and counter Federal coastal incursions wherever they occurred. Naturally these strategic strongholds were to be situated far enough away from the sea to be safely out of gun range of the powerful Federal fleet, and had to be fortified with breastworks to protect the garrison's forces.

Grahamville was chosen as a location for one of Lee's strategic garrisons. This crossroads village surrounded by prosperous low country cotton and rice plantations was located just inland from Port Royal Sound. The crucial railroad joining Charleston and Savannah had just recently been completed; it ran within a mile or so of Grahamville. As a result of the war, geographic circumstances, and fate, the quiet rural plantation country surrounding Grahamville, South Carolina, had become a place of tactical importance to the warring parties. And it was here that the Confederate army's leaders decided to post the green troops of the 25th Regiment N.C.

To reach Grahamville, the regiment traveled along the Wilmington & Manchester Railroad to Florence, South Carolina. From that point, their passage took them to Charleston over the rails of the Northeastern Railroad Line, where they arrived on November 6 and 7 in detachments of several companies, and then to Coosawhatchie on November 8 via the Charleston and Savannah Line. After a brief encampment of six days at Coosawhatchie, the Regiment moved to the vicinity of Grahamville approximately nine miles away. The mountain boys made their living quarters at nearby Camp Lee and spent the winter of 1861-1862 guarding the railroad from potential raiding parties out of the Yankee stronghold on Hilton Head Island. The Federal troops remained relatively quiet that winter and were prevented from breaking out and pushing inland beyond the protective range of their naval artillery.

Although their duty was certainly tedious and boring, the mountain boys of the 25th N.C. applied themselves with an industry second to no other regiment in perfecting their drill and constructing defensive fortifications. Off duty the men passed their time by playing card games and competing in athletic contests or other games of skill or chance. Two log structures that they had fashioned provided a venue for hoedowns, where dancing and singing brought a little cheer and merriment into their lives. There was no want of food during their stay at Grahamville's Camp Lee. Corn, sweet potatoes, rice, beef and bacon were available in abundant quantities from the surrounding plantations. With coffee being in short supply, the mountaineers became appreciative of the stimulating effect and taste of "yeopon tea." This local favorite was brewed from the leaves of the evergreen yaupon shrubs which grew abundantly along the South Carolina coast. Moreover, slaves from the nearby estates frequently wandered through camp vending molasses and vegetables and taking up the soldiers' laundry to wash. Overall, military duty during the Civil War did not get much better than this.[7]

The South Carolina coastal duty would have been idyllic had it not been for one thing—*disease.* Ever-present dysenteries, fevers, and upper respiratory infections pervaded Camp Lee and incapacitated the soldiers in droves. Additionally, childhood infectious diseases such as mumps and measles struck down the boys of the 25th Regiment N.C. as they came in daily contact with a large population of men for the first time in their lives. At Camp Lee, almost one-third of the men of Company F were reported to be on sick leave during the first month or two of service there. And before the South Carolina duty was ended, approximately fifty-six soldiers from the 25th Regiment N.C. died from the ravages of the unseen foe—disease.[8]

While stationed at Camp Lee, the men surely on occasion laid eyes on General Robert E. Lee as he rode by on horseback inspecting the progress of work on the fortifications.[9] He was a man blessed with pleasing physical attributes and a supreme intellect that drew admiration and attention from those in his presence. In addition, he acted with a bearing and humility that quickly earned the respect of the soldiers and officers under his command. Over time, it became a mutual respect. He developed a high esteem and love for the Rebel soldier, especially in the latter phases of the war when they fought so bravely for him against overwhelming odds. However, General Lee was not much impressed with the provincial attitudes of the local populations or with their overall support of the war effort. Sentiments along these lines were expressed to his daughter, Annie, in a letter that he wrote during this time period: "Our

This scene of a Confederate encampment offers a glimpse of living quarters similar to those that the 25th Regiment N.C. would have established near Grahamville, South Carolina (Library of Congress).

people have not been earnest enough, have thought too much of themselves and their ease, and instead of turning out to a man, have been content to nurse themselves and their dimes, and leave the protection of themselves and families to others."[10] During his brief command in South Carolina, Lee was to exert extreme energies and apply his extraordinary intellectual gifts and influence to overcome this attitude. And he took no respite from his endeavors to overhaul the Confederacy's defense preparations along the South Atlantic shores and to push the work forward.

The 25th Regiment N.C. did not engage in significant encounters or skirmishes with the nearby Yankee troops while residing at Camp Lee. However, they were getting closer to the enemy forces and on occasion observed and even fired at some Yankees. One soldier from Company B wrote a letter home to his wife about Camp Lee and the enemy activities: "I can in form you that we have had now fite yet but the yankes Came out nite befor last and kild one of the pickets and Cripeld another but not our men was horsemen that was about tel miles from her and one of the pickets kild three yankes and the yankes went back in the lland."[11]

This Rebel informs his wife that the regiment has had no "fite" yet and he also gives proof that picket duty could be somewhat perilous on occasion. Lt. Garland Ferguson recorded that "doing picket duty, drilling, and building fortifications"[12] were the main occupations of the 25th N.C. while located at Grahamville. They would occupy themselves with such activities for a period of approximately five months, until urgent orders were received to rush back to North Carolina to stave off yet another Union invasion of the coast.

Top: Sleek, speedy blockade runners, such as the one pictured here, were the lifeblood of the South during the Civil War. They carried veritable treasures of war supplies and weaponry from European suppliers to the Confederate army. The Union capture of New Bern and other strategic eastern North Carolina ports was an attempt to interrupt the flow of these war goods and other civilian necessities (Library of Congress). *Above:* Artist's depiction of the Union capture of Roanoke Island by General Ambrose Burnside's Federal Expeditionary Forces (*The War with the South: A History of the Great American Rebellion* by Robert Tomes).

Too Late to New Bern

On March 15, 1862, the 25th Regiment N.C. embarked on railcars and departed from Grahamville in great haste, bound for New Bern, North Carolina. Union forces had gained a beachhead on the North Carolina coastline with the capture of Roanoke Island on February 8, 1862. From this position, Federal General Ambrose Burnside had intentions to exploit his advantage by attacking and capturing New Bern, an important North Carolina port and rail center. Union control of New Bern could facilitate further military advances against Goldsboro some sixty miles to the west, which was a vital Confederate railroad junction. The loss of Goldsboro would be ruinous for the Confederacy, effectually cutting the direct railroad supply lines between the Carolinas, the Deep South and Richmond. In that event, the Southern troops then located in and around Richmond and northern Virginia would be severely crippled.

Early on the morning of March 13, 1862, Union forces disembarked from transport ships and initiated hostile undertakings against New Bern. The South's defensive forces led by General Lawrence Branch offered stubborn resistance for a short while until finally being overwhelmed by the strength of the enemy. General Branch ordered his regimental commanders west to Kinston, North Carolina, where he hoped to regroup and oppose a recommencement of the Federal attack and shield Goldsboro's railroad infrastructure.[13] En route to New Bern and too late to contribute to its defense, the 25th Regiment N.C. received new orders to join the retreating Confederate forces at Kinston. Upon arrival there on March 18, the regiment was assigned to General Branch's Second Brigade, District of Pamlico, in the Department of North Carolina.

It surely was an exciting and anxious time for the men of the 25th Regiment N.C. as they dug in and prepared for the Yankee attack. Given the strategic importance of Goldsboro, an assault was almost certain to fall on the Rebels. After learning of the loss of New Bern, most Southerners felt that Goldsboro was doomed, including Mrs. Mary Boykin Chesnut. This refined Southern lady was the wife of James Chesnut, Jr., who had been a United States Senator from South Carolina before the war and served the Confederacy as an aide to President Jefferson Davis and later as a general in the army. Mrs. Chesnut, who was privileged to be included in the highest level of Southern aristocracy, maintained a wonderful journal of her Civil War experiences. Of the tragedy in North Carolina which befell New Bern and the impending threat to Goldsboro's railroads, she wrote the following:

> Mr. Venable interrupted the fun, which was fast and furious, with the very best of bad news! Newbern shelled and burned, cotton, turpentine — everything. There were 5,000 North Carolinians in the fray, 12,000 Yankees. Now there stands Goldsboro. One more step and we are cut in two. The railroad is our backbone, like the Blue Ridge and the Alleghanies, with which it runs parallel. So many discomforts, no wonder we are down-hearted.[14]

Surprisingly, however, the Union assault on the South's railroad "backbone" never materialized. Instead, while he impatiently awaited orders from Washington to sanction his bold plans to move against Goldsboro, General Burnside whetted an appetite for fame by capturing smaller targets along the Pamlico and Albemarle sounds of North Carolina's coastline.

Meanwhile, further to the North, President Lincoln's fretting and impatience to start his magnificent Army of the Potomac southward was about to be quieted. Throughout the fall and winter, he had relentlessly prodded and encouraged General McClellan to use the idle Union forces, but the "Boy General" steadfastly insisted his army was not ready. In early March 1862, McClellan finally acquiesced and, after obtaining Lincoln's approval of his tactical plans, started the army in motion aboard transport ships headed for a landing in southeastern Virginia. McClellan had chosen a point east of Richmond on the Virginia peninsula (near where the first English settlement was founded at Jamestown) and within close striking distance of that Confederate capital city. The confident McClellan intended to lead his Army of the Potomac from this strategic peninsular landfall on a campaign to capture Richmond, taking advantage of great siege guns mounted on rail cars and secure naval supply lines.

At this point in the war's progression, Southern sentiments were reserved and anxious. Grave concerns were voiced about the direction the war had taken after that first magnificent Rebel victory at Manassas, Virginia. Worrisome were the events unfolding around Richmond and along the Atlantic seaboard. Roanoke Island, New Bern and Port Royal had been captured, and most of the important Southern ports had been effectively picketed by the Union's blockading fleet. Union naval warships commanded by Admiral David Farragut were threatening New Orleans and, in fact, would force the city's surrender before the month of April 1862 was out. In addition, an obscure Federal general by the name of Ulysses S. Grant was scoring impressive victories in the West. The jubilant hysteria which had prevailed the previous year following the surrender of Ft. Sumter had receded from memory, and across the South the people, the politicians, and the governors were clamoring for the Confederate administration to do something.

On April 16, 1862, the Confederate congress, with the support of President Jefferson Davis, took the strong measure of passing the Conscription Act to augment the Southern forces with the hope that the Federal successes could be countered and reversed. The new law required that all able-bodied men in the South between the ages of 18 and 35 be liable for service for a period of three years in the Confederate Armed Forces or for the duration of the war, if shorter than that term. Furthermore, those twelve-month volunteers already serving would be required to remain in the army an additional two years. It was a drastic and calculated move that the Confederate government recognized would be unpopular and possibly create a storm of public controversy. However, it was a necessary expedient and one that targeted to a large degree those men General Robert E. Lee had observed were "content to nurse themselves and their dimes, and leave the protection of themselves and families to others." Mrs. Chesnut recorded a quip regarding conscription which wrings the truth from the matter: "Conscription has waked the Rip Van Winkles. The streets of Columbia were never so crowded with men. To fight and to be made to fight are different things."[15]

This new Confederate conscription law provoked significant repercussions throughout the South and within the Confederate army, including North Carolina's 25th Regiment. All of the regiment's mountaineers had volunteered for a one-year stint the

North Carolinian General Robert Ransom, Jr., took command of Ransom's Brigade in April 1862. The 25th Regiment N.C. was attached to Ransom's Brigade from this point in the war until the final surrender at Appomattox Court House in April 1865 (Massachusetts Commandery Order of the Loyal Legion and the U.S. Army Military History Institute).

Colonel Henry Middleton Rutledge was born to wealth and an aristocratic planter heritage in South Carolina. Upon Colonel Thomas Clingman's promotion to brigadier general in April 1862, Rutledge was elected to command the 25th Regiment N.C. at the age of 22 years. (North Carolina Department of Archives and History, Raleigh)

summer past and their enlistment period was soon to run out. News that they would not be going home to their families, as so many were anxiously anticipating, would come as a dreadful shock to many of those independent mountaineers. After all, they had signed up to fight the Yankees in defense of their individual rights, and this new law was seen as a further invasion of their independence and a diminution of their liberties. Four days after the Conscription Act, Lieutenant Matthew Love (later to be promoted to lieutenant colonel of the 25th Regiment N.C.) of Henderson County wrote to his father: "There is a good deal of dissatisfaction in camp concerning the press [conscription] law. some say they are going home when their time is out regardless of consequences."[16] The level of disaffection was high among the men of the regiment; but whether or not they agreed with the tough Conscription Act, their legal recourses were limited. All men serving in the 25th Regiment N.C. and not under the age of 18 or over 35 were now obliged to serve an additional two years.

The poor military performance at New Bern concerned Confederate authorities, and they moved quickly to assess and remedy the problems in North Carolina's command structure. Colonel Robert Ransom of the 1st Cavalry N.C. was promoted to brigadier general, and in April of 1862 he was ordered from Virginia to Kinston to assist with the reorganization of the troops encamped there and to take command of a brigade. A North Carolinian by birth, General Robert Ransom, Jr., was a West Point graduate of the class of 1850 and served tenure at the academy instructing cadets in cavalry tactics under the tutelage and watchful eyes of then Superintendent Robert E. Lee. It has been noted in one account that Ransom was an esteemed young soldier, yet cursed with ill health.[17] He was a professional soldier through and through and eagerly went about organizing the 2nd Brigade North Carolina which would bear his name. Ransom's Brigade was formed from the combination of the 25th Regiment N.C. along with the Twenty-sixth, Twenty-seventh, and Thirty-fifth North Carolina regiments. In addition, there were a couple of cavalry and five artillery companies attached to Ransom's command, but these would later be detached.

During that spring of 1862, the Confederate army reorganized; and the men mustered in to serve for three years or the duration of the war. Officers of the different regiments again stood for election, which resulted in Colonel Clingman being reelected as the colonel of the 25th Regiment N.C., Major Rutledge being elected as lieutenant colonel, and Captain Samuel C. Bryson of Company C being elected major. Former Lieutenant Colonel Dearing retired from the command while under an anonymous charge of drinking too freely. Two years later, Dearing received an officer's commission in a Confederate cavalry unit after making a personal plea in a letter to President Jefferson Davis, in which he wrote: "Whatever faults I have committed, I trust you will think sufficiently punished by loss of rank for the past two years, and indeed if you could know the agony of mind I have frequently suffered ... I am sure you would no longer withhold this favor."[18]

The ten companies making up the 25th Regiment N.C. also elected new commanders; the following men were selected:

COMPANY	LOCATION	CAPTAIN
COMPANY A	Henderson County	Matthew N. Love
COMPANY B	Jackson County	Harlen A. Boone
COMPANY C	Haywood County	Wesley Freeman
COMPANY D	Cherokee County	Leander B. Tatham
COMPANY E	Transylvania County	Ephriam E. Young
COMPANY F	Haywood County	James M. Cathey
COMPANY G	Georgia, Clay/Macon/Cherokee counties	William S. Grady
COMPANY H	Buncombe/Henderson counties	Solomon Cunningham
COMPANY I	Buncombe County	William Y. Morgan
COMPANY K	Buncombe County	Charles M. Roberts

As it soon turned out, Colonel Clingman was promoted to brigadier general on May 17, 1862, and was assigned his own brigade to lead. Command of the 25th Regiment N.C. was conferred to the regiment's young lieutenant colonel, Henry Middleton Rutledge, who was not yet twenty-three years of age. Rutledge moved up in rank to colonel, Major Bryson was elected lieutenant colonel, and Captain John Francis of Company D was elected major.

It was during this interim, while the army was revamping at Kinston and new conscripts were being assimilated into the army, that Ransom's Brigade acquired the services of a female soldier. Throughout the war, the passionate devotion of women on both sides of the divide impelled many to join an army's van so that they could be closer to loved ones. When permitted, these women lived within the encampments among the soldiers and worked unashamedly at tedious yet essential chores, which included cooking and laundering clothes. It is likely that this highly desired support and female companionship kept many a soldier in the camps and prevented their desertion from the army to join destitute or starving wives and family back home. However, most army commanders prohibited cohabitation with females in their military encampments. In such cases and on rare occasions, unabashed women would take more radical measures to accompany their men at war.

A photograph of Sarah Malinda Blalock (alias "Sam") taken several years after the war. Blalock disguised her gender so that she could join Ransom's Brigade to be with her husband (Wilson Library, University of North Carolina).

4. Carolina Coastal Defense

Although not the norm, it was not unusual for women (and children as evidenced by this photograph) to join their husbands in Civil War encampments (Library of Congress).

A regimental historian wrote of one such instance which occurred with Ransom's Brigade at Kinston:

> While the Twenty-sixth Regiment was in camp in and around Kinston, after the battle of New Bern, many recruits joined the command. Among them were two young men, giving their names as L.M. and Samuel Blalock. They enlisted in Captain Ballew's company (F) and were brought to the regiment by private James D. Moore, of Company F. On the way from their home, in Caldwell County, to join the regiment, Moore was informed in strict confidence by L.M. (Keith) Blalock, that Samuel was his young wife, and that he would only enlist on condition that his wife be allowed to enlist with him. This was agreed to by Moore, who was acting as recruiting officer, and Moore also promised not to divulge the secret. Sam Blalock is described as a good looking boy, aged 16, weight about 130 pounds, height 5 feet and 4 inches, dark hair; her husband (Keith) was over 6 feet in height. Sam Blalock's disguise was never penetrated. She drilled and did the duties of a soldier as any other member of the company, and was very adept at learning the manual and drill. In about two months her husband, who was suffering from hernia and from poison from sumac, was discharged, and Sam informed his Captain and Colonel Vance that he was a woman, whereupon she was discharged and permitted to join her husband.[19]

Although Private "Samuel" Blalock's tenure with Ransom's Brigade was short-lived, there were other instances of women serving and fighting on both sides of the conflict and never being discovered. Whether attributable to devotion to loved ones, zealous belief in the cause, or thirst for adventure, the female combatant is just another example of the extraordinary circumstances and extreme measures brought on by America's civil war.

The newly formed Ransom's Brigade remained in and around Kinston, North Carolina, through the month of April 1862, perfecting its drill and discipline and defending the critical rail lines and bridges. While stationed at Kinston's Camp Ransom, one of the soldiers with the 25th Regiment N.C. wrote home to his wife about his circumstances and thoughts of soon getting out of the army and going home:

> State of NC Lenoir County Kinston
> April the 13 1862
>
> dear wife it is with pleasur that I take the presant opportunity of writing you a few lines to let you now that I am well at this time hoping thes lines will find you in good health I hant any thing strang to rite at this time more then I want to sse you verry bad we hant had any fite yet and I don't think we will have we are stationed 5 miles from kinston and has got Chimneys to our tents and is doing tolerabel well though it does look like that old ransom will drill us to death.... Thar is Chance for us to git off tel our time is out I don't think but forty seven days will soon run Run off and then our time will be out.[20]

This mountain Rebel does not seem to be suffering ill effects from his army experience other than a burning desire to see his wife. He brags that the camp tents have chimneys and complains that "old ransom" is going to drill them to death. In the last sentence it is obvious that the soldier is counting down the days until his volunteer enlistment time runs out, which he expects to be in forty-seven days. Unfortunately, just three days after this letter was penned, the new Confederate Conscription Act would erase his dreams of going home, and those of many thousands of other soldiers like him.

Not quite a year had passed since the mountain men joined together to defend their country. So far, no real opportunities to fight the Yankees had been presented. However, it would not be long before the 25th Regiment N.C. actually learned what war entailed.

5

SEVEN DAYS BATTLES AROUND RICHMOND

In the early spring of 1862, General George McClellan was on the move in Virginia, having initiated his peninsula campaign designed to invest and capture the Confederate capital of Richmond. After getting the heavy siege artillery up and ready to support the army along the railroad, he began the push across coastal marshlands and swamps that lay between the York River carving the northern border of the peninsula and the James River defining the southern extremity. Meandering between these two navigable bodies was the flooding Chickahominy River, which split the peninsula and would effectively hinder the movements of both armies in the coming months.

The Confederate army under the command of General Joseph Johnston made half-hearted and futile attempts to stop the advancing Federal horde. A rear guard of Confederate forces led by General James Longstreet dug in and fought a delaying action near "old" Williamsburg on May 5, 1862. Then on May 31, Johnston, already recoiled as far as President Jefferson Davis would allow, launched a counterattack against the Federals at Seven Pines. In this confused battle, described as "phenomenally mismanaged" by Johnston's chief of ordinance,[1] neither side could claim advantage, although Confederate casualties were higher by some one thousand. The most significant casualty, and one that precipitated a far-reaching consequence on the course of the war, was a severe shoulder wound inflicted upon General Johnston himself. To replace this experienced commander, President Davis turned to a man in whom he had immense confidence — a man who would soon change the fortunes of the Confederate army and cause the sun to shine brighter for a brief while over the South.

On June 1, 1862, General Robert E. Lee assumed command of a dispirited Rebel army accustomed to, and demoralized by, the retreating tactics of their former commander. Immediately, Lee began improving the defensive fortifications in front of Richmond and preparing to give battle to McClellan. He presented an urgent case to President Davis and the secretary of war that more soldiers and workmen were needed to strengthen the Richmond defenses. Inactive troops from North Carolina and South Carolina and elsewhere were rushed to Virginia to support Lee. In a private letter to his daughter-in-law penned on June 22, just three weeks after taking command, Lee wrote, "Our enemy is quietly working within his lines, and collecting additional forces to drive us from our capital. I hope we shall be able yet to disappoint him, and drive him back to his own country."[2] By late June General Lee's prepa-

Confederates attacking a battery on Malvern Hill (*The American Heritage Century Collection of Civil War Art*; artist Thure de Thulstrup).

rations were advanced to such a degree that he finalized battle plans to drive the blue host in his front off the peninsula. Soon began a series of consecutive battles over a week's period of time known as the Seven Days Battles. During these confused and hectic days of maneuvering and massing and fierce fighting in the swampland around Richmond, the 25th Regiment N.C. at last joined the fray.

In early June 1862 General Lee requested the support of North Carolina troops under the command of General T.H. Holmes. Two brigades, General John Walker's and General Robert Ransom's from North Carolina, were directed to Drewry's Bluff in Virginia. This fortification was a naturally strong battery position located approximately seven miles to the southeast of Richmond and overlooking the James River approach to that city. Ransom's regiments left Kinston for Petersburg on June 19 and arrived there

General Robert E. Lee assumed command on June 1, 1862, of the Confederate forces in Virginia. He subsequently led his Southern army through the Seven Days Battles around Richmond and thwarted Union General George McClellan's grandiose Peninsula Campaign to capture the South's capital city (Library of Congress).

by June 21, at which point they marched to the defense works at Drewry's Bluff. During the brief stopover in Petersburg, Ransom's Brigade was strengthened and then included the following regiments: the Twenty-fourth, Twenty-fifth, Twenty-sixth, Thirty-fifth, Forty-eighth, and Forty-ninth North Carolina troops. On June 24, shortly after arriving at Drewry's, General Ransom's Brigade was summoned to Richmond to join General Lee's newly designated Army of Northern Virginia, then girding for battle.

Just a few days before, on June 12, Confederate cavalry forces led by General J.E.B. (Jeb) Stuart undertook a daring circuitous reconnaissance ride around the entire Union army. The young Stuart, a brigadier general at twenty-nine years of age, was of average height, squarely built, with blue eyes and a bushy cinnamon beard. He sported thigh-high boots, a yellow sash, elbow-length gauntlets, a red-lined cape and a soft hat topped with a foot-long ostrich plume.[3] Such a dandy exterior appearance belied the lion-hearted warrior concealed beneath. He was one of General Lee's favorites. Upon his return from the adventurous escapade, bedraggled and showing the effects of two nights in the saddle without any sleep, he appeared in front of his commander and proved once again his worth; and reinforced later claims made by many that he was the finest leader of cavalry forces to serve during the Civil War.

Union General George McClellan, shown in this 1861 carte-de-visite by Mathew B. Brady, commanded the Army of the Potomac in the Virginia Peninsular Campaign and at the Battle of Antietam (Library of Congress).

McClellan's Union Army on the move to Richmond (*Harper's Weekly*, John C. Pace Library, University of West Florida).

Stuart had discovered on his perilous exploit that McClellan's forces were positioned astride the Chickahominy River with their right flank "in the air," or subject to an enemy surrounding movement. This large Yankee contingent north of the river forming the right side of the Union battle front was positioned there to secure the York River Railroad — McClellan's vital lifeline linking his forces with their supply base at White House on the Pamunkey River. The battle plan that Lee devised to thwart the Union's devices involved a complicated series of maneuvers by four army columns to turn the Federal exposed right flank. During the considerable time it would take for Confederate forces under the commands of Generals Stonewall Jackson, D.H. Hill, A.P. Hill and James Longstreet to get into the proper positions north of the Chickahominy River, General John B. Magruder and General Benjamin Huger would remain on the south side of the river. Orders were given to the latter two generals to demonstrate and make such a show in the Yankee front as to discourage an attack below the river. General Lee and his commanding generals committed to June 26, 1862, as the date to launch the Confederate attack.

Engagement at King's School House

General Robert Ransom left Petersburg by train with his six North Carolina regiments and reached Richmond at 10:00 P.M. on the night of June 24. As dawn broke on the morning of June 25, Ransom received orders to rush to the support of Major General Huger's Divi-

5. Seven Days Battles Around Richmond

sion situated in the enemy's front below (south of) the Chickahominy River. The Yankee line stretched southward from the York River Railroad on the north side of the Chickahominy past the Williamsburg road and just beyond the Charles City road on the south side of the river. Huger's position was one of extreme importance, and vulnerability as well, since it manifested the extreme right flank of the Confederate line. Directly opposed to General Huger's forces was Union General Samuel Heintzelman's corps under orders from McClellan to adjust the picket lines and to test the enemy's strength in the vicinity of Seven Pines and the railroad junction of Fair Oaks some seven miles east of Richmond.

The commencement of the Seven Days Battles on June 25, 1862, corresponded with a fierce Federal assault launched by Heintzelman against General Huger's position near King's School House. It was to this inferno along the Williamsburg road that General Ransom and Colonel Henry M. Rutledge were hurrying the mountain boys of the 25th Regiment N.C. Lt. Ferguson recorded an excellent firsthand account of the regiment's initial taste of battle as they met Heintzelman's Yankee troops at King's School House near the crossroads village of Seven Pines, Virginia:

Prior to the Seven Days Battles, Confederate General Jeb Stuart led cavalry forces on a circuitous reconnaissance mission around McClellan's entire Union army to discover the location of the enemy's flank north of the Chickahominy River (Library of Congress).

> [B]y sunrise of the twenty-fifth it [the 25th Regiment] was on the march towards the front and to join the division of General Huger, which was then engaged at Seven Pines on the Williamsburg road. There was heavy fighting of artillery and musketry in front. It had at last come in hearing of the true music of war. About one-half mile from the line the regiment was ordered to double-quick. It was thrown in line on the immediate left of the Williamsburg Road, and when within range of the enemy the regiment halted, the front rank at the command fired and fell to the ground, the rear rank fired over them, then with bayonets fixed we raised the rebel yell and charged; the enemy gave way and the ground which had been lost in the morning had been retaken. The enemy opened a heavy fire of musketry and three times tried, without effect, to retake their lines. At 6 o'clock P.M. a heavy fire of grape shot was opened on the regiment without demoralizing or moving it. It was relieved at dark.[4]

From 11:00 A.M. until sunset the 25th Regiment held the enemy forces in check. On three different occasions the North Carolinians fought off and repelled Yankee attempts to take their forward position in the action that would later be referred to as the engagement at King's School House or Oak Grove. As Lt. Ferguson illuminated, the enemy opened up on the regiment with grape at 6:00 P.M., but the Rebels steadfastly held their position until the Confederate batteries silenced the Union cannon.

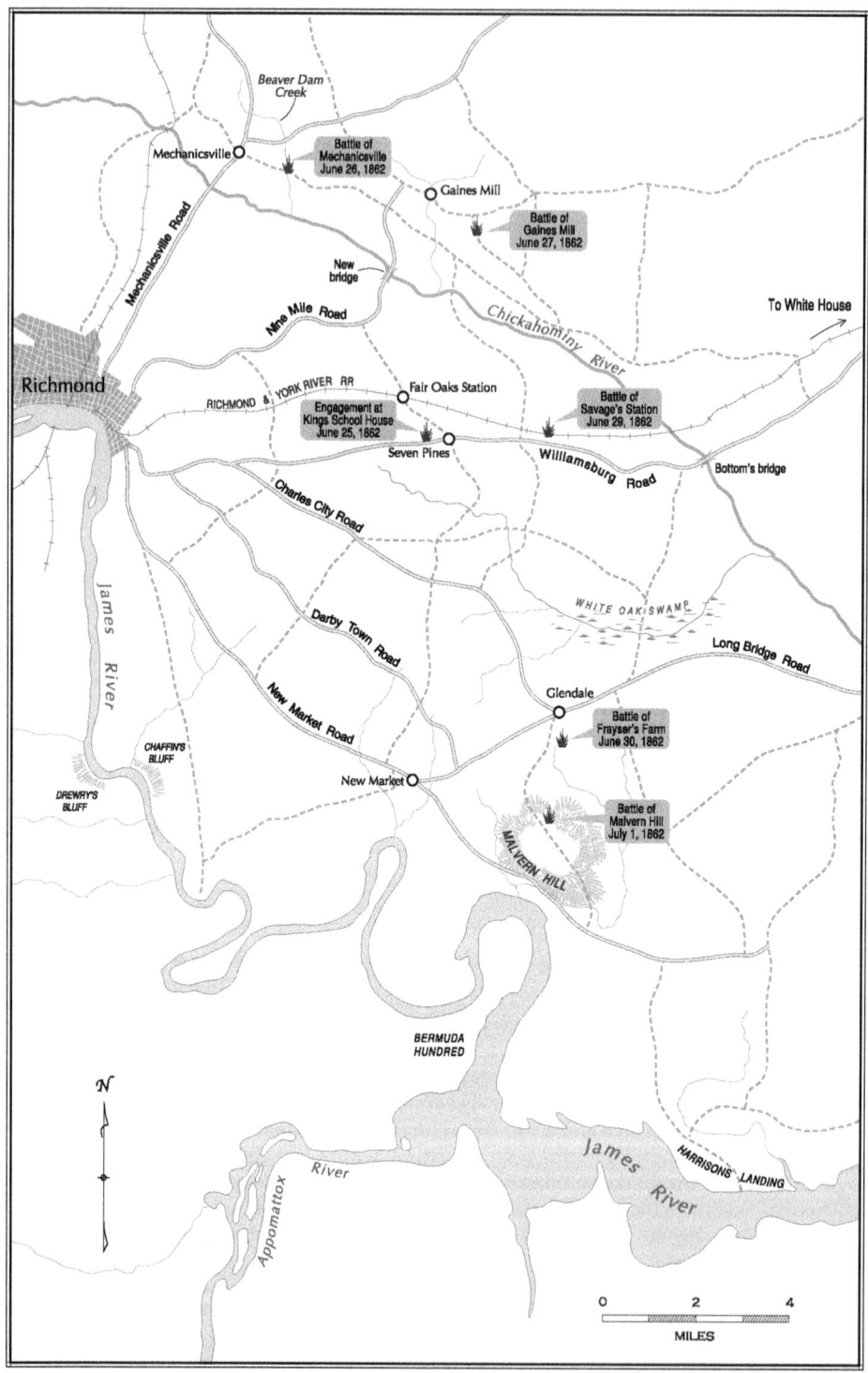

Richmond vicinity and the scene of the Seven Days Battles, contested June 25–July 1, 1862. The 25th Regiment N.C. played conspicuous roles at the engagement near King's School House and the Battle of Malvern Hill (Peter Krafft, Florida State University).

General Ransom reported after the battle: "This was the first time that this regiment (Twenty-fifth N.C.) was ever under fire, although in service for nearly a year. The regiment behaved admirably, and I am proud to bear witness to its unwavering gallantry."[5] Major General Huger commended the 25th Regiment N.C. in his official report of the action, in which he wrote the following: "One of the latter regiments (the Twenty-fifth North Carolina, Colonel [Henry M.] Rutledge) was pushed to the left of the Williamsburg road, where the enemy had advanced, and drove them back in gallant style, holding our original line of pickets."[6]

The gallant action of the regiment helped repel the Union attack and secure Lee's right flank. However, as many as 27 of the regiment's men were wounded, 2 were killed and another 8 would not survive their severe wounds. Private Basil B. Edmondson, from Haywood County's Company C, was promoted to adjutant as a result of his gallantry on the field. In recognition of their distinguished service, General Huger recommended to General Lee that the men of the 25th Regiment N.C. be permitted to inscribe "King's School House" on their banner. Only four other regiments were recognized in such a manner.

Battle of Malvern Hill

Although not part of Lee's offensive battle plan, General Huger's forces helped to halt the Union's savage probing attacks on the lightly guarded Confederate right flank. And they accomplished it in such a convincing manner that McClellan was discouraged from further assaults on that front in the short term. However, General Lee was unaware of the young Union commander's intentions or mindset and pondered whether to proceed with the planned attack on the morrow or defend against further aggressive assaults below the Chickahominy River. After considerable reflection and calculations regarding the Union's probable actions, General Lee made his decision — a decisive conclusion that confirmed an earlier assessment given of him by a former engineer officer who served under his command during the South Carolina coastal defense duty: "If there is one man in either army, Confederate or Federal, head and shoulders above all others in *audacity*, it is General Lee! His name might be Audacity. He will take more desperate chances, and take them quicker than any other general in this country, North or South; and you will live to see it, too."[7]

The next day, June 26, the audacious Lee massed his forces north of the Chickahominy River and launched an assault on the Yankees' right flank near Mechanicsville. However, very little went right on that day for the Confederate army. Stonewall Jackson, the hero of the Shenandoah Valley campaign who had just arrived to join Lee's Army of Northern Virginia, was designated with his three divisions to spearhead the Rebel phalanx. For some inexplicable reason, Jackson failed to get his forces up and initiate the attack. (Some credit this lapse by General Jackson to battle fatigue and the rigors of the Shenandoah campaign.) Finally, in the late afternoon, after waiting most of the day for Jackson to commence the hostilities, an impatient and anxious General A.P. Hill ordered his division to assail the bluecoats lodged strongly behind Beaverdam Creek. The results of Hill's action on the second day of the Seven Days Battles were disastrous for the Confederacy. Nearly 1,500 Rebel casualties were suffered, while the Yankee's lost only 360 men.[8]

McClellan did not welcome the news that the famed Stonewall Jackson was threatening his forces on the right flank, notwithstanding Jackson's weak performance on that second inglorious day. Although McClellan described the Union victory at Mechanicsville to apprehensive ears in Washington as a "complete victory," he nevertheless ordered the forces on the right, commanded by General Fitz-John Porter, to pull back a few miles to high ground east of Boatswain's Swamp near Gaines' Mill. There Porter's troops dug in and formed an even more formidable defensive position than the one most recently occupied and vacated at Beaverdam Creek. Of significant consequence, McClellan also determined that his railroad supply line on the north side of the Chickahominy River was threatened by Confederate operations against his forces protecting that vital road. Consequently, he elected to shift the Union base with all of the army's supplies to the James River. In so doing, he abandoned the railroad and all grandiose plans of siege and bombardment of Richmond by heavy mobile artillery mounted on railcars, effectively transforming his tactical "complete victory" into a strategic success for the southern forces. The "young Napoleon" then turned his attention to defensive preparations and awaited the Confederate army's next move.[9]

On June 27, the third day of the Seven Days Battles, Lee's Army of Northern Virginia again attacked General Porter's Yankee troops on the north side of the Chickahominy at Gaines' Mill. Just as had happened the day before, Jackson was lethargic in supporting the main assault against Porter's center, led again by General A.P. Hill. For most of the day, General Hill's troops fought alone with poorly coordinated and disjointed support from generals Jackson and Longstreet. Near sundown Lee finally was able to orchestrate an assault where all his forces attacked in unison, and the Rebels' ferocious attack penetrated the Union line, forcing its collapse. Timely support from fresh rear guard Federal troops sent from across the river gave General Porter sufficient protection to save his forces and guns and safely recross the Chickahominy River to the south side. At the end of the long day of June 27, a day filled with Southern command blunders, miscommunications, and hapless coordination, Lee's army had wrested a hard-fought, yet costly, victory at Gaines' Mill. More than 9,000 Confederate casualties were sacrificed to extract 2,800 prisoners and 4,000 casualties from the Union army.[10]

After midnight a hysterical and distressed McClellan wired Edwin M. Stanton, Lincoln's war secretary: "I have lost this battle because my force was too small....The Government has not sustained this army.... If I save this army now, I tell you plainly that I owe no thanks to you or to any other persons in Washington. You have done your best to sacrifice this army."[11] Under the illusion that the Southern forces confronting his were superior in number (in actuality, leading into the Seven Days Battles, Lee could muster only about 60,000 men, slightly more than half the numbers available to McClellan), the befuddled McClellan was suddenly searching for scapegoats and a means to extricate himself from his peninsular predicament. Had not a surprised and alert colonel in the War Department telegraph room omitted the last two lines of the ill-advised telegram before sending it on to the war secretary, Stanton and President Lincoln would likely have relieved McClellan of command responsibility for his act of indiscretion.[12]

After the first day's fighting on June 25 near Seven Pines, General Magruder and General Huger had remained on the south side of the Chicahominy River to confront more powerful Yankee forces and hold the right side of the Confederate line. General Huger commented later about the situation he found himself in: "The troops which were in my rear all moved off during the night of the 25th or morning of the 26th to commence that series of brilliant actions which began on the enemy's right. My division alone remained between the enemy and Richmond on this approach."[13] The troops of Ransom's Brigade were still attached to General Huger's Division and participated in the demonstrations and charades of force aimed at keeping the bluecoats at bay. With an enthusiasm reserved only for such theatrical occasions the troops behaved with the most bellicose appearances and threatened and feigned imminent attack at any moment. Apparently the subterfuge worked, since the Federals remained reticent in their front and reports reached McClellan that the Rebels were strong and threatening along the right side of the Confederate line of battle.[14]

On June 29 and 30, Lee attempted to strike the Federal army while it was on the move south of the Chicahominy toward the James River. First, at Savage's Station, Lee devised a complicated plan of maneuver to concentrate his forces in an all-out attack against the Yankees. Again Lee's command and organization proved inept and, hindered by Jackson's continued slowness and timid division commanders, the feeble Confederate assaults by troops under the command of General Magruder were easily repulsed. On June 30, Southern forces undertook yet another complicated strategy to defeat the Federals and similarly met with failure at Frayser's Farm just south of the small village of Glendale. Only Longstreet and Hill's men were able to be thrown at the enemy and they engaged in some fierce fighting which gained a little ground. Casualties resulting from clashes over the two-day period numbered approximately 3,600 on the Union side and more than 4,000 for the Confederates.[15]

On the morning of July 1, Lee snapped at one of his brigadier generals, "If those people get away [it is] because I cannot have my orders carried out!"[16] McClellan had resolved to retreat south to Harrison's Landing on the James River and "save" his army. Pulling back from Glendale, the Federals took up another defensive position at Malvern Hill, a naturally strong geographic feature approximately one hundred and fifty feet in elevation and flanked by deep ravines. General Lee, desperately intent on destroying McClellan before he could escape, attacked the retreating Union army, lodged securely on the formidable Malvern Hill, on July 1, 1862.

The 25th Regiment N.C. had been under fire on several occasions after that first day's battle near King's School House on June 25. And, as fate dictated, they would engage in the last major clash of the Seven Days Battles at Malvern Hill. Lt. Ferguson recorded the following account of the affair at Malvern Hill:

> On 2 July [July 1] at Malvern Hill late in the evening it [the 25th Regiment] made a charge, but for want of support and on account of a galling fire, it was ordered back, and with other regiments of the brigade, was reformed under cover by General Robert Ransom, and again advanced within one hundred yards of the enemy's guns and line, when the men raised a yell and charged in the face of a perfect sheet of fire from musketry and artillery, without wavering, to within twenty yards of the enemy's guns, some going even nearer. At this point General Ransom discovered that he was not supported and that the enemy were heavily massed, very greatly outnumbering his men. Unwilling to sacrifice his men in a hopeless charge and dark coming on he withdrew from the attack.[17]

On that day at Malvern Hill, General Ransom's Brigade had a fighting strength of approximately 3,000. Sometime between 2:00 P.M. and 3:00 P.M., Ransom's regiments were ordered to join General Huger's line of battle formed approximately one and one-quarter miles from the scene of furious fighting then taking place. Ready and waiting in some woods, with shell occasionally bursting around them, the North Carolinians stayed on the alert for directives to move forward against the enemy. Not once, but twice, General Ransom received orders from General Magruder, who was fighting in his front, to come to his support. General Ransom, with endorsement from his superior officer, General Huger, refused both requests by dictating dispatches back to the harried commander that his orders must come through Huger.

By 7:00 P.M. the fighting had intensified along the entire front and General Magruder again summoned support from General Ransom. The plea for help was of such an urgent nature that General Ransom sent forward at once the Twenty-fourth Regiment under Colonel Clarke and informed General Huger of the situation with a request for his orders. Huger's reply was somewhat indecisive and allowed General Ransom to act with discretion without placing himself under General Magruder. Ransom acted immediately and put the brigade in motion by the right flank. One historian offered the following description of General Ransom's actions during these moments: "Ransom, who had been given discretion by Huger, on Magruder's third plea for reinforcements, doubled across the rear of Wright and Mahone, came in on their right and attempted to mount the steep hill from the West. It was not war; it was murder.... Ransom crouched defiantly almost under the mouth of the guns."[18]

As soon as the first three regiments, which included the 25th N.C., arrived at the front, General Magruder threw them into action. Colonel Rutledge's regiment rushed gallantly forward into a ferocious sheet of fire, a fire as fearful as a mind can conceive. The colonel was severely stunned by an exploding artillery round and Major John W. Francis was badly wounded. General Ransom's brother, Colonel Matt Ransom, was wounded twice as he led the Thirty-fifth Regiment forward toward those same gun emplacements on top of Malvern Hill. There was no possibility of further advance against such formidable fire power and the three regiments fell back under cover of some intervening hills. They were met there by General Ransom, who ordered the entire Brigade to the right. Still protected by the high ground in his front, Ransom re-formed the regiments and made the lines he desired within only two hundred yards of the enemy's defenses.

In the twilight, General Ransom put his line into motion and crept as close as one hundred yards from the batteries. And then, riding in front of his line and preparing his troops for an enemy charge, the general commanded the boys to wait until they saw "the whites of their eyes, and d — n it, give it to them."[19] The regiment charged into a perfect sheet of fire from the Yankees' musketry and batteries and closed on the enemy to about twenty yards. However, it was not within the capacity of mortal soldiers to advance further against such a lethal fusillade as that presented by their steely adversaries, and the regiment began to fall back. General Ransom and his troops withdrew in the darkness to the point from which they had begun at 7:00 P.M. As the men slumped to the ground, they glanced around them for their brothers in arms, appraising their condition and accounting for those missing. All told, 24 men from the 25th Regiment N.C. were killed that cruel day on the slopes of Malvern Hill; and of the 94 men who were wounded, 20 would soon be buried in the grounds around the Richmond hospitals.

With dark settling over the scene, the attack was called off and the fought-out Rebels hunkered down to lick their wounds and wait for McClellan's next move. Still convinced that he was facing a Confederate army twice its actual size, the Union general ordered his Federal troops back to the protection of the gunboats at Harrison's Landing on the James River. General Lee had lost more than 20,000 soldiers, dead and wounded, since the Seven Days Battles began. After a week of continuous maneuver and fighting and with the enemy securely protected by strong naval guns, he reluctantly ordered a cessation of further aggressive actions. In a matter of just six weeks following the Battle of Malvern Hill, the Yankee troops boarded their transport vessels and headed back north, effectively aborting the peninsular campaign. Although the Confederate Army of Northern Virginia could claim few tactical successes during the Seven Days Battles, the rebuff of McClellan's grandiose peninsula scheme to capture the South's capital city amounted to an undeniable strategic victory over the Union.

General Robert Ransom credited his regiment's failure to take the enemy's batteries to a lack of support and to darkness, and certainly not for the want of courage and exertion by his troops. In his official report on the day's action, Ransom commended especially the courage and coolness of Colonel Rutledge and Major Francis and had this to say regarding the brigade's behavior in battle: "Although we did not succeed in taking the enemy's guns, I am proud to bear testimony to the resolute and gallant charge of the brigade. Officers and men behaved in every way as becomes the soldier of the Southern Confederacy."[20]

The battles fought over those seven fateful days near Richmond extracted a heavy human toll from the ranks of the 25th Regiment. Fifty-four mountain men had been killed outright or from wounds suffered from Yankee weaponry. Approximately 100 more were wounded and many of these men would not rejoin the regiment, but would eventually hobble back to the Carolina and Georgia highlands badly maimed. Included in the brigade's gruesome tally were three colonels wounded, one lieutenant colonel killed, and several other field officers and company officers killed and wounded. General Ransom witnessed for the first time the bravery and stubbornness of the men under his command, and the general himself demonstrated in battle a martial presence that impressed and inspired his troops. Lt Ferguson later wrote: "After the Battle of Malvern Hill General Ransom had full confidence in the fighting qualities of the 25th Regiment, and the men of the Regiment had full confidence in him as a careful, courageous, and skillful leader in battle."[21]

A full year had transpired since the mountaineers first shook the dirt clods and manure from their boots and began drilling and learning the rudiments of being a soldier. For the first time there on that marshy ground in the Richmond environs, they had aimed and fired their muskets with malicious intent at other human beings. They shot to kill other men just like themselves, the only difference being the color of their uniforms and their political persuasions. It was their first experience in battle where minie balls and grapeshot and shrapnel filled the air with death everywhere around them. Deafening explosions, smoke, and the stench of gunpowder infused their ears, eyes, and nostrils. They learned to duck from the sounds of lethal projectiles whizzing by and heard for the first time the sickening thuds of metal missiles finding their marks in the flesh of men at their sides. It didn't take very long for those mountaineers to determine that war was even worse than they had supposed it to be.

Commendations from Generals Huger and Ransom and the firsthand accounts of Lt. Ferguson attest to the soldierly conduct and "gallant" style demonstrated by the 25th Regiment N.C. It was the men's first battle and their mettle had been tested. Very quickly they transitioned from green troops to seasoned veterans. And, finally, after serving in the Confederate army for a full year, the boys had seen the "elephant."

6

Maryland Campaign

Moving North

Ransom's Brigade fell back to Richmond after the Battle of Malvern Hill and then on July 7, 1862, withdrew to the works at Drewry's Bluff to refit and reorganize. Throughout the Civil War, Drewry's Bluff manifested an important strategic position in the defense lines around Richmond. Since Federal gunboats could navigate the James River all the way to the city's gates, Richmond was vulnerable to Union attack by water as well as by land. To guard against this hazard, a small fort was built seven miles southeast of Richmond on a bluff 90 feet high overlooking the river. There at Drewry's Bluff, the Rebels constructed earthworks, erected barracks, dug artillery emplacements and mounted three large seacoast guns to ward off the Yankee fleet.

During those hot summer months of 1862, General Ransom's brigade was involved in constructing fortifications at Drewry's Bluff and defensive trenches in front of nearby Petersburg, Virginia. Large numbers of troops and over 1,000 slaves were employed in this extensive enterprise.[1] The summer heat and humidity must have been sweltering and barely tolerable to the soldiers garrisoned on the banks of the James River. Subsistence and sanitary conditions in Civil War encampments were notoriously bad; and at Drewry's Bluff, where the soldiers were living within earthworks or in crude barracks, the situation certainly was no different. It was during this period, when the 25th Regiment was stationed at Drewry's Bluff, that many of the men became sick and died from disease. Lt. Ferguson remarked on this fact in his historical account of the regiment: "It was here, in consequence of the exposure just gone through, that army sickness first made its telling effect on the regiment, the loss by death from sickness being eighty-one."[2]

Sickness accounted for a full one-third of all casualties in the Civil War and almost every soldier on both sides reported to sick call multiple times during their service. Unhealthy dietary and sanitary conditions were in large part responsible. Dysenteries, fevers and upper respiratory infections were so prevalent that the average foot soldier was twice as likely to die from a camp disease as he was from a battlefield injury. Another reason was that the rural lifestyles of many of the soldiers had protected them from such childhood diseases as measles, mumps, chickenpox, and scarlet fever. When they came to live together in camps with large groups of men, thousands died of these diseases in the early stages of the war. As Lt. Ferguson's record shows, the men of the 25th Regiment didn't escape the ravages of "camp disease" or other contagious diseases and maladies at Drewry's Bluff.

Union charge at the Dunker Church during the Battle of Antietam (*The American Heritage Century Collection of Civil War Art*; artist Edwin Forbes).

Drewry's Bluff as seen from the James River (*Harper's Weekly*).

General Robert Ransom was becoming better acquainted with the soldiers under his command. He had led them through the battles of the Seven Days, continuously pushed them on the march, and camped among them with few additional creature comforts. Ransom had earned their respect in combat, and the men of the 25th Regiment N.C. valued his leadership abilities and "had confidence in him as a careful, courageous, and skillful leader in battle." But that approbation apparently didn't extend beyond the battlefield for many of his troops. Lt. Ferguson divulged this sentiment when he wrote, "It was only in camp and on the march that any difference existed between the men and their General; this existence amounted to

Above: Rebel encampment at Drewry's Bluff (*Harper's Weekly*).

Opposite Bottom and Above: These two photographs reveal a fortification located at Drewry's Bluff. A soldier is shown in one photograph seated at the door of a bombproof. In the other can be seen one of the three large seacoast guns employed at Drewry's to command the James River (Library of Congress).

positive dislike, in some instances hate." Furthermore, Lt. Ferguson went on to balance the account:

> The men of the 25th Regiment would not have exchanged General Robert Ransom as a leader in battle for any General in the Army of Northern Virginia. His mastery of military tactics, coolness on the field, and judgment of ground enabled him to place his men in action with great rapidity and comparative safety, until they were ready to do execution. If he had understood volunteer soldiers and realized that four-fifths of the men in ranks were as careful of their personal honor, and as anxious for the success of the cause as he, he would have been one of the greatest generals in Lee's army, was the opinion of some, and is still the opinion of the writer.[3]

Lt. Ferguson's complimentary rhetoric does not disguise a deep-seated conviction that General Robert Ransom didn't fully appreciate the motivations and mind-set of the common volunteer soldier. It is obvious that Ferguson believed his brigade commander lacked sympathy for the plight of the common fighting man and was blind to their feelings of honor and loyalty. As a result, General Ransom's penchant for strict rules and discipline angered many of his troops, it appears, and seemingly alienated a certain faction. It was Lt. Ferguson's opinion that this factor alone stood in the way of General Ransom's achieving greatness and rising to the very top echelons of command within Robert E. Lee's Army of Northern Virginia.

In August 1862, while Ransom's Brigade was encamped at Drewry's Bluff, the colonel of the Twenty-sixth Regiment N.C., Zebulon Vance from Buncombe County, was elected governor of North Carolina. General Ransom vehemently opposed promotion of the regiment's young Lieutenant Colonel Harry Burgwyn, Jr., to take Vance's place as colonel, remarking that "he wanted no boy colonel in his brigade." The Twenty-sixth Regiment's men, upon hearing this, were indignant and so resented the general's comment and stance that an application was made through the proper channels for immediate transfer to another brigade.[4] Confederate officials approved the transfer and it would not be until January 1863 before a replacement regiment, the Fifty-sixth N.C., was assigned to Ransom's Brigade.

After the Seven Days Battles, General Lee had no intention of waiting for the Federal army to determine the next initiative or select the ground in which to continue the dispute. He endeavored to carry the war to the North, and in the latter part of August 1862, with General Stonewall Jackson leading the way northward, the Army of Northern Virginia fought and won a battle at Cedar Mountain, Virginia. A few days later, Lee's combined forces scored a tremendous victory over General John Pope's Federal army at Manassas, Virginia, on August 29, 1862. This success occurred in northern Virginia on the same ground where the first battle of Bull Run was fought, just south of the Potomac River, which defined the border between Virginia and Maryland. The thrashing of Pope's army at Manassas had been accomplished within a mere twenty miles of the White House, home to the president of the United States. Lee's Rebel army was now in a position to threaten the northern capital and the border states of Maryland and Pennsylvania.

What a truly amazing turn of events this was, considering that only two short months earlier McClellan had advanced almost within cannon range of Richmond. He, of course, was forced by the Rebel army back into the sea and steaming northward for safety to Washington, D.C. General Robert E. Lee's stature as a military leader rose meteorically across the divided nation as he wrought the stunning reversal of the war's direction in northern Virginia. Now it seemed that Lee and his troops had the wind at their backs as they advanced ever further northward and closer to the enemy's homeland. The question in everyone's mind, including a very anguished and worried President Lincoln, was where General Lee would next lead his great army.

First and foremost in the wily general's mind was the welfare of his troops. He had to feed them, and the fought-over and despoiled Virginia terrain could no longer be relied on to sustain the troops. Maryland offered a virgin food basket potentially filled with unlimited rations for the Army of Northern Virginia. Additionally, Lee wanted to maintain pressure on Lincoln and his administration by harassing the Federal troops in the president's own backyard and threatening Washington, D.C. There was always an outside hope that sufficient political pressure brought to bear on Lincoln might compel him to treat with the South and sue for peace.

Moreover, an invasion of Maryland might be interpreted by certain foreign powers, especially England and France, as a sign of the Confederate army's strength and control of its destiny. In that case, these nations could conceivably be persuaded to recognize the Confederate states as a sovereign country and intervene on its behalf in the war. The South was desperate for this support, which would bring about a resumption of trade, opening up markets for planters' cotton and providing sources where war materials and supplies could be purchased to sustain the war effort. An entry in Mrs. Mary Boykin Chesnut's diary on July 10, 1862, exposes her anxious hope of foreign intervention: "My husband has come. He believes from what he heard in Richmond that we are to be recognized as a nation by the crowned heads across the water, at last." For all of these motives and surely more, General Lee could not be disabused of the merits of a Maryland campaign.

The ever-audacious Lee rode with the van of Rebel forces as they waded across the Potomac River into Maryland. Once on Northern soil the general divided his army and sent a large contingent of troops back across the river to effect the capture of Harpers Ferry, Virginia (now West Virginia). Dividing his forces in such a manner was fraught with risk, as the Southern commander undoubtedly realized. Yet, the ploy anticipated not only short-term tactical objectives but far-reaching strategic purpose, and the fate of the Southern cause seemingly teetered in the balance.

For several weeks following the Seven Days Battles, Ransom's Brigade bounced from Drewry's Bluff to Petersburg to Richmond and back to Drewry's Bluff. However, on or about August 26, 1862, Ransom's Brigade — which then included the Twenty-fourth, Twenty-fifth, Thirty-fifth, and Forty-ninth regiments and comprised a fighting strength of approximately 1,600 men — and General John G. Walker's Brigade received orders to join Lee's army then campaigning in northern Virginia near the Potomac River. The brigades boarded the cars on August 29 bound for Rapidan Station and finally caught up with the Rebel army at Leesburg, Virginia, around September 3, 1862. Arriving too late at the war theatre for a share in the glory at the second battle of Bull Run, the reinforcements were quickly integrated into the Army of Northern Virginia. Brigadier General John Walker (he was promoted to major general in November 1862) was given command of a half-division, which included his own brigade and Ransom's Brigade, and was attached to Lieutenant General James Longstreet's corps of the Army of Northern Virginia.

General Robert E. Lee's weary soldiers are captured in this artwork moving north and crossing the Potomac River (*Harper's Weekly*).

Artist's drawing of Lee's Army of Northern Virginia crossing the Potomac River and being fired on by Union pickets (Library of Congress; artist Alfred Rudolf Waud).

Reaching the Potomac River on September 7, Ransom's Brigade waded across at Point of Rocks—or Check's Ford—where the stream was waist deep and about one-quarter mile wide. As word filtered down to Ransom's Brigade and to the men of the 25th Regiment N.C. that they were moving into Maryland and Northern territory, many of the boys were disappointed at this turn of events. Evidence of this is found in the following account from Lt. Ferguson's regimental history:

> When it was first made known to the men by General Lee's order that the army was to cross the Potomac there was a considerable murmur of disappointment in ranks. The men said they had volunteered to resist invasion and not to invade, some did not believe it right to invade Northern territory, others thought that the same cause that brought the Southern army to the front would increase the Northern army, still others thought the war should be carried into the North; thus the men thought, talked and disagreed. This was the first dissension among the men of the regiment, but all were united in their confidence and love for Lee.[5]

Ferguson's regimental brethren were not the only malcontents. On the march into Maryland, Lee and his commanders were alarmed at the large numbers of stragglers and defectors that were plaguing the army at the time. Many of the desertions surely could be attributed to the lack of shoes and the soldiers' poor diet and harsh lifestyle. However, it is very likely that the sentiment described by Lt. Ferguson and held by some of the boys of the 25th Reg-

6. Maryland Campaign

Walker's Division, which included the 25th Regiment N.C., endeavored to destroy this stone aqueduct of the Chesapeake and Ohio Canal spanning the mouth of the Monocacy River near Harpers Ferry (Library of Congress).

iment N.C. was widespread and contributed significantly to the diminution in Confederate troop strength during that first Maryland campaign.

Capture of Harpers Ferry

Shortly after treading into Maryland and reaching the Monocacy River near Frederick, Maryland, General Walker received specific orders on September 9, 1862, to proceed to the mouth of the Monocacy, some fifteen miles distant from Harpers Ferry, and destroy the aqueduct of the Chesapeake and Ohio Canal. Upon reaching this substantial structure and chasing off the enemy's pickets, Walker's troops set in to accomplish their mission. Working parties were detailed to drill holes in the stone arches for explosives. However, it became evident very soon that their tools were inadequate to the task because of the "extraordinary solidity and massiveness of the masonry." What Walker had reasoned would be a job of hours would take days to complete. Thinking that his forces were too exposed and vulnerable to possible attack from the strong enemy presence in the area, he decided to abandon the demolition efforts. Orders were given for the division to rejoin General Lee's army at Frederick, Maryland.[6]

General Lee had other plans for Walker's Division, however, and sent instructions to Walker for his cooperation with General Jackson and General Lafayette McLaws in the investment and capture of the important river town of Harpers Ferry, West Virginia. A United States arsenal and the scene of an attempted slave insurrection led by John Brown before the war, Harpers Ferry was strategically located at the juncture of the Potomac and Shenandoah rivers on the Virginia-Maryland border. Federal troops in strength were garrisoned at this outpost and could easily threaten and assail the proposed line of communications for Lee's southern army then maneuvering in Maryland and posturing to penetrate into the bountiful Pennsylvania countryside. Walker's assignment was to occupy the Loudoun Heights which overlooked the Shenandoah River and Harpers Ferry from the southeast. Possession of that ground and the surrounding area would allow his division to command the town with its artillery and prevent the Federal garrison's troops from escaping eastward down the right bank (south) of the Potomac River.

After encountering a great deal of difficulty negotiating the steep banks of the Potomac, Walker's Division recrossed the river on September 11 at Point of Rocks, downriver from Harpers Ferry. On the morning of the 13th, Walker's troops reached the foot of the Blue Ridge Mountains near the Loudon Heights just below the river town. At that point, two regiments scaled and occupied the heights without opposition and the remaining forces of the division were strategically positioned to prevent the Union troops garrisoned at Harpers Ferry from escaping down the river. Early on September 14, General Walker's artillery commanders hauled up and placed three Parrott guns and two rifle pieces atop the mountain to command the river town nestled on the opposite bank of the Shenandoah River's junction point with the Potomac.[7] General McLaws finally wrested control of a position on the Maryland Heights to the north, after a sharp encounter with the Union defenders, and General Jackson controlled the Bolivar Heights west of town. All roads were blocked leading out of Harpers Ferry and the Federal troops that remained there were cordoned and trapped by the Rebel aggressors.

In the early morning hours of September 15, a heavy mist hung over the Potomac River flowing by Harpers Ferry and hid the river town from the view of the Confederate artillerists. By around 8:00 A.M., when the last vestiges of the fog had burned away, a severe shelling of the place was commenced from the batteries glaring down at the town from the surrounding heights. The cannon fire was accurate and effective and by 9:30 A.M. the beleaguered Union forces were waving white flags. Some 11,000 prisoners were rounded up and the booty that was captured was enormous—13,000 small arms, 200 wagons, quartermasters' stores and 73 cannon. In addition, there was a tremendous amount of food on hand that the starving Confederates relished and hurriedly devoured. It was first come, first served and, as one historian wrote, those that missed out were not happy: "When Walker's column came over the Shenandoah and McLaws's streamed across the Potomac bridge, on their way back to Lee, there was much grumbling, bitterness even, because the booty had all been devoured or appropriated."[8] Walker's little half-division, which included the 25th Regiment N.C., may not have shared in the booty, but they definitely had a share of the action that culminated in the seizure of Harpers Ferry.

Opposite Top: Photograph overlooking Harpers Ferry, West Virginia. The 25th Regiment N.C. participated in the capture of this strategic river town just days prior to the battle of Antietam (Library of Congress). *Opposite Bottom:* View of the Loudon Heights across the Shenandoah River. General John G. Walker's Division, which included Ransom's Brigade with its 25th Regiment N.C., occupied a position on and around these heights which commanded Harpers Ferry (Library of Congress).

Battle of Antietam

While one part of Lee's Army of Northern Virginia was kept busy capturing Harpers Ferry, the remaining portion operating north of the Potomac River had run into trouble. The Union army, again led by General George McClellan, was maneuvering in force against Lee at Sharpsburg, Maryland. After that army's near destruction at Second Manassas, the Union general had performed a remarkable feat of swiftly reorganizing the scattered and demoralized troops and restoring their fighting capacity. By an extraordinary bit of luck and happenstance, McClellan had discovered a dispatch with Lee's written orders for the Maryland incursion. From these plans, he learned that the Southern army was separated, with large segments of it operating against Harpers Ferry. This was enough information for the usually slow and deliberate McClellan to act upon. He immediately ordered an advance on the Confederate contingent north of the Potomac River with intentions of defeating it before relief from Harpers Ferry could arrive.

When reports of lightning movements and attacks by Federal columns against the Rebel forces guarding the mountain passes north of the Potomac reached Lee, he was confounded. Such swiftness of march and sure tactical maneuver were completely contrary and out of character for an army led by the Union commander he had so recently opposed on the Virginia Peninsula. Little did he suspect at the time that his plans were known to the enemy. Sensing the perilous circumstances of his divided army, Lee quickly abandoned wistful campaign dreams for Maryland and Pennsylvania and issued orders for the entirety of the Army of Northern Virginia to concentrate at Sharpsburg, Maryland, a small village located some fifteen miles to the north of Harpers Ferry. This little town nestled along Antietam Run (a large creek or small river) was destined to host one of the bloodiest battles in the entire war. On September 17, 1862, in the early morning hours, McClellan, with some 90,000 effective troops, attacked the waiting Rebels entrenched along the west bank of the small stream known as Antietam. Lee's forces at the time of the first Federal onslaught numbered only 27,000. Later in the day, after Generals McLaws and A.P. Hill arrived at the battle front from Harpers Ferry, the Confederate force would approach some 40,000.

With a major military conflict imminent north of the Potomac, Walker's Division received urgent orders at Harpers Ferry to join Lee at Sharpsburg. After crossing the Potomac River once again at Shepherdstown and a hurried forced march, Walker united with Lee's forces situated beside Antietam Run on September 16. As early as 3:00 on the morning of September 17, Ransom's Brigade and General Walker's own brigade were moving to their battle positions and entrenching on the right side of the Confederate line approximately one-half mile south of Sharpsburg. This position was selected to cover the ford across Antietam Run and to provide support to General Toombs' command, which was posted in front of a bridge spanning the creek. However, around 9:00 A.M., orders were received from General Lee instructing Walker to rush his two brigades to the support of General Stonewall Jackson, who was attempting to hold the extreme left side of the Confederate battle line against furious Union assaults. There on the opposite side of the battlefield, the North's main thrust under the leadership of generals Sumner and Sedgwick was underway. To that hellish fight, General Robert Ransom led the 25th Regiment N.C. and his other regiments in quick time.

They passed behind the Confederate battle line, reached Sharpsburg and soon left it behind, and made their way through steady streams of wounded men who were being helped to the rear. Rushing into a woods on the Confederate left flank near the little Dunker Church

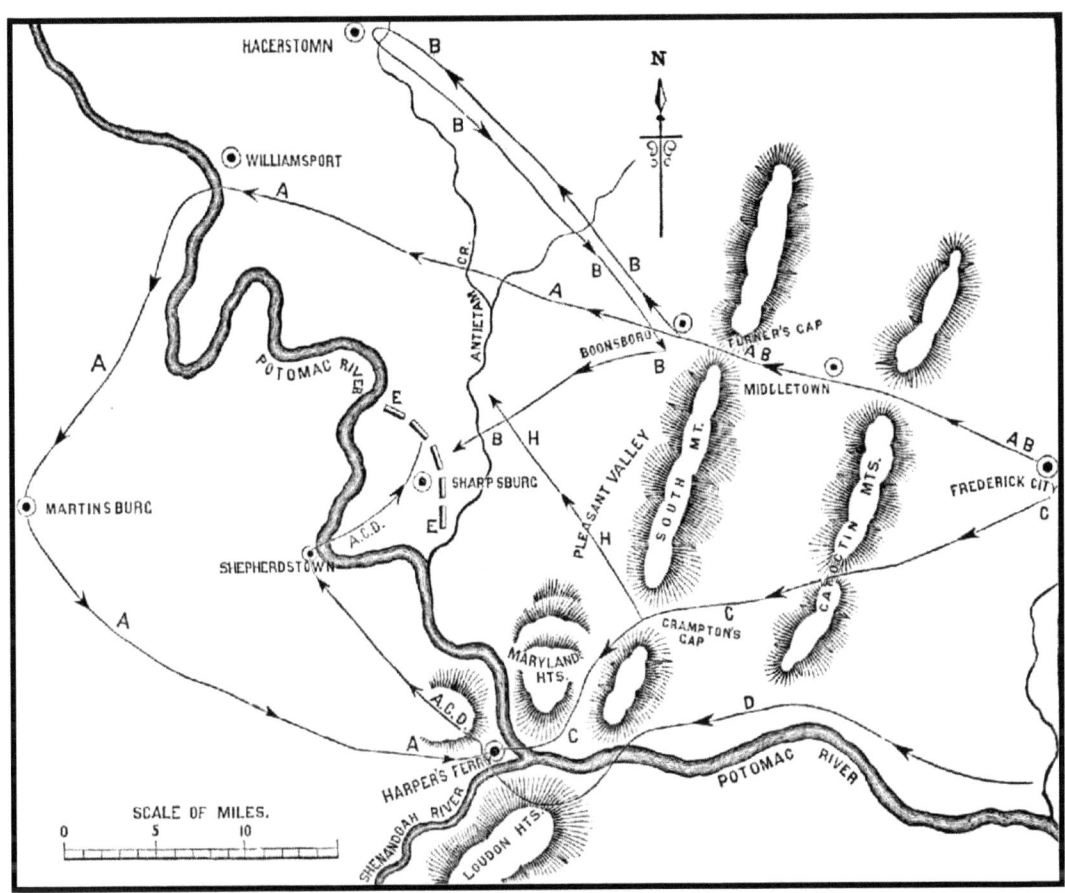

Movements around Harpers Ferry, September 10–17, 1862. (A) Jackson's march from Frederick to Sharpsburg. (B) Longstreet's march from Frederick to Sharpsburg. (C) McLaws and Anderson's march from Frederick to Sharpsburg. (D) Walker's march from Monocacy to Sharpsburg. (E) Confederate position at Antietam. (H) Franklin's march from Pleasant Valley to Antietam. Note: The arrows show the direction of the march. Two or more letters appearing together indicates that more than one body of troops followed the same route (*Harper's Weekly*).

where the commands of generals Hood and Early were committed to a ferocious struggle, General Ransom's troops were quickly formed into a battle line. Sprawled on the ground everywhere or sheltered behind trees, frightened and exhausted Rebel soldiers who had been driven back from more forward positions surrounded the brigade as it charged ahead into battle. A sixteen-year-old adjutant in the Thirty-fifth Regiment N.C. of Ransom's Brigade, Walter Clark, later described the action on Lee's left in a manner that raises one's pulse and adrenalin levels:

> About an hour before day, on the 17th, our division began its march for the position assigned us on the extreme right, where we were to oppose the Federals in any attempt to cross either the bridge (since known as Burnside's) or the ford over the Antietam below it, near Shiveley's [Snavely's].... On taking position, we immediately tore down the fences in our front which might obstruct the line of fire. About 9 A.M., a pressing order came to move to the left; this we did in quick time. As we were leaving our ground, I remember looking up the Antietam, the opposite bank of which was lined with Federal batteries. These were firing at the left wing of our army to the support of which we were moving.

The Federal gunners could be seen with the utmost distinctness as they loaded and fired. Moving northwards, we were passing in rear of our line of battle and met constant streams of the wounded coming out. All this time there was the steady booming of the cannon, the whistling of shells, the pattering of fire-arms, and the occasional yell or cheer rising above the roar of battle as some advantage was gained by either side.

Soon after passing the town the division was deployed in column of regiments. Around and just beyond the Dunker church, in the center of the Confederate left, our line had been broken and was completely swept away. A flood of Federals were pouring in; we were just in time — ten minutes,' five minutes' delay, and our army would have ceased to exist. We were marching up behind our line of battle, with our right flank perpendicular to it. As the first regiment got opposite to the break in our lines it made a wheel to the right and "went in." The next regiment, marching straight on, as soon as it cleared the left of the regiment preceding it, likewise wheeled to the right and took its place in line, and so on in succession. That is, we were marching north, and thus were successively thrown into line of battle facing east. As these regiments came successively into line they struck the Federal lines which were advancing; the crash was deafening. The sound of infantry firing at short distance can be likened to nothing so much as the dropping of a shower of hail-stones on an enormous tin roof.[9]

A pock-marked Dunker Church can be seen in this photograph taken after the battle of Antietam. The area around this church, known as the "West Woods," was the scene of furious fighting in which the 25th Regiment N.C. took part (Library of Congress).

The regimental historian, Lt. Ferguson, offered another description of the fighting at that scene: "At Sharpsburg the regiment was put into action near the extreme left of Lee's line. Our troops were retreating in front of a determined charge of the enemy, the men passed through the retreating troops, raised the yell, and charged with a determination that drove the enemy from the field to cover of his heavy works."[10]

The above remembrances are substantiated in General Walker's official report of the battle, in which he observed that Ransom's Brigade charged the woods that were filled with Yankees who had driven back Hood and Early's men; and the division, with Ransom's Brigade on the left, "advanced in splendid style, firing and cheering as they went, and in a few minutes cleared the woods, strewing it with the enemy dead and wounded." Having witnessed such a charge as this, General Jeb Stuart rode up to General Ransom and remarked that every soldier in that command was worthy to be made a commander. To this, the professional Ransom replied, "God bless the gallant boys, I will never curse them any more."[11]

While the 25th Regiment N.C. was occupying the wooded ground it had taken from the Federals, General Ransom rode off to find his wayward Twenty-fourth N.C. Regiment, which had been diverted and thrown into service by General Stuart. During the brief instance of his absence, enemy forces mounted a fierce assault against the brigade's position, which had been left under the command of Colonel Matt Ransom (General Robert Ransom's brother). After sustaining a "fearful storm of iron missile" for approximately thirty minutes, the Rebels repulsed the enemy, with the gallant Colonel Ransom, whose right arm hung limply from a sling as a result of wounds suffered at Malvern Hill, leading the charge. There were no further Yankee attempts to take Ransom and Walker's position by infantry charges. However, two large Union batteries opened up on Walker's troops and continued to lob artillery rounds at them on an intermittent basis for the remaining hours of the day.

Around 2:00 or 3:00 in the early afternoon, General Ransom received orders to advance and take the batteries in his front, whose incessant fire continued to wreak havoc among the Confederate ranks. With a keen knowledge of the enemy's strength surrounding and protecting the batteries, General Walker forbade the attack as he rode off to clarify the orders with General Longstreet. Shortly thereafter, General Ransom received new orders to hold his position and defer the attack against the enemy batteries until General Jackson's forces made an assault against the Union right flank. General Jackson never attempted that attack and the lethal and persistent fire from batteries in front of General Ransom's troops halted only after darkness enveloped the battlefield.

During the brief interim that Colonel Matt Ransom was in command of Ransom's Brigade, he apparently received a visit from two senior Confederate generals, Stonewall Jackson and Jeb Stuart. The following story as recorded by the Thirty-fifth Regiment's historian explains how General Jackson assessed the enemy's strength opposing Ransom's Brigade and reconsidered an order to assail that point:

> During a lull in the battle, General Jackson, with General J.E.B. Stuart, visited our lines, which were in the famous "West Woods." General Jackson had on an old worn uniform, his slouch hat was pulled down over his eyes, and he was riding a mighty sorry-looking claybank horse. He rode up to where Colonel Ransom was standing and said he wanted him to advance and take a battery that was in sight. Colonel Ransom replied he would do so if he ordered it, but that he was afraid he would fail. Jackson replied he had just witnessed his charge upon that battery and he thought if he would try again he could take it. Colonel Ransom replied he had tried it and when he got on top of the hill he saw what he thought was the greater part of McClellan's army behind it. Jackson asked: "Have you a good climber in your command?" Colonel Ransom called for volunteers, and Private Wm.

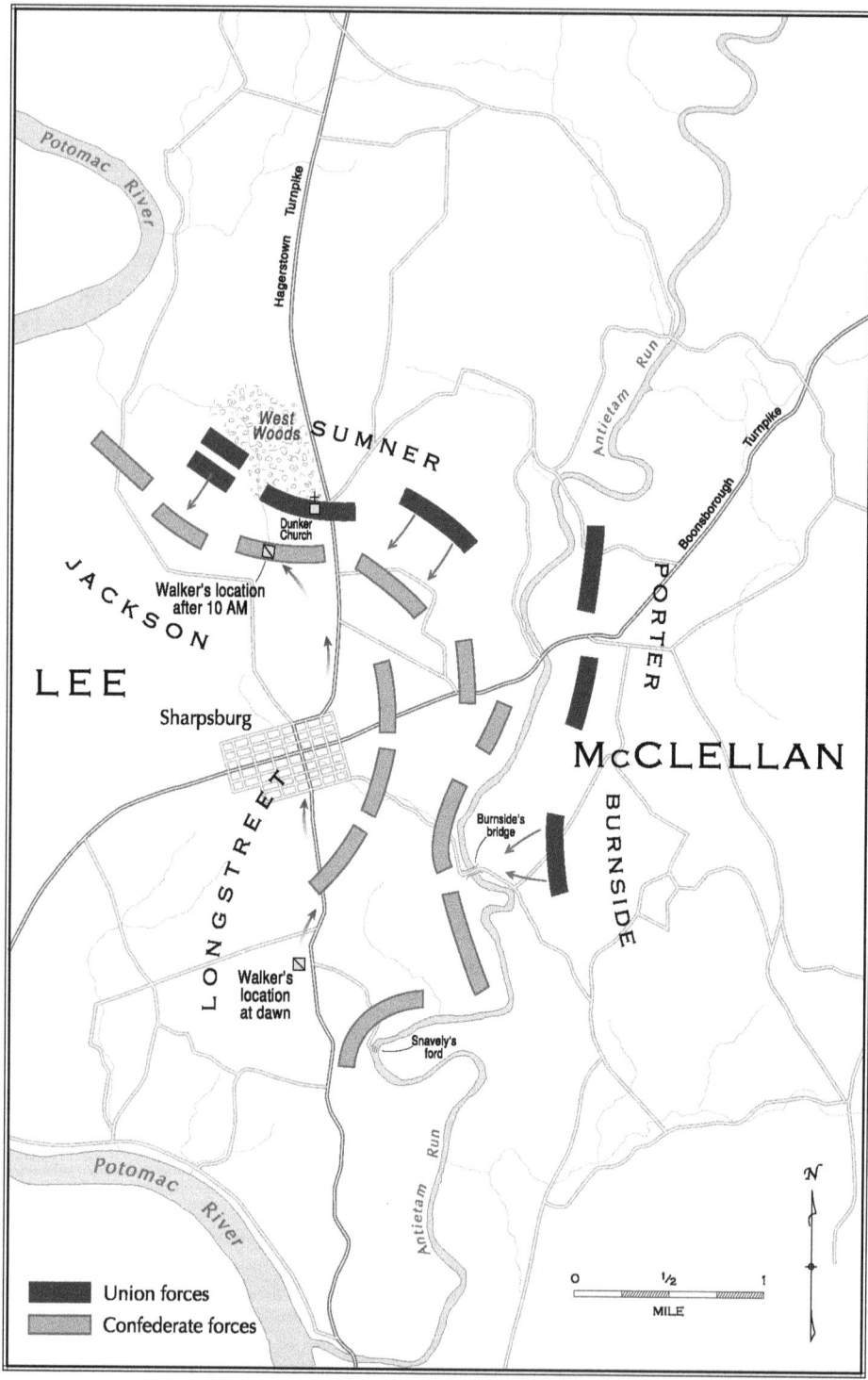

Battle of Antietam: September 17, 1862. The 25th Regiment N.C. battled furiously for much of that bloody September day to repulse Union assaults against the Confederate left near the small Dunker Church in the West Woods (Peter Krafft, Florida State University).

S. Hood, Company H, jumped up and said he could climb. Jackson picked out a tall hickory tree and told him to go up it. Hood pulled off his shoes in a jiffy and went up like a squirrel. When he got near the top, Jackson, sitting on his horse, under the tree, asked him: "How many troops are over there?" Hood, uttering an exclamation of amazement, replied: "Oceans of them." Jackson sternly said: "Count the flags, sir!" Hood began: "One, two, three, four ..." etc., etc., General Jackson repeating after him the numbers until he had counted thirty-nine, when Jackson said: "That will do, come down, sir." All this time the enemy's sharpshooters were firing at Hood.[12]

It was thus that an ill-advised attack against the enemy battery was rescinded, due in a large part to the eagle eyes and daring of the youthful Private William Hood.

General Robert Ransom was filled with pride over the behavior of all his men, not just the young Hood, in the hotly contested fighting at Sharpsburg. The following commentary was included in his official report of the brigade's actions along Antietam Run and attests his satisfaction with the men who he led in that battle:

> I cannot too highly compliment the action of the men and officers for their gallant behavior during the entire day. They formed, under a galling fire, and, in presence of our retiring troops, pressed forward and drove back a far superior force, and, three times afterward, repulsed determined attacks of the enemy and in largely superior numbers to our own; but the highest credit is due for the perfect staunchness exhibited during an eight hours' exposure to an unparalleled cannonade and within canister range.[13]

General Walker in his report also praised the conduct of Ransom's Brigade and of General Robert Ransom in particular. He wrote that Ransom acted coolly in holding the Confed-

Artist's sketch depicts Rebels repulsing a Union attack in the "West Woods" at the Battle of Antietam (Library of Congress, artist: Alfred Rudolf Waud).

erate position on the left and possibly saved the day for the southern forces: "To Brigadier-General Ransom's coolness, judgment, and skill we are in a great degree indebted for the successful maintenance of our position on the left, which, to have been permanently gained by the enemy, would, in all probability, have been to us the loss of the battle."[14]

After being finally repulsed on the Confederate left, the Federals shifted the main force of the attack successively against the center of the Rebel line and to the extreme right side of the battlefield southeast of Sharpsburg. At those contested grounds the fighting was equally ferocious and the powerful surging blue columns received equally stubborn treatment from the Rebels. As night fell and the sound of rifle fire and cannon shot petered out, the exhausted southern army hunkered down and waited in the rain overnight and throughout the next day for McClellan to finish the deadly business that he had started. But he didn't attack on that next day and General Lee was not inclined to give him further opportunity to do so. "In the dark of the night the whole Army stealthily moved off and recrossed the Potomac; the passage of the river being lighted up by torches held by men stationed in the river on horseback. The Army came off safely without arousing the Federal Army, and left not a cannon nor a wagon behind."[15]

Colonel Henry Rutledge, who was wounded during the battle and also suffering from the onslaught of a typhoid fever attack, was in very poor condition to travel. In mid-stream of the Potomac crossing, the colonel fainted and tumbled from his horse into the waist-deep water of the river. Recounting the perilous circumstances years later to his sons, Rutledge remembered being rescued by his black body servant, who accompanied him throughout the war. Ignoring Yankee sharpshooter fire from the banks of the river, the colonel's loyal servant waded to his master, heaved him across his shoulders and bore him to the southern shore and to safety.[16]

The battle of Antietam, or Sharpsburg as referred to in the South, was a heroic struggle between determined foes, and the result hung in the balance all day long. From 10:00 A.M. until dark, the 25th Regiment N.C. and Walker's Division battled on the hard-fought left flank in the West Woods between Jackson's divisions and those led by General John Bell Hood and General Daniel Harvey Hill. In holding that position until reinforcements arrived, a service was rendered by those mountain men that would be difficult to match again. And had not General McLaws and General A.P. Hill arrived at opportune moments from Harpers Ferry with reinforcements, the Confederate army may very likely have been annihilated on the banks of the Potomac. Both sides in this conflict would soon proclaim success and victory. The South's claim that it had repelled McClellan's assaults against all odds and with a disadvantage in troop strength of more than 2 to 1 could not be disclaimed.

Yet, the North had halted the Army of Northern Virginia's incursion and had repelled it to Virginia from whence it had daringly come. All across the North, the battle of Sharpsburg would be hailed as a great victory by the Army of the Potomac and would give President Lincoln the necessary political strength and impetus to pronounce his plans for emancipating the slaves of the South. Dulling any claims of victory by the antagonists, however, was the terrible price paid in manhood. In what is claimed to be the bloodiest and most costly single day of the Civil War, the Union sustained approximately 15,000 casualties at Sharpsburg and Lee's army suffered almost 14,000 as a result of the Maryland expedition. The cost in blood for the 25th Regiment N.C. was 4 men dead and another 14 wounded.

After crossing the river into the Shenandoah Valley, Lee waited for a short interlude while he and his commanders observed the Army of the Potomac and deliberated where next to leverage their veteran troops. The 25th Regiment N.C. waded the Potomac again at Shepherdstown and marched to the environs of Martinsburg, Virginia (now West Virginia) and then on to Winchester, Virginia, where it remained encamped until October 23, 1862. Lt. Ferguson's account of this period gives a flavor of the conditions experienced by the troops while camping in the Shenandoah Valley. "Most of the Regiment's camping equipment had been left behind at Richmond and on the march the men had resorted to using ramrods for baking and forked sticks for the roast. Extra clothing and blankets had been left behind at Sharpsburg so after recrossing the Potomac they were without blankets and during the September nights the beds were roomy but cool."[17]

Colonel Rutledge had so endeared himself to the noncommissioned officers and privates of the 25th Regiment by his élan and courage that they presented him with a fine saddle horse after the Maryland Campaign. The commissioned officers were not allowed to bear any part of the expense or take part in the presentation ceremonies.[18] It made no matter to those mountain men that their colonel was born of a wealthy planter family from the South Carolina low country and had inherited one of the finest plantations in all the Palmetto State. Nor were they bothered to know that his great-great-grandfather was president of the Continental Congress and two of his great-grandfathers had signed the Declaration of Independence. Of more importance to the regiment's men were the courage and leadership that Colonel Rutledge demonstrated in the heat of battle, and the manner in which he treated them and cared for their welfare. It surely must have been a touching presentation ceremony, but one the colonel may not have been able to fully enjoy. The fever which caused the young commander to tumble from his mount into the Potomac River had worsened, and he was hospitalized in October 1862 with "febris typhoides."

When it became a certainty that the bulk of the Federal army had recrossed the Blue Ridge Mountains and was moving toward the Rappahannock River, the 25th Regiment N.C. was ordered with the rest of Ransom's Brigade and Walker's Division to Culpepper Court House via Paris, Virginia, and then on to Madison Court House in Virginia. Arriving there weary and covered with ragged and torn uniform remnants that had barely survived the rigors of the previous months' battles, the mountain boys bivouacked for a brief interlude. At Madison Court House they drew a supply of much needed new clothing and blankets, and were soon on the march again. The 25th Regiment N.C. was ordered with the rest of the Army of Northern Virginia to Fredericksburg, Virginia, where an impending Yankee invasion force was forming on the banks of the Rappahannock River.

7

Heights of Fredericksburg

The Union army had been invigorated with new-found confidence from their success at Sharpsburg, Maryland, and under the continued prodding of President Lincoln plotted to carry the fight to the Confederates once again and capture Richmond. The president was bitterly disappointed with McClellan's lack of aggressiveness in the days following the Battle of Antietam, so much so that he determined to make a command change. He chose General Ambrose Burnside to lead the Union Army of the Potomac, the same general who had captured Roanoke Island and New Bern and had wreaked havoc along North Carolina's eastern coast in early 1862. In very little time, Burnside laid plans for another campaign against Richmond with the main thrust launched from the North. By November 19, 1862, he and an army of some 120,000 men had appeared at Falmouth, Virginia, southeast of Washington, D.C., along the middle reaches of the Rappahannock River.

At Falmouth, where Washington, D.C., was fifty miles in his rear and Richmond, the objective, fifty miles ahead, Burnside dallied for more than two weeks. There he anticipated the arrival of portable pontoons to bridge the Rappahannock River and for supplies to be brought up from the Union base of operations at Acquia Creek on the Potomac River. Opposed across the Rappahannock, just downstream from Falmouth, was the town of Fredericksburg, Virginia, which General Lee reached on November 20 with General Longstreet's First Corps. Just a day or two earlier, Generals Ransom and McLaws had arrived with the vanguard of the Confederate army. So it was that, while the Union forces hesitated and waited for pontoon boats, the remainder of the Army of Northern Virginia rushed to Fredericksburg to block the Federals' river crossing. All along the imposing western heights overlooking the town and the river, Confederate troops, some 78,000 strong, began hastily establishing and fortifying defense lines.

From the high ground he had chosen to confront and block Burnside's invading forces, General Lee was able to peer down upon the quaint old colonial town of Fredericksburg. Picturesque homes and store buildings fashioned from brick, smoke from their chimneys curling upward into a gray winter sky, presented Lee with a dilemma. He was acutely aware that the citizens dwelling there were in imminent danger, and concluded that the scenic village which stood between two great armies would experience devastation on a grand scale. Streets filled with old shops and once harboring the law office of James Monroe would soon have to be vacated by the citizenry and would serve to shelter and shield warriors from both sides. Lee's glances across the valley of the Rappahannock River searched for an old mansion called Chatham. Under the canopy of ancient trees that grew on its grounds, he had wooed his wife,

Rebels behind the stone wall at Fredericksburg (Library of Congress; artist Allen C. Redwood).

Mary Custis, the granddaughter of the woman who married George Washington.[1] He realized that soon the smoke from hundreds of Union cannon firing from the Stafford Heights located beyond the river and commanding Fredericksburg would hide the place of fond youthful memories and signal the beginning of a deadly enterprise to destroy his army. To the enemy's credit must be counted this unfortunate choice of battleground, General Lee rationalized, as he issued orders to have Fredericksburg vacated. Later he wrote the following tribute in which he extolled the virtuous loyalties of the hapless citizens who were forced to abandon their homes and beautiful town:

> The city authorities were informed that, while our forces would not use the place for military purposes, its occupation by the enemy would be resisted, and directions were given for the removal of the women and children as rapidly as possible. The threatened bombardment (by the Union army) did not take place, but, in view of the imminence of a collision between the two armies, the inhabitants were advised to leave the city, and almost the entire population, without a murmur, abandoned

Union General Ambrose Burnside took command of the Army of the Potomac and immediately laid plans to move on Richmond from the north. General Robert E. Lee's Army of Northern Virginia intervened at the old colonial river town of Fredericksburg, Virginia (Library of Congress).

Aquia Landing, pictured here, was the Union base of operations on the Potomac River from which the Army of the Potomac was supplied during its campaign to cross the Rappahannock River at Fredericksburg (Library of Congress).

Photograph showing Fredericksburg as viewed from across the Rappahannock River (Library of Congress).

their homes. History presents no instance of a people exhibiting a purer and more unselfish patriotism or a higher spirit of fortitude and courage than was evinced by the citizens of Fredericksburg. They cheerfully incurred great hardships and privations, and surrendered their homes and property to destruction rather than yield them into the hands of the enemies of their country.[2]

Major General John Walker had been assigned to the Confederate army in the west. Upon his departure, Brigadier General Robert Ransom assumed division leadership responsibility in Lieutenant General James Longstreet's First Corps. Under Ransom's division command at this time were his own brigade and also General John R. Cook's brigade of North Carolina regiments. Ransom positioned his artillery and two brigades, including the 25th Regiment N.C. led by Lieutenant Colonel Samuel C. Bryson (Colonel Henry Rutledge was convalescing from a wound received at Antietam and the effects of typhoid fever), on Marye's Heights some four to six hundred yards in the rear of the stately Brompton mansion, or Marye house, as it was referred to by the combatants. This colonial brick edifice built in the 1830s by John L. Marye, of French Huguenot descent, was fronted with a high portico supported by four large ionic columns extending to the roof line. The imposing Marye house

At Fredericksburg Federal engineers constructed pontoon bridges while under the deadly fire of Rebel sharpshooters (*Harper's Weekly*; artist Alfred Rudolf Waud).

Rebel sharpshooters fire on the Yankee bridge builders at Fredericksburg (*The American Heritage Century Collection of Civil War Art*, artist: Allen C. Redwood).

presided over the bluff given its name and was surrounded with the cannon of the Washington Artillery, infantry troops and other trappings of war.

At the foot of Marye's Heights facing the town and just above the river's flood plain was Telegraph Road, a portion of which ran parallel with the river's course. Generations of wagon traffic had worn the old roadbed lower than the surrounding terrain, and a stone retaining wall had been built along the river side of the roadway to mark and protect the farm fields. As a result, the road's rutted surface was "sunk" a few feet lower than the top of the wall. This

Sunken Road, as it would later be known, provided an ideal entrenchment for the Confederate infantry troops and was quickly occupied as a first line of defense by thousands of General Longstreet's men, including Ransom's Twenty-fourth Regiment N.C.

Eventually Burnside's pontoon boats reached him. The delay in their arrival at the front was apparently due to dual considerations: Burnside's propensity for issuing unclear orders

Top: As seen in this photograph, much of Fredericksburg lay in ruins after the Union cannonade to rid the town of the Rebels (Library of Congress). *Above:* Union troops crossing the Rappahannock River at Fredericksburg on the night of December 11–12, 1862 (Library of Congress; artist Alfred Rudolf Waud).

and uncertainties in Washington regarding the location of the river crossing. Beginning on the morning of December 11 and through the daylight hours, Federal engineers struggled mightily to span the Rappahannock with two bridges at Fredericksburg and a third one located a couple of miles downstream. But it was a mission fraught with danger. The Yankees were exposed and easy targets for a brigade of Mississippi Rebel sharpshooters firing from Fredericksburg's riverfront buildings. As the bridge builders ventured out to throw their pontoons across the narrow river, the Southern marksmen proceeded to easily pick them off one by one. After a few hours of such turkey-shooting, the Union artillery was at last turned on the snipers, but the brave Mississippians continued to fire from behind the rubble and ruins of the shelled buildings. In his report of the battle afterwards, Lieutenant General James Longstreet lauded the service rendered by the Mississippians: "Brigadier-General Barksdale with his brigade held the enemy's entire army at the river bank for sixteen hours, giving us abundance of time to complete our arrangements for battle. A more gallant and worthy service is rarely accomplished by so small a force."[3]

Three Federal regiments finally were able to cross the river in boats and drive the Rebels from town after fierce house-to-house fighting. Hours later when the main Federal army reached Fredericksburg, its troops continued the destruction that the cannoneers had begun. And many of the blue-coated soldiers of less than honorable constitution looted furniture, fixtures and other valuables left behind in the abandoned buildings and generally did a fine job of ransacking the Rebel property.[4]

Through the night the dauntless Yankee engineers worked to lay down their pontoon bridges, and by the cold dawn of December 12 the job was complete. General Burnside immediately began throwing his troops across the river and deploying the Federal columns. Confederate artillery was directed at the blue host assembling on the river's edge, which brought on a reciprocal fire from the powerful Yankee guns. Shortly after 9:00 A.M. on December 13, 1862, after the veil of fog hanging over the river lifted, a Union column struck at General Stonewall Jackson and his forces a few miles downstream from Fredericksburg. Jackson's forces met their Union attackers with obstinate resistance and were eventually able to repulse the enemy, but not without losses.

The main Union thrust was launched around 11:00 A.M. and was aimed toward Marye's Heights and the Sunken Road, where Longstreet's anxious Rebel soldiers waited. Wave after wave of bluecoats marched out of the town, formed ranks and courageously rushed across open fields into a veritable storm of exploding shot and Confederate bullets. Well-positioned in the Sunken Road, lines of Rebel soldiers, one behind the other and protected by the rock wall, alternately took deadly aim and fired at the hordes of stubborn charging Yankees. As if felled by a scythe, the courageous boys in blue fell one on top another in front of the stone fence. The carnage didn't soon stop. Those poor brave Union soldiers continued the onslaught, reportedly coming in waves every quarter hour. In the wake of each receding wave, dead and wounded soldiers lay strewn in piles and contorted positions across the fallow ground in front of the Rebel defenses. In his report of the battle, General McLaws recorded the scene in front of one section of the stone wall:

> The body of one man, believed to be an officer, was found within about 30 yards of the stone wall, and other single bodies were scattered at increased distances until the main mass of the dead lay thickly strewn over the ground at something over 100 yards off, and extending to the ravine, commencing at the point where our men would allow the enemy's column to approach before opening fire, and beyond which no organized body of men was able to pass.[5]

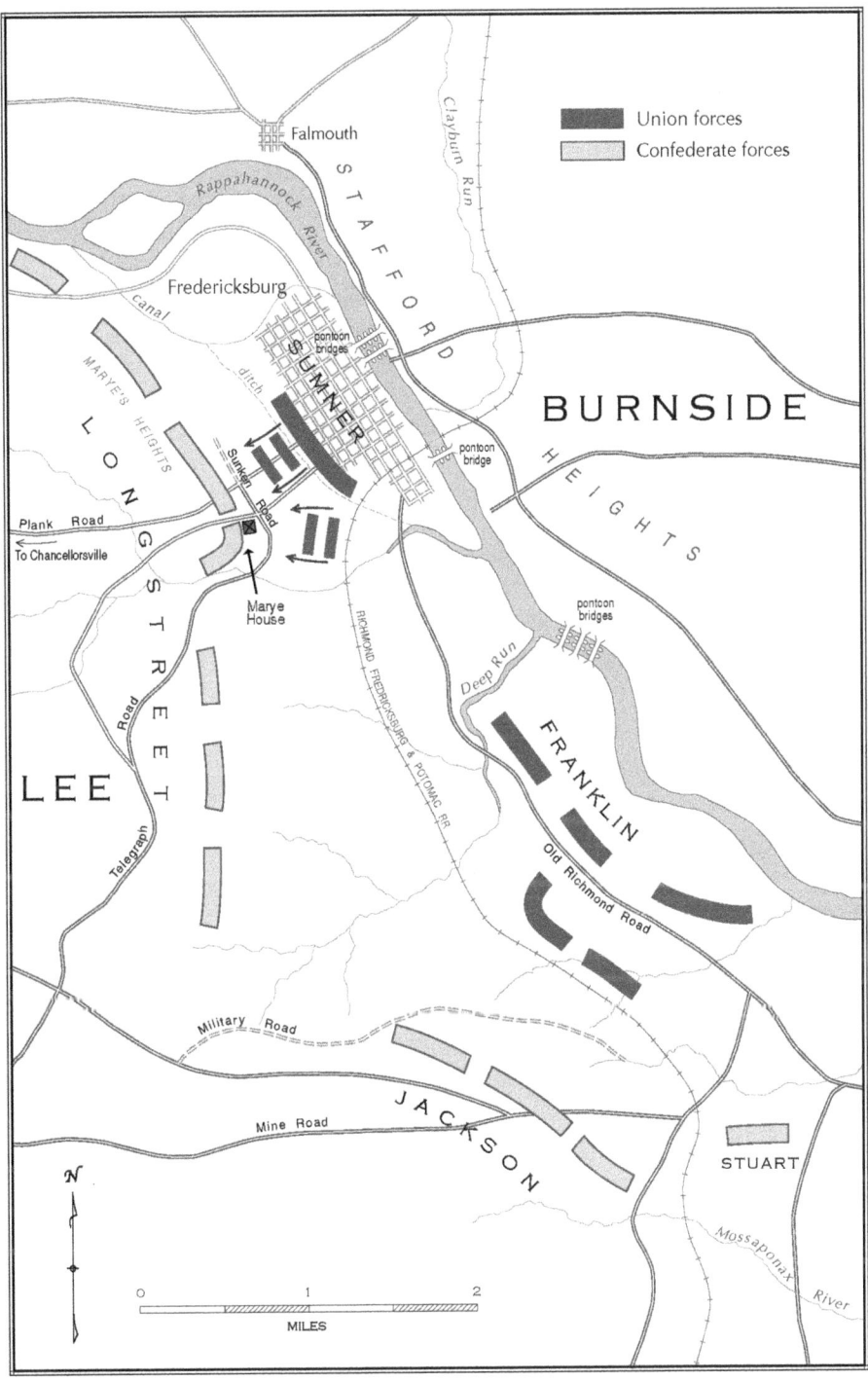

Battle of Fredericksburg: December 13, 1862. From a position on top of Marye's Heights, the 25th Regiment N.C. rushed forward to the Confederate defense line behind the stone wall along the Sunken Road. There they fought off wave after wave of attacking bluecoated soldiers (Peter Krafft, Florida State University).

Rebels positioned at the Sunken Road and atop Marye's Heights maintained a composure that made Longstreet and Lee proud. They kept a continuous and deadly concentrated fire directed at the moving Union masses. Artillery barrages from the Confederate-occupied heights swept the field in front of the Sunken Road and responded to the Union guns firing from new battery positions along the river and from the Stafford Heights beyond. One Confederate general commented afterwards that never had Lee presented so many muskets on so narrow a front. General Lee himself, upon observing the carnage from a vantage point overlooking the battle, was heard to utter the philosophical words, "It is well that war is so terrible — otherwise we would grow too fond of it."[6]

A narrative of the battle written by Lieutenant General James Longstreet and staff was included in his official report to Confederate army headquarters. The general's account provides a summary of the day's action without burdensome detail, and gives insight into the flow of the battle and the movement of troops. Also of note in Longstreet's rendition of the fighting is that, after the first couple of Yankee charges against Marye's Heights, General Robert Ransom was given "immediate care of the point attacked." The following has been excerpted from General Longstreet's report:

Ransom's Brigade, along with the 25th Regiment N.C., was positioned in the rear of the Marye house, shown in this photograph, when the battle of Fredericksburg commenced. Soon after the Union attacks on Marye's Heights were underway, the 25th N.C. was rushed to the support of Rebel defenders behind the stone wall along the Sunken Road (Library of Congress).

One of the main defensive positions of General Lee's army at Fredericksburg was taken below Marye's Heights along the Sunken Road, pictured in these two photographs. Soldiers of the 25th Regiment N.C. stood steadfastly side-by-side behind the low stone wall and fired into the waves of valiant bluecoated soldiers that attacked their position (Library of Congress).

> About 11 A.M. I sent orders for the batteries to play upon the streets and bridges beyond the city, by way of diversion in favor of our right. The batteries had hardly opened when the enemy's infantry began to move out toward my line. Our pickets in front of the Marye house were soon driven in, and the enemy began to deploy his forces in front of that point. Our artillery, being in position, opened fire as soon as the masses became dense enough to warrant it. This fire was very destructive and demoralizing in its effects, and frequently made gaps in the enemy's ranks that could be seen at the distance of a mile. The enemy continued his advance and made his attack at the Marye Hill in handsome style. He did not meet the fire of our infantry with any heart, however, and was therefore readily repulsed. Another effort was speedily made, but with little more success. The attack was again renewed, and again repulsed. Other forces were seen preparing for another attack, when I suggested to General McLaws the propriety of re-enforcing his advanced line by a brigade. He had previously re-enforced with part of General Kershaw's brigade and ordered forward the balance. About this time Brig. Gen. T.R.R. Cobb fell, mortally wounded, and almost simultaneously Brig. Gen. J.R. Cooke was severely wounded. General Kershaw dashed to the front to take the command.
>
> General Ransom, on the Marye Hill, was charged with the immediate care of the point attacked, with orders to send forward additional reinforcements if it should become necessary, and to use Featherston's brigade, Anderson' division, if he should require it.
>
> The attack upon our right seemed to subside about 2 o'clock, when I directed Major-General Pickett to send me two of his brigades. One (Kemper's) was sent to General Ransom, to be placed in some secure position, to be ready in case it should be wanted. The other (Jenkins') was ordered to General McLaws, to replace that of Kershaw in his line. The enemy soon completed his arrangements for a renewed attack, and moved forward with much determination. He met with no better success than he had on the previous occasions. These efforts were repeated and continued from time to time until after night: when he left, the field was literally strewn with his dead and wounded.[7]

At the beginning of the day's action, General Ransom's brigades were positioned in reserve behind the Marye house and the heights. Shortly after the Union forces began their massive offensive and assaulted the Sunken Road and Marye's Heights, Ransom ordered the 25th Regiment N.C. into action. Evidence of the movement of his troops can be found in General Lee's report on the battle:

> In the third assault, the brave and lamented Brig. Gen. Thomas R.R. Cobb fell, at the head of his gallant troops, and, almost at the same moment, Brigadier-General Cooke was borne from the field severely wounded. Fearing that Cobb's brigade might exhaust its ammunition, General Longstreet had directed General Kershaw to take two regiments to its support. Arriving after the fall of General Cobb, he assumed command, his troops taking position on the crest and at the foot of the hill, to which point General Ransom also advanced three other regiments.[8]

Further and more detailed information regarding the action of the 25th Regiment N.C. during the enemy's third assault can be found in the Official Records of the battle as set down by General Robert Ransom himself:

> The enemy now seemed determined to reach our position, and formed apparently a triple line. Observing this movement on his part, I brought up three regiments of my brigade to within 100 yards of the crest of the hills, and pushed forward the Twenty-fifth North Carolina Volunteers to the crest. The enemy, almost massed, moved to the charge heroically, and met the withering fire of our artillery and small-arms with wonderful staunchness. On they came within less than 150 paces of our line, but nothing could live before the sheet of lead that was hurled at them from this distance. They momentarily wavered, broke, and rushed headlong from the field. A few, however, more resolute than the rest, lingered under cover of some fences and houses, and annoyed us with a scattering

but well-directed fire. The Twenty-fifth North Carolina Volunteers reached the crest of the hill just in time to pour into the enemy a few volleys at most deadly range, and then took position shoulder to shoulder with Cobb's and Cook's men in the road.[9]

Throughout that long afternoon the regiment, its soldiers standing "shoulder to shoulder"[10] with the rest of those brave men behind the stone wall, took part in the heavy fighting and was as resolute and unwavering as any other regiment on the field. A firsthand account of the regiment's action and his own experience comes from the pen of Lt. Ferguson. It is not for the squeamish:

> On 11 and 12 December 1862, the regiment was in position back of Marye's House. About 11 o'clock on the morning of the 13th, General Robert Ransom informed the regiment that General Cobb's men, who were holding our line in front of Marye's House, were short of ammunition and must be reinforced, and that the undertaking was a dangerous one; the men fully understanding the importance and danger of the duty, moved forward with a firm and steady step, like patriots, to battle. On reaching the crest of the hill (the regiment having been divided so as to pass the house on either side) it met a fearful fire from the enemy two hundred yards off. In casting an eye along the line men could be seen falling like sheaves before the sickle. In less than two minutes the regiment's loss in killed and wounded was one hundred and twenty. It reached Cobb's line just as his men were emptying their last cartridge, and held the line, repelling six successive assaults until relieved at nightfall.[11]

Lt. Ferguson's record of the battle demonstrates that Fredericksburg was not entirely a one-sided fight. He professes that in less than two minutes after being thrown into action on Marye's Heights, the 25th Regiment N.C. lost 120 men dead and wounded. However, more current estimates of the casualties suffered that day at Fredericksburg dispute Lt. Ferguson's tally and indicate that 12 were killed and approximately 74 suffered wounds, 10 of which would prove to be mortal.[12] Either accounting is a fearful toll and is indeed impressive, but it pales in comparison to the staggering losses experienced by the Union forces. By the end of the day, Union casualties totaled 13,000, while the Confederates suffered less than 5,000. A dispatch from a Northern newspaper correspondent on the scene described the valor demonstrated by the Union troops as well as the lapse in the Union command: "It can hardly be in human nature for men to show more valor, or generals to manifest less judgment."[13]

As previously mentioned, General Robert Ransom submitted a formal report of his division's actions during the Battle of Fredericksburg. It was Confederate policy to do so and all commanders, Confederate and Union, issued these reports at the conclusion of major battles, skirmishes and other significant military actions. Usually they included the details and minutiae regarding the specific military action and were filled with lavish commendations of the performance of various units and laudations for deserving subordinate officers. This was especially true following successful conclusions of major battles when the report writers and their staffs were flushed with victory and eager to record their version of the story for superiors, the public and future generations. General Ransom's report to Lee and Longstreet singles out for special approbation only one infantry regiment, from the eight in his command, for service rendered during the Battle of Fredericksburg. That regiment was the 25th North Carolina, and General Ransom wrote this of the unit, "While I do not disparage any, I cannot fail to mention the splendid and dashing action of the Twenty-fifth North Carolina Volunteers, Lieutenant Colonel (Samuel C.) Bryson commanding, in going into battle."[14]

It is apparent that General Ransom was deeply impressed with the devastating firepower that greeted the 25th Regiment N.C. as they were thrown into action atop the heights. He undoubtedly witnessed their rush to the battle and the terrible scene where Lt. Ferguson recorded that one hundred and twenty mountain men were killed or wounded within a two-minute period.

Until that point in the sectional conflict, Fredericksburg was an unparalleled victory for General Lee and his Army of Northern Virginia. With this success came ever more acclaim for Robert E. Lee. The reputation of his army gleamed brighter and was hailed the world over. On the other hand, the North's Grand Army was defeated once again, this time decisively. Union Commander General Burnside was shaken and crestfallen at his failure as well as his army's. The generals and staff under his command lost any confidence they might have once held in him. There was no follow-up attack on December 14, nor were there further attacks during the rest of the winter months. President Lincoln would ultimately replace Burnside with one of his subordinate generals, Joseph Hooker; and it would be spring before the weather was suitable for further hostile actions by the Army of the Potomac.

One of the brigade's regimental historians wrote of the generosity that General Robert Ransom demonstrated toward the citizens of the war-ravaged town of Fredericksburg:

> [U]pon returning to camp on December 18, General Robert Ransom called the officers of his Brigade to his tent to solicit their charity for the people of Fredericksburg. The general headed the list with one hundred dollars, one-third of his month's pay. This generous example of their commander was generally followed by the officers of the Brigade. I am not aware of an instance of like generosity on the part of a Confederate brigade.[15]

Rebels foraging (Library of Congress; artist Alfred Rudolf Waud).

Rebels roasting corn (Library of Congress; artist Alfred Rudolf Waud).

The winter of 1862–1863 was an unusually cold one at Fredericksburg. The 25th Regiment N.C. remained encamped there after the battle to keep the Federals hemmed up and to guard against more Yankee maneuvering and aggressions. Living conditions were primitive in camp. The men built shelters from pine brush and received blankets and clothing from home to keep them warm by the fire.[16] Family and home would be in the thoughts and dreams of all the mountain boys. It would be their second Christmas away from loved ones, and that surely provoked a powerful homesickness in more than just a few. At least the men of the 25th Regiment had each other to lean on, confide in, and gain strength from; and they now had real war stories to tell and brag about.

8

Back to North Carolina

Eastern Carolina Coastal Defense

In eastern North Carolina the Federals had recently assailed the Confederate transportation facilities at Goldsboro, destroying a key railroad bridge there. At the insistence of Governor Vance and others, General Robert E. Lee reluctantly acquiesced to the demands for more troops to reinforce the scant and beleaguered forces in North Carolina. He started Ransom's Brigade from Fredericksburg on January 3, 1863, to the eastern Carolina defenses. Uprooted from their pine shelters during the cold of winter, one of the Rebel soldiers later wrote:

> The men started to march, ostensibly, for a new camp. The men started out loaded down with camp impediment and winter quarters fixings, but marching past the site selected for the camp, we halted only after a fifteen mile march. As we marched, one by one, the planks, breadtrays, stools, water buckets, etc., etc., were grudgingly discarded until at the end of the day's march, while our impediment was gone, our hearts were light with the hope that we were on the way to North Carolina. This proved to be true, for after marching through Richmond we took the cars at Petersburg for Kenansville, N. C., our destination.[1]

About this same time, Joseph Cathey from Forks of Pigeon in Haywood County received news of the regiment's mountain boys in a letter from a Mr. J.W. Killian of the small western North Carolina community of Davidson's River. Indications are that the troops were in "fine spirits" and must have recently received payment from the Confederate army. They sent home with Mr. Killian "a good large pack of money" to Joseph Cathey's care and distribution to their different families. The letter in part reads as follows:

> Davidson River Jan 19 1863
>
> ____ Cathey Dear Sir
>
> I arrived home last Friday Evening from the army near Fredricksburg I found our mountain Boys general well and in fine Spirits and better clad than I expected to See them Gen Ransom & Gen Cooks Brigagis left there camps on the 4th Jan at 6 o clock a m for part unknown to them at the time while I was at Richmond they marched through the city I went with them out 3 miles the night I was in Petirsburg they were in 2 miles of the city But did not see them I understood they were a waiting for orders where to go I seen Doct Fletcher at Raleigh he told me there were ordered to Goldsboro NC and the Rail Road was making arrangements to transport them from Petersburg to Goldsboro If any

other troops have been ordered from Gen Lees army I did not here it Capt James Cathey and a good many of his Boys sent a good large pack of money to your care and requested you to send an agent after it for them.[2]

Spirits were buoyed as the men entered North Carolina and arrived by train at Warsaw Station, encamping at nearby Kenansville some ten miles distant. This Confederate stronghold, which would soon become a major manufacturing center for war materials, was located along the Wilmington-Weldon Railroad about midway between Goldsboro and Wilmington. From Kenansville, Rebel troops could react to Federal raids out of occupied New Bern against Goldsboro's railroad infrastructure, as well as offer support for the defenders protecting the extremely critical Confederate port city of Wilmington.

In late January 1863, the Fifty-sixth Regiment N.C. was assigned to Ransom's Brigade, which also included at that time the Twenty-fourth, Twenty-fifth, Thirty-fifth and Forty-ninth North Carolina regiments. On February 25 Lieutenant General James Longstreet was assigned the new command of the Department of Virginia and North Carolina, reporting to General Robert E. Lee, with headquarters at Petersburg, Virginia. Major General D.H. Hill was given operational responsibility for North Carolina and he established his command post at Goldsboro. The 25th Regiment and the other regiments of Ransom's Brigade were attached to General Hill and operated at different times out of Weldon, Kenansville, Kinston, Wilmington, Garysburg and other regional hot spots in eastern North Carolina. The Old North State would eventually host some 30,000 Confederate troops to effect the responsibilities tasked to generals Longstreet and Hill. Not only was their military force expected to defend eastern North Carolina from the Yankee invaders and insure the continuance of the vital supply lines in that important theatre, but they were also charged with gathering much needed food supplies from the productive coastal region plantations for General Lee's Army of Northern Virginia.[3]

The 25th N.C. was involved in relatively few hostilities of note during the first several months of 1863. Although the regiment was not engaged directly in General D.H. Hill's siege of Washington, N.C., during this period, it was caught up in ancillary movements on the periphery of that Confederate action. An important port city on the Pamlico River, Washington, N.C., had been in Federal hands since it was captured by General Burnside's naval and infantry forces in the early months of 1862 following the fall of other coastal Carolina territories such as Roanoke Island, New Bern, and Plymouth. Yankee raiding parties oper-

Major General Daniel Harvey Hill, shown in this carte-de-visite by George S. Cook, commanded operations in North Carolina while Ransom's Brigade, and its 25th Regiment N.C., were stationed in eastern North Carolina in 1863 and the early months of 1864. Hill's troops were responsible for defending strategic coastal towns and railroad facilities (South Caroliniana Library, University of South Carolina, Columbia).

ating out of Washington and New Bern were a constant threat to North Carolina's crucial railroad and bridge at Goldsboro, and General Hill devised a plan to rid Washington of its blue host.

Laying siege to the city on March 30, 1863, and corralling the Union forces stationed in that town, Hill's men went to work diligently removing as many stores and as much food as the rich agricultural region along the Pamlico could offer. Hill professed to General P.G.T. Beauregard, who was then in command at Charleston, South Carolina, that he had three main objectives behind his move against Washington: harass the Yankees, get out supplies from the low country, and make a diversion in Beauregard's favor (at the time Federal forces were making an all-out effort to capture Charleston). A dispatch to Hill during this period from one of his brigadier generals, R.B. Garnett, demonstrates the effort involved in gathering foodstuffs from the land and the energies that the diligent Confederate officers exerted to accomplish these endeavors. The general's message dated April 15, 1863, reads in part as follows:

> My train has just arrived from the Pungo River. It brings up 65 barrels of corn and about 8,000 pounds of bacon. Of this lot 2,000 pounds came from Hyde. Captain Swindell, who sent agents into Hyde, reports that most of the bacon remaining in that country is in the hands of persons who have taken the oath of allegiance, and they will not sell it unless it is impressed. I have ordered my train to go to Tranter's Creek Bridge. You do not say in your last dispatch how the surplus meat at Tranter's Bridge is to be transported. I suggested that it should be sent to Greenville or Tarborough by steamboat from Boyd's landing. Please let me have definite instructions in this matter, as I do not think my train can haul the meat in question should we have to move the wagon train all at once. I have no control over the steamboat, and have therefore reported the above facts to you in order that you might give the necessary directions should you deem this mode of transportation preferable.[4]

General Garnett's dispatch shows that vast quantities of food were being purchased from the local farmers around the Pamlico River and Pamlico Sound in Hyde County and transported north to Lee's army. It also reveals the logistical and administrative details and bureaucracy that were involved in running an army and that were forever entangling the Confederate officers. One can imagine General Hill at his headquarters in Goldsboro, surrounded by staff and with the war's burdens weighing heavily upon him, dictating a response to Garnett and, perhaps, a second dispatch to the authorities or owner of the steamboat requesting or impressing its service.

After only a couple of weeks into the investment of Washington, the Federals succeeded in running two ships up the river to replenish their garrison's supplies. In consideration of this and because his troops had drained the locals' fields, barns and warehouses of most of the food resources, General Hill withdrew his troops and abandoned the siege. Back at headquarters in Goldsboro he praised his troops for their "vigilance on duty and good behavior everywhere."[5]

As previously mentioned, the 25th Regiment N.C. was not directly occupied in the Confederate siege of Washington, but its troops were actively moving from one trouble spot to another around eastern North Carolina in the winter/spring of 1863. The schedule below indicates the frequent movements of the regiment during this time period and demonstrates the Confederacy's tactical employ of regimental mobility to overcome a scarcity of troops in reacting to military exigencies. Also, it can be seen just how critical the worn-out railroads were in transporting military units from one theatre of crisis to another.[6]

8. Back to North Carolina

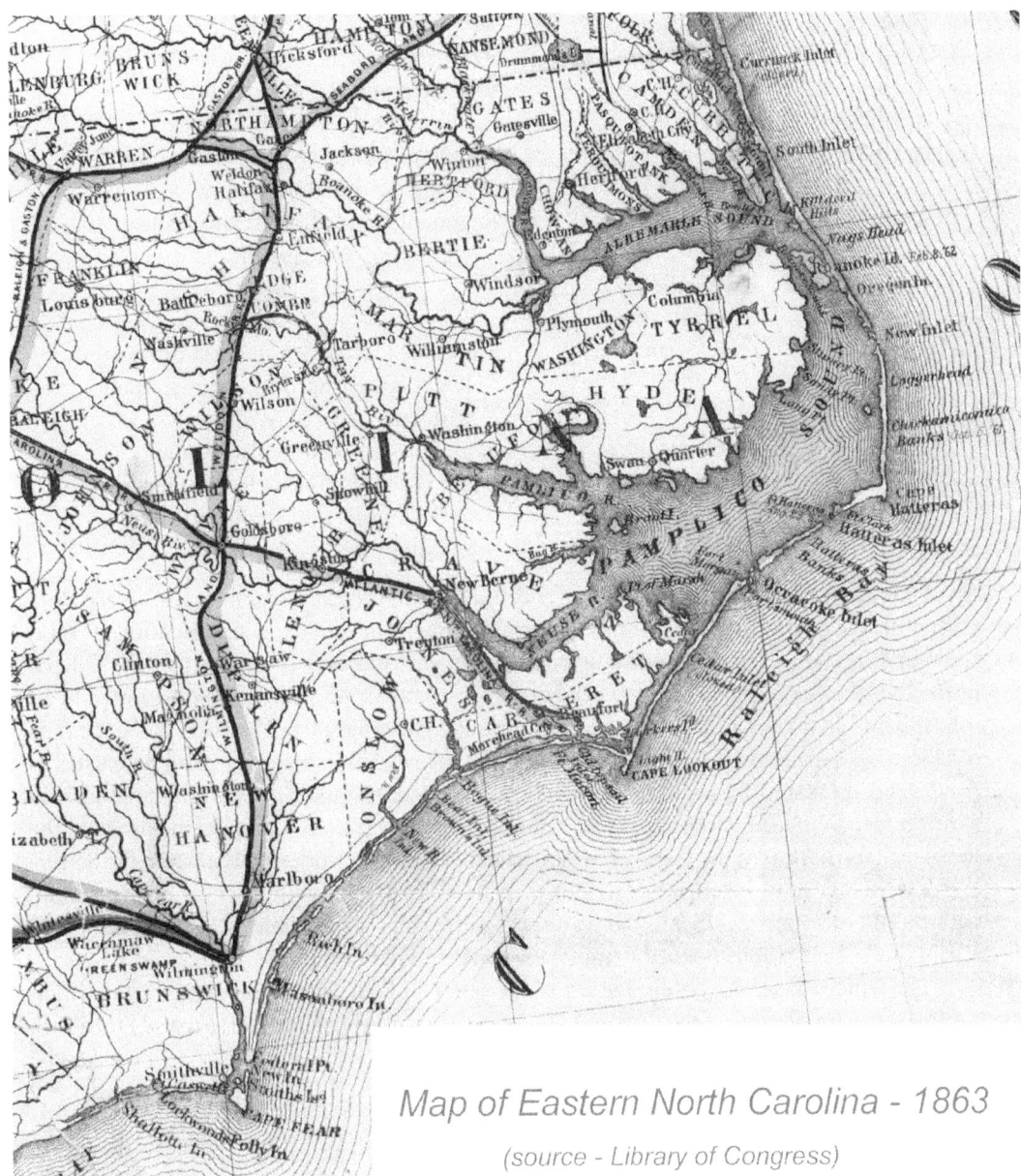

Map of Eastern North Carolina - 1863
(source - Library of Congress)

Map of eastern North Carolina—1863. The 25th Regiment N.C. was stationed at various strategic points throughout eastern North Carolina during 1863 and early 1864 (Library of Congress).

Date (1863)	Stationed At	Remarks
February 22	Wilmington	
February 27	Northeast Station	
March 7	Wilmington	Regiment encamped below Wilmington.
March 10	Topsail Island	
March 28	Goldsboro	Regiment rejoined brigade at Goldsboro.
March 29	Kinston	Marched 7 miles toward Trenton on March 30.

Date (1863)	Stationed At	Remarks
April 1	Kinston	Regiment returned to Kinston.
April 5	Washington	Regiment encamped near town.
April 7	Swift Creek	
April 8	Washington	Regiment moved to crossroads 8 miles above Washington.
April 9–16	Washington	Regiment camped in various spots in vicinity of Washington.
April 17	Greenville	
April 20	Kinston	
April 29	Gum Swamp	Swamp is located 9 miles east of Kinston. Regiment engaged in skirmish there with enemy on May 22.
May 27	Petersburg, Virginia	Regiment took railcars to Virginia.
May 29	Richmond, Virginia	Regiment took railcars from Petersburg to Richmond and went into camp at Camp Lee.

Of note in this listing of movements and activities of the 25th Regiment N.C. is the skirmish with the enemy at Gum Swamp on May 22, 1863. The affair was not mentioned in Lt. Garland Ferguson's historical account of the regiment, nor is it prominent in the Official Records of the Confederate army. It occurred at a remote Confederate outpost located in an inhospitable area known as the Gum Swamp about eight miles east of Kinston along the railroad joining Kinston with New Bern. Earthworks thrown up in a circular pattern protected the Twenty-fifth and Fifty-sixth regiments posted there to guard the railroad approach to Kinston from Yankee incursions. At daylight on May 22 three Union regiments drove in the Rebel pickets in front of the fort and commenced to attack the works. Unknown to the Southern defenders, two more enemy regiments had stolen through the thick cover of the swamp, with the aid of a native guide, to the rear of the outpost to cut off their escape. Around 10:00 A.M. these Yankee troops opened fire and advanced against the surprised Rebels.

The Official Records contain reports of the action at Gum Swamp recorded by the Union commanders involved that day. General J.G. Foster proudly described the surprise rear attack in the following words:

> On arriving in the rear of the enemy's position, Colonel Jones deployed such portions of his command as could be used to advantage, opened fire, and advanced. The enemy fired a few desultory volleys, then broke and fled in great confusion, taking to the swamps and escaping by paths known only to themselves.[7]

The Union forces rushed into the vacated fortifications and succeeded in capturing 165 of the Rebel defenders and almost took General Robert Ransom, who inopportunely was at the post when the attack occurred. Also included in the booty taken from the Rebels that day were 28 horses, 10 mules, 2 baggage wagons, 3 ambulances, 10 sets single harness, 6 artillery harness, 11 saddles, 3 saddles (artillery), 9 bridles, 80 muskets, 80 sets of equipments, 11,000 rounds of ammunition, and one 12-pounder howitzer with limber.[8] All of these trappings of war were of immense value to the Confederate army and it could ill-afford to lose them.

At dusk that same evening, Major General D.H. Hill reached the outpost with the remaining regiments of Ransom's Brigade and Cooke's Brigade and pushed the enemy out of the Confederate works, chasing them back to their fortifications near New Bern. Most of the Rebels taken prisoner that day were from the Fifty-sixth Regiment. The 25th Regiment escaped, for the most part, with only a blemish on its service record. General Lee commented in a note to General Hill, "I regret to hear of the occurrence reported by you (Gum Swamp), and fear that the regiment allowed itself to be surprised. I am gratified, however, that you drove the enemy back so promptly to his intrenchments and did all in your power to retrieve the disaster."[9] Even General Lee termed the events at Gum Swamp a "disaster," and it is understandable that the original historian of the 25th Regiment would omit a recounting of this embarrassing episode.

In late May 1863, General Robert Ransom was promoted to major general. His older brother, Colonel Matthew W. Ransom of the Thirty-fifth Regiment N.C., was elevated to brigadier general and elected to take over his brother's former command on June 15. Matt had just returned to the army after a lengthy convalescence at his home near Warrenton. The valiant service he rendered at Antietam in the "West Woods" had further aggravated the arm wound he suffered previously at Malvern Hill. Matt Ransom was a popular choice, unanimously recommended by officers of the Twenty-fifth, Thirty-fifth, Forty-ninth, and Fifty-sixth Regiments over three senior colonels in the brigade. Officers of the Thirty-fifth Regiment as a group called upon their new general, delivering congratulations while expressing regrets over losing him as their immediate commander. Spokesman for the delegation was Surgeon O'Hagan, whose words caused Matt Ransom to remark to a friend, "[H]e was so much embarrassed by the complimentary things said of him by the eloquent doctor that in his reply he made the meanest speech of his life."[10]

Lt. Ferguson sang high praises of Matt Ransom: "He was a lawyer, very handsome in appearance, of undoubted courage and knew the temper of volunteer soldiers. The men of the 25th Regiment loved him and trusted him."[11] Before the war, Matt Ransom was a plantation and slave owner in eastern North Carolina. However, he was a strong Unionist and, through his elected position in the state's house of commons, worked tirelessly against secessionist forces. Failing in this pursuit, he received orders from the governor of North Carolina to report to Warrenton, where he was to become a lieutenant colonel of the First Regiment Infantry of North Carolina. Instinctively and without hesitation, he accepted the orders to defend his state; and in so doing, he commenced a meritorious military career with the Confederacy. As colonel of the Thirty-fifth Regiment, General Matt Ransom had proven himself to be a warrior and superb leader of men, and had been twice wounded at Malvern Hill during the Seven Days Battles.

Colonel Matthew W. Ransom, a North Carolinian, was elevated to brigadier general and took command of Ransom's Brigade in June 1863 when his brother Robert was promoted to major general (Clark's *Histories of the Several Regiments and Battalions from North Carolina, in the Great War 1861–1865*, vol. 5).

So it was that the old Ransom's Brigade became the new Ransom's Brigade, to which the 25th Regiment N.C. still claimed allegiance. During this interval, while the brigade was seeing light service militarily in eastern North Carolina and undergoing a command change, the Union

Army of the Potomac was spending the winter months near Fredericksburg refitting, reinforcing, reorganizing and licking wounds suffered from the contest for Marye's Heights in December 1862. Late in April 1863 heavy Federal columns began stealthily advancing up the Rappahannock River and crossing over to the south bank into a Virginia wilderness of densely wooded second-growth forests. Over this fateful and highly unsuitable warring ground, just a few miles west of Fredericksburg at a remote crossroads junction known as Chancellorsville, the powerful armies of the North and the South would soon resume their great struggle to destroy each other.

Chancellorsville

In the aftermath of the battle of Fredericksburg in December 1862, the Army of Northern Virginia maintained a heavy presence in and around Fredericksburg and continued to be on heightened alert for further enemy aggressions in that theatre. General Lee remained at his headquarters there,

General Joseph Hooker was reluctantly chosen by President Abraham Lincoln to replace General Burnside after the defeat of the Union army at Fredericksburg. Hooker proceeded to lead the Army of the Potomac in another campaign against the Army of Northern Virginia and suffered similar unfavorable results at Chancellorsville, Virginia (Library of Congress).

where he waited and watched to determine the next move of his Union foe. In April, after the ice had disappeared from the Rappahannock and as the buds and blossoms of spring erupted, Confederate spies and cavalry reconnaissance spotted signs of a buildup in Union forces on the left bank of the Rappahannock River. Lee's highly acute senses were alerted to an imminent assault and he recalled Longstreet's command to him. (These forces eventually arrived too late to participate in the main battle action that followed.) Additionally, he pulled as many troops from General D.H. Hill's North Carolina district as could be afforded and made appeals to the leaders of the Confederacy for all available Rebel warriors. Once again, General Lee feverishly prepared his Army of Northern Virginia to battle a rejuvenated Army of the Potomac under the command of yet another leader.

"Fighting Joe" Hooker was the reluctant choice of President Abraham Lincoln to replace General Ambrose Burnside after the failures at Fredericksburg during the winter of 1862–1863. Hooker, who covertly schemed against Burnside to get the job, received a letter from Lincoln, upon his appointment, which he later described as the kind of missive that a wise father might write to his son. Lincoln wanted Hooker to know that "there are some things in regard to which, I am not quite satisfied in you." Referring to Hooker's running down Burnside, he went on:

> [Y]ou have taken counsel of your ambition ... in which you did a great wrong to the country and to a most meritorious and honorable brother officer. I have heard, in such a way as to believe it, of your recently saying that both the Army and the Government

needed a dictator. Of course it was not for this, but in spite of it, that I have given you the command. Only those generals who gain successes, can set up dictators. What I now ask of you is military successes, and I will risk the dictatorship.[12]

And it was on such a note that General Joseph Hooker took command. During the latter days of April 1863, he confidently set his aggressive plans in motion and unleashed 130,000 Federal troops against Lee's outnumbered Rebel forces.

Several miles above Fredericksburg and beyond the Confederate left flank, some 70,000 blue-coated cavalry and infantrymen surged across the Rappahannock to envelop the Rebel forces. At the town of Fredericksburg, another 40,000 Yankees demonstrated against Lee to hold him there while the flanking movement further developed for a plunge into the left and rear of the gray line. By April 30 Hooker's main force on Lee's left has taken up positions near a crossroads called Chancellorsville, named for the nearby brick Chancellor house which was often used as a tavern. Surprisingly, the South's cunning commander had been outmaneuvered and caught between the lethal pincers of his northern adversary. Divining that the greater threat was above the town, the unflinching and daring Lee divided his army of 60,000 and left a small force of 10,000 infantry troops under the leadership of General Jubal Early to defend against an enemy assault at Fredericksburg. With the remaining forces at his disposal, General Lee brazenly ordered a march to meet the enemy near Chancellorsville.

On May 1, 1863, the Southern Rebel forces collided with the advance units of Hooker's army on open ground near Chancellorsville. Aided by their superior numbers and artillery, the Union army appeared to have the edge when, inexplicably, Hooker ordered his troops back to a thickly overgrown ground, since dubbed "the Wilderness," and into a defensive posi-

Artist's rendering of the Battle of Chancellorsville (*Harper's Weekly*; artist Alfred Rudolf Waud).

tion. That night, General Jeb Stuart, the leader of the Confederate cavalry forces, interrupted a fireside conference where his commander, General Lee, and Stonewall Jackson were seated next to each other on a fallen log and deliberating the morrow's offensive strategy. It was obvious to these renowned military strategists that the Federal's left flank, securely anchored to the Rappahannock, could not be turned. The center — opposite the general's conference setting — had been tested by the gray coats during the day and was found to be held by superior entrenched forces. However, the youthful cavalry leader Stuart brought news of his discovery that the Federal right flank "was in the air" three miles west of Chancellorsville. Immediately seizing on this intelligence godsend, the three opportunistic Southern leaders schemed and drew up plans for one of the boldest and riskiest maneuvers ever undertaken by the daring commander of the Army of Northern Virginia.

Lee endeavored to exploit the Union's weakness uncovered by Stuart to roll up the Union's exposed right flank. He ordered Jackson and his corps of 30,000 infantry and artillery to make a twelve-mile stealthy roundabout march through dense wood thickets behind the screening of Stuart's cavalry. This movement was inherently risky and was a huge gamble for Lee. It left him with only 15,000 soldiers to confront the main army of Hooker, while Jackson's van was strung out to his left and Early was fighting for his life in Lee's rear. It was indeed fortuitous that "Fighting Joe" Hooker had been unnerved by Lee's swift counter movements and apparent willingness to give battle, so much so that he slackened from the accustomed aggressive action he had once been known for. Instead, Lee boldly stole the initiative as he was accustomed to do when given the opportunity.

Their clothes in tatters from an all-day march through the thick woods with its dense thickets and prickly briars, Jackson's forces finally made it to the far left designated position opposite the unsuspecting Federals on the exposed flank. There they quickly and quietly formed a line two miles long and three divisions deep. At 5:15 P.M. on May 2, 1863, those Southern soldiers stormed wildly out of the wilderness woods and set upon the startled Yankees with a pent-up fury as their Rebel yells resonated across the battlefield. Caught by surprise, the Union soldiers offered weak and unorganized resistance before fleeing from the onrushing Confederates. When finally a staunch Federal defense slowed the Confederate advance at "dusky dark," Jackson found that he had driven the blue-

Lieutenant General Thomas "Stonewall" Jackson, pictured here, was one of General Robert E. Lee's ablest and most trusted lieutenants. At the battle of Chancellorsville, he led a surprise attack that rolled up the Union's right flank and set the stage for Lee's most spectacular victory (Library of Congress).

Death of Stonewall Jackson. General Stonewall Jackson suffered a mortal wounding by "friendly fire" from his own troops as darkness settled over the field of his rout of the Union right flank at Chancellorsville (*Wearing of the Gray; Personal Portraits, Scenes, and Adventures of the War*).

coats back some two miles distant. As sporadic fighting continued to flare up throughout the wilderness woods on that moonlit night, the good fortune that had blessed Lee's army quickly turned to tragedy in a most unexpected way.

After darkness had fallen over the battlefield, Jackson was still anxious to take advantage of the momentum gained by the afternoon's highly successful assault. He and several staff officers rode ahead of their lines to reconnoiter and search for potential gaps or other weak points to strike at. As these officers trotted back toward their own lines in the darkness, they were fired on by a group of North Carolina men who mistook them for Union cavalry. General Jackson was hit twice in his left arm by the Rebel sharpshooters and fell wounded from his horse. Later that night his arm was amputated. When notified of the calamity befallen his trusted executive officer General Lee quickly dispatched a courier to Jackson's side with a note expressing regrets: "Could I have directed the events, I would have chosen for the good of the country to be disabled in your stead." He added, "I congratulate you upon the victory, which is due to your skill and energy."[13] The worst was yet to come however. Not uncommonly for the era and circumstances, the bedridden Jackson contracted pneumonia a few days following his surgery and succumbed to its ravages just eight days after the wounding. The mighty Stonewall was gone forever from the Confederate army and Robert E. Lee had lost his greatest lieutenant.

General J.E.B. (Jeb) Stuart assumed the command of Jackson's Corps and on the next day, May 3, after gaining a coveted position from which the Rebel batteries could project their covering firepower over the battlefield, he was able to unite his forces with those led by his commander, General Lee. Battling into the night again in the Chancellorsville wilderness the combined Confederate forces pressed the assault against the Union army until Hooker ordered a general retreat to a stronger defensive position north of Chancellorsville between the Rappahannock and the crossroads. Lee, however, had little time to relish that day's victory for he had received news from the heights of Fredericksburg that the Union army had broken General Jubal Early's defenses.

There the Federal forces, under the leadership of General John Sedgwick, had fought fiercely over the old battleground in front of the Sunken Road and the Marye house, and had pushed Early's forces off Marye's Heights. A division rushing from Chancellorsville under orders to support Early's forces clashed with the oncoming Union army and blunted their advance about halfway between Fredericksburg and Chancellorsville, near the Salem Church. The following day, May 4, saw continued action at this disputed midway ground, with an additional division from Lee's army at Chancellorsville diverted and thrown at the Federals; and the Rebels were repulsed. Yet General Sedgwick, upon learning that Hooker had given up in Lee's front at Chancellorsville, withdrew his troops and marched them back over the pontoon bridges at Fredericksburg and across the Rappahannock River. On the night of May 5–6 in the middle of a rainstorm, the remaining troops of Hooker's Army of the Potomac also retreated to the other side of the river.[14]

Robert E. Lee and his vaunted Army of Northern Virginia had once again defeated in most spectacular fashion Lincoln's Northern army. Confronted and caught between two enemy forces that numbered twice as many as his own, Lee reacted with his usual calculated dar-

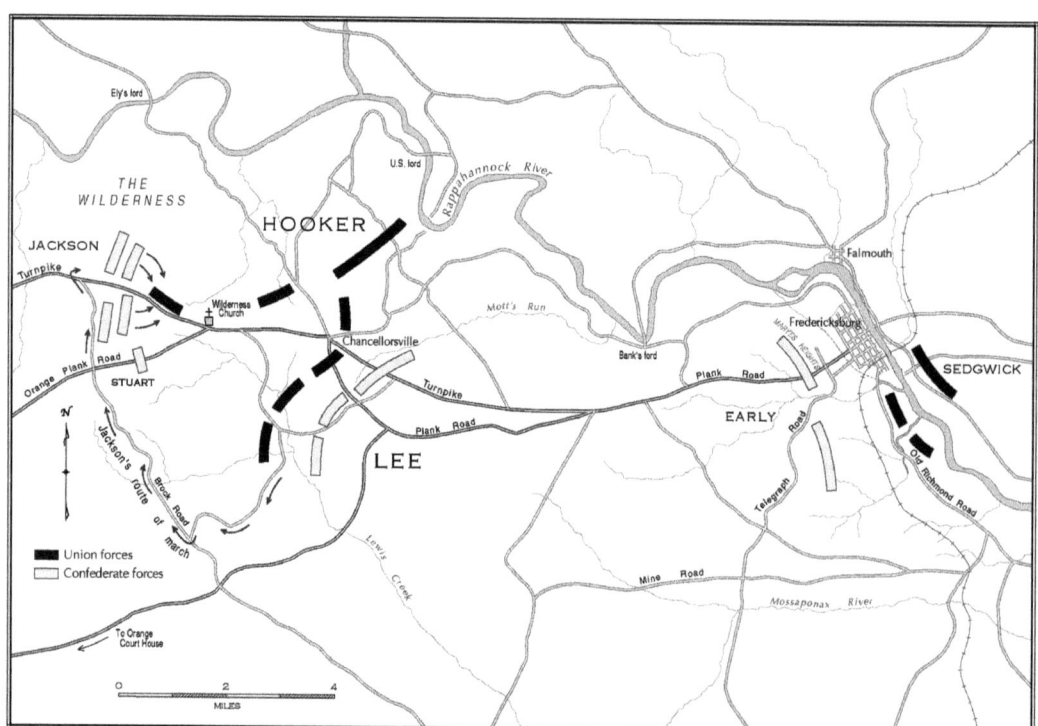

Battle of Chancellorsville: May 1–May 4, 1863. Perhaps the greatest victory achieved by the Army of Northern Virginia was Chancellorsville. Depicted on this map of the Chancellorsville, Virginia, vicinity are the approximate Union and Confederate troop positions on May 2. Late on that fateful day General Stonewall Jackson launched a surprise attack against the vulnerable Union right which was "in the air" (Peter Krafft, Florida State University).

ing. Tactics such as dividing his own army in the enemy's front, not once but on two different occasions, and stealing around the enemy's flank to launch a surprise enfilading attack gained for the South this heralded victory. Fredericksburg and Chancellorsville were General Robert E. Lee's greatest triumphs and marked perhaps the pinnacle of Confederate strength and success during the Civil War. It undoubtedly infused in the Southern population renewed hope and dreams that the rebellion might be won after all. And it demonstrated that the Northern armies, even with their overwhelming advantage in resources, could be dominated and defeated.

The heavy toll in human death at Chancellorsville totaled 13,000 casualties suffered on the Southern side and 17,000 on the North's. The single greatest casualty for the South was, of course, the death of General Stonewall Jackson. Although the eccentric Jackson would be replaced by other Confederate generals, none would be found that could equal his competence and capacity to command. In fact, the very next battle fought by the Army of Northern Virginia at Gettysburg would conclude most unfavorably for the South due in a large part to the absence of Jackson and his instinctive leadership contributions.

Meanwhile, back in North Carolina, the Yankees still threatened incursions on many coastal fronts and lightning assaults at the critical railroads. General D.H. Hill was not at all sympathetic, nor was he happy about losing many of the troops in his North Carolina command to the service of the Army of Northern Virginia or to Richmond's defenses. And the sharp-tongued general was rather vocal about his loss in strength and inability to offer the State of North Carolina adequate protection against the Northern invaders. Contesting one of Lee's requests for troops to be sent to him, General Hill apparently communicated directly to President Davis with his concerns. In a reaction to that conversation, Davis shot off the following dispatch dated May 29, 1863, querying General Lee in regards to the relocation of North Carolina troops:

> General: Hill says he has reported to you as to the condition in North Carolina. To withdraw Ransom's, Cooke's, and Jenkins' brigades is to abandon the country to the enemy, if last information is correct....[15]

General Lee, through correspondence with Secretary of War Seddon and General Hill, was continually pressing for the transfer of Ransom's Brigade to his army in Virginia prior to the battle of Chancellorsville and afterward. Apparently Lee had been sufficiently impressed with General Robert Ransom's performance at Fredericksburg and wanted that general and his veteran troops with him when he again went into battle. In the frenzied efforts to build up his army before Chancellorsville, even while the union troops were crossing the Rappahannock, Lee called upon the adjutant and inspector general of the Confederate army to send the following order to General Hill, dated April 30, 1863:

> Maj. Gen. D.H. Hill, Kinston, N.C.:
>
> Send a brigade immediately to this place; Ransom's preferred, if no loss in time is involved.
>
> S. Cooper
> Adjutant and Inspector General[16]

Ransom's Brigade and the 25th Regiment N.C. were not sent north to Lee's support at Chancellorsville and remained in North Carolina. The communication that follows was made just at the successful conclusion of Lee's engagement against Hooker and shows that the Southern commander was still very much concerned and not certain of the exigencies of his situation:

> War Department, C.S.A.
> Richmond, May 6, 1863
>
> General D.H. Hill, Goldsborough, N.C.:
>
> General Lee urges you should send him Ransom's division. Do so if you can with any safety. Hooker remains on the south side of the Rappahannock in a strong position at Mine Ford. General Longstreet arrived here last night. His forces are yet in Petersburg.
>
> J.A. Seddon
> Secretary of War[17]

Again it is seen that General Lee longed to have Ransom's Brigade join him; but for reasons that are not absolutely clear, General D.H. Hill failed to effect orders given him to transfer Ransom's Brigade. It appears that General Hill was granted discretion in carrying out the orders, and the records suggest that he simply determined that he could not do without Ransom's regiments, delayed their release and transferred other units in their place. In one of Lee's detailed dispatches to General Hill dated May 16, 1863, he queries Hill on the troop strengths in North Carolina, perceived enemy strategies and intentions in the state, and at one point bluntly states to his subordinate general that "Ransom and Cooke I consider as belonging to the Army of Northern Virginia and have relied on their return."[18]

However, in late May 1863, before the leaders of the Confederacy could determine the fate of the respected Ransom's Brigade and the mountain boys of the 25th Regiment N.C., Robert Ransom, Jr., was promoted from brigadier general to major general and given divisional command. He was assigned responsibility for the district that included the Appomattox and Blackwater rivers within Hill's command. In early June 1863, Ransom's Brigade, led by General Matt Ransom, was moved to Petersburg and then to Richmond to offer protection to that city while Lee's Army of Northern Virginia was mounting another foreign campaign in Maryland and Pennsylvania. While in Virginia, Ransom's Brigade briefly joined with those of A.J. Jenkins and John R. Cooke in forming a division under General Robert Ransom's command, all being attached to the Department of North Carolina then under Major General D.H. Hill. On July 4, 1863, General Robert Ransom's Division, which included brother Matt Ransom's Brigade and the 25th N.C., fought and defeated Federal forces advancing on Richmond from Williamsburg near Bottom's Bridge on the Chickahominy River.[19]

Trouble in the Mountains

For Governor Zebulon Vance the summer of 1863 offered little relief for many of the problems facing most North Carolinians. The loss of troops from the state paralyzed his efforts to address the serious issue of violence on the home front. In eastern North Carolina, Federal raiding parties continued to sack and loot private homes, businesses and property. In the western part of the state, Confederate troops for all intents and purposes fought a second civil war against draft evaders, deserters and bushwhackers.

Throughout that year of 1863, the soldiers in the 25th Regiment N.C. received news from home of the unrest and lawlessness that pervaded the western North Carolina mountain region. Many of the mountain people who were initially convinced that secession would lead to greater freedom and more individual and state's rights were unhappy with the current state of affairs. There seemed to be no end to the privations and hardships brought on by the war and news from the war front dampened what little hope there was. In addition, the Confederate government's strict conscription laws and ever-increasing tariffs seemed to favor the wealthy eastern planters at the expense of the poor mountain farmers. As a result of all this, a backlash developed, allying the disgruntled, deserters, conscript evaders, Union sympathizers, and just plain evil men against authority of any kind. Lawless bands roamed the mountains raiding and robbing homesteads and terrorizing innocent women, children and the elderly. Throughout the mountains there settled over the communities and homesteads a heavy cloud of terror.

This terrible state of affairs is vividly described in a letter written to Walter Lenoir, who briefly served in Company F of the 25th Regiment N.C. before transferring out to command a company in the Thirty-seventh Regiment N.C. He was severely wounded at the second battle of Manassas soon after leaving the 25th N.C. While convalescing at his farm near Forks of Pigeon in remote and isolated Haywood County (located in the southwestern mountain region of North Carolina), he received this letter from a family member living in Caldwell County, another mountain county situated in the northeastern highlands of western North Carolina:

Aug 13, 1863
My Dear Walter

> They have a terrible state of things upon the Tennessee line particularly in Watauga [County]. There is a band of robbers & villains who are constantly plundering the people in the night, when resolute and prepared they succeed in driving them off, but a man is occasionally killed on either side. Some ten days ago they attacked the house of Paul Farthing — his brother Young being there. They resisted and fired upon them out of the house & a skirmish ensued. Thomas Farthing heard the firing from his house and hurried over with his gun but unfortunately was discovered & fired upon by a guard stationed on the road side — two balls passing through his heart. You may imagine my distress knowing the high estimation in which I held him. I regarded him decidedly the first man in the County — & I think he was a fast friend of our family. The bad was headed by a man by the name of Guy he has been arrested & released heretofore — They go in bands of 12 or 14 — Nine of Paul Farthing's family were hurt & they found a good deal of blood about the porch & corner of the house: but as they always carry off their wounded the damage done the robbers was not ascertained — The same party robbed Mr. Evans' house while he was down here, carrying off about four or five hundred dollars worth of his & Mr. Skiles's effects — They put his wife under guard & rummaged the house thoroughly — expecting to find money. Evans has since moved his family down here & occupies the Methodist Parsonage.
>
> I have terrible forebodings at times — not that I think that we are not able to defend ourselves and achieve our independence — but fear that the whole strength of the country can not be got out. The men who have heretofore avoided the fight & by coming forward at this crisis & encouraging the remaining conscripts and deserters might restore confidence are increasing the difficulty by crying out for peace which means submission — In the meantime desertion is rife. the men regard their money as worthless & the government is unable to remedy its evil. Thomas says he has seen them give $10 for a water mellon....[20]

This letter conveys the sense of dread and terror that the population of the western mountains of North Carolina held for the raiding bands of bushwhackers. It was such news from home that forced the Confederate army and General Matt Ransom to send a detachment of soldiers from the 25th Regiment to Madison County, North Carolina, to squash a lawless band of bushwhackers operating there.

In Warm Springs, located close to the Tennessee border, it was reported that a Union regiment made up largely of Confederate deserters and Union-supporting area citizens had captured and held the Warm Springs Hotel in the fall of 1863. Lt. Ferguson recorded:

In October 1863 [on October 26, 1863], a detachment of the regiment under Lieutenant Colonel Bryson, had an engagement at Hot Springs, in Madison County, North Carolina. The enemy outnumbered them twenty to one, and the loss of the detachment in killed and wounded was heavy, including Lieutenant Hyatt, of Company F, who was killed on the field.

No further details of this clash are offered or can be found in the *Official Records*, but it can be seen that the outlaw bands were powerful and dangerous—small wonder that the local populations were living in fear for their property and lives. A historical account of the Warm Springs Hotel states that the place served as a Union headquarters until the Northerners were expelled in late October 1863. From that scant information, it is supposed that the Confederate forces finally ousted the outlaws holed up in the hotel and that its assignment was successfully completed, although at a heavy toll of casualties.

Capture of Plymouth

Much had transpired in other war theatres since the 25th Regiment N.C. was detached from the Army of Northern Virginia and detailed to eastern North Carolina. As previously noted, in early May 1863, Lee's army defeated its Northern adversary in a resounding fashion at the battle of Chancellorsville. Replete with increased and justified confidence in his Army of Northern Virginia, Lee once again conspired to cross the Potomac and invade Northern soil. Behind this bold decision was a strong belief that the move into the North might serve to relieve pressure on the Confederate armies operating in Tennessee and Mississippi, which were faring poorly against the Federals. In addition, similar motives as drove the first foreign incursion were in Lee's mind as well—feeding his southern army and forcing the Army of the Potomac to withdraw from Virginia to protect the approaches to Washington.

In June 1863 General Lee led his Rebel warriors on a second campaign north of the Potomac River, quickly passing through Maryland and entering Pennsylvania with loose ambitions of capturing Harrisburg, the state's capital. However, a rare failure by General Jeb Stuart's cavalry units to provide vital intelligence on the movements of the Army of the Potomac allowed that army to concentrate rapidly in Lee's rear. In the first few days of July 1863, the opposing armies collided at Gettysburg, Pennsylvania, and Lee's Army of Northern Virginia sustained its first major setback. General George Meade, yet another Union officer commissioned with the command of the Army of the Potomac, took full advantage of a strong defensive position atop the high ground located just south of Gettysburg. Across those heights the Union's forces massed along a five-mile fishhook-shaped battle line looming high above the Confederates. It curled from Culp's and Cemetery hills and extended in a straight line along Cemetery Ridge to Little and Big Round tops. Well-equipped and with superior numbers, the Federal army beat back successively greater and more determined Confederate attacks against their lines on three consecutive days. At last repulsed and defeated, the Army of Northern Virginia was forced to retreat back across the flooding Potomac's waters to Virginia and barely escaped Meade's pursuing army. The cost in human blood and suffering of the three days of battles was a stunning 28,000 dead, wounded and missing for the South and 23,000 Union casualties. Clearly, Lee was not at his best during the battle of Gettysburg, but he not once offered excuses for the failure or tried to place blame on any other but himself.

In the West, just a day after the Battle of Gettysburg on July 4, 1863, the Mississippi River fortress city of Vicksburg, Mississippi, capitulated to General Ulysses S. Grant's besieging forces. This city, located on a bluff commanding the lazy, broad and meandering naval thor-

Battle of Lookout Mountain at Chattanooga, Tennessee. In late November 1863 Union General U.S. Grant defeated Southern forces investing Chattanooga, Tennessee, and broke out of the besieged city. This opened the way for General William Sherman to lead his Northern army into the Deep South and eventually break the back, and heart, of the Confederacy (Library of Congress, lithograph by Middleton, Strobridge & Co.).

oughfare cutting through the heart of the country, had used its heavy artillery effectively to thwart Federal efforts to seize control of the river. However, a determined Grant mounted a brilliant campaign that culminated in the besiegement and capture of the Confederate stronghold city of Vicksburg. With Vicksburg and the Mississippi River in its grips, the Union continued to pull the noose ever tighter around the South and to gradually squeeze the lifeblood from the Confederacy.

In September 1863 the Confederate Army of Tennessee, led by General Braxton Bragg, scored an impressive victory against Union General William Rosecrans and his Army of the Cumberland. At the battle of Chickamauga near Chattanooga, Tennessee, Federal forces escaped destruction by retreating to Chattanooga, where they holed up and were subsequently invested by Bragg's pursuing Rebel forces. However, on November 24 and 25, 1863, General Ulysses S. Grant, named by President Lincoln to replace the embattled Rosecrans, performed a miraculous hat trick by escaping a seemingly hopeless besiegement at Chattanooga. His Yankee forces, led by Generals Hooker, Thomas and Sherman, assailed Bragg's Rebel army, which was securely and confidently planted along Lookout Mountain and Missionary Ridge, imposing mountain bluffs commanding the town. The intrepid blue-coated soldiers scaled and crawled up the steep slopes in the face of roaring and angry Rebel guns firing down on them and routed the Southern forces from their mountain throne. In doing so, the Union army scored one of the more amazing victories of the Civil War.

Spring of 1864 found the powerful Union Army of the Tennessee advancing toward Atlanta under the generalship of William Tecumseh Sherman. The situation that existed for the Confederacy was more than desperate, and it was such times that desperate measures were required. An entry in Mrs. Chesnut's diary reveals her exasperation at Union tactics leveraging their overwhelming advantage in manpower; and she also exposed another desperate measure taken by the Confederate government of conscripting congressmen to the army's service:

> And now comes a grand announcement made by the Yankee Congress. They vote one million of men to be sent down here to free the prisoners whom they will not take in exchange. I actually thought they left all these Yankees here on our hands as part of their plan to starve us out. All Congressmen under fifty years of age are to leave politics and report for military duty or be conscripted. What enthusiasm there is in their councils! Confusion, rather, it seems to me! Mrs. Ould says "the men who frequent her house are more despondent now than ever since this thing began."

In the months following the July 4, 1863, engagement by the Chickahominy River where Ransom's Brigade stopped a Union thrust toward Richmond, the 25th Regiment N.C. saw very little fighting. However, the regiment stayed on the move providing protection for the Confederate railroads, bridges, towns, and mills in eastern North Carolina and support for the city of Richmond's defenses. The following schedule reflects the various movements of the 25th Regiment during this time frame[21]:

Date (1863)	Stationed At	Remarks
July 20	Weldon	Ordered there to protect vital railroad bridge.
July 23	Petersburg, Virginia	
August 2	Garysburg	
October 16	Warm Springs	Detachment from the regiment sent to Warm Springs, Madison County, where it engaged in skirmish with "Tories."
November 9	Jackson	Moved to a point 13 miles below Jackson.
November 11	Weldon	
November 29	Petersburg, Virginia	
December 16	Weldon	
December 20	Franklin, Virginia	
December 22	Garysburg	Regiment returned to Weldon a few days later.

In January 1864 Ransom's Brigade and the 25th Regiment N.C. were assigned to Major General George Pickett's Department of North Carolina and became involved in an operation masterminded by General Pickett to recapture New Bern. The brigade moved from Weldon to Kinston on January 28–29, where it joined up with other forces under Pickett's command. Much like General D.H. Hill's siege of Washington, this ill-fated plan immediately began to unravel when one of the three Confederate columns sent to attack New Bern on February 1, 1864, failed to do so when confronted with the enemy's strength. Only one of the Rebel spearheads, led by Brigadier General Robert F. Hoke, carried out an assault and it met with limited success. General Pickett soon abandoned the whole operation and recalled his troops to Kinston.

In the schedule below can be seen the movements of Ransom's Brigade during the months of February and March of 1864, preceding a major Confederate action against Plymouth, North Carolina, in April.[22]

Date (1864)	Stationed At	Remarks
February 6	Weldon	Returned to Weldon by rail from Kinston.
Mid-February	Petersburg, Virginia	Regiment encamped at Dunn's Hill.
February 25	Weldon	
February 26	Franklin, Virginia	From Franklin marched to South Mills, Camden County, N.C. Supported by a battalion of cavalry, Ransom's Brigade drove a Federal force down the Dismal Swamp canal toward Suffolk.
March 9	Suffolk, Virginia	Brigade drove Federals out of the city of Suffolk and occupied it for 2 days.
March 12	Weldon	Brigade returned from Suffolk to Weldon.

On March 9, 1864, Ransom's Brigade marched on Suffolk, Virginia, by way of South Mills and drove the Federal forces out of the town, capturing a piece of artillery and quartermaster stores of much value.[23] It was an exciting affair, but most notably it was the first time that the brigade's men had faced unfriendly Union black soldiers in combat. Ransom held the town for two days before continuing his march to Weldon.

In April 1864, Confederate Brigadier General Robert F. Hoke was eager to enhance his reputation and anxious to strike a blow to damage the enemy. Even though he was only twenty-six years of age, Hoke was a veteran, having served with distinction in all the major engagements in the eastern theatre from Big Bethel to Chancellorsville, where he was severely wounded. He, with the encouragement and assistance of General Braxton Bragg, who had been relieved of command duty after the debacle at Chattanooga and subsequently appointed as military advisor to President Davis, formulated tactical plans to recapture Plymouth, North Carolina. Hoke's plan of battle utilized the forces of General Matt Ransom's brigade along with his own and Kemper's brigades and the Eighth and Forty-third North Carolina regiments. In addition, Hoke anticipated the support of the Confederate Ram C.S.S. *Albemarle* then under construction in a cornfield near Hamilton along the Roanoke River. The *Albemarle* was in fact not finished when the time came to move, but Captain James W. Cook had its forges blazing and

Brigadier General Robert F. Hoke commanded a task force comprised of Ransom's Brigade, with its 25th Regiment N.C., and two other brigades. This Confederate force invested and captured Plymouth, North Carolina, in April 1864 (North Carolina Department of Archives and History, Raleigh).

carpenters putting the last work upon the ship as it steamed down the river to take part in the fight.[24]

Matt Ransom received orders on April 12, 1864, to relocate his brigade to Tarboro, North Carolina. Then on April 15, Ransom's Brigade proceeded with General Hoke's other forces toward Plymouth, a strongly fortified strategic supply depot for the Union with a garrison of 2,834 Yankees under the command of General Henry Walton Wessells. By April 17 the town was invested by the Rebel forces on the landward side and the advance began. Ransom's Brigade, forming the right side of the Confederate line, engaged in heavy fighting on April 18 against well-defended breastworks and redoubts guarding the land approaches. They were unsuccessful in forcing the enemy works, but on the next day, April 19, Hoke's Brigade succeeded in taking Fort Wessells, a stronghold on the west side of town. The *Albemarle*, delayed by a broken drive shaft and rudder, river obstructions and low water, finally reached the fighting, whereupon it rammed and sank one Union gunboat, the *Southfield*, and chased three others downriver. During the afternoon and well past sunset, Hoke's well-positioned and coordinated artillery and the pair of 6.4-inch Brooke rifles mounted on the *Albemarle* unleashed a barrage of devastation on the Federal positions ringing Plymouth.

The next morning, April 20, as the Confederate artillery continued to mercilessly pound the enemy, General Ransom readied his men for action. One solider in his brigade later described the battle line employed in that final day's assault:

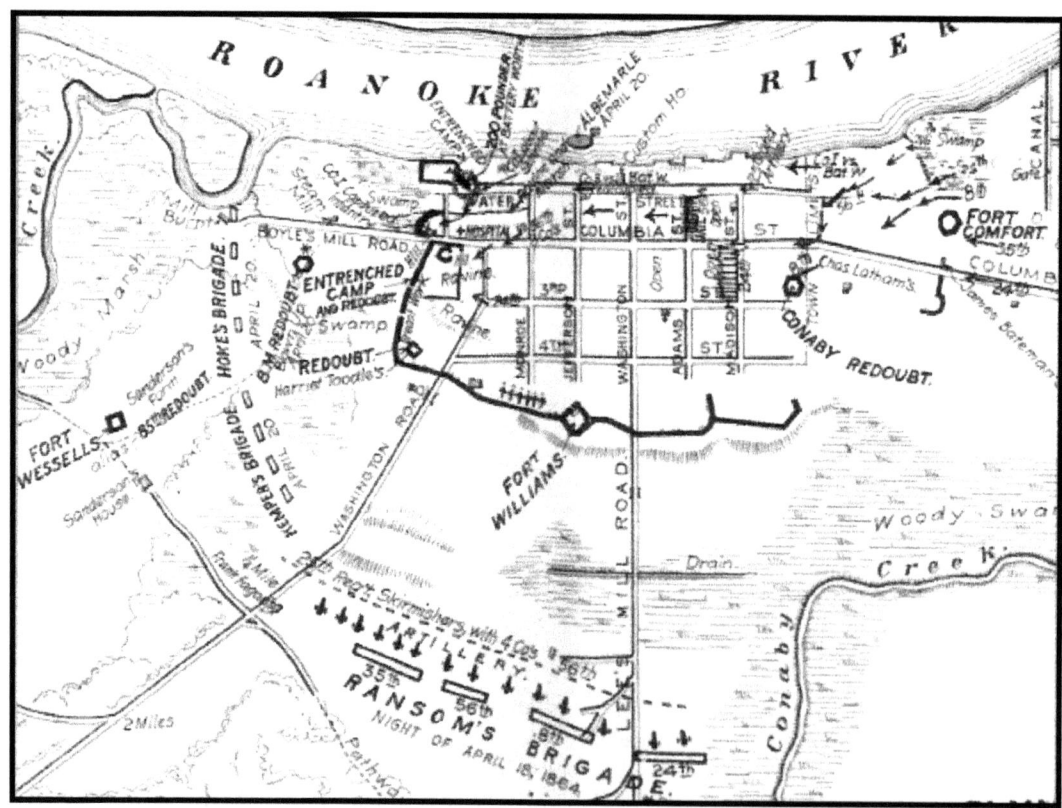

Battle of Plymouth, North Carolina: April 17–20, 1864 (*Histories of the Several Regiments and Battalions From North Carolina, in the Great War 1861–1865*).

At the first break of day Ransom was again in the saddle, and his ringing voice came down the line: "Attention, brigade!" Every man was upon his feet instantly, and the adjusting of twisted blankets across the left shoulder and under the belt at the right hip was only the work of another moment; the line of battle was formed, "Fix bayonets, Trail arms! Forward march!" and the charge began. The alignment was as follows: The Fifty-sixth on the right, flanked by Company I, as sharpshooters, (resting on the Roanoke and near the *Albemarle*, then engaged, as it had been at intervals through the night, with Battery Worth on the river face of the town), and Twenty-fifth, Thirty-fifth, Eighth and Twenty-fourth successively on to the left.[25]

Ransom's Brigade forced the passage of Coneby Creek, a narrow but deep stream to the southeast of the town, and succeeded in capturing the fortifications there. After fighting house-to-house to drive off the enemy and capturing approximately 2,000 prisoners, General Hoke's forces turned their attention to the city's main fortified defense, Fort Williams, where the remaining Federal soldiers and General Wessells were holed up. Hoke demanded the fort's surrender and, after first refusing, Wessells was forced to comply by the effects and threat of the heavy weaponry confronting him. He later reported, "This terrible fire had to be endured without reply, as no man could live at the guns.... This condition of affairs could not be long endured without a reckless sacrifice of life; no relief could be expected, and in compliance with the earnest desire of every officer I consented to hoist a white flag, and at 10:00 A.M. of April 20 I had the mortification of surrendering my post to the enemy with all it contained."[26] According to one report in the Richmond newspaper, the haul netted some 2,500 prisoners, 28 artillery pieces, 500 horses, 5,000 stands of small arms, and masses of ammunition. Federal control of Plymouth was thus relinquished and the portal city beckoned again to the blockade runners laden with extremely critical supplies that a hungry Confederacy craved.[27]

The capture of the port city of Plymouth raised spirits somewhat and was proclaimed one of the most brilliant minor victories of the war. It was, in fact, the last major Confederate victory to be enjoyed by the South before the conclusion of America's Civil War. General Hoke was promoted to major general and the legislature of North Carolina, by formal resolution, thanked Hoke, Commander James Cooke of the *Albemarle*, and the officers and men of their commands for this great feat of arms. Not to be outdone, and in gratitude for the morale-boosting effect the victory had on the people, the Confederate congress passed similar resolutions.

The specific role played by the 25th Regiment N.C. in the battle of Plymouth is not clear. Of the 476 total casualties experienced by Confederate forces at Plymouth, the regiment lost 3 men killed and 20 wounded.[28] Lt. Ferguson writes in his historical account only that the regiment "participated in the assault and capture of

Captain James Cooke used his new Confederate warship, the CSS *Albemarle*, to drive away the Federal gunboats at Plymouth, North Carolina, and to support the capture of that city with a cannonade of the Union fortresses (United States Naval Historical Center).

The CSS *Albemarle* under construction in a cornfield along the Roanoke River in North Carolina (North Carolina Department of Archives and History, Raleigh; artist M. H. Hoke).

Photograph of the CSS *Albemarle* taken after its capture at the end of the war (United States Naval Historical Center).

Plymouth, N.C." However, it is obvious that this was an important tactical victory for the Confederacy and Ransom's Brigade, and the 25th Regiment N.C. lent a hand to make it so.

General Robert Hoke did not intend to sit idly by while he had such a fine military force at his disposal and the Yankees still occupied portions of eastern North Carolina. After the successful venture at Plymouth, he immediately pressed on to Washington, North Carolina. The Federal commander there, alerted to the oncoming danger, torched the town and evacuated his occupying troops. Determined to force the release of more eastern North Carolina territory from the clutches of the enemy, Generals Hoke and Matt Ransom marched their Rebel troops to New Bern and initiated siege operations against that city. However, on May 6, 1864, Hoke received urgent orders to cease all activities in North Carolina and return with his command to Petersburg, Virginia, where a Federal force led by General Benjamin F. Butler threatened Richmond.

9

Richmond and Petersburg Front

Battle of Drewry's Bluff

Beginning in late April 1864, General Robert E. Lee's Army of Northern Virginia engaged in a series of fierce running battles with the Army of the Potomac north of Richmond. While Lee was thus distracted with his back turned, Union General Benjamin F. Butler schemed to attack Richmond. He proceeded to assemble and transport some 30,000 Federal troops up the James River, and on May 5, 1864, his Army of the James landed midway between Richmond and Petersburg at a place called Bermuda Hundred.

President Jefferson Davis, alerted to this new development, summoned General Pierre Beauregard from North Carolina to take command of the Richmond defenses and stave off this latest threat to the capital city. Utilizing troops rushed up from the Carolinas, home guard militia units and even Confederate war department clerks, Beauregard hastily prepared his defense lines to protect Petersburg and Richmond and, most importantly, the railroads. Not until May 12, 1864, did Butler succeed in getting his troops organized and moving, and by that time Beauregard was ready to offer more than token resistance.

Ransom's Brigade reached Kinston at 8:00 A.M. on May 8, 1864, and proceeded from there in railcars through Goldsboro and Weldon towards Petersburg. Recent Union cavalry raids on the railroad had destroyed a twenty-mile section, forcing a night march around the interruption. Finding a train waiting for them at Stoney Creek on May 10, the Brigade boarded and finally arrived at Petersburg several hours later. The troops did not linger long at Petersburg and were hurried to Swift Run Creek. On May 11 General Robert F. Hoke led his three brigades, which included Ransom's Brigade, to Drewry's Bluff, where they took up positions and awaited the Federal assaults.[1]

On May 12, 1864, the 25th Regiment N.C. was engaged in an advance action against Butler's bluecoats. Regarding this fierce struggle Lt. Ferguson recorded, "The regiment was engaged at Drewry's Bluff 12 May, 1864, in which engagement Company F lost Lieutenant Ebed J. Ferguson, killed, and six noncommissioned officers and privates wounded...."[2]

Another participant in the action at Drewry's Bluff attached to Ransom's Brigade remembered: "On 13 May, 1864, while occupying the outer line of works defending Drewry's Bluff, Ransom's Brigade was attacked by Butler's advance with overwhelming force. After gallantly repulsing these attacks, though flanked on the right and in the rear, the brigade held its own and during the night withdrew to the main line of defenses."[3]

Confederate skirmishers (*The American Heritage Century Collection of Civil War Art*; artist William L. Sheppard).

From these accounts and others, it is obvious that on the days of May 12 and 13 overwhelming Federal assaults were launched at the Rebel defenses at Drewry's Bluff, and in every occurrence Ransom's Brigade and the 25th Regiment N.C. were there to offer strong and determined resistance. The fierce fighting continued on May 14 when Brigadier General Matt Ransom was again wounded. A rifle minie ball shattered his left arm, whereupon he was carried off the field to Richmond's Chimborazo Hospital. There, after considerable surgical attention from his old regimental surgeon, Dr. Charles J. O'Hagan, Ransom's arm was spared amputation.[4] Matt again required a furlough to convalesce at his plantation, Verona, on the Roanoke River in Northampton County, North Carolina. He would not rejoin the brigade until October 15, 1864, and until that time the regimental colonels would alternately assume command responsibility for the brigade. Though the continuance of the intense action around Drewry's Bluff, Colonel Henry M. Rutledge of the 25th Regiment led Ransom's Brigade.

Two days later, on May 16, in the main battle of Drewry's Bluff, General Matt Ransom's brigade fought beside troops commanded by Generals Robert Ransom, Hoke and Colquitt. Butler was driven back to his lines but not without a heavy cost paid in casualties on both sides. The 25th Regiment N.C. was heavily engaged in this melee with the other regiments of Ransom's Brigade, as well as in subsequent actions during the ensuing days.

On May 20 Confederate forces attacked Butler's Bermuda Hundred line near Ware Bottom Church, pushing the Yankees back into a neck formed by the James and Appomattox rivers. To contain Butler's forces between the two rivers, Beauregard's Rebels constructed the defensive Howlett Line, which effectively bottled up the Yankees. One of the soldiers in Ransom's Brigade later recorded: "After the battle of Drewry's Bluff, Ransom's brigade occupied the trenches in front of Butler at Bermuda Hundred." General U.S. Grant, upon reading reports of the affairs at Bermuda Hundred, remarked caustically that Butler's army was trapped, "as if it had been in a bottle strongly corked."[5]

General Robert Hoke's division was ordered to the Army of Northern Virginia north of Richmond on May 31, 1864. However, Ransom's Brigade was held back and assigned to General Bushrod R. Johnson's division to keep Butler in check and "bottled up" at Bermuda Hundred. By that time, the 25th Regiment N.C. had been at war for three years. In their service to the Confederate States of America, the regiment's mountain boys had built fortifications in South Carolina, fought in some of the most conspicuous actions in the fiercest battles of the war, guarded railroads, protected eastern North Carolina, captured Plymouth, North Carolina, and most recently fended off marauding Yankee aggressors advancing on Richmond. Certainly they had performed valiantly and could hold their heads as high as their colors. But the ensuing year would prove to be the most trying and difficult of all for the intrepid mountaineers.

Beauregard's Stopgap Defense of Petersburg

President Lincoln brought General Ulysses S. Grant from the west in the spring of 1864 and promoted the successful yet plain and modest officer to the grade of lieutenant general and assigned to him command of all the Union armies. At the time General William T. Sherman wrote a note to his brother about his friend Grant: "Grant is as good a leader as we can find. He has honesty, simplicity of character, singleness of purpose, and no hope or claim to usurp civil power. His character, more than his genius, will reconcile armies and attach the people." Another witness to Grant's presence in Washington, D.C., to receive his country's highest military ranking observed that Grant possessed a "rough dignity" and "habitually wears an expression as if he had determined to drive his head through a brick wall, and was about to do it." General-in-Chief Grant was not familiar to many of the Southern commanders but had been a good friend of General Longstreet at West Point Military Academy. Upon learning of Grant's promotion and new assignment, Longstreet expressed a foreboding assessment of Grant to his fellow Confederate commanders: "We must make up our minds to get into

In May 1864 Confederate General Pierre G.T. Beauregard was summoned to Richmond by President Jefferson Davis to patch together a defense of the South's capital city. Ransom's Brigade, along with its 25th Regiment N.C., was ordered there to bolster the Confederate defenses and stave off Union General Benjamin Butler's advances (Library of Congress).

line of battle and stay there, because that man will fight us every day and every hour until the end of the war." Never were truer words spoken.[6]

Immediately Grant developed plans to destroy General Johnston's Army of Tennessee and loosed General William T. Sherman to fight his way south through Georgia toward Atlanta. General Meade, still in command of the Army of the Potomac after his victory at Gettysburg, Pennsylvania, was given resolute orders to follow Lee wherever he might go. Meade followed Lee and his army into northern Virginia where the blue and gray armies began battering each other with regularity and possibly in the most lethal fighting of the war. Grant vowed that he would fight it out on this line if it took all summer. From April until June 1864, along the Rapidan and North Anna Rivers, this murderous warfare persisted at places such as the Wilderness, Spotsylvania, North Anna, and Cold Harbor, and each time having similar results—thousands and thousands of dead soldiers and Lee still interposed between the Federals and Richmond. But after each clash, Grant managed to maneuver his army farther and farther to his left in a clockwise manner circling ever closer to Richmond.

By June 1864 the bloodletting and human toll were so great that even Grant was dissuaded from a continuation of similar callous tactics to destroy the Army of Northern Virginia. He resolved to bypass Lee and Richmond and attempt to capture Petersburg, an all-important Confederate railroad center which lay just to the south of Richmond. In the early days of June 1864, the Army of the Potomac began a wide flanking movement to the east and then south, sidling around Richmond and behind Lee's forces. After crossing the James River on June 14 utilizing a pontoon bridge 2,100 feet long, Grant's combined armies moved on Petersburg, less than twenty miles away. Waiting there to blunt the Union assault was General Beauregard again, with his skeletal force of shock troops.

The 25th Regiment N.C. had remained in the vicinity of Drewry's Bluff after the violent battles fought there during May 1864 and continued to support the Confederate efforts to protect Petersburg and Richmond. Still attached to Ransom's Brigade (as it was for almost the entirety of the war), the 25th N.C. marched to Bottom's Bridge east of Richmond on June 4, and on June 9 moved to Chaffin's farm opposite Drewry's Bluff across the James River. A clue to the regiment's whereabouts during this crucial period of buildup and posturing by both sides is discovered in a Union intelligence report dated June 9, 1864. The information contained in the communication below was extracted from three deserters from Ransom's Brigade who had been apprehended and questioned; and these disloyal men were, it seems, extremely cooperative:

> We have also 3 men from Ransom's (North Carolina) Brigade (lately belonging to Beauregard's command), who have come to our lines with avowed purpose of availing themselves of President's proclamation. One of them is a sergeant, and a man of considerable intelligence. Ransom's Brigade came from the Bluff on the 4th instant, passed to the right of Richmond, and was seen by the sergeant day before yesterday just below Bottom's Bridge, on the Chickahominy. On arriving there it relieved the Richmond City battalion, which was understood to return within the line of the city defenses. Ransom's Brigade consists of five regiments, which has not seen hard service since it left Lee's army in January, 1863, and averages 450 to 500 men to the regiment. Sergeant estimates the brigade at 3,000. He knows of Hoke's Division (formerly Whiting's) having joined Lee before his brigade left Beauregard. He says it was understood when Ransom left that but one division, of three or four brigades (he does not know which), was left in front of General Butler. He heard his officers generally talk about it, and express themselves to that effect. It is a division known as Bushrod Johnson's. Below position now occupied by Ransom's Brigade he says there is nothing but cavalry.[7]

The intelligence spilled by the obliging deserters confirmed that Ransom's Brigade vacated Drewry's Bluff on June 4 and marched up the James River by Richmond and out to Bottom's Bridge on the Chickahominy River. The North Carolinians relieved the Richmond militia and hurriedly threw up and manned defensive positions between Chaffin's Bluff on the James River and the Chickahominy. In those swampy woods on the same ground where the battles of the Seven Days had taken place, the North Carolinians waited in expectation for Grant's advancing Yankee hoard.

On June 15 Ransom's Brigade was ordered by General Beauregard from Chaffin's Bluff, located downstream a short distance from Drewry's Bluff and on the north side of the James River, back to Petersburg. After crossing the James over a pontoon bridge and an all-night march, the brigade reached the city on the morning of June 16, whereupon it was instantly thrown into the Rebel lines to repel the assaults of Grant's armies already underway. On this day, Beauregard's Rebels, numbering approximately 10,000, fought off more than 48,000 Union forces. A Ransom's Brigade veteran and participant in the action on June 16 later wrote of his rush to Beauregard's aid:

> At 9:30 A.M. on 15 June, Beauregard telegraphed Bragg to send him Ransom's Brigade. The brigade was then at Chaffin's Bluff. It was ordered to report to General Beauregard at once, and marching all night reached Petersburg about sunrise on the 16th. Arriving in sight of the inner line of the works defending Petersburg the enemy were seen advancing upon the same. At a run, through a storm of shot and shell, the Confederates succeeded in getting to the works just in time to meet the enemy's charge and drive them back.[8]

Artist's sketch of Union forces attacking a Confederate fort in front of Petersburg on June 15, 1864 (Library of Congress; artist Edwin Forbes).

The 25th Regiment N.C. fought courageously to repulse the Federal assaults, about which Lt. Ferguson recorded:

> On 16 June, 1864, the regiment crossed to the South of the Appomattox for the defence of Petersburg and entered at once into the fight in front of Avery's House, and checked the advance of the enemy who was driving back the Petersburg militia, the only protection to the city at that time. On the night of the 17th the regiment participated in the engagement at Avery's Farm, and drove the enemy from their breastworks at the point where the 25th made its attack.[9]

During the night of June 16–17 the Rebel forces fell back and closer to Petersburg, where they entrenched and established a new and shorter line of defensive works. A veteran from Ransom's Brigade later wrote, "Early on 17 June the fighting was renewed. Assault after assault was made only to be repulsed, until just at dark a part of the Confederate line was pierced and Battery 14 was captured by Leslie's Division of the Ninth Army Corps. About 11 P.M., Ransom's Brigade was ordered to the support of Wise, who had been driven from the salient occupied by his brigade. Ransom's Brigade was ordered to charge and reestablish the line."[10]

The regiment's actions described above are confirmed through another account from a noted historian of Lee's army:

> The next few hours were decisive. Beauregard had received no relief from the attacks that had begun disastrously at dawn of June 17. Toward evening the assaults became more furious. About dusk a desperate attack by a Division of the IX Corps breached another section of the line and took Battery 14, which had been held by part of Wise's command. The arrival of Archibald Gracie's Brigade prevented deep penetration, but a necessary counterattack by Matt Ransom's North Carolina Brigade cost it many lives. By the time Ransom's men threw the Federals out of the salient they had taken, Beauregard was poised for a withdrawal to new positions.[11]

General Lee arrived with the greater part of the Army of Northern Virginia on June 18 to relieve the exhausted and fought-out men manning the defensive line and safeguarding Petersburg. Lee assumed command of all the Richmond and Petersburg defenses and immediately put the troops into action warding off more uncoordinated Federal attacks, extending the lines and erecting additional works to protect the city and its railroads. Ransom's Brigade, along with the 25th Regiment, would again become formally attached to the Army of Northern Virginia; and for the next nine long months the deadly trenches around Petersburg became home to the mountain boys of the 25th Regiment N.C.

At that particular period in the war, it was also a most difficult time for the civilian population of the South. Southern morale was ebbing lower than ever before. Many harbored little faith of a positive outcome from the Rebellion and worried constantly about loved ones away at war on the infernal battlefields. And there were other troubles that weighed heavily on their minds. The economy was undone, and what industry that existed in the South was primarily devoted to the production of food, clothing, and war materials to sustain the army in the field. The civilian population was under a tremendous strain to secure just the basic commodities and staples to support their existence. Even at the highest levels of society the gentry was challenged by the scarcity and price of food products and other goods. As the value of Confederate money plunged lower and lower with the depletion of the government treasury, wealth was exhausted and a desperation ruled across the South that even the plantations and city mansions did not escape.

Mrs. Mary Boykin Chesnut frequently wrote in her diary of these difficulties and alluded to the rapidly decreasing value of the Confederate currency. The following examples are indicative of the economic problems and concerns inflicted on the civilian population by a cruel war:

> My pink silk dress I have sold for $600, to be paid for in instalments, two hundred a month for three months. And I sell my eggs and butter from home for two hundred dollars a month. Does it not sound well—four hundred dollars a month regularly. But in what? In Confederate money. Hélas!
>
> Mr. Petigru says you take your money to market in the market basket, and bring home what you buy in your pocket-book.
>
> Everybody is in trouble. Mrs. Davis says paper money has depreciated so much in value that they can not live within their income; so they are going to dispense with their carriage and horses.[12]

Mary Boykin Chesnut, the renowned Civil War diarist and witness to the war's destructive social consequences, is depicted here in a reflective moment while penning the latest drama in the South's struggle for independence (*Mary Boykin Chesnut: Witness to War*, Amy V. Lindenberger).

From the diarist's notes, it can be seen that not even the wife of President Jefferson Davis was exempt from the privations brought on by the war. It seems that she, and the president, were strapped to live within the income afforded them by the Confederacy. But the greater burdens by far were heaped on the backs of the entrenched soldiers in front of Petersburg, including those of the 25th Regiment N.C. It would be the most difficult period of their service to the Confederacy and they would experience continuous fighting, fear of surprise attack or bombardment at any time, cold, hunger and adversity unfathomable to those inexperienced in war. Lt. Ferguson recapped the situation thus: "From 16 June, 1864, until April, 1865, the regiment was constantly under fire, with the exception of about ten days in March, occupying the trenches in front of Petersburg."[13]

10

SIEGE OF PETERSBURG

Battle of the Crater

Petersburg was effectively besieged by the Union forces, much to the chagrin of both warring architects, Grant and Lee. General Grant knew very well the difficulty and peril of attacking well-entrenched defensive positions after his unsuccessful attempts to assail the fortified trenches at Vicksburg, Mississippi, and the recent lessons learned at Spotsylvania and Cold Harbor in Virginia. The Army of Northern Virginia was dug in behind strong fortifications which extended southward from the Chickahominy River, near Richmond, in an approximate forty-mile arc circling Petersburg on the eastern and southern sides. Grant resolved to apply relentless pressure and squeeze the Rebels into submission. The South was now forced to defend the approaches to Richmond as well as Petersburg with a numerically inferior army by at least a 2 to 1 ratio. Moreover, the Confederate government lacked the logistical capacity, military supplies, and, most importantly, food to sustain their small army. Grant, mindful of this, coldly calculated that it was only a matter of time before the Southern troops would be weakened beyond the ability to offer strong resistance. And General Lee recognized that unless his army could keep open the lines of supply from the South, there would be "no way of averting the terrible disaster that will ensue."[1]

Ransom's Brigade remained in camp at Petersburg until June 22, 1864, when it was called to the support of General A.P. Hill near the Jones house on the south side of the city and at the right extremity of the Confederate line. General Hill successfully engaged and rebuffed the enemy there along the Jerusalem Plank Road on June 22, while Ransom's Brigade waited in reserve. The next day the brigade returned to the position it formerly held at Petersburg, and on June 24 at midnight they moved into and occupied the trenches south of the Petersburg & Norfolk Railroad (sometimes referred to as the City Point Railroad). Defense of the ground on both sides of this railroad at the outskirts of Petersburg, running from the Appomattox River to the Jerusalem plank road, was charged to General Bushrod Johnson's division, which included Ransom's Brigade and the 25th Regiment N.C.

For the next several weeks, the soldiers of Ransom's Brigade busied themselves fortifying the trenches and defending against a wide array of enemy schemes and techniques to dislodge them. The *Official Records* of the war compiled by the United States government contains daily reports from General Bushrod Johnson highlighting the activities of his brigades during this time. These documents offer insight into the difficulties that the general and his command were facing and the routine that Ransom's Brigade and its 25th Regiment N.C. settled into as the soldiers accustomed themselves to life in the trenches. During the first few days of July 1864, Ransom's Brigade worked on the entrenchments and threw up a timber abatis to obstruct and slow down surprise enemy assaults. Johnson's reports mention more than once the scarcity of tools to work with. The toiling was exhausting and dangerous, even at night, as the Yankees kept up incessant artillery and mortar fire and their sharpshooters fired at any target presented to them.

In those first weeks of July 1864, Colonel P.F. Faison of the Fifty-sixth Regiment N.C. was commanding Ransom's Brigade. (Matt Ransom remained at home in North Carolina to convalesce from the wound received at Drewry's Bluff.) He reported to Johnson that the "enemy mortars annoy him" and that he didn't have the capacity to reply. Hearing similar protests from his other brigades, General Johnson complained to the Confederate army officials about a lack of ammunition to respond to the Union mortar fire. He even recommended the employ of wooden mortars that could utilize ammunition charges which were available in larger quantities.[2] Additional proof that the Confederate forces were desperately short of ammunition can be derived from General Johnson's reports, where he regularly recorded the fruits of his men's daily scavenging efforts around their works. One such day's exertions yielded finds of 12,600 minie balls, 10 pounds of lead, 14 Hotchkiss shells, 18 solid shot and a number of shell fragments.[3] These recovered artifacts of war were turned over to the ordnance officer for recycling and future use against the enemy.

On occasion, General Johnson offered the Confederate war department his thoughtful and unsolicited views on a variety of subjects. Regarding the mortal sacrifice of soldiers in his command being made as a result of the want of ammunition and war equipment, Johnson expressed the following opinions in a report submitted on July 17, 1864:

> The losses and annoyance which the enemy occasion in my lines are simply due, in my opinion, to a want of proper ammunition; from necessity, no doubt. So far as appliances with this army are concerned, we are husbanding our ammunition — that is, men or ammunition; one or the other — the enemy compel us to sacrifice. This is the simple question with us: Which shall we expend, human life or ammunition? We have none of the former material to spare, and the supply of it for future purposes is necessarily limited; of material for manufacturing the latter nature affords a bountiful supply.

Further into his report, the general opined, "I may also be permitted to state the fact that whilst we husband our ammunition and the enemy are thinning our ranks with comparative immunity — our men being

General-in-Chief Ulysses S. Grant was Abraham Lincoln's choice to lead the combined armies of the United States against the Confederate military forces. Fresh from magnificent victories in the West, he took up the challenge to match wits and resources against General Robert E. Lee and the Army of Northern Virginia (Library of Congress).

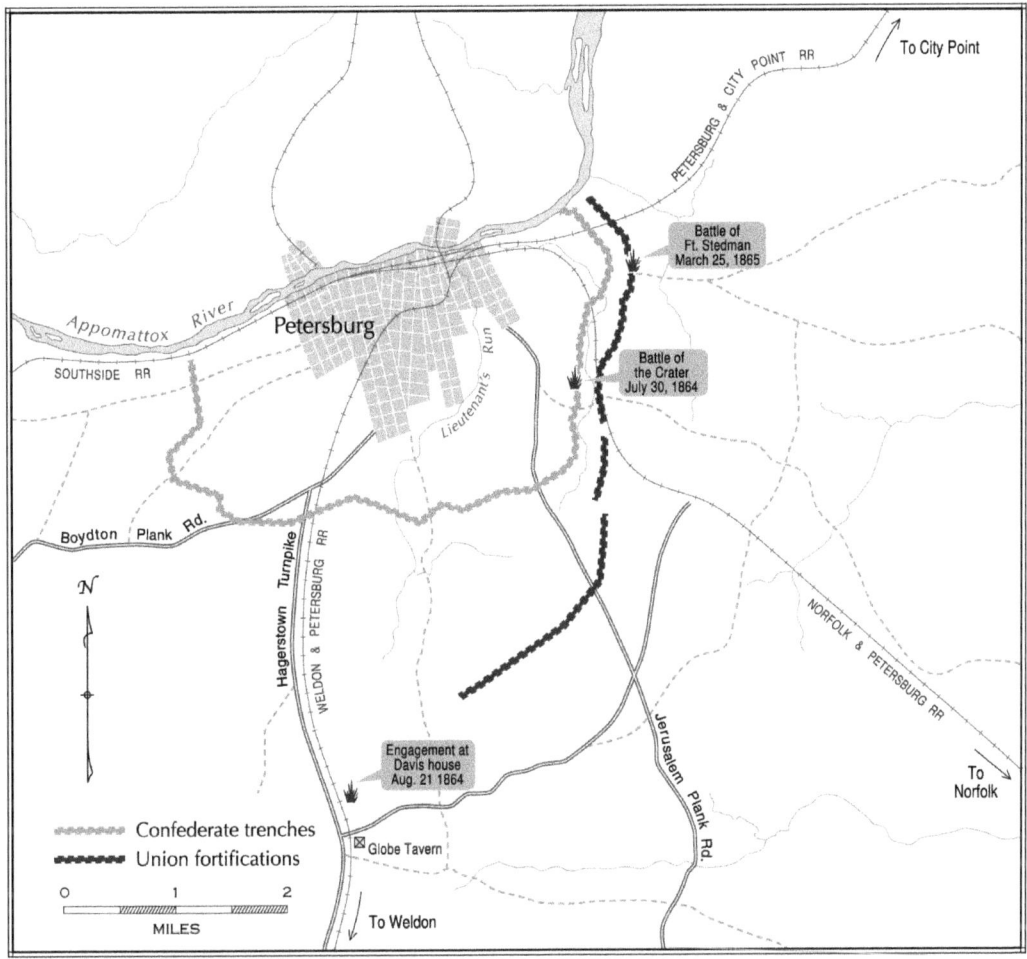

The Siege of Petersburg: June 1864–March 1865. For nine long months, Ransom's Brigade and its Twenty-fifth Regiment N.C., occupied a position in the Confederate trenches between the Appomattox River and the Jerusalem plank road (Peter Krafft, Florida State University).

compelled simply to suffer and endure — a moral effect is being produced which may prove very detrimental to our future success."[4]

As can be seen, the general simply proffers to the Confederate army's adjutant general a simple question: "Shall we expend human life or ammunition?" With the supply of Southern fighting men limited and the materials for manufacturing ammunition abundantly supplied by nature, General Johnson challenges elsewhere in the dispatch the bureaucrat officers to produce and acquire this critical war material. That same daily report shows his division's human sacrifices on the previous day to be 3 men killed and 17 wounded. Ransom's Brigade suffered four men wounded.

Toward the middle of July, the enemy began throwing hand grenades toward the Confederate trenches; but the range proved to be too great and the lethal bombs fell short of the target. To remedy this "shortfall," the Yankees endeavored to extend their trenches closer to the Rebel lines and within hand grenade-throwing distance. For protection from sniper fire while advancing the saps, an ingenious contraption known as a sap roller was devised and constructed. This cylindrically shaped roller, approximately four to five feet in diameter and six to seven feet long, was constructed of tightly interlaced wooden tree limbs, sticks and slats. The density of the wooden materials, woven together in a wicker fashion, made the sap rollers impervious to the Rebel musket fire and thus afforded protection for the Union men laboring behind them as they pushed their trenches ever closer to the Rebel lines. The sap rollers were simply rolled forward and closer to the opposing works as work on the saps progressed.

On July 21 the Confederate records indicate for the first time the use of a sap roller by the enemy. General Johnson recorded that his forces kept up a brisk rifle fire to discourage the Yankees' forward movement of a sap roller. However, on July 25, one of Johnson's brigade commanders communicated that "the enemy No. 2 sap roller advanced eight feet during the darkness of night." General Gracie, commanding one of Johnson's brigades, recommended the use of "Travis fire" to destroy the sap rollers. The reports do not expound further on the notion of utilizing Travis fire other than to indicate that it was prepared by Captain Travis of Mobile, Alabama. Presumably Travis fire was an incendiary substance, akin to the "Greek Fire" first used by the Byzantines in the seventh century A.D. that could be thrown at the sap rollers and cause them to catch fire on impact. It is not clear, however, whether the Rebels ever employed the Alabamian's concoction in order to rid themselves of the Union sap rollers.[5]

During the latter part of July 1864, Colonel Lee M. McAfee from the Forty-ninth Regiment N.C. had assumed command of Ransom's Brigade. His mortars, as well as those of Johnson's other brigades, were responding to the enemy's fire more frequently, undoubtedly at the insistence of General Johnson and as a result of his eloquently expressed and persistent grievances regarding the husbanding of ammunition. Brigadier General Gracie communicated to Johnson on July 27 that he thought the batteries, especially those in rear of and to the left of Ransom's Brigade, "did great execution yesterday." He reported that groans were definitely heard near the sap rollers. Just a few days prior to this successful barrage, on July 21, General Johnson forwarded a request from Gracie that the engineer be sent to his line to sink a mine, as digging was heard in his front, apparently at some depth. The Yankees were up to something and General Gracie and his men could little have suspected the dramatic and tragic consequences of those digging sounds.[6]

Union soldiers planting the mine under the Confederate trenches at Petersburg (Library of Congress; artist Alfred Rudolf Waud).

Soon after the initial Union thrust at Petersburg in June 1864 and the two sides had inhabited opposing trenches and fortifications, the clever Yankees came up with a plot to create a gap in the Confederate defense works. Lieutenant Colonel Henry Pleasants, in command of a Pennsylvania unit, proposed to General Burnside that some of his boys who were coal miners dig a tunnel under the Confederate lines and blow the Rebels up with an underground bomb. Theoretically, a huge explosion would open a breach in the Confederate lines large enough for the waiting Union troops to rush through and overwhelm the surprised Rebel defense forces. General Burnside was taken by the initiative of the Pennsylvania men and championed the novel idea to General Grant. Approval to proceed was quickly given and the Pennsylvanians began digging in late June 1864. By July 17 the mine shaft reached 511 feet and extended under a forward salient in the Rebel defense works. Approximately 8,000 pounds of powder were packed into the end of the tunnel, and by July 28 the mine was armed and ready.[7]

Ransom's Brigade, one of several brigades commanded at that time by General Bushrod Johnson, was positioned in the forward trenches immediately adjacent and to the left of the location where the Yankees had planted their bomb. Directly over that chosen spot was Elliott's Salient, manned by Brigadier General Stephen Elliott's Brigade from South Carolina. The 25th Regiment N.C. represented the extreme right side of Ransom's defense and was the closest unit to Elliott's Salient, less than two hundred yards distant. At 4:55 on the morning of July 30, 1864, the Yankee mine was detonated and instantly the enormous explosion killed or buried 278 of Elliott's unfortunate boys under tons of earth. A crater 170 feet long, 60 to 80 feet wide, and 30 feet deep was blasted open, and into the hole rushed General Burnside's Union troops. These forces, poorly prepared for the mission and with uninspired leadership, poured into the "crater" by the hundreds and even thousands and found themselves confined, as if in a fishbowl, and unable to maneuver. General Grant would later report after the battle that "It was the saddest affair I have witnessed in the war. Such opportunity for carrying fortifications I have never seen and do not expect again to have."[8]

Lt. Ferguson, a participant of the battle of the Crater, expressed his remembrance of the furious action on that eventful day:

> The position of the regiment on 30 June, 1864 [30 July], was on the right of Ransom's brigade and to the left of Elliott's South Carolina brigade. The explosion of Grant's Mine was in the line occupied by the left regiment of the South Carolina brigade. Immediately after the explosion the 25th regiment, then numbering about two hundred and fifty men, moved from the trenches and formed a new line in the rear of the trenches occupied by the South Carolinians, which had been taken at the time of the explosion and which were then occupied by the enemy. The regiment, with a remnant of the Sixth South Carolina, was the only force between the enemy and the city, at that point. The enemy massed his troops in our trenches in front of us until he had sixteen regimental flags in our works. He made several attempts to move forward and force our line, but was successfully repulsed and held in check for several hours, until reinforcements arrived. The regiment led Mahone's men in the charge which retook the works. In retaking the works the fight was hand to hand, with guns, bayonets, and swords, in fact anything a man could fight with. One sixteen year old boy had his gun knocked out of his hands and picked up a cartridge box and fought with that.[9]

It is difficult to imagine a 16-year-old boy picking up a cartridge box and wielding only that as a weapon to fight the Yankees. Grown men with deadly rifles and bayonets were hard pressed to demonstrate such courage, and often did not. Of note in Lt. Ferguson's account above is that the fighting strength of the 25th Regiment N.C. at the battle of the Crater was only two hundred fifty troops, significantly fewer than the 1,600 or more troops whose names appear in the rosters and records of the Regiment.

The explosion of the Yankee mine under the Confederate trench works at Petersburg is depicted in this Civil War–era illustration. On July 30, 1864, this singular action initiated the furious fighting that became known as the Battle of the Crater (*Harper's Weekly*).

For a brief period that chaotic day, the regiment, buoyed with pieces of General William Mahone's division and the remnants of Elliott's Brigade, were the only Rebel forces that stood between the attacking Union troops and the city of Petersburg. With the outcome of the battle hanging in balance, the 25th N.C., along with those units of Elliott and Mahone, charged into the enemy forces occupying the Rebel works and succeeded in retaking their old lines. A Rebel soldier from the Forty-ninth N.C. of Ransom's Brigade witnessed the charge into the Crater by the 25th N.C. and wrote the following account: "I saw the 25th Regiment as they came dashing up the hill towards the Crater. How we cheered them! They rushed up the Crater which was full of the enemy, white and black, fired one volley and then turning the butts of their guns, they let them fall, crushing the skulls ... at every blow."[10]

As meritorious as the action of the Twenty-fifth was, it was not without serious consequences. During the battle, Major William S. Grady, in command of the regiment on that day, was mortally wounded and Captain James M. Cathey of Company F was killed. The exact toll of the regimental casualties is not known, but the battle report submitted by General Bushrod Johnson reveals that Ransom's Brigade suffered 14 men killed, 68 wounded and 8 missing. Elliott's South Carolina brigade manning the Confederate strongpoint directly over Grant's mine on that historic day experienced a casualty rate of almost 700 soldiers. Approximately one-half of those were listed as "missing" and undoubtedly that number includes many of those poor souls blown apart at the instant of the explosion or entombed in an avalanche of earth that fell over them.

Southerners did not take very kindly to this new episode in warfare at Petersburg. Prior to the explosion of the Pennsylvanians' mine, it seems that most Rebels harbored little evil sentiment against the enemy. They were considered more as equals and, as one Johnny Reb remarked, "They fit us, we fit them." However, the "blow-up" and ensuing battle cast a different light on matters, as it was considered a sneaky or mean Yankee trick. Also, at the Crater the Federals employed blacks as combatants, a practice which the South had not yet resorted to. Thus, a new found hatred for the Yankees caused the Rebels to grit their teeth harder and find the will and strength to persevere longer.

Life in the Trenches

The Army of Northern Virginia occupied the trenches and fortified works in front of Petersburg through the foreboding fall and winter of 1864–1865. Assigned to Ransom's Brigade for protection was a stretch of the Confederate defense line extending from a point on the Appomattox River eastward to the Jerusalem road. The brigade, with its 25th Regiment N.C., remained attached to General Bushrod Johnson's division. A renowned historian of Robert E. Lee and the Army of Northern Virginia wrote of the trench warfare and the service rendered in the saps by Johnson's Division: "Bushrod Johnson's Division, moreover, had borne much of the sternest, bitterest day-by-day fighting in the hideous, red trenches of Petersburg."[11]

In the beginning of the siege, troops on both sides were vulnerable to the murderous deadly aim of rifle sharpshooters. Yet, at various times over the duration of the stalemate the sharpshooting was abandoned by common consent of the warring parties. The trenches, or rifle pits, were a complicated system of excavations, with embankments on the front and back sides to protect the men. At regular intervals along these trenches, shorter walls, called traverses, were built to enclose the pits on each end. Traverses offered additional protection for the soldiers from enemy enfilading fire and exploding mortar shells. Small gopher holes were dug into the pit walls and the soldiers would dive into these with astonishing rapidity when lookouts observed shells coming their way.[12]

One soldier from Ransom's Brigade describes his occupancy of the trenches in the following manner:

> [The regiment] was moved to the left, and occupied the line from the iron bridge to the river as before stated. Here it was our daily occupation to watch the enemy through port holes made through sand bags and to dodge mortar shells. At night we did picket duty in the rifle pits between the two lines, in some places not more than forty yards from the Yankee pickets. Often we would meet and exchange tobacco and coffee, and have a social chat with each other.[13]

Yet another Rebel fighter from Ransom's Brigade described the very real dangers and hardships that he and his brethren faced while occupying the red earthen trenches of Petersburg:

> From this date [June 1864] until 16 March 1865, just nine months, in the lines east of Petersburg, occupying at different times positions from the Appomattox river to the Jerusalem plank road, often not a hundred yards from the works of the enemy, constantly exposed to danger and death from mortar and cannon shells and balls, grape, shrapnel and the deadlier minie balls, we engaged in daily battle. Exposed to sun and storm, heat and cold, with scant food and insufficient supplies, the ranks thinning hourly from deaths, wounds and sickness, depressed by the gathering gloom of our falling fortunes, through the dark, bitter and foreboding winter of 1864–65.[14]

Top: This photograph offers a view of the "hideous red trenches" of Petersburg. Note the wooden log traverses constructed to provide more protection from exploding shells and enfilade attacks (Library of Congress). *Above:* In this photograph of the Petersburg trenches, bombproof living quarters can be seen with chimneys made out of mud and wooden barrels (Library of Congress).

Shown in this photograph are the dirt-filled wicker gabions which were used by Union forces to construct their trench fortifications at Petersburg (Library of Congress).

The trenches were home to the soldiers, where shelter was fashioned by stretching blankets and tents across the open pit tops. Underneath these awnings, the soldiers sought refuge from the sun, rain, and snow. Food was generally prepared in cook yards behind the front lines and carried forward across the men's shoulders. One of the brigade's men described the Rebel soldiers living in underground bombproof shelters as scantily clothed, almost barefooted, and half-starved. This same soldier wrote that he once was "invited to a squirrel dinner made of wharf rats."[15]

The privations the soldiers endured were extreme, and as in normal camp life throughout the war, sanitary conditions were abysmal. Many of the soldiers of the 25th Regiment N.C. were stricken with camp disease and other illnesses. For example, the August 1864 records of General Hospital No. 4 confirm that First Lieutenant William H. Hargrove of Company F of the 25th Regiment N.C. was suffering from chronic diarrhea with emaciation dyspepsia, not uncommon disorders during the war. Hargrove was granted a 30-day furlough, whereupon he returned home to Forks of Pigeon in Haywood County to recover. Muster rolls of the regiment indicate he was back and present for duty in the trenches of Petersburg by October 1864.

Clearly shown in this photograph of the Petersburg trenches is the protective abatis breastwork fashioned from wooden poles with sharpened spear-point ends (Library of Congress).

Years after the war was ended, Colonel Henry Rutledge, commander of the 25th Regiment N.C., recalled for his son a visit paid to the saps and his troops one rainy night by General Robert E. Lee. Archibald Rutledge, the first poet laureate of South Carolina, wrote of the conversation afterward and recorded his father's story:

> He told me that, one night of rain and fog, on the dreary and deadly ramparts in front of the trenches at Petersburg, a cloaked figure had suddenly appeared to him out of the mist. It was General Lee. Together they stood talking in the steady downpour, talking of the war, of the coming battle, of those fallen, of those left behind. On leaving, the General said, "I hope your men are well sheltered, Colonel. Keep them dry if you can, and give them extra rations." More than a mile back to his headquarters Lee walked in the rain.[16]

Apparently, the enlisted soldiers were not alone in their suffering. Good commanding officers such as Colonel Henry Rutledge, General Matt Ransom and General Robert E. Lee

Union mortars, such as this one, were located behind the defense lines and were used incessantly and effectively against the Confederate soldiers holed up in the trenches at Petersburg (Library of Congress).

were not oblivious to their conditions and privations and always had the Confederate soldiers' welfare at heart.

Battle of the Weldon Railroad

In the fall of 1864 General Grant determined to move on the Confederate right flank south of Petersburg to capture or destroy the Petersburg-Weldon railroad, the main line linking Richmond and Petersburg with North Carolina and the lower South. A few miles south of Petersburg, Union forces in strength engaged in the destruction of as much Confederate railroad property and trackage as possible in the vicinity of Ream's Station and the Globe Tavern. Upon discovery of this activity, General Lee at once ordered General Beauregard to send Confederate troops to dislodge the Federals from the railroad.

On August 21, 1864, one of several battles to gain control of the Weldon Railroad was fought in the vicinity of Globe Tavern and a farm owned by the Davis family, approximately a mile south of the Confederate trench lines along the railroad. On August 20, Ransom's

Brigade was ordered out of the trenches and to the right of the Confederate line, where it supported General Henry Heth's drive to dislodge the Federals off the railroad. The following day, August 21, the 25th Regiment was ordered to advance and take the enemy's position just to the east of the Weldon Railroad, which was heavily fortified with timber obstructions thrown up to hinder a Rebel assault. Referred to as "abatis" and commonly used during the war, this effective defensive barrier was constructed by crossing the laps of felled trees and hewing the ends of the limbs to sharpened points. Forces charging a position protected by abatis were necessarily slowed down in order to negotiate and penetrate the jumbles of dangerous wooden spear points. The regiment was successful in taking this Federal lodgment, but the mission of the combined Confederate forces to wrest control of the railroad from the Union was not achieved. On August 24 and 25, a larger Confederate contingent, one that did not include the 25th Regiment N.C., attacked the Union defenses at Ream's Station, located a few miles further to the south down the Weldon line toward North Carolina, and succeeded in temporarily driving off the Federals.

Lt. Ferguson, a participant in the action at the Davis House, wrote the following account of the 25th Regiment's fight near the Globe Tavern:

> On 21 August 1864, the regiment participated in the battle of the Weldon Railroad, between Petersburg and Reams' Station. The enemy had entrenched himself behind heavy earthworks and had felled the timber in front, crossing the laps of the trees and sharpening the limbs. In order to reach their works the timber had to be removed so as to make a passway for the men. During this time the enemy kept up a constant fire until our men reached the works. The color-bearer of the regiment was shot down and Sergeant J.B. Hawkins, of Company C, caught the colors, rushed forward and placed them on the works. The works were taken and the enemy driven back under cover of his heavy artillery. The loss of the regiment was heavy in killed and wounded.[17]

Another historian from Ransom's Brigade described the fierce fighting around the Davis House:

> In the latter part of August 1864, Ransom's brigade was ordered to attack and drive back the enemy at the Davis house. They had to charge some distance through an abatis of felled trees. The men had to pick their way through the interlaced timbers and advance without regard to company or regimental formations.
> This advance was so gallantly done as to evoke from General Lee, who witnessed the charge, the remark: "That he had often heard of men straggling to the rear, but he had never before seen men straggle to the attack."[18]

It is apparent from this commentary that the 25th Regiment N.C. behaved in gallant style as they advanced and attacked the Federals entrenched near the Globe Tavern along the Weldon Railroad. General Lee was evidently surprised to see his brave soldiers "straggling to the attack" as they stormed through openings in the timber abatis, and into a formidable wall of rifle and artillery fire from stubborn Yankees, to capture the enemy position. After the 25th Regiment's color bearer was shot down, Sergeant J.B. Hawkins bravely took up the colors and planted them over the breastworks, where they would stay. Losses to the regiment were heavy in killed and wounded, and Lt. Ferguson himself received a wound to the right shoulder but "did not quit the field." The Confederate forces captured 2,100 Union prisoners and suffered an estimated 700 casualties over several days of fighting for control of the Weldon Railroad.

Long Winter of 1864–1865

President Lincoln was reelected for a second term in November 1864, primarily as a result of the growing Union successes on the battlefields. With renewed political strength and a mandate for a continuation of his administration's policies, the president's forceful endeavors to suppress the Southern insurrection seemed unstoppable. News from Georgia portended gloom and doom as it filtered back to the regiment's boys peering over the earthen trench walls or through the slits of their rifle pits at their Northern adversaries. They learned that General Sherman had taken Atlanta and torched a good portion of the city in order to destroy its industrial capacity. By the end of the year, his army had cut a swath to the sea through Georgia culminating in the capture of Savannah in mid–December. Sherman promptly telegraphed President Lincoln: "I beg to present to you, as a Christmas gift, the city of Savannah, with 150 heavy guns and ... about 25,000 bales of Cotton."[19] The mountain boys might also have received news that during Sherman's Savannah campaign the Federals had laid waste to store buildings and plantations around their old stomping grounds at Grahamville, South Carolina. Rumor had it that Charleston would likely be next, and then Sherman would storm through the Carolinas and combine with Grant's forces in Virginia to defeat Lee's army once and finally.

And there were more sad tidings filtering back to the Petersburg trenches. During December of 1864, in a series of fierce battles fought in Tennessee, General George Thomas and his Union army completed the destruction of the remnants of the Confederate Army of Tennessee, recklessly led by General John Bell Hood. Learning of the Tennessee disaster, Confederate war department clerk John B. Jones wrote in his diary: "The darkest and most dismal day ... a crisis such as not been experienced before."[20] Mary Chesnut also bemoaned the news and recorded an entry in her diary on December 19: "The deep waters are closing over us."

The Federals' clutch on the Confederacy was strengthening, and the South's ability to resist and sustain the war effort was dwindling fast. The Carolinas were the only regions of the South still open for the Confederate troops to draw supplies, and the one last remaining southern port, Wilmington, was to be wrested from Confederate control soon after the fall of Fort Fisher on January 15, 1865. Mrs. Mary Chesnut bemoaned the lack of one single port in the South:

> Oh, for one single port! If the *Alabama* had had in the whole wide world a port to take her prizes to and where she could be refitted, I believe she would have borne us through. Oh, for one single port by which we could get at the outside world and refit our whole Confederacy! If we could have hired regiments from Europe, or even have imported ammunition and food for our soldiers![21]

Throughout North Carolina, all of the males of military age were either in service or hiding from it. Western and central counties continued to be plagued by bands of roving, lawless elements and deserters.[22] The Army of Northern Virginia's troops at the Richmond-Petersburg front were haggard and emaciated and barely able to resist the relentless shelling and assaults from a well-supplied and well-fed Federal army. The Rebel soldiers in the trenches were to pass their first winter underground. One of them would later describe the ordeal as follows: "The winter in the trenches was one of great hardship, though scarcely an assault was delivered from either side. Fuel had to be brought in by hand, about a mile, as had been the timber for the bombproofs in the summer. Our winter quarters, as well as chimneys, were made of barrels, boxes, or any material that could be had, and held in place with daubs of mud."[23]

Thoughts of the explosion of Grant's mine, which caused such tremendous destruction and death and initiated the battle of the Crater, lingered in the minds of the Rebels manning the defensive saps at Petersburg. General Bushrod Johnson's daily reports were filled with references to sounds of enemy mining activity, and his officers were constantly alert to suspicious activities and movements in their front. On several occasions Johnson requested the assistance of an engineer or someone familiar with mining work to come forward to his positions to investigate for any signs of such subterranean tunneling. In addition, his men sunk listening tubes into the ground at regular intervals along the front lines to enhance their eavesdropping capability in hopes of detecting the enemy's diabolical plots.[24] The Official Records contain reports of another mine explosion which occurred on August 4, 1864, along General Johnson's defensive line. Apparently this one was of Confederate origin and was exploded in the front of General Gracie's works to destroy a Union sap roller and interrupt continued trenching work by the Yankees. The record indicates "not a gabion or sap-roller was displaced nor much of a crater formed." General Johnson went on to explain the failure: "The mine must have been badly tamped, as the gallery was destroyed as far back as the shaft. Our picket-line was partially filled up, but again dug out."[25]

Every day around the clock, round after round of mortar fire rained down on the entrenched Southern soldiers, and picket sharpshooting kept the air filled with lethal lead projectiles whizzing around them. Not even the protection afforded by gopher holes in the trench walls and bombproof shelters could prevent a steady occurrence of casualties in the Rebel ranks. On a daily basis, General Johnson reported to army headquarters the number of his men wounded and killed the previous day. These communications indicate that troops were dying and being injured with a regularity that matched the movement of celestial bodies. Ransom's Brigade, still anchoring the Confederate left between the Appomattox River and the Jerusalem road and badly exposed to the Yankee barrages, was suffering the loss of one to several soldiers each and every day during its tenancy of the Petersburg trenches.

A severe shortage of ammunition and war supplies on the Confederate side prevented a reciprocal amount of firepower from being directed toward the enemy positions. General Johnson and his officers and men bristled at orders to husband their destructive missiles and warned their leaders of the injurious effects to the morale of the troops and of the shortcomings of such a tactical policy. Johnson submitted to his superiors calculations which demonstrated that the Union soldiers were throwing five times the firepower at his men as the Rebels' limited supplies would allow in response. For example, every man in the 25th Regiment N.C. was given eighteen rounds to fire at the bluecoats each day, whereas Union deserters reported that one hundred rounds were given to them daily to shoot toward the Rebel lines. Johnson's report of these estimates also recorded numerical facts of a much more somber nature: Ransom's Brigade lost 2 men killed and 5 wounded.[26]

Bullets were not the only thing in short supply at Petersburg. There are many testimonies to the fact that Confederate soldiers living in the trenches during that cold winter of 1864–1865 were barefooted. On the last day of the year of 1864, General Johnson communicated to army headquarters: "I would call your attention to the fact that there are a number of barefooted men in this command. The inspector-general of the army inspected Ransom's brigade some ten days or two weeks since, took down the number of barefooted men, and promised the shoes, but they have not been furnished."[27] The Confederate soldier serving loyally and barefooted at Petersburg during the last winter of the Civil War has certainly not received the acclaim or respect given to General Washington's brave Revolutionary War soldiers who weathered the winter snows at Valley Forge. However, the Rebels living in the saps suffered similar extreme weather conditions and severe deprivations for a cause they believed to be equally righteous.

All along the defense lines, the opposing soldiers kept up a somewhat friendly banter back and forth. Although discouraged from, and even ordered from, carrying on in this manner, the Rebels at times were able to gather information of some intelligence value. One evening a bluecoat yelled at a Johnny staring back at him: "Halloo! We are 100-days men. Our time is nearly out and we are going home. We do not want to fight."[28] Proof of their non-bellicose intentions is manifested in the many hundreds of Yankee troops, mostly new raw recruits forced to join the army, who crossed over the lines at Petersburg to surrender themselves to the Confederates. Discourse with the enemy, however, was frowned upon, and Southern soldiers caught fraternizing with the Yankees in their front were dealt punitive treatment that included the commanding officers who allowed the offending communications. For instance, on September 17, 1864, General Bushrod Johnson reported to the Confederate war department: "I placed Colonel Rutledge, commanding Ransom's Brigade, in arrest last evening for permitting communication between men of his command and the enemy and neglect of duty."[29] This very likely is the only blemish on the young colonel's record and reveals his lenient disciplinary approach and sympathy for the plight of the soldiers in his command.

Heretofore in this account of the 25th Regiment N.C. through the great rebellion, little attention has been drawn to the serious problem of desertion. In an earlier chapter addressing Lee's first Maryland campaign, mention was made that the soldiers of the Army of Northern Virginia were disgruntled with the decision to invade Northern territory. This fact, coupled with empty bellies and unshod feet among other things, caused the flight of Rebels from the ranks in epidemic numbers in the fall of 1862. Throughout the conflict, the pull from home and the strain of combat reduced the numbers of both armies by acts of desertion. However, the impact of desertion would never be greater than during the last winter of the war.

At no other time than that cold winter of 1864–1865 in the mud-filled ditches and caves of Petersburg had General Lee's soldiers suffered more or existed on less. Freezing, dirty, barely fed and unshod, the soldiers' miserable existence was almost impossible to bear. In addition, a great many of these souls harbored little faith that the great disparity in resources, human and material, favoring Grant's Federal army could be overcome, especially given their own sorry state of affairs and what they understood of the overall war situation. And that was not all. Letters and tidings from home would only have added to the soldiers' discouragement and worries. With food being hard to come by and currency even scarcer, wives, children, siblings and elderly parents were suffering privations almost as severe as those experienced on the war front. This fact, coupled with the ever-present threat of gangs of bushwhackers roaming the mountains, beckoned the soldiers home to their families. Enormous pressures on the Confederate soldier created by the cumulative physical and psychological effects of all these circumstances made conditions ripe for desertion.

The wholesale disaffection occurring in General Lee's army during this period is evidenced in dispatches from the Southern general-in-chief in which he alerts two Confederate secretaries of war to the alarming circumstances of desertion. The first communication, addressed to James A. Seddon and dated January 27, 1865, elucidates his thoughts regarding the reasons for the high rate of flight from the army:

> Sir: I have the honor to call your attention to the alarming frequency of desertions from this army.... I have endeavored to ascertain the causes, and think that the insufficiency of food and non-payment of the troops have more to do with the dissatisfaction among the troops than anything else. All commanding officers concur in this opinion. I have no

doubt that there is a suffering for want of food. The ration is too small for men who have to undergo so much exposure and labor as ours.[30]

Just one month later, on February 24, 1865, General Lee advised the new Confederate secretary of war, John C. Breckenridge, on the ever-growing evil of desertion in his army:

> Sir: I regret to be obliged to call your attention to the alarming number of desertions that are now occurring in the army.... The desertions are chiefly from the North Carolina regiments, and especially those from the western part of that State. It seems that the men are influenced very much by the representations of their friends at home, who appear to have become very despondent as to our success. They think the cause desperate and write to the soldiers, advising them to take care of themselves, assuring them that if they will return home the bands of deserters so far outnumber the home guards that they will be in no danger of arrest. I do not know what can be done to prevent this evil, unless some changes can be wrought in the state of public sentiment by the influence of prominent citizens of the State. The deserters generally take their arms with them.[31]

The formula for desertion was not complex and simply equated to the sum of the many variables mentioned above — pressure from home, strain of war, nonpayment of salaries, miserable living conditions in the trenches, cold, and hunger. In the Petersburg trenches, the army was literally starving on its feet. A soldier's daily ration consisted of a pint of corn meal and an ounce or two of bacon. If ordered to work with a pick and shovel the victims would simply be overcome with weakness and faintness in a brief time. One unfortunate solider quipped after surviving the war, "I was hungry ... so hungry that I thanked God that I had a backbone for my stomach to lean up against."[32]

General Lee communicated to the secretary of war in February 1865 that his men had been operating against the enemy for days in the winter cold and informed him of their dreadful circumstances:

> Yesterday, the most inclement day of the winter, they had to be retained in the line of battle, having been in the same condition the two previous days and nights. I regret to be obliged to state that under these circumstances, heightened by assaults and fire of the enemy, some of the men had been without meat for three days, and all were suffering from reduced rations and scant clothing, exposed to battle, cold, hail, and sleet.... If some change is not made and the commissary department reorganized, I apprehend dire results. The physical strength of the men, if their courage survives, must fail under this treatment.... Taking these facts in connection with the paucity of our numbers, you must not be surprised if calamity befalls us.[33]

The Southern commander recognized the consequences of the poor treatment his army was receiving at the hands of the Confederate government and warned the authorities of a potential calamity. Barely fed, cold and without hope, many of his soldiers, volunteers and conscripts alike, deserted the Confederate army and crossed over the picket lines to the enemy, just a few yards away. This dishonorable act became so common toward the end of the war that the men joked of "going up" or going over to the enemy. Others sneaked off in the night at opportune moments and beat it for home on long hazardous treks, determined to take their chances of being apprehended by the authorities. One out of every seven Confederates eventually would desert as compared to one out of ten of the Union troops.[34] The desertion rate was even higher for the soldiers from the South's Appalachian highland regions. Historical sociologist Peter Bearman has estimated that approximately 24 percent of all men who enlisted from the mountains deserted. This compares with a 12 percent desertion rate for the state of North Carolina as a whole.[35]

General Bushrod Johnson's division, which included Ransom's Brigade and the 25th Regiment N.C., occupied the trenches at Petersburg that were constructed closest to the enemy. He wrote in one of his daily reports of the occurrence of desertion in his command that one night 20 men from Ransom's Brigade had deserted and that on another night that figure had doubled. Over a ten-day period in February 1865 a total of 1,061 men disappeared from the Army of Northern Virginia. General Lee wrote to the secretary of war at the end of that February: "I am convinced that desertion proceeds from the discouraging sentiment out of the Army, which, unless it can be checked, will bring us calamity." At the end of March 1865 the chief of the Bureau of Conscription estimated that 100,000 deserters from Southern armies were at large.[36]

Desertion afflicted both sides but had a more consequential effect on the welfare of the Confederate army, which did not have the means to replace the wayward men. Both armies tried to discourage the acts of disloyalty without fruitful results. Merciful pardons and amnesty were offered from time to time to entice the soldiers back to the lines. Yet desertion under military law was punishable by death, and throughout the war several hundred deserters from both armies were convicted and executed, including two soldiers from the 25th Regiment's Company H.

A true story concerning General Matt Ransom, as told by one of his regiment's historians, will serve to demonstrate the severe treatment accorded to deserters during the war as well as the compassion of General Ransom:

> One day not far from Petersburg General Ransom rode upon a file of soldiers taking a prisoner out to be shot. He stopped and enquired the cause. The man having been refused a furlough for one night, and encamped only a short distance from his home, ran away for

Union troops employed huge sap rollers, such as the one pictured here, to protect them as they dug their trenches ever closer to the Confederate lines (Library of Congress, artist: Alfred Rudolf Waud).

A GOPHER HOLE.

a few hours to see his wife and children, intending to return to his command the next day, but somehow missed it on the line of march, was arrested, tried and condemned as a deserter. The poor fellow's narrative convinced General Ransom of his innocence of intent to desert.

General Ransom ordered the escort not to shoot him before his return, saying, as he wheeled his horse and spurring to the full run, "I'll try my man. I'll try my poor fellow." In a brief time he returned from General Lee's headquarters, his horse and himself covered with mud, waving the reprieve above his head. It is of pathetic interest to know that this soldier, the next day, was killed by a musket ball through the heart received in the fore front of battle.[37]

On top of all the hardships that the Rebel soldiers at Petersburg had to endure was heaped the humiliation of not being paid their meager salaries by the government. The Confederate treasury was empty, in arrears and in debt. Consequently, it was unable to pay off the soldiers for all the sacrifices and loyal service made for the cause. John C. Breckenridge, having recently replaced James Seddon as secretary of war and upon assumption of his new responsibilities, reported to President Jefferson Davis on February 18, 1865, concerning the calamitous fiscal condition in which he found the army and country:

> The army pay is in arrear for several months—this is an excuse for desertion, the sale of clothing, equipments, and munitions by the soldiers; the operatives in the workshops are suffering and many have deserted; the railroad service is reduced to the lowest point of depression from the same cause; the soldiers in hospitals and who have been furloughed or returned are deprived of many necessities. Throughout the whole country discontent and discredit have arisen from the failure to pay for supplies of food and animals that have been impressed.... It is plainly impracticable for this Department to carry on any of its operations under such a condition of things.[38]

General Lee and Secretary of War Breckenridge were simply overwhelmed with the severity and complexity of the societal and financial problems they found surrounding them and their country. The Union army was one thing and they were resolved to somehow deal with Grant and his bluecoats. However, an insolvent treasury and a starving army with hopelessly few soldiers was another matter altogether. And President Davis, his administration and the Confederate congress were powerless to effect any changes that would right such a floundering ship-of-state as the Confederacy was during the final stages of the war.

Many of the Rebel soldiers forced to burrow into the earth like groundhogs that winter at Petersburg did not "go up" to the enemy or head for home. One of those men who saw the thing through was asked after the war if he and the other boys ever relinquished hope while in the saps, to which he replied:

> [W]e all had the same opinion of General Lee; that he was as humane as he was brave; that he would not uselessly sacrifice the lives of men who always protested against his exposing his own—the protest having been actually enforced at Spottsylvania Court House—that he had often shown his confidence in us, and that we must not prove unworthy of it; that when all was over, he was great enough to say so.[39]

These words are just another testament to the high esteem in which General Robert E. Lee was held in the mind and heart of the Confederate soldier, even during the severe test at Petersburg. Another testimony was pronounced years after the war by Colonel Henry Rutledge to his son: "Lee, of course, was supreme. I do not know that the war ruined the South,

Opposite Top: Firing from the Petersburg Trenches (*Harper's Weekly*). *Opposite Bottom:* Union and Confederate defenders jumped into "gopher holes," such as the one depicted here, for protection from incoming artillery rounds (*Harper's Weekly*).

for it gave her Lee."[40] Many other soldiers were of similar persuasion. It seems that the deep respect and admiration for General Lee was of sufficient weight to tip the balance for a great many men toward perseverance through that long winter of 1864–1865 and fighting it out to the end.

However, the Southern civilian population, not under the direct influence of a revered leader and either not legally obligated to military service or averse to it, was dispirited and had little reason to be confident of a bright destiny. Mrs. Mary Boykin Chesnut had a remarkable ability to see life around her and translate those observations into beautifully worded passages in her diary. But her artistic flair with pen and ink and her keen wit do not hide a deep despair and uneasy conviction that the Confederacy was in its dying throes. The following passage from her journal in early 1865 hints at an abandonment of hope:

> The Bazaar for the benefit of the hospitals opens now. Sherman marches constantly. All the railroads are smashed, and if I laugh at any mortal thing it is that I may not weep. Generals are as plenty as blackberries, but none are in command.

It should not be supposed that the diarist included her husband, General James Chesnut, Jr., with those plentiful generals not in command. The satiric remarks, however, do little to conceal her forlorn sentiments. As the new year of 1865 dawns, she sees that the Confederate lights are going out one by one and those remaining ablaze are barely flickering.

11

WAR ON THE HOME FRONT

In very little time the Civil War thrust the people of the South into a vastly changed environment. The population secluded in the remote depths of the western North Carolina mountains did not escape the tremendous demands and tribulations brought on by the great sectional conflict. Mountain men who could tote a musket and shoot were called upon to defend their homeland and they left in droves to the front. Most of these stalwart mountaineers either signed up by choice or were drafted to fight for the Confederacy. However, more than a few were persuaded that the Union should be preserved and made the difficult choice of "going up" and fighting in Northern military units against their Southern brethren.

The following passage from a letter written by a Confederate soldier in North Carolina in May 1861 gives an excellent example of the conflicting political sentiments that existed throughout the South. Decisions and acts of allegiance to the North created rifts in communities, families and even between husband and wife:

> There are two ladies in town whose husbands are in the Northern Army—One sends to his wife, saying how much he & his friends [miss] her, but says they are coming here to cut all our throats as soon as possible, determined to bring the south [to] its knees if it takes 20 yrs—she folds up the letters & writes on the back—"I want no more of such love neither do I send you anymore of mine"—To what are we coming?[1]

With large numbers of the men away at war, their women, children and parents were left on the homesteads to cope and strive as best they could to survive, and, as they would discover, defend themselves. During the latter half of the war, gangs of immoral men avoiding service in the Confederate army or ruthlessly operating behind the subterfuge of the home guard militia prowled the hills and preyed on those living in isolated cabins and farms. Stealing food, horses and livestock was their primary motive, with the residual effect of terrorizing and sometimes murdering innocent mountain folk. These bands of roaming outlaws that provoked misery on the innocent mountain people effectively brought the war into the Carolina highlands that had been avoided by the great Confederate and Union armies.

Conscription

McClellan's peninsular campaign was a near miss for the Confederacy. Had not General Joseph Johnston been wounded, the fight for Richmond very likely would have concluded

Rebel soldier feasts beside a cornfield (*The Illustrated Confederate Reader* by Rod Gragg).

with unfavorable results for the South. General Robert E. Lee would have remained deeply mired in administrative and advisory duties to President Jefferson Davis while the Union's great army and huge siege guns pushed forward to invest the capital. As is known, however, events transpired in a wholly different manner that exceeded the hopes and expectations of most Southerners. In fact, prior to General Lee's elevation to the command of Richmond's Confederate forces and coincidental with McClellan's initial threatening movements up the

Virginia Peninsula, the direction and progression of the war had cast a pall and sense of doom across the entire South. President Davis and the Confederate congress reacted to the impending crisis with a bold and drastic legislative stroke intended to stem the tide of Union conquests.

On April 16, 1862, a law to conscript fighting men was enacted in an attempt to invigorate the Confederate army to defend the South from Northern invaders and dissuade further campaigns of aggression. The objective of the Conscription Act, the first mandatory draft in American history, was not focused solely on recruiting fresh troops to reinforce the existing army. The primary concern of the Confederate congress and army commanders was that the enlistment periods of approximately one-half of the army's one-year volunteer soldiers were soon to expire. Most of these volunteers were fed up with the war. As one of Stonewall Jackson's soldiers in the Shenandoah Valley said at the time, "The romance of the thing has entirely worn off, not only with myself but with the whole army."[2] Soon the stints of the volunteers would run out and most would simply melt away back to their homes and families. The new Conscription Act of 1862 was designed to prevent that potential disaster by making all able-bodied white male citizens between the ages of eighteen and thirty-five years of age liable for three years of service in the army or for the duration of the conflict if shorter than that term. Of course, this meant that all those one-year volunteers currently serving were obligated to an additional two years of duty.

However, a loophole in the law allowed many to evade service in the army. Those with the financial means could find and hire a substitute outside of the legal age requirements to fulfill their own military obligation. Congress also recognized the need for men of certain

Desertion during the Civil War was a significant problem for both sides. The Confederate army was especially crippled by these desperate acts, which significantly escalated in the latter stages of the war. In this scene the artist depicts Rebel soldiers "going up," or going over to the enemy (*Harper's Weekly*).

East Tennessee Unionists gather around the U. S. flag (*Harper's Weekly*).

skills and professions to remain in the civilian ranks and perform critical work necessary to sustain the war effort. On April 21, 1862, a supplementary law was passed exempting certain categories of the population from military service. These included Confederate and state civil officials, railroad and river workers, telegraph operators, miners, several categories of industrial laborers, hospital personnel, clergymen, apothecaries and teachers. Additionally, the congress concluded that it would be necessary to exempt plantation overseers of twenty or more slaves from the draft in order that a continuing supply of foodstuffs would reach the armies in the field.[3]

Suddenly, wealthy plantation owners became drivers of their own slaves and were thus able to avoid military duty. This was further evidence to the western mountaineers, despite rhetoric to the contrary, that the war was about slavery and the protection of the eastern upper crust. Confederate Captain W.W. Stringfield of Waynesville, North Carolina, later wrote of his contempt of the "press" law: "It was the desperate act of unwise if not desperate men, whose minds were not moulded after the manner or matter of our great Declaration of Independence but rather of the crafty politician and thoughtless slave-holder."[4] More than ever before, the war came to be perceived as "a rich man's war and a poor man's fight."

The impact of the Confederate Conscription Law on the soldiers of the 25th Regiment N.C., their families, and the people of western North Carolina was immediate and far-reaching. Wives, parents, and children expecting their soldiers to return home by the summer of 1862, after the one-year enlistment periods were up, were surely depressed and unhappy. The soldiers themselves were both angered and disheartened with this turn of events and had to summon all their mental fortitude and waning allegiance to the "cause" to endure at least two more long years of perilous war service. One soldier from western North Carolina did not mince his words when writing to President Jefferson Davis about his personal grievances with the new law. In conclusion, he wrote, "And now bastard President of a political abortion, farewell. 'Scalp-hunter,' relic, pole, and chivalrous Confederates in crime, good-bye. Except it be in the army of the Union, you will not again see this conscript."[5]

Certainly most mountaineers liable for military duty did not have the financial capacity to hire substitutes. And only a very few were included in one of the various categories exempting them from service in the Confederate army. Predominantly farmers and sons of farmers, these mountain men had little choice in the matter. Voluntarily enlisting enabled them to join new regiments and elect their own officers just like the volunteers of 1861 had done. Or they could wait to be found by the enrollment officers and conscripted, in which case they would be sent to existing regiments in the field as the government authorities deemed appropriate. As it turned out, many chose another path — one of dodging the draft and military obligations altogether by eluding the enrollment officers and hiding out in the mountains.

By the end of 1863, after stunning setbacks for the Confederate armies at Gettysburg, Vicksburg and Chattanooga, the Confederate congress revised the Conscription Act to eliminate the privilege of hiring substitutes. Additionally, those who were at the end of three-year enlistments were required to remain in the army, and the age limits for eligibility were stretched to seventeen and fifty years of age. By 1864 the effect of the harsh conscription legislation in western North Carolina was that all of the able-bodied men and boys were either serving in the armies, Confederate and Union, or running from service. The problems created by this vacuum of male citizenry in the western Carolina mountain region snowballed into a nightmarish state of affairs for the lonely and defenseless women and children.

Draft Evaders, Deserters and Tories

Beginning about late 1862 into early 1863, lawless men evading service on either side of the conflict began to unite in gangs and roam the mountains of western North Carolina. These outlaw bands terrorized the population as they raided lonely homesteads and small towns and battled Rebel military units sent into the remote fastnesses to capture or destroy them. Sometimes referred to as "bushwhackers" for the guerrilla warfare tactics they employed, these mobs of outliers consisted primarily of draft evaders, deserters, and Unionists, also known as Tories. As the war progressed and invigorated efforts were exerted to enforce the terms of the Confederate conscription law, more and more mountaineers fled to the hills to escape their military obligations. The worst of these men, those of an immoral ilk, joined together with others of their kind and prowled the mountains to prey on the weak. They did much to bring horror and depredation to the mountain people and to create an atmosphere of fear and helplessness that pervaded the region.

The Draft Evaders

The April 1862 Conscription Law enacted by the Confederate congress was intended to remedy the Confederacy's increasing troubles and setbacks in the various war theatres. In fact, it was a measure of absolute necessity to prevent an impending disintegration of the Southern army and the imminent collapse of the Confederacy. Southern politicians in Richmond could have little suspected the overwhelming unpopularity of impressment in Appalachian Carolina or the discord, fear and turmoil that it would create on the home front. By the middle of 1862, the hardships and impoverishment resulting from the rebellion were just beginning to be felt by the highlanders secluded within the mountain recesses. When news of the conscription law reached them and it was learned that the one-year volunteer soldiers would not be returning home as anticipated, sentiments of loyalty to the Rebel government began to erode quickly and disaffection with the war set in with surprising rapidity.

Conscription regulations did not differentiate between married and unmarried men or grant exemptions to fathers of young children. All men between the ages of eighteen and thirty-five years were obliged to either enlist or be drafted for service in the Confederate army. During the euphoric months of 1861, a high proportion of the volunteer troops pouring out of the mountains in response to the faraway war drums were young unmarried men without familial obligations beyond those to their parents and siblings. In fact, one historian wrote of western North Carolina's Sixty-ninth Regiment, which was the first regiment organized west of Asheville: "The twelve companies were made up of those who were the first volunteers from these [western North Carolina] mountains, and were in the bloom of manhood. Ninety percent of them were unmarried."[6]

Although the absence of those first young volunteers was surely lamented, there remained behind plenty of able-bodied men to grow crops and look after the women and children. However, before the ink was dry on the callous words of the new conscription law in 1862, enrollment officers began scouring the hills and valleys in search of all eligible man to send off to the war front. It was the design and intention of the Confederate government to drain the mountains of its manhood and throw it at the invading Yankee forces in other parts of the South. Repeated over and over throughout the hill country were sorrowful scenes of women standing in cabin doorways, with their children hanging at their sides, watching as husbands were trotted off to the cruel business of war. Obvious and often unspoken, of course, was the high probability that they might never see their men again.

Many stubborn and independent highlanders, however, chose for various reasons to dodge their military obligation and not go to war. Instead, they opted to simply "lay out" of sight and avoid the Confederate authorities and troops. Whether motivated by cowardice, binding ties and inescapable devotion to their families, a waning Southern allegiance, or

Unionist loyalties, the draft evaders who made deliberate and unlawful decisions to avoid their responsibilities to the Confederacy became both outlaws and outliers. For the entirety of the rebellion the draft evaders would be hunted down relentlessly by the Confederate infantry and cavalry forces and the Home Guard defense troops.

The Deserters

Deserters were another element who took to the deep woods to hide out and escape their military commitments. The suffering and dangers that the Confederate soldiers were forced to endure were overwhelming and more than many could physically and mentally bear, even those still devoted to the fight for independence. This condition, coupled with the knowledge that their families back home were hungry and wanting for the necessities of life, lured the mountaineers in flocks away from the army camps and trenches and back to their mountain lands.

Desertion was not a rare phenomenon during the Civil War. It was an act hatched mostly from desperation that occurred with alarming frequency and to the general disdain of the commanders on both sides. Over the entire course of the war, one out of every seven soldiers signed up for service in the Confederate army would desert, as compared to one in ten of the Union troops. Even more dramatic was the desertion rate of the Carolina mountain men who joined the Rebel forces. One historian concluded that just over 24 percent of the mountaineers serving in the Confederate army fled from their military responsibilities.[7]

Desertion rates reached an apex during the siege of Petersburg in the last months of the war. Forced to live in muddy trenches and underground warrens, the Rebel forces suffered bitterly through the long cold winter of 1864–1865, with very few rations to eat. During this time General Bushrod Johnson, whose command included Ramson's Brigade and the 25th Regiment N.C., wrote in one of his daily reports of the occurrence of desertion in his ranks: "[T]he previous night twenty men had left from a single regiment of Matt Ransom's Brigade; another night the number was forty."[8] On a daily basis, the soldiers fled the trenches, and many of these deserters found their way back to the Carolina, Georgia and Tennessee mountains where they would hide out with other deserters, draft evaders and general outliers.

The Tories

Another constituent of the bushwhacking outlier bands that populated the secluded mountain coves was a large faction of Unionists, or Tories, as they were frequently and derisively referred to during the war years. In the antebellum days prior to Fort Sumter, the Unionists who remained loyal and supportive of the Federal government probably numbered more than the secessionist rebels. However, with Lincoln's call for troops to put down the Southern insurrection, the thirst for secession exploded, with the prodding and leadership of men such as Thomas Clingman of Asheville. The Unionists withdrew to their cabins and remained relatively quiet for the first year or two of the war. Several regions such as those remote areas bordering pro–Union east Tennessee, Wilkes County and Henderson County's Edneyville were the exception, as these hotbeds of Union support were actively subversive against the Confederacy throughout the sectional conflict. Because the enactment of the Conscription Law of 1862 did not exclude the Tories living within the Southern borders, men filled with loyal Union sentiments were compelled to evade impressment and service in the Confederate army.

Bushwhackers All

All of these disaffected groups—draft evaders, deserters, and tories—became outlaws as a result of their persuasions and actions and were the objects of continuous manhunts to effect their capture or destruction. Many united out of necessity for the protection afforded by an inherent strength in numbers. Banded together within their mountain sanctuaries, these desperados were able to defend against Confederate troops bent on apprehending or killing them, as well as waylay travelers and wagon trains daring to penetrate the mountain gaps and passes where they held sway. William Holland Thomas, a politician and state senator from Jackson County and renowned leader of the Eastern Cherokee Nation, proposed to the governor of North Carolina early in the war that the gaps and passes through the Blue Ridge and Smoky mountains be fortified. His primary concern at that time was the protection of western North Carolina from Federal incursions out of east Tennessee, a region which remained heavily loyal to the Union throughout the war. His words falling mostly on deaf ears, Thomas developed his own strategy and plans to defend the mountains, but these never materialized. However, in November 1862, he became alarmed at another serious threat to his homeland and wrote to Governor Zebulon Vance: "[T]he Western Counties are in danger of being overrun by deserters and renegades who by the hundreds are taking shelter in the mountains."[9]

Bushwhackers exact a toll from a traveler. The mountains of western North Carolina and east Tennessee were filled with deserters, unionists and other men avoiding service in the Confederate army. Many joined together in bands and became bushwhackers, preying on the highlanders living in remote areas (*The Illustrated Confederate Reader* by Rod Gragg).

Even at that early stage in the war (November 1862), the problem of bushwhacker gangs roaming the mountains was manifest to responsible leaders such as William Thomas and Governor Zebulon Vance of North Carolina. In January 1863, shortly after hearing from William Thomas of the treacherous conditions in the western mountains, Governor Vance wrote to the Confederate secretary of war concerning the mounting problem of desertion and its consequences to his mountain constituents:

> The enforcement of the Conscript law in East Tennessee has filled the mountains with disaffected desperados of the worst character, who joining with the deserters from our Army form very formidable bands of outlaws, who hide in the fastnesses, waylay the passes, rob, steal, and destroy as pleased. The evil has become so great that travel has almost been suspended through the mountains.[10]

Vance went on to propose to Secretary James Seddon the creation of a company of regular troops to defend against these very formidable bands of outlaws because the local militia groups had proven inept for the task.

The punitive actions of Confederate regular troops against outliers operating in Madison County led to one of the most egregious episodes ever to take place within the Appalachian Carolina mountains during the war. In the spring of 1863, troops of the Sixty-fourth Regiment N.C. led by Lieutenant Colonel J.A. Keith moved into the Shelton Laurel country of Madison County, hunting for the perpetrators of a raid on the small county seat of Marshall. This wanton attack by Unionists and other disaffected outliers resulted in the looting of stores and harassment and even torture of certain citizens of that town. Most of the band had fled the region, but Keith's troops managed to round up fifteen or so locals who reportedly were involved in the affair at Marshall, two of whom subsequently escaped. The remaining unfortunate captives, ranging in age from twelve years to sixty-five, were led into the woods, where they were separated into a few small groups and forced to kneel on the ground. Then, without pretense of an investigation or trial, the prisoners were summarily executed by gunshot and hastily buried.

The next day, friends and neighbors discovered the bodies concealed in a shallow trench, and news of the outrage quickly reached the governor's office. Governor Vance demanded the resignation of Lieutenant Colonel Keith, who was soon dismissed in disgrace from the Confederate army. At the end of the war, Keith was arrested and jailed for his cruel exploit; but before his case reached the courts, President Andrew Johnson issued his proclamation of amnesty and Keith was released.[11] Certainly the Shelton Laurel Massacre, as it has been called, was one of the more sickening and heinous crimes to be committed in the western mountains of North Carolina during the Civil War. But this event serves to demonstrate the divisive animosities at play within the local mountain populations and the extreme measures that authorities and citizenry took to rid themselves of the bushwhacking elements.

As a direct result of the depravities brought on by the unique ambuscade warfare employed by the outlier posses, in June 1863 the state general assembly provided for the organization of the Guard for Home Defense, or, as better known, the Home Guard. All males between eighteen and fifty years of age and not serving in the Confederate army were required to join the ranks of the Home Guard. Brigadier General John W. McElroy was placed in command of the guard, with his headquarters located in Burnsville, the government seat of Yancey County. It would be proven later that the formation of the Home Guard was too little and too late to provide adequate protection from the bushwhacker gangs roaming the mountains. And in many cases the home guardsmen would prove ineffectual merely at apprehending deserters and sending them back to the front.

Certainly one of the reasons that the Home Guard proved so ineffective in rounding up the outliers was the fact that they were riding against their neighbors and friends and even kindred. In these cases, the home men often managed to arrive too late, overlook known hideouts or simply turn their heads from the wary and elusive evaders. A good example of a dilemma of this sort occurred in Haywood County with Elkanah Turbyfill, a home guardsman whose duty it was to arrest deserters and send them back to the Rebel army. After the War, Turbyfill told a story that his closest friend deserted the ranks and returned to his homeplace. The home guardsman recalled how he, "went into [his] house, took down [his] gun, and said: 'Pluma [his wife], I am going to war. I would rather fight the enemy than my neighbors.'"[12]

On April 12, 1864, Brigadier General McElroy, commander of the Western North Carolina Home Guard, wrote to Governor Vance that a band of tories, headed by Montrevail Ray and numbering about seventy-five men, had surprised the small guard he had left at Burnsville and broken open the magazine and removed all the arms and ammunition. In addition, they had looted Bailey's Store and attacked the local enrolling officer, Captain Lyons, slightly wounding him. Moreover, on the day before, a band of about fifty white women of the county had assembled together and marched in a body to a local storehouse and "pressed," or appropriated, about sixty bushels of government wheat, which they carried off. General McElroy continued in his letter to Governor Vance:

> The county is gone up. It has got to be impossible to get any man out there unless he is dragged out, with but few exceptions. There was but a small guard there, and the citizens all ran on the first approach of the tories. I have 100 men at this place to guard against Kirk, of Laurel, and cannot reduce the force; and to call out any more home guards at this time is only certain destruction to the country eventually. In fact, it seems to me, that there is a determination of the people in the country generally to do no more service in the cause. Swarms of men liable to conscription are gone to the tories or to the Yankees—some men that you have not idea of—while many others are fleeing east of the Blue Ridge for refuge. John S. McElroy and all the cavalry, J.W. Anderson and many others, are gone to Burke for refuge. This discourages those who are left behind, and on the back of that, conscription [is] now going on and a very tyrannical course pursued by the officers charged with the business, and men [are] conscripted and cleaned out as [if] raked with a fine-toothed comb; and if any are left, if they are called upon to do a little home-guard service, they at once apply for a writ of habeas corpus and get off. Some three or four cases have been tried by Judge Read the last two weeks, and the men released.... If something is not done immediately for this county we will all be ruined, for the home-guards now will not do to depend on.[13]

In Yancey County, the Confederate Home Guard forces were spread so thinly that the town of Burnsville could not be protected against either atrocities perpetrated by the tories or groups of irate women deprived of their rightful share of government wheat and provisions. Also of interest in General McElroy's communication to Governor Vance is the fact that conscripted Yancey County civilians were applying for writs of habeas corpus and "getting off," or being relieved of their military obligations. North Carolina was the only Southern state which did not suspend their citizens' legal rights to writ of habeas corpus, which allowed them to seek relief through the courts for unlawful detention. In Yancey County, and surely elsewhere, the mountain folk were using their common-law rights of habeas corpus to their advantage to escape the war.

Similarly, in nearby Wilkes County—a haven of Union loyalist activity during the war—outliers led by John Quincy Adams Bryan brazenly harassed the local population as they easily squelched the feeble protective efforts of the Home Guard. Governor Vance requested from Secretary of War Seddon that a detachment of Robert E. Lee's troops be sent to the area to restore order. Vance wrote, "The vast numbers of deserters in the western counties of this State have so accumulated lately to set the local militia at defiance and exert a very injurious effect upon the community." General Lee responded in the fall of 1863 by sending two infantry regiments and a cavalry squadron under the command of General Robert F. Hoke to Wilkes County to put a stop to the insurrection. Hoke's Confederate forces did manage in a short period of time to round up many outliers and temporarily halt the spree of illegal activities, but they failed to catch up with Bryan and his gang of Unionist outlaws.[14] Additionally, during this same time period, a detachment from the 25th Regiment N.C. was sent into Madison County to apprehend a band of tories which had taken over the town of Warm Springs. Although at a great disadvantage in numbers, it is believed that the Confederate soldiers succeeded in taking back the town and driving this mob of bushwhackers back into hiding in the hills.

About this same time in those closing months of 1863, Union forces led by General Ambrose Burnside had captured and occupied Knoxville, Tennessee, and the surrounding east Tennessee countryside. The Confederate authorities and the civilian population of western North Carolina now had more to fear than just the bushwhacking presence in their hills. The real threat of invasion of the mountain fastness from the Union stronghold of east Tennessee now existed, and the Confederacy reacted by creating the Western Military District of North Carolina. Governor Vance's brother, Brigadier General Robert B. Vance, was appointed to head up this new department and had under his command all the local militia units and what few regular army troops existed in the region.

Although no large expeditions were launched into the Carolina highlands, Federal infantry and cavalry raids from East Tennessee continually harassed the Confederate defenses and mountain population for the rest of the war. Interestingly, in January 1864, General Vance was ordered to east Tennessee with five hundred of his troops to support Confederate General James Longstreet in his efforts to retake Knoxville from the occupying Federal army. In zealous pursuit of defeating the Yankee enemy, General Vance managed, through his own carelessness and a miscommunication with William Holland Thomas, to get himself and fifty of his men captured by Union forces.[15]

The lonely homesteads in remote areas were especially vulnerable to terrorizing raids by outlier gangs. A letter from home to one of the soldiers of the 25th Regiment N.C. (presented earlier in Chapter 8) describes unprovoked attacks against the homesteads in his mountain region by robbers and villains who plundered and murdered indiscriminately. Another incident in Henderson County demonstrates that not even citizens of affluence were aloof from the depravities of bushwhacking vandals. In June 1864, in the resort community of Flat Rock, where many wealthy planters from the South Carolina and Georgia low country retreated and summered, six men paid a visit to Andrew Johnstone at his Beaumont estate. The strangers invited themselves into this fine home, where the rice planter from Georgetown, South Carolina, lived with his family. The unwanted guests demanded to be fed and a nervous Johnstone reluctantly complied. Upon completing his meal, the leader of the bunch suddenly rose up from the table, pulled a firearm from his knapsack and shouted to his cohorts: "Boys, are you ready?" In the confusion that followed, Andrew Johnstone drew his own pistol and was immediately shot dead by the intruders. Elliott Johnstone valiantly rushed to his father's dead body, retrieved the pistol from its side and fired at the scoundrels, killing two and injuring another.[16]

Such episodes of terror-mongering by bushwhackers during the Civil War were repeated many times throughout the Carolina highlands. Outliers avoiding military service and apprehension by the lawful authorities were a curse to the mountain people, creating misery and suffering for all law-abiding persons. These mountain folk, already experiencing privations caused by warfare in faraway theatres and likely grieving for absent husbands and fathers, were forced to suffer the torment of the villains' deeds or the constant threat of them. And just as the Confederacy failed to prevent Union troops from swarming across the South and capturing its cities, it was unsuccessful in providing adequate protection for the Carolina mountain folk from draft evaders, deserters, and tories—bushwhackers all.

12

A Journey Ended

Fort Stedman

With the exception of Lee's Army of Northern Virginia, all of the South's armies were either defeated or powerless to aggressively confront the Union forces opposing them at the close of the year 1864. Through the winter and into early 1865, General Grant continued to fight and launch probing assaults at the Rebel defenses protecting Petersburg. In so doing, he managed to gradually extend the siege lines to the south and west of the town, where the last but one railroad was under Union control. The Rebels stretched their defense works longer and their forces thinner to oppose and resist these calculated Union tactics.

Grant's ploys were not the only worries General Lee contemplated during this time. He was keenly aware that Sherman was marching unchecked through the Carolinas bent on joining the great army in his front to destroy the Confederacy. Before that union was made, Lee knew he had to act and act soon to quit the Richmond-Petersburg front. He determined to take his weakened army and unite with the remaining Southern forces in North Carolina then assembling under General Joseph Johnston. This, of course, would mean giving up Richmond; but better to lose that city, he concluded, than the Army of Northern Virginia, which was the last hope of the Confederacy.

In an effort to loosen Grant's stranglehold on Petersburg and open up sufficient ground to disengage and make an escape to the west, General Lee and Major General John B. Gordon planned and organized an attack against a heavily fortified point in the Union's siege lines. Fort Stedman, as that Yankee stronghold was known, opposed a salient in the Rebel defenses manned by General Bushrod Johnson's division. It was located on Hare's Hill just across from the position held for the previous nine months by Ransom's Brigade. The objective of the mission was to surprise the Federals occupying Stedman and capture those works. Once accomplished, the attack was to continue toward fortifications on both flanks and in the rear of Fort Stedman, where imposing Yankee artillery batteries were positioned. If adequately supported by additional Confederate cavalry and General George Pickett's infantry forces, the breakthrough of the Federal defenses around Hare's Hill might be exploited with follow-up strikes against the rear of the Union lines. Even a partial success could possibly allow the Confederates to seize and hold the commanding ground in the enemy's rear. In that case, Lee and Gordon surmised, the Union besiegers would almost certainly be forced to recall the forces on their left and deploy them defensively against the southern assailants

Grinding corn (*The American Heritage Century Collection of Civil War Art*; artist William L. Sheppard).

securely lodged in newly-gained fortifications. Thus afforded with the opportunity to maneuver beyond his hard-pressed right flank south of Petersburg, Lee's desperate desire for a junction with Johnston's small army in North Carolina might still be effected. The westward roads and rail facilities would be opened for a brief interlude to facilitate the movement of either a portion of his army or a general withdrawal of the entirety of the Army of Northern Virginia from the Richmond-Petersburg theater of war. That was the Confederate plan.

The troops of Ransom's Brigade were ordered on March 16, 1865, to move from their familiar trench positions to Hatcher's Run, located at the extreme right of the Confederate line. Taking respite there for a few short days in some huts built by the army, they relaxed and relished life outside of the trenches for the first time in nine months. The brigade was suddenly ordered back to its old defenses during the night of March 24–25. Upon arriving there and learning of the offensive plans to attack Fort Stedman, the brigade soon formed ranks and the troops moved out against the Federal fortification. A small group of pioneers led the way, clearing paths through the timber abatis and other obstructions. Following close behind, a handpicked assault team proceeded stealthily through the breastworks and captured Fort Stedman without firing a shot.

However, other facets of General Gordon's battle plan were not executed with the same degree of success. Key fortifications surrounding Fort Stedman were either not found in the darkness or not taken. And General George Pickett's troops stationed on the north side of the James River in front of Richmond arrived too late to the battlefront to offer support, having been delayed for hours by the decrepit Confederate railroad system. At the break of dawn, with the Union forces alerted to the Rebel's clandestine movements and positions, a furious Union artillery barrage and counterstroke was launched. The brief tenancy at Fort Stedman was interrupted, and eventually the Confederates were forced to withdraw from the works under orders from General Gordon. Moving back across open ground under a severe shelling and enfilade fire, the boys made it back to their old defense lines, suffering heavy casualties during the retreat. Years after the action on Hare's Hill, Colonel Henry Rutledge described "the storming of Fort Stedman" as the hottest fight in his entire war experience.[1]

The 25th Regiment N.C. played a vital role in the Battle of Fort Stedman on Hare's Hill. Lt. Ferguson recounted the action on that night:

This artwork depicts the Confederate attack on Fort Stedman at Petersburg and shows the Rebel pioneers hacking their way through the abatis constructed of felled trees (*Harper's Weekly*).

On 25 March 1865, a detail of ten men from each regiment of Ransom's brigade, under Lieutenant Burch, was placed in charge of Lieutenant J.B. Hawkins, of Company C, 25th regiment, who received his orders from General Robert Ransom in these words: "I order you to take Fort Stedman, not attack it." Lieutenant Hawkins quietly executed this order and had the fort in possession without the firing of a gun.

The Twenty-fifth was moved forward to the left of Fort Stedman and nearly in front of the position it had occupied in the ditches through the winter; drove in the enemy's pickets, took their first works and held them. The fort of the enemy in the field on the left was not taken, and the enemy from that point poured a fearful enfilading fire into the regiment. Several unsuccessful efforts were made from the front to dislodge the regiment. After the enemy retook Fort Stedman and was advancing in front and while the regiment was suffering the effects of an enfilading fire from the left, the Colonel walked along the line of his regiment with his cap on sword, shouting to his men, "Don't let them take our front, Twenty-fifth, the Twenty-fifth has never had her front taken." At this time orders were received from General Gordon to fall back to our line of works.[2]

Above and opposite: Photographs of the interior of the Union's Fort Stedman at Petersburg (Library of Congress).

This account suggests that Lee and Gordon's vital mission of capturing Fort Stedman was assigned to Ransom's Brigade and that Lt. J.B. Hawkins of the 25th Regiment led the silent assault. Note that Lt. Ferguson mistakenly refers to General Robert Ransom giving the order to take the fort. However, the major general was on duty elsewhere with the Department of South Carolina, Georgia and Florida. General Matt Ransom by then had returned to duty, his wounds from Drewry's Bluff having partially healed, and he commanded both Ransom's Brigade, led at the time by Colonel Rutledge of the 25th Regiment, and William H. Wallace's South Carolina brigade on this crucial operation.

It is truly amazing that without firing a gun the small task force took possession of such an important fortification. This firsthand account is silent on the tactics used by Lt. Hawkins; however, various explanations have been offered over the years by historians. One version explains that the Rebels gained entry to the fort under the pretense of being Southern deserters seeking safe haven in the fort. Another suggests the Confederates feigned Federal pickets driven back to the fort. Today's historians can speculate as to the methods used, but on that night long ago the only matter of consequence to Lt. Hawkins and his handpicked forces was to take the stronghold as ordered by General Matt Ransom. That order they fulfilled. And the beleaguered men held the fort as long as humanly possible under a murderous enfilade fire.

In retrospect, the assault collapsed and failed to give Lee the room he desired to make a breakout to the west over the Southside Railroad, the only remaining railroad not under Union control. Additionally, the Confederate army could ill afford the high cost of the battle. Lee suffered 5,000 casualties, or roughly one-fifth of his army, to Grant's 2,000. Colonel Rutledge, who was commanding Ransom's Brigade during this action, reported the brigade's losses to be 1,364. Diminution of the 25th Regiment's forces was magnified as well by this brief battle. Several commissioned officers were severely wounded, including Lieutenant Garland S. Ferguson of Company F, whose left thigh was broken; and many noncommissioned officers and privates were killed and wounded.

Battle of Five Forks

After the battle of Fort Stedman, the remnants of Ransom's Brigade moved back to Hatcher's Run, located south of the city and at the right extremity of the Confederate line. On March 26, 1865, the Yankees continued their clockwise sidling maneuvers as Grant ordered a corps of infantry and his powerful cavalry, led by General Phil Sheridan, to turn Lee's right flank on the southwestern side of Petersburg. Assisted by Lee's ragged cavalry divisions, led by General Fitzhugh Lee, Robert E. Lee's nephew, Confederate General George Pickett rushed two infantry divisions, including Ransom's Brigade, to blunt the Union push. After the Rebel forces succeeded in driving Sheridan back to Dinwiddie Court House, Pickett retired to the rural crossroads styled Five Forks and established a defensive line to anchor the Confederate army's right.

On April 1, 1865, Federal infantry and cavalry forces numbering no fewer than 30,000 troops moved against no more than 10,000 Rebels forming Pickett's defensive lines at Five Forks. After a short but vicious struggle, the Yankees succeeded in overwhelming and rolling up the Confederate left where General Matt Ransom's and Wallace's brigades were weakly positioned, capturing half of the Rebels and routing the rest. The 25th Regiment N.C. was definitely present and accounted for at Five Forks, fighting with the other regiments of Ransom's Brigade. Colonel Rutledge remembered well the heated action and recorded an account of the affair:

> At Five Forks I was more proud of the regiment than I had ever been before, and that is saying a great deal. I have thought of them and compared them to the "Stonewall" of Manassas. They were surrounded on three sides by many times their own numbers, but there they stood, a solid mass of mountain men, broad sides from the enemy being poured into them, and there they stood like the rock of Gibraltar. When I remember that heroic scene, I cannot fail to compare that gallant company, desperate band, to the line the Great Napoleon saw at Waterloo. Speaking afterwards of the English line of battle, he says: 'I covered them with artillery, I flooded them with infantry, I deluged them with cavalry, but when the smoke of battle rose, there stood the red line yet.' Yes, there stood the gray line, the only line that stood that day, that I saw, and finally, after combating five different and separate times over the same field, pine thickets, broom grass, old fields, all sorts of a place, I was going to win. I was attempting to whip the enemy with the 25th North Car-

olina, and I knew I could do it. I thought I was getting along finely, until I happened to look to front, left and right, and saw we were surrounded with but a small loop hole to get through. We backed through that, emptying into their faces the last cartridge we had.³

The colonel likened his 25th Regiment N.C. to the British line at Waterloo standing firm against everything Napoleon could throw at it. He knew the mountain men forming his gray line could whip the Yankees and indeed believed they were doing it. At last, when he recognized their predicament in being surrounded with only a "small loophole to get through," he backed his remaining troops through it and barely escaped.

Many, however, were left on the field, killed, wounded or captured. Lt. William Hargrove of Company F was one of more than 5,000 Confederate soldiers taken prisoner on that day.⁴ He was sent to Old Capitol Prison and then on to Johnson's Island near Sandusky, Ohio, where he remained until the end of the war. A story is told of one of the North Carolina boys captured in those final days of the war. Upon hearing his Federal captors call out to him, "Surrender, surrender, we've got you!" the ragged and famished Johnny Reb hollered back as he dropped his gun, "Yes, you've got me, and the hell of a git you got!"⁵ This anecdotal response, mythical or not, may well have been shouted by one of those proud mountain boys who bravely fought at Five Forks that day.

The devastating loss at Five Forks exposed the Confederate rear to advances by the enemy and opened a mortal wound in the Petersburg defenses that not even General Lee could heal. He was crestfallen upon hearing of the reverse suffered by Pickett and bitterly remarked to one of his officers, "It has happened as I told them it would at Richmond. The line has been

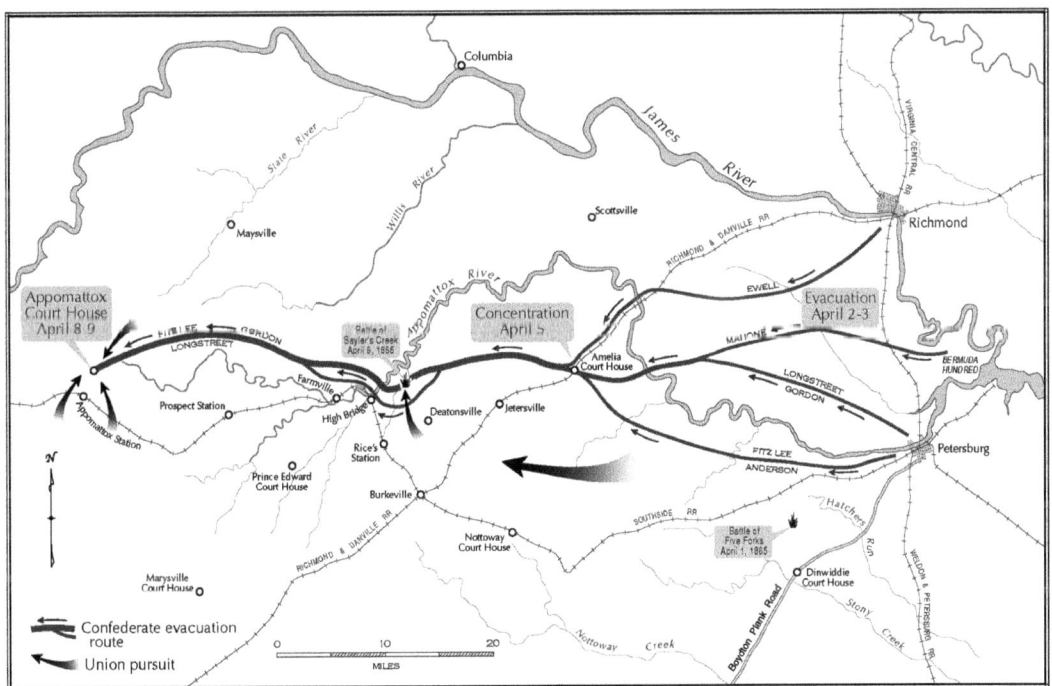

Evacuation route of the Army of Northern Virginia from Richmond and Petersburg: April 2–April 9, 1865. After the Battle of Five Forks on April 1, 1865, General Lee's army attempted to escape the Union stranglehold at Petersburg by taking a route westward up the Appomattox River. However, on April 9 Lee found his weakened Southern army surrounded by superior numbers of Federal troops and was forced to surrender (Peter Krafft, Florida State University).

Confederate prisoners lined up after the Battle of Five Forks (Library of Congress).

stretched until it has broken."[6] When fully informed later of the circumstances and details of the engagement, he learned that generals Pickett and Fitzhugh Lee had been located a couple of miles behind the lines enjoying a shad bake when the Confederate army was outmaneuvered and surprised. Within a matter of days, General Pickett would be relieved of his command and allowed to go home. Similar fates would befall Generals Bushrod Johnson and Richard "Dick" Anderson. Johnson's surviving troops, including those of Matt Ransom's brigade and the 25th Regiment N.C., became attached to General Bryan Grimes' division of General John Gordon's corps.[7]

The defeat impelled Lee to decisive action and he issued orders to make a desperate breakout attempt from the Union's stranglehold around Petersburg. At the same time, on Sunday, April 2, 1865, a dispatch was rushed to President Davis informing him that Richmond could no longer be protected. The hour had arrived for the president's administration and the Confederate government to evacuate the capital city and make their escape to the Carolinas, or wherever safe haven might be found. On the night of April 2–3, 1865, the Confederate forces began slipping out of Richmond and Petersburg to the west toward Danville, Virginia, where needed supplies and trains were scheduled to await them. In the wake of their flight, the soldiers could hear the ironclad gunboats on the James River being blown up and see smoke rising above Richmond from the burning tobacco and army stores warehouses.

Grant was not to be fooled nor denied his prize, however. His army of 110,000 infantry and cavalry troops relentlessly pursued the Confederate columns fleeing westerly along the banks of the Appomattox River. The Union's superb cavalry chased and harassed the Rebels at every opportunity and at every Confederate respite. On April 5, the different elements of Lee's Army of Northern Virginia, a mere shadow of the great army it once had been, united at Amelia Court House, where supplies had been ordered to await them. Alas, the desperately needed sustenance for the Confederate troops had not arrived, and the disheartened and starving soldiers continued the westward flight in front of Grant's pursuing hounds.

The Rebels' rear guard was overtaken at Sayler's Creek the next day, April 6, and subsequently cut off from the rest of the army and destroyed. Gordon's Corps, to which Ransom's Brigade belonged, was severely battered but escaped the total destruction inflicted upon other units.[8] Grant vigorously pressed his forces to charge ahead and contain the remaining two-thirds of Lee's army before it reached the waiting supply trains at Appomattox Station and got away. Finally, on April 9, Lee discovered that his troops were completely surrounded by superior enemy forces, leaving no reasonable options for maneuver or escape. He chose not to sacrifice the Army of Northern Virginia's 35,000 soldiers in a futile and hopeless last gasp battle, and, instead, reluctantly surrendered his once vaunted army.

Sacred Colors

Rumors and whispers spread through the army like wildfire. One cadaverous, ragged, barefooted man grasped the hand of General Bryan Grimes and, with choking sobs, said, "Good-bye, General; God bless you; we will go home, make three more crops and then try them again." Still convinced of their rightful beliefs and committed to the cause, the soldiers surrendered more to grim famine than to the prowess of their enemies.[9]

As Colonel Henry Rutledge of the 25th Regiment N.C. told years later, "At Appomattox when word got out [of the surrender], a lot of my boys smashed their guns against the trees and burst out crying. They were just wild with grief. But when General Lee came riding by, they drew up to him, clung to his boots and stirrups, and tried to kiss his hand. They knew he had done his best for them."[10]

Another cavalryman, upon hearing the news, raised his hand over his head and exclaimed, "If General Lee has had to surrender his army, there is not a just God in heaven!"[11] Though he was no god, Ulysses S. Grant was to prove that he was just. On April 9, 1865, at Appomattox Court House, Robert E. Lee dutifully met with Grant, where the latter demonstrated a courtesy and generosity of spirit beyond anything the Southern commander could have expected. The agreed-upon peace terms allowed the officers and men of the Army of Northern Virginia to retain a degree of self respect and pride in themselves and the "cause" for which they had dearly sacrificed, although it was a cause that Grant later professed to be "one of the worst for which a people ever fought, and one for which there was the least excuse."[12]

As General Lee rode away from the McLean house, a modest brick residence where the surrender terms and agreement were made, many of the soldiers gathered at his side weeping and extolling their revered leader. To such a manifestation of devotion Lee was not unaccustomed, but on this day he was overcome with emotion as he delivered choked remarks: "I have done the best I could for you. My heart is too full to say more."[13] The next day, Lee issued a final written order to his beloved men in which he attempted to express heartfelt sentiments and appreciation for their sacrifices. The 25th Regiment's officers read these words

Confederates surrendering colors and muskets (Library of Congress; artist Alfred Rudolf Waud).

to the small huddle of mountain boys gathered around them in a field near Appomattox Court House:

> General Orders No. 9
> 10 April, 1865
>
> After four years of arduous service, marked by unsurpassed courage and fortitude, the Army of Northern Virginia has been compelled to yield to overwhelming numbers and resources. I need not tell the survivors of so many hard-fought battles, who have remained steadfast to the last, that I have consented to this result from no distrust of them; but feeling that valor and devotion could accomplish nothing that could compensate for the loss that would have attended the continuation of the contest, I have determined to avoid the useless sacrifice of those whose past services have endeared them to their countrymen.
>
> By the terms of agreement officers and men can return to their homes, and remain there until exchanged. You will take with you the satisfaction that proceeds from the consciousness of duty faithfully performed; and I earnestly pray that a merciful God will extend to you His blessing and protection.
>
> With an unceasing admiration for your constancy and devotion to your country, and a grateful remembrance of your kind and generous consideration of myself, I bid you an affectionate farewell.
>
> Robert E. Lee

A total of 28,231 weary and dispirited soldiers were paroled on April 12, 1865, and the once vaunted and powerful Army of Northern Virginia existed no longer. General Matt Ransom and 430 officers and men of Ransom's Brigade are listed on the roll of those who surrendered and took the oath of allegiance at Appomattox. Colonel Henry Middleton Rutledge and Lieutenant Colonel Matthew N. Love walked ahead of only 72 other remaining officers and mountain men of the 25th Regiment N.C. stacking arms on that day. Casualties, capture, disease, desertion, and retirement had reduced the regiment's ranks from more than 1,600 men to those few 74 souls who surrendered with General Lee. Not one soldier from Company F of Haywood County survived the rigors of four long years of war to walk with the regiment down that via dolorosa at Appomattox.

The number of casualties sustained by the 25th Regiment N.C. is sobering to contemplate. An accounting included in Lt. Ferguson's historical record, written in 1901, purports that, from enlistment to surrender, the losses totaled 220 killed in battle and an additional

General Robert E. Lee is depicted in this artwork leaving the McLean House after the surrender of his Army of Northern Virginia (Library of Congress; artist Alfred Rudolf Waud).

The McLean House at Appomattox Court House, Virginia, where Generals Lee and Grant agreed to surrender terms (Library of Congress).

After the surrender at Appomattox Court House, the Rebel troops made their way back to homes and grateful families (*Harper's Weekly*; artist Andrew McCallum).

280 dead from disease. Additionally, it states that 470 soldiers suffered wounds during the war and that 140 of these were wounded more than once.[14] Although current casualty estimates belie the lieutenant's figures, it will be seen in Chapter 14 how the casualties of war slowly and methodically drained the strength and fighting capacity from the 25th Regiment N.C.

Lee's surrender of the Army of Northern Virginia was the precursor to a series of quick and dramatic events that would signal the end to America's War of Rebellion. On April 14, 1865, just two days after Confederate arms were stacked at Appomattox Court House, President Abraham Lincoln was assassinated in Washington, D.C., while enjoying a theatrical performance with his wife at Ford's Theatre. The tragic consequences of this event for the South would eclipse the personal aspects of a nation's loss of its leader. With Lincoln's unfortunate death, his generous and forgiving vision of a united country died also. Reconstruction terms and policies eventually were dictated by Northern politicians who did not share Lincoln's wisdom nor his sentiments and desires. The South suffered their enforcement and implementation for many years afterward.

In North Carolina, General Joseph Johnston and his Confederate forces laid down their arms and capitulated to General William T. Sherman near Raleigh on April 26, 1865. Subsequently, troops in Waynesville, North Carolina, under the direct command of Colonel William Holland Thomas and Lieutenant Colonel James R. Love, surrendered to the Federals in May of 1865, ending all formal hostilities in the state. About this same time in Georgia, near the Florida border, the flight of President Jefferson Davis was interrupted by Union cavalry as he was apprehended stealing out of the country.

The Union army and government quickly took control of the disintegrating Confederacy and began to impose their will across the South. A long period of reconstruction would ensue, and the people would suffer greatly as they strove to regain lifestyles offering some semblance of order and comfort. There was much uncertainty among the Southern folk about their fate, and there were those who looked for scapegoats to blame for their troubles. Mrs. Mary Boykin Chesnut did not have much use for the finger pointers in the war's aftermath. In the following excerpt from her journal, she shares no reverence for the new president of the United States, Andrew Johnson, who had been a tailor in his early years. She also takes a stand for all those brave soldiers who fought to the bitter end and stacked muskets at Appomattox:

> We are scattered and stunned, the remnant of heart left alive within us filled with brotherly hate. We sit and wait until the drunken tailor who rules the United States of America issues a proclamation, and defines our anomalous position.
> Such a hue and cry, but whose fault? Everybody is blamed by somebody else. Only the dead heroes left stiff and stark on the battle-field escape. Blame every man who stayed at home and did not fight. I will not stop to hear excuses. There is not one word against those who stood out until the bitter end, and stacked muskets at Appomattox.[15]

No one in the South, as an adamant Mary Boykin Chesnut avowed, could place blame for their circumstances on the backs of those brave men who took up arms to defend their country from the northern invaders. And that certainly included the mountaineers of the 25th Regiment N.C., who hailed from the lofty reaches of the Appalachian Mountains of western North Carolina and north Georgia. When General Lee's order to surrender was received, the regiment still existed, though greatly reduced in size, and its surviving men continued to hold tightly its sacred colors. As ordered by the terms of the surrender, the flag was taken down and furled. And in so doing, the men were surely filled with heart-wrenching sentiments similar to those captured in the words of a poem written by Father Abram J. Ryan, a Confederate chaplain, upon hearing of the fate of the Army of Northern Virginia:

> Take that banner down! 'tis tattered;
> Broken is its shaft and shattered;
> And the valiant hosts are scattered
> Over whom it floated high.
> Oh! 'tis hard for us to fold it;
> Hard to think there's none to hold it;
> Hard that those who once unrolled it
> Now must furl it with a sigh.[16]

Furl the flag with a sigh they did; however, in disobedience to the Union's dictate, the regimental colors were concealed by the color-sergeant on his person and carried proudly back to North Carolina where they belonged. Their long journey through an uncivil war ended, the Rebels known as the 25th Regiment N.C. held their heads high and returned to their mountain homeland where they would "fight no more forever."

13

CONCLUSION

The Confederate States of America was at no time recognized as a sovereign country by foreign powers, nor had its independence been legitimized by President Lincoln and the United States government. It existed primarily in the minds and actions of the people of the South who sought their independence to better themselves and their circumstances. The confederation fought a war of rebellion against a Union resolved on taking away certain cherished rights of the Southern states and its citizens. After four long years of warfare that brought death, hardship and ruin to the people of the South, the existence of the Confederacy was obliterated. Those hot flames of rebellion, which had been effectively kindled by the North's intolerance of slavery and intransigence toward the South, myopic Southern fire-eater politicians, President Lincoln's bellicose reaction to Ft. Sumter, and a myriad of other complex political and social issues, had finally been extinguished.

The soldiers serving in the 25th Regiment N.C. Infantry Troops followed their regimental banner for four long years through some of the fiercest battles and most critical actions of the Civil War. At the Seven Days Battles they repulsed the first Yankee assault near King's School House and a few days later participated in the last fierce attack against the enemy on Malvern Hill. The regiment's boys stood as the last line of defense holding back wave after wave of Union warriors at Antietam, Drewry's Bluff and Petersburg. Atop Marye's Heights at Fredericksburg, as the mountaineers hurried to join the fray, 120 of the regiment's men were said to have been shot down in less than two minutes' time.

At the "blowup" in front of Petersburg, with the sound of the great explosion still ringing in their ears and clouds of dust settling to earth, the 25th Regiment's troops formed ranks around the brim of a huge smoking cauldron filled with dead Confederates and swarming Yankees. Using muskets, bayonets and even cartridge boxes as weapons, the Rebels gave their famed yell and took the "fite" back to the confused mass of bluecoats trapped within the earthen walls of the Crater. Through it all—constructing fortifications, minor skirmishes, pivotal battles and the hideous red trenches of Petersburg—the 25th Regiment N.C. never gave up its colors, and hoisted them high with honor and pride for friend and foe to see.

Many of those volunteer soldiers who left their secluded homes in the Appalachian Mountains of North Carolina and Georgia in pursuit of the "cause" gave the ultimate sacrifice for the South, never to return to their loved ones. Those who somehow survived the Rebellion managed to find their way home again by one means or another. Slogging along dirt roads, riding in battered railcars over dilapidated tracks, or hitching rides in farm wagons, they eventually made their way back into familiar valleys and to the tops of craggy knobs where anxious families waited.

Lt. William Hargrove was one of those fortunate soldiers of the 25th Regiment N.C. who returned to his home and family in the highlands at the end of the war. He, like the others, was soon enveloped in the bosom of a grateful family and began to reacquaint himself with loved ones—those whose memories had filled his dreams so often at night while he slept by the campfire or during lonely shifts on picket duty. The weary soldiers had left their muskets broken and stacked behind and could now exchange them for the farmer's plough or the miller's apron or the books of the lawyer.

Those returning men of the 25th Regiment N.C. discovered conditions at home much poorer than when they had left four years earlier. The cabins and barns suffered from neglect and had fallen into a shameful state of disrepair. Roads were badly rutted or washed away entirely, and the farm fields lay fallow and grown over with thistle and briars. What little currency was in circulation retained little or no value. And for a period of many months following the end of the war, there was no effective governing authority. Local officials were displaced by the Federal government and, in their stead, carpetbaggers and Unionists were placed in power under the sanction and support of the United States military.

After four long years of ruinous warfare, the economy and commercial foundation of the South lay prostrate, and the Southern people were for the most part demoralized and devoid of thoughts or hopes of future prosperity. The reconstruction period following the war brought more suffering and difficulties for the Southern population than President Lincoln had envisioned or anyone could have expected. Had Lincoln lived, it might have been a kinder and more lenient Federal government that reunited the South with the North. That was not the case, however, and it would take many years for the economy to recover and for new state governments to be formed, state constitutions to be drafted, and the freed black population to be assimilated into society.

After enduring four long years of cruel conflict, the mountaineers who fought with the 25th Regiment N.C. were eager to start their lives anew. And often they thought of the other boys from the regiment with whom they became so closely bonded—the ones they had fought beside in battles and slept next to in camp, men they loved like brothers. Sadly, many of these brave souls would never return to the mountains, and, as Lt. William Hargrove later observed, "now their bones are bleaching far from home or friends and their graves erased, not even a board to mark the lonely spot."[1] Let us never forget those soldiers of the 25th Regiment N.C. Infantry Troops who fought with the bravest of hearts and with the most heroic intent.

A pitchfork steadies this wounded soldier (Library of Congress; artist Edwin Forbes).

14

CASUALTIES OF WAR

Four long years of warfare which gave rise to cruelties, horrors, deprivations, destruction and death on a scale such as mankind had not previously experienced was finally ended. America's Civil War did not turn out as planned by the warmongers and hot-blooded secessionists of the South, or as hoped for by the citizens who had followed them to war. Their ideals of independence and freedom from Northern domination had not been won. Conversely, the consequences of the fateful decisions which led to secession included a shattered Southern economy and a reconstruction darkness that would not soon be illuminated. And the bands of fiercely proud and excited men that had united and marched out of the mountains and off to the battlefields had been severely affected as well. The ten military companies, which were once the stout fabric from which the 25th Regiment N.C. had been formed, were now worn, torn and tattered beyond recognition.

All told, more than 1,670 men signed up with the 25th Regiment N.C. during the entire period that the Civil War raged. Upon General Lee's surrender of the Army of Northern Virginia at Appomattox Court House, only 74 of those highlanders remained to gather together under the colors of the 25th Regiment. The others were dead and buried, disabled, captured or had shamefully stolen back to the mountain recesses to be as far removed from the war as they could get.

Throughout the course of the war, outside influences worked in forceful and subtle ways to drain the manpower from the regiment. Muster rolls of the various companies show that many soldiers were discharged by reason of "disability" or retirement to the Confederate Invalid Corps. Additionally, with the enactment of the Conscription Act of 1862, large numbers of the early volunteers discovered that they fell outside the age limits of the new mandatory draft law. More than a few of these once eager Southern loyalists quickly "unvolunteered" their services, and were legally discharged by reason of being under the age of 18 or over the age of 35. However, the casualties of war attributed to the battlefield, disease, and desertion were the most significant causes by far of the diminution of troops from the regiment. In the pages that follow, it is to these "casualties of war" that attention is drawn.

It is an extremely difficult proposition to quantify the Confederate Civil War casualties with some degree of confidence and legitimacy. Confederate army records, for the last year of the war especially, are incomplete and lack sufficient detail to account fully for most of the individual soldier's actions or service during that crucial period. As the bitter end approached, war department clerks were yanked from their desks at Richmond to join the Rebel soldiers in the saps at Drewry's Bluff and Petersburg to defend against the Yankee foe. The administrative capacity of the war department was surely affected by such drastic action. Also, during this phase of the war, as Lee's Army of Northern Virginia settled into trench warfare, the Southern soldiers were starving, exposed to the elements without proper clothing or shoes, and were the targets of the Yankees' constant sniper fire and bombardment. Moreover, they were receiving letters from home filled with desperate and frightful stories along with pitiful pleas for the Rebel soldiers to return to their loved ones. As a result, the troops began disappearing from the trenches in alarming numbers and the Confederate army was drying up in front of Grant's anxious and waiting Federal forces. The South's officers and staff were simply overwhelmed with the exigencies of such circumstances and the necessity of keeping the Confederate army from disintegrating. Understandably, they were less bothered by meticulous record keeping.

Although the extant records to work from are not ideal, the author has endeavored to determine the approximate casualty rates which befell the 25th Regiment N.C. through the course of the war. This effort included an examination of each individual soldier's service record as contained in *North Carolina Troops, 1861–1865, A Roster*, vol. 7, *Infantry*. First published in 1979 and most recently updated in 2004, this excellent work was compiled over the years by the North Carolina State Department of Archives and History using primary source records, which included company muster rolls, payrolls, rosters, hospital registers, prison registers, parole registers, state records and a variety of other resources. The information for each solider listed with the 25th Regiment N.C. and contained within the pages of *North Carolina Troops* was perused, and any inclusion of casualty data in the record was recorded and tallied into the following categories: wounded, died of wounds, killed, and died of disease.

In addition, an effort was made to glean details from the records to ascertain the desertion rates within each company. It should be restated that the statistics compiled through this process and presented herein are derived from an incomplete database. There were many instances where a soldier's service information was abruptly concluded with the comment "through 1863," "through February 1864," or "through February 1865." In other cases, the record was scant and terminated with the simple declaration "no further records." Thus, the information that has been assembled for the final year or more of the war is sketchy at best and affords the author an opportunity to qualify the findings.

Casualty numbers and desertion rates presented herein should be considered to be on the low side, or understated. It is a certainty that there were casualties suffered yet not recorded, from actions or events extending from about the time of the heated battles around Drewry's Bluff in May of 1864 through the battle of Five Forks on April 1, 1865, and the final surrender at Appomattox eight days later. In addition, the numbers presented for desertion rates, although they appear to be very high, are very likely to be significantly low. The desertion count was derived entirely from the cases in the records where a man was actually declared to have gone over to the enemy or listed as a deserter on the company rolls. Records indicating that a soldier was "absent without leave" with no subsequent explanation or update were not considered desertion, although most assuredly many of these cases were. Also, where men's service records are silent after 1863 or after February 1864, it can be reasonably contemplated that many of those soldiers might have succumbed to the tremendous strains of war and deserted their duties to the Confederate army. Therefore, when examining the seemingly elevated casualty and desertion rates that have been compiled for the 25th Regiment N.C., it should be remembered that the actual incidences were even higher.

Casualty Estimates: Carolina Coastal Defense (September 18, 1861–June 15, 1862)

During the first nine months of its service to the Confederacy, the 25th Regiment N.C. performed defensive duties along the coasts of North Carolina and South Carolina. The regiment left Asheville in September of 1861 and was stationed briefly in Wilmington, North Carolina, before being ordered to Grahamville, South Carolina, near where a Union armada had attacked and captured Hilton Head Island at Port Royal Sound. The Twenty-fifth was garrisoned in the vicinity of Grahamville performing defensive duties and building fortifications until called on March 15, 1862, to New Bern, North Carolina, where Union forces were threatening. Arriving too late to participate in the unsuccessful Confederate attempt to hold New Bern, the regiment remained near Kinston, North Carolina, for approximately three months. While stationed there at Camp Ransom and other nearby locations, it remained in a defensive posture to protect the important railroad facilities at Goldsboro, North Carolina, and to react against further Federal incursions.

A summary of the casualties that befell the 25th Regiment N.C. during this period is given in the following table:

CASUALTY ESTIMATES: CAROLINA COASTAL DEFENSE

COMPANY	WOUNDED	DIED OF WOUNDS	KILLED	DIED
Company A				10
Company B				5
Company C				5
Company D			2	6
Company E	1		1	7
Company F				7
Company G				7
Company H				4
Company I				7
Company K				1
TOTAL	1	0	3	59

As can be determined from the extremely low battlefield casualty numbers, this was a relatively inactive military period for the 25th Regiment, with no significant engagements with the enemy and literally no fighting. One of the three men killed during the coastal Carolina defense was shot while on picket duty and the other two were victims of unfortunate accidents. The significant number of fatalities listed in the "died" column is attributable almost exclusively to disease.

This is not surprising, given the fact that almost one-third of all Civil War casualties were caused by sickness. Ever-present dysenteries, fevers and upper respiratory infections were so prevalent that the average foot soldier was twice as likely to die from a camp disease as he was from a battlefield injury. Another reason — one that was especially true for the mountain men in the 25th Regiment — was that the rural lifestyles of many of the Civil War soldiers had protected them from such childhood diseases as measles, mumps, chickenpox, and scarlet fever. When they came to live together in camps with large groups of men, thousands died of these diseases in the early stages of the war.

The doctors attending the men of the 25th Regiment N.C. who met their unfortunate end by disease diagnosed a wide variety of causes of death during the war. Among the maladies found in the service records that struck down the mountaineers were the following diseases, printed here just as the doctors recorded them many years ago: icterus, diphtheria, dropsy, cerebro miningnitis, diarroea chronic, fistula, febris typhoides, cerebritis, pneumonia, dysentery, continued fever, scurvy, variola, febris remittens, brain fever, pyemia, scarlatina, and bilious fever.

Those raw mountain men were exposed to many "firsts" during their early months of military service. They had seen their first railroad train on the trip to Raleigh. Steamboats running across the sea as far as the eyes could see caught the fancy of most of the men for the very first time at Wilmington. And while garrisoned along the coastlines they were exposed for the first time to deadly bacteria and viruses—lethal enemies they had not sworn to fight.

Casualty Estimates: The Seven Days Battles (June 16, 1862–August 25, 1862)

When Union General George McClellan landed his Army of the Potomac on the Virginia Peninsula with designs of besieging and capturing Richmond, Virginia, the 25th Regiment N.C. was called from North Carolina to join in General Robert E. Lee's defense of the South's capital city. The mountain boys fought the Yankees for the very first time at an engagement near King's School House on June 25, 1862, and again at the battle of Malvern Hill on July 1, 1862. Afterward, the regiment withdrew to Drewry's Bluff on the James River to refit, reorganize and build fortifications in the vicinity of Richmond and Petersburg, Virginia.

An estimate of the casualties suffered by the 25th Regiment N.C. during the Seven Days Battles can be found in the following table:

CASUALTY ESTIMATES: SEVEN DAYS BATTLES

COMPANY	WOUNDED	DIED OF WOUNDS	KILLED	DIED
Company A	20	2	0	5
Company B	20	5	3	9
Company C	11	1	3	7
Company D	8	2	0	3
Company E	12	3	3	9
Company F	7	1	1	6
Company G	12	4	5	5
Company H	13	4	7	3
Company I	13	5	0	6
Company K	10	1	4	6
Field & Staff	3	0	0	0
TOTAL	129	28	26	59

These casualties were the combined result of the engagement fought at King's School House and the major battle contested at Malvern Hill in which the 25th Regiment participated. Also included are the statistics for the subsequent period spent at Drewry's Bluff, where camp diseases proved to be more fatal than Yankee bullets. A further breakdown demonstrat-

Caring for the wounded and burying the dead after the Battle of Antietam (*Harper's Weekly*).

ing the measure of human losses from each of these venues is presented in the following table:

Casualty Estimates: Seven Days Battles

| Company | King's School House | | | Malvern Hill | | | Drewry's Bluff |
	Wounded	Died of Wounds	Killed	Wounded	Died of Wounds	Killed	Died
A	9	1		11	1		5
B	6	2		14	3	3	9
C	5	1	2	6		1	7
D	3	1		5	1		3
E	3			9	3	3	9
F	4	1		3		1	6
G				12	4	5	5
H	2	1		11	3	7	3
I	3	1		10	4		6
K				10	1	4	6
F&S				3			6
Total	35	8	2	94	20	24	59

Although not considered a major battle, the fighting near King's School House was furious and the 25th Regiment experienced loss of life and limb in action for the first time. Ten

Collecting the wounded at Antietam under a flag of truce (*Harper's Weekly*; artist Alfred Rudolf Waud).

mountain men were killed as a result of this action, which initiated the Seven Days Battles. As can be seen from the casualty numbers, Malvern Hill was a conflict of a much larger scale. It manifested the climactic final battle of the Seven Days Battles in which General McClellan and his grand Army of the Potomac were dissuaded by the attacking Rebels from further movements against Richmond. Forty-four men from the 25th Regiment gave their lives in an effort to take the strong Union position atop Malvern Hill. Companies H and G alone sacrificed 10 and 9 men respectively in the futile charges into a wall of cannon fire and lead bullets. Although the resilient Yankees held the hill as night fell, the ferocity of the Rebel attacks persuaded the Northern commanders to withdraw toward their base on the James River and eventually steam off in naval transports back toward Washington, D.C.

During the two months following the battle of Malvern Hill, the 25th Regiment N.C. remained in the Richmond area stationed near Drewry's Bluff. While there, they were employed building fortifications for the defense of Richmond and Petersburg. The casualty statistics indicate that there were no military engagements fought during this time period; however, the men of the 25th Regiment were attacked again by an invisible foe which decimated its ranks. At Drewry's Bluff, 59 men (coincidently the same number that died during the Carolina coastal defense) died of disease during the hot sweltering months of July and August of 1862 — a greater number than had been killed on the battlefields of the Seven Days.

Casualty Estimates: Maryland Campaign (August 26, 1862–October 31, 1862)

When Robert E. Lee invaded Maryland in the late summer of 1862, his Army of Northern Virginia still included the battle-tested 25th Regiment N.C. The regiment participated in the capture of the strategic river town of Harpers Ferry September 11–15, 1862. Then after receiving an urgent summons from General Lee, the mountain boys rushed to his support at Sharpsburg, Maryland, where General McClellan's army was massing superior numbers of troops to throw against the Confederates lodged along Antietam Run. The 25th Regiment N.C. played a conspicuous role in the battle of Antietam on September 17, 1862, as they helped shore up the vulnerable left side of the Confederate battle line in the West Woods near the small Dunker Church. From mid-morning until nightfall, the 25th N.C. repulsed several ferocious Yankee charges and endured an incessant artillery barrage to hold their position and prevent a penetration by the Federal troops.

General McClellan refused to continue the attack the following day, and during the night of September 18–19 the 25th Regiment N.C. withdrew with the remainder of the Army of Northern Virginia across the Potomac River. After moving back into Virginia, the 25th N.C. bivouacked in the vicinity of Winchester in the Shenandoah Valley for a period of several weeks. While there, the troops camped under the stars without adequate clothing, blankets or shelter to protect them from the cool fall weather. Many of the mountaineers, wounded, weakened, and exhausted from their exertions on the battlefield and exposed to the low temperatures at night, succumbed to the ravages of sickness in the aftermath of the battle of Antietam.

The following table reflects the casualties suffered by the 25th Regiment N.C. during the Maryland Campaign:

CASUALTY ESTIMATES: MARYLAND CAMPAIGN

COMPANY	WOUNDED	DIED OF WOUNDS	KILLED	DIED
Company A	2			
Company B	1			1
Company C	2		1	1
Company D			1	2
Company E	1			1
Company F	2			1
Company G	2			2
Company H	3	2		1
Company I	2			2
Company K	1			
TOTAL	16	2	2	11

The battle of Antietam has been referred to as the bloodiest single day of the Civil War. In consideration of this and the desperate fighting in which the 25th Regiment N.C. was engaged, these battlefield casualty statistics seem remarkably low. For instance, 94 men received wounds at the battle of Malvern Hill, compared to only 16 at Antietam. Also, 44 of the regiment's men lost their lives at Malvern Hill, compared to the relatively small number of 4 at the battle of Antietam. Moreover, the number of Antietam casualties falls far below those incurred at the King's School House engagement, which was not considered a major battle. Another perspective can be gained by comparing the low number of casualties suffered by the 25th Regiment N.C. with the grand total of more than 25,000 accredited to the conflict. It is interesting, as well, to note that the number of men who died of disease during the Maryland Campaign was almost three times the number lost in battle.

Top: Rebel casualties at Fredericksburg (Library of Congress; artist Alfred Rudolf Waud). *Bottom:* Wounded soldiers at Fredericksburg (Library of Congress).

Casualty Estimates: Battle of Fredericksburg (November 1, 1862–January 3, 1863)

During the middle of November 1862, the 25th Regiment N.C. and the rest of Ransom's Brigade rushed at the head of the Confederate army van to Fredericksburg, Virginia, to meet a new Union threat. Just across the Rappahannock River from that old colonial town, a new Union army commander, General Ambrose Burnside, was concentrating his forces and preparing for another campaign against Richmond. The Battle of Fredericksburg was soon waged on December 13, 1862, and from the heights known as Marye's and from behind a low stone wall along the Sunken Road, the 25th Regiment N.C. fought to stave off relentless waves of brave bluecoats charging their positions. Thousands of poor Union soldiers fell dead, one on top of another, in the fields opposite the long gray Confederate line. Yet the assaults continued and did not cease until darkness cast its shroud over the field.

As the roar of the cannon and cracking of the musket fire gradually died away, the only sounds penetrating the night were the anguished cries of wounded men calling out for help. Unheard were the laments of General Burnside and his commanders over their flawed battle plan and failed tactics. The Union paid a heavy price of some 13,000 casualties for the decisions made by those officers. Although the South had many fewer casualties—less than 5,000—the 25th Regiment N.C. paid heavily in blood on a scale almost equal to Malvern Hill.

The casualty estimates for the 25th Regiment N.C. at the battle of Fredericksburg are presented in the following table:

CASUALTY ESTIMATES: FREDERICKSBURG

COMPANY	WOUNDED	DIED OF WOUNDS	KILLED	DIED
Company A	3		1	
Company B	8	1	2	
Company C	12	1		
Company D	3	2		
Company E	14	2	1	
Company F	2			
Company G	19	2	2	2
Company H	1	1	2	
Company I	5		1	3
Company K	7	1	3	2
Field & Staff	2	1		
TOTAL	76	11	12	7

Interestingly, the number of casualties experienced by the individual companies of the 25th Regiment varies significantly, so much so that attention is drawn to the disparity between Company G and Company H, for example. Although impossible to know precisely why Company G would have so many more casualties, the fortunes of war surely dictate to some degree such an occurrence. The number of troops in each company, hot spots of intense action or weaponry fire on the battlefield, and the position of the companies in relation to those locations could easily contribute to such an imbalance in the casualty figures. Moreover, one or more well-aimed rounds of exploding shell landing in the midst of a particular company would certainly have a significant impact on the numbers of casualties inflicted on that military unit. Whatever the reason might be, the facts are that all the companies were engaged at Fredericksburg and contributed to a great Southern victory. And all paid a human toll to keep the flames of secession burning a while longer throughout the South.

Casualty Estimates: Eastern North Carolina Defense (January 4, 1863–May 8, 1864)

The 25th Regiment N.C. was dispatched to eastern North Carolina in January 1863 to protect the key railroad facilities and the coastal regions still free from Federal domination. For approximately sixteen months, the regiment moved between encampments and manned outposts near the most strategic eastern towns, including Weldon, Kenansville, Goldsboro, Kinston, Wilmington, and Garysburg. Casualty numbers show that the mountain boys were not engaged in major conflicts with the enemy for the most part, certainly none that approached the scale of those waged in Virginia and Maryland in which they had fought. In the fall of 1863, a detachment of soldiers from the regiment was detailed to Madison County in the western North Carolina mountains to purge the area of a band of bushwhacking "tories." And the mountain boys of the 25th N.C. participated in the last major Confederate victory of the war when they helped capture the key port town of Plymouth in April 1864.

Casualties experienced by the 25th Regiment N.C. during the period of defensive service in eastern North Carolina are presented in the following table:

CASUALTY ESTIMATES:
EASTERN NORTH CAROLINA DEFENSE

COMPANY	WOUNDED	DIED OF WOUNDS	KILLED	DIED
Company A	2		1	
Company B	3			1
Company C	2	1	1	3
Company D	1		1	
Company E	4			1
Company F			1	4
Company G	1			4
Company H	3		1	2
Company I	4	1		4
Company K	2	1	1	2
TOTAL	22	3	6	21

The effects of disease continued to wreak havoc among the ranks of the 25th Regiment N.C. during their tour of duty in North Carolina. And again it can be seen that the mortality rate credited to the Yankees was less than half that attributed to disorders and infections. The records indicate that 5 of the 9 men killed during this period were victims of the tories encountered in a mini-expedition to Warm Springs in Madison County. Regimental historian Lt. Garland Ferguson wrote that the tories had greater numbers by a factor of twenty to one, and "the loss of the detachment in killed and wounded was heavy, including Lieutenant Hyatt, of Company F, who was killed in the field."[1] Three other soldiers were killed in the successful venture to capture Plymouth on April 18–20, 1864.

Casualty Estimates: Richmond and Petersburg Defense (May 9, 1864–April 9, 1865)

In early May 1864, the 25th Regiment N.C. boarded the railcars in Kinston, North Carolina, and headed back to Virginia, for the rest of the war as it turned out. Immediately upon their arrival at Drewry's Bluff, they were pushed into action against General Benjamin Butler's Federal forces making yet another attempt to capture Richmond. After successfully rebuffing this attack, which became known as the battle of Drewry's Bluff, the 25th N.C. joined in the Rebel actions which trapped Butler's army "as if corked in a bottle" at Bermuda Hundred. A short time later, the mountain boys were ordered into action with General Beauregard's meager forces at Petersburg, Virginia, in June 1864 to defend against an assault from General Ulysses S. Grant's combined armies. Fighting from defensive trenches and fortifications, the Rebels were able to hold off the Union forces until General Robert E. Lee arrived with his Army of Northern Virginia.

From that point in the war, June 1864, until the end, when Lee was forced to surrender at Appomattox Court House on April 9, 1865, the 25th Regiment N.C. occupied the defensive saps in front of Petersburg. Those nine months would be the most difficult time of all for the troops, who suffered in the trenches from hunger, severe privations, and enemy bombardment. During this period, the 25th N.C. was involved in major engagements with the enemy at the battles of the Crater, Globe Tavern, Fort Stedman, and Five Forks, and in running battles with Yankee forces along the Appomattox River toward Appomattox Court House.

The following casualty estimates have also been generated from the database of the regiment's roster and service records. There is no doubt that the records during this last year of the war are incomplete and that the extracted casualty figures do not represent the entirety of human loss experienced by the 25th Regiment N.C. It is suggested that this information be considered as the lower threshold of the actual casualties suffered and that the absolute number of men injured and killed during this period was very much higher:

CASUALTY ESTIMATES
RICHMOND AND PETERSBURG DEFENSE

COMPANY	WOUNDED	DIED OF WOUNDS	KILLED	DIED
Company A	16	2	2	5
Company B	19	3	1	6
Company C	23	4	3	5
Company D	19	5	1	5
Company E	13	2	2	3
Company F	16	2	4	1
Company G	23	4	2	3
Company H	12	1	1	4
Company I	26	3	3	2
Company K	9	3	2	1
Field & Staff	4	1		
TOTAL	180	30	21	35

These raw numbers standing alone are impressively high and adequately demonstrate the dangerous and deadly business of the 25th Regiment's service during that last year of the war. The number of men wounded in this period, 180, amounts to 42 percent of all those counted in the "wounded" category for the entirety of the war. Also, the statistics reveal that at least 51 mountaineers lost their lives as a result of enemy action during the last-ditch Confederate efforts to save Richmond and Petersburg. Yet, it is a virtual certainty that there were even more of the regiment's men killed in and around the trenches than has been recorded in the historical service records. Lastly, it can be seen that disease continued to drain soldiers from the ranks. At least 35 deaths were from disease, many of these occurring to men, young and old, recently drafted into service who had not built up immunities to the camp and trench maladies.

Summary of Casualties

A summary of the casualty estimates for the 25th Regiment N.C. during the Civil War is given below. In addition, casualty numbers offered by Lt. Garland Ferguson in his regimental history are presented for comparison:

CASUALTY ESTIMATES: FOR THE WAR

COMPANY	WOUNDED	DIED OF WOUNDS	KILLED	DIED
Company A	43	4	4	20
Company B	51	9	6	22
Company C	50	7	8	21
Company D	31	9	5	16
Company E	45	7	7	21
Company F	27	3	6	19
Company G	57	10	9	23
Company H	32	8	11	14
Company I	50	9	4	24
Company K	29	6	10	12
Field & Staff	9	2		
TOTAL	424	74	70	192
Lt. Ferguson's Estimate	470	220		280

In his history of the 25th Regiment N.C., written in 1901, Lt. Ferguson recorded much higher estimates of casualties inflicted upon the 25th Regiment than the records available today reflect. His numbers for men killed on the battlefield and for those who died of disease are about 50 percent higher than this current accounting indicates. However, the numbers of wounded soldiers are more closely aligned, as the tallies vary by only 11 percent. It is not known how the heroic Lieutenant Ferguson, himself wounded three times in the war, arrived at his approximations of the casualties inflicted on the 25th N.C. With the surety that today's estimates are on the low side, it seems more than likely that the actual number of injured and killed lies somewhere in between.

A reasonable postulation for the total number of soldiers who perished during the war might be closer to 370 — 10 percent more than the current lower threshold estimate of 336 and 25 percent fewer deaths than the 500 reported by Lt. Ferguson. If that is so, this toll of 370 deaths caused by the war would represent approximately 22 percent of the 1,670 or more men who signed up to fight with the 25th Regiment. Or put another way, it signifies that more than 1 out of every 5 of the regiment's soldiers were killed or died of disease during the war. Regardless of the estimations and final metrics, a considerable number of highlanders sacrificed their lives for the Southern cause, and many a mountain homestead hearth would feel their absence in the years following the Civil War.

Desertion in the Ranks

The act of desertion during the Civil War was not an uncommon occurrence, the causes of which have been previously discussed. Although such instances were not strictly considered a casualty of war, the flight of deserting soldiers from the ranks of the 25th Regiment N.C. served equally as well to diminish its effective fighting strength. This writer has extracted the incidences of desertion recorded in the company and regimental records, just as were the casualties, and the resulting count of documented desertions is reflected in the following table:

COMPANY	DESERTIONS
Company A	26
Company B	32
Company C	26
Company D	33
Company E	23
Company F	27
Company G	18
Company H	31
Company I	26
Company K	13
TOTAL	255

The records reveal that more than 255 mountain men deserted from the ten companies of the 25th Regiment N.C. during the war. And since the information for the final 12–16 months is sketchy and incomplete, it is very probable that many more than these numbers abandoned their brethren and broke their sworn loyalties to the Confederate army. Beginning in 1863, the service records abound with references to men who had deserted, were "absent without leave" or had "gone over to the enemy." However, more often than not it was found that they returned to duty a few months later, upon promises of amnesty from the Confederate government. It was not unusual to find records of men who deserted two and three times during the course of the war. And it is obvious, upon studying the service information, that not all the soldiers who in the end deserted were shiftless, cowardly or unprincipled men. Many commissioned and noncommissioned officers deserted, as did brave men who had been wounded more than once in battle or who had been captured in battle and exchanged to fight again for the South.

It is not the objective of this work to pass judgment on the soldiers of the regiment or to question their motives for desertion, although the pressures and hardships that confronted them are very well understood. The intent is only to quantify the level of desertion within the 25th Regiment N.C. and emphasize the tremendous impact that it had in the reduction of the regiment's effective forces. Approximately 1,670 names of individual soldiers are listed in the regiment's roster, and of that total, at least 255, or about 15 percent, deserted or "went

"A Soldier's Dream." Thankful reunions such as the one pictured here occurred throughout the mountains of western North Carolina as the soldiers of the Twenty-fifth Regiment N.C. returned from the Civil War fields of battle (artist: Jack Stuhrman).

over to the enemy." It is not a stretch, in consideration of the lapses in record keeping and the absence of a large amount of information in the Confederate records for the final year of the war, to contemplate that as many as 300–350 men might have finally resorted to desertion. If indeed this was the actual case, as is very likely, the desertion rate then climbs to the range of 18 percent to 21 percent. This would indicate that approximately 1 out of every 5 soldiers who signed up with the 25th Regiment N.C. deserted from the ranks. Therefore, it can be seen that desertion certainly contributed heavily to the decimation of the 25th Regiment, and that almost as many men took flight from the battlefields and trenches as were killed by the Northern invaders and disease.

In the final analysis, the number of men who died in battle or from sickness, combined with the extraordinary number of deserters, stripped the 25th Regiment N.C. of more than 40 percent of its troops. The rest, with the exception of those 74 survivors who surrendered at Appomattox, were victims of severe battlefield wounds, capture by the enemy, or discharged by reason of being over or under age, disability, sickness, infirmity and various other unique circumstances. Thus, it can be seen how the casualties of war took many forms and gradually ate away at the fighting capacity of the 25th Regiment N.C. and the ten companies from which it was formed. Every man lost to the individual companies was like another thread broken, and eventually the resilient fabric of the 25th Regiment N.C. became ripped and tattered and full of holes. The remnants of that fabric, those mountain companies represented at Appomattox Court House on April 9, 1865, bore little resemblance to those which had paraded out of the hills in 1861.

15

THE COLONEL AND HIS LIEUTENANT

Henry Middleton Rutledge and William Harrison Hargrove were two young men caught up in the politics that led to America's Civil War. They both believed strongly that the South's independence from Northern domination was worth fighting for. One was born to wealthy planters from the low country of South Carolina and accustomed to the lifestyle and privileges of the aristocratic slave-holding gentry of the South. The other was a simple mountaineer farmer born and raised along the Pigeon River in Haywood County, North Carolina, and appreciative of the rural and rugged agrarian environment from which he came. The fates of these two youths were joined when they volunteered their services to the State of North Carolina in the summer of 1861 and eventually found their way into the same Confederate military unit—the 25th Regiment North Carolina Infantry Troops.

Rutledge became the "boy colonel" of the 25th Regiment N.C. at the age of twenty-two. Hargrove enlisted as a private in 1861 at the age of twenty and eventually was commissioned 1st lieutenant while serving in the trenches of Petersburg in 1864. The following biographical portraits of these two Confederate warriors are presented so that an appreciation for their diverse heritages can be gained. From these accounts can also be discerned how the two youthful Rebels forged a new beginning to their lives and coped with the obstacles and difficulties of the Reconstruction years subsequent to the great rebellion. Their stories, which converged so dramatically during the Civil War, veered and coursed in opposite directions after the conflict. In the pages that follow, the reader will learn where those diverging paths led and discover the fortunes which befell two brave soldiers who fought with the 25th Regiment N.C.

Henry Middleton Rutledge: "The Boy Colonel"

Colonel walked along the line of his regiment with his cap on sword, shouting to his men, "Don't let them take our front, Twenty-fifth, the Twenty-fifth has never had her front taken!"[1]

The sword-wielding colonel referred to above is Colonel Henry Middleton Rutledge. His fearless leadership during a furious and murderous Union counterattack was vividly recounted years after the battle by the historian of the 25th Regiment North Carolina Infantry Troops. Only twenty-two years old when given command of the 25th N.C., Colonel Rutledge was reputed to be the Confederacy's youngest colonel. He became the embodiment of that superb military unit and inspired his mountain boys to continue their valiant struggle to throw off the Yankee aggressors. Revered by the men he led in battle and admired for his conspicuous bravery and kind disposition, this young colonel who hailed from the South Carolina coastal region and Henderson County, North Carolina, was the essence of a Confederate warrior and officer.

Lineage

Henry Middleton Rutledge was born in Flat Rock, North Carolina, on August 5, 1839, in the midst of Henderson County's scenic Blue Ridge Mountains. His parents, Frederick Rutledge and Henrietta Middleton Rutledge were cousins descended from wealthy planter families that settled in South Carolina during the Colonial period. Both his mother and father's lineages traced back through the Rutledge family for several generations until, interestingly, they shared a common set of great grandparents, John Rutledge and Sara Hext.

Colonel Rutledge's mother, Henrietta, had a heritage deeply rooted in both the Middleton and Rutledge families. Her great-grandfather Henry Middleton served as president of the Continental Congress of the United States; two of her grandfathers, Edward Rutledge and Arthur Middleton, were signers of the Declaration of Independence. In addition to the Rutledge and Middleton families, Colonel Rutledge's ancestry included other prominent South Carolina low country families having the names of Horry, Pinckney, and Williams. This very superficial glimpse of Colonel Rutledge's genealogy shows that he was not born of common stock and indeed boasted an aristocratic parentage of lofty repute.

Frederick Rutledge, Colonel Rutledge's father, was the grandson of old "Dictator John" Rutledge, who had served as the first governor of South Carolina. Fred studied medicine at the University of Dublin and, in addition to his medical training, possessed a high degree of competency in legal affairs and teaching. On October 15, 1825, Frederick married Henrietta on her parents' anniversary date and her mother's birthday. The newlyweds moved to Frederick's ancestral plantation home, Hampton Plantation, located along the South Santee River near Charleston, South Carolina, and soon were gracing the most fashionable circles in the Carolina low country. They enjoyed a lifestyle familiar only to those fortunate few included in the highest level of Southern society.

Early Years

North of Greenville, South Carolina, the Blue Ridge Mountains sprout from the rolling piedmont terrain and begin their magnificent ascent toward the heavens. Frederick Rutledge and a few other visionary friends, including brother-in-law Daniel Blake, endeavored to establish a highland summer resort in that rugged mountainous region. About the year 1829, they began purchasing property in western North Carolina's beautiful "land of the sky" country and promoting the area's beauty and refreshing and healthful climate to the low country rice and cotton planters and Charleston city dwellers. The Flat Rock community of Henderson County (then Buncombe County) very quickly became a mecca for wealthy South Carolinians seeking respite from the summer heat.

Convinced of the benefits of escaping summer's sweltering temperatures and mortal fevers, the low country's gentry began making the two-week long treks to Flat Rock in carriages and caravans. Aristocratic families and slaves driving livestock and hauling clothing, furniture, supplies, and assorted belongings poured into the area. Their journey into the highlands was facilitated greatly by the recently completed Buncombe Turnpike, which offered the best access up the steep ridges and through the mountain ramparts. The construction of fine resort homes and retreats made Flat Rock renowned as the "Little Charleston of the Mountains." Frederick and Henrietta happily divided their time between "Little Charleston" and the magnificent Hampton Plantation as they embarked on their familial pursuit.

Henry Middleton (the colonel) was born in Flat Rock in 1839 and was the next-to-youngest of six children born to Frederick and Henrietta. Most unfortunately, however, when Henry was only three years old, his mother died of a heart attack at the Meadows, the home of her sister, located in the area known today as Fletcher, North Carolina. The death of this beautiful and charming woman, who was said to be fond of wearing a red rose in her hair and humming lullabies to her babies, would leave an eternal void in the lives and hearts of her husband and six children that could never to be completely filled.

Henrietta was interred in a churchyard cemetery associated with the little brick St. John in the Wilderness Church in Flat Rock erected in the mid–1830s. Frederick would never remarry and chose to have his children raised under the guardianship of his mother and mother-in-law. He arranged for the three eldest children, Elizabeth Pinckney (Lise), Sarah Henrietta, and Edward, to return to Hampton Plantation, where his mother, Harriott Pinckney Horry Rutledge, would care for them. Henry Middleton (the colonel) along with sisters Alice Izard and Emma Fredericka (Minna) were sent to Nashville, Tennessee, to be raised by their maternal grandmother, Septima, and Aunt Mary Fogg. Although well along in years, Mrs. Septima Rutledge and her husband, Henry, welcomed the toddlers to Rose Hill, their Tennessee mansion. There they offered the grandchildren the same care and affection that their own beloved daughter, Henrietta, had known growing up.[2]

One can imagine how Rose Hill bloomed with renewed brightness and gaiety with its three new occupants. Sounds of the children at play and the hilarity of the grandparents enjoying their company must have resounded throughout the expansive house. The spacious kitchen once again filled the home with pleasing aromas of baking bread, roasting meat and tantalizing whiffs of fruit pies and pastries cooling in the cupboard or on the windowsills. Approximately twenty acres of property surrounded the house — ample room for the kids to romp and explore in the orchards and terraced gardens. At Rose Hill, Henry and his siblings continued to be reared within an environment and lifestyle that was beyond the reach of most of the citizens of that era. They could not have wanted for more.

Tragedy would again visit young Henry Middleton, however, barely more than a year after he lost his mother. In January 1844, Grandfather Henry Middleton Rutledge was suddenly taken ill while visiting at his daughter Mary Fogg's house and died almost immediately. Mr. Rutledge, sixty-eight years old, was a well-respected gentleman of high stature in Nashville, and the entire city was stunned to hear of his death. He was mourned by the hundreds and a testimony of the good will and generosity that he spread was given in an obituary column in the *Republican Banner* announcing his demise. It read in part as follows:

> Far from the gaze of the multitude and the frivolous agitations of this bustling life, he spent many an hour in visiting the poor and distressed, and pouring into the wounded hearts of widows and orphans the balm of consolation and comfort; and many an humble but aspiring student has had the benefit of his purse, as well as of his counsel and direction.

Eventually young Henry and the rest of the family would overcome this latest loss and become settled in the circumstances and situation created by the absence of another family member. In addition to managing her household affairs at Rose Hill, the widow Septima Rutledge inherited a plantation styled Chilhowee, along with the slaves whose valuable labor was essential to the place's viability. Strapped as she was with these additional burdens, it is very likely that Septima turned to her daughter, Mary Fogg, for assistance in raising the grandchildren and insuring that they received a quality education.

Septima on occasion gave direction for belongings to be packed up and, with the assistance of enslaved servants, made months-long trips to the South Carolina low country. There she visited with kindred at Middleton Place, her father's ancestral plantation which rivaled the Hampton Plantation in beauty, richness and prosperity. Her young wards, surely overflowing with eagerness and excitement to go on these grand treks, were also able to spend time at Hampton Plantation, where they were reunited with their older siblings and paternal grandmother, Harriott Horry Rutledge. And it is likely that Henry's father, Frederick, coordinated his affairs to coincide with the family reunions at Hampton Plantation. The frequency of these pilgrimages was certainly limited to no more than once per year, given the long distance between Charleston and Nashville and the weeks-long journey over the poor roads of the day.

There is little doubt that Septima was a devoted guardian of her three grandchildren and cherished her responsibilities in regard to their welfare and education. Even when she was feeling poorly, the children didn't escape her thoughts and attention. While recovering from a physical infliction at Chilhowee, her plantation in the Cumberland Mountains near Nashville, she wrote to sister Mary Helen about her condition and concern for the children. The following brief excerpts are taken from a very lengthy letter written on October 28, 1847:

> And my restoration at length proved so Lingering, that I could not risk the Journey of two Hundred miles further, to pass the Remainder of the Summer with Dear Emma, for which she was most anxious, & thus I was deprived of the pleasure also of being near, Dear Lise, & Her Father, who always on these Occasions has made the kindest, & most attentive Nurse & Physician, & to my great regret I was prevented gratifying them with a sight of the three Dear Children, who have been long the Objects of our tenderest care.... I truly lamented being the cause of detaining my Children at a Place where there was no attraction except for Invalids, but they readily forgot the sacrifice, & thought only of the benefit I might receive.... Then my sweet little charges put to School, & left them under the care of Aunt Mary, & then stayed but a fortnight in Nashville, as the repairs making to our House, in which Painting was included affected me so much, that I came here for a Purer Atmosphere.[3]

It is a beautifully crafted letter full of items of mutual interest to the two sisters. Importantly, this correspondence gives some insight into young Henry's status and whereabouts at the time he was about eight years old. Septima's correspondence reveals that she and her three wards withdrew to Chilowee where she was to recover from a possible stroke or heart attack through the restorative effects of a nearby spring. Lamentably, she describes how an anticipated summer excursion of some two hundred miles to see her daughter, "Dear Emma [Blake]," and to be near "Dear Lise" and her father was interrupted by the condition of her health. Implicit in her words is that Septima had planned to take Henry and his sisters to Flat Rock, North Carolina, where they could be with their father, Frederick, and seventeen-year-old sister, Lise. Septima regrets her absence from the good doctor's care and granddaughter's devoted attention. It is evident that Henry's father, Frederick, is continuing to reside, at least during the summer seasons, in Flat Rock, where he may have occasionally practiced medicine and lived with his oldest daughter, Lise.

Septima returned to Rose Hill for a brief two-week period, and as mentioned in the letter, "put to School" her three little charges. They were left under the meticulous custody of

Aunt Mary, who, it is suspected, was responsible for nurturing their learning experience through the primary education stages. Mary Fogg was a devout Christian of the Episcopalian faith, who over her lifetime authored seven books, a highly unusual feat for a woman in that age. Henry surely drank with an unquenchable thirst from Aunt Mary's fountain of knowledge and from the taps of the tutors under her employ.

It is likely that Henry would have eclipsed the level of education that Aunt Mary could provide when he reached the age of about ten or eleven years. A search of the United States census data for the year 1850 finds that he was not enumerated in Francis and Mary Fogg's household, although his two sisters were. Nor was Henry living with Septima at Rose Hill or with Frederick and Grandmother Harriott Rutledge at Hampton Plantation. Almost certainly Henry had been packed off to a private boarding school to continue his education in advanced studies. In fact, Septima had dispatched her own two sons, Edward and Henry, when they were of a like age, to St. Mary's Roman Catholic Church in Baltimore, Maryland.

The passage of more than one hundred and sixty years has hidden all vestiges of Henry Middleton Rutledge's teenage years. Documents or records have not been found to illuminate this period of his life to reveal how he filled these crucial formative years. He very possibly left the care of Grandmother Septima and Aunt Mary to further his education at some unknown institution such as the Catholic school in Baltimore, Maryland. Although it is recorded in the history of the 25th Regiment by Lieutenant Garland S. Ferguson that Henry Rutledge possessed a military education, it is believed that he, in fact, did not. The historian wrote: "With the exception of a part of Company G, the regiment was composed of mountain men west of the Ridge, the Colonel was a politician and statesman; the Lieutenant-Colonel a professional soldier; the Major [Henry] a civilian with a military education."[4] However, a letter written by Henry in the spring of 1861 to the Confederate secretary of war, Leroy P. Walker, gives evidence to the contrary.

In this letter Henry wrote of being desirous of entering the army of the Confederate States and "begs" to be permitted to offer himself for a second or third lieutenancy. He continues by presenting the following justification for his request: "I am aware that it is the plan of the government to appoint men who have received a military education rather than civilians but in the event of war it may be necessary to increase the army with those who feel a strong desire to serve the country even without that advantage."[5] From this statement it can be surmised that Henry Rutledge did not have the advantage of a military education. Yet he had an overpowering desire to serve his country and sought appointment to officer's rank from the highest levels of the Confederate War Department.

A Rebel Warrior

Incendiary rhetoric from the state's politicians along with the hot-bloodied fervor demonstrated by southern loyalists increased the drum beat for war in South Carolina during the winter of 1860–1861. At the age of 21 Henry Middleton Rutledge could not have been immune to the political exigencies of the time nor the tide of bellicose sentiment that was rising throughout the coastal region of South Carolina where his ancestral plantation — Hampton Plantation — was located. As a matter of fact it appears that even at this early date Henry was totally persuaded toward the southern cause and had volunteered his services to the South Carolina provincial forces.

Evidence of Henry's early loyalty and conviction can be found in a letter written on his behalf in his quest for an officer's commission. The commissary general of the Confederate army, L.B. Northrop, writes to the Confederate secretary of war testifying to Henry's character and fitness as a military officer. "This young man has been serving on the Islands around the harbour of Charleston during the winter. After the fall of Sumter he got a leave of absence to come on here [Montgomery, Alabama] and present his application in person to you — which he did and then returned to his duty promptly."[6] There is little doubt that Henry was a witness to the reduction and surrender of the Union's Fort Sumter, and it is very plausible to believe that he participated in some minor way in that first act of rebellion by the South.

Northrop's testimonial letter also offers an enlightening description of Henry in the vigor of youthful manhood: "He is tall, robust, well formed, and nimble, with a good eye and modest, self-possessed manner. His education has been good, and his habits hardy: and his rearing that which is the very best for an officer." Still another letter directed to the secretary of war by William Porcher Miles, a prominent Southern politician, lauds Henry's fitness for service and speaks to his heritage: "He is a young gentleman of character and education — and the glorious services rendered by his ancestors to the revolution of '76 entitle him fairly to a chance to show that in aiding the revolution of '61 the stock has not degenerated."[7] The Confederate authorities acted upon these glowing recommendations and on May 21, 1861, Henry M. Rutledge was appointed second lieutenant in the Confederate States Army.

It is not entirely clear why Henry Rutledge decided to join a North Carolina volunteer unit instead of one of those early ones forming around Charleston at the time. Henry and his father were seasonal residents of Henderson County's Flat Rock community, and it is likely that he was enticed by close family friends, the Blakes, to enroll in Captain Frederick Blake's company known as the Cane Creek Rifles. Walter Blake, who was about Henry's age, enlisted as a sergeant in that company. And coincidentally or not, Walter's sister, Anna, must have drawn the early romantic attentions of Henry for she would later be wedded to him.

The Cane Creek Rifles united in Asheville, North Carolina, with the other mountain companies which would eventually form the 25th Regiment North Carolina Infantry Troops. At Camp Patton it didn't take long for the other mountain boys to take note of Henry Rutledge and recognize the leadership skills in him that could serve them well. Henry was elected major of the 25th Regiment N.C. at the relatively young age of 22 years and served under the command of Colonel Thomas Clingman and Lieutenant Colonel St. Clair Dearing. It was primarily due to the knowledge and capabilities of Lieutenant Colonel Dearing and the leadership and dedication of Major Rutledge that the raw volunteers making up the 25th N.C. were molded into a disciplined military unit. As the regimental historian, Lt. Garland Ferguson, later recalled, "Under the mild discipline of the Colonel and skillful training and accurate drill of the Lieutenant Colonel and Major, the regiment was soon thoroughly drilled and disciplined, on duty."

Major Rutledge served at this command level through that first fall and winter at Grahamville, South Carolina, near Port Royal and Hilton Head Island. Because no military actions were undertaken there, Major Rutledge's regiment was primarily occupied building fortifications. After mobilizing to Kinston, North Carolina, in March of 1862, the 25th N.C. was combined with four other North Carolina regiments to form a brigade under the command of General Robert Ransom, Jr. The officers of each regiment again stood for reelection upon the Confederate army's reorganization during that month of April, and Major Rutledge was then elected lieutenant colonel. The 25th remained under the command of Colonel Thomas Clingman, but not for long. In less than a month Colonel Clingman was promoted to brigadier general and given a brigade of his own to lead. In his stead, the boys of the 25th N.C. elected Major Rutledge as their colonel, and the young man of only twenty-two years of age became a true "Boy Colonel." He was one of the youngest colonels in the Confederate army.

Colonel Rutledge and his regiment, associated with Ransom's Brigade, were soon plunged into the midst of a series of confused actions in the vicinity of Richmond, Virginia, known as the Seven Days Battles. On June 25, 1862, near the crossroads village of Seven Pines at King's School House, the 25th Regiment was rushed to the front on the Confederate extreme right flank to help repulse a Union assault. This was the first combat experience for Colonel Rutledge and his boys. Their behavior from all known accounts was exemplary. The regimental historian recorded the following remembrances concerning the action in which he himself participated:

> About one-half mile from the line the regiment was ordered to double-quick. It was thrown in line on the immediate left of the Williamsburg Road, and when within range of the enemy the regiment halted, the front rank at the command fired and fell to the ground, the rear rank fired over them, then with bayonets fixed we raised the rebel yell and charged; the enemy gave way and the ground which had been lost in the morning had been retaken. The enemy opened a heavy fire of musketry and three times tried, without effect, to retake their lines.

The commanding general of the Rebel forces manning the Confederate right flank, Major General Huger, commended the 25th Regiment in his report of the action: "The Twenty-fifth Regiment (Colonel H.M. Rutledge) was pushed to the left of the Williamsburg road, where the enemy had advanced, and drove them back in gallant style." Colonel Rutledge and his regiment had made a difference on that day by preventing a collapse of the Rebel right flank. In doing so, their gallantry had been recognized and commended and notice was taken of the young Colonel Rutledge.

A few short days later, in the final conflict of the Seven Days Battles, Colonel Rutledge again led a spirited attack by the 25th N.C. up Malvern Hill. A glimpse of the action on that day was created by these words from Lt. Ferguson's account of the battle:

> On 2 July [July 1] at Malvern Hill late in the evening it [the 25th Regiment] made a charge, but for want of support and on account of a galling fire, it was ordered back, and with other regiments of the brigade, was reformed under cover by General Robert Ransom, and again advanced within one hundred yards of the enemy's guns and line, when the

Colonel Henry Middleton Rutledge (North Carolina Department of Archives and History, Raleigh).

men raised a yell and charged in the face of a perfect sheet of fire from musketry and artillery, without wavering, to within twenty yards of the enemy's guns, some going even nearer.

The Union position on Malvern Hill was too formidable to be taken, and the boys were finally driven back. Colonel Rutledge, in leading one of the charges, was stunned by an exploding shell. The next day found the Union army in full retreat and the colonel and his regiment would take some time to rest and recover. General Robert Ransom, in his report on the battle of Malvern Hill, praised the troops under his command and commended especially the courage and coolness of Major Francis and Colonel Rutledge. In only his second battle, Colonel Rutledge had once again drawn the attention of a superior officer by his conspicuous actions on the field.

The colonel of the 25th N.C. had proven in a very short time (less than two months) to those in his command, and to himself, that he was possessed of those rare qualities necessary to lead men in battle. One grizzled mountaineer, convinced of the steel and fearlessness of which his commander was made, was queried after the war if he had ever seen the colonel in danger. As his blue eyes brightened with surprise at such a foolish notion, he replied, "The Colonel? If you mean him, he was never out of danger. Didn't he allus lead us? Sometimes he acted as if he wanted to be killed."[8] Colonel Rutledge demonstrated an apathy for his own mortality over and over again throughout the great conflict, and as soon again as mid–September 1862.

On September 17, 1862, the 25th N.C. was thrown into one of the bloodiest and deadliest affairs of the entire Civil War, which played out along a small stream in Maryland known as Antietam Run. Although outnumbered 2 to 1, the Rebels were barely able to repulse the attacks launched by the mighty Union army. The fighting along the Confederate left flank in the vicinity of the little country Dunker Church was especially fierce and the Rebel defense tenuous during the first half of the battle. The 25th N.C. helped to shore up the Rebel lines on that vulnerable Confederate flank and beat back wave after wave of attacking Yankees. On that autumn day in Maryland, the tenacity demonstrated by the North Carolina regiment reached a level that it had not achieved before and one that would be most difficult to attain again.

Colonel Rutledge was wounded at some point during the battle. Many years later his son recounted a story his father told of the repercussions of the day's fighting. Although leavened with humor after the fact, the episode well demonstrates the level of complete exhaustion experienced by warriors in the aftermath of great battles:

> On the first day of that dread September combat, he [the Colonel] had been wounded, and as darkness came on, fever set in. He and his men got together in a little patch of woods for the night. So worn out with the battle was my Colonel that he threw himself on the ground. He was aware that his head was resting on something, which he took for a dead body that he was content to have as a pillow. On awakening the next morning he was surprised to see a circle of men about him, all laughing and pointing to the object on which he had been sleeping. When he sat up and looked around, he discovered that he had been slumbering peacefully all night on a dead hog, which no doubt had been killed by a stray bullet.[9]

After the Battle of Antietam, General Lee ordered his Army of Northern Virginia back across the Potomac River to safe haven in Confederate territory. Colonel Rutledge, suffering from his battle wound and the onslaught of a typhoid attack, was in poor condition to travel. In midstream of the crossing, the colonel fainted and tumbled from his horse into the waist deep water of the river. Recounting the perilous circumstances years later to his sons, the colonel remembered being rescued by his black body servant, who accompanied him throughout the war experience. Ignoring Yankee sharpshooter fire from the banks of the river, the colonel's loyal servant waded to his master, heaved him across his shoulders and bore him to the southern shore and to safety.[10]

After the Maryland campaign, Colonel Rutledge had so endeared himself to the non-commissioned officers and privates of the 25th Regiment N.C. by his courage and élan that they presented him with a fine saddle horse. The commissioned officers were not allowed to bear any part of the expense or take part in the presentation ceremonies.[11] But the colonel may not have been able to enjoy his new mount at the time. The typhoid attack apparently did not let up, and Colonel Rutledge was forced to the care of a hospital in Williamsburg, Virginia, around September 30, 1862. After a three-week stay in the hospital, he was furloughed on October 23 and presumably went home to convalesce for several weeks. The *Official Records* of the war indicate that Colonel Rutledge did not participate in the next great conflict in which the 25th Regiment N.C. engaged.

On December 13, 1862, Colonel Rutledge's 25th N.C. again went into battle; however, the young colonel was not in their front as usual. He was still recovering from the battle wound and fever that had befallen him at the battle of Antietam. In his place leading the regiment was Lieutenant Colonel Samuel C. Bryson, who on that cold December day, presented the 25th N.C. in opposition to the throngs of attacking Yankee bluecoats at Fredericksburg, Virginia. From atop a high ground known as Marye's Heights and from behind a low stone wall running alongside of the Sunken Road, the mountain boys delivered volley after volley of lethal musket fire toward the attacking enemy waves. Union soldiers fell as if before a scythe, one atop another in heaps before that stone fence. Fredericksburg was later to be renowned as one of the South's greatest victories during the war, and the Colonel's veteran troops made a heavy contribution.

The threat of a Union invasion or continued incursions along North Carolina's coastline convinced General Robert E. Lee of the necessity of sending more troops to the state. With the thrill and horror of Fredericksburg still very much in their minds, Colonel Rutledge's now veteran troops were ordered to eastern North Carolina in January 1863 along with the rest of Ransom's Brigade. In May 1863 Matt Ransom took over the command of Ransom's Brigade from his brother, Robert Ransom, who had been promoted to major general. While stationed at various places throughout eastern North Carolina during the year of 1863 protecting the railroads and cities, Colonel Rutledge and the men of the 25th N.C. engaged in no significant battles and relatively few military skirmishes. By April 1864, Generals Robert F. Hoke and Matt Ransom formulated plans and led an attack to recapture the port city of Plymouth, North Carolina. Colonel Rutledge and the mountain boys of the 25th Regiment N.C. took part in this successful venture, which would be the last major Confederate victory of the war.

In the spring of 1864, Union armies were applying significant pressures on the Confederacy, taxing its limited resources. General Sherman was driving toward Atlanta, Georgia, as Confederate General Joseph Johnston offered some resistance but mostly retreated in the Yankees' front. General-in-chief of the Union armies, Ulysses S. Grant, was engaged in a series of murderous running battles in Virginia against General Robert E. Lee's Army of Northern Virginia. With the Confederate forces thinly spread and thus distracted, a third Union army led by General Benjamin Butler threatened Richmond. Commanding the meager and beleaguered forces defending the city was General Pierre Beauregard. Ransom's Brigade was ordered to his support, and Colonel Rutledge rushed his men to the Richmond environs.

From about May 12 until May 20, 1864, the 25th N.C. was constantly engaged in fending off assaults by Butler's superior Federal forces. Although outmanned in every encounter, the Rebels managed to drive the Yankees into a neck of land bounded by the Appomattox and James rivers, where they were very effectively bottled up. The fighting was as fierce as any experienced during the war to that date. Brigadier General Matt Ransom was severely wounded in the action on May 14, and Colonel Rutledge temporarily assumed command of the brigade's four regiments. He led Ransom's Brigade during the next few days of fighting as Old Butler's army was "corked" between the rivers.

A month's time found General Beauregard's still scant Confederate defenses facing the might of General Grant's combined armies. Grant had stealthily circled around General Robert E. Lee's right flank and Richmond to cross over the James River and aim his thrust at the town of Petersburg, Virginia, an all-important Confederate railroad center. Colonel Rutledge and the 25th N.C. were summoned once again by General Beauregard to help stave off this latest Northern aggression. On June 16 and 17, 1864, Beauregard's forces, outnumbered more than 4 to 1, fought valiantly to protect Petersburg and its railroads. By June 18 General Lee had arrived at the front with part of his army whereupon he took over the command of the Petersburg defense from General Beauregard. Grant at that stage called off his general offensive and began making preparations for a lengthy siege of the city.

For the next nine months, Colonel Rutledge and his 25th N.C. Troops were holed up in defensive trenches interposed between Petersburg and the Union army. The colonel would share the misery and privations of trench warfare with his weary troops as they dodged deadly enemy sniper fire and cannon barrages and resisted stealthy assaults. Scorching hot in the summer of 1864, freezing cold during that winter of 1864–1865, and forever hungry, those mountain boys that remained with Colonel Rutledge were a tough and determined bunch of Rebels.

Several significant battles occurred during the long siege of Petersburg in which the Colonel and his men participated. At the battles of the Crater in July 1864 and Weldon Railroad in August 1864 the 25th Regiment N.C. performed commendably. In March 1865, as the end drew near for the Confederacy, Ransom's Brigade, commanded at the time by Colonel Rutledge, and the 25th N.C. led an assault against the Union works of Fort Stedman, which they took without firing a shot. However, failures associated with the execution of other aspects of the Confederate battle plan and a collapse in their support forced Colonel Rutledge and his men to relinquish control of the fort. Years later the colonel was to describe the storming of Fort Stedman as the hottest fight of his war experience.[12]

Following the setback at Fort Stedman, on April 1, 1865, Grant's cavalry and infantry troops, much superior in numbers, managed to outmaneuver the Rebel army and summarily defeat it at a crossroads named Five Forks just a few miles west of Petersburg. Colonel Rutledge was caught in the middle of this battle with his troops and later described the action as follows:

> At Five Forks I was more proud of the regiment than I had ever been before, and that is saying a great deal. I have thought of them and compared them to the "Stonewall" of Manassas. They were surrounded on three sides by many times their own numbers, but there they stood, a solid mass of mountain men, broadsides from the enemy being poured into them, and there they stood like the rock of Gibraltar. When I remember that heroic scene, I cannot fail to compare that gallant company, desperate band, to the line the Great Napoleon saw at Waterloo. Speaking afterwards of the English line of battle, he says: "I covered them with artillery, I flooded them with infantry, I deluged them with cavalry, but when the smoke of battle rose, there stood the red line yet." Yes, there stood the gray line,

> the only line that stood that day, that I saw, and finally, after combating five different and separate times over the same field, pine thickets, broom grass, old fields, all sorts of a place, I was going to win. I was attempting to whip the enemy with the 25th North Carolina, and I knew I could do it. I thought I was getting along finely, until I happened to look to front, left and right, and saw we were surrounded with but a small loop hole to get through. We backed through that, emptying into their faces the last cartridge we had.[13]

The colonel and a few of his soldiers managed to escape capture at Five Forks through that "small loophole." However, most did not, and more than 5,000 Confederate prisoners were rounded up and marched off to Union prisoner-of-war camps. General Robert E. Lee was stunned by the reversal his army suffered at Five Forks and instantly realized that the Union forces had inflicted a mortal wound in the Petersburg defenses that the Federal army would soon exploit. He simultaneously issued orders for his army to escape to the west along the Appomattox River and sent word to President Jefferson Davis at Richmond that he could no longer protect the South's capital city.

After the setback at Five Forks, the end came quickly for Lee's Army of Northern Virginia. Barely more than a week later, on April 9, 1865, and with his army surrounded and no options for maneuver, General Lee surrendered the forces under his command to General Grant at Appomattox Court House. Colonel Rutledge said years later, "At Appomattox, when word got out, a lot of my boys smashed their guns against the trees and burst out crying. They were just wild with grief. But when General Lee came riding by, they drew up to him, clung to his boots and stirrups, and tried to kiss his hand. They knew he had done his best for them."[14]

The Boy Colonel, who spurned the hardships and perils of a horrific war, somehow managed to live through it all. He was there at the end to lead his mountain boys to the surrender point, where they stacked their smashed muskets and signed the parole papers. Out of more than 1,670 men whose names appear on the regimental roster today, only 74 of them, including Colonel Rutledge, survived until the very end at Appomattox. Although the Confederate and Union colonels presented the most conspicuous targets across the fields of battle during the Civil War, Henry Middleton Rutledge eluded all efforts by the Yankees to destroy him as he led the 25th N.C. into battle by waving cap on sword and shouting, "Don't let them take our front, Twenty-fifth, the Twenty-fifth has never had her front taken!"[15]

Return to the Low Country

Bidding farewell to his men after more than three and one-half years of living and fighting together was surely difficult and sad for the colonel. They all had suffered severely, especially during those last nine months spent in the trenches of Petersburg. Seeing brethren shot down to die slow deaths or saving the life of another was a common occurrence and had hardened and numbed those men of the 25th N.C. Yet, for Colonel Rutledge the surviving mountain boys that followed him into battle and had remained at his side were his family, and he would miss them.

After signing his parole papers at Appomattox Court House, the colonel struck out southward toward home, likely with his emancipated body servant by his side. Eventually he made his way back to the low country of South Carolina and his ancestral Hampton Plantation near Charleston on the South Santee River. This once magnificent manor, where Francis Marion, the Swamp Fox of Revolutionary War fame, had hidden out from time to time, was his inheritance from Grandmother Harriott Horry Rutledge. He found it much neglected and in a state of disrepair and ruin. In addition to the house, the colonel's estate included some 2,000 surrounding acres of former rice fields, hardwood and pine forests, and swamps. Also, approximately twenty African-American families recently freed from bondage still lived on the vast plantation lands. They had little means or ability to survive on their own account without continued sustenance from the dwindling plantation assets.

This magnificent Hampton Plantation that the Colonel would call home had once been an amazingly successful rice plantation. Its low-lying land was cleared of huge cypress and gum trees through the backbreaking work of slaves. These same subjugated men and women built canals, earthen dikes and a system of flood control that took advantage of the high and low tidal flows of the Santee River to flood and irrigate the rice fields. The hydraulic systems and agricultural process of planting and harvesting rice required the constant maintenance and attention of many slaves. And as one visitor to the area wrote, "During the summer months, rice crops waved over fields of thousands of acres in extent, and upon a surface so level and unbroken, that in casting one's eye up and down the river, there was not for miles, an intervening object to obstruct the sight."[16]

Growing rice at Hampton Plantation had been a tremendously rewarding proposition through the years, as tons of the cereal crop were exported overseas in exchange for treasure to fill the coffers of the Horry and Rutledge families. However, after the war it was impossible, of course, to compel newly freed slaves to work the fields. As the former plantation slave population gradually melted away, the rice-growing capacity of Hampton Plantation was reduced incrementally, until finally the commercial economics of the enterprise became unprofitable. The challenge of reviving and making his estate prosperous again would occupy much of Colonel Rutledge's energies over the ensuing years. Although he would not discover a method or means to revitalize Hampton Plantation, he would find fulfillment in other pursuits. These included producing and nurturing a large family of his own, enjoying the wild and beautiful land he was blessed to live upon, hunting, fishing and simply living contentedly with the life he had forged.

Colonel Rutledge married Anna Maria Blake not long after the war. She was the niece of Daniel Blake and probably became acquainted with Henry through his father and Aunt Emma's (mother Henrietta's sister) ties to the wealthy Blake family who summered in "Little Charleston," in the North Carolina mountains. The union, blessed with a son, Frederick, was to be short-lived as a result of Anna's premature death in February of 1872. However, in 1873 the Colonel wed again. Margaret Hamilton Seabrook, born on January 24, 1849, in the Beaufort District of South Carolina, became the new mistress of Hampton Plantation, and together the couple would form a lasting partnership in which to share life's pleasures and tribulations. The colonel and his lady, Margaret, became the proud parents of six children: Caroline Phoebe Rutledge, born 1876; Harriott Horry Rutledge, born 1878; Thomas Pinckney Rutledge, born 1879; Henry Middleton Rutledge, born 1881; Archibald Hamilton Rutledge, born 1882; and Mary Pinckney Rutledge, born 1886. This large Rutledge family was the latest of a long line of Rutledge-Horry families to make its home at the beautiful old Hampton Plantation.

Henry and Margaret tried valiantly to revitalize the plantation in the difficult reconstruction years following the war. But without the huge throngs of slave labor to support cultivation of large rice crops, the enterprise proved to be simply unprofitable. Archibald Rutledge, the next to youngest of the children, later wrote, "The freeing of the slaves had dislocated the entire agricultural system of the South.... Life on our plantation went on after the war, but it was a constant and disheartening struggle."[17] As the years went by and the returns from farming significantly diminished, bits and pieces of the land holdings bequeathed to Colonel Rutledge and his wife were sold for the much needed revenues.

In 1915 a traveler who happened upon the plantation was so taken by the experience that he wrote of his visit to the old house and the hospitality extended him. His account offers a lucid description of the stately manor and its hospitable residents:

> I can't remember ever having received such gentle courtesy and hospitality. As we walked up through an avenue of immense trees, I caught glimpses of an outline, until we suddenly faced this noble example of the mansion or big-house of the period. The owners are now impoverished, but proud of their family history. The growing of rice is no longer profitable. They are too far from market to make money on cotton, corn and tobacco, and lack the capital for fertilizer and labor. Ten miles from church and twelve from post office and store.
>
> How I wish I could adequately describe Hampton Hall. The front of the house faces away from the creek and has a portico laid with bricks, the roof being supported by immense wooden pillars in the arc of a circle.
>
> On the lawn a wide-spreading live oak tree provides abundant shade and owes its privilege to remain where it now stands to the fact that General Washington, who was once a guest, advised against a proposed attempt to transplant it to a place directly in front of the portico. Behind the mansion are the ruins of what were once quarters for the slaves, and stable, barns, and granaries....
>
> The bricks were brought from England but the lumber was hewn from these forests and swamps.... The rooms are large and the ceilings high. Tall bookcases line the walls of the living-room in which we sat and above them deer horns are hung in profusion.... One wing of the house is a ballroom of noble dimensions. It contains an immense fireplace, and Mrs. Rutledge said that there had been mirrors between the windows, which were lost during the War Between the States. When I said, "I can think of nothing but Christmas as I look about this house," she said: "Oh, we used to have the most wonderful times at Christmas! Young men and young women would come from miles around, the men to drive deer or fox-hunt or shoot ducks during the day, and we would dance until late in the night. The festivities would go on for days."
>
> There are twenty-three sleeping rooms in the house, the one I occupied being papered in a pattern of many years ago, and furnished with beautiful mahogany of the Colonial period. We were loathe to leave that enchanted place, feeling that we had been in close harmony with times gone by, to return never again — a social era which was hospitable, kindly and generous, made up of chivalrous and manly men and charming women.[18]

The colonel and his wife were impoverished, as the traveler observed, and were living from day to day. But they were still fiercely proud of their heritage and of the lofty station their name once held in Southern society. As the colonel reared his children through the years, they noticed a complacency and passiveness about him and an air of one totally content and at peace. Archibald Rutledge, who would later become a renowned writer of poetry and stories about nature and field sports and the first poet laureate of South Carolina, wrote a book about his mother and father titled *My Colonel and His Lady*. Within his work, Archibald shares intimate conversations with the colonel and reveals some of the philosophical convictions his father held. Here is an example of one such dialog:

> I used to find my Colonel calmly sitting in a chair in his ancient and gently disheveled garden, doing nothing but enjoying the balmy sunshine of the spring morning. Having given me a seat, he would begin to talk, by good fortune, of his philosophy of life.
>
> "People think I'm lazy," he confessed, "but it isn't that. I just don't like to waste too much time working. Hurry shows a lack of poise. I am still young enough and have energy enough to work hard. But I'm not persuaded that those who labor incessantly at anything have chosen the better part. I am a son of Mary. Archie, you must learn to be her son too."

Speaking of the colonel, Archie also wrote, "He had life's greatest gift, that of an understanding and compassionate heart. In that great respect, I never knew a richer human being." Archibald feared that his father might be hidden in the shadows and wrote about him so that others might know the colonel and love him as he himself did. Archie recorded the following words to describe Colonel Rutledge:

> That he was six feet tall; that one shoulder drooped a little because of two old wounds, one from Malvern Hill and one from Antietam; that he always looked and dressed like an English sportsman; that his fine head was regal in its carriage, with its thin aquiline nose, its eyes the color of the blue early-morning sky, its strong and tender mouth, half-hidden under the whit mustache; that the cast of his countenance was gentle, yet with nobility and pride and honor softly suffusing it — all these matters are in a way descriptive. But it was by his behavior that I came to know the real character of this engaging personality. Just as some moments out of the day's routine may take on the long radiance of eternity, so many of the things my Colonel said and many of the things he did are immortal for me. Having Huguenot blood in him, he had the Celtic power to make his slightest gesture count. I have seen him dismiss a great subject with a bare wave of the hand, and slay an imposter with the tilt of an eyebrow.

The colonel enjoyed a long adult life at his Hampton Plantation and the summer home in McClellanville, South Carolina, that his family owned. McClellanville was a small coastal village about ten miles away from the plantation. There the Rutledge clan could escape summer's hot sultry weather and take respite in the refreshing ocean breezes from their struggles to make the noble old plantation profitable. In the end, those struggles were for naught, as the place would never be brought back to its former glory. By one means or another, how-

Photograph of the Hampton Plantation circa 1940 (Library of Congress).

ever, the colonel was able to provide for his family and the former slave families that remained on the estate. He was forever proud of his heritage and of being a Southerner, and when the State of South Carolina made moneys available to its veterans, many years after Appomattox, he refused to apply for his pension. His son wrote, "Although he had fought as much and certainly had lost as much as any other man, my father refused to accept a pension. He said to me later, 'I did not expect to be paid for fighting for what I considered right; besides, some of the other old soldiers may need it more than I do.'"[19]

Although economic success was forever elusive to the colonel, he was blessed in other, less tangible, ways. After all, he beat very long odds and survived four years of a terrible war. And he had a loving family to be proud of—and they of him. The following words written by Archie Rutledge describe a man he cared for deeply and a man he truly admired and respected—his father, Colonel Henry Middleton Rutledge.

> Dr. Johnson once remarked that every man thinks meanly of himself if he has not been a soldier. My Colonel was almost unique in that, by the time he was twenty-four, all his wars were done. Had he lived in these days, he would have been offered (though he would not have accepted) wound-stripes, medals, bonuses, and pensions. He just came home, little more than a lad, with a great record behind him; and throughout his long life (he died at eighty-three) he never sullied that record. His chevrons did not tarnish, and always about him was the fiber of battle alertness and battle strength. Because of the fact that he had been through many cruel experiences, the most tragic of which was the fall of the Confederacy, his nature was made gentle rather than harsh by adversity. I never knew another human being more compassionate in his judgment of humankind. Was it not because his early introduction to passionate suffering and death had given him the power to see life whole, and deeply to discern human nature and human destiny?[20]

After a full life of almost eighty-two years, the colonel finally just faded away in June of 1921, like so many good soldiers, Confederate and Union, before him. He forged a life for himself and his family after the Civil War in the most difficult of Reconstruction circumstances. And as his son testified, he never "sullied" the fine record he forged as a Confederate warrior. Colonel Rutledge was interred next to his mother and father in the Flat Rock, North Carolina, cemetery adjacent to the St. John in the Wilderness Church. "His Lady" Margaret Hamilton Seabrook Rutledge would join the colonel in that final resting place only four years later.

Archibald Rutledge, the colonel and his lady's youngest son, returned to Hampton Plantation, after a career of teaching English at Mercer Academy in Pennsylvania. There he began a restoration process that would breathe new life into the noble old estate, and upon his death the Hampton mansion and plantation were left to the state of South Carolina. The house has been meticulously maintained and is open to the public at the Hampton Plantation State Park.

* * *

William Harrison Hargrove: "A Useful Citizen"

William Harrison Hargrove of Haywood County, along with many other thousands of enthusiastic young men across the South, volunteered his services to defend his homeland against foreign Yankee invaders. He, like most of those early volunteers from western North Carolina, was young and unmarried and the son of a mountaineer farmer. From the day that he signed his name on the enlistment roll, July 18, 1861, his life would forever be changed.

William served with the 25th Regiment N.C. Infantry Troops through the entire war, and rose from the enlistment rank of private to 1st lieutenant by the time he and the other mountain boys manned the hideous red trenches of Petersburg in 1864. Lt. Hargrove was finally captured at the battle of Five Forks on April 1, 1865, less than two weeks before Lee's surrender at Appomattox Court House. There is a story told of one of the North Carolinians apprehended at that particular fracas near Five Forks whose Federal captors shouted out to the unfortunate southern soldier, "Surrender, surrender, we've got you!" To this, the ragged and famished Johnny Reb reportedly hollered back as he dropped his gun, "Yes, you've got me, and the hell of a git you got!"

It is not clear who that distraught but proud North Carolina Rebel was, but it might very well have been Lt. William Hargrove. He was representative of most of the young Southern manhood who gave their hearts and blood for what they considered only the right thing to do. The following biographical sketch of this young mountaineer offers a perspective of the rural setting of his origins along the banks of Haywood County's Pigeon River and a glimpse at his Civil War career with the 25th Regiment N.C. Having survived the war, William returned to the Forks of Pigeon community of his birth and struggled to regain a foothold and start anew. This brief story reveals how Lt. Hargrove overcame reconstruction adversities and forged a successful life for himself, one that was filled with adversity and accomplishment.

Deeply Rooted in the Pigeon Valley

In the midst of the Blue Ridge Mountain Range, whose peaks protrude high into the sky over western North Carolina's Haywood County, a fertile valley lies astraddle the Pigeon River. William Harrison Hargrove was born into this Pigeon Valley in 1841 in a pioneer settlement called Forks of Pigeon. There, where the east and west tributaries of the river are joined, a community of mostly farming homesteads existed.

The first pioneers reached the Pigeon Valley at the onset of the 1800s as the Cherokee Indians retreated further westward into the remotest reaches of the mountains—their migration forced upon them through treaty after treaty with the English colonies and most recently the new government of the United States of America. Those original brave settlers of mostly Scots-Irish, English and German descent claimed the rich bottomlands near the rivers. Others arriving later settled in the coves along smaller streams and creeks and higher up on the mountainsides and along the ridge tops.

In the early years, before the river's power was harnessed by sawmills, the pioneers built small log cabins to live in. They used great care in choosing building sites that were near a good source of water, well-drained, and elevated so the flooding river waters or nearby creeks posed no threat. From the surrounding forests they

William Harrison Hargrove (North Carolina Department of Archives and History, Raleigh).

felled huge trees with axes and built the structures by stacking one log on top of another. The pioneer, wielding only an ax and adze to shape the logs, crafted the corner joints in an interlocking fashion to hold the logs in place. The most important element of the cabin, of course, was the fireplace, which was typically built out of mountain stone or river rock collected nearby and fitted together and fixed with a muddy mixture of clay and straw. Not only was this hearth used to keep the small cabin relatively warm during the cold winters, it also provided the heat for cooking and a source of light at night that beckoned the family to gather and enjoy the company of each other.

Farmers lucky enough to have tracts of bottomland were rewarded with its rich alluvial soil, which was easily broken and readied for planting. Higher up on the mountainsides the settlers were not so fortunate. There the soil was rocky, less productive and more difficult to work. No matter their lot, the valley's pioneer farmers were a hardy and determined sort. They fretted little over hard work, and through tremendous toil and exertions caused the Pigeon Valley to bloom with their precious crops.

Each spring, along about March or April, the valley gradually exchanged its dark gray shroud for a beautiful green veil infinitely spotted with colorful blossoms of the serviceberry, mountain laurel, rhododendron and dogwood trees. It was in this picturesque setting, with the scent of wild onion and damp earth in the air, that the early settlers exerted their energies to break the ground, using horses or mules to pull plows or by simply wielding hoes and crude digging tools. These exhaustive efforts were aimed toward raising corn and wheat crops to feed their families and livestock. Any surplus grain that might be realized could be bartered for necessities that could not be produced at home such as salt, sugar, iron tools, cloth, medicine and other goods. And it was not uncommon in the day for the farmers to trade their hard-won yields for the services of a doctor, hired hand, blacksmith, traveling cobbler, teacher or even a preacher. The grain crops were in this way the valley's treasure and the foundation of the local economy.

In those early days, the roads were important improvements that the Pigeon Valley settlers made to enhance the development of their community. Crops and goods had to be moved into, out of, and throughout the valley to the mills and to markets. This was facilitated somewhat during dry weather by their existing crude roads, which the laws required able-bodied men to work on. Often, however, especially during the winter months, these roads were no more than narrow traces of ruts and muddy washouts that offered little advantage to farmers opting to use them.

Just after the formation of Haywood County in 1808, the newly elected county officials ordered two wagon roads to be "marked out and made" to connect the Pigeon Valley with other outside communities. One road ran from Waynesville across Pigeon Gap (along present day highway 276) into the East Fork area. Another connecting the Beaverdam area (present day Canton) with the Pigeon Valley snaked along the Pigeon River, passing John McDowell's "flowery garden" (or Garden Creek), and connected with the Upper Pigeon Road previously mentioned.[21] In addition, the Western Turnpike, completed sometime around 1850, was the primary umbilical between Asheville and Waynesville and points further west. This critical road passed near where the town of Canton is today and served the Pigeon Valley folk as the principal link to the Buncombe Turnpike and, thereby, the outside markets in Tennessee, South Carolina and Georgia.

A mill and general store owned by "Colonel" Joseph Cathey was in operation in those early years near where the waters of the East Fork and West Fork rivers combine to create the Pigeon River. Cathey has been described as one of the most capable and influential men of his time in the county. His store was reportedly one of the largest and most successful around. It was stocked with a generous variety of supplies needed by the mostly self-sufficient farmers—goods and equipment that the farmers were not able to produce or craft for themselves. Integral to this mercantile business was the local post office, which occupied a small space within the store's walls and had the aptly named postal address of "Forks of Pigeon."

Nearby, the Cathey gristmill, powered by its huge 14-ft diameter undershot wheel and water diverted from the river, groaned continuously as the farmers' "gold" was ground between great granite millstones. The commerce and facility provided by the store and mill made these Cathey enterprises the hub of the local community and economy. It was here that settlers brought their valuable corn and wheat crops to be milled into cornmeal and flour, bought and traded for much needed supplies, and communicated with each other and the outside world.

The blacksmiths provided another essential service to the Pigeon Valley farmers. These were powerful and skilled men with an extraordinary ability to heat, beat, weld, and shape iron into useful implements and hardware over hot forges. Their iron fabrications and repairs were necessary, of course, for the settlers to build and maintain productive homesteads, the underpinning of their community. During the early days in the valley, William Hargrove's uncles, brothers John and Alfred Franklin Hartgrove, were local blacksmiths plying their skills as a livelihood for themselves and to the general benefit of their neighbors.[22]

As the Pigeon Valley settlement grew, at least three different churches were organized in the valley to provide for the spiritual needs and welfare of the people. Many of the hardworking pioneer families were devoted Christians and faithfully received religious and moral guidance at either the Baptist, Presbyterian, or Methodist church. These churches, and their associated camp meetings, were focal points of social activity and congregation during the early days in the Pigeon Valley. Camp meetings were always popular events, held usually in the late summer. Entire families packed up their belongings and traveled to the meeting grounds, where they, along with their neighbors, camped out and worshipped for entire weeks at a time. It was not uncommon for these epic religious revivals to be coordinated around the schedule of some renowned traveling minister or evangelist. In that case, full advantage could be taken of the oratory and spiritual gifts possessed by those dedicated and tireless preachers.

In 1838 a fine two-room schoolhouse was constructed to serve the community on land donated by Elijah Deaver near where the present-day Bethel Junior High School stands. It was a frame and board building with heavy brick fireplaces and chimneys anchoring each end, windows down one side and a door on the other. William's grandfather, William Manson Hartgrove, made the brick and built the two massive chimneys for the schoolhouse. In addition to this school, which was free to all students, subscription schools were not uncommon and parents or guardians could subscribe, or contract, with the teacher for their children's education. Not uncommonly, the teacher's fees would be bartered for bushels of corn or wheat, sides of meat, days of labor, and the like.

Life in the valley during those early times was surely difficult and filled with challenges and hardships not easily imagined today. However, residents of the valley found diversions from their daily work that tended to lighten their spirits and provided sparks of enjoyment and fun to keep their hopes kindled. Womenfolk, for example, could derive satisfaction from their laborious and vital homespun work. Significant amounts of their time and toil were exerted in spinning wool, cotton and flax into yarn and thread. The textiles produced in this manner were in turn woven, sewn and fashioned into artful and practical clothing and coverings for their families. Though tedious and demanding, this essential work surely provided enjoyment and pleasure to the pioneer women as well as a feeling of pride for their creations.

Hunting, trapping and fishing were, of course, vital pursuits of the menfolk which provided food for the table, clothing for the family, and furs to fend off the cold. But for the men and boys, these activities offered a welcome escape from their routine labors and diversions during the long winters. Additionally, the men were frequent visitors at Cathey's store and mill, where they could take delight in passing time with friends and catching up on the latest news, gossip, and tales.

There were plentiful opportunities throughout the year for everyone — men, women, children and young folk — to participate in community gatherings and activities. These proceedings provided excitement and a bit of gaiety and variety in their lives and included church gatherings and singings, corn "huskings" and hoe-downs in the fall, "quiltings" for the women and girls, barn "raisings," molasses-candy pulling in the winter, square dances and such.

Forks of Pigeon was not an extraordinary community, nor was it significantly different from others spread throughout the western North Carolina mountains. It was a typical rural mountain community that possessed the essential elements required for the citizens to work, worship, learn, and prosper. And it was into this setting that William Harrison Hargrove was born on January 31, 1841, more than 160-years ago.

William was the first child born to Augustus Columbus Hartgrove and Ellen Childress. Augustus was a native of Mecklenburg County and came to Haywood County in about 1823 as a 12-year old boy with his parents, William Manson and Mary McKinney Hartgrove. Ellen Childress was from Buncombe County and the daughter of Samuel Childress, who had relocated there from Tennessee. Over the years, as Augustus and Ellen added to their family, William gained the following siblings: Joseph Franklin born in 1844, Mary (Mollie) born in 1848, Augustus Alexander born in 1850, and Althea Caroline born in 1853. Another brother, Thomas, died at the age of one year and a sister, Amanda, died as an infant.[23] For a period of time, Augustus and his family lived in a small log cabin located in the Peter's Cove area in the Forks of Pigeon community.[24] Later he moved his family to lands along the East Fork of Pigeon River while he worked as an overseer on the Lenoir plantation owned by Thomas Lenoir. (Thomas Isaac Lenoir served as the first captain of Company F of the 25th Regiment N.C.)

Much was expected of the oldest son, William Hargrove, as his mother and father struggled to make their small homestead a productive and successful farming venture. Certainly his labors and efforts were primarily employed toward plowing, planting and harvesting crops and hauling them to the mill or market. However, William's mother, Ellen, whose lot around the homestead was not inconsiderable, required his attention and support as well. Her burdensome responsibilities included caring for the babies, cooking, tending the gardens, and producing essential products needed by the family, such as preserves, butter, quilts, and clothing. William undoubtedly helped his mother and lent his growing mind and muscles to these domestic endeavors.

As time allowed, during the long cold winters William was obviously able to acquire a more than satisfactory education, based on the achievements and success that he later enjoyed. It is suspected that for the first several years he attended sessions at Bethel schoolhouse — the same one that his Grandfather William Manson Hartgrove helped construct. Jonathan Plott, an able teacher for years in the area, may have instructed William at one time or another. It surely was apparent early on that William had more than ordinary scholastic ability, for the records indicate that his father sent him over to Waynesville to attend the private school of John M. McIver for more advanced study.

All of William's scholarly learning and innate reasoning capacity would be tapped as his twentieth birthday loomed and passed. State's rights, slavery, and secession were contentious political issues of the day among Southerners and Northerners alike. As a result, in 1860 and 1861, one rebellious Southern state after another voted to secede from the United States of America, and joined together in an independent confederacy to form the Confederate States of America. Throughout the South, young men were being asked to take up arms to defend their states and the Southern "cause." Eventually, the debate reached into the remote recesses of Haywood County's mountain fastness, and the twenty-year-old William Hargrove was forced to contemplate these serious matters, weigh his loyalties and make a difficult and far-reaching decision.

The Farmer's Son Joins the Rebellion

After wavering for several months, North Carolina finally voted to secede from the Union in May of 1861. The sentiment in Haywood County was not completely pro-secession, many sympathizers remaining loyal to the Union throughout the war. But the county moved quickly to form volunteer companies, and on July 18, 1861, William joined with a group of Haywood County men in a company that Joseph Cathey and Captain Thomas Lenoir were assembling. Soon thereafter William marched off to Asheville, North Carolina, where his company was combined with nine other mountain companies to form what would later become the 25th Regiment N.C. Infantry Troops in the service of the Confederate States of America. There at camps Patton and Clingman in Asheville, William began to learn the rudiments of being a soldier.

In September, William's regiment marched eastward from Asheville to a yet to be determined war theatre. Boarding a train in Morganton, the regiment rode to Raleigh, where uniforms were issued to the mountaineers, and then traveled on to Wilmington, N.C. Encamped at Wilmington for a short time, the soldiers were issued muskets and proceeded to hone their skills in musketry and precision drill and military maneuver.

The military actions of the 25th Regiment N.C. during the Civil War have been provided in detail in the earlier chapters of this book. In summary and approximate chronological order, the 25th N.C. fought or served at the following locations during the conflict: defensive duty at Grahamville, South Carolina, near Port Royal; defense of New Bern, N.C.; Seven Days Battles near Richmond, Virginia — Engagement at King's School House and Battle of Malvern Hill; capture of Harpers Ferry, West Virginia; Battle of Antietam at Sharpsburg, Maryland; Battle of Fredericksburg, Virginia; defensive duty in eastern North Carolina and capture of Plymouth; Battle of Drewry's Bluff in Virginia; defense of Richmond, Virginia; siege of Petersburg, Virginia, and associated battles — Battle of the Crater, Battle of Weldon Railroad, Battle of Fort Stedman, and Battle of Five Forks; and finally the surrender at Appomattox Court House.

William Hargrove participated in the entire four-year-long conflict, apparently without being seriously wounded. However, he did suffer from the ravages of camp disease, as did so many others, and was hospitalized twice. On March 21, 1863, 1st Sergeant Hargrove's name appears on the register of the C.S.A. General Hospital, No. 4, in Wilmington, N.C. He had dyspepsia, a malady associated with poor digestion. It appears that he was out of action for several months and spent part of that time on furlough back at Forks of Pigeon.

The second hospitalization was around August 15, 1864 (two weeks after the Battle of the Crater), when 1st Lieutenant Hargrove's name appears on the records of General Hospital No. 4 in Richmond, Virginia. They confirm that he was again suffering from chronic diarrhea with emaciation and dyspepsia and was granted a 30-day furlough, allowing his return to Forks of Pigeon to convalesce and regain his fighting strength. In October 1864, after recovering from the illness, William made his way back to the Petersburg trenches and his name reappears on the muster rolls. Undoubtedly William was on duty in the trenches near Petersburg when on July 30, 1864, Grant's huge mine exploded, triggering the famous Battle of the Crater. Company F and the rest of the 25th Regiment N.C. played a conspicuous role in this melee by helping to hold the tenuous Confederate line protecting the city of Petersburg. Tragically, Captain James Cathey of Forks of Pigeon, and William's close friend, was killed during the fierce fighting around that smoking caldron of confusion and death.

William entered the war as a private, worked his way up to first sergeant in March 1862, and then was commissioned to officer rank as 1st lieutenant in August 1864. From this point until the end of the war, he was sometimes listed as commanding the company in the company records. W.C. Allen gives the following account of "Captain Hargrove" in his book, *The Annals of Haywood County, North Carolina*:

> During the battle of Five Forks he [speaking of Captain Hargrove] rescued Lieutenant G.S. Ferguson, who was desperately wounded. In the affair, however, he was himself captured and sent as a prisoner to Sandusky, Ohio. He was released in June, 1865, and returned to Haywood County.[25]

In an earlier chapter it was noted that Lt. Garland Ferguson was severely wounded with a broken leg at the battle of Fort Stedman, which occurred just one week prior to the Confederate disaster at Five Forks on April 1, 1865. Most assuredly, Ferguson did not participate in the affair at Five Forks, contrary to what Mr. W.C. Allen recorded above. It is very likely that Lieutenant Hargrove performed the heroic act of saving Lt. Ferguson's life at the battle of Fort Stedman, not Five Forks.

Lt. William Hargrove was captured during the battle of Five Forks, which occurred less than two weeks before General Lee's capitulation of the Army of Northern Virginia at Appomattox Court House on April 9, 1865. Records show that he was sent first to City Point, Virginia, and then on to Old Capitol Prison in Washington, D.C. From there he was transferred to Johnson's Island, Ohio, a prisoner-of-war camp for Confederate officers, where he arrived on April 11 and was imprisoned until the end of the war. After signing the Oath of Allegiance to the United States on June 18, 1865, Lt. Hargrove was released from Johnson's Island prison and allowed to return home — for good.

The arduous passage home to the mountains at the end of the war from a northern Ohio prison inspires thoughts of Charles Frazier's novel *Cold Mountain*. During the Civil War, Frazier's heroic mountaineer character, Inman, flees from an eastern North Carolina military hospital and struggles courageously to return to his home on Cold Mountain — a mountain which actually looms over the Pigeon Valley. It is not difficult to imagine the many hazards and obstacles confronting Lt. Hargrove and the extreme hardships that he must have endured simply to make the journey back to western North Carolina. An account of the odyssey taken from his personal memoirs and diary is given below[26]:

- ➢Left Sandusky, OH, on June 19th on train
  - Traveled by train through Newark, OH, to Bellairs, VA, to Martinsburg, VA, and then to Baltimore, MD, arriving on 20th
- ➢Left Baltimore on 21st on a stock boat
  - Traveled on stock boat down Chesapeake Bay to Fort Monroe, VA, arriving on 22nd
- ➢Left Fort Monroe on 23rd on stock boat
  - Traveled on stock boat up the James River to City Point, VA, and then to Pittsburg Landing, VA, arriving on 23rd
  - Stopped off in Petersburg, VA, to look in on friends in hospital. Found all OK except

G.S. Ferguson, who was improving. [William stayed over in Petersburg waiting on his friend Garland Ferguson to get well enough so that he could take him home. After waiting until July 5th and then finding out that it would be another 3 weeks before Garland was well enough to travel, William continued his trip home, alone.]
- Left Petersburg on July 5th on train
  - Traveled by train to Danville, VA, arriving on July 5th
- Left Danville on July 6th on train
  - Traveled by train to Greensboro, N.C., and then to Salisbury, N.C., arriving on July 6th
- Left Salisbury on July 7th by train
  - Traveled by train to Morganton, N.C., arriving on July 7th
- Left Morganton on July 7th at 9pm and arrived home on July 10th at 3pm

A full three weeks were consumed in the trek home from Sandusky, Ohio. Lt. Hargrove relied on trains and stock boats to make his way to Morganton, North Carolina, where the rail lines abruptly ended. From there it can only be surmised that he caught rides on wagons and tromped on foot the rest of the way into the mountains and to his Pigeon Valley. It is a testament to Lt. Hargrove's character that he stopped off in Petersburg, Virginia, to check on friends recovering from wounds in the hospitals there. And he steadfastly remained at the side of his injured friend, Garland Ferguson, for almost two weeks waiting to assist him home. There was no sacrifice too great for those brave young Southern soldiers who had endured such terrible horrors. They fought side by side, slept and ate together, looked after one another, and had in fact developed bonds stronger than those of blood brothers.

Lt. Hargrove apparently returned from the Civil War mentally scarred from the cruelty and horrors he had experienced. And he harbored bitter sentiments toward the men from the South, and the North for that matter, that led the country into war. These intimate feelings he sheltered closely, yet evidence revealing them was left recorded in his notes and a diary that he kept. His diary and reminiscences have survived through the years in the loving care of his family, from which the following short excerpts are respectfully taken:

> Arrived home from this bloody ruthless and unjust war with a very sad heart with the thought of leaving so many dear friends behind me, never again to return.
> In this war just ended I have known many who did not want to enlist or volunteer, but were influenced by some of the above illegitimate influences [the influences Hargrove refers to are "newspapers of the day" and "big mouth politicians" that he mentions elsewhere] and now their bones are bleaching far from home or friends and their graves erased, not even a board to mark the lonely spot and now many of those same persons who influenced them into war are now condemning those poor unfortunate creatures and branding them as hot headed rebels. This is the pay you get for not saying "No."

These words need neither explanation nor interpretation. They express the bitterness and discontentment that the young Lt. William Hargrove felt for those leaders and politicians who tore the country apart. Many thousands of other Rebels would be similarly traumatized and carry home with them significant mental and physical burdens from the Civil War battlefields.

Beginning Anew

The Pigeon Valley that William returned to following the Civil War was much changed from the one he had left four years earlier. Fields lay fallow and overgrown with briars and thistle. Roads had not been maintained and were barely passable. Homes and barns were either derelict or in a state of neglect and ruin uncommon to the proud citizens that made the scenic river valley their home. All of these conditions were the consequence of the extended absence of the many young men who had left their families and homes behind to fight the war just ended. But those native sons were now back at home — the fortunate ones who had survived the war — and quickly began the work of making the fields productive again and rebuilding their community and their lives.

The Augustus Columbus Hartgrove homestead welcomed back from the war not just William but younger brother Joseph Franklin, as well, who had gone to war as an innocent seventeen-year-old youth. It is likely that William lived together with his parents and siblings for the next few years. He continued to labor at farming chores around the homestead, as well as to engage in other pursuits such as teaching school and making regular trips to distant market places. Also, there is evidence of involvement in a social club of sorts by William and some friends from the community. Confirmation of this is found in an old pocket notebook of William's, along with other tidbits and scribblings that reveal many interesting things about his life in the years immediately following the war.[27]

This notebook is identified on the front with the handwritten title *Wm. H. Hartgrove's Book, Lexington, Ky, Nov 9th, 1866*. It is apparent that William intended to dedicate the entire notebook to a trip he made to Lexington, Kentucky, but only eight of approximately forty pages have recordings associated with the trip. There are no clues as to the purpose of the Kentucky venture or who might have accompanied him. It is plausible that William traveled there to teach a subscription school, which for reasons unknown may not have prospered.

The young author begins the records in his notebook with "Kentucky Campaign — Left home on 9th Oct. 1866, Traveled by way of Asheville, Pt. [Paint] Rock & the Asheville road to within 8 miles of Greenville Tenn."

From this point, the notes list the many towns and river crossings that he encountered on the trip to Kentucky, along with distances between the geographical features. William arrived back home from Lexington around November 23, 1866, after a "campaign" of about forty-five days in duration.

The remaining space in the Kentucky notebook is crammed full of other notations that record expenses incurred on trips to markets, track attendance of scholars in the schools he taught, mark accountings of money owed to other people and owed to him, and simply document numerous noteworthy things in William's life. For example, there are records of at least two treks to markets in Augusta, Georgia. His scribbled lines record expenses for tolls, corn & fodder, horse collars, a wagon axel tree, sugar and cheese, and more. These market adventures normally took about one month's time to complete, and William made several of them over the years until the railroad finally penetrated the mountains.

Several pages in the notebook are comprised of attendance records for the subscription and public schools that William taught. In addition, he used the pages to denote the money owed to him by the sponsors of his subscription school scholars. The pages reveal that he opened and taught one subscription school session at Chincapin Grove in 1867. In August 1869 there are notations for another three-month subscription school at Chincapin Grove schoolhouse. It is apparent that he began teaching three classes at the public Bethel schoolhouse on November 22, 1869. Those classes he described as "Class 1st," "Class 2nd," and "Minor Class." A total of approximately 30 "head" of scholars attended that school session, including his sister, Althea.

At the very top of one page was written simply *Ben Franklin's* and under that heading along with the date of Feb 6, 1867, were listed names of club members and credits and debits for club initiation fees. From this scant information, it is surmised that William and several of his young friends founded a club called the Ben Franklin's Club. It may have been fashioned after the famous Junto which Ben Franklin himself formed many years earlier with young friends to discuss topics of the day. That club was dedicated to mutual improvement, which may also have been the inspiration of William and his friends—Jo F. Cathey, A.J. Long, D.B. Nelson, and R.A. Sentelle. Some years later, the Reverend D.B. Nelson became the first grand master of the Masonic Lodge in Waynesville and a principal at Bethel Academy. R.A. Sentelle would become the first county superintendent of schools. It is possible that William's novel club was a forum for these up-and-coming young leaders of the community to discuss politics, reconstruction issues, and other topics of shared interest.

Throughout the pages of William's little journal are many notations inserted in a random fashion which give some insight into the times and the young man's life. A sampling of these is listed below:

> Boar had a calf July 20th 1870
> Disease took the Jack
> Rose took the bull Augt 17th 1870
>
> Christmas Day Dec 25th 1866
> Frost bitten snow last night & cool today
>
> Christmas Day 1867
> Nice & pleasant spent part of the day at Mr. Chambers and the night at Col. J. Cathey's
>
> Deliver the mules to John Summey if he will receive them & the money $475.00. Two one hundred dollar bills U.S. legal tender & at least $175.00 in small bills.
>
> On April 14th, 1870 Jimmie Brown set in to work for a period of one month beginning at 12:00 at a salary of $4.50 per month.
>
> Mr Brown sent two head of cattle here January 5th to winter at 50 cts/per head per month. Took them away March 25th.

Miscellaneous facts, meticulous recordings and mysterious notations from the fascinating old personal notebook that William left behind open a window into his life during the first several years following the war. A glance through it has revealed how he was primarily engaged in farm work and teaching school from the middle of 1865 until the end of 1870. During the fall and winters, he inexplicably made one trip to Lexington, Kentucky, and at least two trips to the markets in Greenville, South Carolina, and Augusta, Georgia. And, odd as it might seem, this young farmer and schoolteacher, along with a few friends, founded and participated in an organization that they dubbed the "Ben Franklin's Club," the purpose or function of which is not clear today.

Another Hargrove and Cathey Union

William married Nancy Louisa Cathey on November 9, 1869. Nannie, as she was known later, was the daughter of William Burton Cathey and Lucinda Moore and the granddaughter of Colonel Joseph Cathey. The Cathey family was one of the very early families to arrive in Haywood County around 1800. William Cathey, Nancy's great-grandfather, broke through the mountain ramparts with the first wave of pioneers and was among the first to settle on the banks of the Pigeon River, near the forks of the east and west branches of that river. A generation later (in the early 1820s) William Manson Hartgrove, William Hargrove's grandfather, found his way into the North Carolina mountains and rooted the Hargrove family to the Pigeon Valley. It was from this pioneer stock that the young William Hargrove and Nancy Cathey were descended. Their marriage was just one of many Cathey/Hargrove unions that occurred over the years in the Pigeon Valley, producing solid working citizens who contributed to the development and prosperity of the community.

Immediately after making their nuptial promises, William and Nancy moved in with Mrs. Lucinda Moore Cathey, Nancy's widowed mother, and commenced to fashion a life together. The house in which they lived was situated in the Cathey Cove on the west side of the Pigeon River and near a large tract of Moore property where Lucinda had been born and raised. During that first growing season, William, along with a hired hand by the name of Jimmie Brown, raised his first crops on a piece of land from the Moore's property. Their efforts apparently were rewarded with a bountiful harvest, as William's notes indicate a month-long venture to the market in Augusta, Georgia, in late 1870. And not to be outdone during that first harvest season, Nancy produced the fruit of her and William's love with the birth of their first child, James Burton, on October 26, 1870.

In his diary, William made a note of building "some" cabins on the Moore place and moving into them during the winter of 1871 and 1872. The use of the word "some" probably refers to a stock shed or barn, in addition to a small log cabin that he, Nancy and baby James moved into. Apparently he had not completed the cabin, nor was the shed ready to shelter livestock. The diary offers the following hint of a tough winter: "moved to them (the cabins) on 29th of Feb. 1872 and then fell a snow 15 in. deep which found us in poor condition to receive it as we had no stables nor cracks filled in our cabin."

It is difficult to contemplate the hardship that the couple and their child suffered during that cold winter — especially poor Nancy. Being a dutiful wife and companion, she faithfully followed her husband, baby in tow and in the midst of a cold winter, to live in a log enclosure which had no mud-filling in the log chinks. During the late February blizzard mentioned in the diary, Nancy and one-year-old James were surely exposed to freezing wintry drafts inside the cabin enclosure. But the young family survived, and as spring finally crept into the Pigeon Valley there was more than warmer weather to be thankful for. On April 15, 1872, Florence Leona poked her head into the world for the very first time in a small rustic log cabin perched on a mountainside overlooking the Pigeon River.

From the following diary note, it appears that William made a crop during that growing season of 1872 on the Moore property, and also managed to purchase a parcel of land for which he took on some debt: "Made a crop on the Moore place but in fall found myself a good deal in debt for land & no visible means to get out." At first the debt must have been worrisome for William and Nancy, as there was "no visible means to get out," but in a short time they were able to come up with a solution to the dilemma. William found work with Nancy's grandfather, Colonel Joseph Cathey, earning a handsome wage of $16.00 per month. After working for the colonel from December 4, 1872, until January 24, 1874, William resumed his farming career and raised another bumper crop on Moore property. He recorded the number of bushels of corn and wheat and the fact that it "was a nice income." That year of 1874 was marked by at least two significant family events. The more pleasant was the birth of Nancy's third child, Joseph Alexander, who arrived on April 12, 1874. On a more somber note, the Pigeon Valley community was plunged into mourning and grief as one of its most revered residents was lost to them. Colonel Joseph Cathey died on June 1, 1874, after a fruitful and unparalleled life of exceptional accomplishment.

It is likely that the land William acquired in 1872 was carved out of William Moore's large tract — possibly the same piece of land where those first crude log cabins were constructed. Nancy's mother, a Moore herself, helped the young couple obtain the property. The county property records reveal that in September 1874 Lucinda deeded another 43-acre tract of land to Nancy, which had been Moore property as well. It is believed that William and Nannie continued to inhabit their small log cabin for a period of time and raise corn and wheat crops on their newly acquired property. In the winter of 1875–1876, William made two trips to the Augusta market in the company of his double brother-in-law, James Webster Cathey (sister Althea's husband and Nannie's brother). When they returned from the second of these trips in late January 1876, William found his father gravely ill, and only a short time later Augustus passed away, on February 18, 1876. Ellen Hartgrove, William's mother, would survive her husband for another twenty years.

William wrote that in June of 1876 heavy rains and a Pigeon River "freshet" flooded the whole valley and did tremendous damage to the crops and fields. Undeterred, he was able to replant the crops and make them in three months, barely completing his harvest in late September ahead of the first white frost tiptoeing down from the mountains. That winter was one of the worst in memory for those living along the Pigeon Valley. A temperature of 20 degrees below zero was recorded — the coldest on record for the valley. It was during this arctic spell that William made a journey to Texas, on January 15, 1877. Although he left no clues regarding the purpose of this trip, William presumably visited his younger brother, Alexander Augustus, who had recently moved to Texas from Haywood County. Likely there were affairs of their father's estate to be discussed and settled. William's diary shows that he returned home from the Texas excursion on February 5, 1877.

With the births of Theodore Augustus on June 6, 1877, and William Walter on September 18, 1879, William and Nancy's family was complete. By that time, they had surely outgrown the small log cabin and moved to larger quarters on their own property that could accommodate the growing family. Farming and making crops were still the primary sources of the family's livelihood, but William's intellectual gifts and personable traits were to open for him entirely different career pursuits.

Hack Hargrove: A Useful Citizen

"Captain Hack" was the name that most of William Hargrove's friends, acquaintances and valley folk used to address him as he progressed in years. There is no evidence to cast light on the origins of the nickname "Hack," but there surely is good reason to believe that the reference to "Captain" acknowledges his officer rank and distinguished service to the Confederate States of America. From this point forward, as the balance of William Hargrove's life endeavors unfold, he will be referred to or identified by his cognomens, "Captain Hack" or just simply "Hack."

Farming and weather were not the only matters preoccupying Hack Hargrove in 1876. The Haywood County records for that year show, surprisingly enough, that he was serving on the board of county commissioners. It is recorded in the archives that Hack voted against a commissioners' order to grant to an individual a license to retail spirituous liquors. This is the first instance found of his involvement in county political affairs. And the vote also demonstrates his strong belief in temperance, which would in later years gain for Hack the state's highest office with the Sons of Temperance organization.

In 1879 the records indicate Hack's appointment by the county commissioners to a five-person committee "whose duty it should be to devise a plan on which to build a courthouse." Obviously, Hack had established by this time an excellent reputation for himself, and the county fathers looked to him to insure that a good and reasonable plan for the erection of a new courthouse was produced. Hack and this committee did develop and deliver an acceptable plan to the commissioners, and their efforts resulted in the construction of the county's third courthouse, a brick structure completed in 1883. In retrospect, Hack's role in this project is surprising, given that it was such an incredible responsibility and undertaking for a simple farmer. After all, it had been just a few short years before that he called a tiny log cabin home and struggled to survive the elements and make a living for his family.

During that same year of 1879, the commissioner's court archives indicate that Hack went before the board of commissioners to "renew his bond as County Surveyor." The bond, in the amount of $500, insured that Hack would reliably and professionally fulfill the responsibilities of his position. The fact that he was renewing the surveyor's bond indicates that Hack was the incumbent County Surveyor, likely having begun as early as 1877. His bond was renewed in 1879 and again in 1881 when he was approved as surveyor for an additional two-year term. However, the commissioners' court records show that Hack resigned from the county surveyor post in 1882 with no explanation given for the resignation. As will be seen, there was good reason that Hack should relinquish such a desirable post.

The year of 1882 saw the arrival of the Western North Carolina Railroad in Haywood County. No longer did the farmers need to depend on long droves down the turnpikes to Greenville and Augusta to reach markets hungry for their grain products, fruit, cattle, and swine. The railroad allowed easy access to the markets beyond the mountains in the North Carolina piedmont and further on into South Carolina and Virginia. Additionally, local industries such as logging and tanning found the railroad a perfect outlet for their products. And the rail service invited other merchants to enter the western mountains and greatly facilitated the travel of tourists desiring to experience the area's beauty and climate.

The railroad would prove to be an economic boon and blessing to Haywood County, as well as to the small town of Pigeon River. This little river village, which later would be named Canton, was the western terminus of the railroad for a year or so, until construction extended the line on to Clyde and Waynesville. One can imagine the level of excitement and activity around the railroad station in Pigeon River as it quickly became the focus of commerce for the entire county. Construction of warehouses and other infrastructure to support the passenger and freight service was hurriedly completed for the coming of the first trains. To manage the railroad's business at Pigeon River, the WNC Railroad Company searched for a competent individual with a good business head, adequate supervisory skills, and proven credibility and influence in the community. They found all these qualities in a local native — Hack Hargrove.

It is now obvious that Hack resigned his coveted county surveyor position to become the first agent for the Western North Carolina Railroad in Pigeon River, N.C., in 1882. He had the total responsibility of running the railroad company's local business and accounting for every passenger and all freight coming in and leaving the station. A statement of account dated October 1882 from the Western North Carolina Railroad auditor's office in Salisbury, N.C. and addressed to "W.H. Hargrove, Agent Pigeon River, N.C.,"[28] lists the monthly credits and debits for passenger, freight and telegraph services. Freight charges to be collected that month totaled $1,514 and passenger ticket sales were valued at $332.

It is believed that Hack held the job of railroad agent for about five years. The circumstances or reasons for his leaving the railroad are not known. However, the railroad company was undergoing a time of fiscal and legal turmoil in 1882. Shortly after its completion to Pigeon River, another company, Richmond & Danville Railroad, acquired ownership; during the next few years they were in dispute with the North Carolina state legislature over the ownership rights to the railroad. This issue would certainly have been distracting and could have influenced Hack's retirement from the railroad business in about 1887.

Back at home, sadly, Nannie Hartgrove died on February 13, 1883. The reasons for her premature death are not known, but the passing of the thirty-four-year-old woman would leave Hack, his family, friends and the entire community in grief for an extended period to come. Not only had Hack lost a life partner but he was now faced with a troublesome dilemma—that of caring for his five young children and carrying on with his professional and political commitments. Although there are no extant records or information to explain how the family coped, it is likely that Hack's mother, Ellen, or mother-in-law, Lucinda Moore, moved to their home and partially filled the void created by Nannie's unfortunate passing. It is also likely that the older children, James, Florence and Joe, would have shared increased responsibilities around the farm, including the care of their younger siblings, Theodore and Walter.

Hack was elected again to the board of county commissioners in 1885, and in June of that same year the commissioners appointed him and two other members to constitute a board of education, possibly the first to be formed in Haywood County. This was surely a demanding and hectic period in Hack's life, for not only was he still farming and working as the railroad station agent at Pigeon River, but he was also fulfilling civic responsibilities with the county.

In June 1887 the records reveal that "Hack Hargrove came into Commissioner's Court and took the oath of County Surveyor." It is believed that this is about the time that Hack left the employment of the railroad company. Apparently he had developed such a high degree of influence in local county politics, as well as with the town of Pigeon River, that it was a relatively easy task to quickly regain the county surveyor job.

In 1888 Hack resigned once again from an appointed position in the county's service. His resignation from the board of education is noted in the records: "Honorable W.H. Hargrove tendered his resignation as a member of the County Board of Education which resignation was accepted with the thanks of this Court in behalf of the educational interest of this County for his valuable services." This action became necessary upon Hack Hargrove's election in 1888 to represent Haywood County in the lower house of the North Carolina state general assembly. In session from January 9 through March 11, 1889, Hack would have traveled to Raleigh by rail to tend to the affairs of the state assembly. It is more than likely that this was Hack's first exodus from the mountains to Raleigh since the Civil War, and undoubtedly he renewed old friendships with veterans from the days of the Rebellion who also were congregated there in the state assembly.

Hack Hargrove was for many years a Mason in Haywood County. Although little publicized, the Masons had a strong influence on the educational, political, financial and religious development in the county. In 1866 the first Masonic Lodge opened in Waynesville, with the Rev. D.B. Nelson elected as the first grand master. Joseph Franklin Hargrove, Hack's brother, was one of the founding members of the Waynesville Masonic Lodge. From this first Waynesville lodge, sprang other Masonic lodges in Pigeon River, Clyde, and Sonoma (Pigeon Valley).

Hack may have first belonged to the Waynesville lodge, but it is known that he was a member of the Pigeon River Masonic Lodge and later moved to the Sonoma lodge when it was created in about 1895. His involvement with the Masons, a fraternal organization which professed to "seek to make good men better and thereby make the world a better place in which to live," offered another avenue to improve the welfare of the community. Throughout most of Hack's adult life and until he was buried with Masonic honors, he devoted his energies through this organization to better the circumstances of those around him.

During the last decade of the 19th century and until his death in 1909, Hack Hargrove's endeavors in political affairs and surveying work continued. He served more terms as a county commissioner. Existing surveys and plats by his hand from this era are evidence of a continued surveying practice. A 1908 newspaper clipping, accidentally discovered between the pages of a musty old book, revealed that Hack was the manager and editor of a publication with the name of the *Canton Vindicator*. By that time, the Champion Fibre Company had constructed and started up one of the world's largest pulp mills in the once sleepy village known as Pigeon River. The town quickly grew into a thriving community around the pulp mill to support the commerce the giant factory provided. Pigeon River civic leaders opted to change the town's name to Canton and the *Vindicator* was one of the first, if not the first, newspapers produced exclusively for the citizenry of Canton. At the helm of this fledgling rag was Hack Hargrove, publishing and feeding news and stories of human interest to his good neighbors of Canton and the Pigeon Valley.

In addition to the *Canton Vindicator*, Hack also helped found another upstart newspaper in 1908 named the *Haywood Enterprise*. He was an associate editor of this weekly publication dedicated primarily to the support of the platform and activities of the Republican Party. Captain Hack's Republican bias very likely ran counter to popular sentiment in Haywood County at that time, so it can be surmised that he was devout in his politics and unafraid to express his political beliefs and thoughts.

In one of the early *Vindicator* editions appears an advertisement for "W.H. Hargrove — Real Estate Agent," in which Hack offered great deals on lots in the booming mill town for $100 to $300, including generous financing terms. There apparently is no end to Hack Hargrove's professional pursuits and interests, and other ventures no doubt remain undiscovered. Until the last year of his life, Hack remained active and prominent in the Canton community, and continued to engage in farming with his son, Joe, publish newspapers, and serve as surveyor for the Town of Canton.

Captain "Hack" Hargrove (courtesy of the Hargrove family).

On April 20, 1909, William Harrison (Hack) Hargrove, age 68 years, departed the world of the living and his beautiful Pigeon Valley. After an extraordinary and productive life, Hack was buried with Masonic honors at Bethel Cemetery. His funeral was widely attended, with the notable exception of Jim (James) Hargrove, his eldest son, who had gone out West in search of gold and adventure. Jim was working mining claims near Beatty, Nevada, when he received a telegram from his brother, Dr. Theodore A. Hargrove, notifying him of Hack's death. In response to this sad message, Jim wrote back to Theodore; the following short passage is taken from that letter: "What makes me feel so bad about it is that I didn't write to poor old Pa oftener. he certainly had a hard time of it through life but if I was only as good a man as he always was I would feel that I was ready to go any time."

Many others surely wished the same — that they were only as good a man as Captain Hack Hargrove. Hack lived an extraordinary life filled with highs and lows, failure and success, and numerous accomplishments. In his obituary published in a local newspaper, Hack was referred to as a "Useful Citizen" and a person who "has been closely identified with the affairs of the county, especially in the welfare and development of Canton." No matter what his pursuits, whether they be Confederate soldier, farmer, teacher, politician, surveyor or newspaperman, Captain Hack gave it his all and accomplished much. He was a useful citizen indeed.

Roster of Troops*

25th Regiment N.C. Troops: Field and Staff

Colonels
CLINGMAN, THOMAS LANIER. Appointed Colonel of Reg. on August 15, 1861; promoted to Brig. Gen. on May 17, 1862.

RUTLEDGE, HENRY MIDDLETON. Appointed Major of Reg. on August 15, 1861; promoted to Lt. Col. on April 29, 1862; promoted to Col. on May 17, 1862; wounded at Malvern Hill, VA; wounded near Petersburg, VA, on June 4, 1864; paroled at Appomattox C.H. in April 1865.

Lieutenant Colonels
DEARING, St. CLAIR. Appointed Lt. Col. of Reg. on August 15, 1861; resigned around April 29, 1862, under "anonymous charge of drinking too freely"; later served in Confederate cavalry.

BRYSON, SAMUEL C. Previously served as Captain of Co. C and appointed Major of this Reg. on April 30, 1862; promoted to Lt. Col. on May 17, 1862; resigned on December 10, 1864, by reason of disability from wounds.

LOVE, MATTHEW NORRIS. Previously served as Captain of Co. A and appointed Major of this Reg. on Nov. 5, 1864; promoted to Lt. Col. on January 1, 1865; paroled at Appomattox Court House in April 1865.

Majors
FRANCIS, JOHN W. Previously served as Captain of Co. D and appointed Major of this Reg. on May 17, 1862; wounded at Malvern Hill, VA; resigned Dec. 6, 1862, to care for family.

GRADY, WILLIAM SAMMONS. Previously served as Captain of Co. G and appointed Major of this Reg. on Dec. 18, 1862; wounded at "the Crater" in Petersburg, VA; died at Greenville, SC, of wounds and fever.

MORGAN, WILLIAM Y. Previously served as Captain of Company I and appointed Major of this Reg. on January 1, 1865; paroled at Appomattox Court House in April 1865.

Adjutants
FREEMAN, WESLEY N. Previously served as 2nd Lt. of Company C and appointed acting Adjutant (2nd Lt.) of this Reg. on August 21, 1861; promoted to Captain and transferred back to Co. C on April 30, 1862.

GRAVES, WILLIAM H. Previously served as 1st Sergeant of Company E and detailed as acting Adjutant of this Reg. in March–April 1862; appointed 1st Lt. and transferred back to Company E around April 28, 1862. Later served as Captain of Company E.

EDMONSTON, BAZIL B. Previously served as Private in Company C and appointed acting Adjutant of this Reg. on June 30, 1862; discharged around October 16, 1864, and re-enlisted as Private in Co. C. of this Reg. on Oct. 17, 1864.

GUDGER, JAMES CASSIUS LOWRY. Previously served as Sergeant in Company I and appointed Adjutant (1st Lt.) of this Reg. on January 26, 1865. Captured at Five Forks, VA, on April 1, 1865, and released from Johnson's Island prison on June 18, 1865, after taking the Oath.

SAWYER, JAMES P. Served as Private in Company A and appointed acting Adjutant of this Reg. around April 1, 1865. Paroled at Appomattox Court House, VA, on April 9, 1865.

Assistant Quartermasters
BRYSON, WILLIAM H. Previously served as Private in Company C and appointed Assistant Quartermaster (Captain) of this Reg. about September 1, 1861. Discharged about May 1, 1862.

MILLER, ANDREW J. Previously served as 1st Lt. of Company E and appointed Assistant Quartermaster (Captain) of this Reg. on May 30, 1862. Dropped from the regimental rolls on October 25, 1862.

---

*Source: North Carolina Troops, 1861–1865, A Roster, volume 7, Infantry, North Carolina Office of Archives and History, 1979, 1991, 2004; reprinted by Broadfoot Publishing Company.

Assistant Commissaries of Subsistence

SAWYER, JAMES P. Previously served as 1st Sergeant of Company A and appointed Assistant Commissary of Subsistence (Captain) of this Reg. in September–October 1861. Reduced to the rank of 1st Sergeant and transferred back to Company A in November–December 1861.

WALKER, JOHN W. Previously served as 3rd Lt. of Company G and appointed Assistant Commissary of Subsistence (Captain) of this Reg. on November 27, 1861. Dropped from the regimental rolls around May 30, 1862, "because of failure to execute bond."

ROBINSON, JOHN C. Previously served as 2nd Lt. and appointed Assistant Commissary of Subsistence (2nd Lt.) of this Reg. on July 8, 1862. Discharged around July 23, 1862, after his appointment was "canceled."

MILLER, WILLIAM D. Previously served as 2nd Lt. of Company I, 16th Regiment N.C. Troops and appointed Assistant Commissary of Subsistence (Captain) of this Reg. around July 25, 1862. Dropped from the rolls of the regiment sometime in 1863.

Surgeons

SATCHWELL, SOLOMON S. Appointed Surgeon of this Reg. on August 15, 1861. Assigned to duty at the military hospital at Wilson on March 26, 1862.

DOAR, STEPHEN D. Reported to duty as Surgeon of this Reg. around January 13, 1862. Later served as Assistant Surgeon of the 10th Battalion NC Heavy Artillery.

LUCKEY, FRANCIS N. Previously served as Assistant Surgeon of the 28th Regiment NC Troops and appointed Surgeon of this Reg. about March 31, 1862. Paroled at Appomattox Court House, VA, on April 9, 1865.

Assistant Surgeons

FLETCHER, GEORGE W. Previously served as 1st Lt. of Company H and appointed Assistant Surgeon of this Reg. on August 15, 1861. Resigned on May 4, 1862.

WEBB, ROBERT T. Previously served as Private in Company G, 41st Regiment NC Troops and appointed Assistant Surgeon of this Reg. on November 18, 1861. Resigned on June 5, 1862, "because (the) Medical Examining Board had reported unfavorably on his examination."

WATKINS, BEVERLY S. Appointed Assistant Surgeon of this Reg. on October 14, 1862. Paroled at Appomattox Court House, VA, on April 9, 1865.

Ensign

HUTCHESON, JOHN W. Previously served as Color Sergeant of Company A and appointed Ensign (1st Lt.) of this Reg. in March–August 1864. Wounded in the right arm near Globe Tavern, VA, on August 21, 1864. Right arm was amputated and he retired to the Invalid Corps.

Sergeants Major

GUDGER, JAMES CASSIUS LOWRY. Previously served as Sergeant in Company I and promoted to Sergeant Major of this Reg. on October 16, 1861. Reduced to the rank of Sergeant and transferred back to Company I on August 6, 1862.

HOWELL, ROBERT H. Previously served as Private in Company C and appointed Sergeant Major of this Reg. on August 1, 1862. Wounded in the neck at Fredericksburg, VA, on December 13, 1862. Dropped from the regimental rolls in January–February 1865, for "continuous absence without leave."

SCOTT, JAMES P. Previously served as Private in Company F and appointed Sergeant Major of this Reg. on January 1, 1865.

Quartermaster Sergeant

JONES, CLINTON A. Previously served as 1st Sergeant of Company G and appointed Quartermaster Sergeant of this Reg. on October 5, 1861. Hospitalized on July 5, 1862, in Richmond, VA, with gunshot wound. Returned to duty on July 15, 1862, and present or accounted for until paroled at Appomattox Court House, VA, on April 9, 1865.

Commissary Sergeants

YOUNG, JULIUS M. Previously served as 1st Sergeant of Company D and promoted to Commissary Sergeant of this Reg. on November 5, 1861. Reduced to ranks in May–August 1862 and transferred back to Company D of this Reg.

SMILEY, ROBERT. Previously served as 1st Sergeant of Company A and promoted to Commissary Sergeant of this Reg. around August 31, 1863. Paroled at Appomattox Court House, VA, on April 9, 1865, after taking the Oath.

Color Sergeant

ALLISON, BENJAMIN F. Previously served as Sergeant in Company D and appointed Color Sergeant of this Reg. on October 5, 1861. Wounded in the thigh at Fredericksburg, VA, on December 13, 1862, and died of wounds at Fredericksburg around January 2, 1863.

Hospital Steward

YOUNG, JULIUS M. Previously served as Private in Company D and promoted to acting Hospital Steward of this Reg. in July–August 1863. Promoted to Hospital Steward on November 23, 1864. Paroled at Appomattox Court House, VA, on April 9, 1865.

Drum Major

RICH, PETER M. Previously served as Musician (Drummer) in Company C and promoted to Drum Major of this Reg. on October 17, 1861. Reduced to the rank of Private in September–October 1863 and transferred back to Company C of this regiment.

Company A — "Edney Greys"

Captains

EDNEY, BALIS M.— Enlisted May 15, 1861, at age 49 in Henderson County. Appointed Captain on May 15,

1861. Declined to stand for reelection as Captain about May 10, 1862.

LOVE, MATTHEW NORRIS — Enlisted May 15, 1861, at age 30 in Henderson County. Appointed 1st Lt. on May 15, 1861, and promoted to Captain on April 30, 1862. Wounded at Malvern Hill, VA, on July 1, 1862. Appointed Major on November 5, 1864, and transferred to the Field and Staff of this Reg.

PLUMBLEE, JOHN S. — Enlisted May 15, 1861, at age 23 in Henderson County. Enlisted as Sergeant and promoted to 1st Sergeant on October 31, 1861. Appointed 1st Lt. on April 30, 1862, and promoted to Captain on November 9, 1864. Killed at Five Forks, VA, on April 1, 1865.

Lieutenants

COOPER, ANDREW, 3rd Lt. — Enlisted May 15, 1861, at age 25. Appointed 3rd Lt. on April 30, 1862. Died at Petersburg, VA, about August 9, 1862, of unreported cause.

EDNEY, JOHN B., 3rd Lt. — Enlisted December 28, 1861, at age 22 at Grahamville, SC. Previously served for six months as Private in Company E, 1st Regiment NC Infantry. Enlisted as Private and promoted to Sergeant on April 30, 1862. Appointed 3rd Lt. on December 29, 1862. Paroled at Appomattox Court House, VA, on April 9, 1865.

EDNEY, JOHN C., 3rd Lt. — Enlisted May 15, 1861, at age 30 in Henderson County. Appointed 3rd Lt. on May 15, 1861. Defeated for reelection on April 30, 1862. Later served in Company E, 62nd Regiment, NC, Troops.

FREEMAN, JOSEPH H., 2nd Lt. — Enlisted May 15, 1861, at age 35 in Henderson County. Appointed 2nd Lt. on May 15, 1861. Defeated for reelection on April 30, 1862.

MAXWELL, ANDREW C., 3rd Lt. — Enlisted May 15, 1861, at age 19 in Henderson County. Promoted to Sergeant on April 30, 1862. Court-martialed about November 12, 1862, and cashiered for unreported reason.

POOR, JULIAS A., 2nd Lt. — Enlisted May 15, 1861, at age 29 in Henderson County. Promoted to Color Corporal on October 31, 1861. Appointed 2nd Lt. on April 30, 1862. Resigned around October 8, 1864, for unreported reason.

Noncommissioned Officers and Privates

ARLEDGE, ELI, Private — Enlisted September 3, 1863, at age 37 in Henderson County. Captured at Petersburg, VA, on April 2, 1865. Released on June 22, 1865, after taking Oath.

BALDWIN, J.R., Private — Enlisted July 23, 1865, at Camp Stokes. Present or accounted for through February 1865.

BALLARD, REUBEN D., Private — Enlisted May 15, 1861, at age 21 in Henderson County. Transferred to Company H of this Reg. on May 6, 1862.

BEARD, JOHN W., Private — Enlisted January 5, 1862, at age 27 at Grahamville, SC. Listed as a deserter on April 23, 1862.

BECKNELL, JOHN L., Private — Enlisted May 15, 1861, at age 22 in Henderson County. Present or accounted for until paroled at Appomattox Court House, VA, on April 9, 1865.

BEDDINGFIELD, GEORGE W., Private — Enlisted May 15, 1861, at age 33 in Henderson County. Discharged on May 17, 1862, after providing Private Benjamin Hensley as a substitute.

BELL, JOHN F., Private — Enlisted May 17, 1861, at age 27 in Henderson County. Died in hospital at Richmond, VA, on December 6, 1862, of "pneumonia" and/or "bronchitis."

BOWEN, ELIJAH, Private — Enlisted May 17, 1861, in Henderson County. Discharged on July 1, 1861, for unknown reason.

BROCK, JOHN, Private — Enlisted May 15, 1861, at age 44 in Henderson County. Discharged on April 30, 1862, by reason of disability.

BROWN, JOHN, Private — Enlisted May 15, 1861, at age 30 in Henderson County. Discharged on June 19, 1862, by reason of disability.

BYERS, JAMES SIMEON, Private — Enlisted May 15, 1861, at age 17 in Henderson County. Discharged on July 16, 1862, under provisions of the Conscription Act for being under age.

BYERS, JOHN HARDY, Private — Enlisted May 15, 1861, at age 19 in Henderson County. Paroled at Appomattox Court House, VA, on April 9, 1865.

CARLISLE, JOEL, Private — Enlisted January 23, 1865, at Camp Stokes. Deserted to the enemy around February 7, 1865.

CASE, JACOB, Private — Enlisted May 15, 1861, at age 45 in Henderson County. Wounded in the head at King's School House, VA, on June 25, 1862. Discharged on July 16, 1862, by reason of being over age.

CASE, JAMES L., Private — Enlisted December 16, 1861, at age 16 at Grahamville, SC. Discharged around July 15, 1862, by reason of being under age. Reenlisted in Company H of this Reg. the same date.

CASE, THOMAS, Private — Enlisted September 3, 1863, at age 43 in Henderson County. Present or accounted for through February, 1864.

COCHRAN, JEPTHA, Private — Enlisted January 23, 1865, at Camp Stokes. Captured in hospital at Richmond, VA, on April 3, 1865.

CONNER, ALEXANDER L., Private. Died at Grahamville, SC, on March 22, 1862, of unreported cause.

CONNER, FRANCIS M., Private — Enlisted October 29, 1863, in Henderson County. Hospitalized at Petersburg, VA, on June 17, 1864, with a gunshot wound.

CONNER, HUMPHREY POSEY, Private — Enlisted May 15, 1861, at age 22 in Henderson County. Wounded in the right leg and in both arms at King's School House, VA, on June 25, 1862. Returned to duty in September–October 1862 and present or accounted for until paroled at Appomattox Court House, VA, on April 9, 1865.

CONNER, McCOY, Private — Enlisted March 14, 1862, at age 22 in Henderson County. Died in hospital at Wilson on July 4, 1862. Cause of death not reported.

CONNER, OBEDIAH GEORGE, Private — Enlisted May 15, 1861, at age 25 in Henderson County. Deserted to the enemy around March 5, 1865.

CONNER, ROBERT J., Private—Enlisted March 11, 1862, at age 22 in Henderson County. Died at Kinston on April 16 or April 22, 1862. Cause of death not reported.

CONNER, WILLIAM A., Private—Enlisted May 15, 1861, at age 29 in Henderson County. Wounded at Plymouth, NC, about April 18–20, 1864. Captured near Petersburg, VA, on June 17, 1864. Confined at Point Lookout, MD, and transferred to Elmira, NY.

CONNER, WILLIAM G., Private—Enlisted May 15, 1861, at age 24 in Henderson County. Furloughed on August 12, 1864, whereupon he failed to rejoin the company. Listed as a deserter on December 12, 1864.

CORN, ROBERT, Private—Enlisted January 23, 1865, at Camp Stokes. Deserted to the enemy on or about February 7, 1865.

CORN, WILLIAM, Private—Enlisted January 18, 1862, at age 38 at Grahamville, SC. Discharged on July 16, 1862, by reason of being over age.

COSTON, WILLIAM BAXTER, Private—Enlisted May 15, 1861, at age 22 in Henderson County. Wounded in the arm at King's School House, VA, on June 25, 1862. Absent wounded or sick until he was discharged on June 17, 1863. Reenlisted in the company on April 18, 1864, and later captured at Five Forks, VA, around April 1, 1865.

CROSS, BARZILLA G., Private—Enlisted May 15, 1861, at age 18 in Henderson County. Reported absent without leave around April 20, 1862, and later listed as deserter on August 1, 1862. Enlisted in Company G, 56th Regiment N.C. Troops on April 12, 1862.

CURTIS, ELIJAH, Private—Enlisted July 30, 1861, at age 26 in Buncombe County. Wounded at Fredericksburg, VA, on December, 13, 1862, and returned to duty prior to March 1, 1863. Wounded at Plymouth, NC, about April 18–20, 1864.

DAVIS, GEORGE W., Musician—Enlisted May 15, 1861, at age 27 in Buncombe County. Present or accounted for until transferring to Company H of this Reg. on November 28, 1861, in exchange for Private James N. McMinn.

DRAKE, ELIAS A., Private—Enlisted May 15, 1861, at age 23 in Henderson County. Wounded at Malvern Hill, VA, on July 1, 1862. Returned to duty in May–June 1863 and no further records after August 1863.

DRAKE, JAMES S., Private. Wounded at the Battle of the Crater near Petersburg, VA, on July 30, 1864. Captured by the enemy and took Oath around October 1864.

DUNCAN, W. HENRY H., Private. Previously served in Company G, 9th Regiment NC State Troops and transferred to this company on October 13, 1864. Captured at Five Forks, VA, around April 1, 1865, and released on June 26, 1865, after taking on Oath.

EARWOOD, JOSEPH P., Private—Enlisted May 15, 1861, at age 28 in Henderson County. Captured at Sharpsburg, MD, around September 17, 1862. Exchanged at Aiken's Landing, James River, VA, on November 10, 1862. Returned to duty and later killed at Fredericksburg, VA, on December 13, 1862.

EDENY, CALVIN, Private—Enlisted May 15, 1861, at age 58 in Henderson County. Discharged on June 18, 1862, by reason of disability.

EDNEY, GEORGE N., Musician—Enlisted May 15, 1861, at age 18 in Henderson County. Enlisted as Private and promoted to Musician in May–June 1863. No further records after February 1864.

EDNEY, HENRY C., Color Corporal. Previously served as Private in Company H, 29th Regiment NC Troops and transferred to this company around January 1, 1863. Promoted to Color Corporal in March–December 1864. Wounded in the left arm at the Battle of the Crater near Petersburg, VA, on July 30, 1864, and again wounded in the left thigh at Fort Stedman, VA, on March 25, 1865. Hospitalized and then captured at Petersburg, VA, on April 3, 1865. Released on June 16, 1865, after taking the Oath.

EDNEY, JAMES H., Private—Enlisted May 15, 1861, at age 16 in Henderson County. Wounded in the head at King's School House, VA, on June 25, 1862. Discharged on July 16, 1862, for being under age.

EDNEY, JOHN O., Private—Enlisted May 15, 1861, at age 24 in Henderson County. Discharged on July 1, 1861, for unknown reason.

EDNEY, JOSEPH L., Private—Enlisted May 15, 1861, at age 23 in Henderson County. Killed at Plymouth, NC, around April 18–20, 1864.

EDNEY, LEWIS M., Sergeant—Enlisted May 15, 1861, at age 18 in Henderson County. Enlisted as Private and was promoted to Sergeant on September 1, 1863. Captured at the Chickahominy River, VA, on June 4, 1864, and confined at Point Lookout, MD, and later Elmira, NY. Released on July 26, 1865, after taking the Oath.

EDNEY, MARVEL F., Private—Enlisted May 15, 1861, at age 19 in Henderson County. Died in hospital at Charleston, SC, on December 8, 1861, of unreported cause.

EDNEY, THOMAS A., Private—Enlisted February 14, 1864 in Northampton County. Paroled at Appomattox Court House, VA, on April 9, 1865.

ELLIS, W., Private. Paroled at Goldsboro in 1865.

ENLOE, ABRAHAM T., Private—Enlisted May 15, 1861, at age 23 in Henderson County. Hospitalized at Petersburg, VA, on December 9, 1863, with gunshot wound. Returned to duty on January 30, 1864, and later detailed as a hospital nurse at Richmond, VA, on October 13, 1864, by reason of disability. Captured by the enemy in hospital at Richmond on April 3, 1865, and paroled on April 24, 1865.

ENLOE, BENJAMIN F., Private—Enlisted May 15, 1861, at age 24 in Henderson County. Deserted in March–December 1864 but returned to duty on February 24, 1865. Later captured near Petersburg, VA, on April 2, 1865, and confined at Point Lookout, MD. Released on June 12, 1865, after taking the Oath.

ENLOE, BENJAMIN M., Private—Enlisted May 15, 1861, at age 53 in Henderson County. Discharged on June 4, 1862, by reason of "imbecility."

ENLOE, THOMAS J., Private—Enlisted May 15, 1861, at age 24 in Henderson County. Wounded in the hip and thigh at Malvern Hill, VA, on July 1, 1862. Returned to duty in January–February 1863 and served until parole at Appomattox Court House, VA, on April 9, 1865.

FEATHERSTON, AMBROSE A., Private — Enlisted May 15, 1861, at age 18 in Henderson County. Enlisted as Sergeant but reduced to ranks on April 30, 1862. Present or accounted for through February 1864.

FEATHERSTON, CALVIN R., Private — Enlisted May 15, 1861, at age 21 in Henderson County. Wounded at Malvern Hill, VA, on July 1, 1862. Returned to duty in September–October 1862 and deserted on May 16, 1863. Returned to duty and subsequently deserted to the enemy on June 4–7, 1864. Confined at Point Lookout, MD, and later Elmira, NY, until release on May 29, 1865, after taking the Oath.

FEATHERSTON, WILLIAM C., Private — Enlisted May 15, 1861, at age 16 in Henderson County. Discharged about July 16, 1862, for being under age. Reenlisted in the company on October 10, 1863, and wounded at Drewry's Bluff, VA, on May 14, 1864. Listed as a deserter but returned to duty on February 8, 1865, and present or accounted for through February 1865.

FLETCHER, LEMUEL J., Private — Enlisted May 15, 1861, at age 38 in Henderson County. Transferred to Company H of this regiment on July 25, 1861.

FORTUNE, JOHN P., Private — Enlisted May 15, 1861, at age 37 in Henderson County. Enlisted as Corporal but was reduced to ranks on April 30, 1862. Discharged on July 16, 1862, for being over age.

FORTUNE, MILLINGTON, Private — Enlisted July 30 1861 at age 28 in Buncombe County. Deserted on May 7 or June 19, 1863, and went over to the enemy. Took the Oath at Knoxville, TN, on March 14, 1865.

FORTUNE, RICHARD, Private — Enlisted May 15, 1861, at age 40 in Henderson County. Discharged around July 16, 1862, for being over age.

FREEMAN, ANDREW ERWIN, Private — Enlisted May 15, 1861, at age 22 in Henderson County. Died at Goldsboro or Kinston on June 21, 1862, of unreported cause.

FREEMAN, CLAIBORNE S., Private — Enlisted May 27, 1862, at age 18 in Lenoir County. Wounded at or near Richmond, VA, on June 28, 1862. Returned to duty prior to September 1, 1862, and present or accounted for through December 1864.

FREEMAN, JOHN TYLER, Musician — Enlisted May 15, 1861, at age 20 in Henderson County. Enlisted as Private and wounded in the right hand at King's School House, VA, on June 25, 1862. Absent wounded until December 3, 1862, when he was discharged. Reenlisted in the company as Musician on March 17, 1864. Paroled at Appomattox Court House, VA, on April 9, 1865.

FREEMAN, LARKIN H., 1st Sergeant — Enlisted March 14, 1862, at age 22 in Haywood County. Promoted to 1st Sergeant on September 1, 1863, and present or accounted for through February 1865.

FREEMAN, ROBERTSON A., Chief Musician — Enlisted May 15, 1861, at age 25 in Henderson County. Enlisted as Sergeant but reduced to ranks on April 30, 1862. Promoted to Musician in September–October 1863 and appointed Chief Musician in January–February 1865. Paroled at Appomattox Court House, VA, on April 9, 1865.

FREEMAN, RUFUS K., Private — Enlisted May 9, 1863, at age 19 in Lenoir County. Deserted in March–November 1864.

FREEMAN, SPENCER M., Private — Enlisted April 16, 1864, in Halifax County. Paroled at Appomattox Court House, VA, on April 9, 1865.

FREEMAN, THOMAS G., Private — Enlisted May 15, 1861, at age 17 in Henderson County. Discharged on December 5, 1861, for unreported reason. Reenlisted in the company on March 14, 1862, and later died in hospital at Drewry's Bluff, VA, on August 4, 1862, of unreported cause.

GARREN, ANDERSON, Private — Enlisted May 15, 1861, at age 35 in Henderson County. Discharged on July 16, 1862, for being over age. Later served in Company G, 34th Regiment NC Troops.

GILBERT, THOMAS W., Private — Enlisted January 5, 1862, at age 36 at Grahamville, SC. Discharged on July 16, 1862, for being over age.

HEAD, ANDERSON C., Corporal — Enlisted May 15, 1861, at age 28 in Henderson County. Wounded in the right thigh at Malvern Hill, VA, on July 1, 1862. Returned on October 14, 1862, and promoted to Corporal on September 1, 1863. Hospitalized at Petersburg, VA, on March 25, 1865, with a gunshot wound of the left eye and/or burn of the face and the head. Captured in hospital at Richmond, VA, on April 3, 1865, and released on June 30, 1865, after taking the Oath.

HEAD, JOHN W., Private — Enlisted July 23, 1863, at age 18 at Petersburg, VA. Hospitalized at Richmond, VA, on May 16, 1864, with a gunshot wound. Returned to duty January–February 1865 and paroled at Appomattox Court House, VA, on April 9, 1865.

HEFNER, SYLVANUS, Private — Enlisted January 23, 1863, at Camp Stokes. Present or accounted for through February 1865.

HENSLEY, BENJAMIN T., Private — Enlisted May 17, 1862, at age 17 in Lenoir County. Enlisted as a substitute for Private George W. Beddingfield. Hospitalized at Richmond, Virginia on May 13, 1864, and no further records.

HENSLEY, CHESTER K., Private — Enlisted May 15, 1861, at age 25 in Henderson County. Promoted to Corporal on April 30, 1862, but reduced to ranks in July 1862. Died in Petersburg, VA, hospital on July 19, 1862, of "typhoid fever."

HUDGINS, LEANDER, Private — Enlisted May 15, 1861, at age 24 in Henderson County. Died in hospital at Petersburg, VA, on June 28, 1862, of "febris remittens."

HUDGINS, RICHARD, Private — Enlisted May 15, 1861, at age 22 in Henderson County. Discharged on January 31, 1862, for unreported reason.

HUTCHESON, JOHN W., Color Sergeant — Enlisted May 15, 1861, at age 20 in Henderson County. Promoted to Color Corporal in September–October 1862 and to Color Sergeant on January 1, 1863. Promoted to Ensign (1st Lieutenant) in March–August 1864 and transferred to Field and Staff of this Reg.

JOHNSON, JOSEPH P., Corporal—Enlisted May 15, 1861, at age 19 in Henderson County. Promoted to Corporal in January–February 1862 and to Sergeant on April 30, 1862. Reduced to ranks in September–October 1863 but promoted to Corporal in March–December 1864. Captured at Amelia Court House, VA, on April 3, 1865, and confined at Point Lookout, MD. Released on June 28, 1865, after taking the Oath.

JONES, JAMES, Private—Enlisted October 28, 1863, at age 38 in Halifax County. No further records.

JONES, JOHN W., Private. Previously served in Company A, 23rd Regiment NC Troops and transferred to this company on January 27, 1865. Captured near Petersburg, VA, on April 1, 1865, and confined at Point Lookout, MD. Released on June 28, 1865, after taking the Oath.

JONES, WILLIAM G., Private—Enlisted May 15, 1861, at age 19 in Henderson County. Died in hospital at Richmond, VA, on November 4, 1862, of "endocarditis."

KING, HIRAM P.M. D., Private. Previously served in Company G, 56th Regiment NC Troops and transferred to this company on February 13 or February 25, 1863. Deserted and went over to the enemy around October 1, 1864. Confined at Louisville, KY, on October 12, 1864, and released around October 14, 1864, after taking the Oath.

KING, JAMES W., Private—Enlisted May 16, 1862, at age 16 in Lenoir County. Enlisted as a substitute for Private John J. King. Wounded in the arm at King's School House, VA, on June 25, 1862, and returned to duty in September–October 1862. Transferred to Company A, 23rd Regiment NC Troops on January 27, 1865.

KING, JOHN J., Private—Enlisted May 15, 1861, at age 36 in Henderson County. Discharged on May 26, 1862, after providing Private James W. King as a substitute. Reenlisted in the company on December 24, 1863. Captured by the enemy in March–December 1864.

KING, JOSEPH U., Private—Enlisted May 15, 1861, at age 36 in Henderson County. Discharged on July 16, 1862, for being over age.

KING, ROBERT J., Private—Enlisted May 15, 1861, at age 21 in Henderson County. Discharged on December 5, 1861, by reason of disability.

KUYKENDALL, JOHN S.—Enlisted March 28, 1864. NC pension records indicate he enlisted on March 28, 1864, for the war. No further records.

LAUGHTER, ALLEN, Private. Discharged on May 30, 1862. No further records.

LAUGHTER, ARTHUR, Private—Enlisted May 15, 1861, at age 16 in Henderson County. Discharged on July 16, 1862, for being under age. Reenlisted in Company F of this Reg. the same date.

LAUGHTER, BIRD A., Private. Previously served in Company I, 16th Regiment NC Troops and enlisted in this company about September 3, 1863. Deserted on February 5, 1864.

LAUGHTER, HAMPTON, Private—Enlisted May 15, 1861, at age 22 in Henderson County. Wounded at Malvern Hill, VA, on July 1, 1862. Absent wounded or absent sick through December 1863 and reported absent on detached service in January–February 1864. No further records.

LAUGHTER, ISAIAH, Private—Enlisted May 15, 1861, at age 21 in Henderson County. Present or accounted for through February 1864. No further records.

LAUGHTER, JOHN R., Private—Enlisted September 15, 1863, in Henderson County. Captured near Petersburg, VA, on April 2, 1865. Confined at Point Lookout, MD, where he died on June 10, 1865, of "dia[rrhoea] chro[nic]."

LAUGHTER, SHADRACH L., Private—Enlisted March 14, 1862, in Henderson County. Discharged on May 30, 1862, by reason of disability.

LEDBETTER, THOMAS Q. North Carolina pension records indicate he enlisted in August 1864. No further records.

LEE, JOHN B., Private—Enlisted September 23, 1863, at Camp Vance. Wounded at Petersburg, VA, around June 17, 1864, and returned to duty prior to January 1, 1865. Captured at Fort Stedman, VA, on March 25, 1865, and confined at Point Lookout, MD. Released on June 28, 1865, after taking the Oath.

LEWIS, HENRY R., Private—Enlisted May 15, 1861, at age 47 in Henderson County. Discharged on July 16, 1862, for being over age.

LEWIS, JOHN G., Private—Enlisted May 15, 1861, at age 20 in Henderson County. Died in hospital at Wilson on June 29, 1862, of unreported cause.

LOVE, JOHN W., Sergeant—Enlisted May 15, 1861, at age 23 in Henderson County. Promoted to Sergeant on August 25, 1862. Captured near Petersburg, VA, on April 2, 1865, and confined at Point Lookout, MD. Released on June 28, 1865, after taking the Oath.

LYDA, ISAAC M., Private—Enlisted May 15, 1861, at age 44 in Henderson County. Enlisted as a Sergeant but reduced to ranks on April 30, 1862. Discharged on July 16, 1862, for being over age.

LYDA, JACOB M., Private—Enlisted May 15, 1861, at age 18 in Henderson County. Discharged on April 22, 1862, by reason of disability. Reenlisted in the company on September 15, 1863, and present or accounted for through February 1865.

LYDA, JAMES W., Jr., Private—Enlisted January 5, 1862, at age 17 in Henderson County. Discharged on July 16, 1862, for being under age.

LYDA, JAMES W., Sr., Private—Enlisted May 15, 1861, at age 57 in Henderson County. Discharged on June 5, 1862, by reason of disability.

LYDA, JOHN W., Private—Enlisted July 30, 1861, at age 17 in Buncombe County. Discharged on July 16, 1862, for being under age.

LYDA, JOSEPH E., Musician—Enlisted May 15, 1861, at age 23 in Henderson County. Promoted to Sergeant on April 30, 1862, and to 1st Sergeant in January–February 1863. Appointed Musician in September–October 1863. Captured at Amelia Court House, VA, on April 3, 1865, and confined at Point Lookout, MD. Released on June 28, 1865, after taking the Oath.

LYDA, LEANDER, Private—Enlisted May 15, 1861, at age 35 in Henderson County. Discharged on July 16, 1862, for being over age.

LYDA, PINKNEY, Private — Enlisted January 8, 1864. Discharged on April 28, 1865. No further records.

McKILLOP, HENRY C., Private — Enlisted September 23, 1864, at Camp Vance. Deserted to the enemy around March 5, 1865, and confined at Washington, D.C. Released around March 8, 1865, after taking the Oath.

McKILLOP, JACOB, Private — Enlisted May 15, 1861, at age 21 in Henderson County. Wounded at Malvern Hill, VA, on July 1, 1862. Died at Richmond, VA, on July 5, 1862, of wounds.

McKILLOP, JOHN A., Sergeant — Enlisted May 15, 1861, at age 20 in Henderson County. Promoted to Corporal on August 1, 1863, and to Sergeant on an unspecified date in 1864. Captured near Petersburg, VA, on June 17, 1864, and confined at Point Lookout, MD. and later transferred to Elmira, NY, around July 28, 1864. Died at Elmira on December 27, 1864, of "pneumonia."

McKILLOP, WILLIAM W., Private — Enlisted March 14, 1862, at age 24 in Henderson County. Died in hospital at Richmond, VA, on November 7, 1862, of "chronic diarrhoea."

McMINN, JAMES N., Private. Previously served in Company H of this Reg. and transferred to this company on November 28, 1861, in exchange for Private George W. Davis. Discharged on July 16, 1862, under provisions of the Conscription Act.

MARSHALL, JOHN H., Private — Enlisted May 15, 1861, at age 25 in Henderson County. Died at Grahamville, SC, on December 17, 1861, of unreported cause.

MAXWELL, ABRAHAM T., Corporal — Enlisted May 15, 1861, at age 18 in Henderson County. Promoted to Corporal on April 30, 1862, and to Sergeant in January–February 1863. Reduced to ranks in September–October 1863 and again promoted to Corporal on an unspecified date in 1864. Captured at Five Forks, VA, on April 1, 1865, and confined at Point Lookout, MD. Released on June 29, 1865, after taking the Oath.

MAXWELL, ALEXANDER LAYAYETTE, Private — Enlisted September 15, 1863, in Henderson County. Wounded in the right shoulder at Drewry's Bluff, VA, on May 16, 1864, and returned to duty prior to January 1, 1865. Captured near Petersburg, VA, on April 2, 1865, and confined at Point Lookout, MD. Released on June 15, 1865, after taking the Oath.

MAXWELL, JAMES H., Private — Enlisted May 15, 1861, at age 21 in Henderson County. Enlisted as Sergeant but was reduced to ranks on April 30, 1862. Promoted to Sergeant in January–February 1863. Appointed Musician in September–October 1863 but reduced to ranks after February 28, 1865. Paroled at Appomattox Court House, VA, on April 9, 1865.

MAXWELL, JAMES M., Private — Enlisted May 15, 1861, at age 26 in Henderson County. Present or accounted for through February 1864 and later killed at Drewry's Bluff, VA (probably in May 1864).

MAXWELL, JESSE, Private — Enlisted May 15, 1861, at age 21 in Henderson County. Present or accounted for through February 1864.

MAXWELL, JONATHAN A., Private — Enlisted May 15, 1861, at age 35 in Buncombe County. Discharged on July 16, 1862, for being over age.

MAXWELL, SAMUEL, Private — Enlisted December 28, 1863, in Halifax County. Present or accounted for through February 1864 and then reported absent without leave in March–December 1864. Dropped from the rolls of the company on February 17, 1865.

MITCHELL, JOSEPH W., Sergeant — Enlisted May 15, 1861, at age 23 in Henderson County. Promoted to Corporal on August 25, 1862, and to Sergeant in March–December 1864. Captured near Petersburg, VA, on April 2, 1865, and confined at Point Lookout, MD. Released on June 29, 1865, after taking the Oath.

MORRISON, DAVID M., Private — Enlisted May 15, 1861, at age 22 in Henderson County. Wounded at Sharpsburg, MD, on September 17, 1862. Returned to duty and deserted around May 16, 1863. Apparently enlisted in the 20th Regiment NC Troops on an unspecified date while absent without leave from this company.

MORRISON, JAMES E., Private — Enlisted July 30, 1861, at age 18 in Buncombe County. Promoted to Corporal in January–February 1863 and reduced to ranks on August 1, 1863. Deserted to the enemy around March 1, 1864, and confined at Fort Monroe, VA. Released around March 14, 1864, after taking the Oath.

MORRISON, JONATHAN, Private — Enlisted September 12, 1861, at age 35 in Buncombe County. Discharged on July 16, 1862, for being over age.

MORRISON, WILLIAM J., Musician — Enlisted November 28, 1861, at age 20 at Grahamville, SC. Captured at Frederick, MD, on September 12, 1862, and confined at Fort Delaware, DE. Paroled and exchanged at Aiken's Landing, James River, VA, on November 10, 1862. Returned to duty prior to January 1, 1863, and promoted to Musician (Fifer) in May–June 1863. Deserted to the enemy around March 17, 1864, and took Oath at Knoxville, TN, on November 14, 1864.

NELSON, WILLIAM D., Private — Enlisted May 15, 1861, at age 24 in Henderson County. Hospitalized at Farmville, VA, on December 21, 1862, with "finger bitten off." Returned to duty on February 9, 1863, and transferred to Company G, 56th Regiment NC Troops on February 13 or February 25, 1863.

NEWSOM, WILLIAM A., Private — Enlisted May 15, 1861, at age 22 in Henderson County. Promoted to 1st Sergeant on April 30, 1862. Wounded at King's School House, VA, on June 25, 1862. Reported absent wounded and absent without leave through September–December 1862. Reduced to ranks in September–October 1862. Returned to duty in January–February 1863 and present or accounted for through February 1864. No further records.

NIX, FRANCIS, Private — Enlisted May 15, 1861, at age 39 in Henderson County. Wounded at Malvern Hill, VA, on July 1, 1862. Discharged on July 16, 1862, for being over age. Reenlisted in the company on September 15, 1863. Reported under arrest in November–December 1864. Returned to duty in January–February 1865. Captured near Petersburg, VA, on

April 2, 1865, and confined at Point Lookout, MD. Released on June 29, 1865, after taking Oath.

NIX, JOHN, Private — Enlisted May 15, 1861, at age 19 in Henderson County. Deserted on April 9, 1863, but reported present and under arrest in May–June 1863. Returned to duty in July–August 1863 and wounded in the right leg at Petersburg, VA, on June 19, 1864. Right leg amputated and reported absent wounded through February 1865.

NIX, JONATHAN P., Private — Enlisted May 15, 1861, at age 25 in Henderson County. Wounded at Sharpsburg, MD, on September 17, 1862.

NIX, WILLIAM, Private — Enlisted May 15, 1861, at age 28 in Henderson County. Died at Goldsboro around April 22, 1862, of unreported cause.

OWENBY, FRANCIS M., Private — Enlisted May 15, 1861, at age 21 in Henderson County. Wounded at Malvern Hill, VA, on July 1, 1862. Died in hospital at Richmond, VA, on August 16 or August 29, 1862. Cause of death not reported.

OWENBY, HAMPTON W.P., Private — Enlisted May 15, 1861, at age 31 in Henderson County. Deserted on April 9, 1863, and apprehended around September 9, 1863. Returned to duty in January–February 1864 and served until parole at Appomattox Court House, VA, on April 9, 1865.

OWENBY, HUMPHREY P., Private — Enlisted May 15, 1861, at age 29 in Henderson County. Discharged on July 16, 1862, under the provisions of the Conscription Act.

OWENBY, JOHN L., Private — Enlisted May 15, 1861, at age 23 in Henderson County. Deserted on September 1, 1862, and returned to duty prior to December 13, 1862, when he was wounded in the right leg at Fredericksburg, VA. Absent wounded through August 1863 and deserted again around September 25, 1863. Went over to the enemy and took the Oath at Knoxville, TN, on May 9, 1864.

OWENS, BUTLER, — Enlisted September 1861. No further records.

PARIS, DAVID, Private — Enlisted January 5, 1862, at age 30 at Grahamville, SC. Died in hospital at Drewry's Bluff, VA, on August 16, 1862, of unreported cause.

PAYNE, CARY J., Private — Enlisted May 15, 1861, at age 22 in Henderson County. Wounded at Malvern Hill, VA, on July 1, 1862, and returned to duty on August 11, 1862. Captured near Petersburg, VA, on June 17, 1864, and confined at Point Lookout, MD, and later transferred to Elmira, NY, on July 27, 1864. Died at Elmira on February 2, 1865, of "pneumonia."

QUINN, JOSEPH F., Private — Enlisted May 15, 1861, at age 22 in Henderson County. Deserted on September 2, 1862.

REECE, DAVID M., Private — Enlisted June 1, 1862, at age 36 in Lenoir County. Enlisted as a substitute. Deserted on October 9, 1862, but returned to duty in March–April 1863. Deserted to the enemy around June 10, 1863, and confined at Washington, D.C. and later transferred to Philadelphia, Pennsylvania on June 21, 1863. Released around June 24, 1863, after taking the Oath.

REED, JOHN C., Corporal — Enlisted May 15, 1861, at age 21 in Henderson County. Promoted to Corporal on April 30, 1862. Died in hospital at Wilson on July 7, 1862, of "typhoid fever."

REESE, HENRY C., Private — Enlisted February 14, 1864, in Halifax County. Hospitalized at Petersburg, VA, on June 17, 1864, with a gunshot wound of the right buttock and died of wound at Petersburg on August 28, 1864.

REESE, JAMES, Corporal — Enlisted May 15, 1861, at age 20 in Henderson County. Promoted to Corporal on April 30, 1862. Captured near Petersburg, VA, on June 17, 1864, and confined at Point Lookout, MD, and later transferred to Elmira, NY, on July 27, 1864. Released at Elmira on July 3, 1865, after taking the Oath.

RHODES, ELI, Private — Enlisted September 15, 1863, at Camp Vance. Wounded near Petersburg, VA, on September 1, 1864, and returned to duty prior to January 1, 1865. Present or accounted for through February 1865.

RHODES, JOHN, Private — Enlisted September 15, 1863, at Camp Vance. Captured at Fort Stedman, VA, on March 25, 1865, and confined at Point Lookout, MD, where he died on June 10, 1865, of "measles."

RICE, WILSON — Enlisted April 1862. No further records.

RIMER, PULASKI, Private — Enlisted June 17, 1864, at Drewry's Bluff, VA. Present or accounted for through February 1864. No further records.

ROBERTSON, ALLEN, Private — Enlisted May 15, 1861, at age 38 in Henderson County. Enlisted as Musician (Fifer) but reduced to ranks in March–April 1862. Reappointed Musician in September–October 1862. Discharged on February 13, 1863, for being over age. Reenlisted in the company with the rank of Private on June 17, 1863, and later wounded in the left thigh at Petersburg, VA, on June 17, 1864. Returned to duty prior to January 1, 1865, and accounted for through February 1865.

ROBESON, WILLIAM M., Private — Enlisted May 15, 1861, at age 24 in Henderson County. Died at Goldsboro on June 16 or June 26, 1862, of unreported cause.

RUFF, HOSEA, Private — Enlisted May 15, 1861, at age 23 in Henderson County. Deserted on April 5, 1863, and reported under arrest in May–June 1863. Returned to duty and later captured near Petersburg, VA, on April 1, 1865, and confined at Point Lookout, MD. Released on June 17, 1865, after taking the Oath. (NC pension records indicate that he was wounded in the left collarbone at Washington, VA, on an unspecified date.)

SALISBURY, WALTER D., Private — Enlisted May 15, 1861, at age 17 in Henderson County. Died at Grahamville, SC, around November 29, 1861, of unreported cause.

SAWYER, JAMES PINKNEY, Private — Enlisted May 15, 1861, at age 24 in Henderson County. Enlisted as 1st Sergeant and appointed Assistant Commissary of Subsistence (Captain) in September–October 1861 and transferred to the Field and Staff of this Reg. Reduced to the rank of 1st Sergeant and transferred back to the company in November–December 1861. Discharged in May–June 1862 after providing a substitute. Transferred to this company from an unspecified unit on November 1, 1864, with the rank of Private. Appointed acting Adjutant around April 1, 1865, and transferred to the Field and Staff of this Reg.

SIMS, JOHN STARK, Private—Enlisted June 17, 1863, at age 38 at Drewry's Bluff, VA. Died at hospital at Petersburg, VA, on March 26, 1865, of unreported cause.

SMILEY, ROBERT, 1st Sergeant—Enlisted September 18, 1861, at age 25 in Buncombe County. Promoted to 1st Sergeant on August 25, 1862. Promoted to Commissary Sergeant around August 31, 1863, and transferred to the Field and Staff of this Reg.

SOUTHER, ALBERT H., Private—Enlisted May 15, 1861, at age 24 in Henderson County. Reported absent without leave around November 1, 1863, but returned to duty around January 1, 1864. Present or accounted for until he deserted on February 26, 1865.

STEPP, COLUMBUS H., Private—Enlisted January 6, 1862, at age 16 at Grahamville, SC. Wounded in the breast at King's School House, VA, on June 25, 1862. Died in hospital at Richmond, Virginia on June 26, 1862, of wounds.

STEPP, FRANCIS A., Private—Enlisted January 5, 1862, at age 17 at Grahamville, SC. Died in hospital at Petersburg, VA, on July 3 or July 8, 1862, of "continued fever."

STEPP, ROBERT J., Private—Enlisted May 15, 1861, at age 25 in Henderson County. Enlisted as Corporal but reduced to ranks in March–April 1862. Deserted around April 5, 1863, and "killed" prior to February 6, 1864, presumably while still a deserter.

SUMMEY, CHRISTOPHER COLUMBUS, Private—Enlisted February 1, 1863, at age 18 in Henderson County. Captured at Lynchburg, VA, on April 7, 1865, and confined at Point Lookout, MD. Released on June 19, 1865, after taking the Oath.

SUMMEY, JOHN S., Private—Enlisted May 15, 1861, at age 24 in Henderson County. Wounded in the left hand at Petersburg, VA, on June 1, 1864, and returned to duty on January 18, 1865. Captured near Petersburg, VA, on April 2, 1865, and confined at Point Lookout, MD. Released on June 19, 1865, after taking the Oath.

SUMMEY, WILLIAM, Private—Enlisted January 5, 1862, at age 16 in Grahamville, SC. Discharged at Drewry's Bluff, VA, on July 16, 1862, for being under age.

SUMNER, JAMES E., Private—Enlisted May 15, 1861, at age 25 in Henderson County. Discharged on July 22, 1861, by reason of disability.

SUMNER, RICHARD RILEY, Private—Enlisted May 15, 1861, at age 27 in Henderson County. Transferred to Company G, 9th Regiment NC State Troops on August 10, 1861.

SUMNER, SAMUEL, Private—Enlisted May 15, 1861, at age 36 in Henderson County. Discharged on July 16, 1862, for being over age.

SURRAT, FRANCIS H., Private—Enlisted September 3, 1863, at age 18 in Henderson County. Deserted on February 5, 1864.

WATSON, DAVID,—Enlisted September 7, 1862. No further records.

WHEELING, ADAM, Private—Enlisted January 5, 1862, at age 25 at Grahamville, SC. Died in Henderson County on July 24, 1862, of unreported cause.

WHEELING, SAMUEL, Private—Enlisted May 15, 1861, at age 18 in Henderson County. Wounded at Malvern Hill, VA, on July 1, 1862, and returned to duty in September–October 1862. Present or accounted for through February 1864. No further records.

WHEELING, WILLIAM A., Private—Enlisted May 15, 1861, at age 26 in Henderson County. Died on the march from Upperville, VA, to Culpeper Court House, VA, around November 2, 1862. Cause of death not reported.

WHITAKER, JOSHUA B., Private—Enlisted May 15, 1861, at age 19 in Henderson County. Enlisted as Corporal but reduced to ranks on April 30, 1862. Present or accounted for through February 1864. No further records.

WHITAKER, JOSIAH L., Private—Enlisted September 16, 1863, in Henderson County. Deserted around July 10, 1864, and went over to the enemy. Took the Oath at Knoxville, TN, on March 21, 1865.

WIHITAKER, ROBERT J., Sergeant—Enlisted July 30, 1861, at age 20 in Buncombe County. Promoted to Corporal in September–October 1862 and to Sergeant on September 1, 1863. Wounded in the left leg near the Petersburg & Weldon Railroad around August 24, 1864. Hospitalized at Richmond, VA, until furloughed on September 3, 1864. Listed as deserter and dropped from the rolls of the company on December 12, 1864, following the expiration of his furlough.

WILLIAMS, GEORGE N., Private—Enlisted May 15, 1861, at age 21 in Henderson County. Discharged on July 1, 1861, for unreported reason.

WILLIAMS, JASPER, Private—Enlisted May 15, 1861, at age 24 in Henderson County. Promoted to Sergeant on September 1, 1863, but reduced to ranks subsequent to February 29, 1864. Deserted around July 17, 1864, and went over to the enemy. Confined at Knoxville, TN, around March 21, 1865, and later transferred to Louisville, KY, on April 2, 1865. Released at Louisville around April 10, 1865, after taking the Oath.

WILLIAMS, JOHN T., Private—Enlisted March 16, 1863, at age 18 in New Hanover County. Deserted to the enemy around February 27–28 1865 and confined at Washington, D.C. Released around March 6, 1865, after taking the Oath.

WILLIAMS, JONAS K., Private—Enlisted May 9, 1863, at age 37 in Lenoir County. Deserted around February 13, 1865, and went over to the enemy. Confined at Knoxville, TN, on March 18, 1865, and transferred to Louisville, KY, on March 26, 1865. Released at Louisville on March 28, 1865, after taking the Oath.

WILLIAMS, MARCUS L., Private—Enlisted May 15, 1861, at age 22 in Henderson County. Wounded in the hand and arm at King's School House, VA, on June 25, 1862. Reported absent wounded until September–October 1862 when he was listed as a deserter. Returned to duty in January–February 1863 and again deserted and went over to the enemy around February 27–28, 1865. Confined at Washington, D.C. until released around March 6, 1865, after taking the Oath.

WILLIAMS, SOLOMON BUXTON, Private. Paroled at Appomattox Court House, VA, on April 9, 1865.

WRIGHT, ALFRED, Private — Enlisted May 27, 1862, at age 24 in Lenoir County. Present or accounted for through February 1865. Reported absent sick during most of that period.

WRIGHT, CHRISTOPHER COLUMBUS, Private — Enlisted September 12, 1861, at age 27 in Buncombe County. Deserted and went over to the enemy around October 1, 1864. Confined at Louisville, Kentucky until released around October 18, 1864, after taking the Oath.

WRIGHT, LEANDER, Private. Previously served in Company H of this Reg. and transferred to this company on May 17, 1862. Deserted on April 9, 1863, but returned to duty and was reported under arrest through June 1863. Rejoined the company in July–August 1863 and served until killed in action in 1864. Place and exact date of death not reported.

WRIGHT, WILLIAM H., Private — Enlisted May 27, 1862, at age 26 in Lenoir County. Died in hospital at Petersburg, VA, around August 3, 1862, of "febris typhoides."

Company B — "Jackson Guards"

Captains

BRYSON, THADDEUS DILLARD — Enlisted May 30, 1861, at age 32 in Jackson County. Elected Captain on May 30, 1861. Discharged on April 30, 1862, after he declined to stand for reelection.

BOONE, HARLEN AURELIUS. Previously served as Private in Company A, 16th Regiment NC Troops and appointed 2nd Lt. of this company on June 7, 1861. Elected Captain on April 28, 1862. Reported absent on attached service from July–August 1863 through February 1864. Resigned on July 23, 1864, probably due to poor health.

ROGERS, DAVID — Enlisted May 30, 1861, at age 31 in Jackson County. Elected 1st Lt. on April 28, 1862. Promoted to Captain in March–December 1864. Wounded in the left leg at Fort Stedman, VA, on March 25, 1865, and hospitalized at Petersburg, VA. Captured by the enemy on April 3, 1865, and confined at various Federal hospitals until confined at Newport News, VA, on May 17, 1865. Released around June 15, 1865, after taking the Oath.

Lieutenants

DILLARD, LYNCH M., 1st Lt. — Enlisted May 30, 1861, at age 32 in Jackson County. Resigned on February 14, 1862, for unreported reason.

FISHER, LUCIUS F., 3rd Lt. — Enlisted May 30, 1861, at age 25 in Jackson County. Appointed 3rd Lt. on May 30, 1861, but defeated for reelection on April 28, 1862.

LONG, SAMUEL M., 3rd Lt. — Enlisted May 30, 1861, at age 22 in Jackson County. Enlisted as 1st Sergeant but reduced to ranks on April 30, 1862. Appointed 3rd Lt. on July 26, 1862. Killed at Fredericksburg, VA, on December 13, 1862.

MOSS, WILLIAM W., 2nd Lt. — Enlisted May 30, 1861, at age 24 in Jackson County. Elected 3rd Lt. on April 28, 1862, and promoted to 2nd Lt. in July–August 1862. Deserted on June 30, 1864, and went over to the enemy around April 1, 1865. Took the Oath at Knoxville, TN, around April 20, 1865. (NC pension records indicate he was wounded in the right thigh at Petersburg, VA, on July 30, 1864.)

NORTON, DAVID, 3rd Lt. — Enlisted July 17, 1862, Jackson County. Promoted to 3rd Lt. on December 29, 1862. Resigned on January 3, 1865. Company records and records of the North Carolina Adjutant General indicate he was dropped from the rolls on the company for desertion on February 12, 1865.

RICE, ISAAC, 1st Lt. — Enlisted May 30, 1861, at age 23 in Jackson County. Elected 1st Lt. on March 6, 1862, but defeated for reelection around April 28, 1862.

SHELTON, SAMUEL P.C., 2nd Lt. — Enlisted May 30, 1861, at age 28 in Jackson County. Elected 2nd Lt. on April 28, 1862, but resigned on July 16, 1862, for unreported reason.

Noncommissioned Officers and Privates

ADAMS, NEWTON J., Private — Enlisted May 30, 1861, at age 18 in Jackson County. Promoted to Corporal on April 30, 1862. Reduced to ranks in July–December 1863. Deserted on August 3, 1863, but returned to duty in November–December 1863. Captured at Fort Stedman, VA, on March 25, 1865, and confined to Point Lookout, MD. Released on June 22, 1865, after taking the Oath.

ADAMS, WILLIAM J., Private — Enlisted May 12, 1864 in Jackson County. Wounded in the shoulder at Fort Stedman, VA, on March 25, 1865, and hospitalized at Richmond, VA. Captured by the enemy on April 3, 1865, and paroled on April 25, 1865.

ALEXANDER JOHN, Sr., Private — Enlisted May 30, 1861, at age 27 in Jackson County. Discharged in May, 1862, for unreported reason.

ALLEN, JOSEPH J., Private — Enlisted May 30, 1861, at age 19 in Jackson County. Wounded at Malvern Hill, VA, on July 1, 1862, and returned to duty in September–October 1862. Captured near Petersburg, VA, on June 17, 1864, and confined to Point Lookout, MD, until transferred to Elmira, NY, on July 27, 1864. Paroled at Elmira on March 14, 1865, and exchanged at Boulware's Wharf, James River, VA. around March 18–21, 1865. Hospitalized at Richmond, VA, on March 22, 1865, with "debilitas" and died in hospital at Richmond on March 28, 1865.

ALLEN, WILLIAM B., 1st Sergeant — Enlisted May 30, 1861, at age 21 in Jackson County. Enlisted as Sergeant and promoted to 1st Sergeant on April 3, 1862.

Wounded at Malvern Hill, VA, on July 1, 1862. Deserted around February 19, 1865.

ALLISON, HENRY R., Private — Enlisted May 30, 1861, at age 19 in Jackson County. Died in a hospital at Petersburg, VA, on July 26, 1862, of "cerebro meningitis."

ALLISON, JOHN B. Jr., Private — Enlisted May 30, 1861, at age 20 in Jackson County. Reported absent without leave in September–October 1862 and court-martialed about December 28, 1862. Returned to duty prior to January 1, 1863. Present or accounted for through February 1865 and reported absent on detached duty as a teamster during much of that period. Paroled at Appomattox Court House, VA, on April 9, 1865.

ALLISON, MONTREVILLE B., Sergeant — Enlisted May 30, 1861, in Jackson County. Present or accounted through February 1863. Transferred to Company H, 62nd Regiment NC Troops prior to June 1, 1863.

ALLISON, SAMUEL N., Private. Previously served in Company H, 62nd Regiment NC Troops and transferred to this company in March–April 1863. Captured at Fort Stedman, VA, on or March 25, 1865, and confined at Point Lookout, MD. Released around June 22, 1865, after taking the Oath.

ALLMAN, JOHN G., Private — Enlisted May 30, 1861, at age 22 in Jackson County. Paroled at Appomattox Court House, VA, on April 9, 1865.

ALLMAN, WILLIAM P., Private — Enlisted April 1, 1864, in Jackson County. Paroled at Appomattox Court House, VA, on April 9, 1865.

ANGOVE, JAMES, Private — Enlisted May 30, 1861, at age 34 in Jackson County. Discharged on June 8, 1862, for unreported reason.

ASHE, WILLIAM H., Private — Enlisted May 30, 1861, at age 21 in Jackson County. Wounded at Fredericksburg, VA, on December 13, 1862, and returned to duty prior to January 1, 1863. Deserted on August 13, 1863, but returned to duty on November 14, 1863. Present or accounted for through February 1865.

BEARD, JAMES, Private — Enlisted May 30, 1861, in Jackson County. Discharged on July 16, 1862, for being under age. Discharge certificate gives age as 17.

BEARD, WILLIAM M., Private — Enlisted May 30, 1861, at age 20 in Jackson County. Promoted to Sergeant on April 30, 1862, but reduced to ranks prior to June 25, 1862. Wounded in the hip at King's School House, VA, on June 25, 1862, and hospitalized at Richmond, VA, where he died around July 7, 1862, of wounds.

BENNETT, JOHN S., Private — Enlisted December 20, 1864, in Jackson County. Captured at Fort Stedman, VA, on March 25, 1865, and confined at Point Lookout, MD. Released on June 24, 1865, after taking the Oath.

BENNETS, JOHN, Private — Enlisted May 30, 1861, at age 21 in Jackson County. Discharged on June 6, 1862, for unreported reason.

BIGHAM, JOHN ROBERT, Private. Previously served in Company C of this Reg. and transferred to this company on May 1, 1862. Present or accounted for through February 1864.

BLANTON, ALVIN R., Private — Enlisted April 20, 1862, in Jackson County. Wounded in both ankles at Fredericksburg, VA, on December 13, 1862. Reported absent wounded until January–February 1864 when he was reported absent without leave.

BOONE, MARCUS T., Private — Enlisted May 30, 1861, in Jackson County. Discharged around July 16, 1862, for being under age. Discharge certificate gives age as 17.

BROWN, ELBERT, 1st Sergeant — Enlisted March 20, 1862, in Jackson County. Promoted to Sergeant on December 11, 1863, and to 1st Sergeant on February 20, 1865. Paroled at Appomattox Court House, VA, on April 9, 1865.

BRYSON, FRANCIS M., Private — Enlisted May 30, 1861, at age 20 in Jackson County. Deserted on August 13, 1863, but returned to duty on December 24, 1863. Present or accounted for through February 1864.

BRYSON, GEORGE W., Private — Enlisted May 30, 1861, at age 20 in Jackson County. Discharged around July 27, 1861, for unreported reason. Later served in Company H, 62nd Regiment NC Troops.

BRYSON, JOSEPH B., Private — Enlisted August 1, 1862, in Jackson County. Enlisted as a substitute. Died in a hospital at Richmond, VA, on November 20, 1862, of "dysentery from measles."

BRYSON, SAMUEL H., Private — Enlisted May 10, 1862, in Jackson County. Reported absent without leave after January–February 1864. (NC pension records indicate he was wounded at Malvern Hill, VA, on an unspecified date.)

BRYSON, WILLIAM H., Jr., Sergeant — Enlisted May 30, 1861, at age 27 in Jackson County. Promoted to Sergeant prior to September 1, 1861. Discharged on October 21, 1861, by reason of "disability to perform the duties of a soldier." Later served as 1st Lt. of Company H, 62nd Regiment NC Troops.

BUCHANAN, BENJAMIN SEBORN, Private — Enlisted May 30, 1861, at age 23 in Jackson County. Enlisted as Corporal and promoted to Sergeant on October 21, 1861. Reduced to ranks on April 30, 1862. Reported absent without leave in November–December 1862 but returned to duty in January–February 1863. Promoted to Sergeant in May–June 1863. Dropped from the rolls of the company on December 12, 1864, after going home on sick furlough on an unspecified date and failing to return. Reduced to ranks in November–December 1864.

BUCHANAN, J.F. — Enlisted August 1863 at age 18 in Jackson County. No further records.

BUCHANAN, JOHN J., Private — Enlisted May 30, 1861, at age 26 in Jackson County. Died in a hospital in Petersburg, Virginia on July 8, 1862, of "chronic diarrhoea."

BUCHANAN, LORENZO D., Private — Enlisted May 30, 1861, at age 21 in Jackson County. Captured at Bermuda Hundred, VA, on June 2, 1864, and confined at Point Lookout, MD, until transferred to Elmira, NY, on July 9, 1864. Died at Elmira on September 12, 1864, of "chronic diarrhoea."

BUCHANAN, THADDEUS M., Private — Enlisted July 17, 1862, in Jackson County. Died at Winchester, VA, in October 1862 of unreported cause.

CARROLL, JAMES, Private — Enlisted July 20, 1862, in Jackson County. Wounded at Fredericksburg, VA, on December 13, 1862, and returned to duty prior to January 1, 1863. Present or accounted for through February 1864. No further records.

CARROLL, JOHN, Private — Enlisted May 30, 1861, at age 20 in Jackson County. Reported absent under arrest in January–February 1864 and confined at E.D.M. Prison in Richmond, VA. Returned to duty prior to June 17, 1864. Captured by the enemy near Petersburg, VA, and confined at Point Lookout, MD, until transferred to Elmira, NY, on July 27, 1864. Released at Elmira on July 11, 1865, after taking the Oath.

CHASTAIN, JOHN, Private — Enlisted May 30, 1861, at age 21 in Jackson County. Reported absent under arrest in January–February 1864. No further records.

COE, LEANDER A., Private — Enlisted April 5, 1863, in Jackson County. Captured at Fort Stedman, VA, on March 25, 1865, and confined at Point Lookout, MD. Released on June 26, 1865, after taking the Oath.

COGDILL, JABLE, Private — Enlisted May 30, 1861, in Jackson County. Discharged on July 16, 1862, for being under age. Discharge certificate gives age as 17.

COGDILL, JOSEPH W., Private — Enlisted May 30, 1861, at age 21 in Jackson County. Wounded at Malvern Hill, VA, on July 1, 1862, and returned to duty in November–December 1862. Deserted on August 13, 1863.

COGGINS, ALFRED C., Private — Enlisted May 30, 1861, at age 21 in Jackson County. Discharged on September 14, 1861, for unreported reason.

COLLINS, JOSEPH A., Private — Enlisted May 30, 1861, at age 18 in Jackson County. Wounded at Malvern Hill, VA, on July 1, 1862, and returned to duty in November–December 1862. Reported absent without leave in January–February 1864.

COLLINS, ROBERT H., Sergeant — Enlisted May 30, 1861, at age 20 in Jackson County. Promoted to Sergeant on April 30, 1862. Received a bayonet wound in battle with a group of "Tory's" near Warm Springs on October 26, 1863. Died on October 27, 1863, of wounds.

CONNER, RUBIN C., Private — Enlisted May 30, 1861, at age 21 in Jackson County. Present or accounted for through February 1864. No further records.

COOK, JAMES P., Private — Enlisted March 20, 1862, in Jackson County. Deserted on August 12, 1863.

COOK, SAMUEL R., Private — Enlisted May 30, 1861, at age 27 in Jackson County. Promoted to Corporal on October 21, 1861, but reduced to ranks on April 30, 1862. Present or accounted for through December 1864 but reported absent sick or absent on detached duty during most of that period. Listed as a deserter on February 19, 1865, and dropped from the rolls of the company.

COOK, WILLIAM J., Private. Previously served in Company I of this Reg. and transferred to this company on May 1, 1862. Died at Drewry's Bluff, VA, on August 7, 1862, of unreported cause.

COPE, WILLIAM, Private — Enlisted May 30, 1861, at age 19 in Jackson County. Transferred to Company A, 16th Regiment NC Troops on July 1, 1862, in exchange for Private George W. Shook.

COURTNEY, JAMES M., Private — Enlisted May 30, 1861, at age 25 in Jackson County. Enlisted as Corporal but reduced to ranks on April 30, 1862. Deserted on May 12–13, 1863, after being sent home on furlough.

COWAN, DAVID L., Private — Enlisted March 20, 1862, in Jackson County. Wounded at Malvern Hill, VA, on July 1, 1862, and returned to duty in January–February 1863. Captured at Fort Stedman, VA, on March 25, 1865, and confined at Point Lookout, MD. Released on June 26, 1865, after taking the Oath. (NC pension records indicate he was wounded in unspecified engagements in 1863 and 1865.)

COWAN, JAMES W., Private — Enlisted May 30, 1861, at age 27 in Jackson County. Wounded at Malvern Hill, VA, on July 1, 1862, and returned to duty prior to September 1, 1862. Hospitalized at Wilmington on March 25, 1863, with a gunshot wound and returned to duty on April 17, 1863. Captured at Fort Stedman, VA, on March 25, 1865, and confined at Point Lookout, MD, until released on June 26, 1865, after taking the Oath.

COWAN, WILLIAM R., Private — Enlisted May 30, 1861, at age 24 in Jackson County. Captured at Fort Stedman, VA, on March 25, 1865, and confined at Point Lookout, MD. Released on June 26, 1865, after taking the Oath. (NC pension records indicate he was wounded in an unspecified engagement.)

COWARD, JAMES R., Private — Enlisted May 30, 1861, at age 19 in Jackson County. Hospitalized at Winchester, VA, in September–October 1862 and failed to rejoin the company. Dropped from the rolls in May–June 1863 on the presumption that he had died at Winchester.

COWARD, WILLIAM, Private — Enlisted May 30, 1861, at age 16 in Jackson County. Discharged on July 16, 1862, for being under age.

CRAWFORD, ANDREW J., Private — Enlisted May 30, 1861, at age 22 in Jackson County. Enlisted as Sergeant but was reduced to ranks on April 30, 1862. Killed at Malvern Hill, VA, on July 1, 1862.

CRAWFORD, JAMES R., Private — Enlisted March 20, 1862, in Jackson County. Died at Richmond, VA, on September 11, 1862, of "measles."

CRAWFORD, JOSEPH P., Private — Enlisted May 30, 1861, at age 18 in Jackson County. Died in a hospital at Petersburg, VA, on July 13, 1862, of "pneumonia."

CRAWFORD, MARTIN W., Private — Enlisted May 30, 1861, at age 18 in Jackson County. Died in a hospital at Goldsboro on March 5, 1863, of "typhoid fever."

CRAWFORD, ROBERT P., Musician — Enlisted May 30, 1861, at age 25 in Jackson County. Enlisted as Musician (Fifer). Deserted on June 17, 1862, but returned to duty in January–February 1863. Deserted again on August 13, 1863.

DAVIS, BENJAMIN P., Private — Enlisted May 30, 1861, at age 32 in Jackson County. Died "at home" on May 14, 1863, of unreported cause.

DILLARD, WILLIAM H.T., Private — Enlisted May 30, 1861, at age 21 in Jackson County. Wounded in the left thumb at Fredericksburg, VA, on December 13, 1862, and returned to duty in March–April 1863. Deserted on an unspecified date after February 1864 and was dropped from the rolls of the company on December 12, 1864.

DILLS, DAVID, Private — Enlisted May 8, 1861(?) at age 22 in Jackson County. Died at Grahamville, SC, about March 21–23, 1862, of disease.

DILLS, GEORGE W., Private — Enlisted May 30, 1861, at age 27 in Jackson County. Transferred to Company H, 62nd Regiment NC Troops in March–April 1863 in exchange for Private James E.S. Slatton.

DILLS, WILLIAM ALLEN, Private — Enlisted May 30, 1861, in Jackson County. Discharged on July 16, 1862, for being under age. Discharge certificate gives age as 17. Later served in Company H, 62nd Regiment NC Troops.

ESTES, JESSE E., Private — Enlisted May 30, 1861, at age 30 in Jackson County. Present or accounted for through February 1864.

EVANS, DANIEL E., Private — Enlisted May 30, 1861, at age 21 in Jackson County. Reported absent wounded in November–December 1864 and through February 1865. (NC pension applications indicate he was wounded at Seven Pines, VA, in 1862.)

FARLEY, WILLIAM V.B., Private — Enlisted September 1, 1861, at age 22 in Buncombe County. Wounded in the right shoulder at Fredericksburg, VA, on December 13, 1862, and returned to duty in March–April 1863. Transferred to Company D of this Reg. on February 12, 1864.

FOWLER, BENJAMIN F., Private — Enlisted May 30, 1861, at age 23 in Jackson County. Discharged in July–August 1862 after providing a substitute.

FOWLER, ELIAS C., Private — Enlisted July 16, 1862, in Jackson County. Enlisted as a substitute. Wounded in the shoulder at Fredericksburg, VA, on December 13, 1862, and died in hospital at Richmond, VA, on January 3–4, 1863, of wounds.

FOWLER, THOMAS J., Corporal — Enlisted May 30, 1861, at age 25 in Jackson County. Promoted to Corporal in July–August 1862 but reduced to ranks in November–December 1862. Promoted to Corporal in January–February 1863 and present or accounted for through February 1864. No further records.

FRADY, JAMES, Private — Enlisted May 30, 1861, at age 20 in Jackson County. Died in hospital at Kinston on May 2, 1862, of disease.

FRIZZLE, JAMES H., Private — Enlisted May 30, 1861, at age 25 in Jackson County. Enlisted as Corporal but reduced to ranks on April 30, 1862. Wounded at Malvern Hill, VA, on July 1, 1862, and returned to duty in September–October 1862. Present or accounted for through February 1864. No further records.

GIBBS, JOSHUA A., Private — Enlisted May 30, 1861, at age 19 in Jackson County. Present or accounted for through February 1864.

GIBBS, WILLIAM H., Private. First listed in the records of this company on June 17, 1864. Died "at home" on October 26, 1864, of unreported cause.

GILSHER, ADAM, Private — Enlisted May 30, 1861, at age 38 in Jackson County. Captured at Hatcher's Run, VA, on April 1, 1865, and confined at Hart's Island, NY. Released on June 21, 1865, after taking the Oath.

GOLDEN, WILLIAM F., Private — Enlisted October 28, 1863, in Jackson County. Captured at Amelia Court House, VA, on April 3, 1865, and confined at Point Lookout, MD. Released on June 27, 1865, after taking the Oath.

GRANT, WILLIAM R., Private — Enlisted May 30, 1861, at age 27 in Jackson County. Present or accounted for through February 1864. Wounded at Plymouth, NC, around April 18–20, 1864. Retired to the Invalid Corps on September 28, 1864.

GREEN, WILLIAM M., Private — Enlisted May 30, 1861, at age 25 in Jackson County. Present or accounted for through February 1864.

HALL, ANSEL J., Private — Enlisted May 30, 1861, at age 18 in Jackson County. Enlisted as Corporal but reduced to ranks on April 30, 1862. Deserted on August 13, 1863, but returned to duty on December 24, 1863. Present or accounted for through February 1864. No further records.

HALL, JOSHUA K., Private — Enlisted October 17, 1861, at age 22 at Camp Davis. Deserted on August 13, 1863.

HALL, LEANDER B., Private — Enlisted May 30, 1861, at age 20 in Jackson County. Wounded in the leg at King's School House, VA, on June 25, 1862. Died at Richmond, VA, on July 12, 1862, of wounds.

HEMPHILL, ROBERT S., Private — Enlisted March 20, 1862, in Jackson County. Wounded at Malvern Hill, VA, on July 1, 1862, and returned to duty prior to September 1, 1862. Died in a hospital at Richmond, VA, on July 16, 1863, of "pneumonia."

HILL, FELIX GRUNDY, Private — Enlisted May 30, 1861, at age 20 in Jackson County. Wounded in the thigh at King's School House, VA, on June 25, 1862, and returned to duty in November–December 1862. Transferred to Company G, 1st Regiment SC Artillery in May–June 1863.

HILL, RICHARD T., Private — Enlisted May 30, 1861, at age 21 in Jackson County. Deserted on January 21, 1864, but returned to duty on an unspecified date. Wounded in the bladder in an unspecified battle and died of wounds in a hospital at Petersburg, VA, on July 13, 1864.

HOLDEN, JOHN, Private — Enlisted July 17, 1862, in Jackson County. Present or accounted for until January–February 1864 when he was reported absent without leave.

HOOPER, DANIEL H., Sergeant — Enlisted May 30, 1861, at age 16 in Jackson County. Promoted to Sergeant on April 30, 1862. Wounded at Malvern Hill, VA, on July 1, 1862. Reduced to ranks in July–August 1862. Returned to duty in November–December 1862. Promoted to Sergeant in January–February 1863. Killed at Petersburg, VA, on June 19, 1864.

HOOPER, THOMAS J., Private — Enlisted December 8, 1863, in Jackson County. Hospitalized at Richmond, VA, on June 14, 1864, with a gunshot wound. Deserted on July 20, 1864.

HOOPER, WLLIAM W., Private — Enlisted April 20, 1862, in Jackson County. Promoted to Musician (Drummer) on August 5, 1863, but reduced to ranks on December 1, 1863. Reported absent without leave in November–December 1863 and through February 1864. No further records.

HOSS, W.W., Private. Records of the Federal Provost Marshal indicate he was a deserter who was confined at Knoxville, TN, on April 20, 1865, and transferred to Chattanooga, TN, the same day. No further records.

HOYLE, JOSEPH, Private — Enlisted May 10, 1862, in Jackson County. Reported absent without leave in September–October 1862 but returned to duty in November–December 1862. Deserted on August 13, 1863.

HOYLE, WILLIAM, Private. Previously served in Company C of this Reg. and transferred to this company on June 2, 1862. Reported absent without leave in September–October 1862 but returned to duty in November–December 1863. Deserted on January 21, 1864.

JAMERSON, THOMAS W., Private — Enlisted May 30, 1861, at age 25 in Jackson County. Present or accounted for through February 1865 but reported on detached service as a teamster during much of the war.

KEENER, DAVID M., Private — Enlisted May 30, 1861, at age 22 in Jackson County. Wounded at Malvern Hill, VA, on July 1, 1862, and returned to duty in November–December 1863. Hospitalized at Richmond, VA, around October 17–18, 1864, with a gunshot wound in the right leg. Reported absent wounded through February 1865.

LONG, ANDREW JACKSON, Private — Enlisted May 5, 1862, in Jackson County. Discharged on July 17, 1862, by reason of disability. Discharge certificate gives age as 18.

LONG, GEORGE M., Private — Enlisted May 30, 1861, at age 21 in Jackson County. Furloughed on an unspecified date subsequent to February 29, 1864, and failed to rejoin the company. Dropped from the rolls on October 19, 1864, for desertion.

LONG, PETER G., Private — Enlisted May 30, 1861, at age 28 in Jackson County. Wounded at Malvern Hill, VA, on July 1, 1862. Died at Richmond, VA, on July 17, 1862, of wounds.

McCALL, FRANCIS C., Private — Enlisted May 30, 1861, at age 27 in Jackson County. Wounded in the left thumb ("with loss of same") at Fredericksburg, VA, on December 13, 1862, and returned to duty in January–February 1863. Reported absent without leave around October 13, 1863, but returned to duty on November 13, 1863. Deserted on January 21, 1864.

MATHIS, ANDREW J., Private — Enlisted May 30, 1861, at age 28 in Jackson County. Promoted to Corporal in May–June 1862 and appointed Musician (Fifer) in July–August 1862. Reduced to ranks in November–December 1862. Appointed Musician (Drummer) in March–April 1863 but reduced to ranks in July–December 1863. Deserted on August 3, 1863, but returned to duty on December 7, 1863. Present or accounted for through February 1864. No further records.

MATHIS, HUGH H., Private — Enlisted May 30, 1861, at age 18 in Jackson County. Deserted on August 3, 1863, but returned to duty on December 7, 1863. Present or accounted for through February 1864. No further records.

MATHIS, JESSE A., Private — Enlisted May 30, 1861, at age 27 in Jackson County. Discharged on July 27, 1861, for unreported reason.

MATHIS, JOHN J., Private — Enlisted May 30, 1861, at age 26 in Jackson County. Present or accounted for through February 1864. No further records.

MATHIS, LEVI J., Private — Enlisted May 30, 1861, at age 21 in Jackson County. Wounded in the neck at King's School House, VA, on June 25, 1862, and returned to duty on July 4, 1862. Paroled at Appomattox Court House, VA, on April 9, 1865. Paroled again at Farmville, VA, on April 11–21, 1865.

MATHIS, THOMAS J., Corporal — Enlisted May 30, 1861, at age 20 in Jackson County. Promoted to Corporal in March–December 1864 and present or accounted for through February 1865.

MILLER, JOHN M., Private — Enlisted May 30, 1861, at age 18 in Jackson County. Died at Grahamville, SC, on March 20–23, 1862, of disease.

MILLER, SAMUEL J., Private — Enlisted May 30, 1861, at age 19 in Jackson County. Discharged on May 9, 1862, by reason of disability.

MILLS, DAVID T., Private — Enlisted June 8, 1861, at age 21 in Jackson County. Discharged in July 1861 for unreported reason. Later served in Company H, 62nd Regiment NC Troops.

MOODY, DANIEL V., Private — Enlisted May 30, 1861, at age 23 in Jackson County. Wounded in the left elbow at Fredericksburg, VA, on December 13, 1862, and returned to duty in July–August 1863. Discharged on September 5, 1863, by reason of disability from wounds.

MOODY, FRANCIS M., Private — Enlisted May 30, 1861, at age 22 in Jackson County. Deserted on May 20, 1863.

MOODY, JOSEPH H., Private — Enlisted May 30, 1861, at age 22 in Jackson County. Enlisted as Musician (Drummer). Wounded in the hand and arm (lost a finger) at Malvern Hill, VA, on July 1, 1862. Reported absent wounded until November–December 1862 when reported absent without leave. Captured by the enemy at Strawberry Plains, TN, on January 17, 1863, and sent to Nashville, TN, and later transferred to Fort McHenry, MD, on February 14, 1863. Paroled and exchanged at City Point, VA, around February 18, 1863. Failed to rejoin the company and was reduced to ranks in March–April 1863. Reported absent without leave in May–June 1863 and listed as a deserter and dropped from the rolls of the company in July–August 1863.

MORROW, ANDREW J., Private — Enlisted April 5, 1862, in Jackson County. Deserted on August 13, 1863.

MOSS, DAVID M., Corporal — Enlisted May 30, 1861, at age 23 in Jackson County. Present or accounted for until confined at a Federal hospital at Frederick, MD, around September 18, 1862. Place and date captured not reported. Paroled and exchanged on an unspecified date and returned to duty prior to December 13, 1862. Wounded in the ankle at Fredericksburg, VA, on December 13, 1863, and returned to duty in January–

February 1863. Deserted on July 22, 1863, but returned to duty in September–December 1863. Promoted to Corporal in March–August 1864. Deserted again around August 25, 1864, and went over to the enemy. Confined at Knoxville, TN, on April 20, 1865, and at Louisville, KY, on April 27, 1865. Released at Louisville around April 28, 1865, after taking the Oath.

MOSS, JAMES E., Corporal — Enlisted May 30, 1861, at age 19 in Jackson County. Wounded in the head at King's School House, VA, on June 25, 1862, and returned to duty in July–August 1862. Deserted on August 15, 1863, but returned to duty in September–December 1863. Promoted to Corporal on December 11, 1863, and present or accounted for through February 1865.

MOSS, JOHN J., Private — Enlisted May 30, 1861, at age 17 in Jackson County. Wounded at Malvern Hill, VA, on July 1, 1862. Died at Richmond, VA, on August 2, 1862, of wounds.

MOSS, MILTON W., Private — Enlisted May 30, 1861, at age 21 in Jackson County. Deserted on July 22, 1863, but returned to duty in September–December 1863. Killed near Petersburg, VA, on June 17, 1864.

MOSS, WILLIAM, Private — Enlisted July 25, 1862, in Jackson County. Wounded at Fredericksburg, VA, on December 13, 1862, and returned to duty prior to January 1, 1863. Deserted on July 22, 1863.

MULL, BRAXTON P., Private — Enlisted May 30, 1861, at age 21 in Jackson County. Discharged on November 25, 1862, by reason of "dislocation of tarsus of eight months standing." Reenlisted in the company on April 1, 1864, and later paroled at Appomattox Court House, VA, on April 9, 1865.

NORTON, FULLER, Private — Enlisted May 30, 1861, at age 23 in Jackson County. Present or accounted for through February 1865 but reported absent on detail as a shoemaker during much of that period.

NORTON, RICHARDSON, Private — Enlisted July 17, 1862, in Jackson County. Killed at Fredericksburg, VA, on December 13, 1862.

NORTON, WILLIAM V., Private — Enlisted May 30, 1861, at age 20 in Jackson County. Killed at Malvern Hill, VA, on July 1, 1862.

PAINTER, JAMES T., Private — Enlisted May 30, 1861, at age 23 in Jackson County. Promoted to Musician (Fifer) on August 15, 1863, but reduced to ranks on December 1, 1863. Present or accounted for through February 1864. Furloughed on an unspecified date and failed to return from furlough. Dropped from the rolls of the company and listed as a deserter on December 12, 1864. (NC pension records indicate he was wounded in the right side at Petersburg, VA, on April 1, 1864.)

PAINTER, OLIVER, Private — Enlisted May 30, 1861, at age 46 in Jackson County. Discharged on August 5, 1861, for unreported reason.

PANNELL, ANDREW J., Private — Enlisted May 30, 1861, at age 21 in Jackson County. Promoted to Corporal on April 30, 1862, but reduced to ranks in July–August 1862. Court-martialed around December 28, 1862, for unknown reason. Returned to duty in January–February 1863 but deserted on April 8, 1863. Records of the Federal Provost Marshal indicate he was captured at Vicksburg, MS, on July 4, 1863, and confined at St. Louis, MO, until "discharged" on August 13, 1863. No further records.

PARKER, HENRY H., Private — Enlisted May 30, 1861, at age 21 in Jackson County. . Enlisted as Sergeant but reduced to ranks on April 30, 1862. Wounded at Malvern Hill, VA, on July 1, 1862, and hospitalized at Richmond, VA. Died of wounds around July 31, 1862.

PARKER, SAMUEL J., Private — Enlisted May 30, 1861, in Jackson County. Wounded at Malvern Hill, VA, on July 1, 1862. Discharged on July 16, 1862, for being under age. Discharge certificate gives age as 17.

PARRIS, ALFRED W., Private — Enlisted May 30, 1861, at age 20 in Jackson County. Wounded in the thigh at Malvern Hill, VA, on July 1, 1862. Reported absent wounded or absent sick through February 1864.

PARRIS, JAMES M., Private — Enlisted May 30, 1861, at age 22 in Jackson County. Promoted to Corporal on July 25, 1863, but reduced to ranks on December 2, 1863. Present or accounted for through February 1864.

PARRIS, MAJOR W., Private — Enlisted May 30, 1861, at age 37 in Jackson County. Discharged on July 16, 1862, for being over age.

PHILLIPS, GEORGE W., Private — Enlisted April 20, 1862, in Jackson County. Deserted on August 13, 1863, but returned to duty in November–December 1863. Captured near Petersburg, VA, on June 17, 1864, and confined at Point Lookout, MD, until transferred to Elmira, NY, on July 27, 1864. Released at Elmira on August 7, 1865, after taking the Oath. (NC pension records indicate he injured his leg at Gum Swamp on June 10, 1863.)

PRESLEY, MONTREVILLE P., Private — Enlisted May 30, 1861, at age 20 in Jackson County. Died at Kinston around May 23, 1862, of disease.

QUEEN, AMERICUS H., Corporal — Enlisted February 7, 1864, in Jackson County. Enlisted as Corporal and present or accounted for through February 1865. (NC pension records indicate he was wounded in the hand at Petersburg, VA, in 1865.)

QUEEN, JOHN B., Private — Enlisted May 30, 1861, at age 25 in Jackson County. Killed at Malvern Hill, VA, on July 1, 1862.

RICE, HENRY H., Private — Enlisted May 30, 1861, at age 21 in Jackson County. Promoted to Corporal on April 30, 1862, but reduced to ranks in January–February 1864. Captured at Petersburg, VA, on June 17, 1864, and confined at Point Lookout, MD, until transferred to Elmira, NY, on July 27, 1864. Died at Elmira on November 16, 1864, of "pneumonia."

RICE, JACOB F., Private. Previously served in Company D, 6th Regiment Alabama Infantry and transferred to this company on November 9, 1862. Failed to report for duty and was listed as a deserter in December 1862.

RICE, WILLIAM R., Private — Enlisted April 5, 1863, in Jackson County. Transferred to Company G, 1st Regiment SC Artillery on June 11, 1863.

SANDERS, ELIJAH, Private. Previously served in Company A, 20th Regiment SC Infantry and transferred to this company on May 28, 1863. Failed to report for duty and was listed as a deserter in June 1863.

SHOOK, GEORGE W., Private. Previously served in Company A, 16th Regiment NC Troops and transferred to this company on July 1, 1862, in exchange for Private William Cope. Deserted on July 20, 1863.

SHOOK, JOSEPH L., Color Corporal — Enlisted May 30, 1861, at age 22 in Jackson County. Promoted to Color Corporal in May–June 1863. Present or accounted for through February 1864.

SHULER, LEANDER, Private — Enlisted May 30, 1861, at age 27 in Jackson County. Died in a hospital at Petersburg, VA, on July 28, 1862, of "typhoid febris."

SLATTON, JAMES E.S., Private. Previously served in Company H, 62nd Regiment NC Troops and transferred to this company in March–April 1863 in exchange for Private George W. Dills. Reported absent under arrest in January–February 1864 and confined at Castle Thunder Prison, Richmond, VA, on May 13, 1864. Rejoined the company on an unspecified date. Hospitalized at Petersburg, VA, on August 21, 1864, with a gunshot wound of the right leg. Died of the wound in hospital at Petersburg on August 24, 1864.

SLATTON, JEPTHA P., Private — Enlisted May 30, 1861, at age 23 in Jackson County. Promoted to Corporal on April 30, 1862, but reduced to ranks in November–December 1862. Present or accounted for until November–December 1864 when wounded in the upper left arm (which required amputation) in the trenches of Petersburg. Reported absent wounded or absent on furlough through March 26, 1865.

SLATTON, JOHN, Private — Enlisted March 20, 1862, in Jackson County. Deserted on August 3, 1863, but returned to duty in September–December 1863. Captured near Petersburg, VA, on June 17, 1864, and confined at Point Lookout, MD, until transferred to Elmira, NY, on July 27, 1864. Paroled at Elmira on March 14, 1865, and exchanged at Boulware's Wharf, James River, VA, around March 18–21.

SLATTON, WARREN D., Private — Enlisted May 30, 1861, at age 25 in Jackson County. Died in a hospital at Petersburg, VA, on July 29, 1862, of disease.

STEWART, JEFFERSON W., Private — Enlisted May 30, 1861, at age 21 in Jackson County. Captured near Petersburg, VA, on June 17, 1864, and confined at Point Lookout, MD, until transferred to Elmira, NY, on July 27, 1864. Died in hospital at Elmira on April 24, 1865, of "pneumonia."

STEWART, JOHN P., Sergeant — Enlisted May 30, 1861, at age 19 in Jackson County. Promoted to Corporal on August 5, 1863, and to Sergeant in March–December 1864. Present or accounted for through February 1865. (NC pension records indicate he was wounded at Fredericksburg, Sharpsburg, and Petersburg.)

STEWART, MILTON M., Private — Enlisted April 6, 1863, in Jackson County. Deserted on August 13, 1863.

STEWART, WILLIAM J., Private — Enlisted July 25, 1862, in Jackson County. Present or accounted for through February 1864.

STILES, JASPER C., Private — Enlisted May 30, 1861, at age 18 in Jackson County. Deserted on August 13, 1863, but returned to duty on November 17, 1863. Captured near Petersburg, VA, on April 2, 1865, and confined at Point Lookout, MD. Released on June 20, 1865, after taking the Oath.

STILES, THOMAS J., Private — Enlisted May 30, 1861, at age 18 in Jackson County. Present or accounted for through February 1864.

SUMMEY, JAMES, Private. Previously served in Company A, 20th Regiment SC Infantry and transferred to this company on May 28, 1863. Reported for duty in July–August 1863 and present or accounted for through February 1865.

TERRELL, JOHN L., Private — Enlisted May 20, 1864, in Jackson County. Present or accounted for until transferred to Company C of this Reg. on November 12, 1864.

TINSLEY, THOMAS J., Private. Deserted in June 1863.

WARD, ISOM J., Private — Enlisted May 30, 1861, at age 30 in Jackson County. Discharged around September 14, 1861, for unreported reason.

WATSON, ALLISON, Private — Enlisted May 30, 1861, in Jackson County. Enlistment date reported as May 30, 1861; however, he was not listed in the records of this company until May–June 1863. Present or accounted for through August 1863. No further records.

WATSON, ARCHIBALD R., Private — Enlisted May 30, 1861, at age 18 in Jackson County. Present or accounted for through July 1863 but reported absent sick during much of that period. Failed to return from furlough on August 10, 1863, and listed as a deserter.

WATSON, BARTLETT N., Private — Enlisted May 30, 1861, at age 21 in Jackson County. Wounded at Fredericksburg, VA, on December 13, 1862, and returned to duty prior to January 1, 1863. Captured at Fort Stedman, VA, on March 25, 1865, and confined at Point Lookout, MD. Released on June 21, 1865, after taking the Oath.

WATSON, BENSON N., Private — Enlisted May 30, 1861, at age 22 in Jackson County. Wounded at Malvern Hill, VA, on July 1, 1862, and returned to duty prior to September 1, 1862. Deserted on August 3, 1863, but returned to duty in September–December 1863. Deserted again on January 21, 1864, and apprehended on January 22, 1864, and confined at Weldon. "Escaped from the guard" on February 17, 1864. No further records.

WATSON, ELBERT, Private — Enlisted May 30, 1861, at age 18 in Jackson County. Wounded in the left arm at Petersburg, VA, on June 17, 1864. Muster rolls do not indicate whether he returned to duty; however, he was listed as a deserter and dropped from the rolls of the company on December 12, 1864, after failing to return from furlough. Went over to the enemy on unspecified date and confined at Knoxville, TN. Took the Oath on April 20, 1865.

WATSON, HENRY, Private — Enlisted April 5, 1863, age in Jackson County. Died in a hospital at Petersburg, VA, on June 18, 1863, of "typhoid fever."

WATSON, JAMES, Private — Enlisted May 30, 1861, at age 29 in Jackson County. Discharged on May 5, 1862, after providing Private Jacob M. Woodring as a substitute.

WATSON, THOMAS M., Private — Enlisted June 1, 1863, in Jackson County. Deserted in August, 1863.

WATSON, WILLIAM L., Private — Enlisted May 30, 1861, at age 25 in Jackson County. Wounded in the right side at Fredericksburg, VA, on December 13, 1862, and rejoined the company in May–June 1863. Present or accounted for through February 1864.

WHITE, ELBERT, Private — Enlisted March 20, 1862, in Jackson County. Died in a hospital at Petersburg, VA, around August 13, 1862, of "continued fever."

WIGGINS, JOHN A., Private — Enlisted May 30, 1861, at age 18 in Jackson County. Wounded in the right shoulder at Petersburg, VA, in July 1864. Listed as a deserter and dropped from the rolls of the company on December 12, 1864, after failing to return from furlough.

WILSON, ANDREW J., Private — Enlisted May 30, 1861, at age 25 in Jackson County. Died at Grahamville, SC, on December 23, 1861, of "typhoid fever."

WILSON, DAVID W., Private — Enlisted May 30, 1861, at age 29 in Jackson County. Died at Petersburg, VA, around July 1, 1862, of "febris continuous communis."

WILSON, HOUSTON M., Color Corporal — Enlisted May 30, 1861, at age 23 in Jackson County. Promoted to Color Corporal in July–August 1862. Present or accounted for until transferred to Company A, 20th Regiment SC Infantry on May 28, 1863.

WILSON, JEREMIAH W., Sergeant — Enlisted May 30, 1861, at age 18 in Jackson County. Promoted to Sergeant in November–December 1862. Present or accounted for until transferred to Company A, 20th Regiment SC Infantry on May 28, 1863.

WILSON, JOHN A., Private — Enlisted May 30, 1861, at age 19 in Jackson County. Died in a hospital at Petersburg, VA, on August 28 or September 25, 1862, of "fever."

WILSON, JOHN C., Private — Enlisted May 30, 1861, at age 29 in Jackson County. Transferred to Company F of this Reg. on May 1, 1862.

WILSON, RICHARD M., Private — Enlisted May 30, 1861, at age 22 in Jackson County. Appointed 3rd Lt. of Company H, 62nd Regiment NC Troops around July 11, 1862.

WOOD, DANIEL H., Private — Enlisted May 30, 1861, at age 20 in Jackson County. Promoted to Sergeant on April 30, 1862, but reduced to ranks in January–February 1863. Present or accounted for through February 1865.

WOOD, HENRY H., Sergeant — Enlisted October 17, 1861, at age 18 at Camp Davis. Promoted to Sergeant on August 10, 1863. Present or accounted for through February 1865.

WOOD, JAMES M., Private — Enlisted July 20, 1863, at Petersburg, VA. Wounded in the left knee at Bermuda Hundred, VA, in June 1864 and returned to duty prior to January 1, 1865. Present or accounted for through February 1865.

WOODRING, JACOB M., Private — Enlisted May 15, 1862, in Jackson County. Enlisted as a substitute for Private James Watson. Captured at Frederick, MD, around September 18, 1862, and confined at Fort McHenry, MD. Paroled at Fort McHenry on November 6, 1862, and exchanged at Aiken's Landing, James River, VA, on November 10, 1862. Returned to duty prior to January 1, 1863. Present or accounted for through February 1864. No further records.

YORK, SAMUEL P.C., Private — Enlisted May 30, 1861, at age 27 in Jackson County. Present or accounted for through February 1864. No further records.

ZACHARY, JAMES MADISON, Private — Enlisted May 30, 1861, at age 18 in Jackson County. Present or accounted for through February 1864.

Company C — "Haywood Invincibles"

Captains

BRYSON, SAMUEL C. — Enlisted May 31, 1861, at age 30 in Haywood County. Appointed Captain on May 31, 1861. Appointed Major on April 30, 1862, and transferred to the Field and Staff of this Reg. Later served as Lieutenant Colonel of this Reg.

FREEMAN, WESLEY N. — Enlisted May 31, 1861, at age 29 in Haywood County. Appointed 2nd Lt. on May 31, 1861. Appointed acting Adjutant (2nd Lt.) on August 21, 1861, and transferred to the Field and Staff of this Reg. Promoted to Captain and transferred back to this company on April 30, 1862. Present or accounted for through February 1865.

Lieutenants

HAWKINS, JOSEPH B., 3rd Lt. Previously served in Company A, 3rd Regiment SC Infantry and transferred to this company on December 18, 1862, with the rank of Private. Promoted to Sergeant on January 14, 1863, and appointed 3rd Lt. on January 1, 1865. Captured at Fort Stedman, VA, on March 25, 1865, and confined at Old Capitol Prison, Washington, D.C. until transferred to Fort Delaware, DE, on March 30, 1865. Released at Fort Delaware on June 17, 1865, after taking the Oath.

SHELTON, STEPHEN JEHU, 1st Lt. — Enlisted May 31, 1861, at age 28 in Haywood County. Appointed 3rd Lt. on May 31, 1861, and promoted to 2nd Lt. on August 20, 1861. Promoted to 1st Lt. on an unspecified date in 1864. Wounded at Fort Stedman, VA, on March 25, 1865, and hospitalized at Petersburg, VA. Returned to duty on April 2, 1865.

SMITH, LEWIS J., 2nd Lt. — Enlisted May 31, 1861, at age 18 in Haywood County. Enlisted as Sergeant and appointed 3rd Lt. on April 30, 1862. Promoted to 2nd Lt. around April 28, 1863. Wounded in the neck and chest at the Battle of the Crater near Petersburg, VA, on July 30, 1864, and returned to duty in November–December 1864. Wounded in the left hip at Fort Stedman, VA, on March 25, 1865, and hospitalized at Petersburg, VA. Captured by the enemy around April 3, 1865, and confined at various Federal hospitals until transferred to Newport News, VA. on May 17, 1865. No further records.

WELCH, WILLIAM PINK, 1st Lt. — Enlisted May 31, 1861, at age 22 in Haywood County. Appointed 1st Lt. on May 31, 1861. Present or accounted for through

December 1863. Detailed as an engineer around May 20, 1864, and assigned to duty with Company H, 2nd Regiment Confederate Engineering Troops in October–December 1864.

Noncommissioned Officers and Privates

ALLEN, DAVID A., Private. Previously served in Company I, 62nd Regiment NC Troops and enlisted in this company in Haywood County at age 27 on April 6, 1863. Paroled at Appomattox Court House, VA, on April 9, 1865.

ALLEN, JEREMIAH M., Private — Enlisted March 22, 1862, at age 36 in Haywood County. Captured near Petersburg, VA, on April 2, 1865, and confined at Point Lookout, MD. Released on June 22, 1865, after taking the Oath.

ALLEN, WILLIAM M., Private — Enlisted March 22, 1862, at age 20 in Haywood County. Wounded at King's School House, VA, on June 25, 1862, and returned to duty in September–October 1862. Present or accounted for through February 1865.

ANDERSON, JAMES S., Private — Enlisted March 22, 1862, at age 21 in Haywood County. Deserted on August 27, 1862.

BEST, SAMUEL B., Private — Enlisted April 12, 1864, at age 17 in Haywood County. Hospitalized at Petersburg, VA, on June 17, 1864, with a gunshot wound and returned to duty prior to January 1, 1865. Paroled at Appomattox Court House, VA, on April 9, 1865.

BIGHAM, JOHN ROBERT, Private — Enlisted May 31, 1861, at age 22 in Haywood County. Transferred to Company B of this Reg. on May 1, 1862.

BIGHAM, WILLIAM B.R., Private — Enlisted May 31, 1861, in Haywood County. Promoted to Corporal on August 16, 1861, but reduced to ranks on April 30, 1862. Discharged on July 16, 1862, for being over age. Discharge certificate gives age as 36.

BRADLEY, JAMES M., Private — Enlisted May 31, 1861, at age 24 in Haywood County. Wounded in the knee at King's School House, VA, on June 25, 1862, and died in hospital at Richmond, VA, around July 18, 1862, of "gangrene."

BRADLEY, WILLIAM J., Private — Enlisted May 31, 1861, at age 22 in Haywood County. Died in hospital at Petersburg, VA, on August 10, 1862, of "febris typhoides."

BRITTAIN, JOHN ROBERT, Private — Enlisted March 22, 1862, at age 17 in Haywood County. Died at Weldon on December 29, 1863, of unreported cause.

BROWN, JOHN W., Private — Enlisted March 1, 1864, in Haywood County. Deserted to the enemy around February 28, 1865, and confined at Washington, D.C. Released around March 6, 1865, after taking the Oath.

BROWN, REUBEN J., Private — Enlisted May 31, 1861, at age 19 in Haywood County. Promoted to Sergeant on April 30, 1862, but reduced to ranks in September–October 1862. Deserted to the enemy around February 28, 1865, and confined at Washington, D.C. Released around March 6, 1865, after taking the Oath.

BROWN, ROBERT G., Private — Enlisted July 1861 in Haywood County. Enlistment date reported as July 1861 but he was not listed in the records of this company until November–December 1864. Deserted to the enemy around February 28, 1865, and confined at Washington, D.C. Released around March 6, 1865, after taking the Oath.

BROWN, WILLIAM H., Private — Enlisted July 1861 in Haywood County. Enlistment date reported as July 1861 but he was not listed in the records of this company until November–December 1864. Retired to the Invalid Corps on January 17, 1865, and assigned to light duty at Richmond, VA. Reported absent on light duty through February 1865.

BRYSON, JOHN L., Private — Enlisted May 31, 1861, at age 20 in Haywood County. Died in hospital at Raleigh around June 11, 1863, of "diarrhea chronic."

BRYSON, JOSEPH Y., Private — Enlisted May 31, 1861, at age 44 in Henderson County. Discharged on October 9, 1861, for unreported reason.

BRYSON, WALTER M., Private. Previously served in Company I, 16th Regiment NC Troops and transferred to this company on December 5, 1861. Appointed Captain and transferred to Company G, 35th Regiment NC Troops on April 21, 1862.

BRYSON, WILLIAM H., Private — Enlisted May 31, 1861, at age 49 in Henderson County. Appointed Assistant Quartermaster (Captain) around September 1, 1861, and transferred to the Field and Staff of this Reg.

BUCHANAN, JULIUS L., Private — Enlisted March 22, 1862, at age 22 in Haywood County. Present or accounted for through February 1865.

BUCHANAN, LUCIUS A., Private — Enlisted May 31, 1861, at age 19 in Haywood County. Killed at Malvern Hill, VA, on July 1, 1862.

BUCHANAN, MOLTON M., Private — Enlisted March 1, 1864, in Haywood County. Captured at Fort Stedman, VA, on March 25, 1865, and confined at Point Lookout, MD. Released on June 24, 1865, after taking the Oath. (NC pension records indicate he was wounded at Petersburg, VA, on an unspecified date.)

BURGESS, JOHN W., Private — Enlisted May 31, 1861, at age 20 in Haywood County. Died at Petersburg, VA, on October 10, 1862, of unreported cause.

BURGNER, DAVID C., Private — Enlisted March 22, 1862, at age 17 in Haywood County. Present or accounted for through December 1863. No further records.

BUTLER, ALBERT T., Private — Enlisted January 14, 1863, at age 18 at Petersburg, VA. Died in hospital at Raleigh on May 14, 1864, of "rubeola."

CALDWELL, JAMES A., Private. Previously served in Company E of this Reg. and transferred to this company on April 28, 1863. Listed as deserter and dropped from the rolls of the company on July 10, 1863.

CALDWELL, DANIEL, Private — Enlisted May 31, 1861, at age 33 in Haywood County. Deserted on September 4, 1861.

CARPENTER, LABAN ALEXANDER, Private — Enlisted May 31, 1861, at age 20 in Haywood County. Captured in hospital at Richmond, VA, on April 3, 1865, and confined at Newport News, VA, on April 24, 1865. Released at Newport News on June 30, 1865, after taking the Oath.

CHAMBERS, ASA, Private — Enlisted May 31, 1861, at age 28 in Haywood County. Reported absent without leave on September 27, 1862, but returned to duty on October 28, 1862. Court-martialed around December 28, 1862. Returned to duty prior to January 1, 1863, and present or accounted for through February 1865.

CHAMBERS, JAMES R., Private — Enlisted May 31, 1861, at age 18 in Haywood County. Deserted on August 8, 1862, but returned to duty on an unspecified date. Deserted again on June 14, 1863, and returned to duty on September 3, 1863. Deserted for third time on December 11, 1863.

CHAMBERS, JOHN H., Private — Enlisted May 31, 1861, at age 26 in Haywood County. Promoted to Sergeant on April 30, 1862. Deserted on August 27, 1862, and reduced to ranks in September 1862. Returned to duty on February 15, 1863, and present or accounted for through December 1863.

CHAMBERS, JOHN M., Private — Enlisted May 31, 1861, at age 31 in Haywood County. Present or accounted for through January 1865 but reported absent on detached duty as a wagon guard or as a teamster during most of this period. Captured near Petersburg, VA, on February 6, 1865, and confined at Point Lookout, MD. Released on June 26, 1865, after taking the Oath.

CHRISTOPHER, JAMES H., Private — Enlisted March 1, 1864, in Haywood County. Wounded in the left lung and/or the left shoulder at Fort Stedman, VA, on March 25, 1865. Hospitalized at Petersburg, VA, where he was captured by the enemy around April 3, 1865. Confined at various Federal hospitals until confined at Camp Hamilton, VA, on May 15, 1865. Released on May 31, 1865, after taking the Oath.

COGGINS, JOHN L., Private — Enlisted May 31, 1861, at age 17 in Haywood County. Killed in action on January 17, 1864. Place of death not reported.

CURRY, JOHN C., Private — Enlisted May 31, 1861, at age 34 in Haywood County. Elected Sergeant on June 13, 1861, but reduced to ranks in January–February 1862. Discharged on July 16, 1862, for being over age.

CURTIS, JOHN M., Private — Enlisted March 1, 1864, in Haywood County. Present or accounted for through February 1865.

DAVIS, JAMES H., Sergeant — Enlisted March 1, 1864, at age 19 in Haywood County. Promoted to Sergeant on September 1, 1862. Wounded at Fredericksburg, VA, on December 13, 1862, and returned to duty in January–February 1863. Present or accounted for through February 1865.

DAVIS, JOHN MILAS, Private — Enlisted November 4, 1863, in Haywood County. Deserted on February 25, 1865, and went over to the enemy. Took Oath at Knoxville, TN, on March 28, 1865.

DEAVER, RUFUS L., Private — Enlisted May 31, 1861, at age 19 in Haywood County. Transferred to Company F of this Reg. on May 1, 1862.

DEAVER, WILLIAM N., Private — Enlisted May 31, 1861, at age 21 in Haywood County. Transferred to Company F of this Reg. on May 1, 1862.

DODSON, ALBERT A., Private — Enlisted May 31, 1861, at age 20 in Haywood County. Enlisted as Corporal but reduced to ranks on April 30, 1862. Present or accounted for through February 1865.

DODSON, DAVID J., Sergeant — Enlisted May 31, 1861, at age 26 in Haywood County. Promoted to Sergeant on April 30, 1862. Died in hospital at Petersburg, VA, on July 29, 1862, of "typhoid fever."

DODSON, JACOB C., Corporal — Enlisted May 31, 1861, at age 22 in Haywood County. Promoted to Corporal on April 30, 1862. Wounded in the back at Sharpsburg, MD, on September 17, 1862, and returned to duty in March–April 1863. Deserted on February 25, 1865.

DODSON, THADDEUS B., Private — Enlisted May 31, 1861, at age 18 in Haywood County. Discharged on April 3, 1862, by reason of disability. Later served in Company A, 62nd Regiment NC Troops.

DODSON, WILLIAM H.H., Private — Enlisted May 31, 1861, at age 20 in Haywood County. Present or accounted for through February 1865.

DUNCAN, JONATHAN N., Private — Enlisted May 31, 1861, at age 18 in Haywood County. Deserted in March–April 1863 but returned to duty on June 27, 1863. Wounded and captured at Five Forks, VA, on April 1, 1865, and confined at Point Lookout, MD. Released on June 26, 1865, after taking the Oath.

EDMONSTON, BAZIL B., Private — Enlisted May 31, 1861, at age 35 in Haywood County. Appointed acting Adjutant on June 30, 1862, and transferred to Field and Staff of this Reg. Appointed Adjutant (Lieutenant) on October 6, 1862, and assigned to permanent duty with the Field and Staff. Discharged around October 16, 1864, for unreported reason. Reenlisted in this company as Private on October 17, 1864, and present or accounted for through February 1865.

EDWARDS, BENJAMIN S., Private — Enlisted May 31, 1861, at age 26 in Haywood County. Promoted to Sergeant on September 1, 1862, but reduced to ranks on an unspecified date. Died in hospital at Huguenot Springs, VA, on February 9, 1863, of "phthisis."

EDWARDS, JAMES L., Private — Enlisted September 17, 1861, at age 23 at Camp Clingman. Discharged around May 1, 1862, after providing a substitute.

ELMORE, HIRAM, Private — Enlisted November 2, 1863, in Haywood County. Hospitalized at Petersburg, VA, on June 18, 1864, with a gunshot wound. Transferred to Farmville, VA, on June 20, 1864, and died in hospital at Farmville on July 20, 1864, of "smallpox."

EVANS, JACOB T., Private — Enlisted May 31, 1861, at age 20 in Haywood County. Wounded in the arm and chest at Fredericksburg, VA, on December 13, 1862, and returned to duty in March–April 1863. Present or accounted for through February 1865.

EVANS, JESSE R., Corporal — Enlisted March 21, 1862, at age 21 in Haywood County. Promoted to Corporal on an unspecified date in 1864. Present or accounted for through February 1865.

FARMER, THOMAS W., Private — Enlisted May 31, 1861, at age 25 in Haywood County. Present or accounted for through April 1862. Detailed for duty in an armory at Richmond, VA, in July–August 1862.

Transferred to Company B, 1st Battalion VA Infantry (Local Defense) on June 15, 1863.

FIE, JOHN C., Private — Enlisted May 31, 1861, at age 17 in Haywood County. Promoted to Corporal on June 30, 1861, but reduced to ranks on August 16, 1861. Wounded at Malvern Hill, VA, on July 1, 1862, and returned to duty in September–October 1862. Deserted to the enemy on December 26, 1864. Took the Oath at City Point, VA, on December 27, 1864, and released around December 30, 1864.

FISHER, SOLOMON C., Private — Enlisted May 31, 1861, at age 21 in Haywood County. Wounded in the foot at Fredericksburg, VA, on December 13, 1862. Discharged on February 16, 1863, by reason of disability from wounds.

FOWLER, DANIEL J., Private — Enlisted March 22, 1862, at age 46 in Haywood County. Captured near Winchester, VA, around December 5, 1862, and confined at Wheeling, (West) VA. Exchanged on March 28, 1863. Transferred to Company B, 35th Regiment NC Troops on November 1, 1863.

FOWLER, JAMES C., Private — Enlisted March 22, 1862, at age 35 in Haywood County. Deserted on October 6, 1863, and apprehended on an unspecified date. Court-martialed and sentenced to death around September 23, 1864, but sentence remitted about October 17, 1864. Reported under arrest through December 1864 and returned to duty in January–February 1865. Captured at Fort Stedman, VA, on March 25, 1865, and confined at Point Lookout, MD. Released on May 13, 1865, after taking the Oath.

FRANKLIN, WILLIAM L., Private — Enlisted May 31, 1861, at age 21 in Haywood County. Killed at King's School House, VA, around June 25, 1862.

FRY, NEELY DAVIDSON, Private — Enlisted March 22, 1862, at age 21 in Haywood County. Wounded at Malvern Hill, VA, on July 1, 1862, and returned to duty in January–February 1863. Paroled at Appomattox Court House, VA, on April 9, 1865.

FULBRIGHT, MARCUS L., Private — Enlisted May 31, 1861, at age 18 in Haywood County. Killed at King's School House, VA, on June 25, 1862.

GIBSON, ADOLPHUS M., Private — Enlisted May 31, 1861, at age 17 in Haywood County. Present or accounted for through December 1863. No further records.

GIBSON, HENRY M., Private — Enlisted May 31, 1861, at age 24 in Haywood County. Present or accounted for through December 1863. No further records (NC pension records indicate he was wounded at Plymouth in October 1864.)

GILLETTE, THOMAS S., Private — Enlisted May 31, 1861, at age 35 in Haywood County. Enlisted as 1st Sergeant but reduced to ranks on April 30, 1862. Wounded in the hand at Fredericksburg, VA, on December 13, 1862, and returned to duty in May–June 1863. Present or accounted for through December 1863. No further war records.

GRASTY, ISRAEL P., Private — Enlisted March 22, 1862, at age 18 in Haywood County. Captured at Frederick, MD, on September 12, 1862, and confined at Fort Delaware, DE. Paroled and exchanged at Aiken's Landing, James River, VA, on November 10, 1862. Returned to duty in January–February 1863. Deserted to the enemy on December 26, 1864, and confined at Washington, D.C. Released about December 30, 1864, after taking the Oath.

GRASTY, JOSEPH J., Private — Enlisted November 7, 1863, in Haywood County. Present or accounted for through February 1865.

GRASTY, WILLIAM F., Private — Enlisted May 31, 1861, at age 21 in Haywood County. Enlisted as Musician (Fifer) but resigned and reduced to ranks on August 1, 1861. Present or accounted for through April 11, 1865.

GREEN, GEORGE W., Private — Enlisted March 22, 1862, at age 25 in Haywood County. Deserted on September 14, 1862, but returned to duty on February 14, 1863. Deserted to the enemy about December 26, 1864, and confined at Washington, D.C. Released around December 30, 1864, after taking the Oath.

GREEN, HENRY L., Private — Enlisted March 22, 1862, at age 20 in Haywood County. Killed at the Battle of the Crater near Petersburg, VA, on July 30, 1864.

GREEN, JEREMIAH, Private — Enlisted May 31, 1861, at age 28 in Haywood County. Wounded in the left thigh at Malvern Hill, VA, on July 1, 1862, and returned to duty prior to September 1, 1862. Wounded in the left wrist near Petersburg, VA, on June 17, 1864, and returned to duty prior to January 1, 1865. Retired to the Invalid Corps on January 17, 1865, by reason of disability from wounds. Captured at hospital at Richmond, VA, on April 3, 1865, and confined at Newport News, VA, on April 24, 1865. Released at Newport News on June 30, 1865, after taking the Oath.

GREEN, MARION P., Private — Enlisted May 31, 1861, at age 19 in Haywood County. Reported absent without leave on August 27, 1862, but returned to duty on October 6, 1862. Deserted to the enemy about December 26, 1864, and confined at Washington, D.C. Released around December 30, 1864, after taking the Oath.

GREEN, WILLIAM H., Private — Enlisted May 31, 1861, at age 19 in Haywood County. Present or accounted for through December 1863. Transferred to Company E, 29th Regiment NC Troops on an unspecified date (probably in January–June 1864).

GREEN, WILLIAM T., Private — Enlisted March 22, 1862, at age 28 in Haywood County. Wounded in the arm at Fredericksburg, VA, on December 13, 1862, and returned to duty in March–April 1863. Present or accounted for through February 1865.

GRIFFITH, WILLIAM D., Corporal — Enlisted May 31, 1861, at age 24 in Haywood County. Wounded at Malvern Hill, VA, on July 1, 1862, and returned to duty prior to September 1, 1862. Promoted to Corporal in May–June 1863 and present or accounted for through February 1865.

HALL, WILLIAM H., Private — Enlisted April 1, 1864, in Haywood County. Present or accounted for through February 1865.

HANNAH, ALEXANDER L., Private — Enlisted May 31, 1861, at age 18 in Haywood County. Wounded in the hand at King's School House, VA, on June 25, 1862, and returned to duty in September–October 1862. Deserted on April 7, 1863. (NC pension records indicate he was wounded at New Bern on an unspecified date.)

HAWKINS, ELKANA, Private — Enlisted January 1, 1865, in Haywood County. Present or accounted for until paroled at Farmville, VA, about April 11–21, 1865.

HAWKINS, GEORGE W., Musician — Enlisted May 31, 1861, at age 20 in Haywood County. Promoted to Musician in September–October 1861. Wounded accidentally in the right shoulder at Weldon on September 3, 1863, and reported absent wounded and "permanently disabled" through February 1865.

HAWKINS, JOSEPH, Private — Enlisted March 22, 1862, at age 60 in Haywood County. Discharged on October 30, 1862, by reason of disability.

HAWKINS, THOMAS M., Private — Enlisted March 22, 1862, at age 26 in Haywood County. Died in hospital at Petersburg, VA, on August 10, 1862, of "meningitis."

HENSON, THOMAS F., Corporal — Enlisted March 22, 1862, at age 31 in Haywood County. Promoted to Corporal on May 1, 1862, and transferred to Company F of this Reg. the same day.

HERREN, ADONIRAM J., Private — Enlisted May 31, 1861, at age 20 in Haywood County. Appointed acting Ordnance Sergeant on July 30, 1862, and transferred to an unspecified unit. Reported absent on detached service as Ordnance Sergeant through August 1863. Reported on duty as acting Ordnance Sergeant of General Ransom's Brigade from September–October 1863 through February 1865. Company records do not indicate whether he rejoined the company but he was captured in hospital at Richmond, VA, on April 3, 1865. Reported in hospital at Point of Rocks, VA, on April 9, 1865.

HIGDON, DAVID, Private — Enlisted May 31, 1861, at age 50 in Haywood County. Discharged on July 16, 1862, for being over age.

HIPPS, WILLIAM E., Private — Enlisted May 31, 1861, at age 19 in Haywood County. Deserted in January 1862.

HOLDER, JOHN P., Private — Enlisted March 22, 1862, at age 17 in Haywood County. Wounded at Sharpsburg, MD, on September 17, 1862, and returned to duty prior to November 1, 1862. Wounded in the arm at Fredericksburg, VA, on December 13, 1862, and returned to duty in March–April 1863. Present or accounted for through February 1865.

HOLDER, WILLIAM H., Private — Enlisted May 31, 1861, at age 22 in Haywood County. Present or accounted for through February 1865. (Records of the United Daughters of the Confederacy indicate he was wounded on September 17, 1862.)

HOLLYFIELD, DANIEL, Private — Enlisted May 31, 1861, at age 18 in Haywood County. Captured at Frederick, MD, on September 12, 1862, and confined at Fort Delaware, DE. Paroled and exchanged at Aiken's Landing, James River, VA, on November 10, 1862. Returned to duty in January–February 1863 and present or accounted for through February 1865.

HOWARD, WILLIAM A., Private — Enlisted May 31, 1861, at age 17 in Haywood County. Deserted on February 25, 1865.

HOWELL, ROBERT H., Sergeant — Enlisted May 31, 1861, at age 18 in Haywood County. Enlisted as Sergeant but reduced to ranks on April 30, 1862. Appointed Sergeant Major on August 1, 1862, and transferred to the Field and Staff of this Reg.

HOYLE, WILLIAM, Private — Enlisted May 10, 1862, in Jackson County. Transferred to Company B of this Reg. on June 2, 1862.

HUNNYCUTT, JAMES F., Private — Enlisted May 31, 1861, at age 18 in Haywood County. Promoted to Corporal on April 30, 1862, but reduced to ranks in May–June 1863. Deserted to the enemy about December 10, 1864, and confined at Washington, D.C. Released around December 15, 1864, after taking the Oath.

HYATT, NATHAN T., Private — Enlisted May 31, 1861, at age 40 in Haywood County. Wounded in the hand at King's School House, VA, on June 25, 1862. Discharged on July 17, 1862, for being over age.

INMAN, JOSEPH L., Private — Enlisted May 31, 1861, at age 18 in Haywood County. Died in a hospital in Petersburg, VA, about August 11–15, 1862, of "meningitis."

JENKINS, JOSEPH M., Private — Enlisted May 31, 1861, at age 21 in Haywood County. Died in a hospital at Lynchburg, VA, on January 17, 1863, of "diarrhea chronic."

JONES, JOHN L., Private — Enlisted March 22, 1862, in Haywood County. Furloughed on September 12, 1862, and failed to return from furlough. Listed as a deserter around November 1, 1862, but returned to duty in November–December 1863. Present or accounted for through December 1863. No further records.

JONES, THOMAS J., Private — Enlisted April 8, 1864, in Haywood County. Paroled at Farmville, VA, about April 11–21, 1865.

JUSTICE, JAMES J., Private — Enlisted May 31, 1861, at age 17 in Haywood County. Wounded in the arm at King's School House, VA, on June 25, 1862, and returned to duty prior to September 1, 1862. Present or accounted for through February 1865.

LEATHERWOOD, E.A., Private — Enlisted April 1, 1864, in Haywood County. Present or accounted for through February 1865.

LEDBETTER, COLEMAN, Private — Enlisted March 22, 1862, at age 43 in Haywood County. Discharged on June 4, 1862, by reason of disability.

LEDFORD, JAMES M., Private — Enlisted September 27, 1861, at age 23 in Wake County. Discharged on June 18, 1862, by reason of disability.

LEMMING, ROBERT H., Private — Enlisted March 22, 1862, at age 29 in Haywood County. Died in hospital at Weldon on April 22–23 1864 of "pneumonia."

LEWIS, J.P., — Enlisted May 1861. NC pension records indicate he enlisted in this company on May 31, 1864. No further records.

LEWIS, PINCKNEY L., Private — Enlisted May 31, 1861, at age 18 in Haywood County. Wounded in the arm/or shoulder at Fredericksburg, VA, on December 13,

1862, and returned to duty in February 1863. Present or accounted for through February 1865.

LEWIS, W.R. — Enlisted February 1861. NC pension records indicate he enlisted on February 15, 1865. No further records.

LINER, MATTHEW, Private — Enlisted March 22, 1862, at age 17 in Haywood County. Deserted on October 9, 1862, and returned to duty on January 9, 1863. Present or accounted for through February 1865.

LOWE, LEANDER P., Private — Enlisted May 31, 1861, at age 35 in Haywood County. Discharged on May 16, 1862, by reason of "inability to perform the duties of a soldier, having but one eye (and) rheumatism."

LOWE, REUBEN B., Private — Enlisted May 31, 1861, at age 21 in Haywood County. Present or accounted for until February 1865.

McCRACKEN, JOSEPH MARCUS L., Private — Enlisted May 31, 1861, at age 22 in Haywood County. Wounded at Malvern Hill, VA, on July 1, 1862, and returned to duty in January–February 1863. Transferred to Company D, 8th Regiment NC State Troops on August 24, 1864.

McCRACKEN, JOSEPH P., Private — Enlisted May 31, 1861, at age 20 in Haywood County. Wounded in the shoulder at Fredericksburg, VA, on December 13, 1862, and returned to duty in March–April 1863. Hospitalized at Petersburg, VA, on September 12, 1864, with a gunshot wound of the head. Died at Petersburg about September 13, 1864, of wounds.

McDANIEL, FRANCIS MARION, Private — Enlisted May 31, 1861, at age 21 in Haywood County. Promoted to Color Corporal in May–June 1863. Hospitalized at Petersburg, VA, on June 18, 1864, with a gunshot wound and returned to duty in August–December 1864. Reduced to ranks in January–February 1865. Present or accounted for through February 1865.

McDANIEL, WILEY A., Sergeant — Enlisted September 17, 1861, in Haywood County. Promoted to Corporal on April 30, 1862, and to Sergeant on April 1, 1863. Captured near Globe Tavern, VA, on August 21, 1864, and confined at Point Lookout, MD. Paroled and exchanged at Boulware's Wharf, James River, VA, on March 18, 1865. Hospitalized at Richmond, VA, on March 19, 1865, with "scorbutus" and furloughed for thirty days on March 24, 1865.

McGEE, WILLIAM C., Private — Enlisted April 18, 1864, in Haywood County. Present or accounted for through February 1865.

MAHAFFEY, JOHN T., Private — Enlisted May 31, 1861, at age 36 in Haywood County. Present or accounted for through February 1862. Detailed for duty in the armory at Richmond, VA, in March–April 1862 and reported absent on detail at Richmond through February 1865.

MESSER, FRANKLIN M., Private — Enlisted May 31, 1861, at age 23 in Haywood County. Enlisted as Corporal but reduced to ranks on April 30, 1862. Promoted to Corporal on April 1, 1863, but again reduced to ranks on an unspecified date in 1864. Wounded in the left foot near Globe Tavern, VA, about August 20, 1864, resulting in amputation of left foot. Reported absent wounded through February 1865.

MESSER, GEORGE S., Private — Enlisted September 17, 1861, at age 28 at Camp Clingman. Wounded in the wrist and/or shoulder at Fredericksburg, VA, on December 13, 1862, and returned to duty in March–April 1863. Deserted on August 5, 1863, but returned to duty prior to January 1, 1864. Captured at Fort Stedman, VA, on March 25, 1865, and confined at Point Lookout, MD. Released on May 14, 1865, after taking the Oath.

MESSER, THADDEUS B., Private — Enlisted May 31, 1861, at age 18 in Haywood County. Captured at Bermuda Hundred, VA, about June 2, 1864, and confined at Point Lookout, MD, until transferred to Elmira, NY, on July 9, 1864. Paroled at Elmira on October 11, 1864, and exchanged at Venus Point, Savannah River, GA, on November 15, 1864. Died at Savannah on November 24, 1864, of unreported cause.

MILLER, JAMES, Private — Enlisted April 1, 1864, in Haywood County. Present or accounted for through February 1865.

MILNER, SAMUEL F., Private — Enlisted May 31, 1861, at age 18 in Haywood County. Deserted to the enemy about February 25, 1865. Took the Oath at Knoxville, TN, on March 28, 1865.

MITCHELL, CHRISTOPHER C., Private — Enlisted May 31, 1861, at age 23 in Haywood County. Present or accounted for through February 1865.

MITCHELL, THOMAS W., Private — Enlisted April 1, 1864, in Haywood County. Present or accounted for through February 1865.

MOODY, ATHALSTON ALEXANDER, Private — Enlisted May 31, 1861, at age 16 in Haywood County. Present or accounted for through February 1865. (NC pension records indicate he was wounded at Petersburg, VA, on August 23, 1863.)

MOODY, JOHN W.D., Private — Enlisted May 31, 1861, at age 20 in Haywood County. Deserted on August 27, 1862, but returned to duty on November 8, 1862. Deserted to the enemy about February 25, 1865, and took Oath at Knoxville, TN, on March 28, 1865. (NC pension records indicate he was wounded in the left hand at Petersburg, VA, about June 24–25, 1864.)

MOORE, W., Private. First listed in the records of this company on February 28, 1865, when hospitalized at Richmond, VA, with a gunshot wound of the right hand. Captured in a hospital at Richmond on April 3, 1865. No further records.

MUSE, DOCTOR F., Private — Enlisted May 31, 1861, at age 20 in Haywood County. Deserted in November–December 1862 but returned to duty on February 15, 1863. Wounded in the hand near Petersburg, VA, about June 17, 1864. Hospitalized at Charlotte on June 24, 1864, and deserted from hospital on July 26, 1864. Dropped from rolls of the company on February 28, 1865.

MUSE, J.A., Private. Paroled at Farmville, VA, about April 11–21, 1865.

MUSE, THOMAS W., Private — Enlisted May 31, 1861, at age 19 in Haywood County. Wounded in the hand near Petersburg, VA, on June 17, 1864. Company records do not indicate whether he returned to duty. (NC pension records indicate he survived the war.)

MYERS, JOHN H., Private. First listed in the records of this company on February 17, 1865, when hospitalized at Chattanooga, TN, with "jaundice." No further records.

NELSON, JESSE B., Private — Enlisted March 22, 1862, at age 22 in Haywood County. Present or accounted for through December 1863. No further records.

NICHOLS, CHRISTOPHER S., Corporal — Enlisted May 31, 1861, at age 21 in Haywood County. Promoted to Corporal on April 30, 1862. Captured at Fort Stedman, VA, on March 25, 1865, and confined at Point Lookout, MD. Released on May 14, 1865, after taking the Oath.

NICHOLS, JAMES S., Private — Enlisted May 31, 1861, at age 36 in Haywood County. Discharged on July 16, 1862, for being over age. Reenlisted in the company on August 15, 1863, and present or accounted for through February 1865.

NICHOLS, JOHN L., Private — Enlisted April 1, 1864, in Haywood County. Present or accounted for through February 1865.

NICHOLS, THOMAS M., Private — Enlisted March 22, 1862, at age 17 in Haywood County. Hospitalized at Petersburg, VA, on June 17, 1864, with a gunshot wound of the head. Reported absent or absent sick through February 1865.

NOLAND, JOHN H., Private — Enlisted May 31, 1861, at age 21 in Haywood County. Died in hospital at Wilson on April 14, 1862, of unreported cause.

NOLAND, WILLIAM RILEY, Private — Enlisted May 31, 1861, at age 22 in Haywood County. Discharged in September–October 1863 for unreported reason.

NORWOOD, JOHN WALL, 1st Sergeant — Enlisted May 31, 1861, at age 18 in Haywood County. Promoted to Sergeant in January–February 1862 and to 1st Sergeant on April 30, 1862. Wounded in the thigh at Fredericksburg, VA, on December 13, 1862. Died in hospital at Fredericksburg on February 2, 1863, of wounds.

PHARR, JOSEPH A., Private. Previously served in Company L, 16th Regiment NC Troops and transferred to this company on August 1, 1862. Killed at Sharpsburg, MD, on September 17, 1862.

RAINS, ALLEN, Private — Enlisted May 31, 1861, in Haywood County. Deserted on August 14, 1861.

RATCLIFF, ALBERT McCONNELL, Sergeant — Enlisted March 22, 1862, at age 22 in Haywood County. Hospitalized at Petersburg, VA, on June 17, 1864, with a gunshot wound of the hand and returned to duty prior to January 1, 1865. Promoted to Sergeant on February 1, 1865, and present or accounted for through February 1865.

RATHBONE, HIRAM, Private — Enlisted May 31, 1861, at age 30 in Haywood County. Discharged on January 8, 1862, for unreported reason. Later served in Company A, 62nd Regiment NC Troops.

RATHBONE, JOHN, Private — Enlisted March 28, 1862, at age 58 in Haywood County. Discharged about March 26, 1863, by reason of "infirmity."

RATHBONE, LORENZO D., Private — Enlisted May 31, 1861, at age 18 in Haywood County. Deserted on June 14, 1863, but returned to duty on August 14, 1863. Hospitalized at Petersburg, VA, around December 1, 1864, with shell wounds of the left thigh, right arm, and right thigh. Died in hospital at Petersburg on December 2, 1864.

REECE, WILLIAM E., Private — Enlisted March 22, 1862, at age 18 in Haywood County. Died in hospital at Petersburg, VA, on July 29, 1862, of "typhoid fever."

RHINEHART, FIDILLA M., Private — Enlisted September 17, 1861, at age 23 at Camp Clingman. Deserted about December 19, 1862, but returned to duty on March 3, 1863. Present or accounted for through December 1863.

RICH, JOSEPH A., Private — Enlisted May 31, 1861, at age 22 in Haywood County. Transferred to Company I of this Reg. on May 1, 1862.

RICH, PETER M., Private — Enlisted May 31, 1861, at age 19 in Haywood County. Enlisted as Musician (Drummer). Promoted to Drum Major on October 17, 1861, and transferred to the Field and Staff of this Reg. Reduced to ranks in September–October 1863 and transferred back to this company. Wounded in the left side at the Battle of the Crater near Petersburg, VA, on July 30, 1864, and returned to duty. Present and accounted for through February 1865.

ROBINSON, AARON B., Private — Enlisted December 2, 1863, at age 21 in Haywood County. Deserted on February 25, 1865.

ROBINSON, JAMES A., Private — Enlisted May 31, 1861, at age 20 in Haywood County. Deserted on February 25, 1865, and went over to the enemy. Took the Oath at Knoxville, TN, on March 28, 1865.

ROBINSON, JOSEPH J., Private — Enlisted March 22, 1862, in Haywood County. Promoted to Musician on April 30, 1862, but reduced to ranks in March–April 1863. Deserted about May 8, 1863, but returned to duty on August 24, 1863. Retired from service on February 17, 1865, by reason of "paralysis of the right side following a severe attack of typhoid fever in the winter of 1862." Retirement certificate gives age as 35.

ROBINSON, REUBEN B., Private — Enlisted May 31, 1861, at age 19 in Haywood County. Detailed as a teamster in November–December 1862 and reported absent on detail through December 1863. Hospitalized at Charlotte on June 24, 1864, with a gunshot wound. Deserted from hospital on July 26, 1864, but rejoined the company prior to January 1, 1865. Deserted again on February 25, 1865.

ROBINSON, WILLIAM W., Private — Enlisted August 15, 1863, at age 18 in Haywood County. Deserted on February 25, 1865. (NC pension records indicate he was wounded in the groin at Seven Pines, VA, on an unspecified date.)

RUSSELL, JAMES H., Private — Enlisted April 1, 1864, in Haywood County. Present or accounted for through November 20, 1864.

SEAY, BENJAMIN, Private — Enlisted May 31, 1861, in Haywood County. Discharged about September 14, 1861, by reason of disability.

SEAY, HENRY DANIEL, Private — Enlisted September 17, 1861, at age 21 in Camp Clingman. Transferred to Company L, 16th Regiment NC Troops on August 1, 1862.

SELLERS, WILLIAM J., Musician — Enlisted May 31, 1861, at age 20 in Haywood County. Promoted to Color Corporal on October 11, 1861, but reduced to ranks in November-December 1861. Promoted to Musician in January-February 1865 and present or accounted for through February 1865.

SHELTON, LEVI, Private — Enlisted May 31, 1861, at age 38 in Haywood County. Discharged on July 16, 1862, for being over age.

SHIELDS, D.J., Private. Paroled at Farmville, VA, about April 11-21, 1865.

SHOOK, RUFUS M., Private — Enlisted May 31, 1861, at age 25 in Haywood County. Died at Wilmington on November 12, 1861, of unreported cause.

SHOTWELL, JOHN, Private. Paroled at Greensboro on May 11, 1865.

SMATHERS, JEREMIAH W., Private — Enlisted May 31, 1861, at age 19 in Haywood County. Wounded at King's School House, VA, on June 25, 1862, and failed to return to duty. Dropped from the rolls and listed as a deserter on February 12, 1863. Returned to duty on February 19, 1863. Died in hospital at Richmond, VA, around August 1, 1864, of unreported cause.

SMATHERS, WILLIAM BURTON, 1st Sergeant — Enlisted May 31, 1861, at age 21 in Haywood County. Promoted to Corporal on January 22, 1862, but reduced to ranks on April 30, 1862. Wounded at Malvern Hill, VA, on July 1, 1862, and returned to duty in September-October 1862. Wounded in head and/or back at Fredericksburg, VA, on December 13, 1862, and returned to duty in January-February 1863. Appointed 1st Sergeant on March 15, 1863. Present or accounted for through February 1865.

SMITH, JOHN A., Private — Enlisted May 31, 1861, at age 22 in Haywood County. Promoted to Musician (Fifer) on August 1, 1861, but reduced to ranks on April 30, 1862. Transferred to Company F of this Reg. on May 1, 1862.

SMITH, JOHN P., Private — Enlisted May 31, 1861, at age 20 in Haywood County. Wounded in the thigh at the Battle of the Crater near Petersburg, VA, on July 30, 1864. Furloughed by the "Medical Board" on August 13, 1864. Dropped from the rolls of the company on February 2, 1865, for unreported reason.

SNIDER, ARCHIBALD M., Private — Enlisted April 8, 1864, in Haywood County. Wounded in the jaw and/or head and captured at Fort Stedman, VA, on March 25, 1865. Died of wounds in hospital at City Point, VA, on April 7, 1865.

SNIDER, FRANCIS M., Private — Enlisted November 1863 at age 17 in Haywood County. NC pension records indicate he enlisted at "Locusfield" in November 1863 at about age 17. Wounded near Petersburg, VA, on July 30, 1864, and discharged in April 1865. No further records.

SNIDER, THOMAS L., Sergeant. Previously served in an unspecified unit and transferred to this company with the rank of Private on January 26, 1863. Promoted to Sergeant in January-August 1864. Wounded with his left foot "shot off" near Globe Tavern, VA, on August 21, 1864. Reported absent wounded through February 1865.

SORRELS, ELIJAH A., Private — Enlisted May 31, 1861, at age 31 in Haywood County. Present or accounted for through February 1865 but reported on detail as a teamster during most of that period. Paroled at Appomattox Court House, VA, on April 9, 1865.

SORRELS, JOSEPH, Private — Enlisted March 22, 1862, in Haywood County. Deserted on May 5, 1864, and went over to the enemy. Took the Oath in eastern Tennessee on December 31, 1864.

SPARKS, GEORGE W., Private — Enlisted April 1, 1864, in Haywood County. Present or accounted for through February 1865.

SPARKS, JOHN T., Private. Previously served in Company G of this Reg. and transferred to this company on May 1, 1862. Wounded in the back at Fredericksburg, VA, on December 13, 1862, and returned to duty in March-April 1863. Present or accounted for through February 1865.

SPIVEY, WILLIAM M., Corporal — Enlisted May 31, 1861, at age 20 in Haywood County. Enlisted as Corporal. Died at Grahamville, SC, on January 19, 1862, of unreported cause.

STEPHENSON, JAMES H., Private — Enlisted at age 18 in Haywood County. Enlisted as Corporal but resigned position and reduced to ranks on June 30, 1861. Died at Grahamville, SC, on January 21, 1862, of unreported cause.

TERRELL, JOHN L., Private. Previously served in Company B of this Reg. and transferred to this company on November 12, 1864. Hospitalized at Richmond, VA, on December 17, 1864, with a gunshot wound. Furloughed for sixty days on January 26, 1865.

TERRELL, WILLIAM STUART, Private — Enlisted May 31, 1861, at age 24 in Haywood County. Transferred to Company A, Infantry Regiment, Thomas Legion on May 13, 1862.

UNDERWOOD, ENOCH D., Private — Enlisted May 31, 1861, at age 39 in Haywood County. Discharged on July 16, 1862, for being over age.

WADE, JAMES M., Private — Enlisted March 22, 1862, at age 18 in Haywood County. Deserted on September 14, 1862, but returned to duty on an unspecified date in 1864. Detailed as a guard at General Johnson's headquarters in November-December 1864. Reported absent on detail through February 1865.

WARREN, THOMAS P., Private — Enlisted April 1, 1864, in Jackson County. Present or accounted for through February 1865.

WELCH, JAMES M., Private — Enlisted January 15, 1863, at age 17 in Haywood County. Died in hospital at Salisbury on August 13, 1864, of a gunshot wound.

WEST, FIDILLIA P., Private — Enlisted May 31, 1861, at age 20 in Haywood County. Enlisted as Sergeant but reduced to ranks on April 30, 1862. Promoted to Sergeant on August 15, 1862, but reduced to ranks on an unspecified date in 1864. Deserted to the enemy on December 10, 1864, and confined at Washington, D.C. Released about December 15, 1864, after taking the Oath.

WHITE, FRANCIS M., Sergeant — Enlisted May 31, 1861, at age 23 in Haywood County. Promoted to

Sergeant on April 30, 1862. Killed "by accident" at Petersburg, VA, about June 11–12, 1863.

WHITE, IRA P., Private — Enlisted May 1864 in Jackson County. Furloughed by the "Medical Board" on July 21, 1864. Company records do not indicate whether he returned to duty. Dropped from the rolls of the company on February 2, 1865, for unreported reason.

WHITE, JAMES V., Private — Enlisted May 31, 1861, at age 25 in Haywood County. Discharged on May 17, 1863, for unreported reason.

WHITE, SAMUEL G.B., Private — Enlisted March 22, 1862, at age 25 in Haywood County. Deserted on September 23, 1862, but returned to duty on March 5, 1863. Present or accounted for through December 1863. No further records.

WHITE, THOMAS ALEX, Private — Enlisted March 22, 1862, at age 29 in Haywood County. Deserted on September 23, 1862, but returned to duty on January 26, 1863. Present or accounted for through December 1863. Paroled at Morganton on May 16, 1865.

WHITEHEAD, HENRY, Private — Enlisted April 6, 1863, at age 39 in Haywood County. Died at Richmond, VA, on July 28, 1864, of unreported cause.

WHITEHEAD, JOSEPH P., Private — Enlisted March 22, 1862, in Haywood County. Died on September 16, 1864. Cause and place of death not reported.

WINCHESTER, JAMES A., Private — Enlisted May 31, 1861, at age 27 in Haywood County. Died at Grahamville, SC, on December 7, 1861, of "measles."

WINES, JAMES F., Private — Enlisted May 31, 1861, at age 19 in Haywood County. Died in hospital near Drewry's Bluff, VA, on August 9, 1862, of unreported cause.

YARBOROUGH, GEORGE W., Private — Enlisted March 22, 1862, in Haywood County. Present or accounted for through November 1864 but reported absent sick or absent on detail as a carpenter during much of that period. Paroled at High Point on May 1, 1865.

Company D — "George's Guards"

Captains

FRANCIS, JOHN W. — Enlisted June 1, 1861, at age 47 in Cherokee County. Appointed Captain on June 1, 1861. Appointed Major on May 17, 1862, and transferred to Field and Staff of this Reg.

TATHAM, LEANDER B. — Enlisted June 1, 1861, at age 30 in Cherokee County. Appointed 2nd Lt. on June 1, 1861. Promoted to 1st Lt. on April 28, 1862, and to Captain on May 17, 1862. Wounded in the head at the Battle of the Crater near Petersburg, VA, on July 30, 1864, and returned to duty. Captured at Fort Stedman, VA, on March 25, 1865, and confined at Old Capitol Prison, Washington, D.C. until transferred to Fort Delaware, DE, on March 30, 1865. Released at Fort Delaware on June 17, 1865, after taking Oath.

Lieutenants

CROMWELL, ZADOC R., 1st Lt. — Enlisted June 1, 1861, at age 23 in Cherokee County. Enlisted as Sergeant and appointed 2nd Lt. on April 28, 1862. Promoted to 1st Lt. on May 21, 1862. Died at Richmond, VA, on July 25, 1862, of "fever."

HALSEY, ANDREW D., 2nd Lt. — Enlisted June 1, 1861, at age 18 in Cherokee County. Appointed 2nd Lt. on July 17, 1862. Court-martialed around September 24, 1864, for unreported reason. Returned to duty in January–February 1865. Deserted to the enemy about February 24, 1865, and confined at Washington, D.C. Released around March 2, 1865, after taking the Oath.

HERBERT, WILLIAM H., 1st Lt. — Enlisted June 1, 1861, at age 28 in Cherokee County. Appointed 1st Lt. on June 1, 1861. Defeated for reelection on April 28, 1862.

PATTERSON, JAMES L., 3rd Lt. — Enlisted August 5, 1861, at age 24 in Buncombe County. Promoted to 1st Sergeant in March–April 1862. Wounded in the breast at King's School House, VA, on June 25, 1862, and returned to duty in July–August 1862. Appointed 3rd Lt. on August 12, 1862, and present or accounted for through February 1864. Deserted on an unspecified date and dropped from the rolls of the company on December 11, 1864.

SETSER, EMANUEL G., 1st Lt. — Enlisted July 15, 1861, at age 27 in Buncombe County. Promoted to Sergeant in September–October 1861 and to 1st Sergeant on November 12, 1861. Appointed 3rd Lt. on April 30, 1862, and promoted to 1st Lt. on May 21, 1862. Resigned on May 25 or August 20, 1864, for unreported reason. Resignation apparently not accepted as he was listed as a deserter and dropped from the rolls of the company on December 16, 1864.

STRANGE, WILLIAM J.A., 3rd Lt. — Enlisted June 1, 1861, at age 24 in Cherokee County. Appointed 3rd Lt. on June 1, 1861. Discharged on April 30, 1862, for unreported reason.

Noncommissioned Officers and Privates

ALDRIDGE, JAMES, Private — Enlisted June 1, 1861, at age 25 in Cherokee County. Wounded in the right arm at Malvern Hill, VA, on July 1, 1862, and returned to duty in September–October 1862. Wounded in the jaw and left thigh near Globe Tavern, VA, about August 21, 1864. Reported absent wounded through December 1864 and then listed as a deserter in January–February 1865.

ALDRIDGE, WILLIAM F., Private — Enlisted June 1, 1861, at age 18 in Cherokee County. Died "at home" around March 25, 1862, of unreported cause.

ALLISON, BENJAMIN F., Sergeant — Enlisted June 1, 1861, at age 29 in Cherokee County. Promoted to Sergeant prior to September 1, 1861. Appointed Color Sergeant on October 5, 1861, and transferred to the Field and Staff of this Reg.

ARNOLD, WILLIAM WASHINGTON, Private — Enlisted June 1, 1864, in Cherokee County. Wounded in the abdomen and captured at Fort Stedman, VA, on March 25, 1865. Died in a Federal field hospital on March 26, 1865, of wounds.

BEVERS, BENJAMIN S., Private — Enlisted April 1864 in Cherokee County. Deserted in January–February 1865.

BIRCHFIELD, WILLIAM M., Private — Enlisted June 1, 1861, at age 21 in Cherokee County. Deserted on August 10, 1863.

BRADLEY, HENRY H., Private — Enlisted June 1, 1861, at age 25 in Cherokee County. Deserted in January–February 1865.

BREWER, JOHN, Private — Enlisted June 1, 1861, at age 25 in Cherokee County. Discharged on September 20, 1861, by reason of "disability."

BROWNING, JOHN E., Private — Enlisted August 15, 1861, at age 21 in Buncombe County. Hospitalized at Richmond, VA, on November 4, 1862, with a gunshot wound of the right shoulder. Reported absent or absent sick through February 1864. No further records.

BRYSON, FRANCIS M., Private — Enlisted June 1, 1861, at age 20 in Cherokee County. Present or accounted for through February 1865.

BRYSON, THOMAS A., Private — Enlisted June 1, 1861, at age 22 in Cherokee County. Died in a hospital at Kittrell's Springs about September 25, 1864, of "cerebro spinal meningitis."

BYRD, ROBERT, Sergeant. Promoted to Sergeant on April 28, 1862. Wounded in the left arm at Malvern Hill, VA, on July 1, 1862, and left arm subsequently amputated. Discharged on September 28, 1864, by reason of disability. Took the Oath at Knoxville, TN, on January 25, 1864.

CAMPBELL, ALFRED C., Private — Enlisted June 1, 1861, at age 41 in Cherokee County. Discharged on June 16, 1862, for unreported reason. Reenlisted in the company on August 1, 1863. Captured near Globe Tavern, VA, about August 21, 1864, and confined to Point Lookout, MD. Died on February 26, 1865, of "diarrhoea chronic."

CAMPBELL, BAXTER B., Private — Enlisted August 15, 1861, at age 44 in Buncombe County. Discharged on July 16, 1862, for being over age.

CARPENTER, THOMAS D., Private — Enlisted June 1, 1861, at age 21 in Cherokee County. Died at Grahamville, SC, around March 3, 1862, of "fever."

CAUDLE, HENRY, Private — Enlisted March 18, 1862, at age 25 in Cherokee County. Captured near Petersburg, VA, on April 2, 1865, and confined at Point Lookout, MD. Released on June 26, 1865, after taking the Oath.

CAWTHAN, WILLIAM L., Private — Enlisted July 15, 1861, at age 21 at Fort Hembree. Deserted on July 20, 1862, but returned to duty on an unspecified date. Deserted again on March 3, 1863, and captured by the enemy in Clay County on February 19, 1864. Confined at Fort Delaware, DE, until released on June 19, 1865, after taking the Oath.

CODY, JAMES, Private — Enlisted June 1, 1861, at age 22 in Cherokee County. Captured at Fort Stedman, VA, on March 25, 1865, and confined at Point Lookout, MD. Released on May 15, 1865, after taking the Oath.

CODY, JOHN A., Private — Enlisted December 28, 1861, at age 20 in Cherokee County. Reported absent without leave in May–June 1862 but returned to duty in July–August 1862. Deserted on May 6, 1863.

CODY, MILES, Private — Enlisted December 28, 1861, at age 17 in Cherokee County. Discharged on July 16, 1862, for being under age.

COLLINS, JOHN W., Private — Enlisted June 1, 1861, at age 19 in Cherokee County. Present or accounted for through February 1864 but reported absent sick or absent on detail during most of that period. Hospitalized at Petersburg, VA, on June 17, 1864, with a gunshot wound of the foot. Reported absent wounded through December 1864 and listed as a deserter in January–February 1865.

COLVARD, JASPER NEWTON, Private — Enlisted August 15, 1861, at age 18 in Buncombe County. Killed at the Battle of the Crater near Petersburg, VA, on July 30, 1864.

CREWS, WILLIAM, Private — Enlisted June 1, 1861, at age 45 in Cherokee County. Discharged around May 14, 1862, by reason of disability.

CRISP, JOEL E., Private — Enlisted June 1, 1861, at age 19 in Cherokee County. Present or accounted for through February 1864. No further records.

DALTON, THOMAS W., Private — Enlisted June 1, 1861, at age 28 in Cherokee County. Deserted on September 1, 1861, but returned to duty prior to November 1, 1861. Reported absent without leave in March–April 1862. Reported absent sick in May–June 1862 and absent without leave in July–August 1862. Returned to duty in September 1862–February 1863. Reported under arrest in July–August 1863. Deserted on September 9, 1863.

DANER, ISAAC, Private — Enlisted March 23, 1862, at age 20 in Cherokee County. Present or accounted for through February 1864. No further records.

DAVIS, JONATHAN M., Private — Enlisted December 28, 1861, at age 17 in Cherokee County. Wounded in the hand at King's School House, VA, on June 25, 1862, and returned to duty prior to July 1, 1862. Deserted in January–February 1865 and went over to the enemy. Took the Oath at Louisville, KY, about April 3, 1865.

DAVIS, WILLIAM H., Private — Enlisted March 28, 1861, at age 24 in Cherokee County. Wounded in the thigh at Fredericksburg, VA, on December 13, 1862, and leg was amputated. Died in hospital at Lynchburg, VA, on January 7, 1863, of wounds and/or "pneumonia."

DITMORE, FRANCIS M., Private — Enlisted August 10, 1861, at age 16 in Buncombe County. Discharged on July 16, 1862, for being under age. Died in hospital at Petersburg, VA, on July 25, 1862, of "cerebro meningitis."

DITMORE, HENRY, Private — Enlisted June 1, 1861, at age 20 in Cherokee County. Captured at Gum Swamp on May 22, 1863, and confined at Fort Monroe, VA. Paroled and exchanged at City Point, VA, on May 28, 1863. Reported absent on detached service until captured in Madison County, TN, on October 25, 1863. Confined at Camp Chase, OH, until transferred to Fort Delaware, DE, on February 29, 1864. Released at Fort Delaware on May 3, 1865, after taking the Oath.

FARLEY, WILLIAM V.B., Private. Previously served in

Company B of this Regiment and transferred to this company on February 12, 1864. Reported absent without leave in January–February 1865.

FARR, JEFFERSON B., Private — Enlisted August 15, 1861, at age 33 in Buncombe County. Captured at Frederick, MD, on September 12, 1862, and confined at Fort Delaware, DE. Transferred to Aiken's Landing, James River, VA, and exchanged on November 10, 1862. Returned to duty prior to February 1, 1863, and present or accounted for through February 1864. No further records.

FLETCHER, JOHN W., Private — Enlisted June 1, 1861, at age 33 in Cherokee County. Discharged in July–August 1862 for unreported reason.

FORE, JOSEPH W., Private — Enlisted June 1, 1861, at age 23 in Cherokee County. Enlisted as Musician (Fifer) but reduced to ranks in September–December 1863. Captured at Gum Swamp on May 22, 1863, and confined at Fort Monroe, VA. Paroled and transferred to City Point, VA, for exchange on May 28, 1863. Present or accounted for through February 1864. No further records.

GANN, BETHEL, Private — Enlisted September 1, 1863, at age 37 in Cherokee County. Captured near Petersburg, VA, on July 30, 1864, and confined at Point Lookout, MD, until transferred to Elmira, NY, on August 8, 1864. Paroled at Elmira on October 11, 1864, and transferred to Venus Point, Savannah River, GA, on November 15, 1864, for exchange.

GASNELL, GEORGE L., Private — Enlisted July 15, 1861, at age 23 in Cherokee County. Wounded in the right thigh at Plymouth on April 20, 1864. Reported absent wounded through December 1864 and then listed as a deserter in January–February 1865.

GEORGE, CHARLES N., Private — Enlisted June 1, 1861, at age 70 in Cherokee County. Enlisted as Sergeant but reduced to ranks on September 15, 1861. Discharged about April 30, 1862, by reason of disability.

GEORGE, JEFFERSON, Private — Enlisted June 1, 1861, at age 24 in Cherokee County. Promoted to Sergeant on October 14, 1861, but reduced to ranks in March–April 1862. Captured near Petersburg, VA, on July 30, 1864, and confined at Point Lookout, MD, until transferred to Elmira, NY, on August 8, 1864. Released at Elmira on July 3, 1865, after taking the Oath.

GIBSON, WESLEY, Private — Enlisted March 18, 1862, at age 28 in Cherokee County. Reported absent without leave in March–April 1863 and under arrest in May–June 1863. Reported absent sick in July–August 1863 but returned to duty prior to January 1, 1864. Captured at Petersburg, VA, on July 30, 1864, and confined at Point Lookout, MD, until transferred to Elmira, NY, on August 8, 1864. Released at Elmira on May 29, 1865, after taking the Oath.

GRIGG, WILLIAM N., Private — Enlisted July 15, 1861, at age 19 in Cherokee County. Captured at Petersburg, VA, on July 30, 1864, and confined at Point Lookout, MD, until transferred to Elmira, NY, on August 8, 1864. Paroled at Elmira about March 2, 1865, and transferred to the James River, VA, for exchange.

HARPER, WILLIAM H., Sergeant. Hospitalized at David's Island, New York Harbor on July 1, 1865. Place and date captured not reported. Released on July 12, 1865, after taking the Oath. Records of the Federal Provost Marshal give his age as 25. No further records.

HASTON, DAVID F., Private — Enlisted June 1, 1861, at age 23 in Cherokee County. No further records.

HEADEN, JEFFREY A., Private — Enlisted June 1, 1861, at age 22 in Cherokee County. Captured at Gum Swamp on May 22, 1863, and confined at Fort Monroe, VA. Paroled and exchanged at City Point, VA, on May 28, 1863. Detailed as an ambulance driver in July–August 1863 and reported absent on detail through February 1865.

HENSLEY, FIELDEN H., Corporal — Enlisted March 23, 1862, at age 19 in Cherokee County. Promoted to Corporal in September–December 1863. Wounded at Plymouth about April 18–20 and subsequently returned to duty. Captured near Petersburg, VA, on April 2, 1865, and confined at Point Lookout, MD. Released on June 27, 1865, after taking the Oath.

HERBERT, DANIEL S., Private — Enlisted June 1, 1861, at age 18 in Cherokee County. Listed as a deserter in January–February 1865.

HOLLAND, JOHN B., Private — Enlisted June 1, 1861, at age 22 in Cherokee County. Died at Kinston or at Richmond, VA, about May 20–26, 1862, of disease.

HOLLAND, JOHN H., Private — Enlisted June 1, 1861, at age 47 in Cherokee County. Enlisted as Musician (Drummer) but reduced to ranks in March–April 1862. Discharged on April 14, 1862, after providing Private Samuel C. Holland (his son) as a substitute.

HOLLAND, SAMUEL C., Private — Enlisted April 14, 1862, at age 20 at Camp Ransom. Enlisted as a substitute for Private John H. Holland (his father). Present or accounted for through August 1863 but was reported absent sick during most of that period. Deserted on September 15, 1863.

HOOPER, GEORGE W., Private — Enlisted June 1, 1861, at age 24 in Cherokee County. Deserted on April 26, 1863.

HOOPER, ISAAC V., Private — Enlisted June 1, 1861, at age 22 in Cherokee County. Reported absent without leave in March–April 1863 and under arrest in May–June 1863. Returned to duty in July–August 1863 and present or accounted for through February 1864. No further records.

HORTON, DAVID F., Sergeant — Enlisted June 1, 1861, at age 21 in Cherokee County. Promoted to Sergeant in March–April 1862 but reduced to ranks in May–June 1862. Again promoted to Sergeant in January–February 1863. Wounded in both legs near Drewry's Bluff, VA, on May 14, 1864, and one leg was amputated. Died in hospital at Richmond, VA, on June 13, 1864, of "pyemia."

HOWARD, WILLIAM H., Private — Enlisted August 5, 1861, at age 28 in Buncombe County. Wounded in the leg at Fredericksburg, VA, on December 13, 1862, and leg was amputated. Hospitalized at Richmond, VA, and died of wounds about December 18, 1862.

HUSKINS, FRANCIS MONROE, Private — Enlisted June 1, 1861, at age 18 in Cherokee County. Killed at Spring Creek on October 25, 1863.

HUSKINS, JAMES, Private — Enlisted June 1, 1861, at age 23 in Cherokee County. Present or accounted for through February 1865.

HUSKINS WILLIAM G., Private — Enlisted June 1, 1861, at age 19 in Cherokee County. Deserted to the enemy in January 1864 and took the Oath of Allegiance at Knoxville, TN, on January 25, 1864.

JOHNSON, BENJAMIN C., Private — Enlisted March 23, 1862, at age 27 in Cherokee County. Wounded at Malvern Hill, VA, on July 1, 1862, and returned to duty on unspecified date. Wounded in the left foot near Petersburg, VA, on June 17, 1864. Reported absent wounded through December 1864.

JOHNSON, WILLIAM HARRISON, Private — Enlisted November 28, 1861, at age 23 at Fort Hembree. Wounded in the head at Fredericksburg, VA, on December 13, 1862. Reported absent wounded or absent sick through February 1865. Paroled at Greensboro on May 5, 1865.

JORDAN, JAMES H., Private — Enlisted June 1, 1861, at age 18 in Cherokee County. Wounded at Malvern Hill, VA, on July 1, 1862. Reported absent wounded or absent sick until being detailed for hospital duty in July–August 1863. Rejoined the company in September–December 1863. Deserted to the enemy on February 18, 1865, and confined at Washington, D.C. Released about February 21, 1865, after taking the Oath.

JORDAN, WILLIAM, Private — Previously served in Company G, 9th Regiment NC State Troops and transferred to this company on October 28, 1864. Captured near Petersburg, VA, on April 2, 1865, and confined at Point Lookout, MD. Released on June 28, 1865, after taking the Oath.

JORDAN, WILLIS E., Sergeant — Enlisted June 1, 1861, at age 18 in Cherokee County. Promoted to Sergeant in March–December 1864. Captured at Fort Stedman, VA, on March 25, 1865, and confined at Point Lookout, MD. Released on May 15, 1865, after taking the Oath.

LANCE, MITCHELL A., Private — Enlisted June 1, 1861, at age 23 in Cherokee County. Discharged on August 15, 1862, for unreported reason.

LANNON, WILLIAM W., Private — Enlisted March 18, 1862, at age 24 in Cherokee County. Wounded in action on an unspecified date after February 1864. Reported absent wounded through December 1864.

LEATHERWOOD, LAFAYETTE L., Private — Enlisted August 10, 1861, at age 21 in Buncombe County. Died in hospital near Petersburg, VA, about August 6, 1862, of "febris typhoides."

LEDFORD, AMOS J., Private — Enlisted August 10, 1861, at age 23 in Buncombe County. Present or accounted for through February 1865.

LEDFORD, ROBERT, Private — Enlisted August 10, 1861, at age 18 in Buncombe County. Discharged on August 15, 1862, for unreported reason.

LEDFORD, TILMAN C., Private — Enlisted June 1, 1861, at age 20 in Cherokee County. Hospitalized at Petersburg, VA, on August 16, 1864, with a gunshot wound of the abdomen. Died of wounds in hospital at Petersburg on August 23, 1864.

LEDFORD, WILLIAM, Private — Enlisted August 10, 1861, at age 18 in Buncombe County. Died in hospital at Grahamville, SC, around January 13, 1862, of "fever."

LOUDERMILK, GEORGE W., Private — Enlisted August 3, 1861, at age 37 in Buncombe County. Discharged on August 15, 1862, for being over age.

LOUDERMILK, WILLIAM W., Private — Enlisted August 3, 1861, at age 45 in Buncombe County. Discharged on August 15, 1862, for being over age.

LOUGHRIDGE, WILLIAM, Private — Enlisted June 1, 1864, in Cherokee County. Deserted in January–February 1865.

LOWRY, THOMAS, Private — Enlisted June 1, 1861, at age 25 in Cherokee County. Deserted in July–August 1863 but returned to duty prior to January 1, 1864. Captured at Five Forks, VA, on April 1, 1865, and confined at Point Lookout, MD. Released on June 28, 1865, after taking the Oath.

McCLURE, JOHN V., Private — Enlisted December 28, 1861, at age 20 at Fort Hembree. Deserted on July 28, 1862.

McCLURE, LUCIUS H., Private — Enlisted August 10, 1861, at age 17 in Buncombe County. Discharged around July 16, 1862, for being under age.

McFALLS, JOHN H., Private — Enlisted June 1, 1861, at age 22 in Cherokee County. Deserted in January–February 1864.

McKEE, WILLIAM J., Private — Enlisted June 1, 1861, at age 18 in Cherokee County. Captured in Madison County, TN, on October 16, 1863, and confined at Camp Chase, OH, on November 14, 1863. Transferred to Rock Island, IL, on January 14, 1864, and paroled at Rock Island about March 20, 1865. Received at Boulware's Wharf, James River, VA, on March 27, 1865, for exchange.

McLELLAN, NEWTON R., Private — Enlisted July 15, 1861, at age 17 in Cherokee County. Discharged on July 16, 1862, for being under age

McLELLAND, GEORGE LEE D., Jr., Private. Previously served as Musician (Bugler) in Company A, 19th Regiment NC Troops and transferred to this company in September–December 1864 with the rank of Private. Deserted to the enemy about February 22, 1865, and confined at Washington, D.C. Released around February 24, 1865, after taking the Oath.

MARTIN, BENJAMIN S., Private — Enlisted June 1, 1861, at age 20 in Cherokee County. Enlisted as Corporal but reduced to ranks in March–April 1862. Reported absent wounded in July–August 1863 and then reported absent wounded or absent sick through February 1865.

MARTIN, HENRY J., Private — Enlisted June 1, 1861, at age 23 in Cherokee County. Enlisted as Corporal but reduced to ranks in March–April 1862. Captured at Hatcher's Run, VA, on April 1, 1865, and confined at Point Lookout, MD. Released on June 29, 1865, after taking the Oath.

MARTIN, JAMES D., Private — Enlisted March 1, 1864, in Cherokee County. Captured at Farmville, VA, on April 6, 1865, and confined at Newport News, VA. Released on June 27, 1865, after taking the Oath.

MARTIN, JOHNSON, Private — Enlisted March 28,

1862, at age 29 in Cherokee County. Reported absent without leave in July–August 1862 but returned to duty in January–February 1863. Deserted to the enemy on an unspecified date after February 1864 and took the Oath at Chattanooga, TN, on June 3, 1865.

MARTIN, WILLIAM JULIUS, Private — Enlisted June 1, 1861, at age 30 in Cherokee County. Wounded at Malvern Hill, VA, on July 1, 1862, and returned to duty prior to September 1, 1862. Paroled at Salisbury on May 2, 1865.

MATHESON, CHRISTOPHER C., Private — Enlisted March 18, 1862, at age 23 in Cherokee County. Present or accounted for through February 1865.

MATHESON, ELISHA D., Private — Enlisted September 1, 1863, at age 18 in Cherokee County. Deserted in January–February 1865.

MATHESON, LEANDER D., Private — Enlisted December 28, 1861, at age 26 at Fort Hembree. Died in hospital at Mount Jackson, VA, on November 3, 1862, of "pneumonia."

MATHESON, RUFUS A., Private — Enlisted June 1, 1861, at age 21 in Cherokee County. Reported absent without leave about January 1, 1863, but returned to duty around March 1, 1863. Present or accounted for through February 1865.

MEADOWS, WILLIAM F., Private — Enlisted March 28, 1862, at age 35 in Cherokee County. Wounded in the thigh at King's School House, VA, on June 25, 1862. Discharged on July 15, 1862, for unreported reason.

MINGUS, JOHN, Private — Enlisted June 1, 1861, at age 42 in Cherokee County. Discharged on July 16, 1862, for being over age.

MINGUS, JOHN L., Private — Enlisted June 1, 1861, at age 16 in Cherokee County. Discharged on August 15, 1862, for being under age.

MONROE, ENOS G., Private — Enlisted June 1, 1861, at age 25 in Cherokee County. Present or accounted for through February 1864. No further records.

MONROE, JEPTHA M., Private — Enlisted June 1, 1861, at age 17 in Cherokee County. Hospitalized at Farmville, VA, on August 28, 1863, with a gunshot wound of the foot. Place and date wounded not reported. Returned to duty around September 21, 1863, and present or accounted for through February 1864. No further records.

MONROE, JETHRO M., Private — Enlisted June 1, 1861, at age 17 in Cherokee County. Discharged in July–August 1862 and reenlisted in the company on May 16, 1863. Present or accounted for through February 1864. No further records.

MONROE, LORENZO D., Private — Enlisted June 1, 1861, at age 23 in Cherokee County. Discharged on July 26, 1862, for unreported reason.

MOORE, ELISHA WARREN, Corporal — Enlisted June 1, 1861, at age 27 in Cherokee County. Enlisted as Corporal. Died in hospital at Grahamville, SC, on February 13, 1862, of "fever."

MOSS, HOWELL M., Private — Enlisted November 28, 1861, at age 20 at Fort Hembree. Hospitalized at Richmond, VA, on June 13, 1864, with a gunshot wound. Reported absent wounded or absent sick through February 1865.

MOSS, LEANDER W., Private — Enlisted November 28, 1861, at age 22 at Fort Hembree. Present or accounted for through February 1863. Reported absent sick from March–April 1863 through February 1864. No further records.

NICHOLS, P. CALVIN, Private — Enlisted March 25, 1862, at age 24 at Fort Hembree. Present or accounted for until January–February 1865 when he was reported absent without leave.

OAR, ANDREW W., Private — Enlisted June 1, 1861, at age 15 in Cherokee County. Present or accounted for until discharged on July 15, 1862, for being under age.

OWENBY, ERASTUS W., Private — Enlisted June 1, 1861, at age 22 in Cherokee County. Transferred to Company I of this Reg. in January–February 1864.

OWENBY, JOHN S., Private — Enlisted June 1, 1861, at age 20 in Cherokee County. Killed at Sharpsburg, MD, on September 17, 1862.

PALMER, JAMES E., Private — Enlisted June 1, 1861, at age 18 in Cherokee County. Wounded in the arm at King's School House, VA, on June 25, 1862. Died at Richmond, VA, about July 11, 1862, of wounds.

PARKER, GEORGE W., Private — Enlisted June 1, 1861, at age 18 in Cherokee County. Present or accounted for through February 1864. No further records.

PARKER, WILLIAM J., Private. Previously served in an unspecified unit and transferred to this company on March 2, 1862. Wounded in the leg at the Battle of the Crater near Petersburg, VA, on July 30, 1864, and leg was amputated. Reported absent wounded from November–December 1864 through February 1865.

PHILLIPS, JAMES M., Private — Enlisted October 5, 1861, at age 28 in New Hanover County. Present or accounted for through February 1864. (NC pension records indicate he was wounded in the left shoulder at Fredericksburg, VA, in November (?) 1863.)

PHILLIPS, NATHANIEL GREENE, Private — Enlisted June 1, 1861, at age 29 in Cherokee County. Discharged on July 30, 1861, for unreported reason. Later served as 2nd Lt. of Company I, Infantry Regiment, Thomas Legion.

RAGLE, HENRY, Private — Enlisted June 1, 1861, at age 45 in Cherokee County. Discharged on April 14, 1862, after providing Private John T. Ragle (his son) as a substitute.

RAGLE, JOHN T., Private — Enlisted April 14, 1862, at age 18 in Cherokee County. Enlisted as a substitute for Private Henry Ragle (his father). Present or accounted for through February 1864. No further records.

REAGAN, JAMES H., Private — Enlisted August 10, 1861, at age 22 in Buncombe County. Promoted to Sergeant in July–August 1862 but reduced to ranks in September–December 1863. Wounded in the thigh at the Battle of the Crater near Petersburg, VA, on July 30, 1864. No further reports until listed as a deserter in January–February 1865.

REAGAN, WILLIAM, Private — Enlisted March 28, 1862, at age 24 in Cherokee County. Present or accounted for through February 1864. Wounded in an unspecified engagement in March–December 1864 and listed as a deserter in January–February 1865.

REDDEN, ALLEN, Private. Paroled at Appomattox Court House, VA, on April 9, 1865.

REEDY, FREDERICK, Private — Enlisted June 1, 1861, at age 18 in Cherokee County. Deserted to the enemy about February 24, 1865, and confined at Washington, D.C. Released around March 1, 1865, after taking the Oath.

RHEA, LEONIDAS W., Private — Enlisted June 1, 1861, at age 16 in Cherokee County. Discharged about March 10, 1862, for unreported reason.

RHEA, WILLIAM, Private — Enlisted June 1, 1861, at age 45 in Cherokee County. Discharged around May 6, 1862, for being over age.

RODGERS, JESSE NEWTON, Private — Enlisted March 27, 1862, at age 25 in Cherokee County. Deserted in January–February 1865.

ROGERS, WILLIAM J., Private — Enlisted August 15, 1861, at age 32 in Buncombe County. Present or accounted for through August 27, 1864.

ROWAN, SAMUEL C., Private — Enlisted March 28, 1862, at age 18 in Cherokee County. Hospitalized at Richmond, VA, on August 17, 1864, with a gunshot wound of the neck and face. Place and date wounded not reported. Died at Richmond on August 19, 1864, of wounds.

RUSSELL, DAVID M., Private — Enlisted August 10, 1861, at age 28 in Buncombe County. Paroled at Appomattox Court House, VA, on April 9, 1865.

RUSSELL, JAMES D., 1st Sergeant — Enlisted July 15, 1861, at age 26 in Buncombe County. Promoted to 1st Sergeant in July–August 1862. Wounded in the left eye near Petersburg, VA, about February 25, 1865, and hospitalized at Richmond, VA. Furloughed for sixty days on March 28, 1865.

RUSSELL, JAMES G., Sergeant — Enlisted August 3, 1861, at age 19 in Buncombe County. Promoted to Corporal in March–December 1864 and to Sergeant subsequent to December 31, 1864. Deserted to the enemy about February 24, 1865, and confined at Washington, D.C. Released around March 1, 1865, after taking the Oath.

RUSSELL, WILLIAM A., Private — Enlisted July 15, 1861, at age 24 in Buncombe County. Died at Goldsboro on July 10 or July 27, 1862, of "fever."

SHARP, RICHARD H., Private — Enlisted July 1, 1861, at age 42 in Cherokee County. "Killed by accident by a sentinel on post" near Grahamville, SC, about February 18, 1862.

SHARP, WILLIAM W., Private — Enlisted June 1, 1861, at age 21 in Cherokee County. Wounded in the abdomen at Malvern Hill, VA, on July 1, 1862. Died of wounds in hospital at Richmond, VA, on July 9, 1862.

SHERMAN, JOHN W., Private — Enlisted June 1, 1861, at age 18 in Cherokee County. Discharged around April 30, 1862, by reason of disability.

SHERRELL, MICHAEL S., Private — Enlisted August 15, 1861, at age 33 in Buncombe County. Promoted to Corporal in March–April 1862. Wounded in an unspecified engagement in March–December 1864. Reduced to ranks and listed as a deserter in January–February 1865.

SMATHERS, JOHN W., Private — Enlisted July 13, 1862, at age 24 in Cherokee County. Present or accounted for through February 1864.

SNIDER, JESSE E., Private — Enlisted July 15, 1862, at age 34 in Cherokee County. Discharged on July 15, 1862, for unreported reason.

SOUTHERLAND, CASWELL J., Private — Enlisted August 15, 1861, at age 48 in Buncombe County. Discharged around September 14, 1861, by reason of "sickness." Reenlisted in the company on August 1, 1863, and present or accounted for through February 1864. No further records.

SOUTHERLAND, JASPER N., Private — Enlisted June 1, 1861, at age 24 in Cherokee County. Present or accounted for through February 1864. No further records.

SUTHERLAND, THOMAS J., Private — Enlisted August 15, 1861, at age 22 in Buncombe County. Present or accounted for through February 1864.

SWINNEY, JAMES H., Private — Enlisted August 15, 1861, at age 25 in Buncombe County. Died in hospital at Grahamville, SC, about March 22, 1862, of unreported cause.

TATHAM, JASPER, Sergeant — Enlisted June 1, 1861, at age 19 in Cherokee County. Enlisted as Sergeant. Present or accounted for through February 1865. Afterward, died of "exposure." Date and place of death unspecified.

TATHAM, JOHN G., Private — Enlisted June 1, 1861, at age 17 in Cherokee County. Present or accounted for through December 1864. "Cut off" from company in January–February 1865 while home on furlough. Attached himself to the cavalry command of General John C. Vaughn and served with that command until the end of the war. "He was with the troops who escorted President (Jefferson) Davis on his journey westward from Richmond, after the evacuation (on April 2, 1865), and, in the capacity of a messenger, was admitted to the last council held by the President and his cabinet."

TATHAM, JULIUS M., Private — Enlisted March 27, 1862, at age 21 in Cherokee County. Died "at home" about January 8, 1863, of "dropsy."

THOMPSON, ROBERT B., Sergeant — Enlisted June 1, 1861, at age 21 in Cherokee County. Promoted to Sergeant in September–December 1863. Captured at Five Forks, VA, on April 1, 1865, and confined at Point Lookout, MD. Released on June 20, 1865, after taking the Oath.

VAUGHN, JOSEPH H., Private — Enlisted December 28, 1861, at age 21 at Fort Hembree. Deserted on August 15, 1863, and reported under arrest in November–December 1863. Deserted again prior to March 1, 1864.

WEBB, JASON C., Sergeant — Enlisted June 1, 1861, at age 18 in Cherokee County. Promoted to Musician (Drummer) in March–April 1862 and promoted to Sergeant in September–December 1863. Hospitalized at Petersburg, VA, on June 20, 1864, with a gunshot wound. Died in hospital at Petersburg on June 26, 1864, of wounds.

WEBB, WILLIAM W., Private—Enlisted June 1, 1861, at age 20 in Cherokee County. Died "at home" on July 15, 1863, of disease.

WEST, WILLIAM B., Private—Enlisted December 28, 1861, at age 20 in Cherokee County. Captured near Globe Tavern, VA, on August 21, 1864, and confined at Point Lookout, MD. Released around October 14, 1864, after joining the U.S. Army. Unit to which assigned not reported.

WILSON, JAMES, Private—Enlisted June 1, 1861, at age 19 in Cherokee County. Enlisted as Corporal but reduced to ranks in March–April 1862. Present or accounted for through February 1864 but died prior to October 7, 1864. Place and cause of death not reported.

YOUNG, GEORGE H., Private—Enlisted June 1, 1861, at age 18 in Cherokee County. Killed in a railroad accident between Florence, SC, and Wilmington about March 17, 1862.

YOUNG, JULIUS M., Private—Enlisted June 1, 1861, at age 29 in Cherokee County. Mustered in as 1st Sergeant. Promoted to Commissary Sergeant on November 5, 1861, and transferred to the Field and Staff of this Reg. Reduced to ranks in May–August 1862 and transferred back to this company. Reported absent without leave in September–October of 1862 but returned to duty in November–December 1862. Promoted to acting Hospital Steward in July–August 1863 and transferred to the Field and Staff of this Reg. Appointed Hospital Steward on November 23, 1864, and assigned to permanent duty with the Field and Staff.

Company E — "Transylvania Volunteers"

Captains

GRAVES, WILLIAM H.—Enlisted June 15, 1861, at age 27 in Henderson County. Enlisted as 1st Sergeant. Detailed as acting Adjutant in March–April 1862 and transferred to Field and Staff of this Reg. Transferred back to this company about April 28, 1862, and appointed 1st Lt. Promoted to Captain on June 22, 1862. Killed near Petersburg, VA, on October 12 or October 17, 1864.

JOHNSTONE, FRANCIS WITHERS—Enlisted June 15, 1861, at age 46 in Transylvania County. Appointed Captain on June 15, 1861. Defeated for reelection on April 28, 1862.

YOUNG, EPHRIAM E.—Enlisted June 15, 1861, at age 26 in Transylvania County. Appointed 3rd Lt. on June 15, 1861, and promoted to Captain on April 30, 1862. Died at Kinston on June 22, 1862, of "fever."

Lieutenants

DEAVER, JAMES P., 3rd Lt.—Enlisted June 15, 1861, at age 17 in Transylvania County. Enlisted as Sergeant and appointed 3rd Lt. around April 30, 1862. Promoted to 1st Lt. on June 22, 1862. Discharged on July 16, 1862, for being under age. Reenlisted in the company with the rank of Private on September 3, 1862. Appointed 3rd Lt. on May 12, 1863, and present or accounted for through February 1864. No further records.

ENGLAND, WILLIAM W., 3rd Lt.—Enlisted June 15, 1861, at age 18 in Transylvania County. Enlisted as Corporal and promoted to Sergeant on July 23, 1862, and to 1st Sergeant on December 31, 1862. Appointed 3rd Lt. in March–December 1864. Wounded in the left arm at Five Forks, VA, on April 1, 1865, resulting in amputation of left arm. Hospitalized at Amelia Springs, VA, and captured on April 9, 1865. Confined at various Federal hospitals until confined at Fort McHenry, MD, about May 10, 1865. Died in hospital at Fort McHenry around May 10, 1865, of "pneumonia following amputation."

HENLEY, ABRAM L., 2nd Lt.—Enlisted June 15, 1861, at age 26 in Henderson County. Appointed 3rd Lt. on August 11, 1862, and promoted to 2nd Lt. on May 12, 1863. Hospitalized at Richmond, VA, on July 14, 1863, with a gunshot wound of the head. Furloughed on July 22, 1863, and resigned on October 10, 1863, by reason of being "a Georgian" and because he wished to join the 23rd Regiment GA Volunteer Infantry.

MILLER, ANDREW J., 1st Lt.—Enlisted June 15, 1861, at age 31 in Transylvania County. Appointed 1st Lt. on June 15, 1861. Declined to stand for reelection and discharged on April 30, 1862. Later served as Assistant Quartermaster (Captain) of this Reg.

MULL, PETER K., 2nd Lt.—Enlisted March 28, 1862, at age 21 in Transylvania County. Appointed 3rd Lt. on December 4, 1863, and promoted to 2nd Lt. in March–December 1864. Paroled at Appomattox Court House, VA, on April 9, 1865.

NEELY, MATTHEW J., 2nd Lt.—Enlisted June 15, 1861, at age 25 in Transylvania County. Promoted to Sergeant on April 30, 1862, and appointed 3rd Lt. on July 23, 1862, and to 2nd Lt. on August 1, 1862. Resigned on February 26, 1863, for unreported reason.

OSBORN, CHARLES LaFAYETTE, 1st Lt.—Enlisted September 8, 1861, at age 27 in Buncombe County. Promoted to Ordnance Sergeant in May–June 1862. Appointed 2nd Lt. on July 23, 1862, and to 1st Lt. on August 1, 1862. Transferred to the 65th Regiment NC Troops because of his inability to "stand infantry service in the summer season."

ROBINSON, JOHN C., 2nd Lt.—Enlisted June 15, 1861, at age 30 in Transylvania County. Discharged about April 30, 1862, after declining to stand for reelection. Later served as Assistant Commissary of Subsistence (2nd Lt.) of this Reg.

SHIPMAN, ANDREW, 1st Lt.—Enlisted June 15, 1861, at age 23 in Transylvania County. Appointed 3rd Lt. about April 30, 1862. Promoted to 2nd Lt. on June 22, 1862, and to 1st Lt. on July 16, 1862. Died near Drewry's Bluff, VA, on August 1, 1862, of disease.

Noncommissioned Officers and Privates

AKINS, ADONIRAUM S., Sergeant—Enlisted January 30, 1862, at age 18 at Grahamville, SC. Promoted to Sergeant on September 27, 1862. Wounded in the right arm at Fredericksburg, VA, on December 13, 1862, and returned to duty in January–February 1863.

Reported absent without leave on February 26, 1865. Reported in hospital in Richmond, VA, on April 22, 1865. Deserted on April 27, 1865.

ALEXANDER, GEORGE W., Private — Enlisted June 15, 1861, at age 22 in Transylvania County. Wounded in the right wrist at Fredericksburg, VA, on December 13, 1862, and returned to duty in January–February 1863. Paroled at Farmville, VA, about April 11–21, 1865.

ALLEN, CHARLES K., Private — Enlisted June 15, 1861, at age 23 in Transylvania County. Died at Kinston on June 3, 1862, of disease.

ALLISON, ADOLPHUS E., Private — Enlisted June 15, 1861, at age 25 in Transylvania County. Reported absent without leave on December 1, 1864.

ALLISON, FRANCIS B., Private — Enlisted June 15, 1861, at age 18 in Transylvania County. "Killed on the picket line" near Petersburg, VA, on December 3, 1864.

ALLISON, FRANCIS H., Private. Previously served in Company F, 8th Regiment GA Infantry and transferred to this company on January 3, 1863. Paroled at Farmville, VA, about April 11–21, 1865. (NC pension records indicate he was wounded in an unspecified engagement on January 20, 1865.)

ALLISON, JAMES M., Private — Enlisted June 15, 1861, at age 17 in Transylvania County. Died near Petersburg, VA, on September 5, 1864, of wounds.

ALLISON, JESSE W., Private — Enlisted June 15, 1861, at age 24 in Transylvania County. Died in hospital at Grahamville, SC, on March 17, 1862.

ALLISON, SAMUEL J., Sergeant — Enlisted June 15, 1861, at age 21 in Transylvania County. Enlisted as Sergeant and died at Goldsboro on April 11, 1862, of disease.

ALLISON, THOMAS A., Private — Enlisted June 15, 1861, at age 25 in Transylvania County. Present or accounted for through February 1864 and reported on detail as a blacksmith during most of that period. No further records.

ANDERS, DAVID B., Private — Enlisted June 15, 1861, at age 19 in Transylvania County. Wounded in the thigh at King's School House, VA, on June 25, 1862, and returned to duty in September–October 1862. Wounded in the abdomen at Fredericksburg, VA, on December 13, 1862, and rejoined the company in March–April 1863. Captured at Gum Swamp on May 22, 1863, and confined at Fort Monroe, VA, until paroled and exchanged at City Point, VA, about May 28, 1863. Returned to duty prior to July 1, 1863, and captured again at Amelia Court House, VA, on April 5, 1865. Confined at Point Lookout, MD, until released on June 23, 1865, after taking the Oath.

ANDERS, LEVI M., Private — Enlisted June 15, 1861, at age 20 in Transylvania County. Killed at Malvern Hill, VA, on July 1, 1862.

BARTON, BENJAMIN P., Private — Enlisted June 15, 1861, at age 20 in Transylvania County. Wounded in both thighs at the Battle of the Crater near Petersburg, VA, on July 30, 1864, and returned to duty on unspecified date. Paroled at Appomattox Court House, VA, on April 9, 1865.

BODENHAMER, WILLIAM A., Private — Enlisted June 15, 1861, at age 17 in Transylvania County. Promoted to Corporal on July 23, 1862, but reduced to ranks on January 24, 1863. Wounded in the right hip near Petersburg, VA, on June 17, 1864, and reported absent wounded until November 14, 1864. Listed as a deserter at that time and dropped from the rolls of the company.

BOWLING, JAMES A., Private — Enlisted March 19, 1862, at age 20 in Transylvania County. Died in hospital at Winchester, VA, on October 30, 1862, of disease.

BOYLE, TERRANCE, Private. Previously served in Company G, 1st Regiment SC Artillery and transferred to this company on June 11, 1863, in exchange for Private Joseph Henry. Reportedly transferred to Company A, 1st Regiment SC Rifles (Orr's) about April 22, 1864, but the records of the 1st Regiment SC Rifles do not indicate his service. Deserted to the enemy around June 1, 1864, and took the Oath at Fort Monroe, VA, on June 11, 1864.

BROWN, HENRY, Sergeant — Enlisted June 15, 1861, at age 26 in Transylvania County. Promoted to Sergeant on April 30, 1862. Died near Drewry's Bluff, VA, about August 27, 1862, of disease.

BURTON, FRANCIS M., Private — Enlisted April 20, 1864, in Pitt County. Furloughed on September 30, 1864. Listed as a deserter and dropped from the rolls of the company on December 31, 1864.

BUSSICK, J.D., Private. Paroled at Greensboro on May 3, 1865.

CAGEL, LEONARD C., Private — Enlisted June 15, 1861, at age 26 in Transylvania County. Wounded at Malvern Hill, VA, on July 1, 1862. Hospitalized at Richmond, VA, where he died on July 12, 1862, of wounds.

CALDWELL, JAMES A., Private. Previously served in an unspecified unit and transferred to this company on April 28, 1863. Transferred to Company C of this Reg. the same day.

CANTRELL, ALEXANDER E., Private. Previously served in Company K, 9th Regiment NC State Troops and enlisted in this company near Petersburg, VA, at age 20 on July 25, 1863. Deserted on an unspecified date after February 1864 and dropped from the rolls of the company on December 5, 1864. Reported under arrest from January 14 through February 28, 1865, and returned to duty on an unspecified date. Captured in Nottoway County, VA, on April 3, 1865, and confined at Point Lookout, MD. Released on June 10, 1865, after taking the Oath.

CANTRELL, JAMES H., Private — Enlisted June 15, 1861, at age 20 in Transylvania County. Deserted on January 28, 1864, and reported under arrest at Weldon on February 28, 1864. Confined at E.D.M. Prison, Richmond, VA, until pardoned and returned to duty in May 1864. Reported absent sick on June 29, 1864. Died at Petersburg, VA, on August 21, 1864, of unreported cause.

CANTRELL, PHYDILA P., Private — Enlisted April 24, 1862, at age 23 at Camp Ransom. Paroled at Appomattox Court House, VA, on April 9, 1865.

CANTRELL, WILLIAM, Private — Enlisted June 15,

1861, at age 23 in Transylvania County. Deserted to the enemy about February 25, 1865, and confined at Washington, D.C. Released around March 1, 1865, after taking the Oath. (NC pension records indicate he was "blown up at Petersburg," VA, on July 10, 1863.)

CASE, ELISHA G., Private — Enlisted June 15, 1861, at age 22 in Transylvania County. Wounded near the kidney at Malvern Hill, VA, on July 1, 1862. Hospitalized at Richmond, VA, where he died on July 13, 1862, of wounds.

CASE, JAMES M., Private — Enlisted June 15, 1861, at age 19 in Transylvania County. Transferred to Company G, 35th Regiment N.C. Troops on November 1, 1861, but transferred back to this company on March 23, 1862. Wounded in the thigh at King's School House, VA, on June 25, 1862, and returned to duty in November–December 1862. Present or accounted for through February 1864. (NC pension records indicate he was mortally wounded near Petersburg, VA, on June 15, 1864.)

CASE, JOHN J., Private. Previously served in Company A, 29th Regiment NC Troops and transferred to this company on August 24, 1861, in exchange for Private George W. Fisher. Transferred to Company G, 35th Regiment NC Troops on November 1, 1861.

CAUL, JAMES H., Private — Enlisted March 28, 1862, at age 46 in Transylvania County. Captured near Petersburg, VA, on April 2, 1865, and confined at Point Lookout, MD. Released on June 26, 1865, after taking the Oath.

CLAYTON, EPHRAIM B., Private. Previously served in Company E, 7th Battalion NC Cavalry and enlisted in this company at Camp Holmes on March 25, 1864. Wounded in an unspecified engagement on July 10, 1864. Dropped from the rolls of the company in November–December 1864 by reason of having returned to the cavalry service without official transfer.

CLAYTON, L.G., Private. First listed in the records of this company in October 1864. Paroled at Farmville, VA, about April 11–21, 1865.

CLAYTON, THOMAS D.L., Private — Enlisted June 15, 1861, at age 18 in Transylvania County. Enlisted as Sergeant but reduced to ranks on April 30, 1862. Wounded in the arm at the Battle of the Crater near Petersburg, VA, on July 30, 1864, and returned to duty on unspecified date. Wounded in the abdomen near Globe Tavern, VA, on August 21, 1864, and reported absent wounded through February 1865.

COUNCIL, R.G., Private. Captured at the South Side Railroad near Richmond, VA, on April 6, 1865, and confined at Newport News, VA, on April 16, 1865. No further records.

COX, JAMES T., Private — Enlisted June 15, 1861, at age 46 in Transylvania County. Discharged on May 29, 1862, by reason of disability.

COX, YANCY M., Private — Enlisted June 15, 1861, at age 19 in Transylvania County. Present or accounted for through February 1864. No further records.

DEMPSEY, JEREMIAH, Private — Enlisted June 15, 1861, at age 17 in Transylvania County. Present or accounted for through February 1865.

DUNN, MARSHALL M., Private — Enlisted March 28, 1862, at age 25 in Transylvania County. Listed as a deserter on February 8, 1864, and dropped from the rolls of the company.

ENGLAND, ALEXANDER S., Private — Enlisted June 15, 1861, in Transylvania County. Discharged on July 16, 1862, for being under age. Discharge certificate gives age as 17. Reenlisted in the company on June 16, 1863, and reported absent on detached service in western North Carolina from August 5, 1863, through February 1864. No further records.

ENGLAND, DAVID H., Private — Enlisted June 15, 1861, at age 17 in Transylvania County. Wounded in the leg at Malvern Hill, VA, on July 1, 1862. Reported absent wounded until February 25, 1863, and then discharged by reason of disability.

ERWIN, LEANDER J., Private — Enlisted June 15, 1861, at age 21 in Transylvania County. Wounded in the leg at King's School House, VA, on June 25, 1862, and returned to duty in July–August 1862. Hospitalized at Richmond, VA, on June 20, 1864, with a gunshot wound of the left foot. Returned to duty prior to January 1, 1865. Died neat Petersburg, VA, on March 30, 1865, of unreported cause.

FISHER, GEORGE W., Private — Enlisted June 15, 1861, at age 20 in Transylvania County. Transferred to Company A, 29th Regiment NC Troops on August 24, 1861, in exchange for Private John J. Case.

FLETCHER, HENRY, Private — Enlisted March 17, 1862, at age 16 in Transylvania County. Died in hospital at Petersburg, VA, on August 29, 1862, of disease.

FORTUNE, RICHARD L., 1st Sergeant — Enlisted June 15, 1861, at age 20 in Transylvania County. Promoted to Sergeant on July 22, 1862, and to 1st Sergeant in March–December 1864. Wounded in the right arm near Petersburg, VA, on August 10, 1864, and returned to duty prior to January 1, 1865. Paroled at Appomattox Court House, VA, on April 9, 1865.

FOWLER, COLUMBUS, Private — Enlisted April 22, 1863, at age 18 at Kingston. Furloughed on August 5, 1864, and listed as a deserter and dropped from the rolls of the company on November 14, 1864.

FOWLER, PERRY, Private — Enlisted June 15, 1861, at age 17 in Transylvania County. Captured at Fort Stedman, VA, on March 25, 1865, and confined at Point Lookout, MD. Released on June 26, 1865, after taking the Oath.

FOWLER, WILLIAM H., Private — Enlisted June 15, 1861, at age 20 in Transylvania County. Wounded in the hip at Malvern Hill, VA, on July 1, 1862, and returned to duty on July 9, 1862. Promoted to Corporal on November 13, 1862. Wounded in the right arm at Fredericksburg, VA, on December 13, 1862, and returned to duty in January–February 1863. Deserted on January 28, 1864, and reported under arrest on February 11, 1864. Reduced to ranks on an unspecified date and returned to duty prior to June 17, 1864, when captured by the enemy near Petersburg, VA. Confined to Point Lookout, MD, until transferred to Elmira, NY. Arrived at Elmira on July 30, 1864, and released at Elmira on July 3, 1865, after taking the Oath.

GALLOWAY, JOHN D., Private — Enlisted May 18,

1862, at age 23 in Lenoir County. Reported under arrest in November–December 1864 for unknown reason. Returned to duty in January–February 1865. Deserted to the enemy about March 15, 1865, and confined at Washington, D.C. Released on or about March 18, 1865, after taking the Oath.

GALLOWAY, JOHN F., Private – Enlisted June 15, 1861, at age 31 in Transylvania County. Wounded in the forehead and captured at Hatcher's Run, VA, on April 1, 1865. Hospitalized at Washington, D.C. on April 8, 1865, and released on June 14, 1865, after taking the Oath.

GALLOWAY, THOMAS C., Private – Enlisted June 15, 1861, at age 21 in Transylvania County. Wounded at Plymouth on April 20, 1864, and reported absent wounded through December 1864. Listed as a deserter and dropped from the rolls of the company on February 1, 1865, after being promoted to an unspecified rank and joining an unspecified unit without proper authorization.

GALLOWAY, THOMAS G., Private – Enlisted September 6, 1863, at age 43 at Camp Vance. Died in hospital at Petersburg, VA, on June 11, 1864, of "febris typhoides."

GILLESPIE, MATTHEW, Corporal – Enlisted April 23, 1862, at age 24 at Camp Ransom. Promoted to Corporal in March–December 1864. Wounded on July 4, 1864, in an unspecified engagement and returned to duty in January–February 1865. Paroled at Appomattox Court House, VA, on April 9, 1865.

GRANT, LEANDER H., Private – Enlisted June 15, 1861, at age 18 in Transylvania County. Furloughed on August 13, 1864, for thirty days. Listed as a deserter and dropped from the rolls of the company on December 1, 1864.

GRANT, THOMAS, Private – Enlisted June 15, 1861, at age 21 in Transylvania County. Deserted to the enemy about February 26, 1865, and confined at Washington, D.C. Released around March 1, 1865, after taking the Oath.

GRANT, WILLIAM L., Private – Enlisted June 15, 1861, at age 23 in Transylvania County. Captured at Amelia Court House, VA, on April 4, 1865, and confined at Point Lookout, MD. Released on June 27, 1865, after taking the Oath.

GRAVES, DAVID H., Private – Enlisted December 29, 1861, at age 21 at Grahamville, SC. Promoted to 1st Sergeant on April 30, 1862, but reduced to ranks on January 1, 1863. Present or accounted for through February 1865.

HAMILTON, WILLIAM C., Private – Enlisted June 15, 1861, at age 20 in Transylvania County. Paroled at Appomattox Court House, VA, on April 9, 1865.

HANLEY, ABRAM S., Private – Enlisted June 15, 1861, in Transylvania County. Present or accounted for through December 1861. No further records.

HARRIS, FLEMMING, Private – Enlisted June 15, 1861, at age 43 in Transylvania County. Discharged on July 16, 1862, for being over age.

HAYES, ADAM C., Private – Enlisted June 15, 1861, at age 25 in Transylvania County. Promoted to Corporal on April 30, 1862, but reduced to ranks about November 9, 1862. Captured near Petersburg, VA, on April 2, 1865, and confined at Point Lookout, MD. Released on June 28, 1865, after taking the Oath.

HAYES, GEORGE W., Private – Enlisted June 15, 1861, at age 20 in Transylvania County. Present or accounted for through February 1864. No further records.

HAYES, THOMAS, Private – Enlisted June 15, 1861, at age 24 in Transylvania County. Wounded in the left leg near Petersburg, VA, about February 15, 1865, resulting in amputation of leg. Hospitalized at Petersburg where presumably captured by the enemy on April 3, 1865. Paroled on May 11, 1865. (Other records indicate he was wounded at Plymouth about April 18–20.)

HEATH, DANIEL M., Private – Enlisted March 29, 1862, at age 16 in Transylvania County. Present or accounted for through December 1863 but reported absent sick during much of that period. Reported absent without leave on January 14, 1864.

HEATH, HEZEKIAH A., Private – Enlisted June 15, 1861, at age 19 in Transylvania County. Discharged on February 18, 1862, by reason of disability. Rejoined the company in November 1863 but was identified as a deserter from the 66th Regiment NC Troops and placed under arrest. Sent back to the 66th Regiment on an unspecified date.

HEATH, ISAAC, Private – Enlisted June 15, 1861, at age 38 in Transylvania County. Discharged on July 16, 1862, for being over age.

HENDERSON, JAMES M., Private – Enlisted June 15, 1861, at age 22 in Transylvania County. Enlisted as Corporal but reduced to ranks on April 30, 1862. Died in hospital at Kinston on May 20, 1862, of disease.

HENRY, JOSEPH, Private – Enlisted June 15, 1861, at age 26 in Transylvania County. Transferred to Company G, 1st Regiment SC Artillery on June 11, 1863, in exchange for Private Terrance Boyle.

HINES, ALLEN L., Private – Enlisted May 18, 1862, at age 27 in Lenoir County. Died in hospital at Petersburg, VA, on August 13, 1862, of "febris typhoides."

HOGSED, WALTER L., Private – Enlisted June 15, 1861, at age 31 in Transylvania County. Enlisted as Sergeant but reduced to ranks on April 30, 1862. Killed at Malvern Hill, VA, on July 1, 1862.

HOGSED, WILLIAM P., Private – Enlisted June 15, 1861, at age 36 in Transylvania County. Discharged on July 16, 1862, for being over age.

HOLDEN, JOSEPH P., Private – Enlisted September 7, 1863, at Camp Vance. Paroled at Appomattox Court House, VA, on April 9, 1865. (NC pension records indicate he was wounded near Petersburg, VA, on July 27, 1864.)

HOLLINGSWORTH, JOHN A., Private – Enlisted June 15, 1861, at age 18 in Transylvania County. Promoted to Corporal on April 30, 1862, but reduced to ranks in September–December 1863. Deserted on January 28, 1864, and reported under arrest on February 11, 1864. Reported in confinement at Castle Thunder Prison, Richmond, VA, about May 14, 1864. Returned to duty prior to January 1, 1865. Paroled at Appomattox Court House, VA, on April 9, 1865. (NC pension records indicate he was wounded near Petersburg, VA, in January 1863.)

JOHNSTON, ROBERT P., Private — Enlisted June 15, 1861, at age 18 in Transylvania County. Transferred to Company A, 27th Regiment SC Infantry on May 21, 1863.

JONES, ISAAC CROCKET, Private — Enlisted June 15, 1861, at age 21 in Transylvania County. Deserted on February 28, 1865.

KENNEMUR, HUMPHREY P., Private — Enlisted June 15, 1861, at age 27 in Transylvania County. Died in hospital at Petersburg, VA, on July 15, 1862, of "cerebro meningitis."

KING, JACOB, Musician — Enlisted January 30, 1862, at age 21 at Grahamville, SC. Promoted to Musician in May 1864. Paroled at Appomattox Court House, VA, on April 9, 1865.

LANCE, JAMES V., Private — Enlisted May 18, 1862, at age 24 in Lenoir County. Died in hospital at Petersburg, VA, on August 4 or August 28, 1862, of "diarrhoea."

LANCE, JOHN H., Private — Enlisted June 15, 1861, at age 20 in Transylvania County. Died in hospital at Petersburg, VA, on September 30, 1862, of disease.

LANNING, ATHAN M., Private — Enlisted June 15, 1861, at age 18 in Transylvania County. Died in hospital at Petersburg, VA, about August 28, 1862, of "icterus."

LANNING, WILLIAM C., Private — Enlisted June 15, 1861, at age 22 in Transylvania County. Wounded in the abdomen at Fredericksburg, VA, on December 13, 1862, and reported absent wounded through April 1863. Failed to return to duty. Listed as deserter and dropped from the rolls of the company on June 14, 1863.

LOCKABY, GEORGE W., Private — Enlisted June 15, 1861, at age 21 in Transylvania County. Enlisted as Musician (Fifer) but reduced to ranks on March 5, 1862. Promoted to Musician (Fifer) on April 30, 1862, but again reduced to ranks on May 6, 1862. Reported absent without leave on November 18, 1862. Apprehended on an unspecified date and confined at Lynchburg, VA, on December 13, 1862. Rejoined the company on December 30, 1862, but reported absent without leave on January 17, 1863. Listed as deserter and dropped from the rolls of the company on February 5, 1863.

LOTTER, I., Private. Deserted to the enemy on an unspecified date and took the Oath at Knoxville, TN, on September 13, 1864.

LYDAY, ISAAC S., Private — Enlisted September 8, 1861, at age 29 in Buncombe County. Discharged on August 19, 1862, after providing Private Moses Watson as a substitute.

LYON, ALBERT R., Private — Enlisted January 30, 1862, at age 19 at Grahamville, SC. Wounded in the thigh at Fredericksburg, VA, on December 13, 1862, and hospitalized at Richmond, VA, until furloughed on January 11, 1863. Died "at home" on January 30, 1863, of wounds.

McCALL, JAMES W., Private — Enlisted June 15, 1861, at age 23 in Transylvania County. Wounded near Globe Tavern, VA, on August 21, 1864, and reported absent wounded through February 1865.

MACKEY, HARRISON P., Musician — Enlisted June 15, 1861, at age 21 in Transylvania County. Promoted to Musician on August 18, 1863. Present or accounted for through February 1865.

MACKEY, JOHN C., Musician — Enlisted June 15, 1861, at age 19 in Transylvania County. Promoted to Musician on April 30, 1862. Died in Transylvania County on December 19, 1864, of disease.

MACKEY, STROB E., Private — Enlisted March 18, 1864, in Halifax County. Present or accounted for through September 16, 1864, but listed as a deserter and dropped from the rolls of the company on November 18, 1864.

MAGAHA, MARTIN A., Private — Enlisted June 15, 1861, at age 17 in Transylvania County. Hospitalized at Richmond, VA, on December 16, 1862, with a gunshot wound and returned to duty on February 13, 1863. Died in hospital at Wilson on February 27, 1864, of "diphtheria."

MAGAHA, THOMAS J., Corporal — Enlisted June 15, 1861, at age 21 in Transylvania County. Promoted to Corporal on April 30, 1862. Killed at Malvern Hill, VA, on July 1, 1862.

MANLY, SILAS W., Private — Enlisted July 22, 1862, at age 46 at Drewry's Bluff, VA. Enlisted as a substitute for Private Harvey E. Mull. Captured at Five Forks, VA, around April 1, 1865, and confined at Point Lookout, MD. Released on June 6, 1865, after taking the Oath.

MANLY, WILLIAM P., Corporal — Enlisted June 15, 1861, at age 18 in Transylvania County. Promoted to Corporal in March–December 1864. Captured at Farmville, VA, on April 6, 1865, and confined at Newport News, VA. Died there on June 17, 1865, of "diarrhoea."

MARLEY, WILLIAM S. — NC pension records indicate he enlisted on July 15, 1863, and died on an unspecified date. Place and cause of death not reported.

MULL, HARVEY E., Private — Enlisted July 21, 1862, at age 25 at Drewry's Bluff, VA. Discharged on July 22, 1862, after providing Private Silas W. Manly as a substitute.

MULL, JACOB C., Private — Enlisted July 21, 1862, at age 19 at Drewry's Bluff, VA. Wounded in the leg or foot at Fredericksburg, VA, on December 13, 1862. Reported absent wounded until September 20, 1863, when he was discharged by reason of disability.

MULL, MARION A., Private — Enlisted March 29, 1862, at age 16 in Transylvania County. Appointed Musician (Fifer) on April 30, 1862, but reduced to ranks on July 9, 1862. Discharged on February 28, 1863, for being under age.

MURRAY, JOHN P., Private — Enlisted June 15, 1861, at age 29 in Transylvania County. "Killed by the falling of a tree" in camp near Kinston on April 28, 1863.

ORR, JABAZ M., Private — Enlisted March 19, 1862, at age 19 in Transylvania County. Died in hospital near Drewry's Bluff, VA, on August 14, 1862, of disease.

ORR, MARTIN J., Musician — Enlisted June 15, 1861, at age 19 in Transylvania County. Promoted to Musician in September–December 1863. Present or accounted for through February 1865.

OSBORN, WILLIAM K., Private — Enlisted September 8, 1861, at age 23 in Buncombe County. Discharged on November 4, 1862, after providing Private John Sims as a substitute.

OSTEEN, THOMAS P., Private — Enlisted June 15, 1861, at age 22 in Transylvania County. Promoted to Musician (Fifer) on March 5, 1862, but reduced to ranks on April 30, 1862. Died in hospital at Kinston on May 16, 1862, of disease.

OWEN, M.J., Private. Paroled at Burkeville Junction, VA, about April 14–17, 1865.

OWENS, RICHARD A.S., Corporal — Enlisted September 9, 1861, at age 21 in Buncombe County. Promoted to Corporal on January 24, 1863. Present or accounted for through February 1864. No further records.

PATTERSON, AMOS L., Private — Enlisted June 15, 1861, at age 19 in Transylvania County. Captured at Farmville, VA, on April 6, 1865, and confined at Newport News, VA. Released on June 27, 1865, after taking the Oath. (NC pension records indicate he was wounded in the left wrist at Petersburg, VA, on an unspecified date.)

PATTERSON, WILLIAM D., Private — Enlisted June 2, 1862, at age 46 at Camp Johnston. Enlisted as a substitute for Private William A. Wilson. Discharged on August 1, 1862, by reason of "fistula."

PATTON, ELI, Private — Enlisted September 8, 1861, at age 39 in Buncombe County. Discharged on July 16, 1862, for being over age.

PATTON, ROBERT W., Private — Enlisted June 15, 1861, at age 42 in Transylvania County. Discharged on July 16, 1862, for being over age.

PAXTON, RUFUS M., Private — Enlisted March 28, 1862, at age 23 in Transylvania County. Present or accounted for through February 1864. No further records.

PETTIT, HARRIS B., Musician — Enlisted June 15, 1861, at age 19 in Transylvania County. Promoted to Corporal on April 30, 1862, and to Musician on November 4, 1863. Paroled at Appomattox Court House, VA, on April 9, 1865.

PETTIT, JOHN M., Private — Enlisted June 15, 1861, at age 21 in Transylvania County. Transferred to Company I of this Reg. on May 1, 1862.

PRITCHARD, JAMES, Private — Enlisted June 15, 1861, at age 17 in Transylvania County. Killed at Fredericksburg, VA, on December 13, 1862.

RAINES, CHRISTOPHER C., Private — Enlisted June 15, 1861, at age 19 in Transylvania County. Wounded at Malvern Hill, VA, on July 1, 1862, and returned to duty prior to September 1, 1862. Wounded in the hip and captured during an unspecified engagement about June 2, 1864. Confined at an unspecified Federal hospital where an "exsection" of the head of the femur was performed. Federal hospital records indicate that he "was almost pulseless when put on the table but after operation rallied and is doing well." Transferred to an unspecified hospital on June 3, 1864. No further records.

RAINES, JOSEPH R., Private — Enlisted April 18, 1862, at age 21 at Camp Ransom. Died in hospital at Drewry's Bluff, VA, about September 7, 1862, of disease.

RANES, ROBERT C., Private — Enlisted September 8, 1861, at age 33 in Buncombe County. Deserted on May 31, 1863, and apprehended on an unspecified date. Rejoined the company on August 9, 1863. Present or accounted for through February 1865.

RAXTER, CHARLES C., Private — Enlisted June 15, 1861, at age 38 in Transylvania County. Discharged on July 16, 1862, for being over age.

RAXTER, WESLEY — Enlisted 1863. NC pension records indicate he enlisted in 1863. Records of the United Daughters of the Confederacy indicate he was captured near Petersburg, VA, on April 2, 1865. No further records.

RAY, WILLIAM C., Private — Enlisted June 15, 1861, at age 18 in Transylvania County. Wounded in the right thigh at Malvern Hill, VA, on July 1, 1862, and returned to duty in November–December 1862. Present or accounted for through February 1864. (NC pension records dated June 21, 1901, indicate that he "was knocked down by shell exploding at Fredericksburg, Virginia ....")

REAVES, JOHN P., Private — Enlisted March 19. 1862 at age 19 in Transylvania County. Discharged on July 21, 1863, by reason of disability.

RICKMAN, WILLIAM R., Private — Enlisted June 15, 1861, at age 19 in Transylvania County. Wounded in the leg and/or right shoulder at Fredericksburg, VA, on December 13, 1862, and returned to duty in March–April 1863. Discharged about September 20, 1863, by reason of smallpox which resulted in the loss of sight in his right eye.

SANDERS, THOMAS, Private — Enlisted June 15, 1861, at age 32 in Transylvania County. Wounded in the arm at Sharpsburg, MD, on September 17, 1862, and returned to duty in May–June 1863. Discharged on August 6, 1863, by reason of disability.

SCERSEY, DAVID W., Private — Enlisted June 15, 1861, at age 24 in Transylvania County. Wounded in the hand at Malvern Hill, VA, on July 1, 1862. When failed to return to duty was listed as a deserter on October 16, 1862. Returned to duty on January 23, 1863. Wounded near Globe Tavern, VA, on August 21, 1864. Failed to return to duty and again listed as a deserter. Dropped from the rolls of the company on November 14, 1864.

SCERSEY, WILLIAM H., Private — Enlisted June 15, 1861, at age 31 in Transylvania County. Reported absent without leave on October 31, 1862. Listed as a deserter and dropped from the rolls of the company on December 1, 1862. Returned to duty on February 12, 1863. Present or accounted for through May 6, 1863. Failed to return from furlough and listed as a deserter on June 14, 1863. Returned to duty on an unspecified date but deserted again on November 14, 1863. Reported under arrest at Weldon on February 5, 1864. No further records.

SCRUGGS, BENJAMIN, Private — Enlisted June 15, 1861, at age 26 in Transylvania County. Deserted around May 31, 1863, and apprehended on an unspecified date. Returned to duty on August 9, 1863. Present or accounted for until furloughed for twenty-five days on February 25, 1864. No further records.

SCRUGGS, RICHARD M., Private—Enlisted March 18, 1862, at age 18 in Transylvania County. Wounded in the hand and/or head at Malvern Hill, VA, on July 1, 1862, and returned to duty in November–December 1862. Deserted about May 31, 1863, and arrested on June 15, 1863. Sent "by mistake" to General Ransom's brigade and his commander was thereafter unable "to learn where he is or what has become of him." No further records.

SHIPMAN, JOHN J., Private—Enlisted June 15, 1861, at age 27 in Transylvania County. Wounded accidentally in the right side near Kinston about June 1, 1862. Discharged on July 31, 1862, by reason of disability.

SHIPMAN, JOHN K., Private—Enlisted June 15, 1861, at age 29 in Transylvania County. Wounded in the lungs at Fredericksburg, VA, on December 13, 1862. Died in hospital at Charlottesville, VA, on January 2, 1863, of wounds.

SHIPMAN, MARION P., Private—Enlisted June 15, 1861, at age 21 in Transylvania County. Transferred to Company G, 35th Regiment NC Troops on November 1, 1861.

SIMS, JOHN, Private—Enlisted November 4, 1862, at age 45 at Culpeper CH, VA. Enlisted as a substitute for Private William K. Osborn. Wounded in the left shoulder at Fredericksburg, VA, on December 13, 1862, and returned to duty in March–April 1863. Present or accounted for through February 1865.

SIMS, SIMPSON, Private—Enlisted June 15, 1861, at age 36 in Transylvania County. Discharged on July 16, 1862, for being over age and reenlisted the same day as a substitute for Private George W. Wilson. Captured at Farmville, VA, on April 6, 1865, and confined at Newport News, VA, on April 14, 1865. No further records.

SMITH, FRANCIS M., Private—Enlisted June 15, 1861, at age 36 in Transylvania County. Wounded in the lungs at Fredericksburg, VA, on December 13, 1862. Reported absent until March–April 1863 when he was reported absent without leave. Returned to duty in May–June 1863. Reported under arrest in July–August 1863. Reported absent sick from November–December 1863 through February 1864. No further records.

SMITH, JAMES D., Private—Enlisted June 15, 1861, at age 23 in Transylvania County. Present or accounted for through February 1864. No further records.

SPENCE, JOHN, Private—Enlisted June 15, 1861, at age 38 in Transylvania County. Discharged on July 16, 1862, for being over age. Reenlisted in the company on November 25, 1863. Died in hospital at Richmond, VA, on September 7, 1864, of "diarrhoea chronic."

STAGGS, ROBERT P., Private—Enlisted June 15, 1861, at age 20 in Transylvania County. Present or accounted for through February 1864. Deserted to the enemy on an unspecified date and took the Oath at Louisville, KY, on August 29, 1864.

STAGGS, WALTON D., Private—Enlisted June 15, 1861, at age 18 in Transylvania County. Present or accounted for through September 16, 1864. Listed as a deserter and dropped from the rolls of the company on November 14, 1864. Returned to duty on an unspecified date. Paroled at Farmville, VA, about April 11–21, 1865.

TEW, M.W., Private. Captured in Sampson County on March 16, 1865, and confined at Hart's Island, New York Harbor where he died on April 26, 1865, of "typhoid fever."

THOMAS, JAMES, Private—Enlisted June 15, 1861, at age 23 in Transylvania County. Died in hospital at Goldsboro on June 24–25, 1862, of disease.

THOMAS, JAMES L., Musician—Enlisted June 15, 1861, at age 18 in Transylvania County. Enlisted as Musician. Discharged about October 25, 1861, by reason of disability.

THOMPSON, HENRY W., Private—Enlisted July 21, 1862, at age 20 at Drewry's Bluff, VA. Present or accounted for through February 1864. No further records.

THOMPSON, JAMES W., Sergeant—Enlisted June 15, 1861, at age 25 in Transylvania County. Enlisted as Corporal but reduced to ranks on April 30, 1862. Promoted to Sergeant on May 6, 1862. Wounded at Malvern Hill, VA, on July 1, 1862, and died near Malvern Hill on July 3, 1862, of wounds.

THOMPSON, NELSON M., Private—Enlisted June 15, 1861, at age 24 in Transylvania County. Enlisted as Corporal but reduced to ranks on April 30, 1862. Promoted to Sergeant on January 1, 1863, but reduced to ranks again in January–February 1865. Deserted to the enemy about February 26, 1865, and confined at Washington, D.C. on February 28, 1865. No further records.

THOMPSON, SAMUEL, Private—Enlisted March 19, 1862, at age 17 in Transylvania County. Reported under arrest in November–December 1863 for unreported reason. Furloughed for twenty-five days on February 11, 1864, and then reported in confinement at E.D.M. Prison in Richmond, VA, about May 1, 1864. Released after volunteering to serve in the defense of Richmond against the Sheridan raid in May 1864. No further records.

THOMPSON, WLLIAM P., Private—Enlisted March 19, 1862, at age 22 in Transylvania County. Present or accounted for through February 1864.

TRAMMELL, JAMES R., Private—Enlisted June 15, 1861, at age 21 in Transylvania County. Present or accounted for through February 1864. Deserted to the enemy on an unspecified date and took the Oath at Knoxville, TN, on September 24, 1864.

TRAMMELL, MONTREVILLE P., Private—Enlisted June 15, 1861, at age 21 in Transylvania County. Transferred to Company H, 2nd Battalion NC Infantry about April 20, 1863.

TUCKER, SAMUEL, D., Private—Enlisted June 15, 1861, at age 19 in Transylvania County. Died in hospital at Grahamville, SC, on December 23, 1861, of disease.

WATSON, MOSES, Private—Enlisted August 19, 1862, at age 17 at Petersburg, VA. Enlisted as a substitute for Private Isaac S. Lyday. Present or accounted for through February 1864. No further records.

WEST, BENJAMIN H., Corporal—Enlisted March 18, 1862, at age 27 in Transylvania County. Promoted to

Corporal on September 10, 1863. Wounded in the mouth and jaw at Warm Springs on October 25, 1863. Reported absent wounded until August 4, 1864, when he retired to the Invalid Corps.

WHITMIRE, HENRY C., Private — Enlisted January 27, 1864, in Halifax County. Reported detailed for duty at Weldon Railroad bridge on February 25, 1864. Wounded at Plymouth about April 18–20, 1864. No further records.

WHITMIRE, JAMES M., Private — Enlisted June 15, 1861, at age 24 in Transylvania County. Promoted to Sergeant on July 23, 1862. Wounded in the leg at Fredericksburg, VA, on December 13, 1862, and returned to duty in January–February 1863. Reduced to ranks subsequent to February 28, 1865. Captured near Petersburg, VA, on April 2, 1865, and confined at Point Lookout, MD. Released on June 21, 1865, after taking the Oath.

WHITTENBURG, JOSEPH W., Private — Enlisted June 15, 1861, at age 17 in Transylvania County. Discharged on July 16, 1862, for being under age.

WILSON, BENJAMIN J., Corporal — Enlisted June 15, 1861, at age 21 in Transylvania County. Promoted to Corporal on November 8, 1863. Paroled at Appomattox Court House, VA, on April 9, 1865. (NC pension records indicate he was wounded in the right lung near Petersburg, VA, in July 1864.)

WILSON, GEORGE W., Sergeant — Enlisted September 8, 1861, at age 21 in Buncombe County. Promoted to Sergeant on April 30, 1862. Discharged on July 16, 1862, after providing Private Simpson Sims as a substitute.

WILSON, JAMES F., Private — Enlisted June 15, 1861, at age 18 in Transylvania County. Listed as a deserter on December 14, 1864, and dropped from the rolls of the company.

WILSON, JOHN C., Private — Enlisted June 15, 1861, at age 21 in Transylvania County. Wounded in the head at Malvern Hill, VA, on July 1, 1862, and returned to duty prior to September 1, 1862. Detached "to hunt deserters" in western North Carolina on October 16, 1863. Deserted about December 20, 1863.

WILSON, JOHN McD., Private — Enlisted June 15, 1861, at age 18 in Transylvania County. Hospitalized at Petersburg, VA, on December 4, 1863, with a gunshot wound of the left hand and returned to duty on January 20, 1864. Present or accounted for through February 1865.

WILSON, JOSEPH H., Private — Enlisted March 29, 1862, at age 24 in Transylvania County. Present or accounted for through December 1864.

WILSON, MATTHEW M., Private — Enlisted June 15, 1861, at age 34 in Transylvania County. Discharged on July 16, 1862, for being over age.

WILSON, ROBERT, Private — Enlisted June 15, 1861, at age 33 in Transylvania County. Wounded in the thigh at Malvern Hill, VA, on July 1, 1862, and returned to duty prior to December 13, 1862. Wounded at Fredericksburg, VA, on December 13, 1862, and returned to duty in March–April 1863. Deserted on July 1, 1863.

WILSON, WILLIAM A., Private — Enlisted June 15, 1861, at age 20 in Transylvania County. Discharged on June 12, 1862, after providing Private William D. Patterson as a substitute.

YOUNG, THOMAS, Private — Enlisted June 15, 1861, at age 20 in Transylvania County. Wounded in an unspecified engagement in January–May 1864. Reported absent wounded or absent on furlough until December 1, 1864, when reported absent without leave. Listed as a deserter and dropped from the rolls of the company on January 2, 1865.

Company F — "Haywood Highlanders"

Captains

BLALOCK, JAMES A — Enlisted June 29, 1861, at age 22 in Haywood County. Enlisted as Sergeant and elected 2nd Lt. on April 28, 1862. Appointed 1st Lt. in November 1863, and promoted to Captain on August 16, 1864. Present or accounted for through April 7, 1865.

CATHEY, JAMES MADISON — Enlisted June 29, 1861, at age 23 in Haywood County. Appointed 3rd Lt. on June 29, 1861, and elected Captain on April 28, 1862. Killed at "the crater" near Petersburg, VA, on July 30, 1864.

LENOIR, THOMAS ISAAC — Enlisted June 29, 1861, at age 43 in Haywood County. Appointed Captain on June 29, 1861, and declined to accept reelection as Captain of the company on April 28, 1862.

Lieutenants

BLALOCK, ETHELDRED H., 1st Lt. — Enlisted June 29, 1861, at age 44 in Haywood County. Appointed 1st Lt. on June 29, 1861, and served until defeated for reelection on April 28, 1862.

BURNETT, JAMES A., 2nd Lt. — Enlisted June 29, 1861, at age 24 in Haywood County. Appointed 2nd Lt. on June 29, 1861, and declined to accept reelection as 2nd Lt. of this company on April 28, 1862. Later served as 2nd Lt. of Company I, 62nd Regiment NC Troops.

CATHEY, JOSEPH T., 3rd Lt. — Enlisted June 29, 1861, at age 26 in Haywood County. Enlisted as 1st Sergeant and elected 3rd Lt. on April 28, 1862. Died in hospital at Wilson on September 8, 1863, of "febris typhoides."

FERGUSON, EBED J., 3rd Lt. — Enlisted June 29, 1861, at age 25 in Haywood County. Promoted to Sergeant on June 23, 1863, and appointed 3rd Lt. around December 4, 1863. Killed at Drewry's Bluff, VA, on or about May 16, 1864.

FERGUSON, GARLAND SEVIER, 2nd Lt. — Enlisted June 29, 1861, at age 18 in Haywood County. Enlisted as Sergeant but reduced to ranks on April 28, 1862. Promoted to Sergeant in September–October 1863. Wounded at Drewry's Bluff, VA, on May 14, 1864, and returned to duty in June 1864. Appointed 2nd Lt. around August 16, 1864. Wounded in the right shoulder near Globe Tavern, VA, on August 21, 1864, and returned to duty prior to January 1, 1865. Wounded in the left leg at Fort Stedman, VA, on March 25, 1865, and hospitalized at Petersburg, VA, where he was presumably captured on April 3, 1865.

Released from Richmond, VA, hospital on August 2, 1865, presumably after taking Oath.

HARTGROVE, WILLIAM HARRISON, 1st Lt.— Enlisted July 18, 1861, at age 20 in Haywood County. Promoted to Sergeant on April 28, 1862, and later appointed 1st Lt. on August 16, 1864. Captured at Five Forks, VA, on April 1, 1865, and confined at Old Capitol Prison, Washington, D.C. until transferred to Johnson's Island, OH, on April 9, 1865. Released on June 18, 1865, after taking the Oath.

HYATT, THADDEUS C.S., 1st Lt.— Enlisted June 29, 1861, at age 23 in Haywood County. Enlisted as Corporal and appointed 1st Lt. on April 28, 1862. Killed at Warm Springs around October 26, 1863.

WRIGHT, WILLIAM M., 2nd Lt.— Enlisted August 22, 1861, at age 18 in Buncombe County. Promoted to Sergeant on May 14, 1863, and appointed 2nd Lt. on September 10, 1863. Resigned on January 21, 1864, for unreported reason.

Noncommissioned Officers and Privates

ABBOTT, GREEN B., Private — Enlisted June 29, 1861, at age 21 in Haywood County. Died in hospital at Petersburg, VA, around July 29, 1862, of "cerebro meningitis."

ALLEN, DAVID, Private — Enlisted July 18, 1861, at age 27 in Haywood County. Discharged on March 8, 1862, by reason of disability.

ALLMAN, WILLIAM N., Private — Enlisted June 29, 1861, at age 19 in Haywood County. Enlisted as Musician but reduced to ranks on April 28, 1862. Deserted on February 24, 1864.

ANDERSON, JASPER N., Private — Enlisted June 29, 1861, at age 22 in Haywood County. Wounded at Malvern Hill, VA, on July 1, 1862, and returned to duty on September 22, 1862. Promoted to Corporal on September 22, 1862, but reduced to ranks on February 17, 1863. Died in hospital at Goldsboro on May 12, 1863, of "febris typhoides."

ANDERSON, JOSIAH McDONALD, Private — Enlisted June 29, 1861, at age 18 in Haywood County. Wounded in the left leg and "disabled for life" at Malvern Hill, VA, on July 1, 1862. Reported absent wounded through February 1865.

BAGGETT, WILLIAM M., Private — Enlisted June 10, 1864, in Moore County. Wounded prior to January 1, 1865, and reported absent wounded or absent sick through February 1865.

BEST, RODOM C., Private — Enlisted September 1, 1863, in Haywood County. Wounded in the back and left hand at Petersburg, VA, and hospitalized at Petersburg on October 12, 1864. Furloughed for sixty days on December 9, 1864.

BLACKBURN, WILLIAM P., Private — Enlisted June 10, 1864, in Lincoln County. Present or accounted for through February 1865.

BLALOCK, GEORGE H., Private — Enlisted April 7, 1863, at age 41 in Haywood County. Present or accounted for until January–February 1865 when reported absent without leave.

BONHAM, WILLIAM, Corporal — Enlisted June 29, 1861, at age 18 in Haywood County. Promoted to Corporal on April 28, 1862. "Killed in the trenches by a shell" near Petersburg, VA, on February 17, 1865.

BROOKSHIRE, HUMPHREY P., Private — Enlisted September 18, 1861, at age 44 in Buncombe County. Discharged on July 16, 1862, for being over age.

BROOKSHIRE, JOHN E., Private — Enlisted June 29, 1861, at age 18 in Haywood County. Died at Winchester, VA, on October 20, 1862, of "fever."

BUGG, HENRY TILMAN, Private — Enlisted June 29, 1861, at age 18 in Haywood County. Wounded in the right leg at the Battle of the Crater near Petersburg, VA, on July 30, 1864. Returned to duty prior to January 1, 1865, and present or accounted for through February 1865.

BUGG, JEREMIAH H., Private — Enlisted June 29, 1861, at age 20 in Haywood County. Wounded in the right arm and captured at Fort Stedman, VA, on March 25, 1865. Confined at various Federal hospitals until confined at Old Capitol Prison, Washington, D.C. on April 24, 1865, and then Elmira, NY, on May 1, 1865. Released at Elmira on August 14, 1865, after taking the Oath.

BURNETT, ALFRED, Private — Enlisted August 14, 1861, at age 26 in Buncombe County. Discharged on January 20, 1862, by reason of "physical disability."

BURNETT, JOHN G., Private — Enlisted June 29, 1861, at age 29 in Haywood County. Enlisted as Corporal but reduced to ranks on April 28, 1862. Discharged on July 16, 1862, after providing a substitute. Later served in Company I, 62nd Regiment NC Troops.

BYERS, WILLIAM, Private — Enlisted June 29, 1861, at age 18 in Haywood County. Present or accounted for through February 1864. No further records.

CATHEY, WILLIAM, Sergeant — Enlisted June 29, 1861, at age 22 in Haywood County. Enlisted as Sergeant and present or accounted for through February 1864.

CHAMBERS, GEORGE W., Private — Enlisted June 29, 1861, at age 22 in Haywood County. Wounded at Malvern Hill, VA, on July 1, 1862, and returned to duty on September 6, 1862. "Killed ... by deserters" on June 10, 1863, while absent on detached duty.

CHRISTOPHER, GEORGE E., Private — Enlisted June 29, 1861, at age 33 in Haywood County. Died at Camp Lee near Grahamville, SC, on February 23, 1862, of "typhoid fever."

CHRISTOPHER, HENRY, Private — Enlisted June 29, 1861, at age 43 in Haywood County. Died in hospital at Wilson, NC, around May 30, 1862, of disease.

CHRISTOPHER, McDANIEL, Private — Enlisted May 1, 1864, in Haywood County. Present or accounted for through February 1865.

CLARK, HIRAM, Private — Enlisted May 1, 1863, at age 38 in Buncombe County. Present or accounted for through February 1865.

CLARK, JOSHUA A., Corporal — Enlisted March 22, 1862, at age 16 in Haywood County. Promoted to Corporal in March–December 1864 and present or accounted for through February 1865.

CLONTS, WILLIAM R., Private — Enlisted June 29, 1861, at age 18 in Haywood County. Promoted to Corporal on May 1, 1862, and reduced to ranks in September–October 1862. Wounded at Sharpsburg, MD, on

September 17, 1862, and returned to duty prior to November 1, 1862. Deserted on February 24, 1865.

COLLINS, ELI, Private — Enlisted August 14, 1861, at age 33 in Buncombe County. Discharged on July 16, 1862, for being over age. Reenlisted in this company on an unspecified date (probably in January 1863) and died at Guinea Station, VA, on February 9, 1863, of "typhoid fever."

CRAWFORD, AMOS A., Private — Enlisted June 29, 1861, at age 26 in Haywood County. Wounded in the hand at King's School House, VA, on June 25, 1862, and returned to duty prior to September 1, 1862. Deserted on September 5, 1862.

DAVIS, JOSEPH N., Private — Enlisted March 22, 1862, at age 23 in Haywood County. Present or accounted for through February 1865 but reported absent sick during much of this period.

DEAVER, RUFUS L., Private. Previously served in Company C of this Reg. and transferred to this company on May 1, 1862. Deserted on the march on February 1, 1864, and went over to the enemy. Took the Oath at Knoxville, TN, around May 22, 1864.

DEAVER, WILLIAM N., Private. Previously served in Company C of this Reg. and transferred to this company on May 1, 1862. Deserted to the enemy on an unspecified date and took the Oath at Knoxville, TN, around May 22, 1864.

EDMONSTON, BENJAMIN F., Private — Enlisted June 29, 1861, at age 25 in Haywood County. Wounded in the leg at King's School House, VA, on June 25, 1862, and returned to duty in July–August 1862. Wounded in the head at the Battle of the Crater near Petersburg, VA, on July 30, 1864. Company muster roll of November–December 1864 indicates he was a prisoner of war.

ESTES, ROBERT J.H., Private — Enlisted February 22, 1863, at age 17 in Haywood County. Present or accounted for through February 1864. No further records.

EVANS, JOHN C., Private — Enlisted October 10, 1863, in McDowell County. Deserted on the march on February 1, 1864, and returned to his home in McDowell County where on June 19, 1864, he assisted two escaped Federal prisoners of war by acting as their guide in crossing Swannanoa Valley. On the morning of June 27, 1864, "his house was surrounded (by Confederate soldiers) ...and he (was) captured and sent to jail in Asheville, North Carolina where he remained 11 days with his hands tied behind his back. Then sent under strong guard to Petersburg to work in the trenches. Captured in the trenches on July 30, 1864, and confined at Elmira, NY, through September 30, 1864. Released on an unspecified date after taking the Oath.

EVANS, WILLIAM J., 1st Sergeant — Enlisted June 29, 1861, at age 18 in Haywood County. Wounded "by a deserter" on June 10, 1862, and returned to duty prior to July 1, 1862. Captured at South Mountain, MD, on September 14, 1862, and confined at Fort Delaware, DE. Exchanged at Aiken's Landing, James River, VA, on November 10, 1862, and returned to duty prior to January 1, 1863. Promoted to Sergeant around November 30, 1863, and promoted to 1st Sergeant in March–September 1864. Deserted on February 4, 1865, while absent on furlough.

FERGUSON, NATHAN J., Private — Enlisted June 29, 1861, at age 29 in Haywood County. Present or accounted for through February 1864.

FRANCIS, WILLIAM F., Private — Enlisted June 10, 1864, in Caswell County. Wounded in the neck and/or right breast and captured at Fort Stedman, VA, on March 25, 1865. Confined at various Federal hospitals until confined at Old Capitol Prison, Washington, D.C. on April 24, 1865, and then transferred to Elmira, NY, on May 11, 1865. Released at Elmira on July 7, 1865, after taking the Oath. (Federal hospital records dated March 1865 give his age as 18.)

FRANKLIN, DAVID N., Private — Enlisted March 22, 1862, at age 30 in Haywood County. Promoted to Corporal on May 23, 1863, but reduced to ranks subsequent to February 29, 1864. Deserted to the enemy on an unspecified date and took the Oath in eastern Tennessee on December 31, 1864.

FRANKLIN, HENRY J., Private — Enlisted June 29, 1861, at age 32 in Haywood County. Deserted around September 23, 1862, and returned to duty in March–June 1863. Present or accounted for through February 1864.

FRANKLIN, PERRY B., Private — Enlisted August 14, 1861, at age 25 in Buncombe County. Discharged on January 20, 1862, by reason of disability. Later served in Company I, 62nd Regiment NC Troops.

GADDIS, DAVID W., Private — Enlisted February 28, 1863, at age 37 in Haywood County. Deserted on January 26, 1865, while absent on furlough.

GLENN, NAPOLEON L., Private — Enlisted June 29, 1861, at age 18 in Haywood County. Present or accounted for until transferred to Company I of this Reg. on May 1, 1862.

GODWIN, LEONARD, Private — Enlisted June 10, 1864, in Sampson County. Captured near Petersburg, VA, on July 30, 1864, and confined at Point Lookout, MD, until transferred to Elmira, NY, on August 8, 1864. Paroled at Elmira on October 11, 1864, and exchanged at Venus Point, Savannah River, GA, on November 15, 1864.

GORDON, ALSON, Private — Enlisted June 29, 1861, at age 36 in Haywood County. Discharged on July 16, 1862, for being over age but reenlisted in the company on August 15, 1863. Wounded in the leg near Petersburg, VA, around August 23, 1864, and left leg amputated above the knee as a result of wounds. Reported absent wounded until December 30, 1864, and then retired to the Invalid Corps.

GREEN, SAMUEL B., Private — Enlisted August 14, 1861, at age 23 in Buncombe County. Deserted on August 14, 1863, and went over to the enemy. Took the Oath at Knoxville, TN, around May 25, 1864.

GREEN, THADDEUS M., Private — Enlisted June 29, 1861, at age 18 in Haywood County. Enlisted in Company C, Infantry Regiment, Thomas Legion in June 1861. Failed to report for duty with that unit and continued to serve in this company through February 1864. Wounded in action on an unspecified date. Reported absent wounded or absent sick until January 26, 1865, and then listed as a deserter.

HALL, GEORGE, Jr., Private — Enlisted June 29, 1861, at age 25 in Haywood County. Present or accounted for through February 1864 but reported absent sick during most of that period. Reported absent without leave in November–December 1864 and then listed as a deserter on February 4, 1865.

HALL, GEORGE R., Private — Enlisted June 29, 1861, at age 17 in Haywood County. Elected Musician (Fifer) on October 16, 1861, but reduced to ranks on April 28, 1862. Died at Drewry's Bluff, VA, around August 25, 1862, of "ulcers."

HARRELL, EZEKIEL T., Private — Enlisted June 29, 1861, at age 18 in Haywood County. Deserted on September 24, 1862, but returned to duty on January 26, 1863. Furloughed on an unspecified date after February 1864 and failed to return to duty. Dropped from the rolls of the company and listed as a deserter on November 3, 1864.

HARTGROVE, RUFUS P., Private — Enlisted September 1, 1863, at age 33 in Haywood County. Deserted on an unspecified date after February 1864 but returned to duty prior to January 1, 1865, after an unauthorized absence of seven months. Captured by the enemy near Petersburg, VA, on April 1, 1865, and confined at Point Lookout, MD. Released on June 14, 1865, after taking the Oath.

HENDERSON, HARPER, Private — Enlisted September 17, 1861, at age 45 in Buncombe County. Discharged on July 16, 1862, for being over age.

HENDERSON, JAMES M., Private — Enlisted June 29, 1861, at age 25 in Haywood County. Wounded in the left lung near Globe Tavern, VA, on August 21, 1864, and died in hospital at Petersburg, VA, two days later.

HENDERSON, WILLIAM, Private — Enlisted June 29, 1861, at age 38 in Haywood County. Enlisted as Sergeant but reduced to ranks on April 28, 1862. Discharged on July 16, 1862, for being over age.

HENSON, BURTON H., Private — Enlisted June 29, 1861, at age 26 in Haywood County. Deserted on the march on November 29, 1863, and went over to the enemy. Took the Oath around May 22, 1864.

HENSON, ELIJAH L., Private — Enlisted June 29, 1861, at age 20 in Haywood County. Deserted to the enemy on an unspecified date after February 1864. Took the Oath at Knoxville, TN, on May 25, 1864.

HENSON, FIDELLIO W., Private — Enlisted June 29, 1861, at age 22 in Haywood County. Died in hospital at Petersburg, VA, on August 4, 1862, of "cerebritis."

HENSON, HENRY, Jr., Private — Enlisted June 29, 1861, at age 25 in Haywood County. Present or accounted for through February 1865.

HENSON, THOMAS F., Corporal. Previously served in Company C of this Reg. and transferred to this company on May 1, 1862, with the rank of Corporal. Deserted on the march on January 28, 1864, and went over to the enemy. Took the Oath at Knoxville, TN, around May 25, 1864.

HENSON, WESLEY, Sergeant — Enlisted June 29, 1861, at age 21 in Haywood County. Promoted to Sergeant on an unspecified date in 1864. Wounded at Drewry's Bluff, VA, around May 20, 1864, and returned to duty prior to January 1, 1865. Captured at Fort Stedman, VA, on March 25, 1865, and confined at Point Lookout, MD. Released on June 14, 1865, after taking the Oath.

HENSON, WILEY, Sergeant — Enlisted June 29, 1861, at age 19 in Haywood County. Captured at Frederick, MD, on September 12, 1862, and confined at Fort Delaware, DE. Exchanged at Aiken's Landing, James River, VA, November 10, 1862, and returned to duty prior to January 1, 1863. Promoted to Sergeant around November 30, 1863. Deserted on February 22, 1864.

HENSON, WILLIAM, Private — Enlisted June 29, 1861, at age 26 in Haywood County. Captured at Frederick, MD, on September 12, 1862, and confined at Fort Delaware, DE. Exchanged at Aiken's Landing, James River, VA, on November 10, 1862, and returned to duty prior to January 1, 1863. Hospitalized at Richmond, VA, on May 11, 1864, with a gunshot wound to the right thigh. Furloughed for sixty days on May 26, 1864, and returned to duty prior to January 1, 1865. Wounded in the left shoulder at Fort Stedman, VA, around March 25, 1865, and hospitalized at Petersburg, VA, where he was presumably captured by the enemy on April 3, 1865. No further records.

HOLLAND, HUMPHREY P., Private — Enlisted June 29, 1861, at age 23 in Haywood County. Enlisted as Color Corporal but reduced to ranks in January–February 1864. Present or accounted for through February 1865.

HOLLAND, MATTHIAS, Private — Enlisted June 29, 1861, at age 21 in Haywood County. Deserted to the enemy on an unspecified date after February 1864. Took the Oath at Knoxville, TN, around May 22, 1864.

HOLLAND, THOMAS, Private. Previously served in Company I, 62nd Regiment NC Troops and enlisted in this company on September 4, 1863. Hospitalized at Petersburg, VA, on July 26, 1864, with a shell wound of the right thigh and died in Petersburg hospital on the same day.

HOOD, PLEASANT B., Private — Enlisted June 29, 1861, at age 35 in Haywood County. Discharged on July 16, 1862, for being over age. Later served in Company I, 62nd Regiment NC Troops.

HOUSE, AMBROSE, Private. Paroled at Farmville, VA, around April 11–21, 1865.

HYATT, ROBERT H., Private — Enlisted August 5, 1861, at age 21 in Buncombe County. Promoted to Sergeant on April 28, 1862, but reduced to ranks on June 23, 1863. Present or accounted for through February 1865.

INMAN, JOSHUA E., Private — Enlisted June 29, 1861, at age 23 in Haywood County. Present or accounted for through February 1864. No further records.

INMAN, LEWIS HEZEKIAH, Private — Enlisted June 29, 1861, at age 19 in Haywood County. Deserted on September 5, 1862, but returned to duty on November 19, 1862. Deserted again on an unspecified date after February 1863 but returned to duty on April 27, 1863. Deserted for third time around August 1, 1864, and went over to the enemy. Took the Oath in eastern Tennessee in December 1864.

INMAN, WILLIAM P., Private — Enlisted June 29, 1861, at age 22 in Haywood County. Wounded at Malvern Hill, VA, on July 1, 1862, and returned to duty on July 15, 1862. Deserted on September 5, 1862, but returned to duty on November 19, 1862. Hospitalized at Petersburg, VA, on August 21, 1864, with a gunshot wound of the neck. Deserted from hospital at Raleigh around November 2, 1864, and went over to the enemy. Took the Oath in eastern Tennessee in December 1864.

JONES, GEORGE W., Private — Enlisted August 12, 1861, at age 29 in Buncombe County. Died in Buncombe or Haywood County on July 4, 1862, of "fever."

JONES, ISAAC W., Private — Enlisted June 10, 1864, in Johnston County. Captured at Fort Stedman, VA, on March 25, 1865, and confined at Point Lookout, MD. Released on June 28, 1865, after taking the Oath.

JONES, JOHN R., Musician — Enlisted June 29, 1861, at age 21 in Haywood County. Appointed Musician on April 28, 1862. Died of wounds on August 13, 1864. Place and date wounded not reported.

LAUGHTER, ARTHUR, Private. Previously served in Company A of this Reg. and enlisted in this company in Henderson County on July 16, 1862, as a substitute. Reported under arrest in January–February 1864 for unknown reason. Confined at E.D.M. Prison in Richmond, VA, until released in May 1864 after volunteering to serve in the defense of Richmond against the Sheridan raid. Deserted to the enemy on February 28, 1865, and confined at Washington, D.C. Released around March 6, 1865, after taking the Oath.

LONG, JOSEPH F., Private — Enlisted June 29, 1861, at age 22 in Haywood County. Deserted on January 28, 1864, but returned to duty on an unspecified date. Hospitalized at Petersburg, VA, with a gunshot wound of the left hand received on August 21, 1864. Reported absent wounded or absent sick through February 1865.

LUTHER, DILLARD T., Private — Enlisted May 1, 1864, in Haywood County. Present or accounted for until discharged "by civil authority" on September 30, 1864.

MAHAFFEY, FRANCIS M., Private — Enlisted September 10, 1861, at age 33 in Buncombe County. Wounded in the arm at Fredericksburg, VA, on December 13, 1862, and returned to duty prior to January 1, 1863. Captured near Petersburg, VA, on April 2, 1865, and confined at Point Lookout, MD. Released on June 29, 1865, after taking the Oath.

MAHAFFEY, JOHN W., Private — Enlisted June 29, 1861, at age 27 in Haywood County. Discharged on April 30, 1862, by reason of disability. Reenlisted in the company on August 15, 1863. Deserted on the march on January 28, 1864, and went over to the enemy. Took the Oath at Knoxville, TN, around May 22, 1864.

MAHAFFEY, JOSEPH H., Private — Enlisted September 1, 1863, at age 42 in Haywood County. Deserted on the march on February 1, 1864, and returned to duty prior to January 1, 1865. Present or accounted for through February 1865.

MANN, JOSEPH B., Sr., Corporal — Enlisted June 29, 1861, at age 18 in Haywood County. Promoted to Corporal on September 10, 1862. Broke his right arm at the Battle of the Crater near Petersburg, VA, on July 30, 1864. Reported absent on furlough through February 1865.

MANN, WILLIAM B., Private — Enlisted August 15, 1863, at age 41 in Haywood County. Reported under arrest in January–February 1864 for unknown reason. Confined at E.D.M. Prison in Richmond, VA, until May 1864 until released after volunteering to serve in the defense of Richmond against the Sheridan raid. No further records.

MEECE, JAMES BRADFORD, Private — Enlisted June 29, 1861, at age 19 in Haywood County. Promoted to Sergeant on April 30, 1862, but reduced to ranks around November 30, 1863. Deserted to the enemy after December 1863. Took the Oath at Knoxville, TN, around May 22, 1864.

MEECE, JOHN M., Private — Enlisted February 14, 1862, at age 21 at Grahamville, SC. Wounded at King's School House, VA, around June 25, 1862, resulting in amputation of index and middle fingers. Reported absent wounded until August 2, 1862, when he was discharged by reason of disability from wounds.

MEECE, MORGAN, Private — Enlisted June 29, 1861, at age 24 in Haywood County. Wounded in an unspecified engagement in March–December 1864. Reported absent wounded through February 1865.

MEECE, WILLIAM R., Private — Enlisted June 29, 1861, at age 18 in Haywood County. Died at Farmville, VA, on March 31, 1863, of "pneumonia" and/or diarrhoea."

MILLER, FRANCIS M., Private — Enlisted March 17, 1862, at age 25 in Haywood County. Died in the hospital at Wilson on April 1 or April 10, 1863, of "typhoid fever."

MOORE, JOHN C., Private — Enlisted June 10, 1864, at age 20 in Moore County. Captured in hospital at Richmond, VA, on April 3, 1865. Paroled around April 18, 1865.

MURRAY, LUTHER W., 1st Sergeant — Enlisted June 29, 1861, at age 17 in Haywood County. Captured at Frederick, MD, on September 12, 1862, and confined at Fort Delaware, DE. Paroled and exchanged at Aiken's Landing, James River, VA, on November 10, 1862. Returned to duty prior to January 1, 1863. Promoted to Sergeant in March–December 1864 and promoted to 1st Sergeant in January–February 1865. Captured near Petersburg, VA, on April 2, 1865, and confined at Point Lookout, MD. Released on June 15, 1865, after taking the Oath.

NORTON, JAMES E., Private — Enlisted June 29, 1861, at age 23 in Haywood County. Present or accounted for through February 1865 but reported absent sick during most of that period.

OSBORNE, ROLAND CALLOWAY, Private — Enlisted June 29, 1861, at age 24 in Haywood County. Died in hospital at Williamsburg, VA, on August 5, 1862, of "febris typhoides."

POSTON, ROBERT, Private — Enlisted June 29, 1861, at age 38 in Haywood County. Discharged on July 16, 1862, for being over age.

PRESSLEY, DANIEL N., Private — Enlisted June 29, 1861, at age 23 in Haywood County. Deserted to the enemy on an unspecified date after February 1864. Took the Oath at Knoxville, TN, around May 22, 1864.

PRESSLEY, JOSHUA A., Private — Enlisted June 29, 1861, at age 18 in Haywood County. Died in hospital at Petersburg, VA, around August 24, 1862, of "febris typhoides."

PRESSLEY, NELSON A., Private — Enlisted June 29, 1861, at age 21 in Haywood County. Died in hospital at Petersburg, VA, on August 21, 1862, of "fever."

QUEEN, ROBERT H., Private — Enlisted March 17, 1862, at age 25 in Haywood County. Deserted on August 29, 1862, but returned to duty on July 1, 1863. Deserted again on August 17, 1863.

REECE, AMOS M., Private — Enlisted June 29, 1861, at age 20 in Haywood County. Died in hospital at Grahamville, SC, on December 25, 1861, of "pneumonia."

REECE, ISAAC N., Private — Enlisted June 29, 1861, at age 21 in Haywood County. Killed at Malvern Hill, VA, on July 1, 1862.

REECE, JOHN V., Musician — Enlisted July 13, 1861, at age 17 in Haywood County. Enlisted as Musician and present or accounted for until discharged around September 14, 1861, by reason of "disability caused by an old cut on his foot." Later served as Corporal in Company I, 62nd Regiment NC Troops.

REECE, JONATHAN K., Private — Enlisted August 6, 1861, at age 23 in Buncombe County. Present or accounted for through February 1865.

REECE, WILLIAM L., Private — Enlisted June 29, 1861, at age 25 in Haywood County. Deserted on August 29, 1862, but returned to duty on an unspecified date. Deserted again around March 27, 1863, and reported under arrest in July–August 1863 and later confined at Castle Thunder Prison, Richmond, VA, in September–October 1863. Reported under arrest at Weldon in November–December 1863. Executed on February 18, 1864, "for murdering G.W. Chambers" while a deserter.

RHODES, WILLIAM B., Private — Enlisted June 29, 1861, at age 24 in Haywood County. Died at Grahamville, SC, on January 30–31, 1862, of "typhoid fever."

ROBERSON, ISAAC W., Private — Enlisted June 29, 1861, at age 20 in Haywood County. Enlisted as Corporal but reduced to ranks on April 28, 1862. Present or accounted for through February 1865.

ROGERS, JOHN C., Private — Enlisted June 29, 1861, at age 23 in Haywood County. Promoted to Sergeant around April 30, 1862, but reduced to ranks on September 30, 1862. Present or accounted for through February 1865.

ROGERS, MATTHEW McA., Private — Enlisted July 18, 1861, at age 22 in Haywood County. Present or accounted for through June 1863 but reported absent sick during much of that period. Listed as a deserter and dropped from the rolls of the company on July 8, 1863. Returned to duty on September 21, 1863. Transferred to Company A, 19th Regiment NC Troops on November 16, 1864, but deserted prior to reporting to new unit. Took the Oath at Knoxville, TN, around March 10, 1865.

SCOTT, JAMES P., Private — Enlisted June 10, 1864, at "Pearson.." Appointed Sergeant Major on January 1, 1865, and transferred to the Field and Staff of this Reg.

SINGLETON, JAMES ANDERSON, Corporal — Enlisted August 14, 1861, at age 21 in Haywood County. Wounded at Sharpsburg, MD, on September 17, 1862, and returned to duty in November–December 1862. Promoted to Corporal in March–December 1864. Present or accounted for through February 1865.

SINGLETON, JAMES M., Private — Enlisted March 18, 1862, at age 20 in Haywood County. Died in hospital at Petersburg, VA, on January 4, 1863, of "typhoid pneumonia."

SINGLETON, JOHN C., Private — Enlisted July 30, 1861, at age 26 in Buncombe County. Promoted to Corporal on October 16, 1861, but reduced to ranks on April 30, 1862. Present or accounted for through February 1865.

SINGLETON, SAMUEL P., Private — Enlisted April 1863 at age 24 in Haywood County. Discharged in June 1863 by reason of disability.

SINGLETON, WILLIAM A.S.C., Private — Enlisted August 14, 1861, at age 17 in Haywood County. Present or accounted for until discharged on July 16, 1862, for being under age.

SMITH, JOHN A., Musician. Previously served as Private in Company C of this Reg. and transferred to this company and appointed Musician (Fifer) on May 1, 1862. Wounded in the jaw at King's School House, VA, on June 25, 1862, and returned to duty on October 11, 1862. Deserted on March 27, 1863.

SORRELLS, HENRY JACKSON, Corporal — Enlisted June 29, 1861, at age 23 in Haywood County. Promoted to Corporal on April 28, 1862. Died in hospital at Petersburg, VA, on July 30, 1862, of "febris typhoides."

STAMEY, JOHN, Private — Enlisted June 29, 1861, at age 21 in Haywood County. Died in hospital at Goldsboro around June 25, 1862, of "fever."

THOMAS, JOHN G., Private — Enlisted June 29, 1861, at age 31 in Haywood County. Deserted on the march on November 27, 1863, and went over to the enemy. Took the Oath at Knoxville, TN, around May 25, 1864.

THOMPSON, JOSEPH M., Private — Enlisted June 29, 1861, at age 18 in Haywood County. Wounded at King's School House, VA, on June 25, 1862. Died of wounds at Richmond, VA, on June 27, 1862.

THOMPSON, WILLIAM, Private — Enlisted June 29, 1861, at age 28 in Haywood County. Died in hospital at Petersburg, VA, on July 30, 1862, of "dysentery" and/or "fever."

TINDLE, J.R., Private. Paroled at Farmville, VA, around April 11–21, 1865.

TRULL, JOHN W., Private — Enlisted June 29, 1861, at age 21 in Haywood County. Wounded in the left foot at Fredericksburg, VA, on December 13, 1862, and returned to duty prior to May 1, 1863. Present or accounted for through February 1865.

VANCE, WILLIAM P., Private — Enlisted July 23, 1861, at age 35 in Buncombe County. Discharged on July 16, 1862, for being over age.

WILLIAMS, WILLIAM H., Private — Enlisted June 29, 1861, at age 20 in Haywood County. Deserted "in front of the enemy" on June 1, 1863.

WILSON, JOHN C., Private. Previously served in Company B of this Reg. and transferred to this company on May 1, 1862. Wounded in the left hand at Fredericksburg, VA, on December 13, 1862, and returned to duty in January–February 1863. Deserted to the enemy around February 28, 1865, and confined at Washington, D.C. Released around March 6, 1865, after taking the Oath.

Company G — "Highland Guards"

Captains

GRADY, WILLIAM S. — Enlisted July 8, 1861, at age 40 in Macon County. Appointed Captain on July 8, 1861. Appointed Major on December 18, 1862, and transferred to the Field and Staff of this Reg.

HAYES, JOHN R. — Enlisted July 8, 1861, at age 27 in Macon County. Appointed 1st Lt. on July 8, 1861, and promoted to Captain on December 18, 1862. Resigned about May 31, 1864, for unreported reason.

PHINIZY, JOHN M. — Enlisted July 8, 1861, at age 38 in Macon County. Appointed 2nd Lt. on July 8, 1861, and promoted to 1st Lt. on December 18, 1862. Promoted to Captain about May 31, 1864. Reported absent without leave in January–February 1865.

Lieutenants

EDMONSTON, RUFUS A., 3rd Lt. — Enlisted July 8, 1861, at age 33 in Macon County. Elected 3rd Lt. on January 4, 1862, but defeated for reelection on April 28, 1862.

HUNNICUTT, THOMAS H., 3rd Lt. — Enlisted July 8, 1861, at age 20 in Macon County. Appointed 3rd Lt. in 1864. Wounded in the left thigh at Fort Stedman, VA, on March 25, 1865, and hospitalized at Petersburg, VA, where he was captured by the enemy on April 3, 1865. Confined at various Federal hospitals until hospitalized at Fort Monroe, VA, on May 17, 1865. Took the Oath about June 21, 1865.

JACKSON, BENJAMIN F.H., 1st Lt. — Enlisted July 8, 1861, at age 22 in Macon County. Promoted to Sergeant prior to September 1, 1861, and to 1st Sergeant prior to November 1, 1861. Elected 3rd Lt. on April 30, 1862, and promoted to 2nd Lt. on December 18, 1862, and to 1st Lt. in March–December 1864. Hospitalized at Danville, VA, about October 2, 1864, with a gunshot wound of the head. Reported absent wounded through February 1865. Captured at Greenville, SC, on May 12, 1865, and paroled on an unspecified date.

MARR, WILLIAM J., 2nd Lt. — Enlisted July 8, 1861, at age 21 in Macon County. Enlisted as Sergeant but reduced to ranks in May–June 1862. Promoted to Sergeant in March–June 1863 and appointed 2nd Lt. on an unspecified date in 1864. Hospitalized at Richmond, VA, on February 23, 1865, with a gunshot wound of the thigh and right hand. Captured in hospital at Richmond on April 3, 1865, and paroled around April 20, 1865.

NETHERLAND, GEORGIA M., 3rd Lt. — Enlisted February 6, 1862, at age 26 at Grahamville, SC. Elected 3rd Lt. on December 29, 1862. Wounded at Malvern Hill, VA, on July 1, 1862, and returned to duty prior to September 1, 1862. Resigned on June 7, 1864, because he had been wounded twice in battle and one of the wounds "fractured my skull and injured my brain so badly that I am absolutely wholly unable for the duties of the office."

WALKER, JOHN W., 3rd Lt. — Enlisted July 8, 1861, at age 37. Appointed 3rd Lt. on July 8, 1861. On November 27, 1861, appointed Assistant Commissary of Subsistence (Captain) and transferred to the Field and Staff of this Reg.

Noncommissioned Officers and Privates

ADAMS, JOHN, Private — Enlisted July 8, 1861, in Macon County. Discharged on May 1, 1862, for being under age. Discharge certificate gives age as 16.

ADAMS, SAMUEL S., Private — Enlisted July 8, 1861, in Macon County. Discharged on May 1, 1862, for being under age. Discharge certificate gives age as 17.

ARIAL, HARVEY O., Private — Enlisted July 20, 1861, at age 18 in Buncombe County. Wounded at Malvern Hill, VA, on July 1, 1862, and returned to duty prior to September 1, 1862. Wounded at Fredericksburg, VA, on December 13, 1862, and returned to duty in May–June 1863. Died in hospital at Richmond, VA, on September 4, 1864, of "febris continued simplex."

ATKINS, ALFRED A., Private — Enlisted July 8, 1861, at age 24 in Macon County. Enlisted as Corporal but reduced to ranks in May–June 1862. Killed at Malvern Hill, VA, on July 1, 1862.

BARTON, DAVID M., Private — Enlisted July 20, 1861, in Buncombe County. Discharged on May 1, 1862, for being under age. Discharge certificate gives age as 16. Reenlisted in the company on May 1, 1863. Reported absent without leave on December 21, 1864, and dropped from the rolls of the company on February 1, 1865, by reason of protracted absence.

BARTON, ROBERT J., Corporal — Enlisted July 20, 1861, at age 18 in Buncombe County. Promoted to Corporal in March 1863. Died in hospital at Richmond, VA, on August 5, 1864, of unreported cause.

BASS, GEORGE F., Private — Enlisted July 8, 1861, in Macon County. Discharged on May 1, 1862, for being under age. Discharge certificate gives age as 17.

BASS, WALTER B., Private — Enlisted July 8, 1861, at age 18 in Macon County. Enlisted as Sergeant but reduced to ranks in May–June 1862. Appointed 1st Sergeant on September 1, 1863, but again reduced to ranks in January–February 1865. Retired to the Invalid Corps on January 13, 1865.

BATTLE, JAMES F., Private — Enlisted July 8, 1861, at age 18 in Macon County. Discharged on September 18, 1861, by reason of disability.

BICE, CHARLES, Private — Enlisted July 8, 1861, at age 26 in Macon County. Wounded in the left eye at Fredericksburg, VA, on December 13, 1862, and returned to duty in September–October 1863. Retired from service on February 14, 1865, by reason of "gunshot wound causing entire disorganization of the left eye, with sympathetic inflammation of the right (eye)."

BIRD, LORENZO W., Private — Enlisted July 8, 1861, at age 18 in Macon County. Died in hospital at Petersburg, VA, about August 7, 1862, of "continued fever."

BIRD, ROBERT, Musician — Enlisted March 1, 1862, at age 13 at Grahamville, SC. Enlisted as Musician and present or accounted for until discharged on May 1, 1862, for being under age.

BLACKMAN, JACOB, Private — Enlisted December 13, 1861, at age 23 at Grahamville, SC. Wounded in the left arm at Malvern Hill, VA, on July 1, 1862, and returned to duty prior to September 1, 1862. Killed at Fredericksburg, VA, on December 13, 1862.

BLACKMAN, LEWIS R.H., Sergeant — Enlisted July 8, 1861, at age 20 in Macon County. Promoted to Sergeant on May 1, 1862. Present or accounted for through February 1865.

BLACKMON, JOAB, Private — Enlisted October 5, 1864, in Wake County. Reported absent wounded in November–December 1864. Retired on February 27, 1865.

BLACKMON, JOSEPH A., Private — Enlisted October 20, 1863, at age 47. Retired to the Invalid Corps on October 7, 1864. Reason not reported.

BONE, GEORGE W., Private — Enlisted July 8, 1861, at age 22 in Macon County. Wounded at Malvern Hill, VA, on July 1, 1862, and returned to duty prior to September 1, 1862. Deserted to the enemy around August 29, 1864. No further records.

BONE, JONATHAN, Private — Enlisted March 21, 1862, at age 43 in Lenoir County. Discharged on May 1, 1862, for being over age.

BONE, MATTHEW, Private — Enlisted April 20, 1862, at age 29 at Athens, GA. Captured near Petersburg, VA, on April 2, 1865, and confined at Point Lookout, MD. Released on June 24, 1865, after taking the Oath.

BRADLEY, JOHN H., Private — Enlisted April 20, 1862, at age 19 in Lenoir County. Captured at Fort Stedman, VA, on March 25, 1865, and confined at Point Lookout, MD, until released on June 23, 1865, after taking the Oath.

BROOKS, CINCINNATUS T., Private — Enlisted July 26, 1864, in Halifax County. Captured and paroled at Athens, GA, about May 8, 1865.

BROOKS, DANIEL W., Private — Enlisted July 20, 1861, at age 18 in Buncombe County. Killed at Malvern Hill, VA, on July 1, 1862.

BROOKS, JAMES L., Private — Enlisted July 20, 1861, at age 20 in Buncombe County. Present or accounted for through February 1864. Reported absent wounded in November–December 1864 and absent without leave in January–February 1865.

BROOKS, REUBEN H., Private — Enlisted December 4, 1861, at age 24 at Grahamville, SC. Present or accounted for through February 1864.

BROWN, ALFRED E., Private — Enlisted July 8, 1861, at age 21 in Macon County. Wounded at Fredericksburg, VA, on December 13, 1862, and subsequently reported absent wounded or absent sick through February 1864. No further records.

BROWN, JACOB W., Private — Enlisted July 8, 1861, at age 18 in Macon County. Discharged on July 25, 1861, by reason of "non compos mentis."

BROWN, JAVAN, Private — Enlisted July 8, 1861, at age 18 in Macon County. Discharged on September 18, 1861, by reason of disability.

BROWN, JOHN M., Private — Enlisted July 8, 1861, at age 21 in Macon County. Present or accounted for through February 1864. No further records.

BURCH, BENJAMIN, Private — Enlisted August 1, 1861, at age 21 in Buncombe County. Promoted to Musician in September–October 1861 but reduced to ranks in March–April 1862. Died at Kinston on June 3, 1862, of unreported cause.

BURNS, RICHARD, Private — Enlisted July 25, 1861, at age 25 in Buncombe County. Promoted to Musician in September–October 1861 but reduced to ranks in May 1862. Discharged on May 27, 1862, after providing Private Alvis Ellington as a substitute.

BYERS, MARION C., Private — Enlisted July 8, 1861, at age 22 in Macon County. Deserted on August 15, 1861.

CABE, JAMES David, Private — Enlisted August 1, 1861, at age 22 in Buncombe County. Killed at Malvern Hill, VA, on July 1, 1862.

CARROLL, AUGUSTUS Y., Private — Enlisted July 8, 1861, at age 21 in Macon County. Died in hospital at Grahamville, SC, on December 8, 1861, of disease.

CARTER, JESSE P., Private — Enlisted January 22, 1862, at age 18 at Grahamville, SC. Wounded in the head and captured at Fort Stedman, VA, on March 25, 1865. Died on board the U.S. Hospital Steamer *Connecticut* on March 28, 1865, of wounds.

CHILDERS, THOMAS R., Private — Enlisted April 20, 1862, at age 22 at Athens, GA. Captured at Amelia Court House, VA, on April 3, 1865, and confined at Point Lookout, MD, until released on June 26, 1865, after taking the Oath.

CHILDERS, WILLIAM A., Private — Enlisted April 20, 1862, at age 22 at Athens, GA. Died in hospital near Gordonsville, VA, on December 9, 1862, of "pneumonia."

COKER, JAMES H., 1st Sergeant — Enlisted July 8, 1861, at age 24 in Macon County. Promoted to 1st Sergeant in May–June 1862. Died in hospital at Petersburg, VA, on April 13, 1863, of "febris typhoides."

COLBERT JAMES S., Color Corporal — Enlisted July 8, 1861, at age 22 in Macon County. Wounded at Fredericksburg, VA, on December 13, 1862, and returned to duty on January 17, 1863. Promoted to Color Corporal in September–October 1863. Wounded in the lungs at Fort Stedman, VA, on March 25, 1865, and died in hospital at Petersburg, VA, on March 31, 1865, of wounds.

COLLEY, LORENZO W., Private — Enlisted April 20, 1862, at age 18 at Athens, GA. Captured near Petersburg, VA, on June 17, 1864, and confined at Point Lookout, MD, until transferred to Elmira, NY, on July 27, 1864. Paroled at Elmira on October 11, 1864, and transferred for exchange. Died in hospital at Baltimore, MD, on October 24, 1864, of "scurvy" and/or "hospital gangrene."

COWARD, EDWARD G., Private—Enlisted July 8, 1861, at age 21 in Macon County. Broke his leg prior to September 1, 1861, and discharged about September 18, 1861, by reason of disability. Later served in Company B, 62nd Regiment NC Troops.

COWARD, ELIHU M., Private—Enlisted April 26, 1864, in Halifax County. Furloughed on August 27, 1864, and then reported absent without leave on December 21, 1864. Dropped from the rolls of the company for "protracted absence" on February 1, 1865.

COWARD, GEORGE W., Private—Enlisted July 8, 1861, at age 31 in Macon County. Died in hospital at Richmond, VA, on January 8, 1863, of "pneumonia."

COWARD, JOHN A., Private—Enlisted July 8, 1861, at age 19 in Macon County. Deserted in January-February 1864.

CROW, JAMES, Private—Enlisted April 20, 1862, at age 35 at Athens, GA. Captured at Fort Stedman, VA, on March 25, 1865, and confined at Point Lookout, MD. Released on June 26, 1865, after taking the Oath.

CURTIS, CHRISTOPHER, Private—Enlisted July 8, 1861, at age 18 in Macon County. Died in hospital at Wilson around April 5, 1862, of disease.

CURTIS, GEORGE W. Sr., Private—Enlisted July 8, 1861, at age 22 in Macon County. Transferred to Company I of this Reg. about March 10, 1862.

DAVENPORT, JOSIAH P., Private—Enlisted July 20, 1861, at age 28 in Buncombe County. Discharged on March 10, 1862, by reason of "physical disability." Later served in Company B, 62nd Regiment NC Troops.

DAVENPORT, SIDNEY S., Private—Enlisted July 20, 1861, at age 18 in Buncombe County. Discharged on March 10, 1862, by reason of "physical disability." Later served in Company B, 62nd Regiment NC Troops.

DAVIS, JOSIAH, Private—Enlisted April 20, 1862, at age 21 at Athens, GA. Present or accounted for through February 1865.

DODGENS, ARCHIBALD J., Private—Enlisted September 27, 1861, at age 26 in Wake County. Promoted to Corporal in July 1862 but reduced to ranks in March-December 1864. Reported absent without leave on December 24, 1864, and dropped from the rolls of the company on February 1, 1865, by reason of "protracted absence."

DODGENS, HIRAM L., Private—Enlisted August 1, 1861, at age 23. Enlisted in Macon or Buncombe counties and present or accounted for until killed "in a fight with Tories" near Warm Springs around October 25, 1863.

DUNAWAY, JAMES H.H., Private—Enlisted July 8, 1861, at age 18 in Macon County. Captured at Amelia Court House, VA, on April 3, 1865, and confined at Point Lookout, MD. Released on June 26, 1865, after taking the Oath.

DUNAWAY, WILLIAM H., Corporal—Enlisted March 11, 1862, at age 26 in Lenoir County. Promoted to Corporal in March-December 1864. Captured at Farmville, VA, on April 6, 1865, and confined at Newport News, VA. Released on June 27, 1865, after taking the Oath.

EDMONDSON, HAMILTON W., Private—Enlisted July 8, 1861, at age 23 in Macon County. Enlisted as Sergeant but reduced to ranks in May-June 1862. Discharged in August 1862 after providing a substitute.

EDMONDSON, JOHN Q., Private—Enlisted July 8, 1861, at age 33 in Macon County. Promoted to Corporal on January 10, 1862, but reduced to ranks in May-June 1862. Deserted in January-February 1864.

EDMONDSON, NAPOLEON B., Private—Enlisted July 8, 1861, at age 21 in Macon County. Discharged on April 30, 1862, by reason of either the "loss of [an] eye" or "disability caused by a gunshot wound in the left hand." Place and date of injury not reported.

ELLER, MARION R., Private—Enlisted January 2, 1862, at age 22 at Grahamville, SC. Wounded in the chest at Drewry's Bluff, VA, on May 16, 1864, and furloughed for sixty days on May 31, 1864. No further records.

ELLINGTON, ALVIS, Private—Enlisted May 27, 1862, in Lenoir County. Enlisted as a substitute for Private Richard Burns. No further records.

FINCANNON, ISAAC D., Private—Enlisted April 8, 1864, in Halifax County. Paroled at Appomattox Court House, VA, on April 9, 1865.

FINCANNON, LEASON W., Private—Enlisted March 22, 1862, at age 17 at Grahamville, SC. Discharged on May 1, 1862, for being under age. Apparently reenlisted in this company subsequent to February 29, 1864, and deserted to the enemy around May 1, 1864. Took the Oath at Louisville, KY, on May 15, 1864.

GARLAND, DAVID N., Private—Enlisted August 1, 1861, at age 22 in Buncombe County. Captured near Petersburg, VA, on April 2, 1865, and confined at Point Lookout, MD. Released on June 27, 1865, after taking the Oath.

GARLAND, GEORGE W., Private—Enlisted August 1, 1861, at age 20 in Buncombe County. Killed at Malvern Hill, VA, on July 1, 1862.

GATES, WILLIAM J., Private—Enlisted March 11, 1862, at age 16 in Lenoir County. Present or accounted for through February 1864. No further records.

GILLESPIE, JAMES L., Corporal—Enlisted August 1, 1861, at age 19 in Buncombe County. Promoted to Corporal in May-June 1862. Wounded at Malvern Hill, VA, on July 1, 1862, and died in hospital at Petersburg, VA, on July 22, 1862, of "typhoid fever."

GILLESPIE, MARSHALL L., Private—Enlisted August 1, 1861, at age 21 in Buncombe County. Present or accounted for through February 1865.

GILLESPIE, WILLIAM H., Private—Enlisted January 22, 1862, at age 23 at Grahamville, SC. Died at Drewry's Bluff, VA, on August 3, 1862, of disease.

GRAHL, JOHN L., Private—Enlisted July 8, 1861, at age 18 in Macon County. Discharged on September 18, 1861, by reason of disability.

GUDGER, KIMSEY, Private—Enlisted July 20, 1861, at age 35 in Buncombe County. Discharged on September 18, 1861, by reason of disability.

HADLEY, FRANCIS M., Sergeant—Enlisted July 8, 1861, at age 20 in Macon County. Enlisted as Corporal and was promoted to Sergeant in May–June 1862. Captured at Amelia Court House, VA, on April 3, 1865, and confined at Point Lookout, MD. Released on June 28, 1865, after taking the Oath.

HARRIS, JOHN, Private — Enlisted April 23, 1862, at age 19 at Athens, GA. Died in hospital at Lynchburg, VA, on December 26, 1862, of "variola."

HARRIS, LIGHTFOOT W., Private — Enlisted March 1, 1862, at age 23 at Grahamville, SC. Present or accounted for through February 1864. Died at Petersburg, VA, prior to September 6, 1864, of unreported cause.

HEMRICK, DAVID, Private — Enlisted April 23, 1862, at age 24 at Athens, GA. Wounded in the knee at Fredericksburg, VA, on December 13, 1862, and reported absent wounded through February 1864. No further records.

HEMRICK, HENRY, Private — Enlisted April 23, 1862, at age 24 at Athens, GA. Promoted to Corporal on May 1, 1863, but reduced to ranks in March–December 1864. Hospitalized at Petersburg, VA, on June 20, 1864, with a gunshot wound of the leg. Returned to duty prior to January 1, 1865. Paroled at Appomattox Court House, VA, on April 9, 1865, and captured and paroled again at Athens about May 8, 1865.

HEMRICK, WILLIAM, Private — Enlisted April 23, 1862, at age 20 at Athens, GA. Captured near Globe Tavern, VA, on August 21, 1864, and confined at Point Lookout, MD. Paroled and transferred to Venus Point, Savannah River, GA, for exchange on November 15, 1864. Returned to duty in January–February 1865 and present or accounted for through February 1865.

HENSLY, WILLIAM C., Private — Enlisted July 20, 1862, at age 30 at Drewry's Bluff, VA. Wounded in both thighs at Five Forks, VA, on April 1, 1865, and hospitalized at Petersburg, VA. Captured there in hospital on April 3, 1865, and then transferred to hospital at Fort Monroe, VA, on an unspecified date. Died at Fort Monroe on July 24, 1865, of "typhoid fever."

HOLDEN, ANDREW J., Private — Enlisted July 8, 1861, at age 27 in Macon County. Present or accounted for until November 15, 1862, when detailed as a shoemaker at Richmond, VA. Transferred to Company B, 2nd Battalion VA Infantry (Local Defense) on June 18, 1863. Later served in Company K, 2nd Regiment VA Infantry (Local Defense).

JACKSON, HENRY T., Private — Enlisted July 8, 1861, at age 18 in Macon County. Captured and paroled at Anderson, SC, around May 3, 1865.

JONES, CLINTON A., 1st Sergeant — Enlisted July 8, 1861, at age 23 in Macon County. Enlisted as 1st Sergeant and appointed Quartermaster Sergeant on October 5, 1861. Transferred to the Field and Staff of this Reg.

JONES, RUSSELL M., Private — Enlisted August 1, 1861, at age 22 in Buncombe County. Captured near Petersburg, VA, on February 6, 1865, and confined at Point Lookout, MD. Released on June 28, 1865, after taking the Oath.

JONES, WILLIAM B., Private — Enlisted August 1, 1861, at age 20 in Buncombe County. Died at Kinston on June 18, 1862, of disease.

KEENER, BENJAMIN F., Private — Enlisted July 8, 1861, at age 18 in Macon County. Present or accounted for through February 1864. Company muster rolls dated November 1864–February 1865 indicate that he was a prisoner of war. Later captured and paroled at Athens, GA, about May 8, 1865.

KELLY, GEORGE W.L., Private — Enlisted January 22, 1862, at age 18 at Grahamville, SC. Wounded at Malvern Hill, VA, on July 1, 1862, and returned to duty prior to September 1, 1862. Present or accounted for through February, 1864. No further records.

KILPATRICK, JACKSON, Sergeant — Enlisted July 8, 1861, at age 24 in Macon County. Promoted to Sergeant in March–December 1864. Wounded in the right leg near Petersburg, VA, on November 18, 1864, and reported absent wounded through February 1865.

KINLEY, JAMES, Private — Enlisted July 8, 1861, at age 31 in Macon County. Promoted to Color Corporal about November 15, 1862. Captured and paroled at Athens, GA, around May 8, 1865.

KIRBY, JAMES K., Private — Enlisted December 22, 1861, at age 25 at Grahamville, SC. Deserted in January–February 1864. Records of the Federal Provost Marshal indicate he was captured and paroled at Athens, GA, about May 8, 1865.

LEDFORD, JAMES A., Private — Enlisted July 8, 1861, at age 22 in Macon County. Deserted in January–February 1864 and went over to the enemy on an unspecified date. Took the Oath at Chattanooga, TN, on March 26, 1864.

LILLEY, JAMES, Private — Enlisted April 20, 1862, at age 17 at Athens, GA. Wounded in both thighs at Fredericksburg, VA, on December 13, 1862, and returned to duty prior to January 1, 1863. Present or accounted for through December 1864 and then dropped from the rolls of the company on February 27, 1865, for "protracted absence." Captured by the enemy and paroled at Athens, GA, around May 8, 1865.

LILLEY, THOMAS, Private — Enlisted April 20, 1862, at age 18 at Athens, GA. Fredericksburg, VA, on December 13, 1862, and returned to duty in March–June 1863. Wounded in action for a third time on an unspecified date prior to January 1, 1865, and returned to duty in January–February 1865. Captured at Amelia Court House, VA, on April 3, 1865, and confined at Point Lookout, MD. Released on June 29, 1865, after taking the Oath.

LOCKABY, WILLIAM C., Private — Enlisted July 8, 1861, at age 21 in Macon County. Wounded at Malvern Hill, VA, on July 1, 1862, and died at Richmond, VA, on July 15, 1862, of wounds.

LONG, HENRY C., Sergeant — Enlisted July 8, 1861, at age 18 in Macon County. Promoted to Sergeant in May–June 1862. Wounded at Malvern Hill, VA, on July 1, 1862, and died at Richmond, VA, on July 15, 1862, of wounds.

LONG, WILLIAM M., Private — Enlisted July 8, 1861, at age 23 in Macon County. Reported missing at Malvern Hill, VA, on July 1, 1862, but returned to duty prior to September 1, 1862. Paroled at Appomattox Court House, VA, on April 9, 1865.

LYLE, ALFRED A., Private — Enlisted April 20, 1862, at age 16 at Athens, GA. Transferred to Company G, 16th Regiment GA Volunteer Infantry on December 9, 1862.

LYLE, GEORGE R., Private — Enlisted April 20, 1862, at age 18 at Athens, GA. Transferred to Company G, 16th Regiment GA Volunteer Infantry on December 9, 1862.

McALLISTER, TIMOTHY S., Private — Enlisted January 22, 1862, at age 20 at Grahamville, SC. Present or accounted for through February 1864. No further records.

McCARTY, FRANCIS J., Private — Enlisted April 20, 1862, at age 25 at Athens, GA. Deserted on August 25, 1862.

McCLAIN, MARTIN V., Private — Enlisted August 1, 1861, at age 24 in Buncombe County. Captured at Farmville, VA, on April 6, 1865, and confined at Newport News, VA. Released on June 27, 1865, after taking the Oath.

McCLURE, HUGH, Private — Enlisted July 8, 1861, at age 18 in Macon County. Died at Wilson around July 10, 1862, of disease.

McCLURE, JOSEPH J., Private — Enlisted July 8, 1861, in Macon County. Discharged on May 1, 1862, for being under age. Discharge certificate gives age as 17. Later served as 2nd Lt. of Company B, 62nd Regiment NC Troops.

McCURRY, AMOS, Private — Enlisted January 22, 1862, at age 22 at Grahamville, SC. Died near Petersburg, VA, about August 17, 1862, of disease.

McDONALD, JAMES T.A., Private — Enlisted July 8, 1861, at age 18 in Macon County. Paroled at Appomattox Court House, VA, on April 9, 1865.

MARTIN, MARION T., Corporal — Enlisted June 1, 1861, at age 18 in Cherokee County. Promoted to Corporal in July–August 1863. Present or accounted for through February 1864. No further records.

MEETS, R.H., Private. Captured near Petersburg, VA, on August 22, 1864, and confined at Old Capitol Prison, Washington, D.C. on September 12, 1864. Released on November 28, 1864.

MOORE, LEANER T., Private — Enlisted August 1, 1861, at age 20 in Buncombe County. Died in hospital at Wilson on August 16, 1863, of "febris remittens."

MOSS, DAVID, Private — Enlisted July 8, 1861, in Franklin County. Discharged on May 1, 1862, for being under age. Discharge certificate gives age as 17.

MURRY, SILAS, Private — Enlisted December 27, 1861, at age 23 at Grahamville, SC. Captured at Boonsboro, MD, on September 14, 1862, and confined at Fort Delaware, DE. Paroled and exchanged at Aiken's Landing, James River, VA, on November 10, 1862. Returned to duty prior to being wounded on December 13, 1862, at Fredericksburg, VA. Returned to duty prior to January 1, 1863. Transferred to Captain Slaten's Company (Macon Light Artillery), GA, Artillery on November 2, 1863.

NELSON, ELISHA, Private — Enlisted July 8, 1861, at age 18 in Macon County. Discharged on September 18, 1861, by reason of disability.

NICHOLS, JAMES A., Private — Enlisted July 8, 1861, at age 21 in Macon County. Died in hospital at Richmond, VA, on January 1, 1863, of "typhoid fever."

PADGETT, WILLIAM S., Private — Enlisted December 27, 1861, at age 23 at Grahamville, SC. Wounded at Fredericksburg, VA, on December 13, 1862, and died on December 15, 1862, of wounds. Place of death not reported.

PARKS, WILLIAM M., Private — Enlisted April 20, 1862, at age 35 at Athens, GA. Present or accounted for through December 1862. Wounded accidentally by Private Silas Murry on an unspecified date. Died in hospital at Petersburg, VA, on January 9, 1863, of wounds.

PEELER, ELISHA M., Private — Enlisted April 20, 1862, at age 42 at Athens, GA. Enlisted as a substitute. Wounded at Fredericksburg, VA, on December 13, 1862, and died in hospital at Richmond, VA, on December 27, 1862, of "variola."

PEELER, JACOB F., Corporal — Enlisted April 20, 1862, at age 36 at Athens, GA. Wounded at Malvern Hill, VA, on July 1, 1862, and returned to duty prior to September 1, 1862. Promoted to Corporal in March–December 1864. Present or accounted for through February 1865.

PEELER, WILEY G., Private — Enlisted March 15, 1862, at age 29 in Lenoir County. Present or accounted for through December 1864 but was reported absent sick during much of that period. Retired to the Invalid Corps on January 5, 1865. Paroled at Athens, GA, on May 24, 1865.

PHIPPS, ANDREW J., Private — Enlisted April 1, 1863, at age 18 in Lenoir County. Present or accounted for through February 1865.

PHIPPS, JAMES W., Private — Enlisted August 1, 1862, at age 22 in Buncombe County. Paroled at Appomattox Court House, VA, on April 9, 1865.

PHIPPS, JOHN K., Private — Enlisted January 1, 1862, at age 20 at Grahamville, SC. Present or accounted for through February 1864. Wounded prior to January 1, 1865, and returned to duty prior to March 1, 1865. Captured at Fort Stedman, VA, on March 25, 1865, and confined at Point Lookout, MD. Released on June 16, 1865, after taking the Oath.

PINKARD, JOHN B., Private — Enlisted July 8, 1861, at age 16 in Macon County. Discharged on May 1, 1862, for being under age.

PLEDGER, ELISHA A., Private — Enlisted March 15, 1862, at age 33 in Lenoir County. Hospitalized at Petersburg, VA, on May 22, 1864, with gunshot wounds of the side and left hand. Returned to duty in January–February 1865. Present or accounted for through February 28, 1865.

PLEDGER, JOHN, Private — Enlisted April 20, 1862, at age 36 at Athens, GA. Hospitalized at Richmond, VA, on December 8, 1864, with a gunshot wound of the right arm. Returned to duty on March 25, 1865. Captured near Petersburg, VA, on April 2, 1865, and confined at Point Lookout, MD. Released on June 16, 1865, after taking the Oath.

PLEDGER, MARSHALL M., Private — Enlisted April 20, 1862, at age 18 at Athens, GA. Wounded at Fredericksburg, VA, on December 13, 1862, and returned to duty prior to January 1, 1863. Captured near Petersburg, VA, on April 2, 1865, and confined at Point Lookout, MD. Released on June 5, 1865, after taking the Oath.

PLEDGER, THOMAS, Private — Enlisted April 20, 1862, at age 24 at Athens, GA. Wounded in action prior to January 1, 1865, and returned to duty prior to April 2, 1865. Captured on that date near Petersburg, VA, and confined at Point Lookout, MD. Released on June 16, 1865, after taking the Oath.

POWELL, CHAMP, Private — Enlisted July 8, 1861, at age 20 in Macon County. Injured his arm on an unspecified date and was furloughed. Discharged on September 18, 1861, by reason of disability.

POWELL, JOHN M.B., Private — Enlisted July 8, 1861, at age 33 in Macon County. Captured near Shepherdstown, VA, in September 1862. Paroled on October 3, 1862. No further records.

POWELL, ROBERT, Private — Enlisted November 12, 1863, at age 17 in Halifax County. Paroled at Appomattox Court House, VA, on April 9, 1865.

POWELL, TILMAN, Private — Enlisted July 8, 1861, at age 20 in Macon County. Present or accounted for through May 16, 1864. No further records.

PRICE, JAMES E., Private — Enlisted July 8, 1861, at age 22 in Macon County. Killed at Malvern Hill, VA, on July 1, 1862.

PRICE, WILLIAM H., Private — Enlisted July 8, 1861, at age 18 in Macon County. Discharged about July 20, 1864, after being "elected to a civil office."

PRICE, WILLIAM J., Private — Enlisted July 8, 1861, at age 18 in Macon County. Promoted to Corporal in September–October 1862. Wounded at Sharpsburg, MD, on September 17, 1862, and returned to duty in January–February 1863. Reduced to ranks in March–June 1863. Reported absent on detached service from May–June 1863 through February 1864. Rejoined the company prior to January 1, 1865. Paroled at Appomattox Court House, VA, on April 9, 1865.

QUEEN, ANDREW M., Private — Enlisted February 6, 1862, at age 17 at Grahamville, SC. Present or accounted for through February 1864 and wounded in action prior to January 1, 1865. Reported absent wounded through February 1865.

QUEEN, JAMES C., Private — Enlisted July 8, 1861, at age 21 in Macon County. Present or accounted for through February 1864. No further records.

QUEEN, JOHN W., Corporal — Enlisted July 8, 1861, at age 23 in Macon County. Enlisted as Corporal. Broke both of his arms at Wilmington in September–November 1861 and discharged on January 10, 1862, by reason of disability.

QUEEN, SAMUEL P., Private — Enlisted July 8, 1861, at age 22 in Macon County. Wounded in the back at Fredericksburg, VA, on December 13, 1862, and returned to duty prior to January 1, 1863. Discharged on May 16, 1863, by reason of disability.

RAMSON, EUGENIUS, Private — Enlisted April 20, 1862, at age 31 at Athens, GA. Killed at Fredericksburg, VA, on December 13, 1862.

REAMES, IRWIN, Private — Enlisted July 8, 1861, at age 23 in Macon County. Wounded at Fredericksburg, VA, on December 13, 1862, and discharged on April 4, 1863, by reason of "total disability" from wounds.

REAMES, JOSHUA, Private — Enlisted July 820, 1861, at age 21 in Buncombe County. Hospitalized at Richmond, VA, on December 16, 1862, with a gunshot wound of the leg and returned to duty in January–February 1863. Wounded at Plymouth about April 18–20, 1864, and returned to duty on an unspecified date. Captured on an unspecified date and reported in confinement in an unspecified Federal prison on August 29, 1864. No further records.

REAMES, REUBEN, Private — Enlisted August 1, 1861, at age 26 in Buncombe County. Wounded in both legs at Fredericksburg, VA, on December 13, 1862, and returned to duty in January–February 1863. Present or accounted for through February, 1865.

ROBERTS, JAMES F., Private — Enlisted July 8, 1861, at age 19 in Macon County. Present or accounted for through February 1864. Company muster rolls dated November 1864–February 1865 indicate he was captured by the enemy on an unspecified date. No further records.

RODGERS, CLARK A., Private — Enlisted January 1, 1862, at age 25 at Grahamville, SC. Died at Kinston on May 20, 1862, of disease.

RODGERS, ELBERT S., Private — Enlisted August 1, 1861, at age 18 in Buncombe County. Wounded at Fredericksburg, VA, on December 13, 1862, and returned to duty on January 20, 1863. Captured near Petersburg, VA, on June 17, 1864, and confined at Point Lookout, MD, until transferred to Elmira, NY, on July 27, 1864. Released at Elmira on July 3, 1864, after taking the Oath.

RUNNION, WILEY J., Private — Enlisted July 8, 1861, at age 36 in Macon County. Discharged on May 1, 1862, for being over age.

SCHEVENELL, JOSEPH H., Corporal — Enlisted July 8, 1861, in Macon County. Enlisted as Corporal. Discharged on May 1, 1862, for being under age. Discharge certificate gives age as 17.

SCHEVENELL, LEONARD, Private — Enlisted April 20, 1862, at age 18 at Athens, GA. Paroled at Appomattox Court House, VA, on April 9, 1865.

SELLERS, FELIX H., Private — Enlisted July 8, 1861, at age 20 in Macon County. Wounded in the hip and/or eye at Malvern Hill, VA, on July 1, 1862, and returned to duty prior to September 1, 1862. Deserted in January–February 1864.

SEUTER, GEORGE W. — Paroled at Appomattox Court House, VA, on April 9, 1865.

SHELTON, JOEL, Private — Enlisted July 8, 1861, in Macon County. Discharged on May 1, 1862, for being over age. Discharge certificate gives age as 37. Reenlisted in the company in August 1862 as a substitute. Deserted to the enemy on an unspecified date and took the Oath at Knoxville, TN, about May 23, 1864.

SINGLETON, WYATT GEORGE, Private — Enlisted July 8, 1861, at age 26 in Macon County. Died at Goldsboro in March 1863 of disease.

SMITH, BENJAMIN, Private — Enlisted July 20, 1861, at age 20 in Buncombe County. Died in hospital at Petersburg, VA, on July 9, 1864, of a gunshot wound of the left thigh.

SMITH, GEORGE W., Private — Enlisted July 8, 1861, at age 25 in Macon County. Wounded at Malvern Hill, VA, on July 1, 1862, and died at Richmond, VA, on July 7, 1862, of wounds.

SMITH, JOHN W.H. H., Private — Enlisted August 1, 1861, at age 20 in Buncombe County. Wounded at Fredericksburg, VA, on December 13, 1862, and returned to duty in November–December 1863. Killed in an unspecified engagement on December 1, 1864.

SPARKS, JOHN T., Private — Enlisted July 20, 1861, at age 20. Transferred to Company C of this Reg. on May 1, 1862.

SPIVEY, SAMUEL M., Private — Enlisted July 8, 1861, at age 23 in Macon County. Discharged on January 10, 1862, by reason of disability.

STAMEY, DARIUS, A., Private — Enlisted September 27, 1861, at age 22 in Wake County. Present or accounted for through February 1864. Wounded in action prior to January 1, 1865, and reported absent wounded through February 1865.

STAMEY, WILLIAM CALVIN, Private — Enlisted March 7, 1862, at age 25 at Grahamville, SC. Paroled at Appomattox Court House, VA, on April 9, 1865.

TEEMS, ABSALOM, Private — Enlisted August 1, 1861, at age 22 in Buncombe County. Wounded in the shoulder at Fredericksburg, VA, on December 13, 1862, and reported absent wounded through December 1863. No further records.

TOLBERT, JAMES M., Private — Enlisted July 8, 1861, at age 42 in Macon County. Discharged on May 1, 1862, for being over age.

TOLBERT, JOHN J., Private — Enlisted March 3, 1862, at age 17 in Lenoir County. Present or accounted for through December 1864. Dropped from the rolls of the company on February 27, 1865, for "protracted absence." Paroled at Augusta, GA, on May 24, 1865.

TOLBERT, THOMAS C., Private — Enlisted April 20, 1862, at age 33 at Athens, GA. Hospitalized at Raleigh on October 3, 1864, with a shell wound of the left leg and reported absent wounded or absent sick through February 1865.

TOLBERT, WILLIAM J., Private — Enlisted July 8, 1861, at age 18 in Macon County. Paroled at Athens, GA, on May 8, 1865.

WALKER, ALLEN, Private — Enlisted July 8, 1861, in Macon County. Discharged on July 16, 1862, for being over age. Discharge certificate gives age as 36.

WATSON, JOHN T., Private — Enlisted July 20, 1861, at age 31 in Buncombe County. Present or accounted for through February 1864. Confined at E.D.M. Prison, Richmond, VA, on an unspecified date and for unknown reason. Released in May 1864 after volunteering to serve in the defense of Richmond against the Sheridan raid. Paroled at Appomattox Court House, VA, on April 9, 1865.

WEATHERFORD, WILLIAM J., Private — Enlisted April 20, 1862, at age 30 at Athens, GA. Hospitalized at Richmond, VA, on June 20, 1864, with gunshot wounds of the hand and left thigh. Died in hospital at Richmond on June 28, 1864, of "gangrene."

WEIL, PETER, Private — Enlisted July 8, 1861, at age 35 in Macon County. Enlisted as Sergeant. Discharged on May 1, 1862, for being over age. Reenlisted in the company on May 27, 1862. Reduced to ranks in May–June 1863. Captured at Petersburg, VA, on April 3, 1865, and confined at Hart's Island, New York Harbor. Released on June 15, 1865, after taking the Oath.

WHEELER, ADAM, Private — Enlisted April 20, 1862, at age 35 at Athens, GA. Died at Drewry's Bluff, VA, on August 9, 1862, of unreported cause.

WHEELER, JAMES, Private — Enlisted April 20, 1862, at age 18 at Athens, GA. Died near Paris, VA, on October 31, 1862, of disease.

WHITE, JOHN W., Private — Enlisted April 20, 1862, at age 19 at Athens, GA. Captured near Globe Tavern, VA, on August 21, 1864, and confined at Point Lookout, MD. Paroled and transferred to Cox's Wharf, James River, VA, for exchange on February 14–15, 1865. Paroled again at Athens, GA, around May 8, 1865.

WILLIAMS, JOHN M., Private — Enlisted July 8, 1861, at age 22 in Macon County. Hospitalized at Petersburg, VA, on June 20, 1864, with a gunshot wound and returned to duty prior to January 1, 1865. Killed in action on January 17, 1865. Place of death not reported.

WILLIAMS, ROBERT, Private — Enlisted July 8, 1861, at age 20 in Macon County. Deserted to the enemy prior to August 29, 1864.

WILLIAMS, WILLIAM A., Private — Enlisted July 8, 1861, in Macon County. Discharged on May 1, 1862, for being under age. Discharge certificate gives age as 17. Reenlisted in the company in May–June 1863. Hospitalized at Petersburg, VA, on June 19, 1864, with a gunshot wound of the right foot. Reported absent wounded until December 21, 1864, and then reported absent without leave. Dropped from the rolls of the company on February 1, for "protracted absence."

WILLIAMS, WILLIAM D., Private — Enlisted July 8, 1861, at age 24 in Macon County. Captured at Farmville, VA, on April 6, 1865, and confined at Newport News, VA. Released on June 27, 1865, after taking the Oath.

WILSON, JESSE E., Private — Enlisted July 8, 1861, at age 23 in Macon County. Deserted to the enemy about November 7, 1863, and took the Oath at Fort Monroe, VA, on January 6, 1864.

WOODS, JOHN N., Sergeant — Enlisted July 8, 1861, at age 21 in Macon County. Promoted to Sergeant in March–December 1864. Captured near Petersburg, VA, on April 2, 1865, and confined at Point Lookout, MD. Released on June 21, 1865, after taking the Oath.

WRIGHT, GEORGE, Private — Enlisted April 20, 1862, at age 17 at Athens, GA. Hospitalized at Charlottesville, VA, on September 23, 1862, with a gunshot wound. Returned to duty on November 16, 1862, and present or accounted for through February 1864. No further records.

YORK, JAMES M., Private — Enlisted September 27, 1861, at age 24 in Wake County. Promoted to Sergeant on May 1, 1862, but reduced to ranks in March–December 1864. Captured at Farmville, VA, on April 6,

1865, and confined at Newport News, VA. Released on June 27, 1865, after taking the Oath.

YORK, JEFFREY S., Private—Enlisted February 6, 1862, at age 20 at Grahamville, SC. Wounded at Malvern Hill, VA, on July 1, 1862. Died at Richmond, VA, on July 16-17, 1862, of wounds.

YORK, JEREMIAH, Private—Enlisted July 8, 1861, at age 22 in Macon County. Present or accounted for until December 24, 1864, when he was reported absent without leave.

Company H — "Cane Creek Rifles"

Captains

BLAKE, FREDERICK R.—Enlisted July 15, 1861, at age 23 in Henderson County. Elected Captain on July 15, 1861. Defeated for reelection on April 30, 1862.

CUNNINGHAM, SOLOMON — Enlisted July 15, 1861, at age 35 in Henderson County. Elected 2nd Lt. on July 15, 1861, and promoted to 1st Lt. in November–December 1861. Elected Captain on April 30, 1862. Wounded at Malvern Hill, VA, on July 1, 1862, and returned to duty prior to September 1, 1862. Wounded at Fredericksburg, VA, on December 13, 1862, and died in hospital at Richmond VA on December 15, 1862, of wounds.

YOUNG, THOMAS J.—Enlisted July 15, 1861, at age 26 in Henderson County. Enlisted as Sergeant and promoted to 1st Sergeant on November 16, 1861. Elected 1st Lt. on April 30, 1862, and promoted to Captain on December 15, 1862. Paroled at Appomattox Court House, VA, on April 9, 1865.

Lieutenants

BLAKE, WALTER, 2nd Lt.—Enlisted July 15, 1861, at age 20 in Henderson County. Enlisted as 1st Sergeant and appointed 2nd Lt. on November 16, 1861. Defeated for reelection on April 30, 1862.

BYERS, JOSEPH R., 1st Lt.—Enlisted July 15, 1861, at age 30 in Henderson County. Promoted to Sergeant on November 16, 1861, appointed 2nd Lt. on April 30, 1862, and promoted to 1st Lt. on December 15, 1862. Paroled at Appomattox Court House, VA, on April 9, 1865.

CLAYTON, WILLIAM L., 3rd Lt.—Enlisted July 15, 1861, at age 37 in Henderson County. Appointed 3rd Lt. on July 15, 1861. Declined to stand for reelection and discharged on April 30, 1862.

FLETCHER, GEORGE WASHINGTON, 1st Lt.—Enlisted July 15, 1861, at age 31 in Henderson County. Appointed 1st Lt. on July 15, 1861. Appointed Assistant Surgeon on August 15, 1861, and transferred to the Field and Staff of this Reg.

LANE, THOMAS P., 2nd Lt.—Enlisted July 15, 1861, at age 17 in Henderson County. Enlisted as Sergeant and elected 3rd Lt. on April 30, 1862. Promoted to 2nd Lt. in January–February 1863. Resigned on July 10, 1864, because "my position in this command is very unpleasant" and because he wished to join the "1st Regiment SC Artillery."

REID, JOHN, 3rd Lt.—Enlisted July 15, 1861, at age 18 in Henderson County. Enlisted as Corporal and promoted to 1st Sergeant on April 30, 1862. Appointed 3rd Lt. on December 29, 1862. Present or accounted for until August 20, 1864, when he "absented himself from his company or regimental commander...." Court-martialed on an unspecified date and resigned on September 12, 1864. Resignation not accepted and listed as a deserter on October 5, 1864.

Noncommissioned Officers and Privates

ALLEN, DAVID J., Private—Enlisted July 15, 1861, at age 26 in Henderson County. Wounded at Malvern Hill, VA, on July 1, 1862, and died on July 7 or July 15, 1862, of wounds.

ALLISON, ISAAC, Private—Enlisted July 15, 1861, at age 28 in Henderson County. Wounded at Malvern Hill, VA, on July 1, 1862, and returned to duty in November–December 1862. Captured at Five Forks, VA, on April 1, 1865, and confined at Hart's Island, New York Harbor. Released on June 18, 1865, after taking the Oath.

ALLISON, NORRIS, Private — Enlisted July 15, 1861, at age 23 in Henderson County. Paroled at Appomattox Court House, VA, on April 9, 1865.

ALLISON, RICHARD, Private—Enlisted July 15, 1861, at age 21 in Henderson County. Wounded in the hand at the Battle of the Crater near Petersburg, VA, on July 30, 1864, and returned to duty on an unspecified date. Paroled at Appomattox Court House, VA, on April 9, 1865.

ANDREWS JOHN, Corporal—Enlisted July 15, 1861, at age 21 in Henderson County. Promoted to Corporal on April 30, 1862. Present or accounted for through December 1863. No further records.

ANDREWS, WILLIAM P., Private—Enlisted May 27, 1862, at age 24 in Lenoir County. Deserted on April 28, 1863, and reported under arrest in May–June 1863. Returned to duty in July–August 1863. Deserted to the enemy about February 16, 1863, and confined at Washington, D.C. Released around February 21, 1865, after taking the Oath.

BALDWIN, WILLIAM C., Private—Enlisted October 23, 1863, in Halifax County. Reported absent without leave on or about August 2, 1864, but returned to duty on February 7, 1865. No further records.

BALLARD, RUBEN D., Private. Previously served in Company A of this Reg. and transferred to this company on May 6, 1862. Wounded at King's School House, VA, on June 25, 1862, and returned to duty prior to November 1, 1862. Wounded in the hip at Fredericksburg, VA, on December 13, 1862, and returned to duty on January 30, 1863. Deserted to the enemy about February 16, 1865, and confined at Washington, D.C. Released around February 21, 1865, after taking the Oath.

BARNWELL, JOHN A., Private — Enlisted July 7, 1862, at age 19 in Henderson County. Wounded in both thighs at Malvern Hill, VA, on July 1, 1862. Reported absent wounded or absent sick until November 22, 1864. Retired to the Invalid Corps on that date by reason of disability.

BARNWELL, JOSHUA DAVID, Private — Enlisted July 15, 1861, at age 32 in Henderson County. Enlisted as Corporal but was reduced to ranks on April 30, 1862. Discharged around May 27, 1862, after providing Private Christopher Columbus Williams as a substitute.

BEDDINGFIELD, LARKIN, Private — Enlisted July 15, 1861, at age 47 in Henderson County. Died in hospital about June 28, 1862, of "typhoid fever."

BELL, FRANK, Private — Enlisted July 15, 1861, at age 19 in Henderson County. Died in hospital at Wilmington on February 2 or February 14, 1862, of disease.

BOWEN, ARTHUR C., Private — Enlisted November 1, 1863, at Camp Vance. Captured at or near Fort Stedman, VA, on March 25, 1862, and confined at Point Lookout, MD. Released on June 23, 1865, after taking the Oath.

BRYSON, ROBERT B., Private — Enlisted July 15, 1861, at age 43 in Henderson County. Discharged on July 15, 1862, by reason of the expiration of his term of service.

BURDETT, REUBEN W., Private — Enlisted July 15, 1861, at age 26 in Henderson County. Died in hospital at Warrenton, VA, on September 28, 1862, of a gunshot wound.

BURNETT, JOSEPH J., Private — Enlisted July 15, 1861, at age 19 in Henderson County. Died at Petersburg, VA, prior to August 23, 1864, of unreported cause.

BURNETT, WILLIAM T., Private — Enlisted July 15, 1861, at age 26 in Henderson County. Present or accounted for through February 1865.

CARLAN, JESSE B., Private — Enlisted September 15, 1863, at Camp Vance. Transferred to Company G, 56th Regiment NC Troops in March–June 1864 in exchange for Private Samuel Dempsey.

CARLAND, FELIX CARSON, Private — Enlisted August 23, 1863, at age 38 in Halifax County. Wounded near Petersburg, VA, on July 26, 1864, and returned to duty prior to January 1, 1865. Paroled at Appomattox Court House, VA, on April 9, 1865.

CARLAND, JAMES M., Private — Enlisted July 15, 1861, at age 24 in Henderson County. Killed at Plymouth about April 18–20, 1864.

CARLAND, LEMUEL J., Private — Enlisted July 15, 1861, at age 28 in Henderson County. Present or accounted for through December 1863. No further records.

CASE, JAMES D., Private — Enlisted March 31, 1862, at age 26 in Henderson County. Deserted on April 28, 1863, and reported under arrest in May–June 1863. Deserted again on June 28, 1863.

CASE, JAMES L., Corporal — Enlisted July 15, 1861, at age 17 in Henderson County. Previously served in Company A of this Reg. and enlisted in this company as a substitute for Private William M. Youngblood. Promoted to Corporal on an unspecified date in 1864 and present or accounted for through February 1864.

CASE, WILLIAM M., Private — Enlisted July 15, 1861, at age 18 in Henderson County. Discharged around November 14, 1861, for unreported reason.

CLARK, NOAH L., Private — Enlisted May 26, 1864, in Halifax County. Captured near Globe Tavern, VA, on August 21, 1864, and confined at Point Lookout, MD. Died at that place on October 12, 1864, of unreported cause.

CLARK, WILLIAM L., Private — Enlisted July 15, 1861, at age 18 in Henderson County. Wounded in the right thigh and captured on the South Side Railroad near Petersburg, VA, on April 1, 1865. Died in hospital at Washington, D.C. on April 9, 1865, of "gangrene."

CLAYTON, GEORGE M., 1st Sergeant — Enlisted July 15, 1861, at age 18 in Henderson County. Promoted to Corporal in March–April 1862 and to Sergeant on June 20, 1863. Promoted to 1st Sergeant on an unspecified date in 1864. Reported absent without leave in November–December 1864 but returned to duty in January–February 1865. Captured at Five Forks, VA, on April 1, 1865, and confined at Hart's Island, New York Harbor. Released on June 18, 1865, after taking the Oath. (NC pension records indicate he was wounded near Petersburg, VA, in June 1864.)

CLAYTON, WILLIAM BENJAMIN, Private — Enlisted April 16, 1864, in Halifax County. Paroled at Appomattox Court House, VA, on April 9, 1865.

CLEMENTS, JOSEPH R., Private — Enlisted July 15, 1861, at age 23 in Henderson County. Wounded at Malvern Hill, VA, on July 1, 1862, and died on July 15–17, 1862, of wounds. Place of death not reported.

COGBURN, JOHN J. — NC pension records indicate he enlisted in this company on an unspecified date in 1864. No further records.

COLE, JESSE W., Private — Enlisted July 15, 1861, at age 29 in Henderson County. Died in hospital at Richmond, VA, on November 21, 1862, of "febris typhoides."

CONNER, AARON W., Private — Enlisted July 15, 1861, at age 29 in Henderson County. Reported absent without leave about July 19, 1862, but returned to duty in January–February 1863. Captured near Petersburg, VA, on February 6, 1865, and confined at Point Lookout, MD, where he died on June 1, 1865, of "chronic diarrhoea."

CONNER, ISAAC W., Private — Enlisted July 15, 1861, at age 19 in Henderson County. Wounded in the left leg and captured at Fort Stedman, VA, on March 25, 1865. Hospitalized at Washington, D.C. until released on August 2, 1865, after taking the Oath.

COOPER, JOHN E., Private — Enlisted July 15, 1861, at age 22 in Henderson County. Discharged on August 20 or September 14, 1861, for unreported reason.

CORDELL, ADOLPHUS, Private — Enlisted July 15, 1861, at age 18 in Henderson County. Present or accounted for through December 1863. No further records.

CORDELL, DANIEL, Private — Enlisted July 15, 1861, at age 20 in Henderson County. Captured at Sharpsburg, MD, on September 17, 1862. Paroled on September 23, 1862, and returned to duty in November–December 1862. Present or accounted for through October 1863. No further records.

CORDELL, ELISHA, Private — Enlisted July 15, 1861, at age 22 in Henderson County. Deserted on August 2, 1862, but returned to duty on an unspecified date. Deserted again on April 9, 1863.

CRAIG, SAMUEL R., Private — Enlisted July 15, 1861, at age 33 in Henderson County. Discharged around January 12, 1862, for unreported reason.

DAVIS, GEORGE W., Private. Previously served in Company A of this Reg. and transferred to this company on November 28, 1861, in exchange for Private James N. McMinn. Transferred to Company G, 35th Regiment NC Troops on February 1, 1863.

DEMPSEY, SAMUEL, Private. Previously served in Company G, 56th Regiment NC Troops and transferred to this company in March–June 1864 in exchange for Private Jesse B. Carlan. Present of accounted for through February 1865.

DEMPSEY, WILLIAM, Private — Enlisted July 15, 1861, at age 24 in Henderson County. Wounded at Plymouth about April 18–20, 1864, and returned to duty. Paroled at Appomattox Court House, VA, on April 9, 1865. (NC pension records indicate he was wounded on April 4, 1865.)

DOTSON, JOSIAH H., Private — Enlisted July 15, 1861, at age 30 in Henderson County. Wounded at Malvern Hill, VA, on July 1, 1862, and returned to duty in November–December 1862. Reported absent without leave in November–December 1864 and dropped from the rolls of the company on January 1, 1865, by reason of prolonged absence. (NC pension records indicate he was wounded on June 16, 1864.)

DOTSON, MARTIN FIFER, Private — Enlisted July 15, 1861, at age 32 in Henderson County. Deserted on April 9, 1863, and reported under arrest in May–June 1863. Returned to duty in July–August 1863. Captured at Farmville, VA, on April 6, 1865, and confined at Newport News, VA. Released on June 27, 1865, after taking the Oath.

DOTSON, NELSON S., Private — Enlisted July 15, 1861, at age 37 in Henderson County. Discharged on July 16, 1862, for being over age. Reenlisted in the company on July 26, 1864. Reported under arrest from November–December 1864 through February 1865.

DUCKER, HEZEKIAH F., Private — Enlisted July 15, 1861, at age 21 in Henderson County. Killed at Fredericksburg, VA, on December 13, 1862.

EARWOOD, HENRY F., Private — Enlisted July 15, 1861, at age 30 in Henderson County. Discharged on September 14, 1861, for unreported reason.

FLETCHER, ANDREW E., Ordnance Sergeant — Enlisted July 15, 1861, at age 30 in Henderson County. Promoted to Ordnance Sergeant in May–June 1862. Wounded in the left hip at Fort Stedman, VA, on March 25, 1865. Hospitalized at Richmond, VA, where he was captured on April 3, 1865. Transferred to hospital at Point Lookout, MD, about May 6, 1865, and released around June 26, 1865, after taking the Oath.

FLETCHER, CHARLES M., Private — Enlisted September 15, 1863, at Camp Vance. Hospitalized at Petersburg, VA, on June 17, 1864, with a gunshot wound of the hip. Returned to duty prior to January 1, 1865. Captured at Five Forks, VA, on April 1, 1865, and confined at Hart's Island, New York Harbor. Released on June 18, 1865, after taking the Oath.

FLETCHER, JOEL H., Private — Enlisted July 15, 1861, at age 18 in Henderson County. Promoted to Sergeant in March–April 1862 and to 1st Sergeant in January–February 1863. Reported absent without leave in November–December 1864 and reduced to ranks on an unspecified date in 1864. Listed as a deserter and dropped from the rolls of the company on February 20, 1865.

FLETCHER, LEMUEL J., Private. Previously served in Company A of this Reg. and transferred to this company on July 25, 1861. Discharged about April 30, 1862, by reason of disability.

FRADY, JULIUS A., Private — Enlisted July 15, 1861, at age 16 in Henderson County. Discharged on July 17, 1862, for being under age.

FRADY, WILLIAM B., Private — Enlisted July 15, 1861, at age 30 in Henderson County. Died on June 17, 1864, of a gunshot wound. Place and date wounded not reported.

GALLIMORE, ASAPH, Private — Enlisted July 15, 1861, at age 39 in Henderson County. Discharged around July 16, 1862, for being over age.

GARREN, DAVID, Private — Enlisted July 15, 1861, at age 28 in Henderson County. Enlisted as Corporal but reduced to ranks on April 30, 1862. (NC pension records indicate he was wounded at Malvern Hill, VA, on June 12, 1862.)

GARREN, ELISHA C., Private — Enlisted July 15, 1861, at age 18 in Henderson County. Killed at Malvern Hill, VA, on July 1, 1862.

GARREN, WILLIAMSON, Private — Enlisted July 15, 1861, at age 28 in Henderson County. Enlisted as Corporal but reduced to ranks on April 30, 1862. Wounded at Malvern Hill, VA, on July 1, 1862. Reported absent wounded until November–December 1862 when he was reported absent without leave. Returned to duty in January–February 1863.

GENTLE, JOSEPH S., Private — Enlisted May 1, 1863, at age 37 at Drewry's Bluff, VA.. Wounded at Plymouth around April 18–20, 1864, and returned to duty prior to January 1, 1865. Captured at Five Forks, VA, on April 1, 1865, and confined at Hart's Island, New York Harbor. Released about June 20, 1865, after taking the Oath.

GUDGER, JESSE SILER, Private — Enlisted February 22, 1862, at age 25 in Henderson County. Wounded at Malvern Hill, VA, on July 1, 1862, and returned to duty in November–December 1863. Company records do not indicate whether he was present for duty during January–October 1864. Reported absent without leave in November–December 1864 and reported absent sick in January–February 1865. Retired to the Invalid Corps on February 14, 1865, by reason of "phthisis pulmonalis."

GWINN, JOHN, Private — Enlisted May 1, 1863, at age 40 in Lenoir County. Captured at Fort Stedman, VA, on March 25, 1865, and confined at Point Lookout, MD. Released on June 27, 1865, after taking the Oath.

HAMMONDS, LEMUEL G., Private — Enlisted July 15, 1861, at age 53 in Buncombe County. Discharged on an unspecified date "shortly after entering service" for unreported reason.

HAMMONS, WILLIAM P., Private — Enlisted April 18, 1864, in Halifax County. Deserted on January 1, 1865.

HAWKINS, HENRY C., Private — Enlisted July 15, 1861, at age 18 in Henderson County. Died in hospital at Petersburg, VA, on August 3, 1863, of "dysenteria."

HENDERSON, LADSON M., Musician — Enlisted July 15, 1861, at age 18 in Henderson County. Enlisted as Musician (Fifer). Deserted to the enemy about April 9, 1865, and confined at Washington, D.C. Released on or about April 12, 1865, after taking the Oath.

HOLDER, LYTTLETON J., Private — Enlisted July 15, 1861, at age 22 in Henderson County. Killed at Malvern Hill, VA, on July 1, 1862.

HOLDER, WILLIAM, Private — Enlisted June 9, 1862, at age 53 in Lenoir County. Enlisted as a substitute for Private Jonathan A. Taylor. Died in November–December 1864. Place and cause of death not reported.

HOLLINGSWORTH, ALEXANDER, Private — Enlisted April 18, 1864, in Halifax County. Deserted to the enemy about February 16, 1865, and confined at Washington, D.C. Released around February 21, 1865, after taking the Oath.

INGRAM, JOEL, Corporal — Enlisted July 15, 1861, at age 18 in Henderson County. Wounded at Malvern Hill, VA, on July 1, 1862, and returned to duty in November–December 1862. Promoted to Corporal on an unspecified date in 1864. Reported absent without leave in November–December 1864. Listed as a deserter and dropped from the rolls of the company on January 1, 1865.

INGRAM, ROBERT, Private — Enlisted July 15, 1861, at age 22 in Henderson County. Killed at Malvern Hill, VA, on July 1, 1862.

ISRAEL, SAMUEL M., Private — Enlisted July 15, 1861, at age 26 in Henderson County. Wounded in the head and left eye at Fort Stedman, VA, on March 25, 1865. Blinded in the left eye and hospitalized at Richmond, VA, where he was captured on April 3, 1865. Transferred to Newport News, VA, about April 24, 1865, and released on June 30, 1865, after taking the Oath.

JENKINS, FIDELLIO, Private — Enlisted July 15, 1861, at age 46 in Henderson County. Discharged on July 16, 1862, for being over age.

JENKINS, JAMES J., Private — Enlisted July 15, 1861, at age 25 in Henderson County. Present or accounted for through December 1863, but was reported absent sick during much of that period. Company records do not indicate whether he was present for duty during January–October 1864. Reported present for duty in November–December 1864. Reported absent sick in January–February 1865.

JENKINS, JOSHUA, Private — Enlisted July 15, 1861, at age 24 in Henderson County. Deserted on July 17, 1864, and went over to the enemy on an unspecified date. Took the Oath at Louisville, KY, on April 3, 1865.

JENKINS, THOMAS A., Private — Enlisted May 1, 1863, at age 18 in Lenoir County. Died on December 1, 1864. Place and cause of death not reported.

JOHNSON, CREED F., Private — Enlisted July 15, 1861, at age 17 in Henderson County. Captured at Malvern Hill, VA, on July 1, 1862, and confined at Fort Columbus, New York Harbor. Paroled and exchanged at Aiken's Landing, James River, VA, on August 5, 1862. Returned to duty in September–October 1862. Captured at Petersburg, VA, on July 30, 1864, and confined at Point Lookout, MD, until transferred to Elmira, NY, on August 8, 1864. Released on May 29, 1865, after taking the Oath.

JOHNSTON, NOBLE P., Private — Enlisted September 14, 1863, in Halifax County. Wounded in the left hand and captured at "the Crater" near Petersburg, VA, on July 30, 1864. Three fingers amputated. Hospitalized at Fort Monroe, VA, until transferred to Point Lookout, MD, around November 25, 1864. Paroled and transferred to Boulware's Wharf, James River, VA, for exchange on March 19, 1865.

JUSTIS, JOSEPH F., Private — Enlisted July 15, 1861, at age 20 in Henderson County. Deserted about August 24, 1863.

KUYKENDALL, EZEKIEL, Private — Enlisted July 15, 1861, at age 27 in Henderson County. Deserted on July 29, 1862, but returned to duty on an unspecified date. Deserted again on September 24, 1862, and "Returned from desertion" on December 16, 1864. "Shot for desertion" on February 14, 1865.

KUYKENDALL, JOHN ALLEN, Private — Enlisted July 15, 1861, at age 24 in Henderson County. Wounded in the right shoulder at Malvern Hill, VA, on July 1, 1862, and returned to duty in November–December 1862. Present or accounted for through February 1865.

KUYKENDALL, JOSEPH, Private — Enlisted July 15, 1861, at age 20 in Henderson County. Deserted on September 24, 1862. Reported under arrest in May–June 1863. Deserted again on June 28, 1863.

KUYKENDALL, LEVI, Private — Enlisted July 15, 1861, at age 28 in Henderson County. Died in hospital at Wilson on June 26, 1862, of disease.

KUYKENDALL, WILLIAM, Private — Enlisted October 5, 1861. Transferred to Company G, 35th Regiment NC Troops on March 24, 1862.

LANCE, JAMES P., Private — Enlisted December 22, 1861, at age 22 in Henderson County. Wounded at Sharpsburg, MD, on September 17, 1862, and returned to duty. Died in hospital at Richmond, VA, on October 14 or October 22, 1862, of a gunshot wound and/or disease.

LANCE, JOHN B., Private — Enlisted July 15, 1861, at age 23 in Henderson County. Promoted to Sergeant in March–April 1862 but reduced to ranks in March–April 1863. Present or accounted for through December 1863. Company muster rolls dated November 1864–February 1865 indicate he was captured by the enemy on an unspecified date. No further records.

LANCE, KIMSEY M., Private — Enlisted December 22, 1861, at age 24 in Henderson County. Deserted on December 11, 1862. Reported under arrest during May–August 1863. Deserted again about September 29, 1863.

LANCE, THOMAS M., Private — Enlisted July 15, 1861, at age 31 in Henderson County. Deserted around December 31, 1862. Reported absent sick in January–February 1863 but deserted again on April 9, 1863.

LEDBETTER, CHARLES W., Private — Enlisted July 15,

1861, at age 18 in Henderson County. Captured at Madison County on October 16, 1863, and confined at Camp Chase, OH, on November 14, 1863. Transferred to Rock Island, IL, on January 14, 1864, and paroled there about March 20, 1865. Transferred to Boulware's Wharf, James River, VA, for exchange on March 27, 1865.

LEVERETT, JOHN, Private. Previously served in Company G, 35th Regiment NC Troops and transferred to this company on February 4, 1863. Deserted on April 28, 1863. Reported under arrest in May–June 1863 and returned to duty in July–August 1863. Present or accounted for through December 1863. Company records do not indicate whether he was present during January–October 1864, but he was reported absent without leave in November–December 1864. Listed as a deserter and dropped from the rolls of the company on January 1, 1865.

LEWIS, WILLIM M., Private — Enlisted July 15, 1861, at age 32 in Henderson County. Died on September 1, 1862, of disease. Place of death not reported.

LISTER, THOMAS R., Private — Enlisted July 15, 1861, at age 16 in Henderson County. Wounded at Malvern Hill, VA, on July 1, 1862. Discharged on July 17, 1862, for being under age. Reenlisted in the company in July–August 1863. Paroled at Appomattox Court House, VA, on April 9, 1863.

LIVINGSTON, JOSEPH FRANK, Private — Enlisted October 19, 1863, in Halifax County. Wounded near Petersburg, VA, on June 18, 1864. Furloughed for sixty days on July 20, 1864. Reported absent without leave in November–December 1864. Listed as a deserter and dropped from the rolls of the company on January 1, 1865.

LOCKMAN, WARREN J., Private — Enlisted July 15, 1861, at age 21 in Henderson County. Deserted on September 24, 1862, but returned to duty on February 12, 1863. Present or accounted for through December 1863.

LYTLE, THOMAS B., Sergeant — Enlisted July 15, 1861, at age 19 in Henderson County. Promoted to Sergeant on April 30, 1862. Reported absent without leave in January–February 1865.

LYTLE, THOMAS L., Private — Enlisted October 18, 1863, in Halifax County. Present or accounted for through February 1865.

McALLISTER, E., Private. Captured on an unspecified date and confined at Elmira, NY. Died at Elmira on April 20, 1865, of unreported cause.

McGINNESS, J.P., Private. Captured on an unspecified date. Hospitalized at Newport News, VA, on May 6, 1865, with "debility" and died on May 14, 1865.

McMINN, JAMES N., Private — Enlisted July 15, 1861, at age 31 in Henderson County. Transferred to Company A of this Reg. on November 28, 1861, in exchange for Private George W. Davis.

MERRILL, HENRY C., Private — Enlisted February 26, 1862, at age 19 in Henderson County. Wounded at Malvern Hill, VA, on July 1, 1862. Died in hospital at Richmond, VA, on July 22, 1862, of wounds. "(He) lay on the battlefield all night. Next day when the wounded were collected and carried to the various hospitals, he and an elder brother (1st Sergeant Benjamin W. Merrill of Company F, 14th Regiment NC Troops) were laid side by side on the same cot. They were both wounded on the same evening, and when the blood was washed off the face of the latter Henry recognized his brother. Thus met the youthful warriors after a separation of fifteen months. They both died in the same hospital, the subject of this notice surviving his brother by 12 days" (*Asheville News*, August 14, 1862).

MINCE, ELISHA, Private — Enlisted March 31, 1862, at age 23 at Grahamville, SC. Deserted on April 28, 1863, and reported under arrest in May–June 1863. Returned to duty in July–August 1863. Present or accounted for through December 1863. (NC pension records indicate he was wounded in the head by the explosion of a shell near Seven Pines, VA, in July 1863.)

MOORE, JOHN, Private — Enlisted May 15, 1863, at age 37 in Lenoir County. Deserted on September 29, 1863, but returned to duty on December 12, 1863. Reported under arrest through December 31, 1863. Rejoined the company on an unspecified date. Reported absent without leave on an unspecified date. Reported in confinement at E.D.M. Prison, Richmond, VA, in May 1864. Released prior to June 1, 1864. Reported absent without leave in November–December 1864. Listed as a deserter and dropped from the rolls of the company on January 1, 1865.

OWENBY, CHARLES, Private — Enlisted July 15, 1861, at age 28 in Henderson County. Listed as a deserter and dropped from the rolls of the company on February 20, 1865.

PADGETT, EDWIN, Private — Enlisted July 15, 1861, at age 18 in Henderson County. Discharged on September 14, 1861, for unreported reason.

PATTON, AARON FRANKLIN, Private — Enlisted July 15, 1861, at age 36 in Henderson County. Discharged about July 16, 1862, for being over age.

PATTON, GEORGE N., Private — Enlisted July 15, 1861, at age 18 in Henderson County. Killed at Fredericksburg, VA, on December 13, 1862.

PEARSON, ROBERT, Private — Enlisted July 15, 1861, at age 18 in Henderson County. Enlisted as Sergeant but reduced to ranks in July–August 1863. Hospitalized at Petersburg, VA, on May 22, 1864, with a gunshot wound of the right hand and returned to duty prior to January 1, 1865. Captured at Fort Stedman, VA, on March 25, 1865, and confined at Point Lookout, MD. Released on June 3, 1865, after taking the Oath.

PEARSON, THOMAS B., Sergeant — Enlisted March 9, 1863, at age 23 in Henderson County. Promoted to Sergeant in January–February 1865. Wounded in the left thigh and right leg and captured at Sayler's Creek, VA, on April 6, 1865. Hospitalized at Washington, D.C. on April 19, 1865. Released about October 9, 1865, after taking the Oath.

PELLY, JOSEPH, Private — Enlisted July 15, 1861, at age 22 in Henderson County. Discharged about July 16, 1862, by reason of being a "foreigner."

PINNER, BENJAMIN, Private — Enlisted July 15, 1861, at age 22 in Henderson County. Paroled at Appomattox Court House, VA, on April 9, 1865.

PINNER, SOLOMON B., Private—Enlisted July 15, 1861, at age 24 in Henderson County. Killed at Malvern Hill, VA, on July 1, 1862.

PLUMBLEE, JAMES M., Private—Enlisted May 1, 1864, in Henderson County. Paroled at Appomattox Court House, VA, on April 9, 1865.

POSEY, COLUMBUS M., Private. Previously served in Company I, 16th Regiment NC Troops and enlisted in this company in Halifax County on October 15, 1863. Present or accounted for through December 1863. No further records.

POTILLO, ALBERT J., Private—Enlisted July 15, 1861, at age 23 in Henderson County. Died in hospital at Petersburg, VA, on June 28 or June 29, 1862, of "febris typhoides."

PRESLEY, ANTHONY, Private—Enlisted July 15, 1861, at age 30 in Henderson County. Promoted to Musician (Drummer) in March–April 1862. Reported absent without leave in November–December 1862 and listed as a deserter on February 12, 1863. Returned to duty in May–June 1863 and reduced to ranks in September–October 1863. Captured at Fort Stedman, VA, on March 25, 1862, and confined at Point Lookout, MD. Released on June 16, 1865, after taking the Oath.

PRESLEY, JOHN R., Private—Enlisted July 15, 1861, at age 40 in Henderson County. Discharged about July 16, 1862, for being over age.

PRESLEY, MITCHELL, Private—Enlisted July 15, 1861, at age 35 in Henderson County. Died at Camp Davis near Wilmington on October 28, 1861, of disease.

PRESLEY, WILLIAMSON, Private—Enlisted May 1, 1863, at age 37 in Lenoir County. Deserted on September 29, 1863, but returned to duty on December 12, 1863. Paroled at Burkeville Junction, VA, about April 14–17, 1865.

RAMSEY, J.F., Private. Paroled at Farmville, VA, about April 11–21, 1865.

RHODES, ANDREW, Private—Enlisted September 5, 1863, in Halifax County. Died in hospital at Richmond, VA, on June 20, 1864, of "febris typhoides."

RHODES, GEORGE W., Private—Enlisted July 15, 1861, at age 47 in Henderson County. Enlisted as Musician (Drummer) but reduced to ranks in November–December 1861. Discharged on January 14, 1862, for unreported reason.

RHODES, JOHN H., Private—Enlisted July 15, 1861, at age 27 in Henderson County. Surrendered to the enemy at Richmond, VA, about April 10, 1865, and confined at Richmond, VA. Released around April 16, 1865, after taking the Oath.

RHODES, WILLIAM J., Private—Enlisted December 5, 1862, at age 19 at Fredericksburg, VA. Present or accounted for through February 1865.

RICKMAN, JOHN, Private—Enlisted July 15, 1861, at age 37 in Henderson County. Discharged on July 16, 1862, for being over age.

ROBINSON, HENRY C., Private—Enlisted July 15, 1861, at age 28 in Henderson County. Present or accounted for through December 1863. No further records.

ROBINSON, WILLIAM E., Private—Enlisted July 15, 1861, at age 21 in Henderson County. Deserted on August 3, 1863, and reported under arrest in September–October 1863. Returned to duty in November–December 1863 and present or accounted for through December 31, 1863. No further records.

RUSSELL, JAMES E., Sergeant—Enlisted July 15, 1861, at age 20 in Henderson County. Promoted to Corporal in May–June 1863 and to Sergeant in July–August 1863. Captured at Farmville, VA, on April 6, 1865, and confined at Newport News, VA. Released on June 27, 1865, after taking the Oath.

RUTH, BRAXTON R., Private—Enlisted July 15, 1861, at age 23 in Henderson County. Promoted to Corporal in May–June 1862. Wounded at Malvern Hill, VA, on July 1, 1862, and returned to duty in January–February 1863. Reduced to ranks in July–August 1863. Deserted on August 3, 1863, and reported under arrest in September–October 1863. Returned to duty in November–December 1863. Hospitalized at Richmond, VA, on March 27, 1865, with a gunshot wound of the hand and then transferred to hospital at Farmville, VA, on April 1, 1865. No further records.

SHAFFER, J.S., Private. Paroled at Farmville, VA, about April 11–21, 1865.

SHROAT, PHILETUS J., Private—Enlisted July 15, 1861, at age 20 in Henderson County. Present or accounted for through December 1863. No further records.

SITTON, JAMES B., Private—Enlisted July 15, 1861, at age 37 in Henderson County. Promoted to Color Sergeant in January–February 1862 and to Sergeant on February 18, 1862. Reduced to ranks in March–April 1862. Discharged on July 17, 1862, for being over age.

SITTON, WILLIAM D., Private—Enlisted July 15, 1861, at age 18 in Henderson County. Wounded in the elbow at King's School House, VA, on June 25, 1862, and died about July 15, 1862, of wounds. Place of death not reported.

SMITH, JOSEPH F., Private—Enlisted July 15, 1861, at age 22 in Henderson County. Hospitalized at Richmond, VA, on June 28, 1862, with a gunshot wound and returned to duty on July 4, 1862. Died in hospital in Wilmington on June 19, 1863, of "febris typhoid."

SOUTHER, THOMAS M., Private—Enlisted June 22, 1864, at Petersburg, VA. Present or accounted for through February 1865.

SOUTHER, WILLIAM H., Private—Enlisted July 15, 1861, at age 21 in Henderson County. Died in hospital at Drewry's Bluff, VA, on August 6, 1862, of disease.

SUMMEY, GEORGE W., Private—Enlisted July 15, 1861, at age 25 in Henderson County. Deserted on December 11, 1862, but returned to duty on an unspecified date. Deserted again on April 9, 1863, and reported under arrest in November–December 1863. Deserted to the enemy about December 20, 1863, and confined at Fort Monroe, VA. Released around January 6, 1864, after taking the Oath.

SUMNER, MARCUS L., Private—Enlisted March 24, 1864, at Greenville, TN. Deserted prior to April 1,

1864, but returned to duty on December 5, 1864, under provisions of an amnesty. Present or accounted for through February 1865.

SUTTLES, STEPHEN, Private — Enlisted July 15, 1861, at age 18 in Henderson County. Deserted to the enemy on February 16, 1865, and confined at Washington, D.C. Released about February 21, 1865, after taking the Oath.

SUTTLES, WILLIAM J., Private — Enlisted May 4, 1864, in Henderson County. Reported absent without leave in November–December 1864. Listed as a deserter and dropped from the rolls of the company on January 1, 1865.

TAYLOR, JESSE W., Private — Enlisted July 15, 1861, in Henderson County. Killed at Malvern Hill, VA, on July 1, 1862.

TAYLOR, JONATHAN A., Private — Enlisted July 15, 1861, at age 32 in Henderson County. Discharged on June 9, 1862, after providing Private William Holder as a substitute.

TAYLOR, WILBOURNE, Private — Enlisted January 2, 1862, at age 24 in Henderson County. Killed at Malvern Hill, VA, on July 1, 1862.

TOW, REUBEN TAYLOR, Private — Enlisted July 15, 1861, at age 35 in Henderson County. Discharged on July 16, 1862, for being over age.

TOW, SAMUEL M., Private — Enlisted July 15, 1861, at age 17 in Henderson County. Discharged about July 16, 1862, for being under age.

TOWNSEND, JOSEPH H., Private — Enlisted July 15, 1861, at age 18 in Henderson County. Wounded in the right knee and left leg and captured at Warm Springs about October 26, 1863. Hospitalized at Knoxville, TN, until transferred to Nashville, TN, around April 12, 1864. Confined at Camp Morton, IN, on May 22, 1864, until released on June 12, 1865, after taking the Oath.

TRAFINSTED, JOSEPH H., Private — Enlisted July 15, 1861, at age 14 in Henderson County. Deserted on August 20, 1863. Reported under arrest from September–October 1863 through December 1863. No further records.

TRAUTHAM, THOMAS S., Sergeant — Enlisted July 15, 1861, at age 26 in Henderson County. Promoted to Corporal in September–October 1862 and to Sergeant in July–August 1863. Present or accounted for through December, 1863. No further records.

VAUGHN, WILLIAM W., Private — Enlisted May 1, 1863, at age 31 in Lenoir County. Deserted on September 29, 1863. Reported under arrest in November–December 1863. Company records do not indicate whether he was present for duty during January–October 1864. Reported absent without leave in November–December 1864. Listed as a deserter and dropped from the rolls of the company on January 1, 1865.

VERMILLION, JAMES M., Private — Enlisted July 15, 1861, at age 36 in Henderson County. Killed at Malvern Hill, VA, on July 1, 1862.

VERMILLION, SAMUEL N., Private — Enlisted June 26, 1864, at Petersburg, VA. Captured at Five Forks, VA, on April 1, 1865, and confined at Hart's Island, New York Harbor. Released on June 14, 1865, after taking the Oath.

WHITAKER, DAVID F., Private — Enlisted July 15, 1861, at age 30 in Henderson County. Enlisted as Sergeant but reduced to ranks on April 30, 1862. Captured at Frederick, MD, on September 12, 1862, and confined at Fort Delaware, DE. Transferred to Aiken's Landing, James River, VA, where he was received on October 6, 1862, and exchanged on November 10, 1862. Returned to duty prior to January 1, 1863. Deserted to the enemy on July 17, 1864, and confined at Knoxville, TN, where he took the Oath about March 21, 1865.

WHITAKER, JOHN, Private — Enlisted May 1, 1863, at age 38 in Lenoir County. Present or accounted for through September 11, 1864, and then deserted on an unspecified date. Listed as a deserter and dropped from the rolls of the company on January 1, 1865.

WHITAKER, WILLIAM NOAH, Private — Enlisted July 15, 1861, at age 21 in Henderson County. Present or accounted for through September 11, 1864, and then deserted on an unspecified date. Listed as a deserter and dropped from the rolls of the company on January 1, 1865.

WHITAKER, WILLIAM R., Private — Enlisted May 1, 1863, at age 39 in Lenoir County. Present or accounted for through December 1863. Company records do not indicate whether he was present during January–October 1864. Reported absent without leave in November–December 1864. Listed as a deserter and dropped from the rolls of the company on January 1, 1865.

WHITAKER, WILLIAM S., Private — Enlisted May 1, 1863, at age 37 in Lenoir County. Wounded in the left thigh at Petersburg, VA, on June 17, 1864. Reported absent without leave in November–December 1864. Listed as a deserter and dropped from the rolls of the company on January 1, 1865.

WILLIAMS, CHRISTOPHER COLUMBUS, Private — Enlisted May 27, 1862, at age 17 in Lenoir County. Enlisted as a substitute for Private Joshua D. Barnwell. Reported absent without leave in December 1862 but returned to duty in January–February 1863. Listed as a deserter and dropped from the rolls of the company on February 20, 1865.

WRIGHT, LEANDER, Private — Enlisted July 15, 1861, at age 23 in Henderson County. Transferred to Company A on this Reg. of May 17, 1862.

YOUNG, SAMUEL, Private — Enlisted July 15, 1861, at age 19 in Henderson County. Deserted on June 11, 1863, and went over to the enemy. Confined at Fort Monroe, VA, until released about January 16, 1864, after taking the Oath.

YOUNGBLOOD, JOSEPH, Private — Enlisted July 15, 1861, at age 20 in Henderson County. Deserted to the enemy on September 24, 1862, and took the Oath at Knoxville, TN, on October 22, 1864.

YOUNGBLOOD, WILLIAM M., Private — Enlisted July 15, 1861, at age 22 in Henderson County. Discharged on July 16, 1862, after providing Private James L. Case as a substitute.

Company I — "Pisgah Guards"

Captains

HOWELL, GEORGE WATSON — Enlisted July 22, 1861, at age 45 in Buncombe County. Appointed Captain on July 22, 1861. Resigned on April 12, 1862, by reason of disability.

MORGAN, WILLIAM Y. — Enlisted July 22, 1861, at age 44 in Buncombe County. Appointed 1st Lt. on July 22, 1861, and promoted to Captain on April 16, 1862. Appointed Major on January 1, 1865, and transferred to the Field and Staff of this Reg.

THRASH, AUGUSTUS BUCKINGHAM — Enlisted July 22, 1861, at age 32 in Buncombe County. Promoted Sergeant prior to October 22, 1861. Reduced to ranks in November–December 1861 but appointed 1st Lt. on April 16, 1862. Promoted to Captain on January 1, 1865. Wounded in the right thigh at Fort Stedman, VA, on March 25, 1865, and hospitalized at Richmond, VA. Transferred to Petersburg, VA, on an unspecified date and captured there on April 3, 1865. Confined at various Federal hospitals until confined at Newport News, VA, on May 17, 1865. Released on June 15, 1865, after taking the Oath.

Lieutenants

HOWELL, FOSTER BENJAMIN, 3rd Lt. — Enlisted July 22, 1861, at age 29 in Buncombe County. Appointed 3rd Lt. on July 22, 1861. Resigned on March 22, 1863, for unreported reason. Reenlisted in the company with the rank of Private on November 1, 1863. (For additional information see service record of Private Benjamin Foster Howell.)

LUTHER, ANDREW A., 2nd Lt. — Enlisted July 22, 1861, at age 38 in Buncombe County. Appointed 2nd Lt. on July 22, 1861. Declined to stand for reelection on April 27, 1863, and discharged. Reenlisted in the company with the rank of Private about April 28, 1863. (For additional information see service record of Private Andrew A. Luther.)

MOORE, ROBERT P., 2nd Lt. — Enlisted July 22, 1861, at age 30 in Buncombe County. Enlisted as Sergeant but reduced to ranks in November–December 1861. Promoted to Corporal on July 11, 1862, and appointed to 2nd Lt. in November–December 1863. Present or accounted for through February 1865.

MORRIS, THOMAS L., 2nd Lt. — Enlisted July 22, 1861, at age 26 in Buncombe County. Enlisted as 1st Sergeant and appointed 2nd Lt. on April 28, 1862. Hospitalized at Petersburg, VA, about April 1, 1865, with a gunshot wound of the right arm. Captured in hospital at Petersburg on April 3, 1865, and confined at various Federal hospitals until confined at Newport News, VA, on May 17, 1865. Released on June 14, 1865, after taking the Oath.

Noncommissioned Officers and Privates

ALEXANDER, AMOS FANNIN, Private. Previously served in Company A, 1st Battalion NC Junior Reserves and transferred to this company on January 30, 1865. Wounded and captured at Fort Stedman, VA, on March 25, 1865. Confined at Point Lookout, MD, until released on June 22, 1865, after taking the Oath.

ALEXANDER, WILLIAM PINK, Private — Enlisted April 15, 1864, in Halifax County. Reported absent without leave in November–December 1864. Listed as a deserter and dropped from the rolls of the company on January 1, 1865. (NC pension records indicate he was wounded in an unspecified engagement on an unspecified date.)

ALLEN, JOHN S., Private — Enlisted July 22, 1861, at age 22 in Buncombe County. Died at Drewry's Bluff, VA, on August 24–25, 1862, of "fever."

ALLEN, RICHARD PINCKNEY, Private — Enlisted July 22, 1861, at age 24 in Buncombe County. Deserted on August 21, 1862, but returned to duty on January 12, 1863. Deserted again on January 24, 1863, and returned to duty in March–August 1863. Deserted for a third time on November 30, 1863. Shot and killed (probably by Home Guard) in Buncombe County on May 16–17, 1864.

BALDWIN, EPHRAIM, Private — Enlisted September 16, 1863, in Buncombe County. Hospitalized at Petersburg, VA, on June 17, 1864, with a gunshot wound of the head. Returned to duty on July 23, 1864. Wounded in the shoulder at the Battle of the Crater near Petersburg, VA, on July 30, 1864. Returned to duty and served until paroled at Burkeville Junction, VA, on April 14–17, 1865.

BARNETT, COLUMBUS V., Corporal — Enlisted July 22, 1861, at age 23 in Buncombe County. Promoted to Corporal in March–April 1862. Wounded at Malvern Hill, VA, on July 1, 1862, and died at Richmond, VA, about July 7, 1862, of wounds.

BLACK, JOHN S., Corporal — Enlisted July 22, 1861, at age 25 in Buncombe County. Wounded at Sharpsburg, MD, on September 17, 1862, and returned to duty in January–February 1863. Promoted to Corporal on an unspecified date in 1864. Deserted to the enemy around March 3, 1865, and confined at Washington, D.C. Released about March 7, 1865, after taking the Oath.

BOLEN, JACKSON B., Private — Enlisted April 27, 1863, at age 38 in Buncombe County. Present or accounted for through March 26, 1865.

BOYD, DANIEL A., Private — Enlisted July 22, 1861, at age 20 in Buncombe County. Wounded at Malvern Hill, VA, on July 1, 1862, and died at Richmond, VA, about July 10–13, 1862, of wounds.

BOYD, JOHN P., Private — Enlisted July 22, 1861, at age 25 in Buncombe County. Promoted to Sergeant in September–October 1861 and reduced to ranks on May 1, 1862. Died in hospital at Richmond, VA, on August 9, 1862, of "typhoid fever."

BROCK, REUBEN, Private — Enlisted February 13, 1865, at Camp Holmes. Present or accounted for through February 28, 1865.

BROOKS, DAVID W., Private — Enlisted March 10, 1862, at age 16 in Lenoir County. Wounded at Malvern Hill, VA, on July 1, 1862, and returned to duty in November–December 1862. Present or accounted for through December 1863. No further records.

BROOKS, GEORGE A., Private — Enlisted March 10,

1862, at age 16 in Buncombe County. Present or accounted for through December 1863.

BROOKS, JOHN, Private — Enlisted March 1, 1864, in Halifax County. Captured in hospital at Richmond, VA, on April 3, 1865, and transferred to Newport News, VA, on April 23, 1865. Released at Newport News on June 30, 1865, after taking the Oath.

BROOKS, S.M., Private. Deserted to the enemy about March 6, 1865, and took the Oath at Washington, D.C. around March 10, 1865.

BROWNING, E.S., Private. Paroled at Farmville, VA, about April 11-21, 1865.

BYNUM, THOMAS H., Private — Enlisted February 13, 1865, at Camp Holmes. Present or accounted for through February 28, 1865.

CANDLER, CHARLES Z., Private — Enlisted July 21, 1861, at age 18 in Buncombe County. Transferred to Company F, 14th Regiment NC Troops about September 24, 1861.

CANNON, WATSON R.A., Sergeant — Enlisted July 22, 1861, at age 20 in Buncombe County. Promoted to Sergeant in March-April 1862. Wounded at Malvern Hill, VA, on July 1, 1862, and died near Richmond, VA, on July 21, 1862, of wounds.

CANNON, WILLIAM M., Private — Enlisted July 22, 1861, at age 32 in Buncombe County. Wounded in the right shoulder at Fort Stedman, VA, on March 25, 1865, and hospitalized at Petersburg, VA. Captured there on April 3, 1865, and transferred to Newport News, VA, about May 17, 1865. Released on June 27, 1865, after taking the Oath.

COOK, JOHN D., Private — Enlisted July 22, 1861, at age 17 in Buncombe County. Present or accounted for through February 1865.

COOK, MARION D., Private — Enlisted May 12, 1862, at age 18 in Lenoir County. Deserted on November 30, 1863.

COOK, MARVELL R., Private — Enlisted July 22, 1861, at age 33 in Buncombe County. Discharged about May 29, 1862, by reason of disability.

COOK, THOMAS B., Private — Enlisted July 22, 1861, at age 46 in Buncombe County. Discharged on April 8, 1862, by reason of disability.

COOK, WILLIAM B., Private — Enlisted July 22, 1861, at age 16 in Buncombe County. Discharged on July 16, 1862, for being under age.

COOK, WILLIAM J., Private. Previously served in Company F, 29th Regiment NC Troops and transferred to this company prior to September 8, 1861. Transferred to Company B of this Reg. on May 1, 1862.

COOK, YOUNG HENRY, Private — Enlisted July 22, 1861, at age 26 in Buncombe County. Captured near Petersburg, VA, on June 17, 1864, and confined at Point Lookout, MD. Transferred to Elmira, NY, on July 27, 1864, and died there on August 20, 1864, of "chronic diarrhoea."

COTHREN, ALFRED, Private — Enlisted March 10, 1862, at age 20 in Lenoir County. Died at Goldsboro on June 22-26, 1862, of disease.

COURTNEY, JOHN HAMILTON, Private — Enlisted July 22, 1861, at age 21 in Buncombe County. Enlisted as Musician. Wounded in the left thigh at Malvern Hill, VA, on July 1, 1862, resulting in amputation of left leg. Reduced to ranks in November 1862. Discharged on November 28, 1862, by reason of disability.

CULBERSON, JOHN W., Private — Enlisted July 22, 1861, at age 37 in Buncombe County. Discharged on December 3, 1861, by reason of disability.

CURTIS, BENJAMIN F., Private — Enlisted July 22, 1861, at age 18 in Buncombe County. Died at Grahamville, SC, on March 23, 1862, of disease.

CURTIS, GEORGE S., Private — Enlisted July 22, 1861, at age 23 in Buncombe County. Present or accounted for through February 1865.

CURTIS, GEORGE WASHINGTON, Jr., Private — Enlisted July 22, 1861, in Buncombe County. Discharged on July 16, 1862, for being under age. Discharge certificate gives age as 17.

CURTIS, GEORGE W., Sr., Private. Previously served in Company G of this Reg. and transferred to this company about March 10, 1862. Deserted on August 21, 1862, but returned to duty on October 3, 1862. Deserted on September 1, 1863, and returned to duty on January 15, 1865. Captured at Fort Stedman, VA, on March 25, 1865, and confined at Point Lookout, MD. Released on June 26, 1865, after taking the Oath.

CURTIS, MADISON ALEXANDER, Private — Enlisted July 22, 1861, at age 22 in Buncombe County. Enlisted as Corporal but reduced to ranks in March-April 1862. Wounded in the left arm at Fredericksburg, VA, on December 13, 1862, and returned to duty in September-October 1863. Killed at the Battle of the Crater near Petersburg, VA, on July 30, 1864.

CURTIS, WASHINGTON HASCUE, Private — Enlisted July 22, 1861, at age 23 in Buncombe County. Present or accounted for through February 1865.

DAVIS, DANIEL M., Private — Enlisted July 22, 1861, at age 18 in Buncombe County. Died at Kinston about April 10, 1862, of "brain fever."

DAVIS, JAMES G.W., Private — Enlisted July 22, 1861, at age 20 in Buncombe County. Captured at Sharpsburg, MD, on September 17, 1862. Paroled on September 20, 1862, and returned to duty in January-February 1863. Present or accounted for through December 1864. Listed as a deserter and dropped from the rolls of the company on February 27, 1865.

DAVIS, JOHN P., Private — Enlisted July 22, 1861, at age 18 in Buncombe County. Present or accounted for through February 1865.

DAVIS, JOSEPH, Private — Enlisted July 22, 1861, at age 20 in Buncombe County. Died in hospital at Petersburg, VA, on June 24, 1864, of a gunshot wound.

DAVIS, JOSHUA, Private — Enlisted July 22, 1861, at age 17 in Buncombe County. Present or accounted for through December, 1863. Wounded in the thigh at the Battle of the Crater near Petersburg, VA, on July 30, 1864, resulting in amputation of the leg. Died near Richmond, VA, about August 23, 1864, of wounds.

DAVIS, URIAH W., Private — Enlisted July 22, 1861, at age 19 in Buncombe County. Died in hospital at Petersburg, VA, on July 17, 1862, of "cerebro meningitis."

DEVOIR, WILLIAM, Private — Enlisted April 27, 1863, at age 25 in Buncombe County. Wounded in the left shoulder at Fort Stedman, VA, on March 25, 1865. Hospitalized at Richmond, VA, and captured there on April 3, 1865. Confined at Camp Hamilton, VA, and released on May 31, 1865, after taking the Oath.

DOCKERY, JAMES, Private — Enlisted July 22, 1861, at age 21 in Buncombe County. Present or accounted for through December 1863. Company records do not indicate whether he was present for duty during January–October 1864. Listed as a deserter on December 26, 1864, but returned to duty on January 2, 1865. No further records.

DOVER, ANDREW E., Private — Enlisted January 1, 1864, in Buncombe County. Captured near Globe Tavern, VA, on August 21, 1864, and confined at Point Lookout, MD. Paroled and transferred to Venus Point, Savannah River, GA, for exchange on November 15, 1864. Company records do not indicate whether he returned to duty, but he was captured by the enemy at Cleveland, TN, on February 10, 1865, and confined at Camp Chase, OH, on March 24, 1865. Released on June 13, 1865, after taking the Oath. Records of the Provost Marshal dated 1865 gives his age as 39.

DRYMAN, JAMES R., Private — Enlisted July 22, 1861, at age 16 in Buncombe County. Discharged on July 16, 1862, for being under age.

DRYMAN, WILLIAM, Private — Enlisted July 22, 1861, at age 29 in Buncombe County. Discharged on May 19, 1862, by reason of disability.

GILLIAN, MILLER E., Private — Enlisted July 21, 1861, at age 36 in Buncombe County. Discharged on July 16, 1862, for being over age. (NC pension records indicate he was wounded on June 4, 1862, and was wounded in both shoulders "at the blow up" near Petersburg, VA, on July 30, 1864. These records also indicate he received a rupture "while lifting at a Pontoon bridge to cross the Potomac River ... near Sharpsburg," MD, September 17, 1862.)

GLENN, NAPOLEON L., Private. Previously served in Company F of this Reg. and transferred to this company on May 1, 1862. Died in hospital at Wilson on July 1, 1862, of "typhoid fever." "He was a generous, noble-hearted boy, and was beloved by all who knew him."

GREEN, THOMAS L., Private — Enlisted September 16, 1863, in Buncombe County. Paroled at Appomattox Court House, VA, on April 9, 1865.

GUDGER, DILLARD F., Private — Enlisted April 15, 1864, at age 18 in Halifax County. Wounded at Washington, NC, about April 27–30, 1864, and returned to duty prior to January 1, 1865. Present or accounted for through February, 1865.

GUDGER, JAMES CASSIUS LOWRY, Sergeant — Enlisted July 21, 1861, at age 24 in Buncombe County. Enlisted as Sergeant. Promoted to Sergeant Major on October 16, 1861, and transferred to the Field and Staff of this Reg. Reduced to the rank of Sergeant and transferred back to this company on August 6, 1862. Appointed Adjutant on January 26, 1865, and transferred to the Field and Staff of this Reg.

HANNA, ZACHARIAH T., Private — Enlisted January 1, 1864, in Buncombe County. Wounded in action on an unspecified date and died in hospital at Richmond, VA, on August 24, 1864.

HAWKINS, GEORGE NEWTON PATTON, Private — Enlisted July 22, 1861, at age 28 in Buncombe County. Present or accounted for through February 1865.

HENSON, THOMAS L., Private — Enlisted September 16, 1863 in Buncombe County. Present or accounted for through February 1865.

HENSON, WILLIAM T., Private. Paroled at Appomattox Court House, VA, on April 9, 1865.

HERRON, WILLIAM, Private — Enlisted July 22, 1861, at age 38 in Buncombe County. Discharged on July 16, 1862, for being over age. Reenlisted in the company on April 27, 1863. Captured near Petersburg, VA, on April 2, 1865, and confined at Point Lookout, MD. Released on June 14, 1865, after taking the Oath.

HOLDEN, GEORGE W., Private — Enlisted July 22, 1861, in Buncombe County. Discharged on July 16, 1862, for being over age. Discharge certificate gives age as 40.

HOLDER, HAMILTON, Private — Enlisted July 22, 1861, at age 18 in Buncombe County. Wounded at Malvern Hill, VA, on July 1, 1862, and returned to duty in May, 1863. Captured at Gum Swamp about May 22, 1863, and confined at Fort Monroe, VA. Paroled and transferred to City Point, VA, for exchange about May 28, 1863. Retired to the Invalid Corps on January 3, 1865.

HOLDER, SAMUEL, Private — Enlisted March 10, 1862, at age 15 in Lenoir County. Deserted on November 30, 1863, but returned to duty on an unspecified date. Discharged on October 31, 1864, by reason of the expiration of his term of service.

HOWELL, FOSTER BENJAMIN, Private. Previously served as 3rd Lt. of this company. Resigned on March 22, 1863, and reenlisted in the company with the rank of Private on November 1, 1863. Captured at Fort Stedman, VA, on March 25, 1865, and confined at Point Lookout, MD. Released on June 14, 1865, after taking the Oath. (For additional information see service record for 3rd Lt. Foster Benjamin Howell.)

HUTCHINSON, ANDREW J., Private — Enlisted May 12, 1862, at age 20 in Lenoir County. Present or accounted for through December 1863. No further records.

HUTCHINSON, THOMAS, Private — Enlisted May 12, 1862, at age 18 in Lenoir County. Killed at Fredericksburg, VA, on December 13, 1862.

ISRAEL, JOHNSTON, Private — Enlisted April 27, 1863, at age 28 in Buncombe County. Captured at Gum Swamp about May 22, 1863, and confined at Fort Monroe, VA. Paroled and transferred to City Point, VA, for exchange around May 28, 1863. Returned to duty in July–August 1863. Deserted on November 30, 1863.

JAMISON, WILLIAM, Private — Enlisted March 10, 1862, at age 15 in Lenoir County. Discharged on October 31, 1864, by reason of expiration of his term of service.

JONES, WILLIAM H., Private — Enlisted September 16, 1863, at Camp Vance. Hospitalized at Richmond, VA, on August 9, 1864, with a gunshot wound to the left hand. Furloughed on October 6, 1864, and returned to duty prior to January 1, 1865. Present or accounted for through February 28, 1865.

JOYCE, RICHARD MARION, Private — Enlisted May 12, 1862, at age 18 in Lenoir County. Wounded at Fredericksburg, VA, on December 13, 1862. Reported absent sick or absent on light duty through February 1865.

JOYCE, WILLIAM MARION, Private — Enlisted July 22, 1861, at age 19 in Buncombe County. Wounded at Malvern Hill, VA, on July 1, 1862, and returned to duty in November–December 1862. Wounded at Fredericksburg, VA, on December 13, 1862, and returned to duty prior to January 1, 1863. Captured at Farmville, VA, on April 6, 1865, and confined at Newport News, VA. Released on June 27, 1865, after taking the Oath.

KNIGHT, JAMES M., Private — Enlisted May 12, 1862, at age 19 in Lenoir County. Died in hospital at Petersburg, VA, on December 4 or December 24, 1862, of "continued febris."

KNIGHT, RICHARD H., Private — Enlisted May 12, 1862, at age 18 in Lenoir County. Captured at Fort Stedman, VA, on March 25, 1865, and confined at Point Lookout, MD. Released on June 14, 1865, after taking the Oath.

KNIGHT, RICHARD M., Private — Enlisted July 21, 1861, at age 23 in Buncombe County. Present or accounted for through December 1863. No further records.

KNIGHT, THOMAS M., Private — Enlisted September 8, 1861, at age 25 in Buncombe County. Wounded at Malvern Hill, VA, on July 1, 1862, and died on July 21, 1862, of wounds.

KNIGHT, WILLIAM H., Private — Enlisted May 12, 1862, at age 30 in Lenoir County. Killed in March–April 1865. Place of death not reported.

LEDFORD, JAMES J., Private — Enlisted July 22, 1861, at age 20 in Buncombe County. Wounded in the thigh at Fredericksburg, VA, on December 13, 1862. Reported absent wounded until May–June 1863 when he was detailed as a quartermaster guard at Goldsboro. Reported absent on detail until November–December 1863 when he rejoined the company. Company records do not indicate whether he was present for duty during January–October 1864. Reported absent sick from November–December 1864 through February 1865.

LUTHER, ANDREW A., Private. Previously served as 2nd Lt. of this company and declined to stand for reelection. Discharged about April 27, 1863, but reenlisted in the company with the rank of Private around April 28, 1863. Present or accounted for through February 1865. (For additional information see service record for 2nd Lt. Andrew A. Luther.)

LUTHER, HAMILTON A., Private — Enlisted September 27, 1863, at age 30 in Buncombe County. Captured near Petersburg, VA, on April 2, 1865, and confined at Point Lookout, MD. Released on June 28, 1865, after taking the Oath.

LUTHER, JAMES H., Sergeant — Enlisted July 22, 1861, at age 22 in Buncombe County. Enlisted as Corporal but reduced to ranks in March–June 1862. Promoted to Sergeant on August 15, 1862, and present or accounted for through February 1865.

LUTHER, JOHN B., Private — Enlisted September 16, 1863, in Buncombe County. Died at Richmond, VA, about September 13, 1864, of unreported cause.

LUTHER, MARTIN DELPHOS, Private — Enlisted January 1, 1864, in Buncombe County. Wounded at Plymouth in April, 1864, and returned to duty on an unspecified date. Wounded twice near Petersburg, VA, on unspecified dates. Paroled on April 9, 1865, at Appomattox Court House, VA, where he "beat the last roal (sic) call in general Lee's army" while serving as a Drummer.

LUTHER, ROBERT H., Corporal — Enlisted July 22, 1861, at age 22 in Buncombe County. Promoted to Corporal on an unspecified date in 1864. Hospitalized at Petersburg, VA, on June 17, 1864, with a gunshot wound and returned to duty on June 19, 1864. Present or accounted for through February 1865.

McFEE, ALEXANDER M., Corporal — Enlisted July 22, 1861, at age 31 in Buncombe County. Promoted to Corporal on May 11, 1863. Reported absent without leave on August 28, 1862, but returned to duty on an unspecified date and subsequently court-martialed. Rejoined the company prior to November 1, 1862. Deserted on August 3, 1863.

McFEE, JOHN F., Private — Enlisted July 22, 1861, at age 20 in Buncombe County. Died near Richmond, VA, about July 27, 1864, of unreported cause.

McFEE, MADISON M., Private — Enlisted April 27, 1863, at age 40 in Buncombe County. Died in Madison County on August 2, 1864, of unreported cause.

MATTHEWS, JAMES MARION, Private — Enlisted March 1, 1863, at age 19 in New Hanover County. Deserted to the enemy on an unspecified date and took the Oath at Chattanooga, TN, on May 12, 1865.

MATTHEWS, JOHN C., Private — Enlisted September 8, 1861, at age 20 in Buncombe County. Discharged on July 28, 1863, by reason of disability.

MEECE, GEORGE W., Private — Enlisted July 22, 1861, at age 40 in Buncombe County. Discharged on July 16, 1862, for being over age. (NC pension records indicate he was wounded at Malvern Hill, VA, in 1863.)

MEECE, MANGRUM, Private — Enlisted July 22, 1861, at age 41 in Buncombe County. Discharged on July 16, 1862, for being over age.

MEECE, WILLIAM R., Private — Enlisted December 1, 1861, at age 19 in Buncombe County. Died near Drewry's Bluff, VA, about August 10–12, 1862, of "fever."

MILLER, JAMES H., Color Corporal — Enlisted July 22, 1861, at age 18 in Buncombe County. Promoted to Color Corporal in March–June 1863. Captured at Farmville, VA, on April 6, 1865, and confined at Newport News, VA. Released on June 27, 1865, after taking the Oath.

MILLER, LEANDER C., Private — Enlisted July 22, 1861, at age 20 in Buncombe County. Listed as a deserter and dropped from the rolls of the company on February 27, 1865.

MILLER, MABERRY M., Private — Enlisted July 22, 1861, at age 18 in Buncombe County. Paroled at Petersburg, VA, on June 26, 1865.

MOORE, JACKSON J., Private — Enlisted September 16, 1863, in Buncombe County. Killed at Petersburg, VA, on an unspecified date.

MOORE, JOHN H., Private — Enlisted July 22, 1861, at age 18 in Buncombe County. Captured near Petersburg, VA, on June 18, 1864, and confined at Point Lookout, MD, until transferred to Elmira, NY, on July 25, 1864. Paroled at Elmira on March 14, 1865, and transferred to Boulware's Wharf, James River, VA, for exchange on March 18–21, 1865.

MOORE, THOMAS L., Private — Enlisted July 22, 1861, at age 40 in Buncombe County. Discharged on July 16, 1862, for being over age. (NC pension records indicate he was killed in Polk County on December 5, 1864, when he fell down and his gun discharged accidentally. These records also indicate he was serving at that time in the 69th Regiment NC Troops; however, records of the 69th Regiment do not reveal his service.)

MORGAN, JAMES M., Sergeant — Enlisted December 1, 1861, at age 29 in Buncombe County. Promoted to Sergeant on April 28, 1862, and present or accounted for through December 1863. No further records.

MORGAN, PERMINTER P., 1st Sergeant — Enlisted July 22, 1861, at age 19 in Buncombe County. Enlisted as Sergeant and promoted to 1st Sergeant on April 28, 1862. Wounded at Malvern Hill, VA, on July 1, 1862, and returned to duty in November–December 1862. Captured near Petersburg, VA, on April 2, 1865, and confined at Point Lookout, MD. Released on June 29, 1865, after taking the Oath.

MORGAN, STEPHEN, Private — Enlisted April 27, 1863, at age 36 in Buncombe County. Hospitalized at Richmond, VA, on March 8, 1865, with a gunshot wound of the left foot. Furloughed for sixty days on March 29, 1865.

MURRY, W.J., Private. Paroled at Farmville, VA, about April 11–21, 1865.

MUSE, WILLIAM H., Private — Enlisted August 17, 1863, at age 40 in Buncombe County. Captured near Petersburg, VA, on April 2, 1865, and confined at Point Lookout, MD. Released on June 29, 1865, after taking the Oath.

NEAL, JOHN H., Private — Enlisted May 12, 1862, at age 20 in Lenoir County. Died at Raleigh on April 3, 1863, of disease.

OGDEN, WILLIAM H., Private — Enlisted June 1, 1864, at Richmond, VA. Deserted to the enemy about February 26, 1865, and confined at Washington, D.C. Released about March 2, 1865, after taking the Oath.

O'KELLY, BENJAMIN F., Private — Enlisted February 10, 1862, at age 25 at Grahamville, SC. Died in hospital at Petersburg, VA, about September 19–26, 1862, of "hypertrophy of heart."

O'KELLY, CHARLES W., Private — Enlisted December 1, 1861, at age 20 in Buncombe County. Enlisted as Sergeant but reduced to ranks in March–April 1862. Wounded at Sharpsburg, MD, on September 17, 1862, and returned to duty in July–August 1863. Present or accounted for through January 1865, but reported absent on detached duty as a nurse most of that period. Retired to the Invalid Corps on February 9, 1865.

O'KELLY, FRANCIS W., Private — Enlisted December 15, 1861, at age 22 at Grahamville, SC. Wounded in the fingers at King's School House, VA, on June 25, 1862. Reported absent wounded through December 1862 and then listed as a deserter on January 24, 1863.

OWENBY, ERASTUS W., Private. Previously served in Company D of this Reg. and transferred to this company in January–February 1864. Wounded in the hips at the Battle of the Crater near Petersburg, VA, on July 30, 1864. No further records.

PARHAM, JOHN, Private — Enlisted April 27, 1863, at age 37 in Buncombe County. Hospitalized at Richmond, VA, on June 13, 1864, with a gunshot wound. Returned to duty on October 1, 1864. Captured near Garrett Station, VA, on April 2, 1865, and confined at Hart's Island, New York Harbor. Released on June 17, 1865, after taking the Oath.

PEARSON, WILLIAM D., Private — Enlisted July 22, 1861, at age 22 in Buncombe County. Enlisted as Corporal but reduced to ranks in March–April 1862. Wounded at Malvern Hill, VA, on July 1, 1862, and returned to duty in September–October 1862. Wounded at Warm Springs about October 25, 1863, and returned to duty prior to January 1, 1865. Present or accounted for through February 28, 1865.

PENLAND, JAMES W., Private. Previously served in Company F, 16th Regiment NC Troops and enlisted in this company in Buncombe County on December 20, 1862. Deserted on August 3, 1863.

PENLAND, JOHN HENRY, Private — Enlisted July 22, 1861, at age 36 in Buncombe County. Died at Goldsboro on June 22, 1862, of "fever."

PENLAND, JOSEPH S., Private — Enlisted March 10, 1862, at age 17 in Lenoir County. Deserted on November 30, 1863.

PENLAND, NEWTON R., Private. Previously served in Company E, 39th Regiment NC Troops and enlisted in this company at Bristol, TN, on February 2, 1865. Deserted to the enemy about March 6, 1865, and confined at Washington, D.C. Released around March 10, 1865, after taking the Oath.

PENLAND, THOMAS M., Private — Enlisted July 22, 1861, at age 20 in Buncombe County. Enlisted as Musician (Drummer) but reduced to ranks in May–June 1862. Listed as a deserter and dropped from the rolls of the company on February 14, 1865.

PEOPLES, GEORGE W., Private — Enlisted July 22, 1861, at age 29 in Buncombe County. Promoted to Sergeant in March–April 1862 but reduced to ranks on August 15, 1862. Deserted on August 28, 1862, and captured by the enemy in Buncombe County on an unspecified date. Confined at Knoxville, TN, on June 15, 1864, and released on June 18, 1864, after taking the Oath. Took the Oath again at Louisville, KY, about June 26, 1864.

PETTIT, JOHN M., Private. Previously served in Company E of this Reg. and transferred to this company on May 1, 1862. Paroled at Appomattox Court House, VA, on April 9, 1865.

POE, ROBERT, Private. Paroled at Farmville, VA, about April 11–21, 1865.

RAYFIELD, AMBROSE R. WINSLOW, Private — Enlisted July 22, 1861, at age 30 in Buncombe County. Deserted to the enemy around December 26, 1864, and confined at Washington, D.C. Released about December 30, 1864, after taking the Oath.

RHODES, GEORGE W., Private — Enlisted July 22, 1861, at age 28 in Buncombe County. Wounded accidentally in the left arm during the retreat from Sharpsburg, MD, on September 19, 1862, resulting in amputation of the arm. Reported absent wounded until July 8, 1863, when he was discharged by reason of disability.

RHODES, WILLIAM, Private — Enlisted May 12, 1862, in Lenoir County. Captured at Frederick, MD, on September 12, 1862, and confined at Fort Delaware, DE. Paroled and transferred to Aiken's Landing, James River, VA, for exchange on October 2, 1862. Exchanged on November 10, 1862, and returned to duty in January–February 1863. Deserted to the enemy about March 3, 1865, and confined at Washington, D.C. Released around March 7, 1865, after taking the Oath.

RICE, JAMES W., Private — Enlisted July 22, 1861, at age 24 in Buncombe County. Reported absent wounded in November–December 1862. Returned to duty in January–February 1863. Deserted on October 16, 1863, and apprehended on an unspecified date. Confined at E.D.M. Prison, Richmond, VA, until released in May 1864 after volunteering to serve in the defense of Richmond against the Sheridan raid. Deserted to the enemy about December 26, 1864, and confined at Washington, D.C. Released around December 30, 1864, after taking the Oath.

RICE, JOHN N., Private — Enlisted May 12, 1862, at age 23 in Lenoir County. Wounded in the left hand at Fredericksburg, VA, on December 13, 1862, and returned to duty in March–June 1863. Hospitalized at Richmond, VA, on July 1, 1864, with a gunshot wound of the left thigh. Returned to duty prior to March 1, 1865. Paroled at Appomattox Court House, VA, on April 9, 1865.

RICE, WILLIAM ALEXANDER, Private — Enlisted September 16, 1863, in Buncombe County. Present or accounted for through February 1865.

RICH, JOSEPH A., Private. Previously served as Private in Company C of this Reg. and transferred to this company on May 1, 1862. Appointed Musician in May–June 1862 but reduced to ranks in July–December 1863. Deserted on August 4, 1863, but returned to duty on November 1, 1863. Present or accounted for through December 1863. (NC pension records indicate he died in VA on June 19, 1864.)

ROLLINS, CHARLES HAMILTON, Private — Enlisted July 22, 1861, at age 24 in Buncombe County. Discharged on November 19, 1861, by reason of disability.

ROLLINS, JOHN F., Private — Enlisted May 12, 1862, at age 24 in Lenoir County. Promoted to Musician in January–February 1863. Captured at Gum Swamp on May 22, 1863, and confined at Fort Monroe, VA. Paroled and transferred to City Point, VA, on May 28, 1863, for exchange. Returned to duty prior to July 1, 1863. Reduced to ranks in January–February 1865. Present or accounted for through February 1865.

RUTHERFORD, JAMES R., Private — Enlisted July 22, 1861, at age 32 in Buncombe County. Deserted on August 4, 1863, but returned to duty on November 1, 1863. Captured at Fort Stedman, VA, on March 25, 1865, and confined at Point Lookout, MD. Released on June 17, 1865, after taking the Oath.

RUTHERFORD, WILLIAM, Private — Enlisted April 27, 1863, at age 38 in Buncombe County. Died in hospital at Petersburg, VA, on August 29, 1863, of "febris typhoides."

SHARP, ELIJAH, Private — Enlisted July 22, 1861, at age 30 in Buncombe County. Captured at Fort Stedman, VA, on March 25, 1865, and confined at Point Lookout, MD. Released on June 20, 1865, after taking the Oath.

SMITH, ANDREW M., Private — Enlisted July 22, 1861, at age 35 in Buncombe County. Discharged on July 16, 1862, for being over age. Reenlisted in the company on April 27, 1863. Deserted on an unspecified date and dropped from the rolls of the company on December 26, 1864.

SMITH, SOLOMON R., Private — Enlisted July 22, 1861, at age 26 in Buncombe County. Wounded in the back at Petersburg, VA, on June 17, 1864, and returned to duty prior to January 1, 1865. Present or accounted for through February 1865.

SNELSON, WILLIAM R., Sergeant — Enlisted July 22, 1861, at age 24 in Buncombe County. Promoted to Color Corporal in January–February 1862 but reduced to ranks in May–June 1862. Promoted to Corporal in January–February 1863 and to Sergeant on an unspecified date in 1864. Deserted to the enemy about February 25, 1865, and confined at Washington, D.C. Released around March 2, 1865, after taking the Oath.

STINES, DILLIARD H., Private — Enlisted July 22, 1861, at age 28 in Buncombe County. Deserted on September 14, 1862, but returned to duty on October 6, 1862. Deserted again on January 24, 1863, but returned to duty prior to July 1, 1863. Present or accounted for through December 1863.

TAYLOR, JAMES M.V., Private — Enlisted July 22, 1861, at age 20 in Buncombe County. Reported absent wounded in July–August 1862. Place and date wounded not reported. Returned to duty and captured on September 17, 1862, at Sharpsburg, MD. Paroled on September 20, 1862, and returned to duty in January–February 1863. Deserted on August 3, 1863.

TAYLOR, SAMUEL, Private — Enlisted December 18, 1864, in Buncombe County. Present or accounted for through February 1865.

TAYLOR, WILLIAM, Private — Enlisted April 27, 1863, at age 36 in Buncombe County. Deserted on August 3, 1863.

THRASH, JOHN MILTON, Private — Enlisted July 22, 1861, at age 16 in Buncombe County. Enlisted as Corporal but reduced to ranks in March–April 1862. Discharged on July 16, 1862, for being under age.

WARREN, ANDREW J., Private — Enlisted July 22, 1861, at age 18 in Buncombe County. Reported absent without leave on August 28, 1862. Rejoined the company prior to November 1, 1862, and was subsequently court-martialed around December 28, 1862. Returned to duty prior to March 1, 1863. Present or accounted for through December 1863. No further records.

WARREN, BENJAMIN F., Private — Enlisted July 22, 1861, at age 25 in Buncombe County. Enlisted as Sergeant but reduced to ranks in March–April 1862. Died at Kinston on May 18–19, 1862, of "fever."

WARREN, GEORGE H., Private — Enlisted July 22, 1861, at age 19 in Buncombe County. Died at Charlottesville, VA, on January 1, 1863, of disease.

WARREN, JAMES M., Private — Enlisted July 22, 1861, at age 18 in Buncombe County. Deserted to the enemy about March 6, 1865, and confined at Washington, D.C. Released around March 10, 1865, after taking the Oath. (NC pension records indicate that he was "shocked by shell" at Petersburg, VA, on and unspecified date.)

WARREN, JOHN, Private — Enlisted July 22, 1861, at age 18 in Buncombe County. Wounded in the right shoulder at King's School House, VA, on June 25, 1862, and returned to duty in January–February 1863. Hospitalized at Farmville, VA, around June 15, 1864, with a gunshot wound of the clavicle and humerus. Furloughed for forty days on September 29, 1864. Listed as a deserter and dropped from the rolls of the company on December 26, 1864.

WARREN, JOHN F., Private — Enlisted July 22, 1861, at age 19 in Buncombe County. Wounded in the hand at Fredericksburg, VA, on December 13, 1862. Reported absent wounded or absent sick through December 1863. Company records do not indicate whether he was present for duty during January–October 1864. Returned to duty prior to January 1, 1865. Captured at Fort Stedman, VA, on March 25, 1865, and confined at Point Lookout, MD. Released on June 21, 1865, after taking the Oath.

WARREN, JOSEPH J., Private — Enlisted April 27, 1863, at age 33 in Buncombe County. Discharged on November 30, 1863, by reason of "dysenteria chronica."

WARREN, JOSHUA, Private — Enlisted July 22, 1861, at age 27 in Buncombe County. Present or accounted for through February 1865.

WARREN, PINKNEY H., Sergeant — Enlisted July 22, 1861, at age 19 in Buncombe County. Promoted to Corporal on April 28, 1862, and to Sergeant on an unspecified date in 1864. Wounded in the right shoulder at Fort Stedman, VA, on March 25, 1865. Hospitalized at Petersburg, VA, on March 25, 1865, and transferred to an unspecified hospital the next day.

WARREN, POSEY U., Private — Enlisted March 10, 1862, at age 17 in Lenoir County. Died in hospital at Petersburg, VA, about July 26, 1862, of "typhoid fever."

WARREN, URIAH, Sergeant — Enlisted July 22, 1861, at age 25 in Buncombe County. Promoted to Sergeant on April 28, 1862. Wounded at Plymouth about April 18–20, 1864. No further records.

WARREN, WESLEY, Private — Enlisted April 27, 1863, at age 40 in Buncombe County. Deserted on October 1, 1863, but returned to duty prior to January 1, 1865. Captured at Fort Stedman, VA, on March 25, 1865, and confined at Point Lookout, MD. Released on June 6, 1865, after taking the Oath.

WARREN, WILLIAM, Private — Enlisted September 16, 1863, in Buncombe County. Present or accounted for through February 1865.

WARREN, WILLIAM H., Private — Enlisted July 22, 1861, at age 23 in Buncombe County. Wounded in the chest at Petersburg, VA, about July 10, 1864. Listed as a deserter and dropped from the rolls of the company on December 26, 1864.

WARREN, WILLIAM K., Private — Enlisted July 22, 1861, at age 27 in Buncombe County. Died at Winchester, VA, about October 8–15, 1862, of "fever."

WAYNE, R.H., Private. Records of the Federal Provost Marshal indicate he was captured in hospital at Richmond, VA, on April 3, 1865. No further records.

WELCH, DANIEL P., Private — Enlisted July 22, 1861, at age 30 in Buncombe County. Present or accounted for until November–December 1862 when he was detailed as a shoemaker at Richmond, VA. Transferred to Company B, 2nd Battalion VA Infantry (Local Defense) on June 18, 1863. Later served in Company K, 2nd Regiment VA Infantry (Local Defense).

WILLIAMS, CHARLES W., Private — Enlisted May 12, 1862, at age 24 in Lenoir County. Wounded at Warm Springs about October 25, 1863. Died at Asheville around November 2, 1863, of wounds.

WILLIAMS, EDWARD J., Private — Enlisted July 22, 1861, at age 30 in Buncombe County. Died at Drewry's Bluff, VA, about August 23–25, 1862, of "fever."

WILLIAMS, JOHN H., Private — Enlisted July 22, 1861, at age 35 in Buncombe County. Discharged on July 16, 1862, for being over age. Reenlisted in the company on August 1, 1863. Wounded in the right arm at Fort Stedman, VA, on March 25, 1865, resulting in amputation of arm. Hospitalized at Petersburg, VA, where he was captured by the enemy on April 3, 1865. Confined at various Federal hospitals until confined at Newport News, VA, on June 6, 1865. Released on June 14, 1865, after taking the Oath.

WILLIAMS, MEREDITH, Private — Enlisted July 22, 1861, at age 19 in Buncombe County. Present or accounted for through February 1865.

WISE, DANIEL A., Private — Enlisted July 22, 1861, at age 19 in Buncombe County. Died at Wilmington on November 24–25, 1861, of "typhoid and pneumonia."

WISE, JAMES M., Private — Enlisted July 22, 1861, at age 26 in Buncombe County. Promoted to Corporal in July–August 1863 and present or accounted for through December 1863. Confined at E.D.M. Prison, Richmond, VA, on an unspecified date and for unreported reason. Reduced to ranks on an unspecified date in 1864. Released from prison about May 1, 1864, after volunteering to serve in the defense of Richmond against the Sheridan raid. Wounded in the left arm at Petersburg, VA, on June 17, 1864. Reported absent wounded until December 7, 1864, when he retired to the Invalid Corps by reason of disability from wounds.

WISE, JASON A., Private — Enlisted July 22, 1861, at age 21 in Buncombe County. Wounded in the foot at King's School House, VA, on June 25, 1862. Died on July 7-10, 1862, of wounds.

YOUNG, ANDERSON W., Private. Previously served in Company E, 24th Regiment GA Volunteer Infantry and transferred to this company on December 10, 1862. Deserted on July 22, 1863, but returned to duty on November 1, 1863. Present or accounted for through December 1863. No further records.

YOUNG, GEORGE W., Private — Enlisted May 12, 1862, at age 29 in Lenoir County. Died at Leesburg, VA, about October 1-15, 1862, of unreported cause.

YOUNG, JAMES M., Private — Enlisted May 12, 1862, at age 25 in Lenoir County. Wounded in the hand at Fredericksburg, VA, on December 13, 1862. Present or accounted for through February 1865.

YOUNG, JOSEPH M., Private — Enlisted July 22, 1861, at age 19 in Buncombe County. Hospitalized at Petersburg, VA, on August 21, 1864, with a shell wound of the back and/or left shoulder. Returned to duty in January-February 1865 and present or accounted for through February 28, 1865.

YOUNG, PINCKNEY RAYBURN, Private — Enlisted September 16, 1863, at age 19 in Buncombe County. Wounded in the left arm at Fort Stedman, VA, on March 25, 1865. Hospitalized at Richmond, VA, and captured by the enemy on April 3, 1865. Paroled on June 9, 1865.

YOUNG, PORTER J., Private — Enlisted May 12, 1862, at age 20 in Lenoir County. Died on December 29, 1864, of disease. Place of death not reported.

YOUNG, THOMAS L., Private — Enlisted May 12, 1862, at age 26 in Lenoir County. Wounded in the left leg at Sharpsburg, MD, on September 17, 1862. Reported absent wounded until November 10, 1864, when he was retired to the Invalid Corps.

YOUNG, WILLIAM H., Private — Enlisted May 12, 1862, at age 26 in Lenoir County. Discharged on August 14, 1862, by reason of disability.

YOUNG, WILLIAM H., Private — Enlisted July 22, 1861, at age 20 in Buncombe County. Promoted to Corporal in November-December 1863. Wounded on an unspecified date in 1864 and reported absent wounded through December 1864. Returned to duty prior to March 1, 1865, and reduced to ranks on an unspecified date. Captured at Fort Stedman, VA, on March 25, 1865, and confined at Point Lookout, MD. Released on June 22, 1865, after taking the Oath.

Company K — "Black Mountain Guards"

Captains

BURLISON, JESSE M., — Enlisted July 23, 1861, at age 22 in Buncombe County. Appointed 3rd Lt. on April 30, 1862, and promoted to 2nd Lt. in November-December 1862. Wounded in the leg at Fredericksburg, VA, on December 13, 1862, and returned to duty in March-June 1863. Promoted to 1st Lt. on April 20, 1863. Reported under arrest in July-August 1863 and absent on furlough in September-October 1863. Reported under arrest in November-December 1863. Company records do not indicate whether he was present for duty during January-October 1864, but he was promoted to Captain on March 23, 1864. Reported absent without leave in November-December 1864 and reported under arrest in January-February 1865. Captured by the enemy at Fort Stedman, VA, on March 25, 1865, and confined at Old Capitol Prison, Washington, D.C. until transferred to Fort Delaware, DE, on March 30, 1865. Released at Fort Delaware on June 17, 1865, after taking the Oath.

ROBERTS, CHARLES McKINNEY — Enlisted July 23, 1861, at age 32 in Buncombe County. Appointed Captain on July 23, 1861. Appointed Major about February 14, 1864, and transferred to the Field and Staff, 69th Regiment NC Troops.

Lieutenants

ANDERS, JOHN, 2nd Lt. — Enlisted July 23, 1861, at age 35 in Buncombe County. Appointed 2nd Lt. on April 30, 1862. Resigned on October 30, 1862, because "I am a poor man and have a large & helpless family."

BARNARD, JOBE DILLINGHAM, 1st Lt. — Enlisted July 23, 1861, at age 26 in Buncombe County. Appointed 1st Lt. on July 23, 1861. Defeated for reelection on April 30, 1862.

BUCKNER, NINEVAH TAYLOR, 3rd Lt. — Enlisted July 23, 1861, at age 22 in Buncombe County. Elected 3rd Lt. on July 23, 1861. Defeated for reelection on April 28, 1862.

GARRISON, THOMAS M., 2nd Lt. — Enlisted July 23, 1861, at age 20 in Buncombe County. Promoted to Sergeant in January-February 1863 and appointed 2nd Lt. on May 25, 1864. Present or accounted for through March 28, 1865.

GENTRY, JOSEPH R., 3rd Lt. — Enlisted July 23, 1861, at age 35 in Buncombe County. Enlisted as 1st Sergeant but reduced to ranks in May-July 1862. Discharged on July 16, 1862, for being over age. Reenlisted in the company on May 16, 1863, with the rank of Private. Elected 3rd Lt. on July 27, 1863, and resigned on January 6, 1864, in order to transfer to the 60th Regiment NC Troops in which his brother and "a large number of relatives & acquaintances" were serving.

HENSLEY, JAMES A., 2nd Lt. — Enlisted July 23, 1861, at age 23 in Buncombe County. Defeated for reelection on April 28, 1862. Continued to serve in this company with the rank of Private. (For additional information see service record for Private James A. Hensley.)

PATTERSON, JAMES R., 3rd Lt. — Enlisted July 23, 1861, at age 16 in Buncombe County. Promoted to Corporal in July-August 1863 and appointed 3rd Lt. in January-July 1864. Wounded in the left arm at "the Crater" near Petersburg, VA, on July 30, 1864, resulting in amputation of arm. Reported absent wounded or absent sick through February 1865. Retired to the Invalid Corps prior to April 9, 1865.

RAY, JAMES M., 1st Lt. — Enlisted July 23, 1861, at age 33 in Buncombe County. Promoted to Color Guard on October 9, 1861, and elected 1st Lt. on April 28,

1862. Dropped from the rolls of the company on an unspecified date after June 1863 for unreported reason.

WILSON, WILLIAM B., 1st Lt.—Enlisted July 23, 1861, at age 23 in Buncombe County. Promoted to 1st Sergeant in May–August 1862 and appointed 3rd Lt. on December 29, 1862. Promoted to 2nd Lt. in July–August 1863 and to 1st Lt. about March 23, 1864. Present or accounted for until January–February 1865 when he was reported absent without leave.

Noncommissioned Officers and Privates

ABBEYNETHE, A.J.—Records of Hollywood Cemetery, Richmond, VA, indicate he died about April 17, 1865. No further records.

ALMON, HENRY C., Private—Enlisted July 23, 1861, at age 22 in Buncombe County. Wounded at Malvern Hill, VA, on July 1, 1862. Died in hospital near Drewry's Bluff, VA, on August 3–5, 1862, of disease.

ANDERS, ALFRED, Corporal—Enlisted July 23, 1861, at age 44 in Buncombe County. Enlisted as Corporal. Discharged on July 16, 1862, for being over age.

ANDERS, DAVID HANSUCKER, Private—Enlisted July 23, 1861, at age 20 in Buncombe County. Wounded and "burned in face and hands with powder" at Malvern Hill, VA, on July 1, 1862. Reported absent wounded through December 1862. Reported under arrest in May–June 1863 but returned to duty in July–August 1863. Present or accounted for through December 1863. No further records.

ANDERS, GEORGE W., Private—Enlisted April 17, 1862, at age 26. Killed at Malvern Hill, VA, on July 1, 1862.

ANDERS, HIRAM J., Private—Enlisted July 23, 1861, at age 28 in Buncombe County. Wounded in the hand at King's School House, VA, on June 25, 1862, and returned to duty prior to September 1, 1862. Reported under arrest in May–June 1863 but returned to duty in July–August 1863. Present or accounted for through December 1863. No further records.

ANDERS, JAMES B., Private—Enlisted July 23, 1861, at age 22 in Buncombe County. Enlisted as Musician (Drummer) but reduced to ranks in May–August 1862. Wounded in the shoulder, arm, and/or thigh at Fredericksburg, VA, on December 13, 1862, and returned to duty in July–August 1863. Present or accounted for through December 1863. No further records.

ANDERS, JOHN G., Private—Enlisted June 15, 1862, at age 17 in Buncombe County. Enlisted as a substitute for Private John M. Carson. Captured near Petersburg, VA, on June 17, 1864, and confined at Point Lookout, MD, until transferred to Elmira, NY, on July 27, 1864. Paroled at Elmira and transferred to the James River, VA, on February 20, 1865, for exchange.

ANDERSON, ALBERT GALLETON, Private—Enlisted July 23, 1861, at age 45 in Buncombe County. Discharged on July 16, 1862, for being over age.

BANKS, HENRY C., Private—Enlisted July 23, 1861, at age 23 in Buncombe County. Wounded in the back at Fredericksburg, VA, on December 13, 1862, and returned to duty prior to January 1, 1863. Deserted on July 22, 1863, and apprehended on an unspecified date and confined at E.D.M. Prison in Richmond, VA. Released about May 1, 1864, after volunteering to serve in the defense of Richmond against the Sheridan raid. (NC pension records indicate he was wounded in July 1864.)

BANKS, HENRY H., Private—Enlisted July 23, 1861, at age 20 in Buncombe County. Wounded at Malvern Hill, VA, on July 1, 1862, and died in hospital at Richmond around August 22, 1862, of wounds.

BANKS, SAMUEL, Private—Enlisted September 7, 1861, at age 17 in Buncombe County. Died in hospital near Drewry's Bluff, VA, on August 5–6, 1862, of disease.

BANKS, WILLIAM H., Private—Enlisted June 15, 1862, at age 25 in Buncombe County. Died at Petersburg, VA, about August 18, 1862, of "diarrhoea."

BARNARD, HEZEKIAH E., 1st Sergeant—Enlisted July 23, 1861, at age 17 in Buncombe County. Promoted to Sergeant in May–August 1862. Wounded in the left arm at Fredericksburg, VA, on December 13, 1862. Promoted to 1st Sergeant in January–February 1863. Returned to duty in March–June 1863. Present or accounted for through December 1863. No further records.

BARNARD, WILLIAM T., Private—Enlisted March 16, 1863, at age 36 in Buncombe County. Present or accounted for through December 1863. Company records do not indicate whether he was present for duty during January–October 1864. Listed as a deserter and dropped from the rolls of the company on December 31, 1864; however returned to duty in January–February 1865. Present or accounted for through April 10, 1865.

BLACK, GEORGE W., Private—Enlisted July 23, 1861, at age 20 in Buncombe County. Killed at Plymouth about April 18–20, 1864.

BLACK, JAMES P., Private—Enlisted July 23, 1861, at age 33 in Buncombe County. Present or accounted for through December 1863. Company records do not indicate whether he was present for duty during January–October 1864; however, other records indicate that he was wounded at Plymouth about April 18–20, 1864. Listed as a deserter and dropped from the rolls of the company on December 31, 1864.

BLACKWELL, BERRY P., Private—Enlisted July 23, 1861, at age 17 in Buncombe County. Captured at Fort Stedman, VA, on March 25, 1865, and confined at Point Lookout, MD. Released on June 23, 1865, after taking the Oath.

BOON, AMOS, Corporal—Enlisted July 23, 1861, at age 32 in Buncombe County. Reported under arrest in May–June 1863 but returned to duty in July–August 1863. Present or accounted for through December 1863. Company records do not indicate whether he was present during January–October 1864; however, other records indicate that he was wounded in the hand at the Battle of the Crater near Petersburg, VA, on July 30, 1864. These records also reveal that he was promoted to Corporal on an unspecified date in 1864. Reported absent without leave in November–December 1864. Listed as a deserter and dropped from the rolls of the company on December 31, 1864.

BOON, JOHN W., Private — Enlisted July 23, 1861, at age 25 in Buncombe County. Discharged on May 27, 1862, by reason of disability.

BROWN, ALFRED W., Private — Enlisted March 16, 1863, at age 37 in Buncombe County. Captured near Petersburg, VA, on April 2, 1865, and confined at Point Lookout, MD. Released on June 23, 1865, after taking the Oath.

BRYANT, COLUMBUS O., Private — Enlisted July 23, 1861, at age 18 in Buncombe County. Wounded at Malvern Hill, VA, on July 1, 1862, and returned to duty prior to September 1, 1862. Killed "in Virginia" on July 10, 1864.

BUCKNER, DAVID, Private — Enlisted July 23, 1861, at age 35 in Buncombe County. Discharged on July 16, 1862, for being over age.

BUCKNER, JAMES ROBERT, Private — Enlisted July 23, 1861, at age 17 in Buncombe County. Discharged on July 16, 1862, for being under age.

BURLISON, EDWARD P., Private — Enlisted September 9, 1861, at age 19 in Buncombe County. Died in hospital at Petersburg, VA, about August 1–10, 1862, of "typhoid fever."

BURLISON, MARION, Private — Enlisted July 23, 1861, at age 27 in Buncombe County. Captured near Petersburg, VA, on April 2, 1865, and confined at Point Lookout, MD. Released on June 23, 1865, after taking the Oath.

CARSON, ANDREW P., Private — Enlisted July 23, 1861, at age 22 in Buncombe County. Deserted on July 22, 1863, but returned to duty in November–December 1863. Deserted to the enemy about September 12, 1864, and confined at Washington, D.C. Released around September 17, 1864, after taking the Oath.

CARSON, HENRY S., Private — Enlisted July 23, 1861, at age 29 in Buncombe County. Present or accounted for through November 1862, but was reported absent sick during most of that period. Returned to duty and wounded at Fredericksburg, VA. Reported absent wounded or absent sick through December 1863. Company records do not indicate whether he was present for duty during January–October 1864, but was listed as a deserter and dropped from the rolls of the company on December 31, 1864.

CARSON, HIRAM B., Private — Enlisted July 23, 1861, in Buncombe County. Not listed in the records of this company until November–December 1864 when he was reported absent without leave. Reported absent sick in January–February 1865. No further records.

CARSON, JOHN M., Private — Enlisted July 23, 1861, at age 31 in Buncombe County. Discharged on June 16, 1862, after providing John G. Anders as a substitute. Reenlisted in the company in January–June 1864 and captured near Petersburg, VA, on June 17, 1864. Confined at Point Lookout, MD, until transferred to Elmira, NY, on July 27, 1864. Died at Elmira on September 2, 1864, of "chronic diarrhoea."

CARSON, NEWTON F., Private — Enlisted July 23, 1861, at age 23 in Buncombe County. Wounded at Malvern Hill, VA, on July 1, 1862, and returned to duty in January–February 1863. Present or accounted for through December 1863. No further records.

CARSON, THOMAS D., Private — Enlisted June 15, 1862, at age 26. Present or accounted for through February 1865.

CARTER, DANIEL W., Private — Enlisted July 23, 1861, at age 23 in Buncombe County. Wounded at Malvern Hill, VA, on July 1, 1862, and returned to duty in November–December 1862. Wounded in an unspecified engagement in 1864 and reported absent wounded in November–December 1864. Reported absent sick in January–February 1865.

CARTER, GARRET D., Private — Enlisted April 27, 1862, at age 40 in Buncombe County. Not listed in the records of this company until May–June 1863. Died in hospital at Petersburg, VA, on September 29, 1864, of "diarrhoea chronic."

CARTER, JASPER S., Private — Enlisted July 23, 1861, at age 30 in Buncombe County. Detailed as a shoemaker on November 15, 1862, and reported absent on detail through February 1865.

CLARK, JACOB M., Private — Enlisted July 23, 1861, at age 26 in Buncombe County. Captured at King's School House, VA, on June 25, 1862, and confined at Fort Columbus, New York Harbor. Paroled there and exchanged at Aiken's Landing, James River, VA, on August 5, 1862. Returned to duty prior to September 1, 1862. Deserted on July 22, 1863.

COLE, GEORGE W., Private — Enlisted July 23, 1861, at age 29 in Buncombe County. Discharged about May 16, 1862, after providing Private Webb Paris as a substitute.

DAVIS, JOSEPH M., Private — Enlisted July 23, 1861, at age 19 in Buncombe County. Present or accounted for through February 1865.

DILLINGHAM, ALBERT G., Private — Enlisted July 23, 1861, at age 28 in Buncombe County. Captured at Gum Swamp on May 22, 1863, and confined at Fort Monroe, VA. Paroled there and exchanged at City Point, VA, about May 28, 1863. Returned to duty prior to July 1, 1863. Wounded in the nose and captured near Five Forks, VA, on April 1, 1865. Hospitalized at Washington, D.C. around April 7, 1865, and released on June 12, 1865, after taking the Oath.

DILLINGHAM, JOHN FOSTER, Private — Enlisted July 23, 1861, at age 25 in Buncombe County. Paroled at Appomattox Court House, VA, on April 9, 1865.

DILLINGHAM, THOMAS S., Private — Enlisted July 23, 1861, at age 19 in Buncombe County. Captured at Madison County on October 16, 1863, and confined at Camp Chase, OH, on November 14, 1863. Transferred to Rock Island, IL, and confined on January 17, 1864. Paroled at Rock Island and transferred to Boulware's and Cox's Wharves, James River, VA, for exchange on March 23, 1865.

DULA, THOMAS M., Corporal — Enlisted July 23, 1861, at age 28 in Buncombe County. Enlisted as Corporal. Discharged on May 27, 1862, by reason of disability.

DUNCAN, WILEY, Private — Enlisted July 23, 1861, at age 18 in Buncombe County. Died on December 23, 1861, of disease at Grahamville, SC.

DUYCK, JAMES M., Private — Enlisted July 23, 1861, at age 23 in Buncombe County. Discharged on June 6, 1862, by reason of being postmaster of Ivy Gap, Madison County.

EDMONDS, SAMUEL R.F., Private — Enlisted July 23, 1861, at age 26 in Buncombe County. Wounded at Malvern Hill, VA, on July 1, 1862, and returned to duty in January–February 1863. Wounded at Plymouth about April 18–20, 1864, and later died in an unspecified North Carolina hospital on July 3, 1864, of a gunshot wound.

EDMONDS, TILMAN W., Private — Enlisted July 23, 1861, at age 20 in Buncombe County. Wounded at Sharpsburg, MD, on September 17, 1862, and returned to duty in January–February 1863. Present or accounted for through September 9, 1863. Listed as a deserter and dropped from the rolls of the company on October 8, 1863.

EDWARDS, MOSES, Private — Enlisted July 23, 1861, at age 38 in Buncombe County. Discharged on July 16, 1862, for being over age.

ELKINS, NATHAN, Private — Enlisted April 27, 1862, at age 36 in Buncombe County. Not listed in the records of this company until May–June 1863. Wounded in the right hip at Drewry's Bluff, VA, in May 1864. Hospitalized at Richmond, VA, on May 16, 1864, and died on May 30, 1864, of "pyemia."

GARRISON, ROBERT N., Private — Enlisted April 27, 1862, at age 20 in Buncombe County. Not listed in the records of this company until May–June 1863. Killed at the Battle of the Crater near Petersburg, VA, on July 30, 1864.

GENTRY, NEWTON A., Private — Enlisted July 23, 1861, at age 29 in Buncombe County. Present or accounted for through December 1863. Company records dated November 1864–February 1865 indicate he was a prisoner of war. No further records.

GOLDSMITH, THOMAS A., Private — Enlisted July 23, 1861, at age 22 in Buncombe County. Present or accounted for through December 1863. No further records.

GREGORY, JAMES O., Private — Enlisted July 23, 1861, at age 18 in Buncombe County. Discharged on May 27, 1862, by reason of disability.

GREGORY, JOHN G., Private — Enlisted July 23, 1861, at age 25 in Buncombe County. Discharged on October 7, 1861, by reason of disability.

GREGORY, WILLIAM M., Private — Enlisted July 23, 1861, at age 20 in Buncombe County. Reported absent without leave in September–October 1862. Court-martialed on an unspecified date and returned to duty in November–December 1862. Present or accounted for through December 1863. No further records.

GUTHRIE, JAMES, Private — Enlisted April 10, 1863, at age 46 in Buncombe County. Enlisted as a substitute. Deserted on August 11, 1863.

HENSLEY, ADOLPHUS E., Musician — Enlisted July 23, 1861, at age 25 in Buncombe County. Enlisted as Musician (Fifer). Present or accounted for through December 1863. No further records.

HENSLEY, ELIJAH P., Private — Enlisted July 23, 1861, at age 17 in Buncombe County. Discharged on July 16, 1862, for being under age.

HENSLEY, EZEKIEL G., Private — Enlisted July 23, 1861, at age 26 in Buncombe County. Captured and paroled at Warrenton, VA, on September 29, 1862. Returned to duty in November–December 1862. Present or accounted for through December 1863. No further records.

HENSLEY, JAMES A., Private. Previously served as 2nd Lt. of this company. Defeated for reelection on April 28, 1862, and reenlisted in the company on the same date with the rank of Private. Reportedly transferred to Company G, 9th Regiment NC State Troops on December 3, 1864. (For additional information see service record for 2nd Lt. James A. Hensley.)

HOLT, ANDREW J., 1st Sergeant — Enlisted July 23, 1861, at age 26 in Buncombe County. Enlisted as Sergeant but reduced to ranks in May–August 1862. Promoted to 1st Sergeant on an unspecified date in 1864. Listed as a deserter and dropped from the rolls of the company on February 28, 1865.

HOPSON, JOSEPH A., Private — Enlisted July 23, 1861, at age 26 in Buncombe County. Wounded in the thigh at Fredericksburg, VA, on December 13, 1862, resulting in amputation of leg above the knee. Reported absent wounded through February 1865.

HURST, JAMES W., 1st Sergeant — Enlisted July 23, 1861, at age 19 in Buncombe County. Enlisted as Corporal but reduced to ranks in May–August 1862. Promoted to Sergeant on an unspecified date in 1864 and promoted to 1st Sergeant in January–February 1865. Captured near Petersburg, VA, on April 2, 1865, and confined at Point Lookout, MD. Released on June 14, 1865, after taking the Oath.

HYATT, PETER G., Private — Enlisted July 23, 1861, at age 19 in Buncombe County. Killed at Fredericksburg, VA, on December 13, 1862.

HYATT, SAMUEL P., Private — Enlisted July 23, 1861, at age 21 in Buncombe County. Wounded at Malvern Hill, VA, on July 1, 1862, and returned to duty in January–February 1863. Hospitalized at Farmville, VA, on April 7, 1865, with a gunshot wound of the right arm. Captured there in hospital on an unspecified date and paroled about April 11–21, 1865. Released from hospital and "transferred home" on June 2, 1865.

HYATT, WILLIAM R., Corporal — Enlisted July 23, 1861, at age 17 in Buncombe County. Promoted to Corporal subsequent to February 28, 1865. Captured at Fort Stedman, VA, on March 25, 1865, and confined at Point Lookout, MD. Released on June 14, 1865, after taking the Oath. (NC pension records indicate he was wounded at Petersburg, VA, in November 1864.)

HYDER, JOSEPH M., Private — Enlisted June 15, 1862, at age 18 in Buncombe County. Wounded at Fredericksburg, VA, on December 13, 1862, and died on December 20, 1862, of wounds. Place of death not reported.

HYDER, WILLIAM D., Private — Enlisted July 23, 1861, at age 40 in Buncombe County. Discharged on July 16, 1862, for being over age.

INGLE, AARON W., Private — Enlisted July 23, 1861, at age 23 in Buncombe County. Promoted to Corporal in May–August 1862. Wounded at Fredericksburg, VA, on December 13, 1862, and returned to duty in January–February 1863. Reduced to ranks in July–

August 1863. Captured at Fort Stedman, VA, on March 25, 1865, and confined at Point Lookout, MD. Released on June 14, 1865, after taking the Oath.

INGLE, ALBERT L., Private — Enlisted July 23, 1861, at age 23 in Buncombe County. Killed at Malvern Hill, VA, on July 1, 1862.

INGLE, ANDREW ERVIN, Private — Enlisted July 23, 1861, in Buncombe County. Discharged on July 16, 1862, for being over age. Discharge certificate gives age as 36.

INGLE, ISAAC, Private — Enlisted July 23, 1861, at age 25 in Buncombe County. Killed at Fredericksburg, VA, on December 13, 1862.

INGLE, SAMUEL, Private — Enlisted May 1, 1863, at age 40 in Madison County. Captured near Petersburg, VA, on April 2, 1865, and confined at Point Lookout, MD. Released on June 14, 1865, after taking the Oath. (NC pension records indicate he was wounded at Petersburg on November 1, 1864.)

JUSTICE, JACOB M., Private — Enlisted July 23, 1861, at age 20 in Buncombe County. Wounded at Sharpsburg, MD, on September 17, 1862, and subsequently returned to duty on unspecified date. Wounded at Plymouth about April 18-20, 1864. Listed as a deserter and dropped from the rolls of the company on December 31, 1864.

JUSTICE, JOHN G.M., Private — Enlisted July 23, 1861, at age 19 in Buncombe County. Present or accounted for through December 1863. Company records do not indicate whether he was present during January-October 1864, but reported under arrest in November-December 1864. Returned to duty in January-February 1865. (NC pension records indicate he was wounded at Fredericksburg, VA, in December 1862.)

JUSTICE, WILLIAM W., Private — Enlisted September 9, 1861, at age 17 in Buncombe County. Wounded at Malvern Hill, VA, on July 1, 1862, and returned to duty in January-February 1863. Present or accounted for through December 1863.

LANKFORD, ROBERT W., Private — Enlisted July 23, 1861, at age 22 in Buncombe County. Paroled at Appomattox Court House, VA, on April 9, 1865.

LANKFORD, WILLIAM R., Private — Enlisted July 23, 1861, at age 18 in Buncombe County. Present or accounted for until July 24, 1864, when he was retired to the Invalid Corps.

LITTLEJOHN, EPHRAIM M., Private — Enlisted July 23, 1861, at age 18 in Buncombe County. Wounded in the left lung in an unspecified engagement on July 5, 1864. Died in the hospital at Petersburg, VA, on July 6, 1864, of wounds.

McKINNEY, CHARLES G., Private — Enlisted July 23, 1861, at age 24 in Buncombe County. Died in hospital at Danville, VA, on February 23, 1863, of "scarlatina."

McKINNEY, JOHN M., Private — Enlisted July 23, 1861, at age 26 in Buncombe County. Present or accounted for through December 1863. No further records.

McKINNEY, WILLIAM A., Private — Enlisted July 23, 1861, at age 26 in Buncombe County. Enlisted as Sergeant but reduced to ranks in May-August 1862. Retired from service on January 20, 1865, by reason of "hypertrophy of the heart and chronic bronchitis."

MANER, JAMES M., Private — Enlisted July 23, 1861, at age 21 in Buncombe County. Furloughed on September 16, 1861, and failed to return to duty. Listed as a deserter on an unspecified date but rejoined the company on January 15, 1862. Captured near Globe Tavern, VA, on August 21, 1864, and confined at Point Lookout, MD, on August 24, 1864. No further records.

MANEY, JAMES H., Private — Enlisted July 23, 1861, at age 21 in Buncombe County. Enlisted as Corporal but reduced to ranks in May-August 1862. Captured near Petersburg, VA, on April 2, 1865, and confined at Point Lookout, MD. Released on June 29, 1865, after taking the Oath.

MANEY, LORENZO M., Private — Enlisted April 17, 1862, at age 25 in Buncombe County. Died in hospital at Petersburg, VA, about August 5, 1862, of "continued fever."

MANEY, MADISON G., Private — Enlisted April 17, 1862, at age 33 in Buncombe County. Deserted around August 28, 1862.

MANEY, WILLIAM R., Private — Enlisted July 23, 1861, at age 21 in Buncombe County. Died at Danville, VA, on May 20, 1863, of "pneumonia."

MORROW, WILLIAM JACKSON, Private — Enlisted July 23, 1861, at age 46 in Buncombe County. Discharged about June 19, 1862, for being over age.

PARRIS, WEBB, Private — Enlisted April 16, 1862, at age 17 in Buncombe County. Enlisted as a substitute for Private George W. Cole. Wounded at Sharpsburg, MD, on September 17, 1862, and returned to duty on an unspecified date. Reported absent wounded in November-December 1864 and absent sick in January-February 1865. No further records.

PATTERSON, JOSEPH M., Private — Enlisted July 23, 1861, at age 24 in Buncombe County. Enlisted as Sergeant but reduced to ranks in November-December 1862. Listed as a deserter and dropped from the rolls of the company on October 1, 1864, but returned to duty in January-February 1865. Paroled at Appomattox Court House, VA, on April 9, 1865.

PENIX, ERVIN, Private — Enlisted September 24, 1861, at age 20 in Buncombe County. Killed at Fredericksburg, VA, on December 13, 1862.

PENLAND, ALEXANDER M., Private — Enlisted September 9, 1861, at age 18 in Buncombe County. Killed at Malvern Hill, VA, on July 1, 1862.

PENLAND, JAMES H., Private — Enlisted July 23, 1861, at age 55 in Buncombe County. Discharged on July 16, 1862, by reason of "age & physical inability."

PENLAND, NEWTON L., Private — Enlisted July 23, 1861, at age 28 in Buncombe County. Died in hospital at Richmond, VA, on December 4, 1862, of "febris typhoides."

PROFFITT, BENJAMIN J., Private — Enlisted July 23, 1861, at age 24 in Buncombe County. Discharged on July 16, 1862, for unreported reason.

PROFFITT, JAMES W., Private — Enlisted July 23, 1861, at age 41 in Buncombe County. Discharged on July 16, 1862, for being over age.

RAMSEY, ANDERSON W., Private — Enlisted July 23, 1861, at age 19 in Buncombe County. Promoted to

Corporal on April 28, 1862. Wounded at Malvern Hill, VA, on July 1, 1862. Reduced to ranks on December 31, 1862. Returned to duty in March–June 1863. Wounded at Plymouth about April 18–20, 1864. Listed as a deserter and dropped from the rolls of the company on December 31, 1864, but returned to duty in January–February 1865. Wounded in the left knee at Fort Stedman, VA, on March 25, 1865. Hospitalized at Richmond, VA, and captured there by enemy on April 3, 1865. No further records.

RAMSEY, JEREMIAH B., Private — Enlisted March 16, 1862, at age 24 in Buncombe County. Present or accounted for through December 1863. However, company records do not indicate whether he was present for duty during January–October 1864. Reported absent without leave in November–December 1864 and listed as a deserter and dropped from the rolls of the company on December 31, 1864.

RIDDLE, MARVIL M., Private — Enlisted July 23, 1861, at age 35 in Buncombe County. Wounded at Malvern Hill, VA, on July 1, 1862. Discharged on July 16, 1862, for being over age.

ROBARDS, ANDREW M., Private — Enlisted July 23, 1861, at age 35 in Buncombe County. Died in hospital at Petersburg, VA, on July 16, 1862, of "bilious fever."

ROBERTS, JACOB W., Sergeant — Enlisted July 23, 1861, at age 26 in Buncombe County. Promoted to Sergeant in November–December 1862. Wounded in the head at Fredericksburg, VA, on December 13, 1862, and returned to duty in January–February 1863. Captured at Fort Stedman, VA, on March 25, 1865, and confined at Point Lookout, MD. Released on June 17, 1865, after taking the Oath.

RUNNIONS, LEWIS P., Private — Enlisted July 23, 1861, at age 22 in Buncombe County. Deserted from hospital at Raleigh on August 26, 1863.

SAGE, JOHN B., Private. Previously served in Company A, 5th Battalion NC Cavalry and transferred to this company on February 17, 1863. However, he failed to report for duty and was listed as a deserter. Rejoined Company A, 5th Battalion NC Cavalry prior to July 1, 1863.

WHITAKER, GEORGE W., Private — Enlisted July 23, 1861, at age 21 in Buncombe County. Wounded at Malvern Hill, VA, on July 1, 1862, and returned to duty in March–June 1863. Present or accounted for through February 1865. (NC pension records indicate he was wounded twice in unspecified battles.)

WHITAKER, RILEY SOLOMON, Private — Enlisted July 23, 1861, at age 22 in Buncombe County. Captured in Madison County on October 16, 1863, and confined at Camp Chase, OH, on November 14, 1863. Transferred to Rock Island, IL, in January 1864 and to New Orleans, LA, on May 3, 1865. Exchanged at New Orleans about May 23, 1865.

WHITT, REUBEN P., Private — Enlisted July 23, 1861, at age 21 in Buncombe County. Present or accounted for through December 1863. Company records do not indicate whether he was present during January–October 1864. Company muster rolls dated November 1864–February 1865 indicate that he was a prisoner of war.

WHITT, RICHARD W., Private — Enlisted July 23, 1861, at age 25 in Buncombe County. Captured at "Noon's Springs" on October 16, 1863, and confined at Louisville, KY, on November 30, 1863. Transferred to Rock Island, IL, and arrived there on December 5, 1863. Paroled at Rock Island and transferred for exchange about February 13, 1865.

WHITTEMORE, GEORGE W., Private — Enlisted July 23, 1861, at age 35 in Buncombe County. Discharged on July 16, 1862, for being over age.

WHITTEMORE, JAMES B., Private — Enlisted July 23, 1861, at age 20 in Buncombe County. Wounded at Malvern Hill, VA, on July 1, 1862, and returned to duty in January–February 1863. Deserted on July 22, 1863.

WHITTEMORE, JOHN A., Private — Enlisted July 23, 1861, at age 25 in Buncombe County. Died in hospital at Richmond, VA, on December 5, 1862, of "typhoid fever."

WHITTEMORE, MARTEN, Sergeant — Enlisted July 23, 1861, at age 36 in Buncombe County. Enlisted as Sergeant. Discharged on July 16, 1862, for being over age.

WILLIAMS, JAMES G., Private. Previously served in Company G, 9th Regiment NC State Troops and transferred to this company on December 3, 1864. Paroled at Appomattox Court House, VA, on April 9, 1865.

WILLIAMS, JOHN H., Private — Enlisted July 23, 1861, at age 26 in Buncombe County. Present or accounted for through December 1863. Company records do not indicate whether he was present for duty during January–October 1864. Reported absent without leave in November–December 1864 and listed as a deserter and dropped from the rolls of the company on December 31, 1864.

WILLIAMS, LEWIS D., Private — Enlisted July 23, 1861, at age 22 in Buncombe County. Killed at Malvern Hill, VA, on July 1, 1862.

WILLIAMS, SIDNEY H., Private — Enlisted July 23, 1861, at age 20 in Buncombe County. Paroled at Appomattox Court House, VA, on April 9, 1865.

WYATT, ALFRED A., Corporal — Enlisted July 23, 1861, at age 17 in Buncombe County. Promoted to Corporal in November–December 1862. Present or accounted for through December 1863. No further records

Company Affiliation Unknown

Civil War records indicate that the following soldiers served in the 25th Regiment N.C. Troops; however, the companies in which they served are not reported.

ALLEN, JOHN, Private. Took the Oath at Point Lookout, MD, on June 23, 1865.

BEEVLER, J.F., Private. Captured and paroled at Athens, GA, about May 8, 1865.

CLYER, E.A., Private. Captured and paroled at Athens, GA, about May 8, 1865.

EDNEY, G.P. NC pension records indicate he enlisted in this Reg. in March 1865. No further records.

GARDNER, S.A., Private. Captured and paroled at Athens, GA, about May 8, 1865.

GREEN, J.W., Private. Deserted to the enemy on an unspecified date. Took the Oath at Washington, D.C. about December 30, 1864.

HILL, J.L., Private. Captured and paroled at Athens, GA, about May 8, 1865.

McNEILL, HECTOR. NC pension records indicate he enlisted in this Reg. on an unspecified date in 1864 and served for "about ten months." No further records.

MOORE, JAMES MURRY, Private. Records of Company E, 18th Regiment NC Troops indicate he was transferred to this Reg. about March 4, 1863. However, records of this Reg. do not reveal his service.

O'CONNER, _____, Private. Deserted to the enemy or was captured at Petersburg, VA, on March 5, 1865. Confined at Washington, D.C. until released about March 8, 1865, after taking the Oath.

RHODES, S.B., Private. Deserted to the enemy on an unspecified date. Took the Oath at Knoxville, TN, about May 25, 1865.

STEVENS, J.B., Private. Captured and paroled at Athens, GA, about May 8, 1865.

SUMMIT, WILLIAM. Deserted to the enemy about December 26, 1863, and confined at Norfolk, VA. Transferred to Baltimore, MD, about January 16, 1864. No further records.

TURWELL, S.W., Private. Captured and paroled at Athens, GA, about May 8, 1865.

WIGHT, S.M., Private. Captured and paroled at Athens, GA, about May 8, 1865.

WILLIAMS, S.R., Corporal. Paroled at Richmond, VA, about April 22, 1865.

APPENDIX A:
COMMAND STRUCTURE

Colonel   Thomas Lanier Clingman (promoted to brigadier general); Henry Middleton Rutledge (paroled at Appomattox)

Lieutenant Colonel   St. Clair Dearing (resigned from service); Samuel C. Bryson (wounded at Petersburg 1864); Matthew Norris Love (paroled at Appomattox)

Major   Henry Middleton Rutledge (promoted to colonel); Samuel C. Bryson (promoted to lt. colonel); John W. Francis (wounded at Malvern Hill, 1862); William S. Grady (wounded at Petersburg, 1864); William Y. Morgan (paroled at Appomattox)

Adjutant   Wesley N. Freeman (promoted to captain Company C); William H. Graves (became captain of Company E); Bazil B. Edmonston (resigned); James C.L. Gudger (captured at Five Forks); James P. Sawyer ((paroled at Appomattox)

Assistant Quartermaster   William H. Bryson (discharged 1862); Andrew J. Miller (dropped from rolls 1862)

Assistant Commissary of Subsistence   James P. Sawyer (transferred back to Company A); John W. Walker (dropped from rolls, 1862); John C. Robinson (discharged, 1862); William D. Miller (dropped from rolls, 1863)

Surgeon   Solomon S. Satchwell (assigned to hospital duty in 1862); Stephen D. Doar (transferred out of Regiment); Francis N. Luckey (paroled at Appomattox)

Assistant Surgeon   George W. Fletcher (resigned, 1862); Robert T. Webb (resigned, 1862); Beverly S. Watkins (paroled at Appomattox)

Sergeant Major   James C.L. Gudger (promoted to adjutant); Robert H. Howell (wounded at Fredericksburg, 1862); James P. Scott

Quartermaster Sergeant   Clinton A. Jones (paroled at Appomattox)

Commissary Sergeant   Julius M. Young (reduced in ranks/paroled at Appomattox); Robert Smiley (paroled at Appomattox)

Color Sergeant   Benjamin F. Allison (died of wounds at Fredericksburg, 1863)

Hospital Steward   Julius M. Young (paroled at Appomattox)

Drum Major   Peter M. Rich (transferred back to Company C)

Company Commanders (Captains)

Company A (Edney Greys)   Baylis M. Edney (declined to stand for reelection); Matthew N. Love (promoted to major and then to lt. colonel) John S. Plumblee (killed at Five Forks)

Company B (Jackson Guards) Thaddeus D. Bryson (declined to stand for reelection); Harlen A. Boone (resigned, probably due to poor health); David Rogers (wounded at Ft. Stedman)

Company C (Haywood Invincibles) Samuel C. Bryson (promoted to major and then to lt. colonel); Wesley N. Freeman

Company D (George's Guards) John W. Francis (promoted to major); Leander B. Tatham (captured at Ft. Stedman)

Company E (Transylvania Volunteers) Francis W. Johnstone (defeated for reelection); Young, Ephriam E. (died at Kinston of "fever"); William H. Graves (killed at Petersburg)

Company F (Haywood Highlanders) Thomas I. Lenoir (declined to stand for reelection and resigned); James M. Cathey (killed at "the Crater" in Petersburg); James A. Blalock

Company G (Highland Guards) William S. Grady (promoted to Major); John R. Hayes (resigned); John M. Phinizy

Company H (Cane Creek Rifles) Frederick R. Blake (defeated for reelection); Solomon Cunningham (killed at Fredericksburg); Thomas J. Young (paroled at Appomattox)

Company I (Pisgah Guards) George W. Howell (resigned from service); William Y. Morgan (promoted to major); Augustus B. Thrash (wounded at Ft. Stedman)

Company K (Black Mountain Guards) Charles M. Roberts (promoted to major of battalion); Jesse M. Burlison (captured at Ft. Stedman)

Appendix B: Parolees at Appomattox

25th Regiment Officers
Henry M. Rutledge, Colonel 25th N.C.
Matthew N. Love, Lt.-Colonel 25th N.C.
Joseph R. Byers, 1st Lt. Co. H, 25th N.C.
Thomas J. Young, Capt. Co. H, 25th N.C.
Peter K. Mull, 2d Lt. Co. E, 25th N.C.
John B. Edney, 2d Lt. Co. A, 25th N.C.
Francis N. Luckey, Surgeon 25th N.C.
Beverly S. Watkins, Assistant Surgeon 25th N.C.

Noncommissioned Staff
Robert Smiley, Commissary Sergeant (Co. A)
Julius M. Young, Hospital Steward (Co. D)
Clinton A. Jones, Quarter Master Sergeant (Co. G)

Company A
Privates
James P. Sawyer
John H. Byers
Thomas A. Edney
Spencer M. Freeman
Thomas J. Enloe
John L. Becknell
James H. Maxwell
Solomon B. Williams
John W. Head
Robertson A. Freeman
John T. Freeman
Humphrey P. Conner

Company B
Sergeant
Elbert Brown

Privates
John G. Allman
William P. Allman
Braxton P. Mull
John B. Allison, Jr.
Levi J. Mathis

Company C
Privates
Samuel B. Best
David A. Allen
Elijah A. Sorrells
Neely D. Fry

Company D
Privates
David M. Russell
Allen Redden
Porter R. Murrell

Company E
Sergeant
Richard L. Fortune

Privates
Benjamin J. Wilson
Benjamin P. Barton
Phydila P. Cantrell
Matthew Gillespie
Jacob King
John A. Hollingsworth
Joseph P. Holden
Harris B. Pettit
William C. Hamilton

Company F (none)

Company G
Privates
Isaac D. Fincannon

Henry Hemrick
William M. Long
Leonard Schevenell
George W. Seuter
John T. Watson
James W. Phipps
James T. McDonald
William C. Stamey
Robert Powell
William J. Price

Company H
Privates
Norris Allison

Richard Allison
Thomas. R. Lister
James M. Plumblee
Felix C. Carland
William Dempsey
Benjamin Pinner

Company I
Privates
Martin D. Luther
William T. Henson
John N. Rice
John M. Pettit
Thomas L. Green

Company K
Privates
Joseph M. Patterson
James G. Williams
Robert W. Lankford
John F. Dillingham
Sidney H. Williams

APPENDIX C:
DEPLOYMENT OF 25TH N.C. TROOPS DURING THE CIVIL WAR

CAROLINA COASTAL DEFENSE

DATE/LOCATION: 9/18/1861, Asheville, N.C. MOVEMENT: Marched by foot to Morganton, N.C., arriving about 9/20. REMARKS: Morganton was the railroad's western terminus in N.C. during the Civil War.

DATE/LOCATION: about 9/21/1861, Morganton, N.C. MOVEMENT: Marched by train to Raleigh, N.C., stopping for a couple of days to be outfitted with uniforms. Entrained again and marched by railroad to Wilmington, N.C., arriving about 9/28. REMARKS: Encamped at Camp Davis near Wilmington, N.C.

DATE/LOCATION: 11/5/1861, Wilmington, N.C. MOVEMENT: Marched by train to Charleston, S.C., arriving on 11/7.

DATE/LOCATION: 11/8/1861, Charleston, S.C. MOVEMENT: Marched by train to Coosawhatchie, S.C., arriving the same day. REMARKS: Encamped in vicinity of Fort Beauregard.

DATE/LOCATION: 11/14/1861, Fort Beauregard. MOVEMENT: Marched by foot about 9 miles to Grahamville, S.C., arriving the same day. REMARKS: Encamped at Camp Lee.

DATE/LOCATION: 3/15/1862, Grahamville, S.C. MOVEMENT: Marched by train to Kinston, N.C., arriving on 3/18.

DATE/LOCATION: 3/21/1862, Kinston, N.C. MOVEMENT: Marched by foot about 8 miles west toward Goldsboro, N.C. REMARKS: Encamped at Camp Johnston near railroad.

DATE/LOCATION: 3/23/1862, Kinston, N.C. vicinity. MOVEMENT: Marched by foot back to Kinston, N.C. REMARKS: Encamped for 2 nights and performed guard duty.

DATE/LOCATION: 3/25/1862, Kinston, N.C. MOVEMENT: Marched by foot back to camp arriving same day. REMARKS: Encamped near Kinston, N.C.

DATE/LOCATION: 3/28/1862, Kinston, N.C. vicinity. MOVEMENT: Marched by foot back to Kinston, N.C., arriving same day.

DATE/LOCATION: 3/29/1862, Kinston, N.C. MOVEMENT: Marched by foot about 5 miles in direction of New Bern, N.C. REMARKS: Encamped at Camp Ransom.

DATE/LOCATION: 5/2/1862, Camp Ransom. MOVEMENT: Marched by foot to Kinston, N.C.

DATE/LOCATION: 6/1/1862, Kinston, N.C. MOVEMENT: Marched by foot about 8 miles west toward Goldsboro, N.C. REMARKS: Encamped at Camp Johnston.

THE SEVEN DAYS BATTLES

DATE/LOCATION: 6/19/1862, Kinston, N.C. MOVEMENT: Marched by train to Petersburg, Va., arriving on 6/21/1862. Marched by foot 2 miles north and encamped. REMARKS: Encamped near Petersburg, Va.

DATE/LOCATION: 6/24/1862, Petersburg, Va., vicinity. MOVEMENT: Marched by foot to vicinity of Richmond, Va., arriving on 6/25. REMARKS: Regiment rushed down Williamsburg Road to participate in the engagement at King's School House on 6/25/1862.

DATE/LOCATION: 6/26/1862 to 7/1/1862, Richmond, Va., vicinity. MOVEMENT: Regiment fought several skirmishes with the retreating enemy forces on the south side of the Chickahominy River. On 7/1/1862 the regiment fought in the Battle of Malvern Hill and subsequent to that action followed the enemy to Harrison's Landing on the James River. At that safe harbor the Union gunboats kept the pursuing Confederate army and the 25th Regiment's troops at a distance. REMARKS: Participated in the final hours of the Battle of Malvern Hill.

DATE/LOCATION: 7/6/1862, Richmond, Va., vicinity. MOVEMENT: Marched by foot to Drewry's Bluff, Va., arriving by 7/7. REMARKS: Encamped at Drewry's Bluff, Va.

DATE/LOCATION: 7/30/1862, Drewry's Bluff, Va. MOVEMENT: Marched by foot to below Petersburg, Va., and encamped. REMARKS: Encamped near Petersburg, Va.

DATE/LOCATION: 8/19/1862, Petersburg, Va., vicinity. MOVEMENT: Marched to the vicinity of Richmond, Va.

MARYLAND CAMPAIGN

DATE/LOCATION: 8/27/1862, Richmond, Va. MOVEMENT: Marched by Virginia Central Railroad to Rapidan Station, Va., arriving on 8/28.

DATE/LOCATION: 8/31/1862, Rapidan Station, Va., vicinity. MOVEMENT: Marched by foot toward Maryland via Culpeper, Jefferson, Warrenton, and Leesburg, Va. Crossed the Potomac River on 9/7 and reached Frederick, Md., on 9/9. REMARKS: Encamped near Frederick, Md.

DATE/LOCATION: 9/10/1862, Frederick, Md., vicinity. MOVEMENT: Marched by foot back across the Potomac River at Point of Rocks on 9/11 and continued march until reaching Harpers Ferry, Va. (now West Virginia), on 9/13. REMARKS: Regiment participated in the siege and capture of Harpers Ferry on 9/13 – 9/15/1862.

DATE/LOCATION: 9/16/1862, Harpers Ferry, Va., vicinity. MOVEMENT: Marched by foot across the Potomac River at Shepherdstown, Va., and arrived late on the night of 9/16 at Sharpsburg, Md. REMARKS: Regiment participated in the Battle of Sharpsburg (Antietam Run) on 9/17/1862 and played a key role in the Confederate victory.

DATE/LOCATION: 9/18/1862, Sharpsburg, Md. MOVEMENT: Left the battlefield on the night of 9/18 – 9/19 and marched by foot back across the Potomac River at Shepherdstown, Va., to the environs of Martinsburg, Va. (now West Virginia), arriving there about 9/20. REMARKS: Encamped near Martinsburg, Va.

DATE/LOCATION: 10/1/1862, Martinsburg, Va., vicinity. MOVEMENT: Marched by foot to Winchester, Va. REMARKS: Encamped near Winchester, Va.

DATE/LOCATION: 10/23/1862, Winchester, Va., vicinity. MOVEMENT: Marched by foot to Paris, Va., arriving on 10/25. REMARKS: Encamped near Paris, Va.

HEIGHTS OF FREDERICKSBURG

DATE/LOCATION: 10/31/1862, Paris, Va., vicinity. MOVEMENT: Marched by foot via Culpeper Courthouse, Va., and encamped briefly. REMARKS: Encamped at Culpeper Courthouse, Va.

DATE/LOCATION: 11/8/1862, Culpeper Courthouse, Va. MOVEMENT: Marched by foot to Madison Courthouse, Va., and encamped for a few days. REMARKS: Encamped at Madison Courthouse, Va.

DATE/LOCATION: 11/18/1862, Madison Courthouse, Va. MOVEMENT: Marched by foot to the vicinity of Fredericksburg, Va., arriving there about 11/19-11/20. REMARKS: Encamped in the Fredericksburg, Va., vicinity until the end of the year 1862. On 12/13/1862 the regiment participated meritoriously in the Battle of Fredericksburg.

EASTERN NORTH CAROLINA COASTAL DEFENSE

DATE/LOCATION: 1/3/1863, Fredericksburg, Va. MOVEMENT: Marched by foot to Petersburg, Va., via Hanover Junction and Richmond, Va. arriving about 1/7. REMARKS: Encamped near Petersburg, Va.

DATE/LOCATION: 1/17/1863, Petersburg, Va. MOVEMENT: Marched by Petersburg & Weldon Railroad to Warsaw Station, N.C., located 40 miles below Goldsboro, N.C., arriving on 1/18. REMARKS: Encamped near Warsaw Station, N.C.

DATE/LOCATION: 1/20/1863, Warsaw Station, N.C., vicinity. MOVEMENT: Marched by foot 10 miles southeastward to Kenansville, N.C., arriving same day. REMARKS: Encamped near Kenansville, N.C.

DATE/LOCATION: 2/22/1863, Kenansville, N.C., vicinity. MOVEMENT: Marched by foot 8 miles to train depot at Magnolia, N.C. Entrained there and marched by Wilmington & Weldon Railroad to Wilmington, N.C., arriving same day. REMARKS: Encamped at Wilmington, N.C.

DATE/LOCATION: 2/24/1863, Wilmington, N.C. MOVEMENT: Marched by foot approximately 2 or 3 miles east of Wilmington, N.C. REMARKS: Encamped near Wilmington, N.C.

DATE/LOCATION: 2/27/1863, Wilmington, N.C., vicinity. MOVEMENT: Marched 9 miles north of Wilmington, N.C., to railroad bridge over Northeast (Cape Fear) River arriving same day. REMARKS: Encamped at Northeast River Station, N.C. and guarded the railroad bridge.

DATE/LOCATION: 3/7/1863, Northeast River railroad bridge. MOVEMENT: Marched by foot to camp below Wilmington, N.C., arriving same day. REMARKS: Encamped near Wilmington, N.C.

DATE/LOCATION: 3/10/1863, Wilmington, N.C., vicinity. MOVEMENT: Marched by foot to Topsail Sound, N.C. REMARKS: Encamped at Topsail Sound, N.C.

DATE/LOCATION: 3/25/1863, Topsail Sound, N.C. MOVEMENT: Marched by foot to Wilmington, N.C. Entrained there and marched by railroad to Goldsboro, N.C., arriving at night on 3/28.

DATE/LOCATION: 3/29/1863, Goldsboro, N.C. MOVEMENT: Marched by train to Kinston, N.C., arriving on same day.

DATE/LOCATION: 3/30/1863, Kinston, N.C. MOVEMENT: Marched by foot about 7 miles in the direction of Trenton, N.C. REMARKS: Encamped near Trenton, N.C.

Appendix C: Deployment During the Civil War

Date/Location: 4/1/1863, Trenton, N.C., vicinity. Movement: Marched by foot to Kinston, N.C.

Date/Location: 4/2/1863, Kinston, N.C. Movement: Marched by foot to the vicinity of Washington, N.C., arriving on 4/5. Remarks: Encamped near Washington, N.C.

Date/Location: 4/7/1863, Washington, N.C., vicinity. Movement: Marched by foot to Swift Creek, N.C., approximately 13 miles south of Washington, N.C., arriving the same day. Remarks: Encamped at Swift Creek, N.C.

Date/Location: 4/8/1863, Swift Creek, N.C. Movement: Marched by foot to Cross Roads, 8 miles above Washington, N.C., arriving same day. Remarks: Encamped near Washington, N.C. Regiment participated in Confederate General D.H. Hill's ill-fated siege and attempt to capture Union-held Washington, N.C.

Date/Location: 4/9/1863, Washington, N.C., vicinity. Movement: Marched by foot and crossed over to the north side of the Tar River near Washington, N.C. Remarks: Encamped near Washington, N.C.

Date/Location: 4/10/1863, Washington, N.C., vicinity. Movement: Marched by foot and re-crossed to the south side of the Tar River near Washington, N.C. Remarks: Encamped near Washington, N.C.

Date/Location: 4/17/1863, Washington, N.C., vicinity. Movement: Marched by foot in the direction of Greenville, N.C. eventually arriving in Kinston, N.C. on 4/20. Remarks: Encamped near Kinston, N.C.

Date/Location: 4/29/1863, near Kinston, N.C. Movement: Marched by foot to Gum Swamp about 9 miles southeast of Kinston, N.C., and arrived same day. Remarks: Encamped in fort at Gum Swamp. On 4/30/1863 the 25th Regiment repulsed a small force of enemy troops at Gum Swamp. However, on 5/22/1863 a larger Union assault surprised and routed the 25th and 56th regiments stationed at Gum Swamp.

Date/Location: 5/27/1863, Kinston, N.C. Movement: Marched by railroad to Petersburg, Va., arriving on 5/28.

Date/Location: 5/28/1863, Petersburg, Va. Movement: Marched by railroad to Richmond, Va., arriving on same day.

Date/Location: 6/2/1863, Richmond, Va. Movement: Marched by railroad to Petersburg, Va., and then on to Ivor Station near the Blackwater River in Va. Remarks: Encamped in the vicinity of Ivor Station near the Blackwater River in Va.

Date/Location: 6/12/1863, Ivor Station near the Blackwater River in Va. Movement: Marched by railroad to Petersburg, Va., and then on to a point near Drewry's Bluff, Va., arriving the same day. Remarks: Encamped at Drewry's Bluff, Va.

Date/Location: 6/17/1863, Drewry's Bluff, Va. Movement: Marched by railroad to Petersburg, Va. Remarks: Encamped near Petersburg, Va.

Date/Location: 6/21/1863, Petersburg, Va. Movement: Marched by railroad to a point near Drewry's Bluff, Va. Remarks: Encamped at Drewry's Bluff, Va.

Date/Location: 6/25/1863, Drewry's Bluff, Va. Movement: Marched by foot via pontoon bridge to north side of James River and then on to the vicinity of Seven Pines, Va. Remarks: Encamped near Seven Pines, Va. and on 7/4 repulsed Union forces advancing toward Richmond.

Date/Location: 7/12/1863, Seven Pines, Va., vicinity. Movement: Marched by foot and railroad to Petersburg, Va. Remarks: Encamped near Petersburg, Va.

Date/Location: 7/20/1863, Petersburg, Va. Movement: Marched by railroad to Weldon, N.C. Remarks: Encamped near Weldon, N.C.

Appendix C: Deployment During the Civil War

DATE/LOCATION: 7/22/1863, Weldon, N.C. MOVEMENT: Marched by railroad back to Petersburg, Va.

DATE/LOCATION: 7/28/1863, Petersburg, Va. MOVEMENT: Marched by railroad to Garysburg, N.C.

DATE/LOCATION: 7/29/1863, Garysburg, N.C. MOVEMENT: Marched by foot to Jackson, N.C., arriving on 7/30. REMARKS: Encamped 3 miles west of Jackson, N.C.

DATE/LOCATION: 8/1/1863, Jackson, N.C., vicinity. MOVEMENT: Marched by foot to Garysburg, N.C. REMARKS: Encamped at Garysburg, N.C.

DATE/LOCATION: 8/3/1863, Garysburg, N.C. MOVEMENT: Marched by foot to camp 2 miles west of Garysburg, N.C. REMARKS: Encamped 2 miles west of Garysburg, N.C.

DATE/LOCATION: 10/16/1863, Weldon, N.C., and Garysburg, N.C., vicinity. REMARKS: A large detachment of troops from the 25th Regiment was deployed to western N.C. to combat a band of Tories near Warm Springs, N.C.

DATE/LOCATION: 11/9/1863, Weldon, N.C., vicinity. MOVEMENT: Marched by foot 13 miles on scout below Jackson, N.C., and returned to Weldon, N.C. on 11/11. REMARKS: Encamped near Weldon, N.C.

DATE/LOCATION: 11/29/1863, Weldon, N.C. MOVEMENT: Marched by railroad to Petersburg, Va.

DATE/LOCATION: 12/16/1863, Petersburg, Va. MOVEMENT: Marched by railroad back to Weldon, N.C.

DATE/LOCATION: 12/20/1863, Weldon, N.C. MOVEMENT: Marched by railroad to a point near Franklin, Va.

DATE/LOCATION: 12/22/1863, Franklin, Va. MOVEMENT: Marched by railroad to Weldon, N.C. REMARKS: Encamped near Weldon, N.C.

DATE/LOCATION: 1/28/1864, Weldon, N.C. MOVEMENT: Marched by railroad to Goldsboro, N.C., arriving the same day.

DATE/LOCATION: 1/29/1864, Goldsboro, N.C. MOVEMENT: Marched by railroad to Kinston, N.C., arriving the same day.

DATE/LOCATION: 1/30/1864, Kinston, N.C. MOVEMENT: Marched by foot to the vicinity of New Bern, N.C., arriving on 1/31. REMARKS: Regiment participated in Confederate General George Picket's unsuccessful attempt to re-take New Bern from Federal forces on 2/1–2/2/1864.

DATE/LOCATION: 2/3/1864, New Bern, N.C. MOVEMENT: Marched by foot back to Kinston, N.C., arriving on 2/5.

DATE/LOCATION: 2/6/1864, Kinston, N.C. MOVEMENT: Marched by railroad to Weldon, N.C., arriving same day. REMARKS: Encamped near Weldon, N.C.

DATE/LOCATION: 2/25/1864, Weldon, N.C. MOVEMENT: Marched by railroad to Franklin, Va., arriving same day. REMARKS: Encamped near Franklin, N.C.

DATE/LOCATION: 2/27/1864, Franklin, Va. MOVEMENT: Marched by foot through Gates and Pasquotank counties on 2/27 and 2/28 and marched to South Mills, N.C. (near Elizabeth City, N.C.), on 2/29. REMARKS: Regiment participated in the Confederate action at Suffolk, Va. on 3/9/1864 where the Federals were driven out of the town.

DATE/LOCATION: 3/12/1864, Suffolk, Va., vicinity. MOVEMENT: Regiment returned to Weldon, N.C.

DATE/LOCATION: 4/12/1864, Weldon, N.C. MOVEMENT: Regiment moved to vicinity of Tarboro, N.C.

DATE/LOCATION: 4/15/1864, Tarboro, N.C., vicinity. MOVEMENT: Regiment marched to Plymouth, N.C., arriving about 4/17/1864. REMARKS: Regiment participated in Confederate General Robert F. Hoke's capture of Plymouth, N.C. on 4/17 — 4/20/1864.

DATE/LOCATION: 4/21/1864, Plymouth, N.C. MOVEMENT: Regiment marched by foot to Washington, N.C., and then on to New Bern, N.C. REMARKS: Regiment participated in General Hoke's plans to re-take these important Confederate towns. However, Hoke received orders on 5/6/1864 to come with his troops to Petersburg, Va. to fend off a pending Union assault on Richmond, Va.

RICHMOND AND PETERSBURG DEFENSE

DATE/LOCATION: 5/7/1864, New Bern, N.C., vicinity. MOVEMENT: Regiment marched by foot to Kinston, N.C., arriving on the morning of 5/8.

DATE/LOCATION: 5/8/1864, Kinston, N.C. MOVEMENT: Marched by railroad via Goldsboro, N.C., and Weldon, N.C., to a point where the railroad was interrupted some 20 miles south of Stony Creek Station, Va. Marched by foot through the night around the interruption and to Stony Creek Station. Entrained there on 5/10 and marched by railroad to Petersburg, Va., arriving on the same day.

DATE/LOCATION: 5/10/1864, Petersburg, Va. MOVEMENT: Regiment was hurried to Swift Run Creek, Va., and then on to Drewry's Bluff, Va., arriving on 5/11/1864. REMARKS: Regiment immediately engaged in continuous fighting around Drewry's Bluff for the ensuing several days and then was assigned to keep Union General Benjamin Butler's forces bottled-up at Bermuda Hundred.

DATE/LOCATION: 6/4/1864, Drewry's Bluff, Va., vicinity. MOVEMENT: Marched by foot to Bottom's Bridge near Richmond, Va. REMARKS: Encamped near Bottom's Bridge.

DATE/LOCATION: 6/9/1864, Bottom's Bridge near Richmond, Va. MOVEMENT: Marched by foot to Chaffin's Farm, Va., located across the James River from Drewry's Bluff, Va. REMARKS: Encamped near Chaffin's Bluff, Va.

DATE/LOCATION: 6/15/1864, Chaffin's Farm, Va., on the James River. MOVEMENT: Marched by foot through the night crossing the pontoon bridge over the James River and reaching Petersburg, Va. on 6/16. REMARKS: Regiment was instantly thrown into furious fighting then taking place on 6/16 and 6/17/1864 as Confederate General Beauregard defended Petersburg, Va., from heavy Union assaults.

After successfully defending against the Union attacks on Petersburg, Virginia, on June 16 and June 17, 1864, the 25th Regiment N.C. remained in the Petersburg area for the rest of the war. Its troops dug, fortified, and manned the "hideous red" trenches protecting the city throughout the hot summer of 1864 and the bitter cold winter of 1864–1865. Deprivations, danger, homesickness, and hunger would be constant companions of the mountaineers from western North Carolina; and many were those who could not bear the suffering and chose to go back to their families and the seclusion of the Carolina highlands. The men of the 25th who remained in the ditches participated in the great battles and lesser engagements that were waged during the long Petersburg siege including the battles of the Crater, Weldon Railroad, Fort Stedman, Five Forks, and the final running fights along the Appomattox River.

Chapter Notes

1. Flames of Secession

1. John C. Inscoe and Gordon B. McKinney, *The Heart of Confederate Appalachia: Western North Carolina in the Civil War* (2000), 44.
2. USGenWeb/NC/Henderson/Letters/Edney; Internet Website, http://ftp.rootsweb.com/pub/usgenweb/nc/henderson/letters/edney09.txt.
3. Inscoe and McKinney, *The Heart of Confederate Appalachia*, 43.
4. Hunter Library, Western Carolina University, Special Collections: Civil War Letters, Cathey Collection; Joseph Cathey to the Rev. L.F. Siler, February 22, 1861.
5. James McPherson, *Battle Cry of Freedom* (1988), 274.
6. Inscoe and McKinney, *The Heart of Confederate Appalachia*, 60.
7. McPherson, *Battle Cry of Freedom*, 276.
8. Ibid., 277.
9. Ibid., 283.

2. Farmers Join the Rebellion

1. James McPherson, *Battle Cry of Freedom* (1988), 62.
2. John W. Moore, *Roster of North Carolina Troops in the War Between the States* (1882).
3. Foster A. Sondley, *A History of Buncombe County* (1977, reprint), 690.
4. Garland S. Ferguson, "Twenty-Fifth Regiment," *Histories of the Several Regiments and Battalions from North Carolina, In the Great War 1861–1865*, vol. 2, Walter Clark, ed. (1901), 291.
5. Ibid.

3. The Fabric of the 25th Regiment N.C.

1. Information regarding county origins of troops compiled from John W. Moore's *Roster of North Carolina Troops* (1882).
2. Information regarding officers' service records taken from Louis H. Manarin's *North Carolina Troops, 1861–1865, A Roster*, vol. 7, *Infantry* (2004).

4. Carolina Coastal Defense

1. Major A. Gordon, "Quartermaster-General's Department," *Histories of the Several Regiments and Battalions from North Carolina, In the Great War 1861–1865*, vol. 1, Walter Clark, ed. (1901), 23.
2. Shelby Foote, *The Civil War: A Narrative, Fort Sumter to Perryville* (1958), 352.
3. Hunter Library, Western Carolina University, Special Collections: Civil War Letters, Estes Collection; R.P. Crawford to Wm. Eastis [or Estes], September 29, 1861.
4. E.A. Pollard, *The Lost Cause* (1867), 194.
5. Time-Life Books, *The Blockade: Runners and Raiders* (1983) 34.
6. *Pensacola News Journal*, "Confederate General Lee's Letters Sell for $61,000," September 30, 2007.
7. William L. Barney, *The Making of a Confederate* (2008), 60.
8. Ibid., 58.
9. Douglas S. Freeman, *Robert E. Lee: A Biography*, vol. 1 (1934), 615.
10. Clifford Dowdey, *Lee* (1965), 176.
11. Hunter Library, Western Carolina University, Special Collections: Civil War Letters, Parris Collection, Major Wiley Parris to Jane Parris, February 6, 1862.
12. Garland S. Ferguson, "Twenty-Fifth Regiment," *Histories of the Several Regiments and Battalions from North Carolina, In the Great War 1861–1865*, vol. 2, Walter Clark, ed. (1901), 291.
13. Peter M. Chaitin, *The Coastal War* (Time-Life Books), 37.
14. Mary Boykin Chesnut, *A Diary from Dixie* (1905).
15. Ibid.
16. John C. Inscoe and Gordon B. McKinney, *The Heart of Confederate Appalachia: Western North Carolina in the Civil War* (2000), 113.
17. Douglas S. Freeman, *Lee's Lieutenants*, vol. 1 (1942), 273.
18. Louis H. Manarin, *North Carolina Troops, 1861–1865, A Roster*, vol. 7, *Infantry* (2004).
19. George C. Underwood, "Twenty-Sixth Regiment," *Histories of the Several Regiments and Battalions*, vol. 2, Walter Clark, ed. (1901), 303.
20. Hunter Library: Paris Collection, Major Wiley Parris to Jane Parris, April 13, 1862.

5. Seven Days Battles Around Richmond

1. James McPherson, *Battle Cry of Freedom* (1988), 461.
2. Douglas S. Freeman, *Robert E. Lee: A Biography*, vol. 2 (1934), 107.

3. Shelby Foote, *The Civil War: A Narrative, Fort Sumter to Perryville* (1958), 471.
4. Garland S. Ferguson, "Twenty-Fifth Regiment," *Histories of the Several Regiments and Battalions from North Carolina, In the Great War 1861–1865*, vol. 2, Walter Clark, ed. (1901), 291.
5. General Robert Ransom, Official Report of Brigade's Actions at King's School House or Oak Grove, and Battle of Malvern Hill, O.R., Series I, Vol. XI, Part II, Chapter 23, 792.
6. General Benjamin Huger, Official Report of Division's Actions at King's School House or Oak Grove, O.R., Series I, Vol. XI, Part II, Chapter 23, 787.
7. Freeman, *Robert E. Lee*, 92.
8. James McPherson, *Battle Cry of Freedom* (1988), 466.
9. Ibid.
10. Ibid., 467.
11. Ibid., 468.
12. Ibid.
13. Huger, Official Report of Division's Actions at King's School House or Oak Grove, 788.
14. McPherson, *Battle Cry of Freedom*, 467.
15. Frances H. Kennedy, *The Civil War Battlefield Guide* (1998), 98, 101.
16. McPherson, *Battle Cry of Freedom*, 469.
17. Ferguson, *Histories of the Several Regiments and Battalions*, 291.
18. Douglas S. Freeman, *Lee's Lieutenants*, vol. 1 (1942), 602.
19. W.N. Rose, "Twenty-Fourth Regiment," *Histories of the Several Regiments and Battalions from North Carolina In the Great War 1861–1865*, vol. 2, Walter Clark, ed. (1901), 269.
20. General Robert Ransom, Official Report of Brigade's Actions at King's School House or Oak Grove, and Battle of Malvern Hill, O.R., Series I, Vol. XI, Part II, Chapter XXIII, 795.
21. Ferguson, "Twenty-Fifth Regiment," 291.

6. Maryland Campaign

1. Clayton Marlow, *Matt W. Ransom: Confederate General from North Carolina* (1996), 55.
2. Garland S. Ferguson, "Twenty-Fifth Regiment," *Histories of the Several Regiments and Battalions from North Carolina, In the Great War 1861–1865*, vol. 2, Walter Clark, ed. (1901), 291.
3. Ibid.
4. George C. Underwood, "Twenty-Sixth Regiment," *Histories of the Several Regiments and Battalions*, vol. 2, Walter Clark, ed. (1901), 303.
5. Ferguson, "Twenty-Fifth Regiment," 291.
6. General John Walker, Official Report of Division's Actions at Harpers Ferry on 9/17/1862, O.R., Series I, Vol. XIX, Part I, Chapter XXXI, 913.
7. Ibid.
8. Douglas S. Freeman, *Lee's Lieutenants*, vol. 2 (1942), 201.
9. Walter Clark, "Sharpsburg (or Antietam)," *Histories of the Several Regiments and Battalions*, vol. 5, Walter Clark, ed. (1901), 71.
10. Ferguson, "Twenty-Fifth Regiment," 291.
11. W.N. Rose, "Twenty-Fourth Regiment," *Histories of the Several Regiments and Battalions from North Carolina In the Great War 1861–1865*, vol. 2, Walter Clark, ed. (1901), 269.
12. William H.S. Burgwyn, "Thirty-Fifth Regiment," *Histories of the Several Regiments and Battalions*, vol. 2, Walter Clark, ed. (1901), 591.

13. General Robert Ransom, Official Report of Brigade's Actions at Sharpsburg on 9/17/1862, O.R., Series I, Vol. XIX, Part I, Chapter XXXI, 920.
14. General John Walker, Official Report of Division's Actions at Sharpsburg of 9/9–9/19/1862, O.R., Series I, Vol. XIX, Part I, Chapter XXXI, 917.
15. Clark, "Sharpsburg (or Antietam)," 71.
16. Archibald Rutledge, *My Colonel and His Lady* (1937), 88.
17. Ferguson, "Twenty-Fifth Regiment," 291.
18. Ibid.

7. Heights of Fredericksburg

1. Douglas S. Freeman, *Robert E. Lee: A Biography*, vol. 2 (1934), 461.
2. General Robert E. Lee's Report on Battle of Fredericksburg, April 10, 1863, O.R., Series I, Vol. XXI, Chapter XXXIII, 551.
3. General James Longstreet's Report on Battle of Fredericksburg, Va., December 14, 1862, O.R., Series I, Vol. XXI, Chapter XXXIII, 571.
4. James McPherson, *Battle Cry of Freedom* (1988), 571.
5. General Lafayette McLaws' Report on Battle of Fredericksburg, December 30, 1862, O.R., Series I, Vol. XXI, Chapter XXXIII, 581.
6. Freeman, *Robert E. Lee*, 462.
7. General James Longstreet's Report on Battle of Fredericksburg, December 11–15, 1862, O.R., Series I, Vol. XXI, Chapter XXXIII, 570.
8. General Robert E. Lee's Report on Battle of Fredericksburg, April 10, 1863, O.R., Series I, Vol. XXI, Chapter XXXIII, 625.
9. General Robert Ransom's Report on Battle of Fredericksburg, December 20, 1862, O.R., Series I, Vol. XXI, Chapter XXXIII, 625.
10. General Robert Ransom's Report on Battle of Fredericksburg, December 20, 1862, O.R., Series I, Vol. XXI, Chapter XXXIII, 626.
11. Garland S. Ferguson, "Twenty-Fifth Regiment," *Histories of the Several Regiments and Battalions from North Carolina, In the Great War 1861–1865*, vol. 2, Walter Clark, ed. (1901), 291.
12. Louis H. Manarin, *North Carolina Troops, 1861–1865, A Roster*, vol. 7, *Infantry* (2004).
13. Douglas S. Freeman, *Lee's Lieutenants*, vol. 2 (1942), 368.
14. General Robert Ransom's Report on Battle of Fredericksburg, December 20, 1862, O.R., Series I, Vol. XXI, Chapter XXXIII, 627.
15. William H.S. Burgwyn, "Thirty-Fifth Regiment," *Histories of the Several Regiments and Battalions*, vol. 2, Walter Clark, ed. (1901), 591.
16. Ferguson, "Twenty-Fifth Regiment," 291.

8. Back to North Carolina

1. William H.S. Burgwyn, "Thirty-Fifth Regiment," *Histories of the Several Regiments and Battalions*, vol. 2, Walter Clark, ed. (1901), 591.
2. Hunter Library, Western Carolina University, Special Collections: Civil War Letters, Cathey Collection, J.W. Killian to Joseph Cathey, January 19, 1863
3. Clayton Marlow, *Matt W. Ransom: Confederate General from North Carolina* (1996), 72.
4. Dispatch from Brig. Gen. R.B. Garnett to Maj. Gen. D.H. Hill, April 15, 1863, O.R., Series I, Vol. XVIII, Chapter XXX, 988.

5. Shelby Foote, *The Civil War: A Narrative, Fredericksburg to Meridian* (1963), 259.
6. Louis H. Manarin, *North Carolina Troops, 1861–1865: A Roster*, vol. 7, *Infantry* (2004).
7. Dispatch from Major-General J.G. Foster to Maj. Gen. H.W. Halleck, June 2, 1863, O.R., Series I, Vol. XVIII, Chapter XXX, 363.
8. Dispatch from Colonel George H. Pierson to Lt. Colonel Southard Hoffman, Assistant Adjutant General, May 27, 1863, O.R., Series I, Vol. XVIII, Chapter XXX, 365.
9. Dispatch from General R.E. Lee to General D.H. Hill, May 28, 1863, O.R., Series I, Vol. XVIII, Chapter XXX, 1075.
10. Clayton Marlow, *Matt W. Ransom: Confederate General from North Carolina* (1996), 77.
11. Garland S. Ferguson, "Twenty-Fifth Regiment," *Histories of the Several Regiments and Battalions from North Carolina, In the Great War 1861–1865*, vol. 2, Walter Clark, ed. (1901), 291.
12. James McPherson, *Battle Cry of Freedom* (1988), 585.
13. Shelby Foote, *The Civil War: A Narrative, Fredericksburg to Meridian* (1963), 306.
14. Ibid., 282–314.
15. Dispatch from President Jefferson Davis to R.E. Lee, May 29, 1863, O.R., Series I, Vol. XVIII, Chapter XXX, 1077.
16. Dispatch from S. Cooper to Maj. Gen. D.H. Hill, April 30, 1863, O.R., Series I, Vol. XVIII, Chapter XXX, 1032.
17. Dispatch from J.A. Seddon to Gen. D.H. Hill, May 6, 1863, O.R., Series I, Vol. XVIII, Chapter XXX, 1047.
18. Dispatch from Gen. R.E. Lee to Maj. Gen. D.H. Hill, May16, 1863, O.R., Series I, Vol. XVIII, Chapter, XXX, 1063.
19. Clayton Marlow, *Matt W. Ransom: Confederate General from North Carolina* (1996), 78.
20. Wilson Library, University of North Carolina, Southern Historical Collection, Documenting the American South: Lenoir Family Papers, Jos. C. Norwood to Walter Lenoir, August 13, 1863.
21. Louis H. Manarin, *North Carolina Troops, 1861–1865, A Roster*, vol. 7, *Infantry* (2004).
22. Ibid.
23. Marlow, *Matt W. Ransom*, 86.
24. Burgwyn, "Thirty-Fifth Regiment," 591.
25. Robert D. Graham, "Fifty-Sixth Regiment," *Histories of the Several Regiments and Battalions*, vol. 3, Walter Clark, ed. (1901), 313.
26. Shelby Foote, *The Civil War: A Narrative, Red River to Appomattox* (1974), 115.
27. Peter M. Chaitin, *The Coastal War* (1984), 96.
28. Graham, "Fifty-Sixth Regiment," 313.

9. Richmond and Petersburg Front

1. Clayton Marlow, *Matt W. Ransom: Confederate General from North Carolina* (1996), 97.
2. Garland S. Ferguson, "Twenty-Fifth Regiment," *Histories of the Several Regiments and Battalions from North Carolina, In the Great War 1861–1865*, vol. 2, Walter Clark, ed. (1901), 291.
3. William H.S. Burgwyn, "Thirty-Fifth Regiment," *Histories of the Several Regiments and Battalions*, vol. 2, Walter Clark, ed. (1901), 591.
4. Marlow, *Matt W. Ransom*, 99.
5. Shelby Foote, *The Civil War: A Narrative, Red River to Appomattox* (1974), 264.
6. Ibid., 5, 21, 123.
7. Dispatch from C.A. Dana, June 9, 1863, O.R., Series I, Vol. XXXVI, Part I, Chapter XLVIII, 93.
8. Burgwyn, "Thirty-Fifth Regiment," 591.
9. Ferguson, "Twenty-Fifth Regiment," 291.
10. Burgwyn, "Thirty-Fifth Regiment," 591.
11. Douglas S. Freeman, *Lee's Lieutenants*, vol. 3 (1942), 535.
12. Mary Boykin Chesnut, *A Diary from Dixie* (1905).
13. Ferguson, "Twenty-Fifth Regiment," 291.

10. Siege of Petersburg

1. Douglas S. Freeman, *Lee's Lieutenants*, vol. 3 (1942), 538.
2. Report from General B.R. Johnson, July 12, 1864, O.R., Series I, Vol. XL, Part I, Chapter LII, 779.
3. Report from General B.R. Johnson, July 27, 1864, O.R., Series I, Vol. XL, Part I, Chapter LII, 785.
4. Report from General B.R. Johnson, July 15, 1864, O.R., Series I, Vol. XL, Part I, Chapter LII, 780.
5. Report from General B.R. Johnson, July 23, 1864, O.R., Series I, Vol. XL, Part I, Chapter LII, 784.
6. Reports from General B.R. Johnson, July 20–28, 1864, O.R., Series I, Vol. XL Part I, Chapter LII, 783, 786.
7. James McPherson, *Battle Cry of Freedom* (1988), 759.
8. Report from Lieutenant General U.S. Grant, August 1, 1864, O.R., Series I, Vol. XL, Part I, Chapter LII, 17.
9. Garland S. Ferguson, "Twenty-Fifth Regiment," *Histories of the Several Regiments and Battalions from North Carolina, In the Great War 1861–1865*, vol. 2, Walter Clark, ed. (1901), 291.
10. B.F. Dixon, "Additional Sketch—Forty-Ninth Regiment," *Histories of the Several Regiments and Battalions*, vol. 3, Walter Clark, ed. (1901), 151.
11. Douglas S. Freeman, *Lee's Lieutenants*, vol. 3 (1942), 748–749.
12. University of West Florida Library Special Collections Department, *Harper's Weekly*, August 6, 1864.
13. W.N. Rose, "Twenty-Fourth Regiment," *Histories of the Several Regiments and Battalions from North Carolina In the Great War 1861–1865*, vol. 2, Walter Clark, ed. (1901), 269.
14. Thomas R. Roulhac, "Forty-Ninth Regiment," *Histories of the Several Regiments and Battalions from North Carolina, In the Great War 1861–1865*, vol. 3, Walter Clark, ed. (1901), 125.
15. Robert D. Graham, "Fifty-Sixth Regiment," *Histories of the Several Regiments and Battalions*, vol. 3, Walter Clark, ed. (1901), 313.
16. Archibald Rutledge, *My Colonel and His Lady* (1937), 86.
17. Ferguson, "Twenty-Fifth Regiment," 291.
18. William H.S. Burgwyn, "Thirty-Fifth Regiment," *Histories of the Several Regiments and Battalions*, vol. 2, Walter Clark, ed. (1901), 591.
19. James McPherson, *Battle Cry of Freedom* (1988), 811.
20. Ibid., 815.
21. Mary Boykin Chesnut, *A Diary from Dixie* (1905).
22. Clayton Marlow, *Matt W. Ransom: Confederate General from North Carolina* (1996), 115.
23. Graham, "Fifty-Sixth Regiment," 313.
24. Dispatch from General B.R. Johnson to Col. G.W. Brent, Assistant Adjutant General, August 11, 1864, O.R., Series I, Vol. XLII, Chapter LIV, 887.
25. Report from General B.R. Johnson to Col. G. W. Brent, Assistant Adjutant General, August 6, 1864, O.R., Series I, Vol. XLII, Chapter LIV, 885.
26. Report from General B.R. Johnson to Major Duncan, Assistant Adjutant General, Dec. 2, 1864, O.R., Series I, Vol. XLII, Chapter LIV, 918.
27. Dispatch from General B.R. Johnson to Major Dun-

can, Assistant Adjutant General, Dec. 31, 1864, O.R., Series I, Vol. XLII, Chapter LIV, 925.
  28. Dispatch from General B.R. Johnson to Col. G.W. Brent, Assistant Adjutant General, Sept. 17, 1864, O.R., Series I, Vol. XLII, Chapter LIV, 892.
  29. Ibid.
  30. Dispatch from General R.E. Lee to Secretary of War, James A. Seddon, Feb. 24, 1865, O.R., Series I, Vol. XLVI, Part II, Chapter LVII, 1143.
  31. Dispatch from General R.E. Lee to Secretary of War John C. Breckenridge, Feb. 24, 1865, O.R., Series I, Vol. XLVI, Part II, Chapter LVII, 1254.
  32. Douglas S. Freeman, *Lee's Lieutenants*, vol. 3 (1942), 621.
  33. Dispatch from General R.E. Lee to Secretary of War James A. Seddon, Feb. 8, 1865, O.R., Series I, Vol. XLVI, Part II, Chapter LVII, 1209.
  34. James I. Robertson, *Tenting Tonight* (Time-Life Books, 1984), 153.
  35. John C. Inscoe and Gordon B. McKinney, *The Confederate Appalachia: Western North Carolina in the Civil War* (2000), 114.
  36. Douglas S. Freeman, *Lee's Lieutenants*, vol. 3 (1942), 624.
  37. Wm. H.S. Burgwyn, An Address on the Military Services of General Matt W. Ransom, Delivered in the Senate Chamber at Raleigh, N.C., on May 10, 1906.
  38. Dispatch from John C. Breckenridge to President Jefferson Davis, February 18, 1865, O.R., Series I, Vol. XLVI, Part II, Chapter LVII, 1239.
  39. Graham, "Fifty-Sixth Regiment," 313.
  40. Rutledge, *My Colonel and His Lady*, 87.

11. War on the Home Front

  1. Wilson Library, University of North Carolina, Southern Historical Collection, Documenting the American South: Lenoir Family Papers, letter from Louis to Mame, May 2, 1861.
  2. James McPherson, *Battle Cry of Freedom* (1988), 429.
  3. Ora Blackmun, *Western North Carolina: Its Mountains and Its People to 1880* (1977), 340.
  4. John C. Inscoe and Gordon B. McKinney, *The Heart of Confederate Appalachia: Western North Carolina in the Civil War* (2000), 111.
  5. Ibid., 113.
  6. W. Clark Medford, *The Early History of Haywood County* (1961), 142.
  7. Inscoe and McKinney, *The Heart of Confederate Appalachia*, 114.
  8. Douglas S. Freeman, *Lee's Lieutenants*, vol. 3 (1942), 624.
  9. Inscoe and McKinney, *The Heart of Confederate Appalachia*, 110.
  10. Ibid., 114.
  11. John Preston Arthur, *Western North Carolina: A History From 1730 to 1913* (1914), 603.
  12. Inscoe and McKinney, *The Heart of Confederate Appalachia*, 130.
  13. Arthur, *Western North Carolina: A History*, 604.
  14. Inscoe and McKinney, *The Heart of Confederate Appalachia*, 127.
  15. Ibid., 131.
  16. Ibid., 128.

12. A Journey Ended

  1. Archibald Rutledge, *My Colonel and His Lady* (1937), 94.
  2. Garland S. Ferguson, "Twenty-Fifth Regiment," *Histories of the Several Regiments and Battalions from North Carolina, In the Great War 1861–1865*, vol. 2, Walter Clark, ed. (1901), 291.
  3. Ibid.
  4. Douglas S. Freeman, *Lee's Lieutenants*, vol. 3 (1942), 671.
  5. Ibid., 718.
  6. Richard Wheeler, *Witness to Appomattox* (1989), 87.
  7. Freeman, *Lee's Lieutenants*, 721.
  8. Louis H. Manarin, *North Carolina Troops, 1861–1865, A Roster, vol. 7, Infantry* (2004).
  9. Bryan Grimes, "Surrender at Appomattox," *Histories of the Several Regiments and Battalions*, vol. 5, Walter Clark, ed., 247.
  10. Rutledge, *My Colonel and His Lady*, 95.
  11. Freeman, *Lee's Lieutenants*, 740.
  12. Ulysses S. Grant, *Personal Memoirs: Ulysses S. Grant* (1999), 580.
  13. Wheeler, *Witness to Appomattox*, 231.
  14. Ferguson, "Twenty-Fifth Regiment," 291.
  15. Mary Boykin Chesnut, *A Diary from Dixie* (1905).
  16. Abram Joseph Ryan (1838–1886), "The Conquered Banner," *New York Freedman's Journal* (June 24, 1865).

13. Conclusion

  1. *Diary and Reminiscences of W.H. Hargrove* (Sweetwater, TX: Hattie Rue and Dale Campbell, 1938).

14. Casualties of War

  1. Garland S. Ferguson, "Twenty-Fifth Regiment," *Histories of the Several Regiments and Battalions from North Carolina, In the Great War 1861–1865*, vol. 2, Walter Clark, ed. (1901), 291.

15. The Colonel and His Lieutenant

  1. Garland S. Ferguson, "Twenty-Fifth Regiment," *Histories of the Several Regiments and Battalions from North Carolina, In the Great War 1861–1865*, vol. 2, Walter Clark, ed. (1901), 291.
  2. Mary Bray Wheeler and Genon Hickerson Neblett, *Chosen Exile* (1942), 111–113.
  3. Ibid., 120.
  4. Ferguson, "Twenty-Fifth Regiment," 291.
  5. Letter from Henry M. Rutledge to the Honorable L. P. Walker, Confederate Secretary of War, undated, with note indicating receipt on April 21, 1861, the National Archives, document image found at www.footnote.com.
  6. Letter from L. B. Northrop to the Honorable L. P. Walker, Confederate Secretary of War, dated May 17, 1861, with note indicating receipt on May 20, 1861, the National Archives, document image found at www.footnote.com.
  7. Letter from Wm. Porcher Miles to the Honorable L. P. Walker, Confederate Secretary of War, dated April 17, 1861, with note indicating receipt on April 19, 1861, the National Archives, document image found at www.footnote.com.
  8. Archibald Rutledge, *My Colonel and His Lady* (1937), 91.
  9. Ibid., 93–94.
  10. Ibid., 88.
  11. Ferguson, "Twenty-Fifth Regiment," 291.

12. Rutledge, *My Colonel and His Lady*, 94.
13. Ferguson, "Twenty-Fifth Regiment," 291.
14. Rutledge, *My Colonel and His Lady*, 95.
15. Ferguson, "Twenty-Fifth Regiment," 291.
16. G.S.S., "Sketches of the Santee River," *American Monthly* (October 1836).
17. Rutledge, *My Colonel and His Lady*, 130.
18. Ibid., 28–36.
19. Ibid., 45.
20. Rutledge, *My Colonel and His Lady*, 97.
21. W. Clark Medford, *Early History of Haywood County* (1961), 21.
22. Cathey and Hargrove genealogy records compiled by Tony Jones.
23. Ibid.
24. Thomas Erwin, *Thomas Erwin History*, n.d., n.p.
25. W.C. Allen, *Annals of Haywood County North Carolina* (1935), 148.
26. W.H. Hargrove, *Diary and Reminiscences of W.H. Hargrove* (Sweetwater, TX: Hattie Rue and Dale Campbell, 1938).
27. W.H. Hargrove's personal notebook, dated 1866.
28. Cathey and Hargrove genealogy records compiled by Tony Jones.

BIBLIOGRAPHY

Books

Allen, W.C. *The Annals of Haywood County North Carolina.* Spartanburg, SC: North Carolina State Library, 1935. Reprinted. Reprint Company, 1977.

Arthur, John Preston. *Western North Carolina: A History from 1730 to 1913.* Asheville, NC: The Edward Buncombe Chapter of the Daughters of the American Revolution of Asheville, North Carolina, 1914. Reprinted. Johnson City, TN: Overmountain Press, 1996.

Barney, William L. *The Making of a Confederate: Walter Lenoir's Civil War.* New York: Oxford University Press, 2008.

Blackmun, Ora. *Western North Carolina: Its Mountains and Its People to 1880.* Boone, NC: Appalachian Consortium Press, 1977.

Chaitin, Peter M. *The Civil War: The Coastal War.* Alexandria, VA: Time-Life Books, 1984.

Chesnut, Mary Boykin. *A Diary from Dixie.* New York: D. Appleton, 1905.

Clark, Walter, ed. *Histories of the Several Regiments and Battalions from North Carolina, In the Great War 1861–1865,* Vol. 2. Goldsboro, NC: Nash Brothers Book and Job Printers, 1901.

Dowdey, Clifford. *Lee.* New York: Bonanza Books, 1965.

Esposito, Brigadier General Vincent J. *The West Point Atlas of War: The Civil War.* New York: Tess Press, 1995.

Foote, Shelby. *The Civil War, A Narrative: Fort Sumter to Perryville.* New York: Random House, 1958, 1974.

———. *The Civil War, A Narrative: Red River to Appomattox.* New York: Random House, 1963.

Freeman, Douglas Southall. *Lee's Lieutenants: A Study in Command.* Vols. 1–3. New York: Scribner's, 1942.

———. *R.E. Lee: A Biography.* Vols. 1–4. New York: Scribner's, 1934.

Grant, Ulysses S. *Personal Memoirs: Ulysses S. Grant.* New York: The Modern Library, New York, 1999. First published 1887 by Charles Webster.

Inscoe, John C., and Gordon B. McKinney. *The Heart of Confederate Appalachia: Western North Carolina in the Civil War.* Chapel Hill and London: University of North Carolina Press, 2000.

Jordan, Weymouth T., Jr. *North Carolina Troops, 1861–1865: A Roster.* Vol. 7, *Infantry.* North Carolina Office of Archives and History, 1979, 1991, 2004. Reprinted by Broadfoot Publishing, Wilmington, North Carolina.

Kennedy, Frances H. *The Civil War Battlefield Guide.* New York and Boston: Houghton Mifflin, 1988.

Marlow, Clayton Charles. *Matt W. Ransom: Confederate General from North Carolina.* London and Jefferson, NC: McFarland, 1996.

McCaslin, Richard B. *Portraits of Conflict: A Photographic History of North Carolina in the Civil War.* Fayetteville: University of Arkansas Press, 1997.

McPherson, James. *Battle Cry of Freedom: The Civil War Era.* New York: Oxford University Press, 1988.

Medford, W. Clark. *The Early History of Haywood County.* Asheville, NC: Miller Printing, Asheville, 1961.

Moore, John W. *Roster of North Carolina Troops in the War Between the States.* Raleigh, NC: Raleigh state printer, 1882.

Pollard, E.A. *The Lost Cause.* New York: E.B. Treat, 1867. Reprinted by Bonanza Books.

Robertson, James I. *The Civil War: Tenting Tonight.* Alexandria, VA: Time-Life Books, 1984.

Rutledge, Archibald. *My Colonel and His Lady.* New York and Indianapolis: Bobbs-Merrill, 1937.

Sondley, Foster A. *A History of Buncombe County North Carolina.* Advocate Printing, 1930. Reprinted in 1977 by Reprint Co., Spartanburg, SC.

Time-Life Books. *The Blockade: Runners and Raiders.* Alexandria, VA: Time-Life Books, 1983.

United States War Department. *The War of the Rebellion: A Compilation of the Official Records of the*

Union and Confederate Armies. Washington, DC: Government Printing Office, 1881 (date of commencement of issue).

Wheeler, Mary Bray, and Genon Hickerson Neblett. *Chosen Exile: The Life and Times of Septima Sexta Middleton Rutledge, American Cultural Pioneer.* Nashville, TN: Rutledge Hill Press, 1980.

Wheeler, Richard. *Witness to Appomattox.* New York: Harper & Row, 1989.

Special Collections

Hunter Library, Western Carolina University, Special Collections, Civil War Letters: Cathey, Paris and Estes Collections.

John C. Pace Library Special Collections Department, University of West Florida, Collection of *Harper's Weekly* publications through the Civil War period.

Wilson Library, University of North Carolina, Southern Historical Collection, Documenting the American South — Lenoir Family Papers.

Newspapers and Magazines

Canton Vindicator, miscellaneous 1908 and 1909 publications on microfilm, North Carolina State Archives and Records, Raleigh, N.C.

"Confederate Gen. Lee's Letters Sell for $61,000." *Pensacola News Journal*, September 30, 2007.

Ray, Fred L. "Fort Stedman." *American Civil War Magazine* (May 2005).

Ross, Kathy. "Haywood History, 1809 — Civil War." *Waynesville Mountain Newspaper,* date 2005.@@@

Other

Erwin, Thomas. *Thomas Erwin History.* N.p., n.d.

Haywood County North Carolina Commissioners' Court Records.

Hargrove, W.H. *Diary and Reminiscences of W. H. Hargrove.* Sweetwater, TX: Hattie Rue and Dale Campbell, 1938.

_____. Personal notebook in the possession of Carroll Jones.

Jones, Tony. Genealogy records of the Cathey and Hargrove families of Haywood County, North Carolina.

Ryan, Abram Joseph (1838–1886). "The Conquered Banner." *New York Freeman's Journal*, June 24, 1865.

INDEX

Numbers in *bold italics* refer to pages with illustrations.

abatis breastworks 122, *130*, 132, *155*
C.S.S. *Albemarle*: at the Battle of Plymouth 110–11; construction of 109, *112*
Allen, W.C. (*The Annals of Haywood County, North Carolina*) 203
Amelia Court House, Va. 161
ammunition *see* guns and ammunition
Anders, John (Company K) 32
Anderson, Richard "Dick" 160
The Annals of Haywood County, North Carolina (Allen) 203
Antietam Run, Sharpsburg, Md. *see* Battle of Antietam
Appomattox Court House, Va.: "Lee's leaving McLean House..." (Waud) *164*; Lee's surrender at (Apr. 9–12, 1865) 161–64, 193; stacking of arms at 165, 193
Appomattox River: Confederate defense lines 121, 127, 134, 137, 179; Lee's escape route *159*, 161, 193
Appomattox Station, Va. 161
Aquia Landing, Union army base at *80*
Arkansas, secession by 10
Army of Northern Virginia (Confederate): desertions from 137; evacuation route *159*; Grant's efforts to destroy 117; headquarters at Petersburg 98; joining of Ransom's Brigade to 51; Lee's attempts to save 153; number of troops, 56; *see also specific battles and actions*
Army of Tennessee (Confederate): at battle of Chickamauga 107; destruction of 133
Army of the Cumberland (Union), at battle of Chickamauga 107
Army of the James (Union), landing of at Bermuda Hundred 114

Army of the Potomac (Union): camp at Aquia Landing *80*; following the First Battle of Manassas 14; refitting of during winter of 1863 98; replacement of Burnside with Hooker 98; replacement of McClellan with Burnside 78; retreat from Chancellorsville/Fredericksburg 102; *see also specific battles and actions*
Ashe County, N.C., volunteers from 9, 13
Asheville, N.C., road to Waynesville from 199
Atlanta, Ga.: Sherman's march toward 107–8; Union capture and destruction of 133
Augusta, Ga., Hargrove's trips to, 205, 208

Barksdale, William 84
Barnard, Jobe D. (Company K) 32
Battery 14, near Petersburg, Union capture of 119
Battle Cry of Freedom (McPherson) 3
Battle of Antietam (Sharpsburg, Md.; Antietam Run) (Sept. 17, 1862): caring for the wounded and dead *173*, *174*; casualties 76–77, 174–75; description of 70–77; fighting at the Dunker Church *61*, 71, *72*; map *74*; Ransom's Brigade at 72–73; the 25th Regiment at 72–73, 190; Union view of 76
Battle of Bottom's Bridge, Va. (July 4, 1863) 104, 117–18
Battle of Cedar Mountain, Va. (August 9, 1862) 64
Battle of Chancellorsville, Va. (May 1–4, 1863): artist's rendering *99*; casualties 103; description 98–104; map *102*
Battle of Chickamauga, Tenn. (Sept. 1863) 107

Battle of Drewry's Bluff, Va. (May 12, 1864): casualties 114, 173–74; description 114–15; the 25th Regiment N.C. at 192
Battle of First Bull Run (First Manassas) (July 21, 1861), 14, 44
Battle of Five Forks, Va. (April 1, 1865): casualties, prisoners 21, 27, 38, 159, *160*; description 158–60; Hargrove's capture at 203; the 25th Regiment N.C. at 158–60, 192–93
Battle of Fort Stedman, Va. (March 25, 1865): artist's rendering *155*; casualties 32, 158, 203; description 153–56; strategy used in capture of 157–58; the 25th Regiment N.C. at 155–57, 192
Battle of Frayser's Farm, Va., during Seven Days Battles (June 30, 1862) 57
Battle of Fredericksburg, Va. (Dec. 13, 1862): casualties 21, 23, 30, 32, 84, 88, 89, 177–78; Longstreet's report on 86–88; map *85*; opening attack 84; the 25th Regiment N.C. at 88–89, 191; valor of Confederate forces during 86; view of as Confederate success 90
Battle of Gaines Mill, Va., during Seven Days Battles (June 27, 1862) 56
Battle of Gettysburg, Pennsylvania (July 1863) 106
Battle of King's School House (Oak Grove), Va., during Seven Days Battles (June 26, 1862): casualties 25, 55, 172–73, 175; description 52–55; map *54*; Rutledge's leadership at 189; the 25th Regiment N.C. at 55, 57
Battle of Lookout Mountain, Chattanooga, Tenn. (Nov. 1863) 107, *107*

303

Battle of Malvern Hill, Va., during Seven Days Battles (July 1, 1862): artist's rendering *50*; casualties 21, 29, 30, 57, 105, 172–74; description 55–59; Lee's strategy at 57; map *54*; the 25th Regiment N.C. at 59, 189–90
Battle of Mechanicsville, Va. during Seven Days Battles (June 26, 1862) 55–56
Battle of Plymouth, N.C. (Apr. 17–20, 1864): casualties 111; description 110–11; map *110*; the 25th Regiment N.C. at 111, 191
Battle of Port Royal Sound, S. C. (Nov. 7, 1861) *35*, 36
Battle of Savage's Station, Va., during Seven Days Battles (June 29, 1862) 57
Battle of Sayler's Creek, Va. (April 6, 1864) 161
Battle of Second Bull Run (Second Manassas) (August 29, 1862) 64, 70
Battle of Seven Pines, Va. (May 31–June 1, 1862): description 53–55; Johnston's command at 49; Rutledge's leadership at 189; the 25th Regiment N.C. at 53
Battle of the Crater, Va. (July 30, 1864): casualties 125; explosion of mine below Confederate trenches 125; the 25th Regiment N.C. at 192, 203
Battle of the Weldon Railroad, Va. (Aug. 20–21, 1864): casualties 132; description 131–32; the 25th Regiment N.C. at 192
Beauregard, Pierre G.T. 5, 14, 94, 114, *116*, 118
"Ben Franklin's Club," Pigeon Forks, N.C. 205–6
Bermuda Hundred, Va.: Confederate attack on Union line at 115–16; landing of Army of the James at 114
Bethel Cemetery, near Waynesville, N.C. 211
Bethel schoolhouse, near Waynesville, N.C. 200, 201
Black Mountain Guards *see* Company K
Blackwater River defense 104
Blake, Daniel 184
Blake, Frederick R. (Company H) 12, 30, 188
Blake, Walter (Company H) 30
Blalock, L.M. (Keith) (Company F) 47
Blalock, Samuel ("Sam," Sarah Melinda) (Company F): enlistment and service 46–47; photograph of *46*
Blaylock, James A. (Company F) *22*, 28
blockade runners 35, *42*, 111
Board of Education, Haywood County 210
bombproof shelters: at Drewry's Bluff *63*; in trenches 134

Boone, Harlan A. (Company B) 23, 46
Bottom's Bridge, Va., Ransom's Brigade at 117–18
Brady, Matthew B., portrait of McClellan *51*
Bragg, Braxton 107, 109
Branch, Lawrence 43
Breckenridge, John C. 136, 139
Brompton Mansion (Marye house), Marye's Heights, Va. 81
Brooke rifles 110
Bryan, John Quincy Adams 150
Bryson, Samuel C. (Company C): at Battle of Fredericksburg 81, 89, 191; election as captain 12; election as lieutenant colonel 46; election as major 45; service history 24
Bryson, Thaddeus D. (Company B): election as captain 12; photograph of *22*; service history 21
Bryson, William H. 15
Buckner, Ninevah T. (Company K) 32
"Building Pontoon Bridges at Fredericksburg" (Waud) *81*
Bull Run, first battle of *see* Battle of Manassas, first
Buncombe County, N.C.: Childress family 201; members of Company A from 20; members of Company E from 25; members of Company F from 27; members of Company H from 29; members of Company I from 30; members of Company K from 31; response to attack on Ft. Sumter in 6, 12; volunteers from *19*; *see also* Vance, Zebulon
Buncombe Turnpike 199
Burch, Benjamin (Company G), at Battle of Fort Stedman 156
Burgwyn, Harry, Jr. 64
Burlison, Jesse M. (Company K) 32
Burnett, Ethelred H. (Company F) 28
Burnside, Ambrose: at Battle of Fredericksburg 89; capture of Knoxville 151; capture of Roanoke Island 42; communications problems, delayed actions 43, 83; photograph of *79*; replacement of by Joseph Hooker 98; replacement of McClellan by 78; at Siege of Petersburg 125
Burnsville, N.C.: headquarters of Home Guard at 149; tory attacks in 150
bushwhacker outlier bands, outlaws: attacks by 104–5, 135, 145–46, 151–52; "Bushwhackers Exact a Toll from a Traveler" (Gragg) *148*; reasons for banding together 148–49; tories among 147; use of the 25th Regiment N.C. to counter 105
Butler, Benjamin 113, 114, 192
Byers, Joseph R. (Company H) 30

camp life: bombproof shelters *63*, 134; at Camp Davis, Wilmington, N.C. 34–36; camp diseases 40, 60; at Camp Lee, Grahamville, S.C. 40–41; daily rations 136; in Fredericksburg, Va. 91; at Kinston, N.C. 48; at Martinsburg, W. Va. 77; in the trenches at Petersburg *128*, 129, 133, 134–35
Camps Patton and Clingman, Asheville, N.C.: assembly of Ransom's Brigade at 13–15; impact of news of Bull Run victory at 14; striking camp 16; training at 16, 188, 202
Cane Creek Rifles *see* Company H
Canton (earlier, Pigeon River), N.C.: Hack Hargrove's prominence in 211; name change 211; railroad at 209; wagon roads 199
Canton Vindicator (newspaper) 211
Cape Fear District, Confederate Department of North Carolina 35
captains *see* officers, commissioned
"Capture of Lee's soldiers as they crossed the Potomac" *65*
Carolina Coastal Defense (Sept. 18, 1861–June 15, 1862): blockade runners 41; casualty estimates 171; Lee's strategy 40–41; New Bern area defenses 43–48; Port Royal Sound area defenses 33–42; role of the 25th Regiment N.C. in 191; South Atlantic blockade 38
cartridge box *2*
casualties: official estimates 171–180; quantifying, challenges of 169–70; 25th Regiment, N.C., Ferguson's summary 180–81; *see also* disease; *specific battles*
Cathey, James M. (Company F): death at the Battle of the Crater 125, 203; photograph of *22*; service record 28
Cathey, James Webster 208
Cathey, Joseph F. 205–6
Cathey, Joseph T. (Company F): death 207; election as captain 46; employment of Hargrove after the war 207; formation of Company F 202; mill and general store 199–200, 201; photograph of *26*; service with Company F 28; views on secession 8–9; visit with 25th in Petersburg 92–93
Cathey, Lucinda Moore 206, 208
Cathey, William 206
Cathey Cove, N.C. 207
Cedar Mountain, Va., Confederate victory at 64
Chaffin's Bluff, Va., Ransom's Brigade at 118
Chancellorsville, Va., resumption of war at 98
Charleston, S.C.: attack on Ft. Sumter 5; Port Royal Sound area *39*
Charleston & Savannah Railroad: near Grahamville, S.C. 40; strate-

gic importance 37; troop transport on 40
Chatham Plantation, Fredericksburg, Va. 78
Chattanooga, Tenn.: battle of Chickamauga 107; Battle of Lookout Mountain *107*
Cherokee County, N.C.: members of Company D from 24; members of Company E from 25; members of Company G from 28; 25th Regiment N.C. troops from 12, *19*
Chesapeake and Ohio Railroad, efforts to destroy bridges used by 67, 67–68
Chesnut, James, Jr. 43, 140
Chesnut, Mary Boykin (*A Diary from Dixie*): abandonment of hopes for Confederate victory 135–39; on the Conscription Act 44; on defeat of the Confederacy 165; on defeat of the Confederate Army of Tennessee 133; on financial difficulties faced by civilians 120; on the lack of Southern ports 133; on loss of New Bern and threat to Goldsboro 43; on pending foreign recognition of the Confederacy 64; portrait of 120; as source of information 3; on Yankee tactics and Confederate conscription 108
Chickahominy River: positioning of Union troops on 52; role in Peninsular Campaign 49
Childress, Samuel 201
Chilhowee plantation, near Knoxville, Tenn. 185–86
Chimborazo Hospital, Richmond, Va. 115
City Point, Va., Union prison at 203
The Civil War: A Narrative (Foote) 3
civilian life: loss of able-bodied men to the war effort 145–46; poverty among farmers 105; scarcity and privation 135, 150; in South, during summer of 1864 119–20; vulnerability to attack 151; "yeopon tea" 40; *see also* bushwhacker outlier bands, outlaws; farmers, small
Clark, Walter 72–73
Clarke, Col., at Battle of Malvern Hill 57–58
Clay County, N.C.: members of Company G from 28; 25th Regiment N.C. troops from 12, *19*
Clayton, William L. (Company H) 30
Clingman, Thomas Lanier: background and political career 15–16; dispute with Mitchell 16; dispute with Yancey 16; election as colonel 15; enlistment and service 15; photographs of *15, 22*; promotion to brigadier general 45, 46, 188; reelection as colonel 45; support for secession 7, 147

Clingman's Dome 16
clothing, shoes and blankets: "A Confederate Soldier standing barefoot..." (Taber) *2*; difficulties of traveling with 77; Johnson's complaints about barefoot soldiers 134; lack of, among Army of Northern Virginia 136, 170, 175; lack of, desertions and 66; from loved ones 91; production of, as focus of Confederate economy 119; sale of, among deserters 139; sources and provision of 33–34
Cobb, Thomas R.R. 88–89
Cold Mountain (Frazier) 203
Colquitt, Alfred Holt 115
commissioned officers *see* officers, commissioned
Company A (Edney Greys) 12; commissioned officers 21, 46; raising, enlisting and mustering 20; troop origins 20–21
Company B (Jackson Guards): commissioned officers 21–23, 46; location and captain 12; raising, enlisting and mustering 21; skirmishes with Yankees during stay at Camp Lee 41; troop origins 21
Company C (Haywood Invincibles) 12; commissioned officers 24, 46; raising, enlisting and mustering 23; troop origins 23
Company D (George's Guards) 12; commissioned officers 24–25, 46; raising, enlisting and mustering 24; troop origins 24
Company E (Transylvania Volunteers) 12; commissioned officers 25–27, 46; raising, enlisting and mustering 25
Company F (Haywood Highlanders) 12; at the Battle of Drewry's Bluff 114; at the Battle of the Crater 203; casualties 163; commissioned officers 28, 46, 201; formation of 202; Hargrove's joining of 202; raising, enlisting and mustering 27; sick leave among, while at Camp Lee 40; troop origins 27; Walter Lenoir 105; woman soldier in 47
Company G (Highland Guards) 12; at the Battle of Fredericksburg 178; commissioned officers 29, 46; raising, enlisting and mustering 28; at the Seven Days Battle 174; troop origins 28–29; volunteers from Georgia in 18
Company H (Cane Creek Rifles) 12; at the Battle of Fredericksburg 178; commissioned officers 30, 46, 188; execution of deserters from 137; raising, enlisting and mustering 29; Rutledge's joining of 188; at the Seven Days Battle 174; troop origins 29–30
Company I (Pisgah Guards) 12; commissioned officers 31, 46; raising, enlisting and mustering 30; troop origins 30–31

Company K (Black Mountain Guards) 12; commissioned officers 31–32, 46; raising, enlisting and mustering 31; troop origins 31
Coneby Creek, N.C. 111
Confederate Department of North Carolina, Cape Fear District 35
Confederate Invalid Corps 169
"Confederate Skirmishers" (Sheppard) *115*
Confederate soldiers *10*
Conscription Act of 1862 17; desertion among 147; dissatisfaction of, as one reason for Conscription Act 143; dissatisfaction of, following capture of Harpers Ferry 69–70; hardships experienced by 2; highlander volunteers 17; moral of, during winter of 1864–65 133; pride among *12*; return home following surrender *164*; *see also* desertions, deserters
Confederate States Army: artist's rendering of Confederate encampment *41*; commissioning of Rutledge in 188; "Confederate Troops Leaving for the Front" (Gragg) *34*; "Confederates Attacking a Battery on Malvern Hill" (Thulstrap) *50*; "Confederates Surrendering Colors and Muskets" (Waud) *162*; Department of North Carolina 104; Department of North Carolina-South Carolina-Georgia-Florida 39; Department of Virginia and North Carolina 93; desertions from 136–37; disintegration of in April 1865 160; reorganization of 45; western Military District of North Carolina 151
Confederate States of America: conditions in at end of the war 168; economic stress in 119–20; evacuation of government from Richmond 160–61; formation of 202; insolvency of, impact on military operations 139; morale in at start of war 5–9, 142–43; morale in during early 1862 44; morale in during summer of 1864 119–20; morale in during winter of 1864–1865 133; records kept by 18; tariffs 104–5
Conscription Act of 1862 17; amendment of to include Confederate congressmen, 1864 108; factors leading to 143; impact of, in western North Carolina 146; long-term impact on home front 104–5; loopholes and exemptions from 143–45, 169; requirements of 44; response to among soldiers 44–45; revisions eliminating privilege of hiring substitutes 145
Cook, George S., portrait of Daniel Harvey Hill *93*
Cooke, James W., captain of the CSS *Albemarle* 109, *111*

Cooke, John R. 88, 104
Cooke's Brigade (Twenty-seventh Regiment N.C.): Ransom's assumption of command over 81; at retaking of Gum Swamp outpost 97
Cooper, Andrew (Company A) 21
Coosawhatchie, S.C., Lee headquarters at 38–39
cotton, seizing and destruction of: during capture of Savannah 133; at New Bern 53
County Commissioner, Hack Hargrove's service as 208–9, 210
County Surveyor, Hack Hargrove's service as 209, 210
Crawford, R.P. (Company B) 35
Crittenden, John J. 9
Cromwell, Zadoc R. (Company D) 24
"The CSS *Albemarle* Under Construction in a Cornfield" (M.H. Hoke) *112*
Culpepper Court House, Va. 77
Cunningham, Solomon (Company H) 30, 46
Custis, Mary 79

Davis, Jefferson: assignment of Lee to head Carolina coastal defenses 36; Breckenridge report to on army's financial problems 139; Dearing's letter to requesting a commission 45–46; D.H. Hill letter to complaining about Lee 103; escape attempt from Richmond 160, 165; naming of Lee as commander of Confederate army 49; photograph of *9*; *see also* Conscription Act of 1862
Davis, Mrs. Jefferson 120
Davis house, battle at (Aug. 21, 1864) 132
Dearing, St. Clair: army experience 16; election as lieutenant colonel 15; request for commission in a cavalry unit 45–46; retirement from command 45; training troops at Camp Patton 188
Deaver, Elijah 200
Deaver, James P. (Company E) 27
Democrat, N.C., enlistment of Company K at 31
Department of North Carolina, assignment of Ransom's Division to 104
Department of North Carolina-South Carolina-Georgia-Florida, establishment of 39
Department of Virginia and North Carolina, assignment of Longstreet to 93
desertions, deserters: among Confederate *vs.* Union troops 147; Confederate, illustration showing *143*; escalation of, at the end of the war 2, 133, 135–37, 146; executions of 137; during the fall of 1862 135; and lawlessness on the N.C. home front 104, 105–6, 151;

during Maryland campaign 66; quantifying, challenges of 170; from Ransom's Brigade 117; role of Home Guard in arresting 150; the 25th Regiment N.C. 181–82
A Diary from Dixie (Chestnut) 3
Dillard, Lynch M. (Company B) 23
disease: camp diseases 60; deaths from, among the 25th Regiment N.C. 165, 171; deaths from at Camp Lee, Grahamville, S.C. 40; deaths from, at Drewry's Bluff 60; deaths from, during the Maryland Campaign 175; Hargrove's bouts with 202–3; Hargrove's hospitalizations for 202; in the trenches at Petersburg 129
District of North Carolina, Second Brigade, District of Pamlico 43
draft evaders: as bushwhackers 148, 152; hiding by 147; hunting of 104, 146–47
Drewry's Bluff, Va.: fortifications 50–51, *62*, *63*; Ransom's Brigade at 60, 117–18; "Rebel Encampment" at *62*; strategic importance 60; view of from James River *61*; *see also* Battle of Drewry's Bluff
Dunker Church, Sharpsburg, Md.: effects on following Battle of Antietam *72*; Union charge at during Battle of Antietam *61*, 70, 71

Early, Jubel: at Battle of Chancellorsville 102; at defense of Fredericksburg 99
East Fork area, Pigeon Valley, 199
East Tennessee: cavalry raids from 151; "East Tennessee Unions gather around the U.S. Flag" *144*; Union support in 148; western North Carolina fears of invasion from 151
eastern Cherokee Nation 148
eastern North Carolina: in 1863 (map) *95*; federal raiding parties 104
Edmonson, Basil B. (Company A) 55
Edmonston, Rufus A. (Company G) 29
Edney, Baylis M. (Company A) 12, 21
Edney, John B. (Company A) 21
Edney, John C. (Company A) 21
Edney, Thomas A. 6
Edney Greys *see* Company A
Edneyville, N.C., enlistment of Company A at 20
Elliott, Stephen 125
Elliott's Brigade, explosion of Union mine beneath 125–26
Ellis, John, call for North Carolina volunteers 11
Enfield rifle *2*
England, William M.(Company E) 27
England, Confederate efforts to win support from 64

executions: of bushwhackers 149; of deserters 137
"Explosion of Yankee mine under Confederate trench works at Petersburg" *126*

Faison, P.F., command responsibility for Ransom's Brigade 122
Falmouth, Va., Burnside's army at 78
farmers, small: conscript evaders, bushwhackers among 105; enthusiasm about enlisting 11, 17; food supplied by 94; in Pigeon Valley, N.C. 199–200; views on secession 7
Farragut, David 44
Federal Expeditionary Forces, capture of Roanoke Island *42*
Ferguson, Ebed J. (Company F) 114
Ferguson, Garland Sevier (Company F): on characteristics of 25th Regiment volunteers 11; on the defense of Petersburg 118–19; enlistment and service 15; final tally of 25th Regiment casualties 163–65; Hargrove's rescue of 1; Hargrove's visit to in Petersburg hospital 204; in impact of camp diseases on the 25th 60; on Matt Ransom 97; photographs of *15*, *26*; on picket duties and other activities at Camp Lee 41; on plans to invade Maryland 66; regimental history 1–3; report on skirmish near the Globe Tavern 132; report on the Battle at King's School House 53; report on the Battle of Antietam 73; report on the Battle of Fort Stedman 155–57; report on the Battle of Fredericksburg 89–90; report on the Battle of Malvern Hill 57, 189–90; report on the Battle of the Crater 125; rescue of, by William Hargrove 203; on Robert Ransom 61–63; service history 28; summary of 25th Regiment N.C. casualties 180–81; tribute to the dead 168; wounding of, at Battle of Fort Stedman 158
15th Volunteers North Carolina 15
Fifty-sixth Regiment N.C.: at the Battle of Plymouth 111; in command rotation for Ransom's Brigade 122; in Ransom's Brigade 64, 93; at skirmish near Gum Swamp, N.C. 96–97
"Firing from the Petersburg Trenches" *138*
First Corps (Confederate), at Fredericksburg, Va. 78, 82–83
Fisher, Locus F. (Company B) 23
Flat Rock, N.C.: attacks on Johnstone's property 151; Henry Middle Rutledge's burial in 197; Henry Middle Rutledge's childhood in 186; summer community at 184–85

Fletcher, George W. (Company H): appointment as asst. surgeon 15; service history 30
Fletcher, N.C., Henrietta Rutledge's death at 185
Fogg, Mary, care for Rutledge children 185, 186–87
food: at Camp Lee, Grahamville, S.C. 40; exemptions from conscription for food suppliers 145; "Grinding Corn" (Sheppard) *154*; hunger, at end of the war 161; lack of, impact on troops 170; from local farmers 94; in Maryland, as a motive behind Maryland Campaign 64; purchase of from Pamlico River area 94; "Rebel Soldier Feasts Beside a Cornfield" (Gragg) *142*; "Rebels Foraging" (Waud) *90*; "Rebels Roasting Corn" (Waud) *91*; removal of from Washington, N.C. 94; scarcity of, among civilians 150; scarcity of, and desertions 66, 136; seizing of, at Harpers Ferry 69; seizing of, from Washington, N.C. 94; starvation, among the Confederate soldiers 121, 136; in the trenches at Petersburg 129; "yeopon tea" 40
Foote, Shelby (*The Civil War, a Narrative*) 3
Forbes, Edwin: "A Pitchfork Steadies This Wounded Soldier" *168*; "Union Charge at the Dunker Church during Battle of Antietam" *61*; "Union Forces Attacking a Confederate Fort in Front of Petersburg" *118*
Forks of Pigeon, N.C.: community activities 201; 1863 report on conditions at 105; enlisting of Company F at 27; Hargrove's return to after war 203–4; response to Ft. Sumter, secession in 5, 8–9; settlement of 200; *see also* Pigeon Valley, N.C.
Forsyth County, N.C.: members of Company A from 20; 25th Regiment N.C. troops from 19
Fort Beauregard, Port Royal Harbor, S.C.: photograph of *36*; Union capture of 38
Fort Fisher, Wilmington, N.C. 133
Fort Stedman, Petersburg, Va.: Confederate attack on 153–54, *155*; interior *156, 157*; Union counter-attack 155
Fort Sumter, Charleston, S.C.: attack on 5–6, *6*; surrender of, Rutledge's presence at 188
Fort Walker, Port Royal Harbor, S.C., Union capture of, *37*
fortifications: abatis breastworks 122, *130*, 132, *155*; at Camp Lee 41; at Drewry's Bluff 50–51, 60, *62*, *63*; around Petersburg 122; use of sap rollers for building 123–24; *see also* trenches, Petersburg

Forty-eighth N.C. Regiment, in Ransom's Brigade 61
Forty-ninth N.C. Regiment: participation in command rotation for Ransom's Brigade 124; in Ransom's Brigade 61, 93
Foster, J.G., on Union attack at Gum Swamp 96
4th Military District of South Carolina 36
France, Confederate efforts to win support from 64
Francis, John W. (Company D): commendations following Battle of Malvern Hill 59, 190; election as captain 12; election as major 46; service history 24
Franklin, N.C. (Company G) 28
Frayser's Farm (Glendale), battle at during Seven Days Battles 57
Frazier, Charles (*Cold Mountain*) 203
Fredericksburg, Va.: Confederate defense forces at 78; impact of war on 78, 90; Union capture and destruction of *84*, 84; view from across the Rappahannock River *80*; wounded soldiers at *176*; *see also* Battle of Fredericksburg
Freeman, Douglas Southall (*Lee's Lieutenants*) 3
Freeman, Joseph H. (Company A) 21
Freeman, Wesley N. (Company C): election as adjutant 15; election as captain 46; service history 24
furling the flag, as symbol of surrender 165–66

Gaines' Mill, Va., fortifications and battles at during Seven Days Battles 56
Garnett, R.B. 94
Garrison, Thomas M. (Company K) 32
General Hospital 4, Richmond, Virginia 202–3
Gentry, James 9–10
Gentry, Joseph R. (Company K) 32
George's Guards *see* Company D
Georgia: members of Company D from 24; members of Company E from 25; members of Company G from 28; members of Company I from 30; 25th Regiment N.C. troops from, 12, 18, *19*
Gettysburg, Pa. *see* Battle of Gettysburg
Glendale, Va., 1862 battle at 57
Globe Tavern, Davis House, 1864 battle at 131–32
Goldsboro, N.C.: destruction of railroad bridge at 92; 1862 defense of 43; North Carolina Division command post at 93
gopher holes, in trenches 127, 134, *138*
Gordon, John B. 153
Gordon's Corps: attachment of

Ransom's Brigade to 160; escape to Appomattox 161
Gracie, Archibald 119, 124, 134
Grady, William S. (Company G): election as captain 12, 46; mortal wound at Battle of the Crater 125; service history 29
Gragg, Ron: "Bushwhackers Exact a Toll from a Traveler" *148*; "Confederate Troops Leaving for the Front" *34*; "Rebel Soldier Feasts Beside a Cornfield" *142*
Grahamville, S.C.: Rutledge's service at 188; strategic importance 39–40; 25th Regiment N.C. move to 36; Union capture and destruction of 133
Grant, Ulysses S.: on Battle of the Crater 125; on Butler's position at Bermuda Hundred 116; character 116; at Chattanooga, Tenn. *107*, 107; as commander of the Army of the Cumberland 107; courtesies shown surrendering Confederate troops 161; at Petersburg 161; photograph of 122; promotion to head of Union armies 116; strategy decisions 117, 121, 131–32; at Vicksburg, Miss. 106; western battles 44
Graves, William H. (Company E) 25
Grimes, Bryan: division of, attachment to Ransom's Brigade 160; soldiers' farewell to 161
"Grinding Corn" (Sheppard) *154*
gristmills, Pigeon Valley, N.C. 199, 200
Gudger, James Cassius Lowry 22
Gum Swamp, N.C., skirmish at (May 22, 1863) 96–97
guns and ammunition: artillery on Loudon Heights, W. Va. 69; Brooke rifles 110; Enfield rifle *2*; Grahamville, S.C. garrison 39; hand grenades 123; mines 124–25, 127, 134; mortars 122, 124, 127, *131*, 134; Parrott guns 69; at Petersburg 122, 134; scarcity and shortages of in Confederate army 122–23; scavenging for 122; seized by Union, during Battle of Plymouth 111; seized by Union, during capture of Savannah 133; Travis fire 124; *see also* sharpshooters, snipers

habeas corpus rights, maintenance of in North Carolina 150
Halsey, Andrew D. (Company D) 25
Hampton Plantation, McClellanville, S.C.: current status 197; efforts to revitalize 193–95; hospitality offer at 195; photograph of *196*; rice production on 194; Rutledge home at 184
hand grenades 123
Hargrove, Alfred Franklin 200
Hargrove, Althea Caroline 201

Hargrove, Amanda 201
Hargrove, Augustus Alexander 201, 205, 208
Hargrove, Augustus Columbus 201, 205, 208
Hargrove, Ellen Childress 201, 208
Hargrove, Florence Leona 207
Hargrove, James Burton (Jim) 207, 211–12
Hargrove, John 200
Hargrove, Joseph Alexander 207
Hargrove, Joseph Franklin 201, 205
Hargrove, Mary (Mollie) 201
Hargrove, Nancy Louisa Cathey (Nannie, Mrs. William Harrison) 206–8, 210
Hargrove, Theodore Augustus 208, 211
Hargrove, Thomas 201
Hargrove, William Harrison ("Captain Hack") (Company F): acts of bravery 1; background 3; "Ben Franklin's Club" 205–6; birth and childhood 201; capture, during Battle of Five Forks 159, 198, 203; community/political activities 208–9, 211; death and burial 211; education and work on homestead 201–2; election to North Carolina General Assembly 210; employment by Joseph Cathey 207; enlistment and service 197–98, 202; farming career 207–8; hospitalizations during the war 129, 202; marriage and family 206, 210; membership in Pigeon River Masonic Lodge 210–11; newspapers founded and edited by 211; photographs of *26*, *198*, *211*; promotions 203; property owned by 207–8; as railroad agent 209–10; real estate transactions 211; rescue by Garland Ferguson 203; response to war experience 204; return home at end of war 168, 203–4; service history 28; support for the Republican Party 211; travels 205–6, 208
Hargrove, William Manson 200, 206
Hargrove, William Walter 208
Harpers Ferry, W. Va.: Confederate investment and capture of 65–70, *71*; strategic importance 67, 69; view of *68*
Hartgrove *see under* Hargrove
Hawkins, Joseph B. (Company G): at Battle of Fort Stedman 156; at Battle of the Weldon Railroad 132; service history 24
Hayes, John R. (Company G) 29
Haywood County, N.C.: Board of Education 210; members of Company C from 23; members of Company E from 25; members of Company F from 27; members of Company G from 29; railroad in 209; response to attack on Ft. Sumter in 5; settlement of 199; 25th Regiment N.C. troops from

11, 12, *19*; views about secession in 8, 202
Haywood Enterprise (newspaper) 211
Haywood Highlanders *see* Company F
The Heart of Confederate Appalachia: Western North Carolina in the Civil War (Inscoe and McKinney) 3
Heintzelman, Samuel 53
Henderson (later Buncombe) County, N.C.: bushwhacker attacks in 151; Flat Rock summer community 184–85; members of Company A from 20; members of Company C from 23; members of Company E from 25; members of Company H from 29; members of Company K from 31; 25th Regiment N.C. troops from 12, *19*
Henley, Abram L. (Company E) 27
Hensley, James A. (Company K) 32
Herbert, William H. (Company D) 25
Heth, Henry 132
Highland Guards *see* Company G
highlanders, mountaineers: avoidance of service by 146–47; occupations of 17; *see also* volunteers, highlander (mountaineers); western North Carolina
Hill, Ambrose Powell (A.P.): at the Battle of Antietam 70, 76; at the Battle of Mechanicsville 55; Ransom's Brigade support for 121; role during the Seven Days Battles 52
Hill, Daniel Harvey (D.H.): at the Battle of Antietam 76; complaints about casualties 103; at Gum Swamp battle 97; photograph of *93*; role during the Seven Days Battles 52; at the siege of Washington, N.C. 93–94; support for North Carolina troops 93, 104
Hilton Head Island, S.C., Union capture of 36, 38, *38*
Hoke, M.H., "The CSS *Albemarle* Under Construction in a Cornfield" *112*
Hoke, Robert F. (Hoke's Brigade): assignment to the Army of Northern Virginia 116; at the Battle of Drewry's Bluff 115; at the Battle of Plymouth 109–10; photograph of *109*; role in putting down unrest in Wilkes County, N.C. 151; role in Washington, N.C. defenses 113
Holmes, T. H., during defense of Richmond 50–51
Home Guard (Guard for Home Defense) 147; establishment of 149; ineffectiveness of 150–52
home guard militia: deserters and bushwhackers among 141; use of in defense of Petersburg and Richmond 124

Hood, John Bell: at the Battle of Antietam 76; Confederate Army of Tennessee command 133
Hood, William S. 75
Hooker, Joseph: at the Battle of Chancellorsville 101–2; at the Battle of Lookout Mountain 107; replacement of Burnside by 98
Hot Springs, N.C., response to bushwhackers and deserters in 105–6
Howell, Foster B. (Company I) 31
Howell, George W. (Company I): election as captain 12; service history 31
Huger, Benjamin: at the Battle of Malvern Hall 57; praise for Rutledge and the 25th Regiment N.C. 55, 189; Ransom's Brigade's support of 52; role in defense of Richmond 53; role during the Seven Days Battles 52, 56
Hunnicutt, Thomas H. (Company G) 29
Hyatt, Thaddeus C.S. (Company F): death during Warm Springs expedition 178; service history 28

Icard Station, Morganton, N.C., march to 33
Inscoe, John C. (*The Heart of Confederate Appalachia*) 3

Jackson, Benjamin F.H. (Company G) 29
Jackson, Thomas "Stonewall": at the Battle of Antietam 73; at the Battle of Chancellorsville 100–101; at the Battle of Fredericksburg 84; at the Battle of Mechanicsville 55; at the capture of Harpers Ferry 69; on morale 143; mortal wounding, death of *101*, 101; performance problems 57; photograph of *100*; role during the Seven Days Battles 52; during the Shenandoah Valley campaign 64; strategy decisions 100
Jackson County, N.C.: members of Company B from 21; members of Company C from 23; members of Company F from 27; members of Company G from 29; members of Company I from 30; 25th Regiment N.C. troops from 12, *19*
Jackson Guards *see* Company B
James River: Drewry's Bluff *61*, *63*; Harrison's Landing 57–58; ironclads on 160; strategic importance 49, 50, 56, 60, 155, 192; Union crossing and use of 114, 117–18, 174
Jenkins, A.J., brigade of 104
Johnson, Andrew 149, 165
Johnson, Bushrod R.: assignment of Ransom's Brigade to 116, 127; casualty reports by 134; complaints about casualties 122–23; defense of Petersburg & Norfolk Railroad 121–22; on desertions

136–37, 147; on mining activities during the Siege of Petersburg 134; punishment of Rutledge for lax discipline 135; relieving of from command 160
Johnson's Island, Oh., Union prison camp 159, 203
Johnston, Joseph: actions against McClellan 49; at the first Battle of Manassas 14; North Carolina forces under 153; surrender to Sherman 165; wounding, replacement of with Lee 49
Johnstone, Andrew 151
Johnstone, Elliott 151
Johnstone, Francis W. (Company E): election as captain 12; service history 25
Jones, Clinton A. 15
Jones, Edmund W. 11
Jones, John B. 133

Keith, J.A. 149
Kenansville, N.C.: strategic importance 93; 25th Regiment N.C. move to 92
Kentucky, refusal to provide troops to Lincoln 10
Killian, J.W. 92–93
King's School House, Va.: battle at during Seven Days Battles 53, 189; casualties at 172–73
Kinston, N.C.: Ransom's Brigade at 45, 48; 25th Regiment N.C. move to 43; 25th Regiment N.C. reorganization at 45–48
Knoxville, Tenn., battles at 151

Lane, Thomas P. (Company H) 30
Lee, Fitzhugh 160
Lee, Robert E.: audacity 55, 102–3; on concerns about condition of the troops 136; Department of North Carolina-South Carolina-Georgia-Florida 39; on desertions 135–36; devotion to among Confederate soldiers 63, 161; final order 161–62; headquarters at Coosawhatchie, S.C. 38–39, 40; importance of Fredericksburg to 78–79; Maryland campaign 64–65; at Petersburg and Richmond defenses 119; photograph of *50*; praise for Stonewall Jackson 101; replacement of Johnston as commander of the Confederate States Army 49; request for support from Ransom's Brigade 103; respect of troops for 40, 139–40; response to Peninsular Campaign 52, 142–43; on skirmish at Gum Swamp 97; South Carolina command 36, 40–41; strategy decisions 49–50, 78–79, 106, 99–100, 102, 114, 153; surrender at Appomattox,–63, *164*, 193; tribute to people of Fredericksburg 79–81; victory at Gaines' Mill 56; visit to the 25th Regiment N.C. at Petersburg 130; at West Point 45

Lee's Lieutenants (Freeman) 3
Lenoir, Thomas Isaac (Company F): election as captain 12; Hargrove's work for 201; service history 28
Lenoir, Walter, letter to about lawlessness in Caldwell County 105
Leslie's Division, Ninth Army Corps (Union), at Petersburg 119
Lexington, Ky., Hargrove's trip to 205
lieutenants *see* officers, commissioned
Lincoln, Abraham: assassination 165, 168; assignment of McClellan to head Army of the Potomac 43–44; call for militiamen by 9–10, 11, 147, 166; 1864 reelection 133; Lee's efforts to pressure 64; photograph of *9*; replacement of Burnside with Hooker 80, 98–99; replacement of McClellan with Burnside 78; replacement of Rosecrans with Grant 116, 122; response to defeat at Manassas 14; responses to 1860 election of 7–9; worries about military performance 56, 64, 76
living quarters *see* camp life
Long, A.J. 206
Long, Samuel M. (Company B) 23
Longstreet, James: actions near Williamsburg, Va. 49; assessment of Grant 116–17; at the Battle of Antietam 73; at the Battle of Fredericksburg 84, 86–88; command of the Department of Virginia and North Carolina 93; efforts to recapture Knoxville 151; First Corps of 78; joining of Walker's forces to 65; Ransom's promotion to division command under 81; role during the Seven Days Battles 52
looting, seizing of property: by bushwhacker bands 105, 151; following Gum Swamp skirmish 96; at Fredericksburg 84, at Harpers Ferry 69–70; in Madison County, N.C. 149; at Washington, N.C. 94
Loudon Heights, W. Va., occupation of by Walker's Division 68, *68*, 69
Love, James R. 165
Love, Matthew N. (Company A): on the Conscription Act 45; election as captain 46; service history 21; surrender at Appomattox 163
Luther, Andrew A. (Company I) 31

Macon County, N.C.: members of Company B from 21; members of Company D from 24; members of Company G from 28; members of Company I from 30; volunteers from 12, *19*
Madison County, N.C.: members of Company E from 25; members of Company K from 31; 25th Regiment N.C. troops from *19*; use of the 25th Regiment to counter lawlessness in 105–6, 149, 151
Madison Court House, Va., transfer of Walker's Division to 77
Magruder, John B.: request for support from Ransom's Brigade 57–58; role during the Seven Days Battles 52, 56
Malvern Hill, Va.: battle at 57–58; casualties at 172–73; *see also* Battle of Malvern Hill
Manassas, Va.: first battle of Bull Run 13–14, 44; second battle of Bull Run 64, 70, 105
Manson, William 201
maps: Battle of Antietam *74*; Battle of Chancellorsville *102*; Battle of Fredericksburg *85*; Battle of Malvern Hill *54*; Battle of Plymouth *110*; eastern North Carolina *95*; Evacuation Route of the Army of Northern Virginia *159*; Port Royal Sound including Grahamville *39*; Siege of Petersburg *123*; Seven Days Battles *54*; 25th Regiment N.C. majors theaters of operation *14*; 25th Regiment N.C. movement during the Civil War *13*; 25th Regiment N.C., troop origins *20*
Marlow, Clayton (*Matt W. Ransom: Confederate General from North Carolina*) 3
Marr, William J. (Company G) 29
Marshall, N.C., bushwhacker raids in 149
Martin, James 33
Martinsburg, W. Va., encampment at 77
Marye, John L. 81
Marye house *86*
Marye's Heights, Va.: battles at 102, 191; Union attack on, Dec. 1862 84; *see also* Battle of Chancellorsville; Battle of Fredericksburg
Maryland Campaign (Aug 26, 1862 Oct 31, 1862): casualties 174–75; dissension among troops about 66; Lee's strategy 64–65, 70; *see also* Battle of Antietam; Harpers Ferry, W. Va.
Masons 210–11
Matt W. Ransom: Confederate General from North Carolina (Marlow) 3
Maxwell, Andrew C. (Company A) 21
McAfee, Lee M., command of Ransom's Brigade 124
McCallum, Andrew, "Rebel troops returning home after surrender" *164*
McClellan, George: appointment as commander of the Army of the Potomac 14; at the Battle of Mechanicsville 55–56; at the Battle of Sharpsburg. 70; miscalculations by 56, 58; Peninsular Campaign 43–44, 49, 56, 58; photograph of *51*; replacement of by

Burnside 78; during the Seven Days Battles 50
McClellanville, S.C., Rutledge summer home at 196
McDowell, John 199
McElroy, John W., Home Guard command 149, 150
McGruder, John B. 57
McIver, John M. 201
McKinney, Gordon B. (*The Heart of Confederate Appalachia*) 3
McKinney, Mary 201
McLaws, Lafayette: at the Battle of Antietam 70, 76; at the Battle of Fredericksburg 78; at the capture of Harpers Ferry 69; on valor of the defenders of Sunken Road 84
McLean House, Appomattox Court House, Va. **164**
McPherson, James (*Battle Cry of Freedom*) 3
Meade, George: strategy against the Army of Northern Virginia 117; strategy during Battle of Gettysburg 106
Mechanicsville, Va., assault on Union forces at during Seven Days Battles 55
Middleton, Arthur 184
Middleton, Henry 184
Middleton Place plantation, Charleston, S.C. 186
Miles, William Porcher 188
militia companies, Appalachian: assembly and organization of 13–14; enlistments in 12; training 12–13, 16; *see also* 25th Regiment N.C.; volunteers, highlander (mountain soldiers)
Miller, Andrew J. (Company E) 27
mines: Confederate use of 134; impact on Confederate morale 127, 134; Union use of 124–25
Mississippi Rebel sharpshooters 84
Mitchell, Elisha 16
money, decreasing value of in the South 105, 119–20
Monocacy River railroad bridge: photograph showing **67**; Walker's Division efforts to destroy 67–69
Monroe, James 78
Moore, James D. (Company F) 47
Moore, John W. 12, 18
Moore, Robert P. (Company I) 31
Moore's farm, Cathey Cove, N.C. 207
Morgan, William Y. (Company I): election as captain 46; service history 31
Morganton, N.C., railroad at 33
Morris, Thomas L. (Company I) 31
mortars 122, 124, 127, **131**; at the Siege of Petersburg 134
Moss, William W. (Company B) 23
mountain soldiers *see* volunteers, highlander (mountain soldiers)
Mull, Peter K. (Company E) 27
munitions *see* guns and ammunition

Nashville, Tenn., Rutledge family in 185
Neely, Matthew J. (Company E) 27
Nelson, D.B.: "Ben Franklin's Club" 206; Pigeon River Masonic Lodge 210
Netherland, Georgia M. (Company G) 29
New Bern, N.C.: defense of 43, 113; Union capture of 43
New Orleans, La., Union capture of 44
North Carolina: authorization for ten volunteer regiments 11; conditions in during winter of 1865 133; Hargrove's election to state assembly 210; maintenance of habeas corpus rights in 150; secession by 5, 10, 202
North Carolina Defense, Jan 4, 1863–May 8, 1864, casualty estimates 178
North Carolina Office of Archives and History 3
North Carolina Troops 1861–1865: A Roster (North Carolina Office of Archives and History) 3, 170
Northeastern Railroad Line, troop transport on 40
Northrop, L.B. 187–88
Norton, David (Company B) 23
Norwood, John W. **26**

officers, commissioned: Company A (Edney Greys) 21; Company B (Jackson Guards) 21–23; Company C (Haywood Invincibles) 24; Company D (George's Guards) 24–25; Company F (Haywood Highlanders) 28; Company G (Highland Guards) 29; Company H (Cane Creek Rifles) 30; Company I (Pisgah Guards) 31; Company K (Black Mountain Guards) 31–32; remaining, at end of war 163; *see also* Ransom's Brigade; 25th Regiment N.C.; *specific battles*
Official Records of the Union and Confederate Armies 3
O'Hagen, Charles J. 97, 115
Old Capitol Prison, Washington, D.C. 159, 203
"One Confederate Is Equal of Ten Yankees!" (Silvette) **12**
Osborn, Charles L. (Company E) 27
outliers *see* bushwhacker outlier bands, outlaws

parolees at Appomattox 162, 287–88
Parrott guns 69
Patterson, James L. (Company D) 25
Patterson, James R. (Company K) 32
Peninsular Campaign: impact on Confederate morale 141–43; Lee's countering of 50; McClellan's strategy 43–44, 49, 58; spring floods and 49; troop movements during 52
Pennsylvania coal miners, at Petersburg 125
Petersburg, Va.: Confederate command post at 93; defense of, casualty estimates 179–80; fighting near, during Battle of Chancellorsville 102; order of Walker's Division to 77; Ransom's Brigade's role in defense of 114, 117–18; Union strategy at 117–19; *see also* the Siege of Petersburg
Petersburg & Norfolk Railroad, defense of 121
Petersburg-Weldon railroad line, defense of 132
Phinizy, John M. (Company G) 29
picket duty 41, 127, 168, 181
Pickett, George: at the Battle of Five Forks 160; at the Battle of Fort Stedman 155; relieving of from command 160; at the Siege of Petersburg 158
Pigeon River, N.C. *see* Canton (earlier Pigeon River), N.C.
Pigeon River Masonic Lodge 210–11
Pigeon Valley, North Carolina: blacksmiths 200; churches 200; conditions in after the war 204–5; early settlers 198–99, 206–7; farmers, farm work 199; roads 199; winter of 1872 207
Pisgah Guards *see* Company I
"A Pitchfork Steadies This Wounded Solider" (Forbes) **168**
Pleasants, Henry 125
Plott, Jonathan 201
Plumblee, John S. (Company A) 21
Plymouth, N.C., Confederate recapture of 109–11, 178
Polk County, N.C.: members of Company E from 25; 25th Regiment N.C. troops from **19**
pontoon bridges 78, 81, 83–84
Poor, Julius A. (Company A) 21
Pope, John 64
Port Royal, S.C.: Fort Beauregard **36**; Fort Walker **37**; Union capture of 37–38
Porter, Fitz-John, at Gaines' Mill 55–56
Potomac River, crossing by Lee's army **65**, 65, **66**
Railroads: defense of 96, 103, 108, 114, 116, 119, 191; destruction of 92, 140; in Haywood County, N.C. 209; strategic importance 36, 43, 94, 103; troop transport on 33–34, 94, 114
Raleigh, N.C.: Hargrove in state assembly at 210; Johnston's surrender to Sherman at 165
Ransom, Matthew W. (Matt): amputation 115; at the Battle of Antietam 73; at the Battle of Drewry's Bluff 115, 192; at the

Battle of Fort Stedman 157; at the Battle of Malvern Hill 58; at the Battle of Plymouth 110–11; deployment to Madison, N.C. 105; photograph of *97*; promotion to head Ransom's Brigade 97, 191; response to a deserter 137–39; surrender at Appomattox 162; *see also* Ransom's Brigade 25th Regiment N.C.

Ransom, Robert, Jr.: background and training 45; at the Battle of Antietam 73–75; at the Battle of Fredericksburg 88–89; at the Battle of Malvern Hill 57–59; concern for people of Fredericksburg 90; conflicts with troops 64; criticisms of 63; defense of Marye's Heights 86, 88; at Gum Swamp skirmish 96; leadership skills 59, 61, 75–76; photograph of *44*; praise for the 25th Regiment, N.C. 55, 73, 75, 89, 190; promotion to brigadier general 45; promotion to division command 81; promotion to major general 97, 104; *see also* Ransom's Brigade

Ransom's Brigade: actions in eastern North Carolina 93; addition of troops to 51, 93; assignment to Johnson's Division 116; attachment of the 25th Regiment N.C. to 44; barefooted soldiers 134; at the Battle of Antietam 73, 75–76; at the Battle of Bottom's Bridge 104; at the Battle of Drewry's Bluff 60; at the Battle of Five Forks 158; at the Battle of Fort Stedman 154–55, 157–58; at the Battle of Fredericksburg 77–78; at the Battle of Plymouth 110; at the Battle of the Weldon Railroad 131–32; in Bermuda Hundred 116; command changes 97, 115, 122, 124, 160, 191, 192; crossing of the Potomac 66; deserters from 117, 137, 147; formation of 45; at Gum Swamp battles 97; integration into Army of Northern Virginia 51, 65, 103–4; at Kinston, N.C. 48; movements of, July 1863 to March 1864 108–9; movements of, summer 1864 117; moves to Petersburg 50, 104, 114; during the Seven Days Battles 52–53, 65; at the Siege of New Bern 113; at the Siege of Petersburg 119, 121–22, 123, 127, 134; size of 117; surrender at Appomattox 162

Ransom's Division: formation of 81; Lee's request for 104

Rappahannock River: Union efforts to cross 77–78, 98; "Union Troops Crossing, Dec. 11–12, 1862" (Waud) *84*; view of Fredericksburg from *80*

Ray, James M. (Company K) 32
Ray, Montrevail 150
Ream's Station, battle at, August 1864 132

"Rebel Picket's Death at Fredericksburg" (Waud) *176*
"Rebel Sharpshooters Firing on Yankee Bridge Builders at Fredericksburg" (Redwood) *82*
"Rebel Soldier Feasts Beside a Cornfield" (Gragg) *142*
"Rebels Behind the Stone Fall at Fredericksburg" (Redwood) *79*
"Rebels Foraging" (Waud) *90*
"Rebels Roasting Corn" (Waud) *91*
"Rebs" (Waub) *18*
Reconstruction 165, 168, 193, 194, 197–98
record keeping, Confederate 170
Redwood, Allen C.: "Rebel Sharpshooters Firing on Yankee Bridge Builders at Fredericksburg" *82*; "Rebels Behind the Stone Fall at Fredericksburg" *79*
Reid, John (Company H) 30
reprieves, for deserters 139
Republican Party: Chicago Platform 9; Hargrove's support for 211
Rice, Isaac (Company B) 23
Rich, Peter M. 15
Richmond, Va.: Confederate defenses 49, 50–51, 60, 114, 121; defense of, casualty estimates 179–80; evacuation of Confederate government and troops from 160–61; Seven Days Battles area (map) *54*; 25th Regiment N.C. service in support of Huger's Division 52–53; Union efforts to capture 44, 49, 78, 113, 114
Richmond & Danville Railroad 209–10
road construction, Pigeon Valley 199
Roanoke Island, N.C., Union capture of 43
Roanoke Island, Union capture of *42*
Roanoke River 109
Roberts, Charles M. (Company K): election as captain 12, 46; service history 31
Robinson, John C. (Company E) 27
Rogers, David (Company B) 23
Rose Hill Plantation, Nashville, Tenn., Rutledge childhood in 185–87
Rosecrans, William, defeat at battle of Chicamauga 107
Roster of North Carolina Troops in the War Between the States (Moore) 12, 18
Rutland, Anna Maria Black 194
Rutledge, Alice Izard 185
Rutledge, Archibald Hamilton ("Archie") 130, 194; descriptions of his father 195–96; tribute to his father 197
Rutledge, Caroline Phoebe 194
Rutledge, "Dictator John" 184
Rutledge, Edward 184, 185
Rutledge, Elizabeth Pinckney (Lise) 185

Rutledge, Emma Fredericka (Minna) 185
Rutledge, Frederick 184, 194
Rutledge, Harriott Horry 194
Rutledge, Harriott Pinckney Horry 185
Rutledge, Henrietta Middleton 184, 185
Rutledge, Henry Middleton ("Boy Colonel"): appointment as second lieutenant 188; assumption of command of 25th Regiment N.C. 46; assumption of command over Ransom's Brigade 115, 192; on attack of Fort Stedman 155; background, lineage 3, 45, 77, 184; at the Battle of Antietam 190; at the Battle of Five Forks 158–59, 192–93; at the Battle of Fort Stedman 192; at the Battle of King's School House 55, 189; at the Battle of Malvern Hill 58–59; at the Battle of Plymouth 191; birth and childhood 185; black servant of, heroism shown during retreat from Sharpsburg 76, 191; childhood and education 185–87; convalescences and furloughs 81, 191; death and burial 197; descriptions of 195–96; election as captain 45; election as colonel 183, 188–89; election as lieutenant colonel 45, 188; election as major 15; enlistment 187–88; establishment of summer community at Flat Rock, N.C. 184–85; later years 195–97; leadership skills 16, 192; Lee's visit to in Petersburg 130; loyalty to the Confederate cause 187–88; marriages and family 194; photographs of *22*, *45*, *189*; punishment of for allowing conversations with Union troops 135; return to South Carolina after the war 193–94; service at Grahamville, S.C. 188; surrender at Appomattox 163; training of troops at Camp Patton 188; in the trenches at Petersburg 192; troops' affection and respect for 77, 183–84, 190–91; on troops' response to surrender 161, 193; typhoid fever 77, 190–91; wounds and injuries 58, 76
Rutledge, Henry Middleton (the colonel's grandfather) 185
Rutledge, Henry Middleton (the colonel's son) 194
Rutledge, Margaret Hamilton Seabrook 194, 197
Rutledge, Mary Pinckney 194
Rutledge, Sarah Henrietta 185
Rutledge, Septima: devotion to Rutledge grandchildren 185, 186; family trips to South Carolina 186; inheritance of Chilhowee plantation 185–86
Rutledge, Thomas Pinckney 194
Ryan, Abram J. 166

St. John Wilderness Church, Flat Rock, N.C. 185, 197
sanitation: at Drewry's Bluff 60; at Petersburg 129, 135
sap rollers 123–24, 134, **137**
Satchwell, Solomon S. 15
Savage's Station, Va., attack on Union forces at during Seven Days Battles 57
Savannah, Ga.: celebration of secession in **8**; Union capture and destruction of 133
Sayler's Creek, Va., battle at 161
Seabrook, Margaret Hamilton 197
secession: Cathey's views on 8–9; following Lincoln's call for troops 10; in North Carolina vs. other Southern states 5–7
Second Brigade, District of Pamlico: reorganization of 45; 25th Regiment N.C. in 43
Seddon, James A.: Lee letter to about desertions 135–36; letter requesting transfer of Ransom's Brigade to Lee 104; Vance letter to about desertions 149; Vance letter to requesting help with deserters 151
Sedgwick, John, at Battle of Chancellorsville 102
Sentelle, R.A. 205–6
Setser, Emanuel G. (Company D) 25
Seven Days Battles, Richmond, Va. area (June 25–Jul 1, 1862): attack on fortifications at Gaines' Mill 56; Battle at Glendale 57; Battle of Frayser's Farm 57; Battle of Gaines Mill 56; Battle of Kings School House (Oak Grove) 25, 52–55, **54**, 172–73, 175 ; Battle of Malvern Hill 21, 29, 30, 55–59, **54**, 105, 172–74, 189–90; Battle of Mechanicsville 55–56; Battle of Savage's Station 57; casualties 58, 59, 105, 172; Lee's leadership at 50, 57; map **54**
Seven Pines, Va. 25th Regiment N.C. first battle near 53
Sharpsburg, Md. see Battle of Antietam
sharpshooters, snipers: at the Battle of Antietam 75, 76, 201; at the Battle of Chancellorsville 101; at the Battle of Fredericksburg 81, **82**, 84; at the Battle of Plymouth 111; at the Siege of Petersburg 122, 123, 127, 134, 192; casualties from, at Drewry's Bluff 170
Shelton, Samuel P.C. (Company B) 23
Shelton, Stephen J. (Company C) 24, **26**
Shelton Laurel Massacre 149
Shenandoah Campaign 55
Sheppard, William L.: "Confederate Skirmishers" **115**; "Grinding Corn" **154**
Sheridan, Phil 158
Sherman, William Tecumseh: at Battle of Lookout Mountain 107; capture of Atlanta and Savannah 133; Johnston's surrender to 165; march through Georgia 107–8, 117
Shipman, Andrew (Company E) 27
ships and boats: ironclad gunboats 58, 60, 110–11, 160; steam ships, supplies brought by 35, 94
shoes see clothing, shoes and blankets
Siege of Petersburg, Va. (June 1864–April 1865): artist's rendering **131**; Battle of the Crater 120; Battle of the Weldon Railroad 131–32; casualties 123, 134, 179–80; Confederate morale during 139–40; desertions 135–39, 147; Grant's strategy during 153; life in the trenches 127–31, 133–40; map **123**; the 25th Regiment N.C. at 120, 192; Union sap rollers and mines 123–25
Siler, L.F. 8–9
Silvette, David ("One Confederate Is Equal of Ten Yankees!") **12**
Sixth Carolina, impact of Union mine explosion on 125
Sixty-fourth Regiment N.C. 149
Sixty-ninth Regiment N.C. 146
slaves, slavery: freed, at Hampton Plantation 194; Rutledge's body servant 76, 191; services to the 25th Regiment N.C. 40; slaveholder benefits from Conscription Law 145; 36°30' demarcation line for 9
Smith, Lewis J. (Company C) 24
"A Soldier's Dream" (Stuhrman) **182**
South Carolina: coastal defenses 36; life in following surrender 165; members of Company E from 25; members of Company G from 28; prominence of Rutledge and Middleton families in 184; 25th Regiment N.C. troops from 18, **19**; see also Carolina Coastal Defense
Southern Historical Collection: Documenting the American South 3
U.S.S. *Southfield* 110
Special Collections — Civil War Letters 3
Stanton, Edward 56
Starvation: among the civilian population 46; among Confederate troops 69, 136, 139, 161, 170; see also food
Stokes County, N.C., members of Company D from 24
Strange, William J. (Company D) 25
Stringfield, W.W. 145
Stuart, J.E.B. (Jeb): at Battle of Chancellorsville 101–2; at Battle of Gettysburg 106; command of Jackson's Corps 101; intelligence work at Chancellorsville 100; reconnaissance rides 51, 53; visit to Ransom's Brigade during Battle of Antietam 73
Stuhrman, Jack, "A Soldier's Dream" **182**
substitutes, hiring of, under Conscription Act 145
Suffolk, Va., defeat of black Union soldiers at 109
Sunken Road (Telegraph Road), near Fredericksburg, Va.: battles at 84, 102, 191; Longstreet's First Corps fortifications along 82–83; photographs showing **87**; see also Battle of Fredericksburg
supplies, equipment: at Camp Davis 35; clothing production and supplies 33–34; role of blockade runners 42; role of railroads 52, 94; role of steam ships and boats 35, 94; see also clothing, shoes and blankets; food; guns and ammunition
surrender see Appomattox surrender

Taber, Walton, "portrait of a barefoot Confederate soldier" **2**
Tatham, Leander B. (Company D): election as captain 46; service history 24
Tennessee: members of Company A from 20; secession convention 10; 25th Regiment N.C. troops from 18, **19**
Thirty-fifth Regiment N.C.: at the Battle of Antietam 71–75; at the Battle of Malvern Hill 58; at the Battle of Plymouth 111; deployment during Battle of Malvern Hill 58; inclusion in Ransom's Brigade 45, 51, 65, 93, 97; promotion of Matt Ransom from 97; in Ransom's Brigade 55, 61, 93; at the retaking of Harpers Ferry 71–72
Thomas, George 133
Thomas, William Holland 148; surrender at Waynesville, N.C. 165
Thrash, Augustus B. (Company I) 31
Thulstrap, Thure de **50**
tories (unionists): among bushwhacker bands 147; efforts to avoid conscription 146–47; as outlaws 148, 150–52; skirmishes with 108; in Tennessee **144**, 148; in western North Carolina 105, 141, 150
training, drilling: at Camp Davis 36; at Camp Lee 41; at Camps Patton and Clingman 13, 16, 188, 202
Transylvania County, N.C.: members of Company A from 20; members of Company E from 25; 25th Regiment N.C. troops from 12, **19**
Transylvania Volunteers see Company E
traverses 127, **128**

Travis fire 124
trenches, at Petersburg: abatis breastworks 130; conversations between Union and Confederate soldiers 135; living conditions 122, 127, 128, 133, 170; wicker gabions 129
trenches, Petersburg see fortifications
Turbyfill, Elkanah 150
Twenty-fourth Regiment N.C.: at the Battle of Antietam 73; at the Battle of Fredericksburg 83; at the Battle of Malvern Hill 57–58; at the Battle of Plymouth 111; diversion from Ransom's Brigade 73; inclusion in Ransom's Brigade 51, 65, 93
25th Regiment N.C.: actions against bushwhackers and tories 105–6, 151; actions during Carolina Coastal Defense 171; actions during North Carolina Defense 178; appending of 15th Volunteers, N.C. to 15; attachment to Department of N.C., Second Brigade, District of Pamlico 43; attachment to 4th Military District of South Carolina 36; attachment to Ransom's Brigade 44–45, 93, 192; at the Battle of Antietam 70–71, 73, 77, 175; at the Battle of Bottom's Bridge 104; at the Battle of Drewry's Bluff 114, 192; at the Battle of Five Forks 158; at the Battle of Fort Stedman 155–57, 158, 192; at the Battle of Fredericksburg 82–83, 88–89, 178; at the Battle of King's School House 53, 55, 189; at the Battle of Malvern Hill 57–58; at the Battle of Plymouth 110–11; at the Battle of the Crater 125–26, 192; at the Battle of the Weldon Railroad 132, 192; at Camp Davis 34–36; at Camp Lee 40, 41; carrying of flag of, back to North Carolina 166; casualty estimates 125, 163–65, 171–81; command changes 59, 188; companies and commanding officers 12, 15, 17, 20–29; desertions from 2, 137, 181–82; disease among 40, 60, 129; during the Seven Days Battles 50, 52–53, 172; duties during winter 1861–62, 40; elections of officers 45, 188; female soldier in 47; Killian's report on to Cathey 92–93; at Kinston, N.C. 48; Lee's visit to at Petersburg 130; march to defend of New Bern 43; march to Fredericksburg 77, 81; march to Martinsburg, W. Va. 77; march to Morganton 33; march to Petersburg and Richmond 104; march to Tarboro, N.C. 109; movement of, after Kings School House battle 56–57; movement of, from July 1863 through March 1864, 108–9; movement of, through eastern North Carolina 93–96; organization 12–15, 202; original vs. final troop strength 169; privations experienced by 120; relocation of to Kenansville, N.C. 92; reorganization 45–48; response to news of surrender 161; response to plans to invade Maryland 66; response to the Conscription Act 44–45; role in defending Wilmington 35; routes taken during the war (map) 13; at the Siege of Petersburg 118–19, 121–22, 179–80, 192; at skirmish at Gum Swamp, N.C. 96; source materials about 3; surrender at Appomattox 162–63; surviving members of 165; theaters of operation (map) 14; training of 16; volunteers for, characteristics 11, 17, 18–20, 19, 20; winter encampment at Fredericksburg 91; see also Ransom, Matthew; Ransom, Robert, Jr., Ransom's Brigade; specific companies
Twenty-sixth Regiment N.C.: application for removal from Ransom's Brigade 64; female soldier in 57; inclusion in Ransom's Brigade 55, 61
Twenty-seventh Regiment N.C., inclusion in Ransom's Brigade 45, 55

Union army: counter-attack at Fort Stedman 155; desertions from 136, 147; soldiers from western North Carolina in 141; voluntary surrender by, at Petersburg 135; see also Army of the Potomac
"Union Charge at Dunker Church during Battle of Antietam" 61
"Union Forces Attacking a Confederate Fort in Front of Petersburg" (Forces) 118
Union Navy, attack on South Carolina coast 36–37
"Union Soldiers Planting the Mine under the Confederate Trenches at Petersburg" (Waud) 124
"Union Troops Crossing the Rappahannock, Dec. 11–12, 1862" (Waud) 84
Union troops digging a trench under cover of a sap roller (Waud) 137
unionists see tories (unionists)
University of North Carolina, Wilson Library 3

Valley Town, N.C., enlistment of Company D at 24
Vance, Robert B. 151
Vance, Zebulon: election as governor of North Carolina 64; letter to about deserters and gangs 148–49; letter to Seddon about deserters and gangs 149; photograph of 7; problems on the home front 104; reluctance to support secession 6, 7; request for troops to help with lawlessness 92, 151
Verona, N.C., Ransom plantation at 115
Vicksburg, Miss., Grant's capture of 106–7
Virginia: members of Company C from 23; ordinances of secession 10; 25th Regiment N.C. troops from 18, 19; see also specific battles
volunteers, highlander (mountain soldiers): backlash among 104–5; bravery during first battles 58–59; desire to return home 48; early enlistees, enthusiasm of 11; honoring of, in home communities at start of war 13; militia companies, training 12–13; motivations, sense of threat 17; origins and characteristics 17–18, 19, 146; response to Conscription Act 44–45; from western North Carolina 12, 145

wages, failure to pay 139
Walker, John G. (Company G): appointment as Commissary 15; service history 29
Walker, John W.: at the Battle of Antietam 73, 75–76; command of Ransom's Brigade 65; reassignment to command in the west 81; support for Lee during Seven Days Battles 50
Walker, Leroy P. 187
Walker's Brigade 65
Walker's Division: at the Battle of Antietam 70–71; establishment of 65; at the investment and capture of Harpers Ferry 67–69; return to Frederick, Md. 69
Wallace, William H., South Carolina brigade 157
Washington, D.C., Lee's threats against 64
Washington, N.C.: D.H. Hill's Siege of 93–94; Hoke's efforts to recapture 113
Waub, Alfred Rudolf ("Rebs") 18
Waud, Alfred Rudolf: "Building Pontoon Bridges at Fredericksburg" 81; "Confederates Surrendering Colors and Muskets" 162; "Lee leaving McLean House following surrender" 164; "Rebel Pickets Death at Fredericksburg" 176; "Rebels Foraging" 90; "Rebels Roasting Corn" 91; "Union Soldiers Planting the Mine under the Confederate Trenches at Petersburg" 124; "Union Troops Crossing the Rappahannock, Dec. 11–12, 1862" 84; Union troops digging a trench under cover of a sap roller 137; "West Woods battle" during Battle of Antietam 75
Waynesville, N.C.: early roads to 199; enlistment of Company C at

23; schools 200, 201; Thomas' and Love's surrender at 165
Webster, N.C., enlistment of Company B at 21
Welch, William Pink: description of the 25th Regiment N.C. 24; photograph of *22*
Wessells, Henry Walton 110–11
"West Woods battle" during Battle of Antietam *72*, 73, *75*, 76, 97, 175
western Carolina University, Hunter Library 3
western Military District of North Carolina: appoint of Robert B. Vance as commander 151; creation of 151
western North Carolina: agricultural products 7, 199–200; anti–Confederate backlash 105; conditions in at end of the war 168, 197–98; conflicting political sentiments 141; conflicts about secession and war 5–6, 9, 145; desertions among soldiers from 136; enthusiasm of early enlistees 11–12; fears of Union invasion in 151; impact of Conscription Law in 145; pro–Union sentiment in 6–7; support for individual property rights in 7; Thomas's plan for protection of 148; ultra-secessionists 7; *see also* bushwhacker outlier bands, outlaws; volunteers, highlander (mountaineers)
western North Carolina Railroad 209–10
wicker gabions *129*
Wilderness battles (spring 1864) 99
Wilkes County, N.C.: tory activities in 150–51; use of troops in to put down unrest 151
Wilmington, N.C.: amphibious assaults on 35; Confederate support for 93; outfitting and training of the 25th at 202; troop train to 34; Union capture of 133
Wilmington & Manchester Railroad, troop transport 40
Wilson, William B. (Company K) 32

Wise, Henry A. 119
Wm. H. Hargrove's Book, Lexington, Ky. 205–6
women: attack by on Burnsville storehouse 150; as combatants 46–48; services in the camps 46, *47*
wooden mortars 122
Wright, William M. (Company F) 28

Yancey, William 16
Yancey County, N.C.: avoidance of conscription in 150; members of Company K from 31; 25th Regiment N.C. troops from *19*
"yeopon tea" 40
York River Railroad, strategic importance 52
Young, Ephraim E. (Company E): election as captain 46; service history 25
Young, Julius M., appointment as Commissary Sergeant 15
Young, Thomas J. (Company H) 30

www.ingramcontent.com/pod-product-compliance
Ingram Content Group UK Ltd.
Pitfield, Milton Keynes, MK11 3LW, UK
UKHW050542150426
5217IPUK00026B/2042